S. Ichimura · Y. Matsumoto (Eds.)

Econometric Models of Asian-Pacific Countries

Springer-Verlag
Tokyo Berlin Heidelberg
New York London Paris Hong Kong
Barcelona Budapest

Dr. Shinichi Ichimura
Professor Emeritus, Kyoto University,
Professor, Osaka International University, 50-1 Sugi 3, Hirakata, Osaka, 573-01 Japan

Dr. Yasumi Matsumoto
Associate Professor,
International School of Economics and Business Administration, Reitaku University,
2-1-1, Hikariga-oka, Kashiwa City, Chiba, 277 Japan

This publication was supported, in part, by a Grant-in-Aid for the Publication of Scientific Research Results, this being one of the Grants-in-Aid for Scientific Research given by the Ministry of Education, Science, and Culture of Japan.

ISBN-13:978-4-431-70134-7 e-ISBN-13:978-4-431-68258-5

DOI: 10.1007/978-4-431-68258-5

Printed on acid-free paper

Reprint of the original edition 1994

Preface

This book is a sequel to our first report of ASIAN LINK PROJECT in 1985: *Econometric Models of Asian LINK,* Springer-Verlag, Tokyo - Berlin - New York. Now the scope is expanded to Asian-Pacific Countries in coverage, so that this monograph presents the econometric models of Japan, the United States, Canada, China, Korea, Taiwan, Hong Kong, Thailand, the Philippines, Malaysia, Singapore, Indonesia, Australia and the European Community. We are particularly happy to have included the excellent models of Australia and Canada whose economies are essential parts of the Asian-Pacific Economic Community. Most of those models were presented at the Workshop of Asian Link Project held in Bandung, Indonesia at the time of the Second Convention of the East Asian Economic Association, 1990. Those models have been up-dated since then, and several other important models were added. Unlike our previous book, we have not tried here to link these national models as a regional or global model in any way, except for the model by S. Kinoshita which offers a regional linkage for Pacific-basin economies by linking the US, Japan, Canada, the European Community countries as a group, Asian NIEs (Korea, Hong Kong, Taiwan), ASEAN (Indonesia, Malaysia, the Philippines, Singapore) and East Asian economies.

As we argued in our previous publication, we tried to publish these econometric models again with the statistical data as much as we could, so as to enable the reader examine the estimation and performance of the models by himself. Due to the shortage of space permitted to this monograph, however, we regret that we could not fulfill this requirement for big Canadian and Australian models. The statistical time series will be made available to those who wish seriously to work on those models from the authors' or editors' offices. We believe that the scientific progress of econometric research depends crucially on the availability of models and data at the same time, so that other researchers can trace the findings of original econometricians and share the common empirical results, as theoretical and experimental Physicists do in their scientific works.

After the publication of *Econometric Models of Asian LINK,* the most remarkable development of econometric research in East Asian countries is that the applications of macroeconometric models and input-output tables have become routine work in almost all government offices, and that the teaching of those subjects have become the standard cources at most representative universities. Now it is almost impossible in most countries to trace all the publications in these fields. Even China is no exception. If, however, the quality of the models and statistical data are questioned, there remains much to be desired. That is why we are editing this monograph and hoping that the interested academic and government economists in developing Asian countries will quickly learn the best works available in the Asian-Pacific countries and try to improve the quality of their modeling and applications to policy-making. After all, as J. R. Hicks once remarked in his preface to *Value and Capital,* the place of economic theory – or econometric research for that matter – is the servant of applied economics.

The next stage of our research is to find a better way of linking these national models and to analyze the interdependence of the Asian-Pacific economies. The ordinary way of linking them through trading relations such as the use of trade matrix in the most recent past does not seem to be sufficiently satisfactory at the comtemporary world, when overseas capital investment, financial transactions, and Official Development Aid play such important roles in influencing the international economic relations. However difficult it may be, some devices must be made. N. Oguchi's contribution in this book is an attempt toward that end. We are trying also to find a better program of international telecommunication to exchange the model simulations through an international network of linked national models. We sincerely hope that we shall be able to publish our third monograph containing these results in a few years.

We wish to express at this opportunity our wholeheated gratitude for the generous support of our research at several stages from the Kansai Economic Research Center and for the grant to this publication from the Ministry of Education. We are very grateful for the contributors and owe some of them apologies for the delay of this publication which is mainly due to the responsibility of the editors.

Osaka, Japan

August 25, 1993

Shinichi Ichimura

Yasumi Matsumoto

Table of Contents

Chapter 1

Development of Econometric Models in Asian-Pacific Countries

Shinichi Ichimura[1]

A survey of econometric model-building experiences in East and Southeast Asian countries up to 1985 was provided in detail by Chapter 1 in *Econometric Models of Asian LINK,* Springer-Verlag, 1985. Since then, there have appeared a number of new models in most Asian-Pacific countries in addition to the works continued at the institutions mentioned in my survey quoted above. Each chapter of this book contains a list of references to econometric models in each country. There are a number of other models, however, that are not quoted by the author. The following survey is intended mainly to provide the reader some other important works which came to the attention of this editor.

In *Korea,* the Korea Development Institute and the Bank of Korea continued to maintain their own models and played the leading roles in practical applications of econometric models. Several new academic models have been constructed to analyze the recent liberalization of foreign trade and investment and the monetary sector. The model by N. Oguchi here is one example; another is Sung Y. Kwak's "Sterilization of the Monetary Effects of Current Account Surpluses and its Consequences: Korea, 1986 – 1990," in *Exchange Rate Policy and Interdependence: Prospective of the Pacific-Basin,* edited by Reuben Glick and Michael Hutchison, Cambridge University Press, 1994.

In *Taiwan,* interests in econometric models seems to have shifted from the Council of Development Planning to other government academic research institutes like Chung Hua Institute for Economic Research and the Central Bank of China. The former held an international conference in Hong Kong in June, 1992, and its proceedings: *Conference On Global Interdependence And Asia-Pacific Cooperation,* Chung-Hua Institute for Economic Research, Taipei, December, 1992 includes some models for the Taiwan economic studies. There are other models as well in the Institution. The Central Bank's Institute of Economic Research maintains a model constructed for financial analysis. The role of international and domestic firms' investment has been interestingly analyzed by Eric D. Ramstetter, "The Macroeconomic Effects of Inward Direct Investment in Taiwan: an multiform econometric analysis," in *Projections for Asian Industrializing Region I,* listed below.

In *the Philippines,* the Central Bank and School of Economics, University of the Philippines have not kept up with their excellent works quoted in my 1985 survey. The Philippine Economic Development Center keeps its model in cooperation

[1] Osaka International University

with visiting scholars from abroad, but their practical applications to government policy-making seem to be rather limited. The Asian Development Bank maintains a model to analyze the Philippine economy in its research department. That model is based on that of Central Bank published in our previous book of Asian LINK. Roberto Mariano's model published here is an up-to-date development of the ADB research department model and the previous UP School of Economics Model. A CGE model of the Philippines was constructed by Shoichi Ito: "A CGE Analysis of the Philippine Economy," *Bulletin of the University of Osaka Prefecture,* Series D, vol. XXXI, 1987.

In *Thailand,* neither the Bank of Thailand nor any government office itself does not seem to rely on econometric models for its own policy-making any longer. The Thai Development Research Center – a semi-governmental and internationally supported think tank for the government as well as the private businesses – maintains a task force for the forecast and analysis of the Thai national economy. There are several econometric models developed by university economists. Professor Kitti's model published here is one of the outstanding models now available and used for policy suggestions. Some other words are quoted in his reference.

In *Malaysia,* several research institutes are engaged in the economic analysis and forecast of the Malaysian economy. The Institute for Strategic and International Studies, directed by Dr. Nordin Sopiee, and Institute for Economic Research, directed by Dr. Kamal Salih, are two leading institutions and serve the government for economic analysis and policy suggestions. Bank Negara Malaysia used to maintain an econometric model but no longer does so.

In *Indonesia,* the most pragmatic model is the one maintained by the Team Quantitative, National Development and Planning Agency (BAPPENAS). But its current model is not readily available to outsiders. Its old version is almost the same as Sei Kuribayashi's (1987) model, "A Medium-Term Macro-Econometric Model for Economic Planning in Indonesia," *South East Asian Studies,* vol. XXIV, No.4, (March, 1987). This model has been up-dated and adjusted to the new statistical data based on New National Income Accounts by several Japanese and Indonesian experts at BAPPENAS. A CGE model of Indonesia was constructed by Mitsuo Ezaki: "Oil Price Declines and Structural Adjustment Policies in Indonesia," *The Philippine Review of Economics and Business,* vol. XXXI, No.2, (December, 1989).

In *Singapore,* a model presented here is the basic model for the Singapore economy. Similar models produced by Dr. Toh Mun Heng and Dr. Linda Low has been used to present their prediction at the Economic Outlook Conference mentioned below. A CGE model was constructed by Shoichi Ito and Tay Boon Nga, "The Impacts of Oil Shocks on Singapore Economy," *The Asian Economic Journal,* vol. VII, No.3, (November, 1993). There are several other models on the Singapore economy, but they are not applied to practice.

Econometric Models in *China* did not exist around 1985, except for the ones constructed outside China. Since 1986, there have been a number of models inside and outside China, including Tang Quoxing (Fudan University, visiting Kyoto University), Haruki Niwa (Kyoto Sangyo University) and Lawrence J. Lau (Stanford

University). In recent years, however, the Planning Commission of the Chinese government, and several institutes of the Chinese Academy of Social Sciences, the Chinese Academy of Sciences, the Shanghai Academy of Social Sciences and several universities in various provinces joined the band wagon of model-building including the Input-Output models as well as econometric models. One example is: Li Jingwen, Qi Jianuo, Wang Tengsan, and Shen Lisheng, *The Relationship Between Industrial Development Policy and Economic Growth in China (1978-1988),* Institute of Quantitative and Technical Economics, Chinese Academy of Social Sciences, 1993. It is impressive that even a remote Yunnan province's government has produced an econometric model and is trying to use it for its own development plan. A CGE model by Mitsuo Ezaki and Shoichi Ito makes use of the Interindustrial Table produced by the Chinese government in cooperation with the World Bank experts: "A CGE Analysis of the Chinese Economy," in *Market and the Role of Government: Experiences of Japan and China,* edited by Mitsuo Ezaki, Graduate School of International Development, Nagoya University, March, 1993.

Econometrics models in *Australia* have gone through ups and downs at several places. The university of Melbourne group seems to maintain a model on which basis its experts report their forecast and analysis at the Economic Outlook Conference mentioned above. But the most practical model in use is the one published here: the Treasury Model. There have been several other models available, but they are no longer maintained.

In *Canada,* the one summarized here is the most authoritative model and is maintained up-to-date at the Institute for Policy Analysis, University of Toronto.

In *the US and Japan,* there are so many models produced by many econometricians. It would require a separate survey. In practical applications in Japan the most important one is the model maintained at the Institute of Economic Research, Economic Planning Agency in Japan whose essential part is published in the Annual White Paper of the EPA. Another best known is the NEEDS Model of the Japan Economic Research Center, whose prediction is published regularly in the Nihon Keizai Shinbun (Japan Economic Newspapers). The Japan Economic Research Center publishes quarterly another forecast of the Japanese economy on the basis of what they call a successive approach model. The Bank of Japan and the Ministry of Finance maintain their own econometric models and make use of them for their own applications. In addition, almost all major banks and a few securities companies have their own research departments or separate research institute associated with them and are engaged in the applications of econometric models. Their predictions are announced at least several times a year and offered to their customers as well as for their internal use. The summary of their forecasts are reviewed in the *Monthly Report of the Japan Economic Research Center* every year. Another regular and reliable forecast is offered by the Kansai Economic Research Center in Osaka on the basis of excellent econometric model, whose chief architects are Professors Chikashi Moriguchi and Kanemi Ban, Osaka University. The regional models for Asian-Pacific economies linking these national models are not many. About the same time as our previous model of Asian LINK was out,

Economic Planning Agency published two volumes of The World Model: The EPA World Model, vol. I and vol. II, whose chief architects were Professors A. Amano and M. Toyota, Kobe University and Dr. M. Yoshitomi, EPA, and it is maintained by a team of staff at EPA Institute of Economic Research. The latest version is available in *Keizai Bunseki (Economic Analysis)*, No.124, July, 1990. It contains the models of the US, Japan, Canada, Australia and Korea as well as major developed economies in Europe. The Institute of Developing Economies in Tokyo is also maintaining a set of econometric models of Asian NIEs (except for Hong Kong) and ASEAN (except for Brunei) and holds a regional forum from time to time. The papers presented at the conference in 1990 and a model on China are published in *The Economic Prediction and Analysis of ASEAN and Asian NIEs*, edited by Mitsuru Toda, Institute of Developing Economies, March, 1991. Another report of IDE is very useful: *Projections for Asian Industrializing Region I*, March, 1992. Kinoshita's Model published here is an excellent single man's work of this type. Another type of research needed to analyze the development process of Asian developing countries is to make a comparative study of several economies, one of such types was provided by M. Ezaki and S. Ito's "Oil Shocks and Tax Policy : an international comparison of CGE analyses on Indonesia, the Philippines, Thailand and Japan, " *The Economic Review*, January, 1988. In order to promote a global and regional modeling and its applications, it is essential to have a forum for the exchange of experiences and analyses among applied econometricians. As such the most noteworthy development of further research and applications is the *Economic Outlook Conference of PECC (the Pacific Economic Cooperation Council)* and its workshop preceding the Conference which is regularly held in Osaka, Japan every year. In this workshop a number of econometricians from the Pacific-basin countries present the lastest forecast of the macro conditions of their own national economies and exchange the observations and opinions on the latest problems of their respective countries. Some predictions are based on the models of participants like Iwan Azis' Indonesian Model and KDI's Model published in this book, but most of the predictions are not based on the strict findings from the models. Those interested in those alternative models may be able to obtain them from the secretariat of the Economic Outlook Conference.[2] The well known Project LINK led by Lawrence R. Klein in recent years cover several Asian-Pacific economies. But the closest to the ideal place for model-building and its practical applications to an East Asian economies are offered by a newly established International Center for the Study of East Asian Development (ICSEAD), Kitakyushu, Japan in cooperation with the University of Pennsylvania. It publishes the main statistical data and its model predictions every year. Its annual publication, *Asian Data Handbook*, is the most handy statistical handbook for macroeconomic time series for all the East Asian economies. The recent significant conference report: *Exports, Foreign Investment, and Growth in East and Southeast Asia, 1992*, vol. I and vol. II, edited by F.G. Adams and R.F. Wescott, contain many national and regional econometric models.

---

[2] Secretariat is located at the Kansai Economic Research Center, Nakanoshima Center Building, Nakanoshima 6, Kita-Ku, Osaka, Japan.

Chapter 2
The ICSEAD Japan-U.S.-ROW Model

Yosihisa Inada[1] and Robert F. Wescott[2]

1 Background

The ICSEAD Japan-U.S.-ROW Model is a linked macro model of Japan, the United States, and the Rest of the World. It has been built as a tool for analyzing economic policy issues in Japan and the United States and is intended to serve as a platform for the development of further linked models of the East Asia region at the International Center for the Study of East Asian Development (ICSEAD). The 464 equation model is in the Keynesian tradition. It draws on previous work by Y. Inada (1987) and also consists of a part of Japan, the United States, China and the rest of the world quadrilateral model which was jointly developed by Klein, Lau, and Chinese Academy of Social Science (1988).

Supply side responses are incorporated through an implicit production function, whereby increases in the private capital stock lead to increases in potential GNP. This decreases the rate of capacity utilization, which in turn puts downward pressure on the producer price index – the key determinant of prices in the model. The monetary sector of each country relies on a key short-term interest rate equation that uses basic monetary policy instruments as right-hand side variables. Countries are linked through trade flows. Separate bilateral import and export functions explain the trade of merchandise goods between countries. Service trade in two categories is explained. The model is estimated over the period 1960-1989 using mainly standard OLS techniques.

The model is well equipped to study many of the macroeconomic policy options being debated in the United States and Japan, including fiscal stimulus measures and policies designed to reduce the bilateral trade gap between the two countries. These include such options as increases in Japanese public capital formation, U.S. federal budget deficit reduction measures, tariff reduction measures, and various degrees of monetary policy coordination. It is also a useful tool for assessing the macroeconomic effects of various oil price assumptions on the two countries, and for analyzing the impacts of Japanese direct foreign investment on U.S. economic activity and the bilateral trade balance. The dollar/yen exchange rate is exogenous in the model, and must be managed in the creation of various scenarios. Aggregate rest-of-world GNP growth and prices are endogenous.

[1] Associate Professor, Ritsumeikan University
[2] Research Fellow, International Center for the Study of East Asian Develpment

This paper includes:
1. a sector-by-sector overview of each model block, with a brief description of the underlying theoretical roots of the model blocks.
2. results of a series of validation tests on the model, including history of forecast graphs, a description of the model's responses to a battery of exogenous shocks, a report of key model multiplier properties, and a report of its import elasticities.
3. a description of the trade linkages that connect economic activity and prices in the three trade blocks: Japan, the United States, and the rest of the world. 4. an equation listing and variables listing.

2 Theoretical Roots of the Model

The theoretical roots of the U.S. and the Japan component models are very similar. They share the same general theoretical specifications and the same general categorization of final demand components, etc. However, there are a number of differences because of the differing structures of the national accounts, the different policy instruments favored by the central banks, and the differing power (or lack of power) of the data to support the theoretically preferred specifications.

2.1 Final Demand Block

2.1.1 Consumption

Consumption is divided into three main categories for each country – durables, nondurables, and services. Some extra detail available in the U.S. model: durables are split into motor vehicles/parts, and other; nondurables are split into gasoline/oil and other. In general terms the consumption functions are specified as:

(2.1) $$C = f(mpc * \frac{YPD}{PC}, \frac{PCi}{PC}, KD_{-1}, Timetrend)$$
where:

MPC	=	marginal propensity to consume
	=	$f(interestincome/stockofsaving_{-1})$
YPD	=	household disposable income price deflator for all
PC	=	price deflator for all consumption goods
PCi	=	price deflator for the i-th comsumption category
KD	=	stock of durable goods (used for durable equation only)
$Timetrend$	=	time trend (used for services equations only)

These equations are standard formulations. Consumption depends positively on real disposable income and the stock of durables (durables equations only), and negatively on the relative price of the i-th consumption sector to all consumer prices. The marginal propensity to consume is essentially a function of an effective interest rate, so if the effective interest rate increases, households are expected to increase their saving, and consumption is expected to fall.

2.1.2 Residential Investment

Investment is split into residential and non-residential components. There is also an inventory equation for each country. Residential investment is specified as follows:

(2.2) $$IR = f\left(\frac{YPD}{PC}, \frac{depr}{KIR+i} * \frac{PIR}{PC}, KIR_{-1}\right)$$

where:

IR	=	residential investment
YPD	=	household disposable income
PC	=	price deflator for all consumption goods
$depr$	=	depreciation rate for housing
KIR	=	stock of residential housing
i	=	short term interest rate
PIR	=	price deflator for IR

The first term is real disposable income and it is positively related to residential investment. The second term is a cost of capital term, composed of an interest rate, a depreciation rate, and a price index for residential investment. Its movement relative to general consumption inflation determines this investment. If interest rates rise, the price of housing rises, or the price of general consumption goods falls, then residential investment will fall. Also, residential investment is positively related to the capital stock of housing.

2.1.3 Non-Residential Investment

Non-residential investment uses a mixture of the above type of cost of capital formulation and a real cashflow measure. In short, it is a modified Jorgensonian investment function. Generally speaking:

(2.3) $$INR = f\left(\frac{Cashflow}{PINR}, \frac{Sales}{PINR*UCC}, INR_{-1}, KINR_{-1}\right)$$

where:

INR	=	non-residential investment
$Cashflow$	=	cash flow, defined as business income plus depreciation allowances, plus stock valuation adjustment, less taxes
$PINR$	=	price deflator for non-residential investment
$Sales$	=	total sales of the economy, defined as nominal GNP less gross domestic capital formation
UCC	=	short term interest plus an average depreciation factor for non-residential investment goods
$KINR$	=	stock of non-residential plant and equipment

Non-residential investment increases as corporate cashflow in an economy increases, as the relative price of non-residential investment falls, as overall sales in the economy increase, or as interest rates fall.

2.1.4 Inventory Investment

Inventory investment is a function of the rate of capacity utilization, a real interest rate, the inflation rate, final sales, and the previous stock of inventories:

(2.4) $$IV = f(CU, i - inflationrate, inflationrate, Sales, KIV_{-1})$$

where:

IV	=	inventory investment
CU	=	capacity utilization rate
i	=	short-term interest rate
$inflation\ rate$	=	deflator for domestic demand categories
$Sales$	=	total sales of the economy, defined as nominal GNP less gross domestic capital formation
KIV	=	stock of inventories

Theoretically, businesses will hold more inventories if the economy is operating at a high level of capacity (to ensure supplies in tight times), if the real rate of interest is low (lower carrying costs), if the rate of inflation is high (to make inventory profits), if the rate of sales is high (do not miss sales by not having enough product to sell), and if previous period inventory stocks were low (replenish supplies to maintain sales).

2.1.5 Imports and Exports

Nominal exports and imports are determined in the international transactions block. A separate section of this paper addresses the specification of the trade linkages in the model.

2.2 Income Distribution and Fiscal Block

This bloc is handled largely by identities that follow standard government accounting guidelines.

2.2.1 Income Distribution by Sector

Income is broken down into the following sectors:

Households:

Wages and Salaries
Interest and Dividend Income
Proprietors' Income

Goverment:

Interest and Dividends (State and Local, and Federal)

Businesses:

Corporate Profits

Non-profit organizations:

Entrepreneurial Income
Property Income (Japan)

2.2.2 Government Detail

On the expenditure side, the following breakdown is provided:

United States:

Defense
Non-defense
State and Local
Social Security Benefits
Other Transfers
Subsiders

Japan:

Public Consumption
Public Non-residential Investment
Public Residential Investment
Public Land Purchases
Social Security Benefits
Other Transfers
Subsiders

The following breakdown is provided on the government receipts side:

United States:

Personal Income Taxes (Federal, State and Local)
Corporate Income Taxes (Federal, State and Local)
Indirect Business Taxes (State and Local Sales Taxes, etc.)
Indirect Business Taxes (Federal Gasoline Tax)
Indirect Business Taxes (Federal Excise Taxes including Liquor, Tabacco, Windfall Profits Tax, etc.)
Indirect Business Taxes (Customs Duties)
Indirect Business Taxes (State and Local Sales Taxes, etc.)
Indirect Business Taxes (State and Local Property Taxes)
Employers' Contribution for Social Insurance (Federal, State and Local)
Personal Contribution for Social Insurance (Federal, State and Local)
Government Receipts for Health Charges, Fines, etc.
Non Tax Items

Japan:

Personal Income Taxes
Corporate Income Taxes
Indirect Taxes (Customs Duties)
Indirect Taxes (other than Customs Duties)
Indirect Taxes (Consumption Tax)
Social Security Contribution
Social Assistance

2.3 Production and Employment Block

Supply side responses are incorporated through an implicit production function. Increases in private capital stock lead to increases in potential production. This decreases the rate of capacity utilization, which in turn puts downward pressure on the producer price index – the key determinant of prices in the model.

2.3.1 Potential Production

Potential production is modeled as follows:

(2.5) $$PP = f(Max(Hours) * LF, Max(CU) * KINR_{-1}, Timetrend)$$
where:

PP	=	potential production
$Hours$	=	maximum possible working hours
LF	=	labor force
CU	=	maximum possible capacity utilization
$KINR$	=	stock of non-residential capital
$Timetrend$	=	time trend

Potential production would increase if the labor force, the maximum possible hours worked, or capacity utilization where to increase. More investment would also lead to increases in potential production. Finally, it is assumed that this concept increases over time, other things being equal. Capacity utilization is determined as a simple ratio of actual output to this measure of potential output:

(2.6) $$CU = f(\frac{Output}{PP})$$
where:

$Output$	=	GNP plus Imports
PP	=	potential production

2.3.2 Labor Force

The labor force is a function of the non-institutionalized population aged 15 years and older, and a lagged dependent term:

(2.7) $$LF = f(POP, LF_{-1})$$

where:

POP	=	non-institutionalized population, over 15 years old
LF	=	labor force

2.3.3 Employment

Total employment is a function of the overall level of economic activity, the wage level relative to the overall price level, and a lagged dependent variable. The number of working hours per week is also a function of these same factors, except that contemporaneous employment is also used as an explanatory factor.

(2.8) $$EMP = f(GNP, \frac{WAGES}{PDD}, EMP_{-1})$$

and

(2.9) $$HOURS = f(GNP, \frac{WAGES}{PDD}, EMP)$$

where:

EMP	=	total employment
GNP	=	gross national product
$WAGES$	=	national wage level
PDD	=	price deflator for domestic demand
$HOURS$	=	average workweek (in hours)

As GNP increases, so do employment and hours worked. As wages increase relative to overall prices in the economy, businesses will find it relatively unattractive to add workers, and they will try to reduce the number of hours worked. Also, *ceteris paribus,* as employment goes up, the number of hours worked will go down, because more workers substitute for more hours of work.

2.4 Wage and Price Block

The key price indicator in both the U.S. and Japan models is the wholesale price index (producer price index). It is explained by labor costs, labor productivity, capacity utilization, and import prices. Thus it is also implicitly influenced by the exchange rate. Some exogenous price assumptions feed into the wholesale price index, such as oil prices. The other price indices and deflators in the models are in turn driven by these wholesale price index variables and various appropriate measures of market tightness. Certain taxes also have an impact on some consumer prices. Following is the formulation of the general wholesale price index equations:

(2.10) $$WPI = f(WAGES, PROD, CU, PIMP)$$

where:

WPI	=	wholesale price index
$WAGES$	=	national wage level
$PROD$	=	labor productivity (output per man hour)
CU	=	capacity utilization
$PIMP$	=	unit price index for imports

All of these factors except labor productivity are positively associated with WPI – because labor markets are getting tighter, industrial capacity is more strained, or imported inputs cost more. If productivity is higher it means less price pressure.

The typical final demand price deflator is expressed as a function of the wholesale price index, the national wage level, and a lagged dependent variable:

(2.11) $$P = f(WPI, WAGES, P_{-1})$$

where:

P	=	price deflator
$WAGES$	=	national wage level

Import and export prices are discussed in the special trade linkages section of this paper.

3 Model Validation

This section attempts to validate the econometric model by systematically assessing it's overall properties and the reasonableness of its simulation properties. Four tests are considered: 1) the models' ability to dynamically track history over the 1980s, 2) the separate U.S. and Japan models' GNP multipliers in response to standard government spending shocks, 3) the models' import elasticities, and 4) the models' full simulation responses to a set of standard policy scenarios.

3.1 Forecast of History Test

Appendix A presents a battery of graphs that show the U.S. and Japan component models' abilities to track history over the 1980s in a dynamic "forecast of history" test. Both the level and the annual percentage change of the variables are presented; in all cases the solid line represents actual history, and the dotted line represents the models' forecast of history. The U.S. model does a generally good job of tracking most components of aggregate demand. It does an excellent job hitting the turning points in consumption, non-residential investment, and imports and exports. Over the latter 1980s, the model slightly under-predicts U.S. exports, and over-predicts non-residential investment. Over most of the 1980s it over-predicts the GNP price deflator, although not by a wide margin. Producer prices are under-predicted from 1982 to 1986, and then over-predicted. The employment, wages per hour, import price index, and interest rate and money supply equations all track history quite closely.

The Japan model does a credible job tracking imports, exports, consumption, and non-residential investment, but it over-predicts residential investment over the late 1980s. The model's biggest difficulty is in tracking the GNP price deflator over the 1980s. The model over-predicts inflation from 1982 to 1985, and then under-predicts it from 1986 through 1988. Very likely the model has too big of an estimated exchange rate effect in certain key price equations. During the period of weak yen, the Japanese economy was more immune than expected against imported inflation, and then over the period of "endaka" or "high yen", higher inflation than expected was experienced. In fact, the Japanese economy has perhaps been more insulated from foreign exchange swings than would have been expected. The model does an excellent job tracking both short and long term interest rates, and also the M2 money supply.

3.2 Standard Multiplier Tests

Standard multiplier tests were performed on both the U.S. and Japan models over the period from 1982 to 1988. For the tests the models were run in independent mode – that is, dis-engaged from trading partners via the trade linkages. This was done to provide GNP multipliers more readily comparable to other reported national multipliers that usually do not include cross-country feedback effects. All multipliers reported are real multipliers, not nominal multipliers. For the U.S. model, a simulation that added an additional 1% of historical GNP to the government spending profile (split between defense and non-defense) was produced in two variations: without any monetary accommodation and with monetary accommodation. The monetary accommodation scenario exogenized both the critical short-term and long-term interest rates and assumed that the monetary authorities would pump into additional reserves to completely offset the tendency for interest rates to be bid up with the higher level of economic activity.

The same type of simulations were produced with the Japan model, except that the 1% of historical GNP was added into the public investment category. The same definition of accommodation was made.

3.2.1 U.S. Multiplier Results

U.S. model real GNP multipliers in the 1.5 to 2 range (with accommodation) that peak after a couple of years, and then decline monotonically are well supported in the U.S. modeling literature. And the U.S. model pattern of the multiplier falling monotonically without any accommodation seems reasonable. The difference between the two multipliers, at about a half a percent, also seems reasonable.

U.S. Model Real GNP Multiplier

Year	No Monetary Accommodation	Monetary Accommodation
1	1.62	1.71
2	1.63	1.88
3	1.59	1.98
4	1.53	2.07
5	1.46	2.00
6	1.32	1.77
7	1.22	1.54

3.2.2 Japan Multiplier Results

Most Japanese models show sharply lower GNP multipliers than U.S. models, and the result here fit into the middle range. With a lower marginal propensity to consume than in other OECD-type economies (i.e., a higher propensity to save) it is to be expected that Japan should have lower GNP multipliers from most shocks that increase aggregate demand. In addition to lower multiplier, there is little difference in the multiplier between the case of monetary accommodation and no monetary accommodation.

Japan Model Real GNP Multiplier

Year	No Monetary Accommodation	Monetary Accommodation
1	1.09	1.10
2	1.12	1.13
3	1.03	1.05
4	0.86	0.89
5	0.76	0.81
6	0.59	0.65
7	0.42	0.47

3.3 Import Elasticity Measures

The sensitivity of the U.S. and Japan economies to imports is a critical model property, given that the aggregate model will be used for trade studies. Generally speaking, the lower the import response to higher domestic economic growth, the less leakage from the economy, and the higher the associated activity multipliers, *ceteris paribus.*

The import elasticities were measured from the same simulations used to measure the government spending GNP multipliers (no accommodation cases). Reported measures show percentage change of real imports divided by percentage change in real GNP.

Aggregate Import Elasticities

Year	U.S.	Japan
1	1.32	0.90
2	1.62	1.16
3	1.94	1.45
4	2.35	1.95
5	2.98	2.45
6	3.80	3.69
7	4.75	5.15

3.4 Simulation Properties

Six simulation tests have been performed with the U.S. model: 1) faster non-borrowed reserves growth 2) high interest rates 3) lower dollar 4) increase in Federal government spending 5) Federal personal income tax hike 6) gasoline tax increase

Three simulations have been performed with the Japan model: 1) increase in government infrastructure spending 2) official discount rate cut 3) yen appreciation

A description of the scenarios and their results follows. Each scenario was run from 1982-1988 against a baseline that used add-factors to exactly match history over the period. All differences are expressed as relative to this baseline case.

3.4.1 Simulation Properties in the U.S. Model

(1) High Reserves Growth

a. Assumption: NBRMU (Nonborrowed reserves) increased by $2 billion each year (1982-1988).

b. Comments: The key short rate, INRFFU (Federal funds rate) only falls by about 50 basis points, whereas some other models show a decline of 100 basis points or even more. (Note: over this period non-borrowed reserves were only on the order of $30 billion - $38 billion, so a $2 increase would have represented about a 6% increase – a large boost.) As a result, the economy does not really move much. There is an historical tendency of interest changes by the Federal Reserve to be achieved by a combination of open market operations (roughly 2/3 impact) and official discount rate adjustments (about 1/3 impact). If a corresponding adjustment is made to the discount rate in creating scenarios, the monetary sector is considered to behave appropriately.

(2) Higher Interest Rates

a. Assumption: INRFFU (Federal funds rate) excluded from the model and increased by 200 basis points.

b. Comments: The economy's response is reasonable for CPEU (aggregate consumption) and IFNRU (non-residential investment), if somewhat subdued. Average impact (years 1 to 5): CPEU – Consumption down 0.3% in the first year, with a peak impact of 1.7% in the fourth year. IFNRU – Non-residential investment down 1% in the first year, and 4% to 7.5% thereafter. IFRU – Residential investment down 5% to 11% over the first five years. Imports rise slightly in first year, and then are down 1% to 2% in years three to five. Generally imports should fall by a percentage somewhere between the CPEU and IFNRU percentage declines, not less than both of them, as is the case here.

(3) A 10% Depreciation of the Dollar

a. Assumptions: Multiplied RATEJ (exchange rate of yen/$, etc.), RATEC, RATEG, RATEI, RATEF, RATEUK by 0.9 to effect a 10% depreciation. The effect can be confirmed by noting that ERATEU (effective U.S. exchange rate) did in fact drop by 10%. Note: all these currencies are expressed as units per dollar – even UK rate is expressed this way. Multiplied PEXMR (effective export price of goods from the rest of the world to the U.S.) by 1.05 (i.e., assumed that imports from the rest of the world would cost U.S. importers 5% more if the dollar depreciated 10%). This is based on an assumption that roughly 50% of U.S. imports from the rest of the world are dollar denominated and therefore only 50% of the 10% depreciation (5%) would show up in import prices. Some analysts might argue that even assuming a 50% pass-through is too high, and that 30% would be better.

b. Comments: Things generally move in the right direction. Imports are down 3.5%-4.5% from baseline, and exports are up 1% in the first two years, then are actually lower that the baseline from year four onward – a somewhat curious result. An upward adjustment of the Rest-of-World GNP might make a more reasonable scenario.

The 10% depreciation of the dollar adds 0.4 points to the rate of GNP deflator inflation over years two through five. With other U.S. models (WEFA models, for example) a 10% depreciation only added about 0.5 points in the first year, and then maybe only 0.3 points thereafter. This was a good result based on historical experience in the 1980s. The inflation effect could be mitigated some by only assuming a 30% pass-through of PEXMR prices, instead of the 50% pass-through assumed in this scenario.

(4) Federal Spending Increases by 1% of Historical GNP

a. Assumption: Increased GFNDU (non-defense government spending), GF DU (defense spending), and GSLU (state and local government spending) by an aggregate 1% of historical real GNP, 1982-1988. Assume no monetary accommodation, i.e., assume that interest rates should rise and some crowding out will occur.

b. Comments: The multipliers and import elasticities are reported above. These multipliers seem reasonable without monetary accommodation. With higher interest rates, there should be some crowding out. Note that other models of the U.S. economy have tended to show import elasticities on the order of 3 after about three year – somewhat higher than these results.

(5) A $20 Billion Increase in Federal Personal Taxes

a. Assumptions: TPFIU (federal personal income tax receipts) is excluded and increased by $20 billion relative to baseline in each year.

b. Comments: Model seems to give generally good results here. The GNP multiplier after 1 year is about 1.5. Other results: GNP–down about 0.7% over years one through four; CPEU–Aggregate consumption down about 1.0% over years one through four; IFNRU–Non-residential investment down about 1% years one through four; then little change; IFRU–Residential investment down 11% first year, then down 3%-6%; Exports–no real change; Imports–down 2%-2.5% (reasonable); INRFFU–Federal funds down 20 basis points; PGNPU–rate of deflator inflation down 0.2% points years one through five.

(6) A 20% Increase in Gasoline Tax

a.Assumptions: Increase RTGASU (rate of gasoline tax) by 20, i.e., a 20% increase in gasoline taxes.

b. Comments: All key variables move in the right direction–GNP falls, inflation is nudged up, consumption, investment, and imports fall, and the federal budget deficit shrinks. Overall consumption falls by about 1%, a reasonable amount. Interest rates drift downward with the softening economy.

3.4.2 Simulation Properties in Japan Model

(1) Higher Government Spending

a. Assumptions: Increased IGGJ (Central government investment spending) by 1% of historical GNP.

b. Comments: The GNP multipliers and import elasticities are reported above. These multipliers are in line with other estimates for Japanese model multipliers. The multipliers seem to fall reasonably over time. There is a strong possibility that over the period of the early 1990s, the import to income elasticity in Japan will be higher than the 0.9 short-run elasticity found with the model. This reflects the changes taking place in Japanese buying patterns and responses to international pressures.

Other results: IMJ–Imports increase 0.5% in the first two years, and 1.5% in years three through seven; INRCJ–Call Money rate is up only about 10 basis points relative to baseline over years two through six–that is, there is little impact on short-run financial variables. It could be argued that there should be more movement of interest rates as higher levels of government spending crowd out some private sector activity. The longerinterest rates (INRBJ) increases 22 basis points–a better response.

(2) A cut of 100 Basis Points in the Official Discount Rate

a. Assumption: Cut thc ODRJ (official Japanese discount rate) by 100 basis points, 1982-1988.

b. Comments: Virtually 100% of this cut shows up in market short-term interest rates from the first year on–i.e., the elasticity is about 100%.

(3) A 10% Appreciation of the Yen

a. Assumption: RATEJ (yen/$, exchange rate) is multiplied by 10%, i.e., a 10% appreciation of the yen against the dollar.

Note: there is no need to make an analogous assumption about rest of world prices (as in the U.S. model), because they are all divided by the RATEJ variable in all the key trade equations–i.e., it is assumed that all Japanese imports are dollar denominated.

b. Comments: Imports in the first year, though only slightly. This is counter-intuitive, but seems to be due to a productivity effect. They then fall 2% in years two and three, and then 4%-6% in years five through eight. EXJ–exports fall about 5% over years one through six. This was significantly more than the apparent elasticity of exports in the Japanese experience over the late 1980s. Historically, even as the yen appreciated by almost 100% against the dollar between 1985 and 1989, Japanese exports in yen terms actually increased by roughly 18%. Indeed, this apparent insensitivity of Japanese exports to such a major shift in exchange rates is one of the most bewildering economic events of the decades of the 1980s. INCRJ–Call money rate falls 46 basis points in the first year, then is down about 20 basis points. With real GNP down 1% to 1.5% over years one through six, this seems like a reasonable response. CPEJ–Consumption is basically unaffected–down just slightly.

4 Trade Linkages

At the heart of the Japan-U.S.-Rest of World Model are the trade linkages, where activity and price effects in the model's three trade blocks are transmitted to other blocks. In simplest terms, the level of domestic activity in each trade block determines that block's demand for imports, and this in turn drives exports from the other trade blocs. Relative export prices in each trade block determine the competitiveness of each block's exports, and influence the trade flows. All effects are fully simultaneous. For example, more export demand for the products of a particular trade block lead to more activity and higher prices in that economy, which in turn makes its exports somewhat less competitive; it would also cause it to import more, which in turn would reduce the current account gain from what it otherwise might be from the initial shock.

This section describes the formulation of the key trade equations. The sector starts with key national income accounts trade data, and then uses a series of accounting-type equations to link this national data to internationally comparable data–in this case, the International Monetary Fund's Directions of Trade Statistics.

Imports into the United States are split into two categories: imports from Japan and imports from the rest of the world. Imports from the rest of the world are then split into two categories: petroleum imports and non-petroleum imports. Japanese imports are handled in analagous fashion, with the major split being into imports from the United States and imports from the rest of the world. Likewise both the United States and Japan have two destinations for their exports: the other country and the rest of the world.

The following discussion begins with national income account trade for exports, explains the transformation of this national data into standardized international trade data concepts (particularly the International Monetary Fund's Directions of Trade data). It then discusses the import side, starting from these international data concepts–the heart of the trade bloc–and then works back to the national trade data concepts. Finally, the development of international trade prices are discussed.

4.1 Exports

The beginning (within country) nominal export identity for each trade block is:

(4.1) $$EXIN_i = EXMIN_i + TRMR_i + EOS_i + FAR_i$$

where:

$EXIN_i$ = nominal exports of goods and services by country i

$EXMIN_i$ = nominal exports of non-military merchandise goods by country i

$TRMR_i$	=	nominal exports of military goods and services by country i
EOS_i	=	nominal exports of services, other than factor income, by country i
FAR_i	=	nominal exports of factor income by country i

Military exports (if any) are not broken out separately in the accounts for Japan, and so this term does not appear in the Japanese identity. They are taken as exogenous for the U.S. economy. Nominal exports of merchandise goods (EXMIN) are then linked to Directions of Trade (DOT)-defined nominal exports (EXMND) via an identity where the ratio of the national concept to the DOT concept is an exogenous assumption, based on its historical pattern.

4.1.1 Merchandise Exports

Total trade block DOT-based exports are then split into those to the two other trade blocks via this identity:

(4.2) $$EXMND_i = EXMND_{ji} + EXMND_{ik}$$

where:

$EXMND_i$	=	total DOT-based nominal merchandise exports from trade block i
$EXMND_{ij,ik}$	=	DOT-based nominal merchandise exports from trade block i to trade block j, and from trade block i to trade block k

The heart of the trade sector is that these exports are then determined by the other trade blocs' import demands, based on the near-identities:

(4.3) $$EXMND_{ij} = f(IMMND_{ji})$$

and

(4.4) $$EXMND_{ik} = f(IMMND_{ki})$$

where:

$IMMND_{ji,ki}$	=	trade block j's merchandise imports from trade block i, and trade block K's merchandise imports from trade block i

4.1.2 Invisible Exports

Service sector exports of non-factor income, EOS, are determined by the general level of foreign activity:

(4.5) $$EOS = f(EOS_{-1}, GNPAWD)$$

where:

EOS	=	nominal exports of services, other than factor income
EOS_{-1}	=	lagged dependent value of EOS
$GNPAWD$	=	world GNP, weighted by activity (with zero weight for the exporting country)

The more foreign activity, the more exports of services.

Factor income exports are based on the quantity of the country's assets abroad, foreign rates of return on assets, and the exchange rate:

(4.6) $FAR = f(INRAB * KRPA, ERATE, INRED * KROA)$

where:

FAR	=	nominal factor income exports
$INRAB$	=	foreign average bond yield
$KRPAU$	=	country's private assets abroad
$RATE$	=	exchange rate
$INRED$	=	3-month Eurodollar rate
$KROA$	=	country's official foreign reserves

The country's assets abroad are split into private and public components, and each is multiplied by the most appropriate interest rate. The exchange rate is present to capture changes in the value of the foreign earnings as they are repatriated back to the home country. The more foreign assets held or the higher the interest rate they earn, the more the exports of factor income.

4.2 Imports

4.2.1 Merchandise Imports

Each country's imports are determined by domestic demand and relative prices–export prices from other countries (adjusted by exchange rates) relative to domestic prices. For the U.S. and Japan models, however, there is first a split between petroleum and non-petroleum imports, with petroleum imports always assumed to come from the rest of the world. For example:

(4.7) $IMMND_i = IMMND_{ij} + IMMND_{ik}$

where:

$IMMND_i$	=	total DOT-basis merchandise imports into country i
$IMMND_{ij}$	=	DOT-basis merchandise imports into country i from country j
$IMMND_{ik}$	=	DOT-basis merchandise imports into country i from country k (the rest of the world)

and:

(4.8) $IMMND_{ik} = IMMNDP_{ik} + IMMNDO_{ik}$

where:

$IMMNDP_{ik}$	=	DOT-basis petroleum imports into country i from country k (rest of world)
$IMMNDO_{ik}$	=	DOT-basis non-petroleum imports into country i from country k (the rest of the world)

The key import equations in the model are for U.S. and Japanese imports from each other. All values at this stage are adjusted so they are dollar based. The equations have the form:

$$\frac{IMMND_{ij}}{PEXC_j} * ERATE = f(DD_i, PEXC_j/ERATE_j/PDD_i) \tag{4.9}$$

where:

$IMMND_{ij}$ = DOT-basis merchandise imports to country i from country j
$PEXC_j$ = export price index for country j
$ERATE$ = exchange rate
DD_i = real domestic demand in country i
PDD_i = domestic price deflator for domestic demand

The left-hand-side term is effectively real merchandise imports, in dollar terms. This is explained as a function of real domestic demand in the importing country, and the relative price of exports in the exporting country to domestic prices–with export prices adjusted for exchange rate changes. The signs are all conventional. Real imports from this exporter are higher if domestic demand is stronger, if the exporters' prices are lower, if the exchange rate is stronger (for the importer), and if overall domestic prices are higher.

Imports from the rest of the world are similar in spirit, but are all assumed to be dollar-denominated from the start:

$$\frac{IMMNDP_{ri}}{POIL} = f(DD_i, \frac{POIL}{PDD_i}, \frac{POIL}{PDD_i}(lagged)) \tag{4.10}$$

where:

$IMMNDP_{ri}$ = DOT-basis petroleum imports into country i from the rest of the world
$POIL$ = average crude oil price

and

$$\frac{IMMNDO_{ir}}{PEXWIND} = f(DD_i, \frac{PEXWIND}{PDD_i}, \frac{PEXWIND}{PDD_i}(lagged)) \tag{4.11}$$

where:

$IMMNDP_{ir}$ = DOT-basis non-petroleum imports into country i from the rest of the World
$PEXWIND$ = non-petroleum price index for exports from industrial countries, excluding U.S. and Japan
DD_i = real domestic demand in country i
PDD_i = domestic price deflator for domestic demand

Thus, real non-petroleum imports from the rest of the world are a function of domestic demand and the relative price of foreign goods to domestic goods. Again, the signs are the usual ones.

A series of accounting-type bridging equations then convert these merchandise imports from DOT-basis concepts to national account concepts.

4.2.2 Invisible Imports

Imports of non-factor income services, IOS, are then calculated as a function of the nominal domestic gross national product:

(4.12) $$IOS = f(GNPN, IOS_{-1})$$

where:

IOS	=	nominal imports of non-factor income services
$GNPN$	=	nominal gross national product

As gross national product increases, a country's imports of general services increases.

Imports of factor income services, FAO, are specified like exports of factor income services, except that there is no exchange rate adjustment, because all transactions are by definition in the domestic currency:

(4.13) $$FAO = f(INRCB * KRPL, INRTB * KROL)$$

where:

FAO	=	nominal factor income imports
$INRCB$	=	domestic corporate bond yield
$KRPL$	=	stock of foreign private assets
$INRTB$	=	domestic government bond yield
$KROL$	=	stock of foreign official assets

If the stock of foreign assets–either private or official–goes up, or if the yield on either type of asset goes up, then the domestic country implicitly imports more factor income from abroad.

Total nominal imports are then defined in national terms by the following identity:

(4.14) $$IMIN_i = IMMIN_i + TRMO_i + IOS_i + FAO_i$$

where:

$IMIN_i$	=	total nominal imports into country i
$IMMIN_i$	=	non-military merchandise imports into country i
$TRMO_i$	=	military imports into country i
IOS_i	=	non-factor income service imports into country i
FAO_i	=	factor income service imports into country i

Again, Japan's trade accounts do not have any breakdown for military merchandise, so this term does not appear in its identity. Bridging equations then convert this import total to necessary national real total import concepts.

4.3 Trade Prices

There are three key price variables in the model–the export price indices for the three trade blocks. When these variables are compared to each other, and relative to domestic prices, they determine the underlying competitiveness of each block and help explain exports. Easiest to explain is the merchandise goods export price index for the rest of the world trade block:

(4.15) $PEXMR = f(POIL, PEXWIND)$

where:

$PEXMR$	=	export price index, merchandise goods (rest of the world)
$POIL$	=	average crude oil price
$PEXWIND$	=	export price index of non-petroleum goods from industrial countries

Both of these right-hand-side terms–the oil price and industrial countries export prices are exogenous in the model.

Export prices for the United States and Japan are endogenously determined. They are a function of two key factors: the level of domestic inflation, and a constructed price index that might be called "competitors' export prices facing the domestic exporters". This says that domestic exporters do not set prices purely in a vacuum, looking only at domestic pricing factors, but that they are aware of international price competition, and will do their best to compete in world markets. The general export price index can be specified as:

(4.16) $PEXM_i = f(PDD_i, PEXWC_i, PEXM_i(lagged))$

where:

$PEXM_i$	=	export price index of merchandise goods for country i
PDD_i	=	price deflator for domestic activity in country i
$PEXWC_i$	=	weighted average of competitors' export price facing country i

and:

(4.17) $PEXWC_i = f(WC_{ji} * (\frac{PEXM_j}{RATE_j}) + WC_{ri} * PEXMR)$

where:

WC_{ji}	=	export price weight for country j in country i's export prices
$PEXC_j$	=	export price index for country j
$RATE$	=	exchange rate
WC_{ri}	=	export price weight for rest of world in country i's export prices
$PEXMR$	=	export price index, merchandise goods (rest of world)

Therefore, as domestic inflation increases, a country's exports would get more expensive, and hence less competitive in world markets. But as competitors' export prices go down relative to domestic export prices, there will be some tendency for the domestic producers to lower prices somewhat to stay competitive, and so the overall loss of competitiveness will be partially offset. Indeed, especially in the case of Japan in the period from 1985 to 1990 this seems to have happened. Japanese firms sacrificed profit margins on exports in order to remain competitive in overseas markets.

4.4 The Rest of the World GDP

In the model, we have endogenized the rest of the world GDP function in order to take the repercussion of the world economy (excluding Japan and the United States) into consideration. The rest of the world GDP can be specified as:

(4.18) $$GDPROW = f(GDPROW(lagged), EXMNDR, IMMNDR)$$

where:

$GDPROW$ = rest of the world GDP
$EXMNDR$ = rest of the world exports
$IMMNDR$ = rest of the world imports

5 Remarks

This chapter was written based on our activity as of 1991. Now ICSEAD LINK model consists of Japan, USA, Taiwan, South Korea, China, EC, ROW models and a trade linkage model. The trade linkage model plays a role of interface linking these countries and regions. As still described, Japan and U.S. models are full-fledged core model but Taiwan, South Korea, China, EC models are very simple and composed of only

(1) GNP/GDP components in nominal and real bloc,
(2) production and employment bloc, and
(3) deflators bloc.

In addition, Japan model has a top down regional model with which we can grasp impacts of foreign shocks on regional economy.

References

[1] Klein, L. R., L. J. Lau, Shen Lisheng, Xu Leilei (1990) "Quadrilateral Trading Patterns: China-Japan-USA and Rest of the World," mimeo.

[2] Inada, Y. and K. Fujikawa (1993) "Outline of ICSEAD's Japan Model," ICSEAD Working Paper Series (A) No.93-1, January

[3] Inada, Y. and K. Fujikawa (1993) "Outline of ICSEAD's Trade Linkage Model and Simulation," ICSEAD Working Paper Series (A) No.93-2, January

[4] Inada, Y. and K. Fujikawa (1993) "Outline of ICSEAD's U.S. Model," ICSEAD's Working Paper (A) No.93-3, June

[5] Inada, Y. and K. Fujukawa (1993) "Development and Application of ICSEAD World Link Model – Empirical Analysis of Impact of a Free Trade Area –," ICSEAD Working Paper Series (A) No.93-4, June

Chapter 3

Economy of China: 1969–1989 A Macro–Econometric Model (CMD90)[1]

Tang Guoxing

1 Introduction

1.1 The Economy of China

The Economy of China has been growing at a high rate of about 8.1% in the past two decades. This represents 2.5 points more than in the two decades prior to 1970. Since 1979, the economic reform and open policies were implemented, the economy has been growing particularly much faster and the labor productivity improved, due to the progressive introduction of the market mechanism.

In the countryside, the reform of productive organizations, the price system and the form of distribution increased the supply of agricultural goods.

The figures for agricultural growth rate has reached 5.9% between 1979 and 1989, which is 2.6 points higher than between 1970 and 1978. The promotion of efficiency in agriculture has resulted into a shift of the labor force from the agricultural sector to other industrial sectors of rural areas.

Therefore, the rural industry has seen a rapid development. The share of agriculture in the rural gross output, 68.6% in 1978, has significantly declined in the past ten years, it became less than 50% in 1987 and reached 45.1% in 1989. In the countryside, important changes in the industrial structure have become a relevant reason to make the farmers' income level rapidly go upwards.

Also the farmers increasing demands for commodities became strong pulling force for the market. As for the industrial sector, its pattern of growth was based on fixed investments reserved previously to the heavy industry before 1979. The growing of the heavy industry had indeed far exceeded that of the light industry.

Due to this development strategy the fixed investment rose rapidly by 11.4%, but the consumption rose only by 4.9% between 1970 and 1978, the shortage of the consumer goods was very serious during that long period. Since 1979 the government has paid more attention in raising people's standards of living. This is how the industry of consumer goods developed faster and we can note a reverse pattern as for the growth rate of heavy versus light industry(Table 1).

[1]This research is supported by Natural Sceince Fundation of China. Fudan University, People's Republic of China

Table 1. Outlook of China's Economy through different time periods
(Average annual increase rate %)

Item	1953–1969	1970–1978	1979–1989
Agriculture	2.38	3.30	5.92
Industry	11.13	11.93	12.39
Light industry	9.05	9.72	14.33
Heavy industry	13.85	13.69	10.70
Construction	9.18	9.34	9.03
Transport	7.39	8.48	10.43
Commerce	3.78	6.93	8.89
National income	5.26	7.37	8.69
Consumption	4.25	4.92	8.90
Fixed accumulation	10.14	11.38	6.72
Total exports&imports	4.39	19.9	16.6
Retail price index	0.97	0.34	6.07

Foreign trade had increased by the rate of about 18% from 1970 to 1989, which exceeds the growth rate of the national income during the same period as shown in table 1.

After 1979, however, the balance between imports and exports has been disturbed by excessive import demands and the trade deficits reached progressively 47 billion U.S.dollars in eleven years from 1979 to 1989. The impact of progressively negative balance of payments has been greatly alleviated by introduction of foreign capitals including foreign loans and foreigndirect investment, which amounts to about 57.8 billion U.S. dollars between 1979 and 1989.

Due to the fast increase of money supply, prices grew on them in the past ten years, particularly food prices went up by 23% in 1988. Tight policies were implemented about one year ago and have, as a result effectively relaxed high inflation, but the economic benefits have represented remarkable decline.

As an objective, the government plans to maintain the economic growth at a rate of 7–8% until year 2000. The problem remains in agriculture. It has been noted that agricultural growth has been showing a trend of slowdown, so that agriculture will again call for attention.

1.2 Statistical Data

The account of national income in China follows MPS (Material Product System), in which the total output value of the material production sectors, including agriculture, industry, construction, transport & communication and commerce, constitute the Total Gross Output Value (TGO), and the value added comes to the National Income(NI). It is taken as one of the main economic indicators today.

GNP is also published by the State Statistical Bureau from 1985. There is a good statistical relationship between GNP and NI shown as the following estimation:

$$\log GNP = -0.09 + 1.0337 * \log NI$$

(-1.8) (178.03)

R^2=0.9997 (1978-1989)

where GNP and NI are all at 1980's price.

The data on the trade are the statistics from the Foreign Trade Ministry (FTM) and the customs office. But the data from the latter is available on 1980 and after. There exsist differences between these two statistics, which particularly become notable since 1983 due perhaps to the increase of the joint ventures.

The statistics of the balance of payments are available from 1982, which have been published by the People's Bank of China since 1985.

Price indices currently published basically have some relation with the retail price of goods and services. Therefore, many price deflators need to be estimated in another way. For example, the deflator for consumption (PC) is estimated by

$$PC = \frac{C}{IC} * \frac{IC_{1970}}{C_{1970}}$$

(1970=100)

where C is consumption at current price and IC is the index of consumption.

The price indices of imports and exports can be obtained from the FTM statistics but can not be classified.

Because debts, foreign loans and repayments are included in the financial revenues and expenditures, the published figures of deficits are more less than the actual.

Regarding the money and the bank's credit we can use the state banks sheets and the data of deposits and loans of rural credit cooperatives. The main tools of the People's Bank of China to control the money supply are the interests and the amount of loans.

2 Structure of the Model

2.1 Framework of the Model

CMD90 is an annual model, in which the production functions of agriculture and industry are the central parts. The framework of the model is similar to that early published [1][2][3], but the money sector and the sector of balance of payments are implemented and the price sector is processed to be more detailed.

Although outputs are determined by the production factors in the long–term Chinese economy, it however ,may be observed that there exist remarkable fluctuations in the short–term, which are strongly depending on the demand situations, except agriculture.

The national income, which is composed of the value added of five material production sectors, is considered as a main development indicator. It is classified into personal incomes, retaining of enterprises and government revenue, all of which become the income factors variously affecting final demand.

The final demand is differenciated to consumptions (household consumption, CH and social consumption, CS), accumulations (fixed, AFC and circulating, ACC) and net export, EX—IM. Here consumption and accumulation make available national income, NIU. Considering the balance between the total added value and the final expenditure, the circulating accumulation, which is nearly equivalent to inventory in SNA, is determined as a residual in the model as follows

$$ACC = NI - (CH + CS + AFC + EX - IM) + ER$$

where ER is statistical error.

The purpose of the model is for the annual forecasting as well as for the analysis of the effects of the policies of public expenditure, money supply, price, and so on. The main exogenous variables are classified to the groups as follows

Public finance

Q1	share of expenditure on capital construction in financial expenditure
Q7	share of expenditure for supporting agriculture in financial expenditure
QSW	share of expenditure on education, culture, welfare in financialexpenditure
QD	share of expenditure on defense in financial expenditure
QAD	share of administrative expenditure in financial expenditure
QO	ratio of extrabudgetary receipts to financial revenue
RDB	debts and borrowings

Money

R1	one year interest
LOANA	agricultural loan
LOANE	loan for fixed investment
LOAN	amount of loans

Domestic price and exchange rate

REXCN	exchange rate of RMB to U.S. Dollar
PIA	purchasing price index of farm products
PGRN	purchasing price of grain
PCF	price of chemical fertilizer

World trade

EXW	total world exports in value
POIL	price of petroleum
PEF	unit value index of world food exports
PEWM	unit value index of world exports of manufactures
PIMGR	import price of grain

Others

PT	population
LW	number of staff and workers
ADD	disaster affected area
RSAGRN	share of grain sown area

The interrelationship of the variables and blocks are shown in following Diagram 1.

2.2 Production

Agriculture is important in Chinese economy in the sense of its large labor share of about 60% as well as its net output share of over 30%.

The factors affecting the agriculture as may be considered follows: (a)production factors like sown area, labor, fixed capital stock, (b)techniques like the use of chemical fertilizer, pesticide, electricity, irrigation facility, and so on. (c)improvement of breeds and adjustment of crops structure, (d)weather condition, and (e)price of agricultural products.

The effects by the above factors show the notable diferences between before and after 1979. This is the year that the economic reform in the rural areas started, that is the influences of "hard factors" became weaker than before and the effect of the "soft factors" such as the price of farm goods and the change of inner structure of agricultural sector was remarkably improved. The effect by the reform is shown in Table 2.

There exists a glut of labor force in the rural area of China, so it may not be considered that the labor force would be a factor to contain the growth of Agriculture but only a reservoir of labor force for the industrial sector.

The production function of agriculture depends on the farming machines used (KFM), chemical fertilizer consumed(CF), area affected by disaster(ADD), relative price of grain to chemical fertilizer(RGNCF) and time trend (TIME) respecting the improvement of other factors as the explanatory variables. Meanwhile sown area was neglected because of its very small change in the sample period.

Diargm 1.   Flowchart of the Model

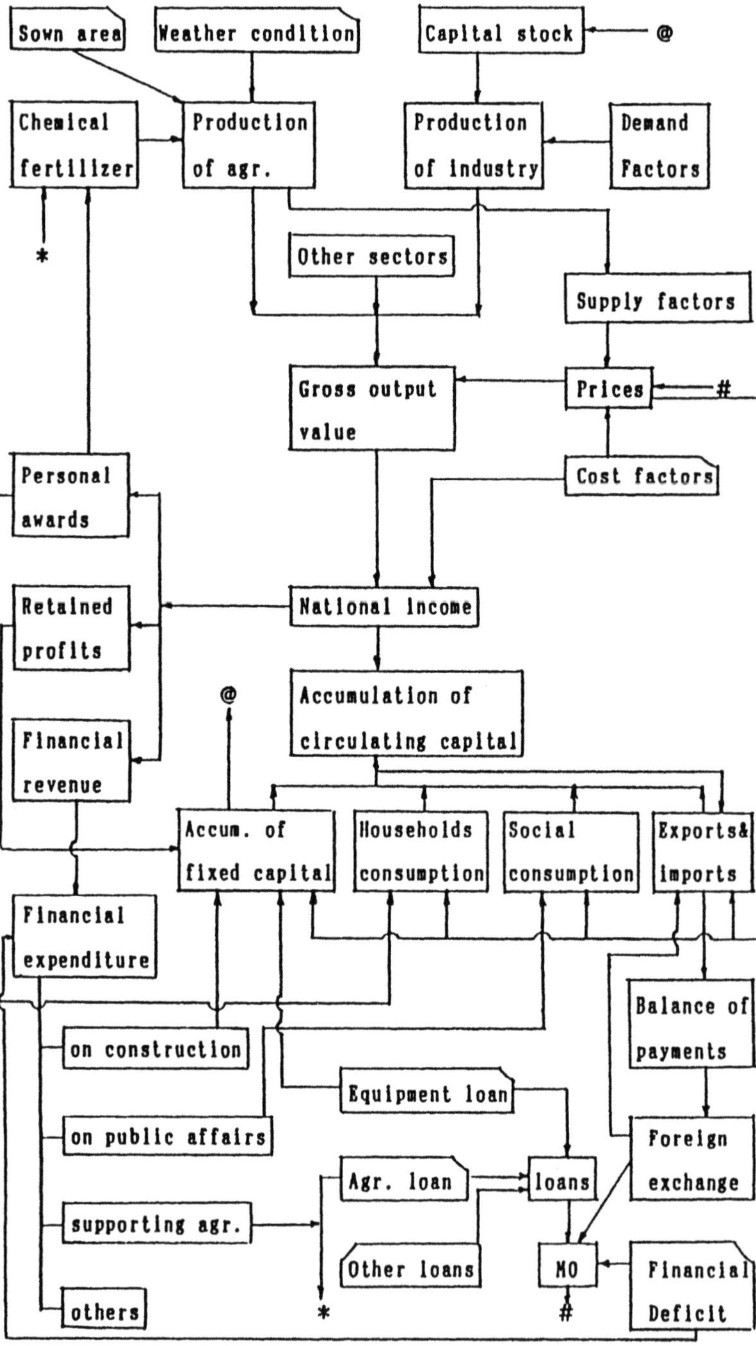

Table 2. Comparison of factors of agricultural growth

(Average increase rate %)

	Output and Factors	1970–1978	1979–1989
	Gross Output of Agr.	3.88	6.19
F	Labor Force	0.50	1.46
a	Farm Machinery	22.32	8.24
c	Sown Area	0.70	-0.22
t	Irrigated Area	2.40	-0.00
o	Fertilizer Input	13.95	9.33
r	Disaster Affected Area* (in average, million hectares)	11.20	19.90
	Price of Farm Products	1.22	9.86
	Proportion of Farming* (in average, %)	77.1	65.8

* not increase rate

Industrial production is under control of capital stock in long–term but varies according to the change of demands.

It is known that there existed cycles of about 5–6 years in the fluctuation of industrial production and the fixed investment before 1979.

However, two features have been shown in the industrial growth after 1979, one is the pace down of the growth in light and havy industry and another is very fast growing of the countryside industry, which is coming up mainly according to the market principles.

The production function of industry is specified as

$$IGI = f(K, \delta)$$

where K is the real capital stock and δ represents the factors of short term change such as fixed investment, retail sales, exports, circulating funds supplied by banks, price, and so on.

The missing of labor force is due to considering the existance of hidden unemployment and supposing that the real participation of labor force is dependent on above shortterm factors.

2.3 Final Demands

The classification of Consumption and its composition in 1989 are as follows.

The ratio of self–sufficiency of consumption has greatly decreased, from 60% of 1978 to 31% of 1989. It may be shown that there exists a large difference in consumption between peasant and non–peasant and that the non–peasant households have greatly increased their expenditure on the durable goods while the peasant households on the housing.

Let us suppose the self-sufficient part of consumption depends on the net output of agriculture(NIAR) while the commodity consumption on the money income(YP), which is obtained by selling the farm products.

Retail price index of industrial products in rural areas(PIR), also affect the peasant consumption (index) function. Thus,

$$ICHP = f(NIAR, YP, PIR)$$

The source of income of non–peasant households is mainly the wage, although the self–employed income has been fast increasing in recent years. Suppose the non–peasant consumption is specified according to the theory of consumption custom as follows

$$ICHNP = f(\frac{YW}{PIU}, ICHNP_{-1})$$

Capital accumulation is defined as investment minus depreciation and divided into the accumulation of fixed capital(AFC) and the accumulation of circulating capital(ACC). The accumulation of fixed capital is formed with the investment carried out by the state–owned and collective owned units and the personal housing construction mainly in rural areas.

The composition of investments by the form of ownership in recent years is shown in Table 3. It may be realized from the table that the share of state–owned investment is gradually decreasing although occupying more than 60% yet.

The function of capital fixed accumulation function is a statistical equation such as

$$AFC = f(IFS, YP - YP_{-1}, GIN - GIN_{-1})$$

where IFS is investment of state-owned units,$YP - YP_{-1}$ is used to explain added personal investment in housing in the rural area and $GIN - GIN_{-1}$ is applied to reflect the influence of economic growth on the behaviour of investor.

The state–owned investment is divided into the investment in capital construction (ICC) and the investment in renovation (IR), whose sources are the financial allocation, bank loarns for investment with foreign capital and retained profits.

As mentioned below, the circulating accumulation is considered as a residual of income minus other expenditures.

Table 3. Shares of investment by forms of ownership

	Total Value	Composition (%)		
Period	(billion yuan)	State-owned	Collective	Personal
1981	96.1	69.5	12.0	18.0
1982	123.0	68.7	14.2	17.1
1983	143.0	66.6	10.9	22.5
1984	183.2	64.7	13.0	22.3
1985	254.3	66.1	12.9	21.0
1986	301.9	65.5	13.0	21.5
1987	364.0	63.1	15.0	21.9
1988	449.6	61.4	15.8	22.7
1989	413.7	61.3	13.8	24.9

Source: Statistical Yearbook of China, 1981–1990

2.4 Public Finance and Money

Government Revenue includes profits from state–owned enterprises, taxes from industries and commerce, tariff, agricultural tax, debts and foreign borrowings. The reforming of public finance, such as increase the retained profits of state–owned enterprises since 1984, has resulted the role of public finance gradually weaken. Therefore, the extra budgetary revenue, mainly consisting of retained profits and depreciation funds, was fast increasing.

The amount of the profit from state–owned enterpries and the taxes from industries and commerce (REV1), which occupy the major part of the revenue, is specified as follows

$$REV1 = f(+NII, +PIS, -PIA, +EEC1)$$

where NII is added value of industry, and PIS is price index of retail sales. PIA, purchasing price index of farm goods, is used to reflect price subsidies for purchasing farm products. EEC1, financial allocation for capital construction, is a variable to illustrate the force of administrative control.

The expenditure is differentiated into that on the economic construction including the capital construction (EEC1), renovation, supporting agriculture (EEC7), and the public affairs such as education(ESW), defence (ED), administration (EAD). Their shares in expenditure are considered as the exogenous variables in the model.

The balance sheet of national banks is shown in Table 4. According to the differences of liquidity we define

M0	=	Currency in circulation
M1	=	Deposits of enterprises, government agencies and organization
	=	M2 - (KSR+KSH)

after considering no cheque is available in personal deposits accounts and neglecting the balance of foreign accounts, and

$$M2 = LOAN + FEX + (LOANG - DEPG) - FUNDB$$

M0 is strongly dependent on M1 and the inflation rate, and M1 is relating to M2 and one year interest, so that the money may be controlled by the amount of loans and the interest.

Table 4. Balance Sheet of National Banks

	Sources (Liabilities)		Applications (Assets)
1.	Domestic deposits Enterprises deposits Budgetary deposits(DEPG) Deposits of government agencies and organizations Urban savings deposits(KSU) Rural savings deposits(KSR)	1.	Domestic Loans(LOAN) Loans to Industrial Productive enterprises(LOANI) Loans to industrial supply and material supply dept. Commercial loans(LOANC) Loans to agriculture (LOANA) Equipment loans(LOANE)
2.	Deposits of international monetary institutions	2.	Foreign exchange(FEX)
3.	Currency in circulation(M0)	3.	Claims on government (LOANG)
4.	Funds of banks(FUNDB)	4.	Gold
5.	Current balance of profit and loss accounts	5.	Assets in IMF
6.	Others		

2.5 Prices and Wage

Published price indices are as follows

PIS	General retail price index
PIU	General price index of living cost of staff and workers
PIR	General retail price index of industrial products in rural areas
PIA	General purchasing price index of farm and sideline products (printed in Statistical Yearbook of China) and
PEX	Price index of exports
PIM	Price index of imports (printed in Almanac of China's Foreign Economic Relations

Retail goods include consumer goods and means of agricultural production, where prices are represended by PICG and PAPM respectively.

Consumer goods price is dependent on (a) supply factors, mainly the supply of agricultural goods, (b) cost factors, such as PIA, (c)demand factor,reflected by M0, and is specified as follows

$$PICG = (-IGA, +MO, +MO_{-1}, +PIA, +PIA_{-1})$$

The price of means of agricultural production is in great deal controlled by government, and can be considered to be statistically relating to the price of chemical fertilizer(PCF), because it holds a large share in the sales of means of agricultural production.

2.6 Foreign Trade and Balance of Payments

Imports are classified into following items according to the FTM statistics

IMME	machinary and equipment
IMMI	raw and intermediate materials for industrial use
IMMA	raw and intermediate materials for agricultural use
IMNGR	non–grain consumer goods
IMGR	grain

and exports are

EXAP	agricultural and sideline products
EXTA	textile products
EXLP	other light industrial products
EXHP	heavy industrial products

We have considered that the imports are dependent on (a) domestic demands, (b)import prices, (c)exchange rate (REXCN), (d)foreign exchange stock of government (KFXG) and (e)ability of import substitution, which is represented by lags of RIMEQ, the ratio of equipment imports value to investment on capital construction, defined as follows

$$RIMEQ = \frac{IMME * REXCN}{ICC} * 100$$

Following factors are considered as the explanatory variables of the export functions: (a) world exports,(b) prices, (c)exchange rate and (d)abilities of supply, represented by agricultural output index (IGA) in the case of EXAP and by lags of RIMEQ in other cases.

The converting from total imports and exports of FTM to that of the customs is made by statistical equations, while the difference between two statistics is considered to be partly introduced by differencial accounts for the import and export goods of joint ventures, where values are supposed to be relating to the accumulative direct investment (KDI).

Because only small sample data from 1982 to 1988 are available, modelling the balance of payments is difficult. In the model two statistical equations are estimated for the merchandise trade balance and the services trade balance, and capital accounts are considered exogenously, about which we have presented more detailed discussions in [4].

3 Simulation

The structural equations were estimated by OLS within the sample period 1970–1989, except ones relating to the foreign trade and the balance of payments. The model was simulated(final test) for the period of 1980–1988, within which the data of allvariables are available. Table 5 shows the results of final test for main variables and Table 6 shows detailed results for some important indicators.

From Table 5 we find that the average rate of errors rates for IGA, IGI and INI, the variables relating to production, as well as for price vairiables are all about 1%. The error rates about exports, government revenue, and money are from 2% to 5%. The variables which average error rate is about 5–10% are those relating to the investment and the imports. The results of final test for balance of payments are poor, particularly for the services balance SB.

Table 5. Results of final test for main variables (1980-1988)

Variable	CORR.	A.E.R	R.M.S.R.
DGA	0.9759	0.2834	0.4213
DGI	0.9206	0.1794	0.2199
DNI	0.8914	0.1184	0.1589
IGA	0.9972	0.0143	0.0180
GRAIN	0.9931	0.0132	0.0170
IGI	0.9994	0.0118	0.0143
IGT	0.9986	0.0133	0.0183
IGCN	0.9870	0.0460	0.0564
IGCM	0.9961	0.0277	0.0379
INI	0.9993	0.0099	0.0124
NI	0.9995	0.0124	0.0160
NIU	0.9990	0.0194	0.0246
ICHP	0.9972	0.0138	0.0171
ICHNP	0.9993	0.0092	0.0119
ICS	0.9960	0.0537	0.0593
IAFC	0.9824	0.0637	0.0750
IACC	0.6668	0.1728	0.2181
EXDOL	0.9980	0.0265	0.0310
IMDOL	0.9773	0.0819	0.0998
YP	0.9985	0.0229	0.0296
YW	0.9989	0.0177	0.0217
W	0.9983	0.0171	0.0206
PLV80	0.9958	0.0159	0.0187
LIN	0.9963	0.0108	0.0126
PIS	0.9980	0.0105	0.0121
CF	0.9975	0.0270	0.0325
FM	0.9443	0.1472	0.1881
IFS	0.9935	0.0546	0.0773
ICC	0.9948	0.0463	0.0656
IR	0.9868	0.0953	0.1211
FIR	0.9869	0.0719	0.0943
REV	0.9956	0.0279	0.0327
MO	0.9958	0.0463	0.0571
SALE	0.9995	0.0099	0.0120
FSPP	0.9963	0.0346	0.0420
TB	0.8465	45.4822	134.6460
SB	0.3665	0.3893	0.6620
KFX	0.8905	0.4406	0.5334

CORR. = Correlation coefficient of Y and Y^P

A.E.R. = $1/n * \sum \left|(Y - Y^P)/Y\right|$

R.M.S.R. = $(1/n * \sum((Y - Y^P)/Y)^2)^{1/2}$

Y = Actual

Y^P = Predicted

Table 6. Detailed results of final test for important variables

IGA

Period	Actual	Predicted	Error	Rate%
1980	217.9	214.67	3.23	1.48
1981	230.5	230.78	-0.28	-0.12
1982	256.5	260.91	-4.40	-1.72
1983	276.5	285.04	-8.53	-3.08
1984	310.4	320.80	-10.40	-3.35
1985	321.0	325.39	-4.38	-1.37
1986	331.8	335.36	-3.56	-1.07
1987	351.0	352.66	-1.66	-0.47
1988	364.9	365.72	-0.82	-0.23

IGI

Period	Actual	Predicted	Error	Rate%
1980	1972.3	1972.0	0.26	0.01
1981	2057.1	2093.4	-36.31	-1.76
1982	2217.7	2219.2	-1.46	-0.07
1983	2465.8	2521.7	-55.89	-2.27
1984	2867.3	2912.6	-45.25	-1.58
1985	3480.7	3426.0	54.75	1.57
1986	3886.8	3948.4	-61.57	-1.58
1987	4574.5	4571.0	3.49	0.08
1988	5525.4	5433.4	92.00	1.67

INI

Period	Actual	Predicted	Error	Rate%
1980	516.3	512.75	3.54	0.69
1981	541.4	546.72	-5.32	-0.98
1982	585.8	593.78	-7.98	-1.36
1983	644.2	659.72	-15.52	-2.41
1984	731.9	746.15	-14.26	-1.95
1985	830.6	823.42	7.18	0.86
1986	894.5	893.13	1.37	0.15
1987	985.7	985.43	0.27	0.02
1988	1097.2	1092.25	4.95	0.45

IC

Period	Actual	Predicted	Error	Rate%
1980	380.8	386.1	-5.27	-1.38
1981	411.0	412.1	-1.08	-0.26
1982	441.4	445.1	-3.70	-0.84
1983	479.2	490.4	-11.24	-2.34
1984	547.4	562.7	-15.27	-2.79
1985	633.8	624.5	9.26	1.46
1986	682.9	678.7	4.22	0.62
1987	737.5	729.7	7.76	1.05
1988	798.7	779.6	19.14	2.40

IAFC

Period	Actual	Predicted	Error	Rate%
1980	1476.9	1372.9	104.0	7.04
1981	1247.0	1309.6	-62.6	-5.02
1982	1518.2	1285.6	232.6	15.32
1983	1720.1	1762.4	-42.3	-2.46
1984	2134.7	2346.0	-211.3	-9.90
1985	2623.5	2755.3	-131.8	-5.02
1986	2858.6	2890.5	-31.9	-1.11
1987	3311.4	3103.5	207.9	6.27
1988	2582.8	3396.7	186.2	5.20

ACC

Period	Actual	Predicted	Error	Rate%
1980	272.0	272.9	-0.94	-0.34
1981	328.0	256.5	71.54	21.81
1982	267.0	381.1	-114.06	-42.72
1983	296.0	383.8	-87.82	-29.67
1984	343.0	375.9	-32.90	-9.59
1985	745.0	535.6	209.44	28.11
1986	748.0	687.2	60.80	8.13
1987	580.0	511.9	68.14	11.75
1988	871.0	900.9	-29.15	-3.43

EXDOL

Period	Actual	Predicted	Error	Rate%
1980	182.7	179.01	3.69	2.02
1981	220.1	207.21	12.89	5.86
1982	223.2	218.96	4.24	1.90
1983	222.3	226.56	-4.26	-1.92
1984	261.4	252.82	8.58	3.28
1985	273.5	272.86	0.64	0.23
1986	309.4	314.63	-5.23	-1.69
1987	394.4	413.00	-18.60	-4.72
1988	475.2	485.90	-10.70	-2.25

IMDOL

Period	Actual	Predicted	Error	Rate%
1980	195.5	205.9	-10.4	-5.32
1981	220.1	200.9	19.2	8.72
1982	192.8	161.0	31.8	16.50
1983	213.9	229.1	-15.2	-7.09
1984	274.1	326.7	-52.6	-19.17
1985	422.5	418.4	4.1	0.96
1986	429.1	418.4	10.7	2.49
1987	432.1	409.5	22.6	5.22
1988	552.7	507.2	45.5	8.24

W

Period	Actual	Predicted	Error	Rate%
1980	762	764.3	-2.26	-0.30
1981	772	799.6	-27.55	-3.57
1982	798	795.7	2.30	0.29
1983	826	835.3	-9.54	-1.15
1984	974	939.5	34.51	3.54
1985	1148	1130.3	17.70	1.54
1986	1329	1298.6	30.38	2.29
1987	1459	1477.2	-18.23	-1.25
1988	1747	1721.3	25.75	1.47

PIS

Period	Actual	Predicted	Error	Rate%
1980	146.9	147.4	-0.46	-0.31
1981	150.4	152.0	-1.60	-1.06
1982	153.3	152.6	0.68	0.44
1983	155.6	153.0	2.62	1.68
1984	160.0	157.9	2.06	1.29
1985	174.1	172.2	1.94	1.12
1986	184.5	184.1	0.39	0.21
1987	198.0	202.2	-4.18	-2.11
1988	234.6	237.5	-2.87	-1.23

REV

Period	Actual	Predicted	Error	Rate%
1980	1085.2	1106.0	-20.8	-1.92
1981	1089.6	1111.5	-21.9	-2.01
1982	1124.0	1127.1	-3.1	-0.27
1983	1249.0	1295.1	-46.1	-3.69
1984	1501.9	1543.5	-41.6	-2.77
1985	1866.4	1771.7	94.7	5.07
1986	2260.3	2130.4	129.9	5.74
1987	2368.9	2302.0	66.9	2.83
1988	2628.0	2648.8	-20.8	-0.79

MO

Period	Actual	Predicted	Error	Rate%
1980	346.20	375.29	-29.09	-8.40
1981	396.34	422.22	-25.88	-6.53
1982	439.12	442.31	-3.20	-0.73
1983	529.78	492.20	37.58	7.09
1984	792.11	758.71	33.40	4.22
1985	987.83	983.10	4.72	0.48
1986	1218.36	1253.31	-34.95	-2.87
1987	1454.48	1600.91	-146.42	-10.06
1988	2134.03	2107.42	26.60	1.24

References

[1] C.Moriguchi and Tang Guoxing (1984) "An econometric model of PRC," LINK Project meeting, Stanford University, Aug.

[2] Tang Guoxing (1984) "Long-term Multi-Sectoral Econometric Model of China," Quantitative & Technical Economics, NO. 10

[3] Tang Guoxing (1990) "Macro-Economic Model 1," the Development Research Centre of the State Council ed., *Economic Development and Econometric Model of China,* China: Finance & economy Press, pp. 60-87.

[4] Tang Guoxing (1988) "Opening to Foreign Investment and Economic Growth of China," Discussion Paper KIER 8801, Kyoto Institute of Economic Research

Appendix

A China Model System (CMD90)

Growth Rate of Agriculture

(1) $$DGA = -38.2913 + \underset{(6.92)}{0.568436} * DKFM + \underset{(11.7)}{0.30967} * DCF - \underset{(-4.18)}{0.0271569}$$

$$* DADD - \underset{(-6.82)}{6.12242E - 0.3} * ADD + \underset{(11.3)}{0.240208} * (0.6 * RGNCF_{-1}$$

$$+ 0.4 * RGNCF_{-2}) - \underset{(-4.72)}{4.9889} * DD83 + \underset{(9.00)}{1.2593} * TIME$$

RR = 0.946182 DW = 2.29745 SE = 0.8694 (1971 - 1989)

Growth Rate of Industry

(2) $$DGI = (\frac{IGI}{IGI_{-1}} - 1.0) * 100$$

Index of Agricultural Gross Output

(3) $$IGA = (1 + \frac{DGA}{100.0}) * IGA_{-1}$$

Output of Grain

(4) $$GRAIN = 165665 * IGA^{\underset{(14.7)}{0.937975}} * PGRN^{\underset{(2.18)}{0.127537}} * PGRN_{-1}^{\underset{(-2.29)}{-0.173952}}$$

$$* PCF^{\underset{(-6.13)}{-0.20517}} * RSAGRN^{\underset{(4.38)}{1.94199}}$$

RR = 0.989403 DW = 2.03191 SE = 0.0143577 (1970 – 1989)

Index of Industrial Gross Outoput

(5) $$IGI = 0.0109469(\frac{KFIR + KFIR_{-1}}{2})^{\underset{(10.2)}{0.602426}} * (\frac{IFS}{PAFC} * 100)^{\underset{(4.84)}{0.214621}}$$

$$* (\frac{SALE}{PIS} * 100)^{\underset{(2.49)}{0.21444}} * PIN^{\underset{(14.6)}{0.90865}} * DD76E^{\underset{(-3.6)}{0.0618}}$$

$$* DD74E^{\underset{(-4.3)}{-0.0740}}$$

RR = 0.999258 DW = 1.9559 SE = 0.0161182 (1970 – 1989)

Gross Output Value of Agriculture

$$(6) \quad GAG = \frac{IGA * PAG * 10.21}{157.8}$$

Gross Output Value of Industry

$$(7) \quad GIN = \frac{IGI * PIN * 21.17}{798.1}$$

Index of Gross Output of Transport

$$(8) \quad IGT = -22.8807 + \underset{(10.4)}{0.176917} * IGI + \underset{(9.75)}{1.28552} * IC$$

RR = 0.998428 DW = 2.3399 SE = 210.1503 (1969 – 1989)

Gross Output Value of Transport

$$(9) \quad GTR = \frac{IGT * PTR * 1.17}{400}$$

Index of Gross Output of Construction

$$(10) \quad IGCN = 3.1256\left(\frac{IFS}{PAFC} * 100\right)^{\underset{(4.21)}{0.353655}} * \left(\frac{YP}{PIR} * 100\right)^{\underset{(9.75)}{0.531236}}$$

RR = 0.995151 DW = 1.30407 SE = 0.03877 (1969 – 1989)

Gross Output Value of Construction

$$(11) \quad GCN = \frac{IGCN * PCN * 2.71}{543.9}$$

Index of Commercial Gross Output

$$(12) \quad IGCM = -22.5302 + \underset{(75.2)}{0.312973}\left(\frac{SALE}{PIS} * 100\right)$$

RR = 0.996655 DW = 1.05029 SE = 15.0414 (1969 – 1989)

Gross Output Value of Commerce

$$(13) \quad GCM = \frac{IGCM * PCM * 2.74}{210.4}$$

Growth Rate of National Income

(14) $DNI = (\frac{INI}{INI_{-1}} - 1) * 100$

Index of National Income

(15) $INI = 6.6174 * NI^{1.00895} * PAG^{-0.384457} * PIN^{-0.148323} * PTR^{-0.160287}$

(58.3) (-10.7) (-2.02) (-3.80)

$* PCM^{-0.139748}$

(-8.48)

RR = 0.999931 DW = 2.28899 SE = 3.62589E-03 (1969 – 1989)

Net Output Value of Agriculture

(16) $NIA = 1.47856 * GAG^{1.00132} * (CF * PAPM)^{-0.0640078}$

(42.4) (-3.60)

RR = 0.999416 DW = 1.3743 SE = 0.0137077 (1969 – 1989)

Net Output of Industry

(17) $NII = 0.0498312 * IGI^{0.907955} * PIN^{0.781546} * DD76E^{-0.05963}$

(105.0) (14.1) (-3.98)

RR = 0.999461 DW = 1.68986 SE = 0.0143795 (1969 – 1989)

Net Output Value of Construction

(18) $NICN = -7.69916 + 0.282288 * NICN_{-1} + 0.200629 * GCN$

(4.09) (12.5)

RR = 0.996874 DW = 1.18227 SE = 12.9533 (1970 – 1989)

Net Output Value of Transport

(19) $NIT = 68.146 + 0.640866 * GTR - 0.360731 * PIA_{-1}$

(29.0) (-5.92)

RR = 0.99840 DW = 1.70465 SE = 5.34834 (1970 – 1989)

Net Output Value of Commerce

(20) $NICM = 198.447 + 0.817371 * GCM - 1.21738 * PIA_{-1}$

(37.8) (-9.3)

RR = 0.997951 DW = 1.40935 SE = 16.2521 (1970 – 1989)

National Income

(21) $NI = NIA + NII + NICN + NIT + NICM$

Available National Income

(22) $NIU = NI - EX + IM - ER$

Index of Peasant Household Consumption

(23) $ICHP = 21.9523 * YP^{0.379164} * PIR^{-0.156815}$

(28.0) (-4.51)

$$* \left(\frac{0.7 * NIA + 0.3 * NIA_{-1}}{PIA}\right)^{0.494488}$$

(10.9)

RR = 0.999275 DW = 2.24719 SE = 0.01083 (1969 – 1989)

Peasant Consumption (Nominal)

(24) $$CHP = \frac{ICHP * PCHP * 7.70}{199.5}$$

Index of Non-Peasant Household Consumption

(25) $$ICHNP = 1.14932\left(\frac{YW}{PIU} * 100\right)^{0.525449} * ICHNP_{-1}^{0.450285}$$

$$* \left(\frac{PIU}{PIU_{-1}}\right)^{0.588474}$$

RR = 0.99938 DW = 2.11286 SE = 0.010735 (1970 – 1989)

Non–Peasant Consumption (Nominal)

(26) $$CHNP = \frac{ICHNP * PCHNP * 3.75}{239.5}$$

Hpusehold Consumption (Nominal)

(27) $CH = CHP + CHNP$

Index of Social Consumption

(28) $ICS = 66.6726 * (ESW + ED + EAD)^{0.822182} * PCS^{-1.32197} * ICS_{-1}^{0.545658}$

(8.81) (-9.37) (7.93)

RR = 0.998335 DW = 2.19299 SE = 0.0273089 (1970 – 1989)

Social Consumption (Nominal)

(29) $CS = \frac{ICS * PCS}{266.8} * 1.13$

Consumption Fund (Nominal)

(30) $C = CH + CS$

Index of Consumption

(31) $IC = -1.56857 + 0.674278 * ICHP + 0.274101 * ICHNP + 0.065937 * ICS$

(118.0) (59.0) (36.0)

RR = 0.999995 DW = 1.19723 SE = 0.459279 (1969 – 1989)

Index of Fixed Capital Accumulation

(32) $IAFC = \frac{AFC}{PAFC} * \frac{778}{4.19}$

Accumulation of Fixed Capital (Nominal)

(33) $AFC = 125.689 + 0.673891 * ICC + 1.47166 * IR + 0.184317 * (YP - YP_{-1})$

(5.10) (9.71) (2.31)

$+ 0.0586624 * (GIN - GIN_{-1})$

(2.22)

RR = 0.998466 DW = 1.59536 SE = 35.6249 (1970 – 1989)

Index of Circulating Capital Accumulation

(34) $IACC = \frac{ACC}{PACC} * \frac{306.5}{1.99}$

Accumulation of Circulating Capital

(35) $ACC = NIU - C - AFC$

Exports (Yuan)

(36) $EX = 1.10367 * EXDOL^{0.976103} * REXCN^{1.03209}$

$$\qquad\qquad (182.0) \qquad\qquad (60.3)$$

RR = 0.999673 DW = 2.21969 SE = 0.019972 (1969 – 1989)

Imports (Yuan)

(37) $IM = 0.998051 * IMDOL^{1.00195} * REXCN^{0.990144}$

$$\qquad\qquad (185.0) \qquad\qquad (52.1)$$

RR = 0.999673 DW = 1.16409 SE = 0.0218956 (1969 – 1989)

Exports (US$)

(38) $EXDOL = 0.685226 + 0.987178 * EXF + 0.6402 * KDI_{-1}$

$$\qquad\qquad (54.69) \qquad\qquad (10.0)$$

RR = 0.998987 DW = 2.62315 SE = 4.16693 (1978 – 1988)

Imports (US$)

(39) $IMDOL = -2.48148 + 1.02568 * IMF + 0.970512 * KDI$

$$\qquad\qquad (26.1) \qquad\qquad (8.849)$$

RR = 0.996801 DW = 2.66811 SE = 9.18282 (1978 – 1988)

Exports (US$, FTM)

(40) $EXF = EXAP + EXTP + EXLP + EXHP$

Exports of Agricultural Produsts (US$, FTM)

(41) $EXAP = 2.60518E - 03 * IGA^{0.84964} * REXCN^{0.421988}$

$$\qquad\qquad (3.53) \qquad\qquad (2.12)$$

$$* PEF^{1.03607}$$

$$(6.72)$$

RR = 0.969069 DW = 1.29846 SE = 0.10381 (1969 – 1988)

Exports of Textiles (US$, FTM)

$$(42)\quad EXTP = -35.068 + 2.13774E-03 * EXW + 14.5096 * REXCN$$

(12.7) (12.3)

$$+ 0.466891 * RIMEQ_{-3}$$

(2.80)

RR = 0.988947 DW = 1.87721 SE = 2.66688 (1972 – 1988)

Exports of Light Industrial Products (US$, FTM)

$$(43)\quad EXLP = -26.7533 + 2.36068E-03 * EXW + 9.20748 * REXCN$$

(9.31) (4.41)

$$+ 0.836932 * RIMEQ_{-2}$$

(3.38)

RR = 0.977547 DW = 1.01086 SE = 4.24105 (1971 – 1988)

Exports of Heavy Industrial Products (US$, FTM)

$$(44)\quad EXHP = -87.419 + 2.75466 * POIL + 32.1647 * REXCN$$

(15.2) (9.63)

$$+ 2.01783 * RIMEQ_{-3}$$

(5.81)

RR = 0.975389 DW = 1.5735 SE = 6.98651 (1972 – 1988)

Imports (US$, FTM)

$$(45)\quad IMF = IMME + IMMI + IMMA + IMSNG + IMGR$$

Imports of Equipments (US$, FTM)

$$(46)\quad MME = 54.5707 + 0.0891759 * IFS + 0.0201684 * IFS_{-1} + 0.376534$$

(4.76) (1.03) (6.10)

$$* KFXG_{-2} - 39.592 * REXCN - 3.28766 * RIMEQ_{-3}$$

(-6.84) (-8.23)

RR = 0.981822 DW = 2.48691 SE = 5.33633 (1972 – 1988)

Imports of Materials for Industrial Use (US$, FTM)

$$(47)\quad IMMI = 30.5629 + \underset{(17.7)}{0.0527935} * IGI - \underset{(-11.5)}{27.3887} * REXCN + \underset{(7.58)}{0.424627} * KFXG_{-2} - \underset{(-3.75)}{1.29879} * RIMEQ_{-2}$$

RR = 0.994795 DW = 2.68771 SE = 3.8679 (1972 – 1988)

Imports of Materials for Agricultural Use (US$)

$$(48)\quad IMMA = -5.90134 + \underset{(5.54)}{7.17E-03} * CF_{-1} + \underset{(3.79)}{0.117} * PEWM + \underset{(7.25)}{0.09886} * (EXF_{-1} - IMF_{-1})$$

RR = 0.950486 DW = 1.56636 SE = 1.58258 (1972 – 1988)

Imports of Non-Grain Consumer Goods (US$, FTM)

$$(49)\quad IMSNG = -8.94456 + \underset{(10.1)}{0.017316}(\frac{SALE}{PIS} * 100) + \underset{(4.43)}{1.28325} * DPIS - \underset{(-2.12)}{0.190964} * DPEWM$$

RR = 0.976748 DW = 2.60994 SE = 2.96027 (1972 – 1988)

Imports of Grain (US$, FTM)

$$(50)\quad IMGR = \frac{IMGRQ * PIMGR}{10000}$$

Quantum of Grain Imports

$$(51)\quad IMGRQ = -13829 - \underset{(-2.799)}{0.09327} * GRAIN_{-1} - \underset{(-3.19)}{0.109356} * GRAIN_{-2} + \underset{(7.07)}{0.206419} * PT + \underset{(4.11)}{682.408}\frac{\frac{PGRN_{-1}}{REXCN_{-1}}}{PIMGR_{-1}}$$

RR = 0.832295 DW = 2.04991 SE = 187.896 (1975 – 1988)

Monetary Income of Peasants

$$(52)\quad YP = -573.028 + 0.951506 * NIA + 0.0757141 * NII + 0.78566 * NICM$$

(15.0) (1.26) (6.76)

RR = 0.99936 DW = 1.74287 SE = 35.3306 (1969 – 1989)

Wage Bill of Staff and Workers

$$(53)\quad YW = 8.83294E - 05 * LW^{1.01492} * W^{0.994466}$$

(77.5) (124.0)

RR = 0.999879 DW = 0.926451 SE = 7.00615E-03 (1969 – 1989)

Wage Rate

$$(54)\quad W = -142.343 + 0.708805 * W_{-1} + 3.04551 * PIU - 5.24161$$

(4.94) (3.38) (-3.78)

$$* PIU_{-1} + 0.0324681 * PLV80 + 0.0488176 * PLV80_{-1}$$

(3.29) (3.48)

RR = 0.9977 DW = 3.21289 SE = 20.2017 (1970 – 1989)

Labor Productivity of Industry

$$(55)\quad PLV80 = 503.951 * PLV80_{-1}^{0.357735} * IGI^{0.992914}$$

(4.57) (19.1)

$$* IGI_{-1}^{-0.473907} * LIN^{-0.492882}$$

(-7.45) (-5.34)

RR = 0.998011 DW = 1.22724 SE = 0.01557 (1970 – 1989)

Number of Industrial Labor

$$(56)\quad LIN = 0.143135 * LW^{1.10892} * IFSR^{0.0759246} * DD76E^{0.0669675}$$

(27.5) (3.59) (4.11)

RR = 0.99746 DW = 1.02646 SE = 0.0155698 (1970 – 1989)

Deflator for Agricultural Gross Output

$$(57)\quad PAG = 0.721717 * \underset{(7.43)}{PIA^{0.543783}} * \underset{(2.86)}{PIA_{-1}^{0.212336}} * \underset{(3.61)}{W^{0.148813}}$$

RR = 0.998126 DW = 1.77748 SE = 0.0136424 (1970 – 1989)

Deflator for Industrial Gross Output

$$(58)\quad PIN = 1.35807 + \underset{(8.29)}{0.738997 * PIN_{-1}} + \underset{(7.81)}{0.24736 * PIS} - \underset{(-5.27)}{0.0436244 * PIA_{-1}}$$

RR = 0.998205 DW = 1.78861 SE =0.586441 (1970 – 1989)

Deflator for Construction Gross Output

$$(59)\quad PCN = 0.0893402 + \underset{(3.42)}{0.492325 * PCN_{-1}} + \underset{(4.21)}{0.347988 * PIS} + \underset{(6.27)}{0.0196456 * \frac{IFS}{PAFC} * 100}$$

RR = 0.998201 DW = 2.29129 SE = 1.48556 (1970 – 1989)

Deflator for Commercial Gross Output

$$(60)\quad PCM = -72.2465 + \underset{(14.1)}{2.14404 * PIS} - \underset{(-5.52)}{0.461253 * PIA} - \underset{(-2.40)}{0.172797 * PIA_{-1}} + \underset{(3.04)}{6.69257 * REXCN} + \underset{(3.95)}{0.100051 * IMDOL} - \underset{(-2.94)}{0.0855885 * IMDOL_{-1}}$$

RR = 0.983731 DW = 1.52428 SE = 3.35947 (1970 – 1989)

Deflator for Peasant Consumption

$$(61)\quad PCHP = 51.2525 + \underset{(4.7)}{0.128685 * PICG} + \underset{(10.4)}{0.113342 * PIA} + \underset{(6.1)}{0.014917 * W}$$

RR = 0.99914 DW = 1.68597 SE = 0.744773 (1969 – 1989)

Deflator for Non-Peasant Consumption

(62) $PCHNP = 13.2104 + 0.500696 * PICG + 0.027802 * W$

(10.6) (5.45)

RR = 0.997497 DW = 1.61031 SE = 1.71957 (1969 – 1989)

Deflator for Social Consumption

(63) $PCS = 61.6172 + 0.296254 * PICG - 8.24446E - 0.3 * (\frac{IFS}{PAFC} * 100)$

(53.0) (-13.0)

RR = 0.997303 DW = 1.75715 SE = 0.558477 (1969 – 1989)

Deflator for Accumulation of Fixed Capital

(64) $PAFC = 1.53583 * PIS^{0.561712} * PCN^{0.313282}$

(15.9) (9.89)

RR = 0.999058 DW = 1.94155 SE = 5.90527E-03 (1970 – 1989)

Rising Rate of Purchasing Price of Farm and Sideline Products

(65) $DPIA = (\frac{PIA}{PIA_{-1}} - 1) * 100$

Price Index of Retail Sales

(66) $PIS = 0.929814 * PICG^{0.72005} * PAPM^{0.300335}$

(50.8) (16.0)

RR = 0.999723 DW = 1.32676 SE = 3.53049E-03 (1969 – 1989)

Rate of Retail Price

(67) $DPIS = (\frac{PIS}{PIS_{-1}} - 1) * 100$

Price Index of Living Cost in Urban Areas

(68) $PIU = 10.3513 + 0.684768 * PIU_{-1} + 0.979355 * PICG$

(6.51) (17.9)

$- 0.817285 * PICG_{-1} + 0.01704 * W$

(-8.1) (5.2)

RR = 0.999518 DW = 2.42114 SE = 1.08577 (1970 – 1989)

Retail Price Index of Industrial Products in Rural Areas

(69) $PIR = -11.2169 + 0.817513 * PIN + 0.405897 * PAPM$

(3.36) (3.46)

RR = 0.989324 DW = 0.849835 SE = 1.85838 (1969 – 1989)

Retail Price Index of Consumer Goods

(70) $PICG = 99.8412 - 0.166414 * IGA + 0.0110877 * MO + 0.0266276$

(-6.5) (1.79) (3.77)

$* MO_{-1} + 0.221489 * PIA + 0.09920 * PIA_{-1} + 6.952 * DD78$

(5.52) (1.94) (3.32)

RR = 0.998194 DW = 1.91072 SE = 1.94881 (1970 – 1989)

Retail Price Index of Means of Agribultural Production

(71) $PAPM = -4.92647 + 0.116789 * PCF + 0.808983 * PIN$

(6.3) (4.0)

Chemical Fertilizer Applied

(72) $CF = -356485 + 0.966069 * CF_{-1} + 6.52931$

(45.1) (5.34)

$* (EEC7 - EEC7_{-1}) + 3.55 * RGNCF$

(4.7)

RR = 0.995224 DW = 1.6233 SE = 46.7166 (1970 – 1989)

Farm Machinary Increase

(73) $FM = 601.745 + 0.179858 * NIA_{-1} + 2.33439 * EEC7$

(4.67) (6.4)

$- 6.45098 * PAPM - 0.171565 * CF$

(-6.1) (-5.15)

RR = 0.820767 DW = 2.12131 SE = 18.2536 (1970 – 1989)

Stock of Farm Machinary

(74) $KFM = KFM_{-1} + FM$

Investment by State-Owned Units

$$(75) \quad IFS = ICC + IR$$

Real IFS

$$(76) \quad IFSR = \frac{IFS}{PAFC} * 100$$

Investment in Capital Construction

$$(77) \quad ICC = 823.395 + \underset{(4.99)}{0.61869 * ECC1} + \underset{(2.87)}{0.248568 * REVO_{-1}} + 0.455042$$

$$* LOANE + \underset{(4.57)}{17.9675 * DPIS} - \underset{(-3.18)}{6.81531 * PAFC}$$

RR = 0.995103 DW = 2.71846 SE = 29.8371 (1970 – 1989)

Investment in Renovation

$$(78) \quad IR = 1143.9 + \underset{(9.29)}{0.648979 * REVO_{-1}} + \underset{(2.79)}{0.254751 * LOANE}$$

$$- \underset{(-3.95)}{9.81674 * PAFC_{-1}} + \underset{(2.52)}{6.71452 * DPIS} - \underset{(-3.35)}{42.4824 * R1}$$

RR = 0.995133 DW = 1.65894 SE = 24.52 (1970 – 1989)

Formation of Industrial Fixed Capital

$$(79) \quad FI = -100.214 + \underset{(5.09)}{0.55245 * IFS_{-1}} + \underset{(1.19)}{0.161445 * IFS_{-2}}$$

$$+ \underset{(5.89)}{261.622 * DD85}$$

RR = 0.992665 DW = 1.8445 SE = 42.2163 (1971 – 1989)

Real FI

$$(80) \quad FIR = \frac{FI}{PAFC} * 100$$

Real Capital Stock in Industrial Sector

$$(81) \quad KFIR = KFIR_{-1} + FIR$$

Financial Expenditure

(82) $EXPE = REV - BG$

Financial Revenue

(83) $REV = REV1 + TAG + TAR + RDB$

REV-TAG-TAR-RDB

(84) $$REV1 = 0.345506 * \underset{(7.97)}{NII^{0.635136}} * \underset{(6.31)}{PIS_{-1}^{0.998632}}$$

$$* \underset{(-5.05)}{PIA^{-0.724258}} * \underset{(7.59)}{EEC1^{0.391704}}$$

RR = 0.995192 DW = 1.11946 SE = 0.0286 (1970 – 1989)

Agricultural Tax

(85) $$TAG = -1.66548 + \underset{(9.5)}{1.09144 * TAG_{-1}} + \underset{(5.14)}{0.0193343 * GAG}$$

$$- \underset{(-4.1)}{0.0198847 * GAG_{-1}} - \underset{(-1.6)}{1.88 * ADD}$$

RR = 0.979261 DW = 2.68418 SE = 2.2301 (1970 – 1989)

Tariff

(86) $$TAR = -174.873 + \underset{(5.76)}{0.855766 * IMMI} + \underset{(4.45)}{2.5363 * IMSNG} + \underset{(8.12)}{71.78}$$

$$* REXCN - \underset{(-6.77)}{1.805 * KDI}$$

RR = 0.976846 DW = 1.42755 SE = 9.41308 (1970 – 1989)

Financial Expenditure on Capital Construction

(87) $$EEC1 = \frac{Q1 * EXPE}{100}$$

Financial Expenditure for Supporting Agriculture

(88) $$EEC7 = \frac{Q7 * EXPE}{100}$$

Financial Expenditure on Culture, Education, Public Health, etc.

$$(89)\quad ESW = \frac{QSW * EXPE}{100}$$

Financial Expenditure on Defense

$$(90)\quad ED = \frac{QD * EXPE}{100}$$

Financial Expenditure on Administration

$$(91)\quad EAD = \frac{QAD * EXPE}{100}$$

Extra-Budgetary Receipts

$$(92)\quad REVO = \frac{QO * (REV1 + TAG + TAR + RDB - RDBF)}{100}$$

Currency in Circulation

$$(93)\quad M0 = 0.190394 * MI^{1.02397} * (\frac{PIS}{PIS_{-1}})^{1.858}$$

(72.4) (8.15)

RR = 0.999191 DW = 2.00216 SE = 0.026738 (1970 – 1989)

Money M1

$$(94)\quad M1 = M2 - (KSR + KSU)$$

Money M2

$$(95)\quad M2 = LOAN + FEX - KSG - FUNDB$$

Foreign Exchange

$$(96)\quad FEX = FEX_{-1} + SFEX$$

Increase of Foreign Exchange

$$(97)\quad SFEX = 2.4553 + 1.041 * (KFXG - KFXG_{-1}) * REXCN$$

(14.89)

$$+ 0.27647 * (KFX - KFX_{-1}) * REXCN$$

(4.36)

RR = 0.962272 DW = 2.60809 SE = 12.5574 (1970 – 1989)

Net Savings of Public Finance

$$(98)\quad KSG = 34.1231 + \underset{(7.58)}{0.792491 * KSG_{-1}} + \underset{(4.37)}{1.16142 * BG}$$

RR = 0.845308 DW = 1.86102 SE = 59.1201 (1970 – 1989)

Rural Savings Deposits

$$(99)\quad KSR = 23.6194 + \underset{(21.6)}{1.16197 * (DRCC - LRCC)} - \underset{(-6.24)}{0.0155512 * GIN}$$

$$+ \underset{(8.02)}{0.428001 * LOANA}$$

RR = 0.997764 DW = 1.35456 SE = 9.91212 (1970 – 1989)

Urban Savings Deposits

$$(100)\quad KSU = 0.0241302 * \underset{(7.69)}{KSU_{-1}^{0.575497}} * \underset{(6.24)}{YW^{0.903058}}$$

$$* \underset{(-4.27)}{\left(\frac{PIS}{PIS_{-1}}\right)^{-1.23132}} * \underset{(3.73)}{R1^{0.213287}}$$

RR = 0.999455 DW = 2.08254 SE = 0.0301567 (1970 – 1989)

Funds of Banks

$$(101)\quad FINDB = 36.2838 + \underset{(29.3)}{1.04638 * FUNDB_{-1}} - \underset{(-3.26)}{6.75936 * DPIS}$$

$$+ \underset{(4.0)}{8.6799 * DPIS_{-1}}$$

RR = 0.994729 DW = 2.75817 SE = 23.4683 (1972 – 1989)

Deposits of Rural Credit Cooperatives

$$(102)\quad DRCC = 0.160074 * \underset{(4.26)}{DRCC_{-1}^{0.497889}} * \underset{(4.80)}{YP^{0.650068}}$$

$$* \underset{(1.77)}{EEC7^{0.0594239}} * \underset{(-3.71)}{\left(\frac{PIS}{PIS_{-1}}\right)^{-1.29135}}$$

RR = 0.998414 DW = 2.51501 SE = 0.0398951 (1970 – 1989)

Total Retail Sales

$$(103)\ SALE = 4.7327 * SALE_{-1}^{0.43943} * YP^{0.285826} * YW^{0.341108}$$

(11.4) (10.1) (6.0)

$$* PIS^{0.54977} * PIS_{-1}^{-0.825615} * R1^{-0.0671597}$$

(6.56) (-7.43) (-4.37)

RR = 0.999919 DW = 1.9967 SE = 6.35199E-03 (1970 – 1989)

Farm and Sideline Products Purchases

$$(104)\ FSPP = 0.166339 * GAG^{1.18144} * PIA^{0.214321} * PAPM^{-0.353882}$$

(15.3) (1.40) (-3.77)

RR = 0.998671 DW = 1.20191 SE = 0.02702 (1969 – 1989)

Merchandise Trade Balance

$$(105)\ TB = 4.41436 + 0.985216 * EXDOL - 0.948771 * IMDOL$$

(25.9) (-35.5)

RR = 0.995727 DW = 2.48839 SE = 4.07636 (1980 – 1988)

Services Trade Balamce

$$(106)\ SB = 9.85332 - 0.0357779 * (EXDOL + IMDOL) + 2.08237 * XTR$$

(-2.47) (2.97)

$$+ 0.07564 * (0.2 * KFX + 0.8 * KFX_{-1}) - 0.232947 * LAS$$

(5.62) (-1.89)

RR = 0.8252 DW = 2.68317 SE = 1.36959 (1980 – 1988)

Foreign Exchange by Tourism

$$(107)\ XTR = 0.0329468 * (EXDOL + IMDOL)^{0.639871} * REXCN^{-0.822656}$$

(3.37) (-4.53)

$$* TIMEE^{0.179976} * DD89E^{-0.48345}$$

(4.71) (-6.71)

RR = 0.991697 DW = 2.42125 SE = 0.0577176 (1980 – 1989)

Balance of Current Account

$$(108)\; CB = TB + SB + TRS$$

Accumulative Direct Investment

$$(109)\; KDI = KDI_{-1} + DINV$$

Balance of Long-Term Capital Account

$$(110)\; LC = LLI - LAS$$

Basic Balance of Payments

$$(111)\; BB = CB + LC$$

Overall Balance of Paymants

$$(112)\; OB = BB + SC + ERR$$

Foreign Exchange Reserves

$$(113)\; KFX = 0.966675 + \underset{(22.2)}{0.995402} * KFX_{-1} + \underset{(20.2)}{0.992668} * OB$$

RR = 0.988727 DW = 3.02369 SE = 2.6696 (1980 – 1988)

$$(114)\; RIMEQ = IMME * \frac{REXCN}{ICC} * 100$$

$$(115)\; DADD = (\frac{ADD}{ADD_{-1}} - 1) * 100$$

$$(116)\; DCF = (\frac{CF}{CF_{-1}} - 1) * 100$$

$$(117)\; DSA = (\frac{SA}{SA_{-1}} - 1) * 100$$

$$(118)\; RGNCF = \frac{PGRN}{PCF} * 100$$

$$(119)\; DKFM = (\frac{KFM}{KFM_{-1}} - 1) * 100$$

$$(120)\; DPEWM = (\frac{PEWM}{PEWM_{-1}} - 1) * 100$$

B List of Variables–China Model CMD9O

	VARIABLE	UNIT	
ACC	Accumulation of Circulating Capital(Nominal)	10^8 Yuan	a
ADD	Disaster affected area	10^4 Hec.	a
AFC	Accumulation of Fixed Capital(Nominal)	10^8 Yuan	a
BB	Basic Balance of Payments	10^8 \$	ik
BG	Balance on Government Finance	10^8 Yuan	a
C	Consumption (Nominal)	10^8 Yuan	a
CB	Current Balance	10^8 \$	ik
CF	Input of Chemical Fertilizer	10^4 Ton	ab
CH	Consumption of Households (Nominal)	10^8 Yuan	a
CHNP	Consumption: Non–peasant Households	10^8 Yuan	a
CHP	Consumption: Peasant Households	10^8 Yuan	a
CS	Social Consumption	10^8 Yuan	a
DADD	$(ADD/ADD_{-}-1)*100$	%	
DCF	$(CF/CF_{-1}-1)*100$	%	
DGA	Growth Rate of Agriculture	%	
DGI	Growth Rate of Industry	%	
DINV	Direct Investment	10^8 \$	g
DKFM	$(KFM/KFM_{-1}-1)*100$	%	
DNI	Growth Rate of National Income	%	
DPIA	$(PIA/PIA_{-1}-1)*100$	%	
DPIS	$(PIS/PlS_{-1}-1)*100$	%	
DRCC	Deposits of Rural Credit Cooperatives	10^8 Yuan	i
EAD	Administrative Expenditure	10^8 Yuan	a
ED	Expenditure on Defense	10^8 Yuan	a
EDB	Expenditure for Returning Debts	10^8 Yuan	a
EEC1	Expenditure on Construction Investment	10^8 Yuan	a
EEC7	Expenditure for Supporting Agriculture	10^8 Yuan	a
EO	Other Financial Expenditure	10^8 Yuan	a
ER	Account Error	10^8 Yuan	a
ERR	Error and Omission	10^8 \$	ik
ESW	Expenditure on Education,Culture,Welfare,etc.	10^8 Yuan	a
EX	Exports (Nominal ,in Yuan)	10^8 Yuan	a
EXAP	Exports of Agricultural Products (FTM)	10^8 \$	g
EXDOL	Exports (Nominal,in U.S.Dollar)	10^8 \$	a
EXF	Exports (FTM)	10^8 \$	g
EXHP	Exports of Heavy Industrial Products (FTM)	10^8 \$	g
EXLP	Exports of Light Industrial Products (FTM)	10^8 \$	g
EXPE	Firiancial Expenditure(FTM)	10^8 Yuan	a
EXTP	Exports of Textile(FTM)	10^8 \$	g
EXW	World Exports	10^8 \$	ag
FEX	Buyirig of Foreign Exchange	10^8 Yuan	i

	VARIABLE	UNIT	
FI	Fixed lnvestment in Industry (Nominal)	10^8 Yuan	c
FIR	Fixed Investment in Industry (at 1970 price)		
FM	Increase of Farm Macninary	10^8 Wt	ab
FSPP	Purchase of Farm and Sideline Products	10^8 Yuan	a
FUNDB	Funds of Banks	10^8 Yuan	i
GAG	Gross Output Value of Agriculture (Nomirial)	10^8 Yuan	a
GCM	Gross Output Value of Commerce (Nominal)	10^8 Yuan	a
GCN	Gross Output Value of Construction (Nominal)	10^8 Yuan	a
GIN	Gross Output Value of Industry (Nominal)	10^8 Yuan	a
GTR	Gross Output Value of Transport (Nominal)	10^8 Yuan	a
GRAIN	Output of Grain	10^4 Ton	a
IC	Consumption Index	1952=100	a
ICC	Investment in Capital Construction (Nominal)	10^8 Yuan	a
ICHP	Consumption Index (Peasant Households)	1952=100	a
ICHNP	Consumption lndex (Non–peasant Households)	1952=100	a
IFS	Fixed Investment (State–owned Units,Nominal)	10^8 Yuan	a
IGA	Index of Agricultural Gross Output	1952=100	a
lGCM	Index of Commercial Gross Output	1952=100	a
IGCN	lndex of Gross Output of Construction	1952=100	a
IGI	Index of Industrial Output	1952=100	a
IGT	Index of Gross Output of Transport	1952=100	a
IM	Imports (in Yuan)	10^8 Yuan	a
IMDOL	Imports (in U.S.Dollar)	10^8 \$	a
IMF	Imports (FTM)	10^8 \$	g
IMGR	Imports of Grain in Value(FTM)	10^8 \$	ag
IMGRQ	Quantum of Grain Imports	10^4 Ton	ag
IMMA	Imports of Agricultural Materials (FTM)	10^8 \$	g
IMME	Imports of Equipments(FTM)	10^8 \$	g
IMMI	Imports of Industrial Materials(FTM)	10^8 \$	g
IMSNG	Imports of Non–grain Consumer Goods(FTM)	10^8 \$	g
INI	Index of National Income	1952=100	a
IR	Investment in Renovation (Nominal ,State–owned)	10^8 Yuan	a
KDI	$=KDI_{-1}+DINV$		
KFIR	Fixed Capital Stock in Industry (Real)	10^8 Yuan	
KFM	Farm Machi nary Stock	10^8 Wt	a
KFX	Foreign Exchange Reserves	10^8 \$	i
KFXG	Foreign Exchange Reserves of Government	10^8 \$	i
KSG	Net Savings of Public Finance	10^8 Yuan	i
KSR	Rural Savings Deposits	10^8 Yuan	i
KSU	Urban Savings Deposits	10^8 Yuan	i
LAS	Long–term Capital (Assets)	10^8 \$	ik
LC	Balance of Long–term Capital	10^8 \$	ik
LIN	Number of Industrial Labor	10^4 Ps	ac

	VARIABLE	UNIT	
LLI	Long-term Capital (Liabilities)	10^8 $	ik
LOAN	Bank's Loan	10^8 Yuan	i
LOANA	Agricultural Loan	10^8 Yuan	i
LOANE	Loan for Fixed Investment	10^8 Yuan	i
LRCC	Loan of Rural Credit Cooperatives	10^8 Yuan	
LW	Number of Staff and Workers	10^4 Ps	a
MO	Currency in Circulation	10^8 Yuan	i
M1	Money M1	10^8 Yuan	i
M2	Money M2	10^8 Yuan	i
NI	National Income (Nominal)	10^8 Yuan	a
NIA	Net Output Value of Agriculture	10^8 Yuan	a
NICM	Net Output Value of Commerce (Nominal)	10^8 Yuan	a
NICN	Net Output Value of Construction (Nominal)	10^8 Yuan	a
NII	Net Output Value of Industry (Nominal)	10^8 Yuan	a
NIT	Net Output Value of Transport (Nominal)	10^8 Yuan	a
NIU	Available National Income (Nominal)	10^8 Yuan	a
OB	Overall Balance	10^8 $	ik
PAFC	Deflator for Accumulation of Fixed Capital	1970=100	j
PAG	Deflator for Agricultural Output	1970=100	a
PAPM	Price Index of Goods for Agri. Production	1950=100	a
PCF	Price of Chemical Fertilizer	Yuan/Ton	ak
PCHP	Deflator for Peasant Consumption	1970=100	a
PCHNP	Deflator for Non-peasant Consumption	1970=100	a
PCM	Deflator for Commercial Gross Output	1970=100	a
PCN	Deflator for Constructive Gross Output	1970=100	a
PCS	Deflator for Social Consumption	1970=100	a
PEF	Price Index of World Food Exports	1980=100	m
PEWM	Price Index of World Exports (Manufactures)	1980=100	m
PGRN	Purchasing Price of Grain	Yuan/Ton	a
PIA	Purchasing Price Index of Farm Products	1950=100	a
PICG	Retail Price Index of Consumer Goods	1950=100	a
PIMGR	Price of Import Grain =IMGR/IMGRQ*10000	$/Ton	
PIN	Deflator for Industrial Gross Output	1970=100	a
PIR	Price Index of Manuf. Goods in Rural Areas	1950=100	a
PIS	Price Index of Total Retail Sales	1950=100	a
PIU	Price Index of Living Cost in Urban Areas	1950=100	a
POIL	Price of Petroleum (Libya)	$/Barrel	n
PT	Population	10^4 Ps	a
PTR	Deflator for Transport Gross Output	1970=100	a
PVL80	Labor Productivity of Industry	Yuan/Ps	ac
Q1	EEC1/EXPE*100	10^8Yuan	
Q7	EEC7/EXPE*100	%	
QAD	EAD/EXPE*100	%	

	VARIABLE	UNIT	
QD	ED/EXPE*100	%	
QSW	ESW/EXPE*100	%	
QO	REV0/(REV1+TAR+TAG+RDBD)*100	%	
R1	One Year Interest	%	
REV	Financial Revenue	10^8 Yuan	an
REV1	REV–TAG–TAR–RDB	10^8 Yuan	an
RDB	Debts	10^8 Yuan	an
RDBD	Domestic Debts	10^8 Yuan	an
RDBF	Foreign Borrowings	10^8 Yuan	an
REVO	Extra-budgetary Receipts	10^8 Yuan	an
REXCN	Exchange Rate of Yuan to U.S.Dollar	Yuan/$	ik
RGNCF	=PGRN/PCF*100		
RIMEQ	=IMME*REXCN/ICC*100		
RSAGRN	Share of Grain Sown Area	%	a
SA	Sown Area	10^4 Hec.	a
SALE	Total Retail Sales	10^8 Yuan	a
SB	Services Balance	10^8 $	i
SC	Short–term Capital Balance	10^8 $	ik
SFEX	FEX–FEX_{-1}		
TAG	Agricultural Tax	10^8 Yuan	an
TAR	Tariff	10^8 Yuan	ah
TB	Trade Balance	10^8 $	ik
TRS	Unrequited Transfers	10^8 $	ik
W	Average Wage	Yuan	a
XTR	Foreign Exchange Earnings by Tourism	10^8 $	af
YP	Monetary Income of Peasants	10^8 Yuan	a
YW	Wage Bill	10^8 Yuan	a
DDnn	=1, if 19nn, =0, else		
DDnnE	=Exp(DDnn)		
Dnn	=1, if 19nn and after , =0, else		
DnnE	=Exp(Dnn)		
TIMEE	=Exp(TIME), TIME=Year–1970		

Note:

a: Statistics Yearbook of China
b: Agricultural Almanac of China
c: Industrial Economic Statistics of China
d: Journal of Chinese Finance
e: Peking Review, 8 Sept 1987, 18 Oct 1988
f: Statistics of China's Trade and Prices (1952–1983)
g: Almanac of China's Foreign Economic Relations and Trade (1984–1989)
h: China Finance Statistics (1950–1988)
i: China Financial Statistics (1952–1987)

j: National Income Statistics (1949–1985)
k: Statistics of China's Trade, Foreign Economic Relatioris (1952–1988)
l: Monthly Bulletin of Statistics U.N.
m: International Financial Statistics IMF
n: Statistics Yearbook of China's Rural Area

C Data List (1969–1989)

Year	ACC	ADD	AFC	BB	BG	C	CB	CF	CH	CHNP
1969	79	1500	278	....	0.9	1180	....	273.1	1068	363
1970	199	330	419	....	13.5	1258	....	351.2	1145	375
1971	216	745	468	....	12.5	1324	....	410.4	1195	391
1972	169	1718	479	....	0.2	1404	....	455.9	1263	439
1973	239	762	502	....	0.4	1511	....	502.8	1364	466
1974	188	653	553	....	-7.7	1550	....	476.6	1396	481
1975	182	1024	648	....	-5.3	1621	....	489.0	1450	504
1976	125	1144	623	....	-29.6	1676	....	528.8	1502	537
1977	187	1516	654	....	31.0	1741	....	595.9	1553	579
1978	304	2180	783	....	10.1	1888	....	884.0	1673	630
1979	323	1512	838	....	-170.6	2195	....	1086.3	1910	698
1980	272	2232	893	11.24	-127.5	2531	-5.56	1269.4	2223	839
1981	328	1874	778	51.48	-25.4	2799	47.87	1334.9	2473	901
1982	267	1612	969	60.63	-29.3	3054	56.74	1513.4	2688	951
1983	296	1621	1125	42.89	-43.5	3358	42.40	1659.8	2957	1016
1984	343	1526	1453	19.17	-44.5	3905	20.30	1739.8	3395	1163
1985	745	2271	1883	-47.16	21.6	4879	-114.17	1775.8	4240	1512
1986	748	2366	2196	12.03	-70.5	5552	-70.35	1930.6	4773	1779
1987	580	2039	2718	61.00	-79.5	6386	3.00	1999.7	5502	2121
1988	871	2394	3360	32.54	-78.6	8038	-38.02	2141.5	6995	2829
1989	1721	2445	2953	9.23	-95.4	8903	-43.17	2357.1	7730	3188

Year	CHP	CS	DINV	DRCC	EAD	ED	EDB	EEC1	EEC7	EO
1969	705	112	0	73.3	24.78	126.18	0	206.22	14.87	50.38
1970	770	113	0	76.4	25.27	145.26	0	298.36	15.91	53.07
1971	804	129	0	90.3	30.89	169.47	0	309.56	19.65	64.50
1972	824	141	0	90.9	34.63	159.35	0	309.06	25.10	80.35
1973	898	147	0	104.8	35.58	145.39	0	307.17	35.49	94.91
1974	915	154	0	121.2	36.92	133.39	0	312.83	38.23	88.64
1975	946	171	0	135.1	38.83	142.46	0	326.96	42.53	75.72
1976	965	174	0	141.2	41.01	134.45	0	311.25	46.01	55.14
1977	974	188	0	151.3	43.32	149.04	0	300.88	50.68	53.80
1978	1043	215	0	166.0	49.09	167.84	0	451.92	76.95	65.85
1979	1212	285	2.98	215.9	56.87	222.66	0	514.69	90.11	68.55
1980	1384	308	3.58	272.3	66.79	193.84	28.5	419.39	82.12	82.83
1981	1572	326	4.65	319.6	70.88	167.97	62.8	330.63	73.68	82.20
1982	1737	366	6.49	389.9	81.60	176.35	55.5	309.15	79.88	92.88
1983	1941	401	9.61	487.4	102.20	177.13	42.4	382.81	86.66	110.57
1984	2232	510	14.19	624.5	137.28	180.76	28.9	488.93	95.93	147.65
1985	2728	639	19.56	724.9	143.58	191.53	39.5	583.80	101.04	254.98
1986	2994	779	22.44	962.3	182.43	200.75	50.1	671.82	124.30	478.88
1987	3381	884	26.47	225.2	195.48	209.62	79.8	628.12	134.16	557.89
1988	4166	1043	37.40	339.8	239.35	218.00	76.7	633.37	158.74	14.89
1989	4542	1173	37.73	669.5	289.70	251.46	72.5	612.58	199.07	681.14

(continued)

Year	ER	ERR	ESW	EX	EXAP	EXDOL	EXF	EXHP	EXLP	EXPE
1969	67.3	....	47.64	59.8	8.24	22.0	22.04	4.72	4.19	525.9
1970	49.3	....	50.18	56.8	8.29	22.6	22.60	3.54	5.94	649.4
1971	52.9	....	59.14	68.5	9.55	26.4	26.36	4.95	6.59	732.2
1972	65.1	....	70.16	82.9	10.77	34.4	34.43	6.07	9.54	766.4
1973	52.7	....	79.85	116.9	20.80	58.2	58.19	9.12	15.01	809.3
1974	70.5	....	85.65	139.4	25.30	69.5	69.49	16.22	16.24	790.8
1975	56.4	....	94.17	143.0	21.50	72.6	72.64	20.76	17.41	820.9
1976	-2.5	....	109.56	134.8	19.46	68.6	68.55	18.64	16.64	806.2
1977	64.1	....	108.96	139.7	20.96	75.9	75.90	20.02	19.71	843.5
1978	54.8	....	131.57	167.6	26.91	97.5	97.45	24.85	24.31	1111.0
1979	25.2	....	154.23	211.7	31.57	136.6	136.58	43.57	32.68	1273.9
1980	11.0	2.39	176.57	272.4	34.19	182.7	182.72	72.06	43.79	1212.7
1981	36.1	-2.22	193.08	367.6	36.81	220.1	208.93	90.56	46.64	1115.0
1982	-88.0	1.44	218.39	413.8	32.43	223.2	218.19	103.66	45.50	1153.3
1983	-59.5	-6.01	247.58	438.3	35.29	222.3	221.97	95.39	49.50	1292.5
1984	-9.1	-13.68	288.33	580.6	41.20	261.4	244.16	106.59	47.08	1546.4
1985	-38.1	0.33	347.85	808.9	45.32	273.5	259.15	110.81	51.98	1844.8
1986	-220.8	-2.63	415.51	1082.1	52.02	309.4	270.14	87.48	65.47	2330.8
1987	-226.8	-14.50	410.15	1470.0	58.78	394.4	347.11	116.52	89.83	2448.5
1988	-242.4	-10.94	527.87	1766.7	69.54	475.2	406.40	132.10	111.6	2706.6
1989	-208.1	1.17	608.49	1956.0	66.11	525.4	430.40	138.32	122.13	3014.6

Year	EXTP	EXW	FEX	FI	FIR	FM	FSPP	FUNDB	GAG	GCM
1969	4.89	2435	16.3	....	....	191.7	324	193.1	948	250
1970	4.83	3146	6.5	177.9	177.9	24.8	348	220.3	1021	274
1971	5.27	3885	4.9	165.7	163.9	65.5	369	152.3	1068	282
1972	8.05	4340	8.7	227.2	222.0	95.0	377	138.9	1075	297
1973	13.26	5730	5.9	242.8	237.0	101.3	436	183.1	1173	330
1974	11.73	8417	10.2	182.1	177.5	114.7	446	222.6	1215	334
1975	12.97	8745	9.8	252.2	242.8	154.8	479	258.1	1260	315
1976	13.81	9896	12.3	247.5	236.7	115.1	470	303.0	1258	307
1977	15.21	11269	23.8	289.2	272.5	163.2	495	359.9	1253	384
1978	21.38	13009	14.3	263.4	340.4	148.8	558	421.9	1397	438
1979	28.76	16439	20.6	326.2	299.2	163.0	714	471.1	1698	409
1980	32.68	19905	-8.5	330.2	293.9	136.7	842	496.9	1923	440
1981	34.92	19718	89.6	372.7	321.5	93.4	955	621.5	2181	490
1982	36.60	18327	217.7	420.0	354.1	93.4	1083	674.5	2483	474
1983	41.79	18086	266.1	472.7	388.9	140.8	1265	720.7	2750	549
1984	49.29	19028	263.6	516.6	408.4	147.5	1440	776.1	3214	689
1985	51.04	19244	93.1	969.9	727.2	141.6	1680	856.4	3620	1103
1986	65.17	21277	38.1	1035.6	725.4	203.7	1990	951.8	4013	1202
1987	81.98	24977	132.1	1236.8	810.9	188.6	2369	1074.0	4676	1412
1988	93.21	28340	158.4	1482.9	850.9	173.9	2998	1196.9	5865	1914
1989	107.84	30307	264.5	1832.8	933.8	149.2	3386	1315.8	6535	2204

(continued)

Year	GCN	GIN	GTR	GRAIN	IC	ICC	ICHP	ICHNP	IFS	IGA
1969	222	1665	99	21097	203.0	200.83	182.9	231.3	246.92	149.2
1970	271	2117	117	23996	216.0	312.55	199.5	239.5	368.08	157.8
1971	311	2414	128	25014	226.5	340.84	206.8	250.0	417.31	162.9
1972	323	2565	136	24048	239.6	327.98	211.3	279.6	412.81	161.2
1973	335	2794	144	26496	257.1	338.10	229.5	296.5	438.12	174.5
1974	376	2792	142	27527	262.8	347.71	233.0	304.4	463.19	180.7
1975	437	3207	160	28452	274.3	409.32	240.7	317.6	544.94	186.3
1976	435	3278	155	28631	283.1	376.44	245.1	337.6	523.94	185.5
1977	462	3725	179	28273	291.5	382.37	247.6	354.0	548.30	184.8
1978	569	4237	205	30477	312.7	500.99	261.4	382.7	668.72	199.8
1979	645	4681	209	33212	346.7	523.48	281.5	416.0	699.36	214.8
1980	767	5155	250	32056	380.8	558.89	310.5	465.2	745.90	217.9
1981	747	5400	257	32502	411.0	442.91	342.6	487.9	667.51	230.5
1982	912	5811	286	35450	441.4	555.53	371.9	504.5	845.31	256.5
1983	1053	6461	318	38728	479.2	594.13	410.7	528.0	951.96	276.5
1984	1263	7617	388	40731	547.4	743.15	464.0	588.6	1185.18	310.4
1985	1656	9717	488	37911	633.8	1074.37	528.8	684.0	1680.51	321.0
1986	2038	11194	592	39151	682.9	1176.11	548.1	752.2	1978.50	331.8
1987	2431	13813	702	40298	737.5	1343.10	582.2	824.4	2297.99	351.0
1988	2967	18224	837	39408	798.7	1574.31	625.5	911.5	2761.33	364.9
1989	2834	22017	1014	40755	799.2	1551.74	623.3	923.2	2535.49	376.2

Year	IGCM	IGCN	IGI	IGT	IM	IMDOL	IMF	IMGR	IMGRQ	IMMA
1969	188.6	445.6	601.6	336.7	47.1	18.3	18.25	2.20	378.6	2.44
1970	210.4	543.9	798.1	400.0	56.1	23.3	23.26	2.77	536.0	2.20
1971	216.5	614.2	915.3	437.6	52.4	22.0	22.05	1.96	317.0	2.04
1972	228.1	630.2	978.2	465.0	64.0	28.6	28.58	3.03	475.6	2.51
1973	253.4	640.3	1071.3	492.3	103.6	51.6	51.57	8.31	812.8	3.26
1974	256.5	702.5	1077.7	485.5	152.9	76.2	76.19	12.36	812.2	3.85
1975	266.5	800.8	1244.7	547.0	147.4	74.9	74.87	5.75	373.5	5.70
1976	275.7	784.8	1274.9	529.9	129.3	65.8	65.78	3.54	236.6	3.75
1977	303.3	820.9	1461.1	612.0	132.8	72.1	72.14	7.79	734.5	4.92
1978	344.8	995.5	1659.0	700.9	187.4	108.9	108.93	10.02	883.2	6.89
1979	376.3	1101.9	1805.3	714.5	242.9	156.7	156.95	16.44	1235.5	9.23
1980	400.1	1282.6	1972.3	844.4	291.4	195.5	195.50	24.80	1287.0	14.25
1981	469.2	1212.3	2057.1	868.1	367.7	220.1	194.82	32.43	1448.0	14.09
1982	499.2	1438.1	2217.7	966.0	357.8	192.8	174.78	34.07	1615.0	13.82
1983	551.9	1588.6	2465.8	1053.9	421.8	213.9	185.30	24.77	1353.0	17.84
1984	617.4	1800.9	2867.3	1172.1	620.5	274.1	253.56	18.32	1041.0	20.87
1985	741.0	2167.1	3480.7	1405.2	1257.8	422.5	343.31	9.97	600.0	14.91
1986	822.0	2469.8	3886.8	1553.8	1498.3	429.1	330.83	10.82	773.0	9.09
1987	899.2	2717.3	4574.5	1726.0	1614.2	432.1	333.99	17.54	1628.0	15.89
1988	981.0	2914.8	5525.4	1945.6	2055.3	552.7	398.50	18.95	1533.0	26.29
1989	913.4	2576.5	5995.0	2087.6	2199.9	591.4	391.43	29.90	1658.0	27.63

(continued)

Year	IMME	IMMI	IMSNG	INI	IR	KDI	KFIR	KFM	KFX	KFXG
1969	2.17	10.43	0.99	239.0	46.09	0	1330	192	4.98	4.83
1970	3.69	13.36	1.24	294.6	55.53	0	1508	217	1.91	0.88
1971	4.84	11.63	1.58	315.3	76.47	0	1671	282	2.02	0.37
1972	5.57	14.62	2.85	324.3	84.83	0	1893	377	5.43	2.36
1973	7.88	28.26	3.86	351.2	100.02	0	2130	478	0.83	-0.81
1974	15.85	37.95	6.18	355.2	115.48	0	2308	593	3.69	0.00
1975	24.06	34.17	5.19	384.7	135.62	0	2550	748	8.99	1.83
1976	20.37	32.99	5.13	374.5	147.50	0	2787	863	12.55	5.81
1977	12.77	37.23	9.43	403.7	165.93	0	3060	1026	23.45	9.52
1978	19.03	62.72	10.27	453.4	167.73	0	3400	1175	15.57	1.67
1979	39.57	78.67	12.84	485.1	175.88	2.98	3700	1338	21.45	8.40
1980	53.75	86.20	18.72	516.3	187.01	6.38	3993	1475	22.62	-12.96
1981	51.05	76.69	25.63	541.4	224.60	11.03	4315	1568	47.83	27.08
1982	33.94	75.96	24.82	585.8	289.78	17.52	4669	1661	111.35	69.26
1983	32.54	95.37	20.20	644.2	357.83	26.68	5058	1802	143.42	89.01
1984	51.96	132.61	32.00	731.9	442.03	40.87	5466	1950	144.20	82.20
1985	109.65	159.83	50.34	830.6	606.14	60.43	6193	2091	119.13	26.40
1986	122.92	152.74	37.89	894.5	802.39	82.87	6919	2295	105.14	20.72
1987	108.03	142.66	51.49	985.7	954.89	109.34	7730	2484	152.36	29.23
1988	108.18	181.82	67.10	1097.2	1187.02	146.74	8581	2658	175.48	33.72
1989	120.72	167.01	50.47	1133.4	983.75	184.47	9515	2807	170.40	55.50

Year	KSG	KSR	KSU	LAS	LC	LIN	LLI	LOAN	LOANA	LOANE
1969	119.60	78.4	61.0	....	....	2932	....	945.5	84.0	0
1970	176.80	83.3	64.5	....	....	3519	....	1033.4	85.1	0
1971	188.90	93.5	73.3	....	....	3939	....	1113.9	51.6	0
1972	172.60	91.4	85.1	....	....	4240	....	1145.6	56.6	0
1973	160.80	107.3	94.1	....	....	4445	....	1269.0	58.8	0
1974	137.30	123.4	105.8	....	....	4697	....	1353.5	64.0	0
1975	140.20	136.9	114.6	....	....	5107	....	1462.7	72.4	0
1976	97.90	136.7	122.2	....	....	5714	....	1541.8	90.4	0
1977	151.90	143.2	135.1	....	....	5843	....	1663.3	98.3	0
1978	187.40	154.4	154.9	....	....	6091	....	1850.0	115.6	0
1979	58.45	203.7	202.6	....	....	6298	....	2039.6	136.7	7.9
1980	-8.21	239.8	282.5	8.36	16.80	6714	25.16	2414.3	175.9	55.5
1981	24.71	278.4	354.1	14.24	3.61	6975	17.85	2860.2	189.7	132.9
1982	5.53	329.9	447.3	29.23	3.89	7204	33.12	3180.6	212.5	238.1
1983	-5.88	391.3	572.6	26.53	0.49	7397	27.02	3589.9	231.2	307.1
1984	-94.90	372.4	776.6	42.41	-1.13	7930	41.28	4766.1	368.1	451.7
1985	93.32	449.6	1057.8	28.30	67.01	8349	95.31	5905.6	416.6	705.3
1986	58.60	559.6	1471.5	31.55	82.38	8980	113.93	7590.8	570.4	1005.8
1987	-207.98	626.3	2067.6	39.40	58.00	9342	97.40	9032.5	685.8	1286.8
1988	-305.38	669.6	2659.2	40.58	70.56	9661	111.14	10551.3	814.2	1559.2
1989	-246.57	716.3	3734.8	68.93	52.40	9568	121.33	12409.3	895.1	1776.0

(continued)

Year	LRCC	LW	M0	M1	M2	NI	NIA	NICM	NICN	NII
1969	17.8	5714	137.00	509.70	649.10	1617	722	186	60	587
1970	18.8	6216	132.20	495.00	642.80	1926	778	205	80	789
1971	19.4	6787	136.20	610.80	777.60	2077	808	207	91	891
1972	21.1	7134	151.20	666.30	842.80	2136	808	214	88	942
1973	20.8	7337	166.20	729.60	931.00	2318	886	231	92	1020
1974	22.0	7651	176.60	774.60	1003.80	2348	922	227	99	1015
1975	26.7	8198	182.60	822.70	1074.20	2503	946	196	113	1152
1976	35.8	8673	203.90	894.30	1153.20	2427	940	169	120	1106
1977	39.7	9112	195.40	897.00	1175.30	2644	913	238	124	1263
1978	45.1	9499	212.00	945.70	1255.00	3010	986	294	125	1487
1979	47.5	9967	267.71	1124.36	1530.66	3350	1226	245	130	1628
1980	81.6	10444	346.20	1394.84	1917.14	3688	1326	247	185	1804
1981	96.4	10940	396.34	1671.06	2303.56	3941	1509	268	193	1840
1982	121.2	11281	439.12	1941.06	2718.26	4258	1723	231	209	1948
1983	163.7	11515	529.78	2177.25	3141.15	4736	1921	254	259	2136
1984	354.5	11890	792.11	3199.46	4348.46	5652	2251	377	303	2516
1985	400.0	12358	987.83	3541.58	5048.98	7020	2492	697	409	3163
1986	568.5	12809	1218.36	4704.60	6735.70	7859	2720	732	514	3573
1987	771.4	13214	1454.48	5604.68	8298.58	9313	3154	876	637	4262
1988	908.6	13608	2134.03	6612.80	9941.55	11738	3818	1261	783	5416
1989	1094.6	13742	2344.02	7272.36	11723.50	13125	4209	1388	774	624

Year	NIT	NIU	OB	PAFC	PAG	PAPM	PCF	PCHP	PCHNP	PCM
1969	62	1537	....	99.98	98.20	103.9	228	99.87	100.23	101.79
1970	74	1876	....	100.00	100.00	103.9	228	100.00	100.00	100.00
1971	80	2008	....	101.08	101.33	101.7	222	100.73	99.89	100.02
1972	84	2052	....	102.33	103.07	99.9	222	101.04	100.28	99.98
1973	89	2252	....	102.43	103.89	99.9	222	101.38	100.38	100.00
1974	85	2291	....	102.59	103.92	100.1	226	101.75	100.92	99.99
1975	96	2451	....	103.87	104.53	100.0	226	101.83	101.35	90.76
1976	92	2424	....	104.57	104.81	100.1	236	102.01	101.59	85.50
1977	106	2573	....	106.14	104.79	100.2	223	101.92	104.46	97.22
1978	118	2975	....	106.76	108.06	100.1	231	103.38	105.14	97.54
1979	121	3356	....	109.03	122.18	100.5	236	111.55	107.16	83.46
1980	126	3696	15.19	112.36	136.40	101.5	237	115.49	115.19	84.45
1981	131	3905	50.67	115.94	146.24	103.2	243	118.88	117.94	80.19
1982	147	4290	61.56	118.60	149.61	105.2	260	121.01	120.39	72.91
1983	166	4779	34.13	121.53	153.72	108.4	259	122.45	122.90	76.38
1984	205	5701	-3.41	126.48	160.03	118.0	322	124.63	126.19	85.69
1985	259	7507	-24.12	133.37	174.30	123.7	369.5	133.66	141.18	114.30
1986	320	8496	-13.55	142.75	186.93	125.1	381.2	141.53	151.05	112.29
1987	384	9684	48.62	152.52	205.90	133.9	427.7	150.46	164.32	120.58
1988	460	12269	22.36	174.27	248.41	155.6	539.9	172.56	198.22	149.80
1989	513	13577	-4.78	196.27	268.48	185.0	636.8	188.80	220.55	185.29

(continued)

Year	PCN	PCS	PEF	PEWM	PGRN	PIA	PICG	PIMGR	PIN	PIR
1969	99.99	100.05	27.0	32.4	240.8	194.9	138.0	58.64	104.34	112.1
1970	100.00	100.00	28.6	35.2	241.2	195.1	137.8	51.68	100.00	111.9
1971	101.63	99.73	30.2	37.0	252.2	198.3	139.7	61.77	99.43	110.2
1972	102.87	99.49	34.2	40.1	256.0	201.1	139.4	63.71	98.85	109.6
1973	105.01	99.91	50.3	46.8	253.8	202.8	141.7	102.24	98.32	109.6
1974	107.42	99.97	66.6	57.0	252.0	204.5	141.9	152.18	97.67	109.6
1975	109.52	100.28	62.8	64.1	254.4	208.7	143.0	153.95	97.13	109.6
1976	111.25	99.98	66.0	64.4	255.6	209.7	143.3	149.62	96.93	109.7
1977	112.95	100.33	75.4	70.1	256.6	209.2	147.8	106.06	96.11	109.8
1978	114.72	100.48	76.2	79.6	263.4	217.4	150.0	113.45	96.28	109.8
1979	117.48	101.36	85.6	90.4	330.7	265.5	153.2	133.06	97.75	109.9
1980	120.02	106.02	100.0	100.0	360.6	284.4	164.0	192.72	98.53	110.8
1981	123.67	106.53	89.0	94.0	381.7	301.2	168.3	223.99	98.96	111.9
1982	127.28	106.02	78.0	92.0	392.2	307.8	171.5	210.96	98.78	113.7
1983	133.03	105.81	77.0	89.0	392.6	321.3	173.6	183.07	98.78	114.8
1984	140.76	106.29	74.0	86.0	395.1	334.2	176.6	175.95	100.15	118.4
1985	153.37	108.90	66.0	87.0	416.0	362.9	193.2	166.18	105.24	122.2
1986	165.61	111.76	74.0	103.0	465.0	386.1	205.8	140.03	108.58	126.1
1987	179.56	114.29	75.0	116.0	508.5	432.4	221.0	107.74	113.84	132.2
1988	204.30	126.08	87.0	123.0	563.7	531.9	263.0	123.64	124.34	152.3
1989	220.76	142.77	87.0	125.0	750.0	611.7	309.0	180.38	138.45	180.8

Year	PIS	PIU	POIL	PT	PTR	PLV80	Q1	Q7	QAD	QD
1969	131.8	137.8	2.23	80671	100.52	7006	39.21	2.83	4.71	23.99
1970	131.5	137.8	2.33	82992	100.00	7888	45.94	2.45	3.89	22.37
1971	130.5	137.7	3.23	85229	100.00	7761	42.28	2.68	4.22	23.15
1972	130.2	137.9	3.62	87177	99.99	7429	40.33	3.28	4.52	20.79
1973	131.0	138.0	5.15	89211	100.00	7603	39.19	4.39	4.40	17.96
1974	131.7	138.9	15.77	90859	99.99	7220	39.56	4.83	4.67	16.87
1975	131.9	139.5	15.32	92420	100.00	7722	39.83	5.18	4.73	17.35
1976	132.3	139.9	16.20	93717	100.00	7132	38.61	5.70	5.09	16.68
1977	135.0	143.7	14.00	94974	99.99	7701	35.67	6.00	5.14	17.67
1978	135.9	144.7	13.90	96259	99.99	8458	40.68	6.93	4.42	15.11
1979	138.6	147.4	19.91	97542	100.00	8706	40.40	7.07	4.46	17.48
1980	146.9	158.5	35.93	98705	101.22	8952	34.58	6.77	5.51	15.98
1981	150.4	162.5	39.83	100072	101.21	8946	29.65	6.61	6.36	15.06
1982	153.3	165.8	35.49	101590	101.22	9364	26.81	6.93	7.08	15.29
1983	155.6	169.1	30.89	102764	103.16	10151	29.62	6.70	7.91	13.70
1984	160.0	173.7	30.15	103876	113.17	11190	31.62	6.20	8.88	11.69
1985	174.1	194.4	30.15	105044	118.73	12372	31.63	5.48	7.78	10.38
1986	184.5	208.0	14.60	106529	131.58	12609	28.82	5.33	7.83	8.61
1987	198.0	226.3	18.52	108073	139.05	13961	25.65	5.47	7.98	8.56
1988	234.6	273.1	14.15	109614	147.08	15835	23.40	5.86	8.84	8.05
1989	276.4	317.6	17.16	111191	166.06	16568	20.32	6.60	9.61	8.34

(continued)

Year	QSW	QO	R1	REV	REV1	RDB	RDBD	RDBF	REVO	REXCN
1969	9.06	16.59	3.96	526.8	490.9	0	0	0	87.42	2.4618
1970	7.73	15.23	3.96	662.9	623.9	0	0	0	100.94	2.4618
1971	8.08	15.92	3.24	744.7	708.8	0	0	0	118.56	2.4611
1972	9.15	17.51	3.24	766.6	733.2	0	0	0	134.24	2.2451
1973	9.87	23.62	3.24	809.7	770.2	0	0	0	191.29	1.9894
1974	10.83	28.06	3.24	783.1	739.0	0	0	0	219.72	1.9612
1975	11.47	30.83	3.24	815.6	771.2	0	0	0	251.48	1.8598
1976	13.59	35.45	3.24	776.6	732.5	0	0	0	275.32	1.9419
1977	12.92	35.60	3.24	874.5	818.9	0	0	0	311.31	1.8578
1978	11.84	30.96	3.24	1121.1	1063.9	0	0	0	347.11	1.6836
1979	12.11	42.40	3.96	1103.3	1012.5	35.31	0	35.31	452.85	1.5549
1980	14.56	53.48	5.40	1085.2	981.0	43.01	0	43.01	557.40	1.4984
1981	17.32	59.13	5.40	1089.6	934.1	73.08	0	73.08	601.07	1.7050
1982	18.94	74.06	5.76	1124.0	963.3	83.86	43.83	40.03	802.74	1.8925
1983	19.16	79.90	5.76	1249.0	1082.8	79.41	41.58	37.83	967.68	1.9757
1984	18.65	81.01	5.76	1501.9	1286.7	77.34	42.53	34.81	1188.48	2.3270
1985	18.86	83.28	6.72	1866.4	1529.3	89.85	60.61	29.24	1530.03	2.9367
1986	17.82	79.52	7.20	2260.3	1925.9	138.25	62.51	75.74	1737.30	3.4523
1987	17.98	89.67	7.20	2368.9	2005.2	169.55	63.07	106.48	2028.80	3.7221
1988	19.50	91.19	7.68	2628.0	2128.5	270.78	92.17	138.61	2270.00	3.7221
1989	20.18	91.99	11.12	2919.2	2382.6	274.30	56.26	134.30	2562.00	3.7659

Year	RGNCF	RIMEQ	RSAGRN	SA	SALE	SB	SC	SFEX	TAG	TAI
1969	105.61	2.66	83.4	14094.4	801.5	....	....	....	29.56	6.3
1970	105.79	2.90	83.1	14348.7	858.0	....	....	-9.80	31.98	7.0
1971	113.60	3.49	83.1	14568.4	929.2	....	....	-1.60	30.86	5.0
1972	115.32	3.81	81.9	14791.9	1023.3	....	....	3.80	28.37	5.0
1973	114.32	4.64	81.6	14858.1	1106.7	....	....	-2.80	30.52	9.0
1974	111.50	8.94	81.4	14863.5	1163.6	....	....	4.30	30.06	14.0
1975	112.57	10.93	80.9	14954.5	1271.1	....	....	0.40	29.45	15.0
1976	108.30	10.51	80.6	14972.3	1339.4	....	....	2.50	29.14	15.0
1977	115.07	6.20	80.6	14933.3	1432.8	....	....	11.50	29.33	26.2
1978	114.03	6.40	80.3	15010.4	1558.6	....	....	-9.50	28.40	28.7
1979	140.13	11.75	80.3	14847.7	1800.0	....	....	6.28	29.51	26.0
1980	152.15	14.41	80.1	14637.9	2140.0	7.42	1.56	-29.05	27.67	33.5
1981	157.08	19.65	79.2	14515.7	2350.0	8.11	1.41	98.04	28.35	54.0
1982	150.85	11.56	78.4	14475.5	2570.0	9.39	-0.51	128.12	29.38	47.4
1983	151.58	10.82	79.2	14399.3	2849.4	17.39	-2.75	48.38	32.96	53.8
1984	122.70	16.27	79.3	14422.1	3376.4	15.74	-8.90	-2.51	34.84	103.0
1985	112.59	29.97	75.8	14362.1	4305.0	14.63	22.71	-170.46	42.05	205.2
1986	121.98	36.09	76.9	14420.4	4950.0	17.27	-22.95	-55.00	44.52	151.6
1987	118.89	29.94	76.8	14495.7	5820.0	17.37	2.12	94.00	51.81	142.3
1988	104.41	25.58	76.0	14486.9	7440.0	10.94	0.58	26.34	73.69	155.0
1989	117.78	29.29	76.6	14655.4	8101.4	9.22	-15.18	106.10	83.20	179.1

(continued)

Year	TB	TRS	W	XTR	YP	YW
1969	....	....	575	....	362.5	322.6
1970	....	....	561	....	394.0	334.3
1971	....	....	560	....	425.7	364.0
1972	....	....	588	....	439.3	409.6
1973	....	....	587	....	497.7	429.1
1974	....	....	584	....	519.1	441.9
1975	....	1.34	580	1.20	558.8	463.5
1976	....	2.37	575	1.40	558.4	489.2
1977	....	3.10	576	1.80	609.1	514.8
1978	....	3.80	615	2.63	698.7	568.9
1979	....	4.64	668	4.50	887.2	646.7
1980	-18.68	5.70	762	6.17	1079.6	772.4
1981	34.01	5.75	772	7.85	1204.4	820.0
1982	42.49	4.86	798	8.43	1352.0	882.0
1983	19.90	5.11	826	9.41	1593.2	934.6
1984	0.14	4.42	974	11.31	2079.5	1133.4
1985	-131.23	2.43	1148	12.50	2671.0	1383.0
1986	-91.41	3.79	1329	15.31	2855.2	1659.7
1987	-16.61	2.24	1459	18.62	3438.0	1881.1
1988	-53.15	4.19	1747	22.47	4426.0	2316.2
1989	-56.20	3.81	1935	18.60	4953.0	2618.2

Chapter 4

A Quarterly Econometric Model of the Korean Economy

Yoonha Yoo[1]

1 Introduction

This paper presents a preliminary report of the KDI quarterly econometric model which is presently under extensive revision. The initial KDI quarterly model was developed in 1979 and has since been revised and reestimated annually. Since 1986, however, the Korean economy has undergone sweeping structural changes in various sectors. As an example, for the first time in Korean history, the balance of payments turned into surplus in 1986 and increased further to $14 billion in 1988. The financial sectors, as a natural consequence of these developments in the external trade sector, also had experienced both qualitative and quantitative shifts and changes as well. Along with these external developments, there has been a substantial restructuring in the Korean financial markets towards more liberalization and deregulations.

Since these external and internal changes gradually affected the decision–making processes of the various economic agents in the economy, such as individuals, firms and even the government itself, it now seems necessary to take a fresh look at the way the economy is working in this new environment and to incorporate these changes formally into the model.

In what follows, we describe the basic structure of the latest version of the revised model and report the simulation results. We also provide the policy simulation results.

For policy simulation analysis, we subjected the system to an increase in government expenditure by 1% of nominal GNP and followed the resulting path of the economy by differentiating the methods of financing the increased expenditures, such as money financing, bond financing and tax financing, and by the composition of the expenditures such as consumption and investment.

2 Structure of the Model

The model consists of six blocks: the balance of payments, the money market, the GNP or final demand, the labor market, the government, and wages and prices. A rough flow chart description of the model is given below in Figure 1.

[1]Korea Development Institute

The balance of payments block shows how the Korean economy is linked to the rest of the world. Since the Korean economy is small and open, the outside world directly affects the economy, without being similarly affected by what happens in Korea. This block has eight equations, four of which determine the real volume of commodity exports and oil and non-oil imports, and the unit prices of commodity exports. The unit prices of commodity imports are assumed to be exogeneous. The remaining four equations determine the volume and unit prices of non-factor services.

The final demand block has 5 equations for private consumption, total fixed investments, changes in inventories, and commodity exports and imports. The last two equations are simply bridge equations which convert the dollar volume of commodity exports and improts in the balance of payments block into 1985 won. An additional GNP identity closes the block, with the government consumption being treated as exogeneous.

The private consumption function incorporates the permanent income concept by including lagged personal disposable income in the equation following Friedman's (1957) adaptive expectations model. In addition, the equation takes into account the effect of changes in real wealth, which is proxied by total real money supply, and the effect of interest rate changes on saving. However, a distinction between durables and non-durables is not made, mainly because consumption of durable goods occupies only less than 5 percent of total consumption expenditure in Korea. Consequently, the distinction between consumption expenditures and consumption flow is not made, either.

The fixed investment is assumed to be influenced by changes in real GNP and credit availability with the latter being proxied by changes in the real money supply. The real interest rate was initially expected to play a major role in determining the fixed investment, but actually proved to be statistically insignificant during the sample period from the first quarter of 1973 to the 4th quarter of 1989. One possible reason why investment demand is independent of the real interest rate is that the credit market in Korea has long been strictly controlled by the government, and as a consequence, the market interest rate could not respond to the changing supply and demand for loanable funds.

Recently, however, the credit markets have been in the process of being liberalized, rendering it more likely that investment responds more actively to changes in the real interest rate. The net fixed investment–gross investment less depreciation–in the current period adds to the existing capital stock.

A division of investment into private and public components is not made due to the unavailability of the public investment series on a quarterly basis in the new SNA. A division of the total fixed investment into different types of investment, such as machinery and equipment, residential construction and non-residential construction, is not made either, mainly due to a lack of appropriate disaggregated stock data.

The government sector determines the amount of taxes, which are divided into internal taxes and custom duties, and the volume of government credit. Changes in the amount of total taxes affects private disposable income, and thereby the total aggregate demand through its effects on private consumption. The gap between government expenditure and government revenue, which comes from taxes, is reflected in the government budget surplus and deficit. Those in turn determine the volume of government credit.

The labor sector has two equations which determine the unemployment rate in the non-agricultural sector and labor forces. Unemployment rate in the non-agricultural sector is assumed to be a function of GNP gap, and the labor forces as a function of population and distributed lags of past real GNP. The latter variable is expected to capture the discouraged worker effects. Transforming the labor force by unemployment rate generates employment. The employment level determined here is then combined with the non-agricultural GNP and the hours worked in the manufacturing sector to determine labor productivity, which is then used to explain wages and prices. The labor force obtained in this block, together with the capital stock which comes from the final demand block is formulated to determine the future potential GNP. Employment in the agricultural sector is assumed to be exogeneous.

The price block determines wages, the wholesale price index(WPI),the consumer price index(CPI), the price deflator for private consumption, the price deflator for fixed investment, and the GNP deflator. Wages are assumed to be explained in terms of labor productivity, unemployment level and consumer prices.

The WPI, which is explained by wages, import prices, labor productivity and the capacity utilization ratio, plays the most basic role in this block in that all the remaining price equations are dependent on it. Since the behavior of the WPI in the 1980s is significantly different from that of the 1970s, we introduced slope dummy variables into the wage and import price variables. The capacity utilization ratio is measured by the relative magnitude of actual GNP to the potential growth path, and is intended to capture the demand pressure in the economy. The CPI is set as dependent on WPI, the nominal money supply. The price deflator for private consumption is explained by CPI, and the deflator for fixed investment by WPI, import prices, and wages. Finally, the GNP deflator is determined by the ratio of nominal GNP to real GNP, with the former being determined as a sum of disaggregated nominal components such as nominal consumption expenditure and nominal fixed investment.

The financial sector comprises one equation and one identity: an equation measuring the demand for real money and an identity which defines the money supply process. The demand for money equation is estimated with a dependent interest rate variable. The money supply is endogenized by allowing the effects of the government budget constraint and overall balance of payments position. The real and financial sectors are linked through the following channels: the total money stock included in the consumption function and the consumer price equation, and the credit availablity in the investment function, and the money supply process. Therefore, the conventional linkage through the real interest rate variable is not established in this model.

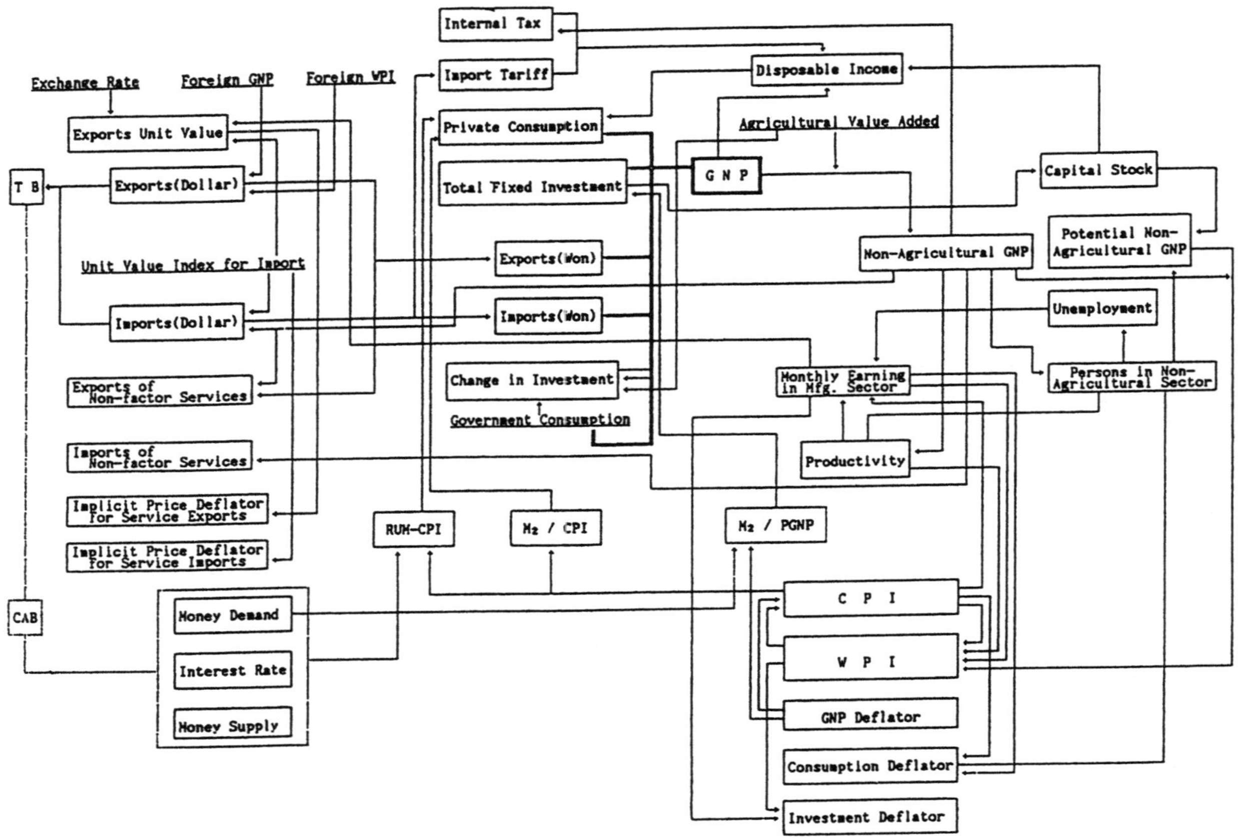

Figure Flow Chart of the KDI Model

3 Estimation

The exact specification of the model and the estimation results are given in the Appendix A, along with a list of the variables.

The model uses data from 1973:I to 1989:IV. With the exception of the capital stock data, which was derived by our own method, data was mostly obtained from monthly bulletins and the economic statistics yearbook of the Bank of Korea. Data in real terms are measured in 1985 prices. Some series are adjusted for seasonality by dummies.

For estimation, the ordinary least square method is used, along with some serial corrections where needed. Despite the fact that the OLS estimations could be subject to a simultaneity bias problem, these methods were chosen for their ease and because the results from alternative two–stage least square method were not significantly different from the OLS estimates . The system estimates, such as the three–stage least square estimates, have been also tried, but with results which were very sensitive to the specifications of the entire model system.

Equations that showed very low or high Durbin-Watson statistics have been reestimated using the Cochrane-Orcutt iterative method (or the Hildreth-Lu methods for equations with lagged dependent variables). For these cases, we reported rho statistics.

4 Historical Simulation

The historical simulation results are reported in Table 1. The model has been simulated over the period from 1981:I to 1989:IV, using the dynamic Gauss–Seidel method to solve the nonlinear simultaneous equations. As shown in Table 1, the simulated values of each endogenous variable trace the actual data very closely. Both root–mean square (RMS) errors and RMS percentage errors, which is RMS as a percentage of the mean, are reported. The RMS percentage errors are in the range of 2 to 7%, except for the three variables for trade balance, and government budget surplus and deficit and NFA.

Table 1. Dynamic Simultaneous Simulation Statistics of Predicted Values

(1980:I to 1989:IV)

Variables	RMSE	AAE	RMSPE	AAPE
GNP	438.85	355.62	2.52	1.94
CP	230.07	194.86	1.98	1.69
IF	292.93	237.26	4.98	4.06
NFA	766.85	621.66	59.84	23.93
X	447.16	343.70	5.74	4.48
XG	411.94	322.76	6.29	5.01
XGS	458.36	360.38	6.18	4.94
XGSV	515.09	388.69	6.42	4.97
M	417.00	332.15	5.68	4.46
MG	391.73	295.80	5.61	4.20
MGS	439.56	347.51	5.77	4.54
MGSV	466.41	372.86	5.81	4.60
WPI	3.37	2.77	3.62	2.92
CPI	3.26	2.74	3.34	2.83
PGNP	.04	.03	4.65	3.52
PXGS	1.87	1.50	1.65	1.34
TB	370.90	275.55	130.38	56.36
BSD	177.68	140.91	106.25	57.47
LEN	127.24	99.13	1.28	.97
Mz	915.22	633.10	2.68	2.14

RMSE = root-mean-square-error
AAE = average-absolute-error
RMSPE = root-mean-square-percentage-error
AAPE = average-absolute-percentage-error

5 Policy Simulations

To see how the system reacts to an external shock, we subjected the model to an increase in the government expenditures by 1% of the nominal GNP in 1983 and traced the resulting paths of the economy. Since the method of financing is crucial in analyzing the effects of increased government expenditures, we distinguished the following three cases: money financing, bond financing and tax financing. Furthermore, we treated investment expenditures differently from consumption expenditures to separate the capacity enhancing effects of investment expenditures.

The simulations were conducted over the 1983:I – 1989:IV period. The major results are presented in Table 2 to Table 3 and Figure 2 or 3, which reports the percentage deviations of the simulated values from the baseline values.

a) Government Consumption Expenditure

In response to an increase in government consumption with monetary accommodation, the real GNP increases by 1.2% in the first year and 0.07% in the second year, as shown in Table 2. Since then, the real GNP rapidly approaches the long run equilibrium path with weak cyclical fluctuation. Consumption expenditures without monetary accommodation bring smaller gains in the output and smaller cyclical fluctuations.

Table 2. Elasticities of Government Consumption Expenditure

Year	GNP(%)			WPI(%)		
	M	B	T	M	B	T
1983	1.204	0.919	0.727	0.655	0.454	0.365
1984	0.074	-0.157	-0.113	0.338	0.033	0.041
1985	-0.158	-0.161	-0.116	-0.123	-0.193	-0.136
1986	0.008	0.020	0.016	-0.048	-0.046	-0.032
1987	0.036	0.021	0.017	0.001	-0.006	-0.004
1988	0.009	-0.001	0.000	-0.017	-0.020	-0.14
1989	0.008	0.003	0.003	-0.020	-0.015	-0.012

Year	LEN(%)			TB(millon dollars)		
	M	B	T	M	B	T
1983	0.302	0.233	0.184	-198.7	-78.6	4.4
1984	0.141	0.043	0.036	-154.3	11.5	6.1
1985	-0.055	-0.067	-0.048	-91.9	21.0	5.2
1986	-0.017	-0.008	-0.006	-7.6	55.3	35.0
1987	0.009	0.007	0.006	0.8	31.2	19.5
1988	0.001	-0.001	-0.001	-12.3	9.3	4.5
1989	-0.001	-0.002	-0.001	-7.7	8.2	4.5

Note: M, B and T are defined as money, bond and tax financing respectively.

Following an increase in consumption accompanied by monetary expansion, the wholesale prices rise 0.66% in the first year and 0.34% in the second year. The expansionary effects of tax financed consumption are much smaller than those of money finacing and bond financing. Prices in this case increase by only 0.37% in the first year.

Trade balance deteriorates substantially in the first year following the expansionary policies. A setback in commodity exports due to an increase in domestic prices and an increase in commodity imports caused by increased income contributes to the trade balance deficit.

b) Government Investment Expenditures

The short-run paths after the expansionary shock are similar to the case when expenditures take the form of consumption, whereas the long-run paths diverge significantly.

Table 3. Elasticities of Government Investment Expenditure

Year	GNP(%) M	GNP(%) B	GNP(%) T	WPI(%) M	WPI(%) B	WPI(%) T
1983	1.215	0.934	0.743	0.614	0.414	0.325
1984	0.277	0.046	0.091	0.322	0.017	0.027
1985	-0.255	-0.257	-0.213	-0.401	-0.473	-0.416
1986	0.022	0.035	0.030	-0.245	-0.243	-0.230
1987	0.100	0.085	0.081	-0.125	-0.131	-0.129
1988	0.059	0.050	0.051	-0.124	-0.126	-0.122
1989	0.052	0.048	0.048	-0.103	-0.099	-0.096

Year	LEN(%) M	LEN(%) B	LEN(%) T	TB(millon dollars) M	TB(millon dollars) B	TB(millon dollars) T
1983	0.297	0.229	0.181	-406.8	-286.5	-202.9
1984	0.202	0.105	0.098	-205.0	-38.9	-45.2
1985	-0.109	-0.121	-0.102	-22.0	91.4	74.9
1986	-0.048	-0.039	-0.037	61.0	123.5	103.3
1987	0.007	0.006	0.004	51.3	81.2	69.7
1988	0.002	0.000	0.000	7.4	28.4	23.7
1989	0.000	0.000	0.000	3.8	19.6	16.0

Note: M, B and T are defined as money, bond and tax financing respectively.

Investment expenditures expand the future production capacities of the economy by increasing the capital stock, thereby contributing a larger gain in output without invoking price increases. In the case of tax financed investment, the initial price raising effects of government investment expenditures are more than offset by the cumulative price stabilizing effects in the third year, at which point prices actually begin to drop below the original level.

References

[1] Friedman, M. (1957) *A Theory of the Consumption Function*, Princeton: Princeton University Press

[2] Lee, S. (1984) "Annual Econometric Model for Korea," Korea Development Review, pp.136-60 (in Korean)

[3] Nam, S. W. and O. H. Chang (1984) "A Quarterly Macroeconometric Model for the Korean Economy: Specifications and Estimated Results," mimeo., Korea Development Institute

[4] Park, W. A. (1987) "A Quarterly Macroeconometric Model for the Korean Economy," KDI Working Paper No. 8716, Korea Development Institute

Appendix

A Model Specification and Estimation Results of the Quarterly KDI Model

A.1 Balance of Payments

Commodity Exports (Real) (2nd Degree PDL, Far Restriction)

(1) $\log XGS = 0.1258 + 3.2064 \log FGNP + 0.1989 \log \frac{FWPI}{PXGS}$

(11.12) (10.29) (1.36)

$+ 0.2713 \log \frac{FWPI}{PXGS_{-1}} + 0.3015 \log \frac{FWPI}{PXGS_{-2}}$

(3.20) (3.81)

$+ 0.2895 \log \frac{FWPI}{PXGS_{-3}} + 0.2352 \log \frac{FWPI}{PXGS_{-4}}$

(3.20) (3.81)

$+ 0.1387 \log \frac{FWPJ}{PXGS_{-5}} + 0.12575 D_2$

(2.46) (11.12)

$+ 0.1317 D_3 + 0.1657 D_4$

(10.10) (14.60)

R^2=0.9942 DW=1.99 SE=0.0499
ρ=0.8513

(2) $$FGNP = GNPAME^{0.6257} * \frac{GNPJAP}{238.54}^{0.2643} * \frac{GNPGER}{2.944}^{0.057} * \frac{GDPBRI}{0.7714}^{0.053}$$

(3) $$FWPI = WPIAME^{0.6257} * (WPIJAP * \frac{238.54}{RTJAP})^{0.2643} * (WPIGEA * \frac{2.944}{RTGER})^{0.057} * \frac{\frac{WPIBRI}{0.7714}}{RTBRI}^{0.053}$$

Non-Oil Imports (Real)

$$(4)\quad \log MCSNO = -0.6494 + 0.72149\log CP + 0.2460\log IF + 0.1200\log XG$$

(-0.91) (4.85) (2.75) (1.53)

$$- 0.3311\log PMGSNO * \frac{E}{WPI} + 0.1915\log MGSNO_{-1}$$

(-3.90) (2.33)

$$- 0.3507D75III + 0.2109D78IV + 0.0126D_2 - 0.0702D_3$$

(-5.03) (3.13) (0.30) (-2.17)

$$- 0.1115D_4$$

(-2.80)

R^2=0.9908 DW=1.61 SE=0.0638

Oil Imports (Real)

$$(5)\quad \log MGSO = 1.8164 + 0.5640\log\frac{1}{2}\sum_{i=0}^{3}(GNPN - NFI)_{-i} - 0.0405\log\frac{WPIO}{WPI}$$

(6.10) (18.18) (-0.93)

$$- 0.2105DMGSO - 0.0402D_2 - 0.0446D_3 - 0.0112D_4$$

(-5.53) (-1.07) (-1.19) (-0.30)

R^2=0.8696 DW=2.10 SE=0.1088

Unit Value Index for Commodity Exports (Real)

$$(6)\quad \log PXGS = 2.2339 + 0.2746\log\frac{1}{4}\sum_{i=0}^{3}WM_{-i}$$

(20.45) (25.91)

$$- 0.4409\log E + 0.4227\log PMGS - 0.0540DPXGS$$

(-16.17) (17.34) (-3.76)

R^2=0.9915 DW=0.93 SE=0.0251

Commodity Exports (Value)

$$(7)\quad XGSV = XGS\frac{PXGS}{100}$$

Commodity Imports (Real)

(8) $MGS = MGSO + MGSNO$

Oil Imports (Value)

(9) $MGSOV = MGSO \frac{PMGSO}{100}$

Non-oil Imports (Value)

(10) $MGSNOV = MGSNO \frac{PMGSNO}{100}$

Commodiry Imports (Value)

(11) $MGSV = MGSOV + MGSNOV$

Unit Value Index for Commodity Imports

(12) $PMGS = \frac{MGSV}{MGS} * 100$

Trade Balance

(13) $TB = XGSV - MGSV$

Exports of Non-Factor Services (Value)

(14) $\log XSNSV = -3.3828 + 1.1077 \log \frac{1}{2} \sum_{i=0}^{1} XGSV + MGSV_{-i}$

$$\begin{array}{ll} (-4.59) & (14.02) \end{array}$$

$$+ 0.1293D_2 + 0.0475D_3 + 0.0869D_4$$

$$\begin{array}{lll} (7.23) & (2.28) & (4.71) \end{array}$$

R^2=0.9928 DW=1.86 SE=0.0778
ρ =0.8305

Imports of Non-Factor Services (Value)

(15) $\log MSNSV = -0.5693 + 0.1592 \log \frac{GNPNV}{E} * 870.02$

$$\begin{array}{ll} (-2.04) & (2.62) \end{array}$$

$$+ 0.8425 \log MSNSV_{-1} + 0.1520D_2 + 0.0918D_3 + 0.1509D_4$$

$$\begin{array}{llll} (16.88) & (4.00) & (2.47) & (4.05) \end{array}$$

R^2=0.9890 DW=2.55 SE=0.1067

Price Deflator for Exports of Non-Factor Services

$$(16)\quad \log PXSN = \underset{(-3.62)}{-3.7702} + \underset{(3.64)}{0.3342} \log PXGS * E + \underset{(7.81)}{0.6581} \log PXSN_{-1} \underset{(-2.22)}{- 0.0434} D_3$$

R^2=0.9837 DW=1.94 SE=0.0688

Price Deflator for Imports of Non-Factor Services

$$(17)\quad \log PMSN = \underset{(-4.66)}{-1.8012} + \underset{(4.70)}{0.1597} \log PMGS + \underset{(28.96)}{0.8380} \log PMSN_{-1} \underset{(-1.88)}{-0.0174} D_3$$

R^2=0.9967 DW=1.71 SE=0.0330

Factor Income Paid Abroad (2nd Degree PDL, Far Restriction)

$$(18)\quad MSFSV = \underset{(0.19)}{16.2715} + \underset{(6.50)}{0.0169} \frac{GNPV}{E} * 1000$$

$$+ \underset{(7.80)}{0.0613} \frac{REU * (FLS + FLNM + FLM)_{-1}}{100}$$

$$+ \underset{(7.80)}{0.0511} \left(\frac{REU(FLS + FLNM + FLM)_{-1}}{100} \right)_{-1}$$

$$+ \underset{(7.80)}{0.0409} \left(\frac{REU * (FLS + FLNM + FLM)_{-1}}{100} \right)_{-2}$$

$$+ \underset{(7.80)}{0.0307} \left(\frac{REU * (FLS + FLNM + FLM)_{-1}}{100} \right)_{-3}$$

$$+ \underset{(7.80)}{0.0205} \left(\frac{REU * (FLS + FLNM + FLM)_{-1}}{100} \right)_{-4}$$

$$+ \underset{(2.37)}{0.01022} \left(\frac{REU * (FLS + FLNM + FLM)_{-1}}{100} \right)_{-5}$$

$$+ \underset{(3.76)}{116.050} D_2 \underset{(-1.12)}{- 39.698} D_3 + \underset{(1.93)}{69.9291} D_4$$

R^2=0.9439 DW=2.71 SE=118.444

Currrent Balance

(19) $CB = TB + XSNSV - MSNSV + XSFSV - MSFSV + NTR$

Capital Balance

(20) $CAPSV = LCB + SCB$

Overall Balance

(21) $OB = CB + CAPSV + EOBP$

A.2 Final Demand

Private Consumption

$$(22)\quad CP = \underset{(4.88)}{2425.0} + \underset{(4.65)}{0.2443}YDP + \underset{(3.13)}{0.1463}\frac{M2}{CPI} * 100 - \underset{(-1.60)}{10.9664}(RUM - \dot{CPI})$$

$$+ \underset{(1.96)}{0.1881}CP_{-1} + \underset{(2.69)}{277.0183}D_3 - \underset{(-1.82)}{552.5133}D_4$$

R^2=0.9930 DW=1.34 SE=294.881

Total Consumption

(23) $C = CP + CG$

Nominal Private Consumption

(24) $CPV = CP * PCP$

Nominal Total Consumption

(25) $CV = CPV + CGV$

Total Fixed Investment

$$(26)\quad IF = \underset{(-16.06)}{-1815.5790} + \underset{(6.75)}{0.1968}\frac{1}{4}\sum_{i=0}^{3} GNP_{-i} + \underset{(1.32)}{0.0645}\Delta\frac{M2}{PGNP} + \underset{(6.01)}{0.4826}IF_{-1}$$

$$+ \underset{(14.48)}{2003.3090}D_2 + \underset{(10.62)}{1048.6070}D_3 + \underset{(16.37)}{1517.7810}D_4$$

R^2=0.9915 DW=1.98 SE=239.394

Changes in Inventories

$$(27)\quad IS = -554.392 + 0.5080GNPA - 0.1918(CP + CG + IF + X) + 0.6365M$$

(-5.14) (3.74) (-6.47) (6.76)

$$- 201.063D_2 - 298.818D_3 + 951.272D_4$$

(-1.47) (-1.50) (1.34)

R^2=0.9643 DW=1.36 SE=290.851

Commodity Exports (Real)

$$(28)\quad XG = -75.1104 + 1.0137XGS\frac{870.02}{1000}$$

(-5.78) (426.89)

R^2=0.9996 DW=0.702 SE=53.51

Commodity Imports (Real)

$$(29)\quad MG = 211.960 + 1.0238MGS\frac{870.02}{1000}$$

(8.18) (224.0)

R^2=0.9987 DW=1.24 SE=95.9743

Export of Non-Factor Services (Real)

$$(30)\quad XSN = \frac{XSNSV * E}{PXSN * 1000}$$

Import of Non-Factor Services (Real)

$$(31)\quad MSN = \frac{MSNSV * E}{PMSN * 1000}$$

Export of Goods and Services (Real)

$$(32)\quad X = XG + XSN$$

Import of Goods and Services (Real)

$$(33)\quad M = MG + MSN$$

Gross Domestic Products

$$(34)\quad GDP = CP + CG + IF + IS + X - M + STD$$

Gross National Products

(35) $GNP = GDP + NFI$

Non-Agricultural Value-Added

(36) $GNPN = GNP - GNPA$

Proxy for Disposable Personal Income

(37) $YDP = GNP - CCA - \frac{TX}{PCP}$

Nominal Gross National Products

(38) $GNPV = GNP * PGNP$

Nominal Total Fixed Investment

(39) $IFV = IF * PIF$

Nominal Non-Agricultural Value-Added

(40) $GNPNV = GNPV - GNPAV$

Total Capital Stock (Real, End of Quarter)

(41) $K = IF + K_{-1} - CCA$

Capital Consumption Allowance

(42) $CCA = 0.0125 * K_{-1}$

A.3 Labor Market

Employment in Non-Agricultural Sector

(43) $LEN = (1 - 0.01 * UN) * LFN$

Total Employment

(44) $LE = LEN + LEA$

Labor Force in Non-Agricultural Sector

$$(45)\quad LFN = -16773.060 + 194.2531 D_2 - 320.0766 D_4 + 0.6362 POP$$

$$(-30.61) \qquad (5.44) \qquad (-8.95) \qquad (38.36)$$

$$+ 0.1465 \frac{1}{4} \sum_{i=0}^{3} GNP_{-i}$$

$$(19.23)$$

R^2=0.9980 DW=1.38 SE=120.299

Unemployment Rate in Non-Agricultural Sector

$$(46)\quad \log(UN) = 6.0874 - 2.3820 D_2 - 2.0049 D_3 - 1.6108 D_4$$

$$(8.24) \qquad (-8.24) \qquad (-9.28) \qquad (-7.34)$$

$$+ 0.1041 \left(\frac{GNPNFP - GNPNF}{GNPNFP} * 100 \right) + 0.77121 DMUN$$

$$(4.50) \qquad\qquad\qquad (3.21)$$

$$- 3.03544 TR$$

$$(-5.22)$$

R^2=0.8766 DW=2.02 SE=0.6259

Potential Non-Agricultural Value-Added Excluding Net Factor Income from Abroad

$$(47)\quad \log GNPNFP = -2.6980 + 0.9994 \log K_{-1} + 0.0567 \log K_{-2} + 0.0472 \log K_{-3}$$

$$(-5.62) \qquad (8.92) \qquad (5.47) \qquad (5.47)$$

$$+ 0.0378 \log K_{-4} + 0.0283 \log K_{-5} + 0.0189 \log K_{-6}$$

$$(5.47) \qquad (5.47) \qquad (5.47)$$

$$+ 0.0095 \log k_{-7} + 1.0010 \log LFN + 0.0640 D_2 + 0.0722 D_3$$

$$(5.47) \qquad (8.92) \qquad (8.40) \qquad (9.86)$$

$$+ 0.1253 D_4$$

$$(15.12)$$

R^2=0.9979 DW=1.01 SE=0.0213

A.4 Wages and Prices

Nominal Monthly Earnings per Person in Manufacturing Sector

$$(48)\quad \log WM = 9.8820 + 0.0363D_2 + 0.0785D_3 + 0.1171D_4 - 0.2051\log\frac{1}{4}\sum_{i=0}^{3} UN_{-i}$$

(8.43) (4.56) (8.47) (14.13) (-1.67)

$$+\,0.9268\log\frac{1}{4}\sum_{i=0}^{3}\left(\frac{\frac{GNPN}{LEN}}{HWN}\right)_{-i} + 1.3364\log CPI$$

(3.10) (16.48)

R^2=0.9986 DW=2.09 SE=0.0350

Wholesale Price Index

$$(49)\quad \log WPI = -2.2855 + 0.2455\log WPIO + 0.4226\log WM * D70AF$$

(-5.21) (10.64) (13.57)

$$+\,0.2460\log WM * D82AF + 0.0576\log PMGSNO * E$$

(5.52) (1.13)

$$-\,0.2896\log\frac{GNPN}{LEN} + 0.4822\log\frac{GNPNF}{GNPNFP} * 100 * D82AF$$

(-5.14) (3.97)

R^2=0.9987 DW=1.83 SE=0.0196
ρ =0.7377

Wholesale Price Index in Oil Sector

$$(50)\quad \log WPIO = 0.3325 + 0.4643\log\frac{1}{2}\sum_{i=0}^{1} PMGSO * \frac{E}{870.02}_{-i}$$

(7.21) (7.74)

$$+\,0.4658\log WPIO_{-1} + 0.1380DWPIO$$

(7.38) (3.77)

R^2=0.9909 DW=0.97 SE=0.0780

Consumer Price Index

$$(51)\quad \log CPI = -0.7637 + 0.5706 \log \frac{1}{2}\sum_{i=0}^{1} WPI_{-i} + 0.1264 \log \frac{1}{2}\sum_{i=0}^{1} M2_{-i}$$

(-4.61) (25.10) (4.11)

$$+ 0.1171 \log \frac{1}{2}\sum_{i=0}^{1} WM_{-i}$$

(2.81)

R^2=0.9984 DW=0.42 SE=0.0244

Price Deflator for Private Consumption

$$(52)\quad \log PCP = -4.9869 + 1.0794 \log CPI$$

(-131.85) (119.73)

R^2=0.9954 DW=0.17 SE=0.0412

Price Deflator for Fixed Investment

$$(53)\quad \log PIF = -7.0964 + 0.4118 \log WPI + 0.2114 \log WM$$

(-19.64) (7.23) (14.67)

$$+ 0.2259 \log PMGS * E$$

(5.00)

R^2=0.9980 DW=1.67 SE=0.0242

GNP Deflator

$$(54)\quad PGNP = 0.0044 + 0.9808 WAPGNP$$

(0.90) (159.87)

R^2=0.9974 DW=1.35 SE=0.0173

$$(55)\quad WAPGNP = \frac{CPV + CGV + IFV + XG\frac{PXGS}{100} * \frac{E}{870.02}}{CP + CG + IF + XG - MG}$$

$$- \frac{MG * \frac{PMGS}{100} * \frac{E}{870.02}}{CP + CG + IF + XG - MG}$$

A.5 Government Sector

Internal Tax Revenues

$$(56)\quad TXIN = \underset{(50.33)}{0.1189}GNPNV * D_1 + \underset{(53.13)}{0.1158}GNPNV * D_2 + \underset{(57.91)}{0.1208}GNPNV * D_3 + \underset{(50.05)}{0.0988}GNPNV * D_4$$

R^2=0.9853 DW=1.37 SE=131.592

Import Tariffs

$$(57)\quad TXIM = \underset{(30.34)}{0.0752}MGSV * \frac{E}{1000} * D_1 + \underset{(32.19)}{0.0724}MGSV * \frac{E}{1000} * D_2 + \underset{(33.05)}{0.0749}MGSV * \frac{E}{1000} * D_3 + \underset{(33.95)}{0.0729}MGSV * \frac{E}{1000} * D_4 - \underset{(-7.08)}{179.04}DTXIM - \underset{(-2.17)}{71.4339}DTXIM3$$

R^2=0.9584 DW=0.47 SE=44.0711

Total Tax Revenues

$$(58)\quad TX = TXIN + TXIM + TXO$$

Total Government Revenues

$$(59)\quad GR = TX + GRO$$

Government Budget Surplus

$$(60)\quad BSD = GR - GE - GLDMB$$

A.6 Money Market

Interest Rate in Unorganized Money Market

(61) $\log RUM = 4.0570 + 0.1219 \log RD - 0.4399 \log \frac{M2}{PGNP}$

(5.31) (1.91) (-2.68)

$+ 0.2135 \log \frac{1}{4} \sum_{i=0}^{3} GNP_{-i} + 0.3389 \log RUM_{-1}$

(1.02) (3.08)

$+ 0.0967 \log DRUM$

(3.02)

R^2=0.9433 DW=2.02 SE=0.0713

Broadly Defined Money Supply

(62) $M2 = DCG + DCP + NFA + OL$

Net Foreign Assets of BOK and DMB

(63) $NFA = 9.2073 + 0.8878 OB * \frac{E}{1000} + 1.0000 NFA_{-1}$

(0.27) (19.20) (NC)

R^2=0.9954 DW=2.49 SE=275.282

Claims on Government and Government Agency of BOK and DMB

(64) $DCG = DCG_{-1} - BSD + BSDOTH$

B List of Variables

"*" denotes exogenous variables

	Notation	Definition	Unit
	BSD	Budget Surplus	billion won
	BSDOTH	Other Budget Deficit Financed Through Borrowing from BOK and DMB	do
	C	Total Consumption (real)	1985 billion won
	CAPSV	Capital Account Balance	million U.S. dollars
	CB	Current Account Balance	do
	CCA	Capital Consumption Allowances (real)	1985 billion won
*	CG	Government Consumption (real)	do
*	CGV	Government Consumption (value)	billion won
	CP	Private Consumption (real)	1985 billion won
	CPI	Consumer Price Index	1985ī00
	CPV	Private Consumption (value)	billion won
	CV	Total Consumption (valuc)	do
	DCG	Claims on Government and Government Agency of BOK and DMB, End of Month Average	do
*	DCP	Claims on Private Sector of DMB, End of Month Average	
*	D1	Seasonal Dummy for the First Quarter	
*	D2	Seasonal Dummy for the Second Quarter	
*	D3	Seasonal Dummy for the Third Quarter	
*	D4	Seasonal Dummy for the Fourth Quarter	
*	D70AF	Dummy for WPI	1 70I-81II 0 Otherwise
*	D75III	Dummy for IF	1 75III 0 Otherwise
*	D78IV	Dummy for IF	1 78IV 0 Otherwise
*	D82AF	Dummy for WPI	1 81III-89IV 0 Otherwise
*	DMGSO	Dummy for MGSO	1 73III-74I, 75IV, 83I-83III, 87I-87IV 0 Otherwise
*	DMUN	Dummy for UN	1 79I-80IV 0 Otherwise
*	DPXGS	Dummy for PXGS	1 75I IV 0 Otherwise

	Notation	Definition	Unit
*	DRUM	Dummy for RUM	1 78I-80IV 0 Otherwise
*	DTXIM	Dummy for TXIM	1 89I-IV 0 Otherwtse
*	DTXIM3	Dummy for TXIM	1 85III-IV 0 Otherwise
*	E	Exchange Rate, Won per Dollar, Average	won
*	EOBP	Errors and Omission for BOP	million U.S. dollars
*	FGNP	Foreign GNP (real)	1985 billion U.S. dollars
*	FLM	Bank Foreign Debt, $17,566 for 1983.4	million U.S. dollars
*	FLNM	Non-Bank Long-Term Foreign Debt, $16,538 for 1983.4	do
*	FLS	Short-Term Debt (private), $4,947 for 1983.4	do
*	FWPI	Foreign WPI	1985=100, dollars base
	GDP	Gross Domestic Product (real)	1985 billion won
*	GDPBRI	GDP of U.K. (real)	1985 billion pounds
*	GE	Government Expenditures (value)	billion won
*	GLDMB	Central Government's Net Lending	do
	GNP	Gross National Product (real)	1985 billion won
*	GNPA	Agricultural Value Added (real)	do
*	GNPAME	GNP of U.S. (real)	1985 billion U.S. dollars
*	GNPAV	Agricultural Value Added (value)	billion won
*	GNPGER	GNP of Germany (real)	1985 billion marks
*	GNPJAP	GNP of Japan (real)	1985 billion yen
	GNPN	Non-Agricultural Value Added (real)	1985 billion won
	GNPNFP	Potential Non-Agricultural Value-Added, Excluding Net Factor Income from Abroad (real)	do
	GNPNV	Non-Agricultural Value Added (value)	billion won
	GNPV	Gross National Product (value)	do
	GR	Central Government Revenue (value)	do
*	GRO	Non-Tax Government Revenue (value)	do
*	HWN	Average Manhours Worked in Manufacturing Sector	hours per week
	IF	Total Fixed Investment (real)	1985 billion won
	IFV	Total Fixed Investment (value)	billion won
	IS	Change in Inventories (real)	1985 billion won
	K	Total Capital Stock (real, end of quarter)	do
*	LCB	Long–Term Capital Balance	million U.S. dollars

	Notation	Definition	Unit
	LE	Total Employment	1000 persons
*	LEA	Number of Persons Employed in Agricultural Sector	do
	LEN	Number of Persons Employed in Non-Agricultural Sector	do
	LFN	Economically Active Population in Non-Agricultural Sector	do
	M	Imports of Goods and Services in NIA (real)	1985 billion won
	MG	Imports of Commodities (real)	do
	MGS	Commodity Imports (real)	1985 million U.S. dollars
	MGSNO	Non-oil Imports (real)	do
	MGSNOV	Non-oil Imports (value)	million U.S. dollars
	MGSO	Oil Imports (real)	1985 million U.S. dollars
	MGSOV	Oil Imports (value)	million U.S. dollars
	MGSV	Commodity Import (value)	million U.S. dollars
	MSN	Imports of Non-Factor Services (real)	1985 billion won
	MSNSV	Imports of Non-Factor Services	million U.S. dollars
	M2	Broadly Defined Money Supply, End of Month, Average	billion won
	NFA	Net Foreign Assets of BOK and DMB	do
*	NFI	Net Factor Income Received from Abroad in NIA (real)	1985 billion won
*	NTR	Net Transfer from Abroad in BOP	million U.S. dollars
	OB	Overall Balance	million U.S. dollars
*	OL	Other Assets in Monetary Survey, End of Month Average	billion won
	PCP	Price Deflator for Private Consumption	1985=1
	PGNP	Price Deflator for GNP	do
	PIF	Price Deflator for Fixed Investment	do
	PMGS	Unit Value Index for Commodity Imports	1985=100, dollars base
*	PMGSNO	Unit Value Index for Non-oil Imports	do
*	PMGSO	Petroleum Import Price Index	do
	PMSN	Implicit Price Deflator for Service Imports	1985 = 100
*	POP	Total Population	1000 person
	PXGS	Unit Value Index for Commodity Exports	1985=100, dollars base
	PXSN	Implicit Price Deflator for Service Exports	1985 = 100
*	RD	Bank Deposit Rate, One-year Time Deposits	% per annum

	Notation	Definition	Unit
*	RTBRI	Exchange Rate U.K. Pound per Dollar, Average	pound
*	RTGER	Exchange Rate West German Mark per Dollar, Average	mark
*	RTJAP	Exchange Rate, Japanese Yen per Dollar, Average	yen
	RUM	Interest Rate in Unorganized Money Market	% per annum
*	SCB	Short-Term Capital Balance	million U.S. dollars
*	STD	Statistical Discrepancy in NIA	1985 billion won
	TB	Trade Balance	million U.S. dollars
*	TR	Time Trend	1973I=1
	TX	Total Tax Revenue	billion won
	TXIM	Import Tariff	do
	TXIN	Total Internal Tax	do
*	TXO	Other Tax Revenue	do
	UN	Unemployment Rate in Non-Agricultural Sector	%
	WM	Nominal Monthly Earnings per Person in Manufacturing Sector	won
	WPI	Wholesale Price Index	1985 = 100
	WPIO	Wholesale Price Index in Oil Sector	1985 = 100
*	WPIAME	U.S. WPI	do
*	WPIBRI	U.X. WPI	do
*	WPIGER	West German WPI	do
*	WPIJAP	Japanese WPI	do
	X	Exports of Goods and Services in NIA (real)	1985 billion won
	XG	Commodity Exports in NIA (real)	do
	XGS	Commodity Exports (real)	1985 million U.S. dollars
	XGSV	Commodity Exports (value)	million U.S. dollars
	XSN	Exports of Non-Factor Services in NIA (real)	1985 billion won
	XSNSV	Exports of Non-Factor Services	million U.S. dollars
	YDP	Proxy for Disposable Personal Income	1985 billion won

C The Data Used in KDI Quaterly Model 1991.3.28

		GNP	GNPV	GNPNFP	GDP	GDPV	CP1	CP2	CP1V
80:	1	10874.4	7022.8	11725.6	11191.7	7241.30	8015.2	96.800	5180.80
80:	2	12411.9	8684.2	13054.4	12905.4	9042.20	8224.6	95.900	5694.90
80:	3	13004.2	9214.3	13124.1	13332.8	9460.60	8592.9	94.900	6313.70
80:	4	15970.2	11828.4	13695.7	16558.7	12297.0	9151.6	94.100	7153.50
81:	1	11081.5	8733.5	12752.8	11479.8	9064.80	8165.8	92.500	6556.60
81:	2	12787.6	10600.2	14153.1	13454.3	11177.0	8614.4	92.000	7257.60
81:	3	13667.4	11341.5	14271.5	14157.4	11767.7	9033.5	91.200	7879.60
81:	4	17817.9	14852.9	14863.7	18523.9	15472.5	9823.2	87.600	8649.60
82:	1	11777.9	10441.1	13869.4	12282.7	10901.7	8591.7	96.000	7600.50
82:	2	13662.1	12241.0	15358.5	14332.1	12852.4	9153.1	97.400	8251.40
82:	3	14662.5	12938.3	15510.2	15175.1	13406.0	9809.0	95.100	8913.30
82:	4	19219.6	16561.8	16124.5	20030.9	17282.6	10401.7	92.600	9445.00
83:	1	13269.6	12567.4	15086.3	13770.8	12999.6	9358.8	125.200	8738.50
83:	2	15444.1	14482.3	16683.4	16083.7	15074.9	9946.4	130.100	9289.00
83:	3	16791.9	15523.7	16840.7	17247.2	15948.3	10688.2	121.500	9841.80
83:	4	21297.3	19148.9	17487.3	21999.2	19810.0	11341.2	119.700	10389.2
84:	1	15238.0	14614.0	16417.7	15714.1	15070.1	10101.5	159.500	9644.00
84:	2	17136.5	16526.8	18132.2	17846.6	17217.5	10706.6	159.900	10235.6
84:	3	18133.0	17650.9	18269.5	18758.5	18263.0	11575.3	154.700	11123.7
84:	4	22496.5	21292.2	18968.0	23287.2	22093.7	11994.8	153.200	11590.6
85:	1	16219.3	16103.7	17880.2	16785.9	16672.4	10698.4	182.500	10595.8
85:	2	18382.5	18120.6	19689.7	19136.3	18881.9	11350.6	192.000	11263.6
85:	3	19400.5	19550.3	19814.5	20083.3	20222.8	12236.2	186.100	12325.5
85:	4	24086.2	24313.9	20599.9	24841.5	25069.7	12846.2	182.900	12946.5
86:	1	17873.9	18456.4	19470.2	18564.8	19153.4	11534.2	193.200	11711.5
86:	2	20677.7	21095.6	21354.0	21462.5	21913.4	12267.8	201.300	12384.8
86:	3	22541.4	23020.7	21487.3	23098.8	23613.4	13289.3	190.600	13423.9
86:	4	27080.4	28026.0	22413.3	27741.6	28745.6	13848.4	187.200	13976.2
87:	1	20754.7	22006.6	21193.3	21238.8	22546.8	12461.8	215.000	12800.8
87:	2	23935.4	24796.9	23121.0	24535.0	25442.1	13396.1	214.500	13700.5
87:	3	25257.7	26394.1	23365.6	25693.9	26871.6	14347.2	204.000	14821.2
87:	4	29663.9	32826.8	24527.3	30335.9	33567.8	14979.7	201.700	15790.1
88:	1	24285.9	26803.3	23212.0	24726.7	27288.7	13758.8	248.900	14686.1
88:	2	26101.3	28923.7	25251.4	26539.4	29409.5	14636.3	246.800	15702.9
88:	3	28179.3	31450.7	25591.6	28486.3	31821.3	15754.0	232.900	16887.0
88:	4	33413.5	39052.8	26961.7	33739.9	39443.2	16416.4	225.700	18133.6
89:	1	25790.5	29602.2	25473.3	26052.1	29914.6	15168.2	267.600	16739.6
89:	2	28047.1	32505.9	27585.6	28318.0	32847.6	16108.7	268.000	17958.9
89:	3	29837.5	34698.4	28040.8	30023.6	34973.9	17250.4	250.600	19079.4
89:	4	35859.6	44259.7	29618.9	36034.7	44530.6	17977.9	245.600	20636.8

(continued)

		CP2V	IF	IFV	IS	X	XV	M	MV
80:	1	57.8000	3277.80	2341.4	-659.30	3771.1	2602.8	4932.9	3424.1
80:	2	58.3000	4248.20	3324.8	-437.10	4231.5	3076.8	5113.3	3750.9
80:	3	62.1000	4006.10	3092.5	-473.70	4395.8	3338.4	5092.9	3995.9
80:	4	63.5000	4238.5	3466.9	1705.90	4879.2	3925.5	5522.4	4603.2
81:	1	71.8000	3112.7	2659.7	-1171.10	4482.0	3814.0	5017.3	4492.7
81:	2	70.1000	4054.2	3547.2	-650.90	5127.6	4482.6	5612.7	5091.1
81:	3	73.7000	3667.2	3276.0	-102.00	5114.4	4475.2	5584.7	4972.7
81:	4	73.6000	4292.3	3792.7	3006.00	5165.9	4568.8	5655.9	5162.2
82:	1	88.2000	3135.1	2868.7	-997.00	4684.7	4248.5	4953.7	4425.7
82:	2	84.3000	4381.9	4035.3	-920.70	5416.4	4928.9	5629.8	5075.7
82:	3	85.8000	4343.4	4056.8	-479.60	5303.9	4813.1	5892.7	5274.4
82:	4	85.5000	4832.7	4484.8	3171.20	5375.0	4779.0	6051.7	5397.8
83:	1	120.900	3595.9	3409.6	-544.80	5156.0	4505.3	5834.3	5253.1
83:	2	118.200	5309.7	4960.1	-1052.20	6019.4	5534.2	6237.3	5573.2
83:	3	115.700	5130.7	4848.7	-1093.80	6602.8	6109.9	6130.6	5568.6
83:	4	114.800	5625.4	5450.4	2860.10	6997.9	6599.0	7030.9	6653.7
84:	1	157.000	4170.5	3989.6	-123.80	6029.2	5758.7	6466.0	6138.7
84:	2	149.700	6058.5	5793.0	-879.10	6661.1	6459.0	6820.0	6537.2
84:	3	150.300	5636.9	5431.5	-349.50	6797.9	6643.0	6926.2	6734.9
84:	4	150.100	5945.7	5784.0	2336.60	7256.0	7265.1	6878.0	6628.1
85:	1	190.300	4530.2	4423.0	-236.60	5957.0	5911.8	6399.0	6186.7
85:	2	186.700	5853.0	5806.4	-478.20	6935.9	7003.6	6707.1	6761.8
85:	3	184.100	5924.1	5952.1	-898.40	7254.2	7205.5	6456.3	6554.9
85:	4	182.400	6529.3	6655.0	2449.70	7790.1	7816.3	7357.0	7416.0
86:	1	203.000	4997.6	5037.8	-236.20	7225.6	7236.5	7304.3	7180.7
86:	2	199.900	6836.6	6950.4	-882.20	8744.6	8891.2	7911.7	7566.4
86:	3	195.400	6671.8	6764.6	-794.00	9319.0	9555.5	7943.7	7526.5
86:	4	191.100	7062.4	7240.6	2591.20	9949.3	10351.0	8553.9	8091.8
87:	1	226.200	5687.9	5834.8	-377.10	9126.8	9628.8	8187.2	7785.5
87:	2	221.200	7667.5	7927.3	-703.50	11172.9	11597.0	9677.7	9311.8
87:	3	215.100	7792.4	8086.1	-315.60	10873.5	11364.8	9692.8	9206.6
87:	4	213.500	8651.8	9283.1	2489.40	11675.5	12460.1	10313.7	10052.2
88:	1	276.500	6680.3	7237.7	-79.40	11220.7	11769.2	9876.2	9513.6
88:	2	267.700	8585.6	9362.6	-580.20	11740.5	12335.4	10530.4	10106.8
88:	3	258.800	8895.2	9985.2	-330.80	12144.5	13125.4	11109.8	10500.2
88:	4	255.100	9645.0	10769.1	2767.30	13103.6	13871.3	11215.8	10446.4
89:	1	310.400	7421.9	8241.4	631.70	10914.1	11177.0	11236.8	10221.1
89:	2	306.400	9724.0	10966.4	125.60	11314.4	11972.6	11976.0	10995.4
89:	3	298.100	10390.0	11817.5	394.20	11498.9	12277.5	12817.5	11404.4
89:	4	295.500	11745.4	13753.0	3566.10	12555.4	13287.0	13667.6	12169.7

(continued)

		XG	XGV	MG	MGV	K	CPI	WPI	XGSV
80:	1	3115.1	2110.2	4388.8	3117.2	89817.1	64.8000	70.5000	3705.2
80:	2	3499.2	2452.3	4559.4	3410.0	92942.6	69.5000	77.2000	4130.8
80:	3	3624.1	2698.2	4451.2	3580.4	95786.9	72.6000	79.9000	4435.0
80:	4	4056.8	3159.0	4855.5	4129.8	98828.1	77.0000	84.3000	4943.0
81:	1	3695.4	3047.1	4383.4	4014.0	100705.	81.0000	88.8000	4671.5
81:	2	4240.0	3601.3	4858.1	4502.6	103501.	85.1000	94.0000	5317.9
81:	3	4245.8	3629.6	4788.5	4354.0	105874.	89.2000	96.3000	5375.2
81:	4	4240.2	3607.4	4934.1	4592.9	108843.	89.7000	96.3000	5306.2
82:	1	3832.3	3348.2	4309.8	3916.4	110618.	90.5000	97.7000	4889.5
82:	2	4449.5	3909.5	4927.1	4506.5	113617.	92.1000	98.0000	5476.0
82:	3	4306.5	3801.0	5121.1	4646.4	116540.	93.2000	98.5000	5313.2
82:	4	4261.5	3700.5	5349.5	4823.6	119916.	93.4000	98.7000	5200.5
83:	1	4108.7	3510.1	5212.8	4733.0	122013.	95.1000	99.2000	4658.4
83:	2	4948.4	4405.0	5449.0	4898.9	125797.	95.5000	98.4000	5724.1
83:	3	5382.4	4888.6	5519.6	5038.3	129356.	95.6000	98.0000	6226.1
83:	4	5651.0	5242.9	6265.8	5956.2	133364.	95.6000	98.1000	6595.3
84:	1	5001.9	4663.3	5801.0	5530.2	135868.	97.0000	98.5000	5860.8
84:	2	5510.3	5269.8	6208.1	5971.2	140228.	97.5000	98.8000	6602.0
84:	3	5511.0	5387.3	6273.8	6127.0	144112.	97.8000	99.6000	6647.2
84:	4	6030.0	5920.4	6136.5	5932.5	148256.	98.1000	99.7000	7224.6
85:	1	4918.7	4842.9	5799.1	5621.0	150933.	98.8000	99.8000	5790.1
85:	2	5735.9	5777.5	6106.2	6168.1	154899.	99.7000	99.9000	6673.1
85:	3	5997.0	5967.9	5866.5	5956.8	158887.	100.500	100.100	6771.8
85:	4	6366.5	6429.8	6733.0	6758.9	163431.	101.000	100.200	7206.5
86:	1	5934.5	6035.3	6724.5	6564.5	166385.	102.400	99.7000	6803.5
86:	2	7206.9	7395.0	7268.3	6880.3	171142.	102.900	98.4000	8336.8
86:	3	7661.2	7904.1	7328.8	6863.0	175675.	103.200	98.4000	8959.0
86:	4	8144.2	8531.9	7903.3	7403.4	180541.	102.500	97.7000	9813.9
87:	1	7561.9	8019.3	7539.7	7076.7	183972.	103.200	98.0000	9372.9
87:	2	9310.5	9723.1	9040.2	8606.9	189340.	105.400	99.1000	11743.5
87:	3	9058.8	9537.7	9010.1	8475.1	194766.	106.800	99.2000	11810.8
87:	4	9874.4	10639.3	9516.1	9179.1	200983.	108.100	99.6000	13316.6
88:	1	9488.2	9995.0	9138.5	8705.4	205151.	110.900	101.200	12960.4
88:	2	9884.8	10458.7	9740.6	9251.8	211172.	113.000	101.300	14218.7
88:	3	10276.9	11162.0	10241.1	9591.2	217428.	114.400	102.100	15437.9
88:	4	11169.3	11841.8	10307.8	9500.8	224355.	115.400	102.100	17031.2
89:	1	9156.3	9478.4	10274.5	9240.9	228972.	117.100	102.500	14001.2
89:	2	9435.7	10013.3	10873.7	9892.6	235834.	119.400	103.300	15069.0
89:	3	9566.5	10391.7	11580.2	10175.6	243276.	120.900	103.200	15528.4
89:	4	10525.8	11258.2	12337.5	10855.6	251981.	122.300	103.700	16810.1

(continued)

		MGSV	XSSV	MSSV	PXGS	LF	LFA	LE	LEA
80:	1	5022.90	1116.30	1403.90	103.100	14584.0	5324.00	13760.0	5242.00
80:	2	5214.50	1293.60	1698.60	102.700	15408.0	6075.00	14736.0	6044.00
80:	3	5464.20	1389.70	1579.20	105.700	15053.0	5681.00	14361.0	5641.00
80:	4	5896.50	1563.70	2067.50	104.000	12679.0	3573.00	11876.0	3506.00
81:	1	5637.80	1434.40	1669.70	107.600	14641.0	5281.00	13827.0	5218.00
81:	2	6212.30	1642.30	2191.30	108.600	15726.0	6064.00	15118.0	6037.00
81:	3	6083.70	1606.80	1952.60	108.500	15386.0	5827.00	14760.0	5793.00
81:	4	6365.30	1914.60	2302.90	107.300	12978.0	3616.00	12387.0	3564.00
82:	1	5309.90	1820.30	1814.10	107.100	14909.0	4944.00	14079.0	4881.00
82:	2	5882.00	1957.90	2078.50	105.000	15939.0	5646.00	15339.0	5625.00
82:	3	6023.10	1902.80	1971.40	103.600	15591.0	5291.00	15039.0	5263.00
82:	4	6258.60	1795.30	2166.50	101.500	13690.0	3488.00	13059.0	3434.00
83:	1	5928.10	1636.60	1737.90	98.7000	14937.0	4496.00	14121.0	4438.00
83:	2	5985.30	1758.10	2077.80	100.700	16159.0	5384.00	15621.0	5364.00
83:	3	6010.00	1828.00	1666.40	100.700	15885.0	5102.00	15358.0	5078.00
83:	4	7044.00	1956.00	2131.20	101.600	13789.0	3152.00	13197.0	3109.00
84:	1	6503.30	1707.50	1850.00	102.000	14315.0	3568.00	13570.0	3514.00
84:	2	6999.60	1804.10	2020.40	104.300	16122.0	4947.00	15627.0	4927.00
84:	3	7073.60	1814.50	1979.80	105.000	15777.0	4587.00	15266.0	4565.00
84:	4	6794.00	1990.20	2343.70	104.300	14166.0	2993.00	13641.0	2961.00
85:	1	6311.30	1646.40	1899.80	102.400	15061.0	3498.00	14321.0	3432.00
85:	2	6678.90	1618.00	2123.00	101.300	16622.0	4596.00	16049.0	4560.00
85:	3	6358.50	1640.20	1948.30	98.3000	16239.0	4298.00	15665.0	4261.00
85:	4	7111.80	1759.80	2139.40	98.7000	14554.0	2758.00	13937.0	2715.00
86:	1	6979.50	1607.90	2047.70	99.8000	15461.0	3408.00	14626.0	3340.00
86:	2	7329.20	1974.50	2314.90	100.700	16959.0	4420.00	16444.0	4400.00
86:	3	7356.60	2064.00	1982.10	101.800	16601.0	4147.00	16098.0	4122.00
86:	4	8042.00	2405.30	2334.50	104.900	15305.0	2912.00	14784.0	2889.00
87:	1	7811.30	2338.40	2019.40	107.900	16588.0	3654.00	15888.0	3612.00
87:	2	9882.00	2670.70	2334.80	109.800	17740.0	4332.00	17273.0	4312.00
87:	3	9958.60	2498.70	2043.60	113.500	17448.0	4065.00	17013.0	4047.00
87:	4	10932.9	2502.20	2634.80	117.400	16047.0	2863.00	15665.0	2840.00
88:	1	10702.0	2485.80	2322.70	119.500	16903.0	3419.00	16429.0	3392.00
88:	2	11932.5	2788.00	2506.10	126.000	17970.0	4123.00	17593.0	4108.00
88:	3	12607.3	2866.70	2442.70	131.400	18051.0	4141.00	17626.0	4124.00
88:	4	12961.0	3111.40	2713.20	133.900	16536.0	2660.00	16108.0	2636.00
89:	1	12907.6	2871.00	2767.30	134.900	17656.0	3464.00	17107.0	3423.00
89:	2	14033.3	3159.50	3043.00	141.100	18631.0	4177.00	18216.0	4158.00
89:	3	14595.3	3174.30	3190.10	142.400	18453.0	3996.00	18052.0	3980.00
89:	4	15275.3	3436.40	3430.40	142.400	17467.0	3028.00	17014.0	3000.00

(continued)

		PMGS	DC	TX	TXIN	TXIM	RUM	WM	M2
80:	1	108.100	12710.5	1469.50	958.30	194.000	50.7600	127752.	10045.8
80:	2	109.600	13581.8	1434.80	908.80	193.200	48.8400	141982.	10455.9
80:	3	114.200	14467.4	1589.80	1000.20	194.800	42.4800	156690.	11012.5
80:	4	113.600	15808.8	1302.00	802.70	170.400	37.6800	161744.	11923.0
81:	1	119.500	17429.1	1761.70	1131.90	223.100	36.6000	154921.	12792.0
81:	2	118.500	18674.0	1743.40	1066.20	228.500	35.1600	169811.	13263.9
81:	3	115.400	19525.3	2042.60	1249.90	241.500	33.8400	186674.	13867.7
81:	4	117.400	21074.5	1812.80	1183.20	245.900	35.4000	192960.	14973.9
82:	1	111.400	22657.1	1743.90	1104.40	230.400	32.6400	182054.	16077.0
82:	2	109.300	23905.0	2040.20	1244.40	248.300	33.1200	192945.	16949.1
82:	3	106.500	25578.0	2340.90	1452.60	250.300	27.4800	213550.	18311.8
82:	4	105.400	26909.3	2274.80	1449.30	283.600	29.0400	220495.	19421.8
83:	1	104.900	28056.9	2143.10	1339.80	294.800	24.1200	205917.	20050.9
83:	2	101.700	29112.8	2432.20	1452.50	375.400	27.4800	220698.	20661.8
83:	3	101.200	30111.4	2787.10	1694.50	381.800	26.7600	236640.	21550.7
83:	4	104.100	31108.5	2717.80	1701.60	411.500	24.7200	242931.	22435.7
84:	1	104.300	32417.4	2489.90	1498.20	407.700	24.7200	224956.	22997.9
84:	2	104.900	33019.8	2748.70	1666.20	396.000	25.6800	236063.	22793.7
84:	3	104.900	34249.0	2907.90	1765.50	408.800	23.5200	254636.	23316.7
84:	4	102.700	35358.8	2806.60	1767.50	381.200	25.4400	265952.	24284.1
85:	1	100.700	36689.7	2741.00	1721.70	405.600	24.7200	242857.	24751.6
85:	2	101.500	37957.7	3142.20	1948.30	420.500	24.1200	258262.	25242.7
85:	3	100.200	40064.1	3232.00	2049.30	358.100	23.7600	283239.	26595.0
85:	4	98.000	41615.1	2793.10	1777.70	381.800	23.4000	295002.	27817.5
86:	1	95.800	43193.5	3161.40	2066.00	389.500	22.9200	268100.	28504.5
86:	2	92.900	44175.5	3428.00	2106.20	484.100	23.1600	285925.	29911.2
86:	3	92.400	45334.9	3733.60	2250.70	530.800	23.1600	306867.	31293.8
86:	4	93.800	47149.1	3318.80	2041.10	538.100	23.2800	322025.	32941.3
87:	1	95.500	48287.9	3848.20	2384.60	602.600	22.8000	287722.	33739.1
87:	2	100.100	50541.8	4142.90	2581.50	673.600	22.4400	306368.	35196.8
87:	3	101.400	52241.9	4372.60	2655.10	699.500	24.3600	331173.	36993.3
87:	4	105.100	55079.0	4026.50	2390.80	720.700	22.2000	388287.	39126.1
88:	1	105.900	55482.5	4811.30	3054.40	689.600	23.2800	343364.	39651.6
88:	2	110.900	56707.2	4767.80	3083.20	602.500	24.0000	369048.	41048.7
88:	3	112.700	58114.7	5301.40	3445.20	642.500	22.2000	424794.	43690.2
88:	4	116.100	60525.0	4602.40	2962.20	638.600	21.2400	436483.	46892.3
89:	1	114.800	61373.3	5175.20	3681.50	434.500	17.0800	410354.	47383.5
89:	2	113.200	63208.5	5474.20	3931.70	498.500	20.6400	471927.	48667.1
89:	3	113.100	65329.3	6016.00	4299.10	560.000	19.7600	492761.	51307.5
89:	4	113.700	71594.0	4757.40	3298.80	606.000	18.9000	506320.	55196.6

(continued)

		IFM	TEXO	NFI	FA	FL	MGSOV	IFC	REU
80:	1	1726.30	65.000	-317.300	3259.6	3242.50	1389.40	1551.50	19.9000
80:	2	1836.20	130.000	-493.500	3426.1	3765.30	1189.80	2412.00	9.8000
80:	3	1757.50	150.000	-328.600	4033.3	4425.60	1355.50	2248.60	12.1000
80:	4	1924.50	165.000	-588.500	4459.5	4977.10	1703.40	2314.00	18.1000
81:	1	1618.80	80.000	-398.300	4431.1	5371.20	1912.90	1494.00	15.0000
81:	2	2037.90	200.000	-666.700	4439.6	5939.70	1451.50	2016.30	18.7000
81:	3	1603.60	240.000	-490.000	4321.1	6257.10	1371.60	2063.70	17.3000
81:	4	1985.30	160.000	-706.000	4901.1	7152.70	1639.80	2307.00	13.9000
82:	1	1522.90	110.000	-504.800	4879.9	7572.10	1463.00	1612.20	15.0000
82:	2	1977.20	210.000	-670.000	5123.1	8236.60	1494.80	2404.60	15.1000
82:	3	1865.80	240.000	-512.600	4971.2	8590.70	1426.00	2477.60	12.6000
82:	4	1995.20	190.000	-811.300	5448.3	9562.70	1719.00	2837.50	9.9000
83:	1	1624.40	155.000	-501.200	5168.5	10016.4	1597.10	1971.50	9.1000
83:	2	2207.20	200.000	-639.600	5254.5	10405.5	1133.30	3102.50	9.3000
83:	3	1948.20	265.000	-455.300	5637.4	10977.1	1085.70	3182.50	10.0000
83:	4	2240.10	210.000	-701.900	5947.8	11270.8	1760.60	3385.30	9.8000
84:	1	1922.60	155.000	-476.100	6025.9	11506.1	1484.00	2247.90	10.0000
84:	2	2742.60	225.000	-710.100	6200.6	12042.2	1359.90	3316.00	11.3000
84:	3	2312.30	255.000	-625.500	6500.9	12534.2	1579.90	3324.60	11.8000
84:	4	2327.90	231.000	-790.700	6953.0	12998.9	1366.30	3617.80	9.7000
85:	1	2144.70	137.000	-566.600	6800.5	13341.5	1494.90	2385.50	8.9000
85:	2	2435.00	235.000	-753.800	6821.1	14138.0	1372.00	3417.90	8.2000
85:	3	2429.70	260.000	-682.800	7066.7	14995.1	1236.70	3494.40	8.0000
85:	4	2710.30	197.000	-755.300	7987.4	15612.9	1485.10	3819.00	8.0000
86:	1	2563.20	165.000	-690.900	7483.4	15526.1	1382.30	2434.50	7.8000
86:	2	3116.70	250.000	-784.800	7699.7	15480.5	626.60	3719.90	6.9000
86:	3	2987.10	335.000	-557.400	8505.5	15612.7	552.10	3684.70	6.2000
86:	4	3374.50	234.000	-661.200	8451.4	14541.7	784.40	3687.90	6.0000
87:	1	2918.60	207.300	-484.100	8419.0	13450.4	760.30	2769.30	6.4000
87:	2	3646.30	171.500	-599.600	8086.3	12338.9	931.00	4021.10	7.2000
87:	3	3583.40	246.100	-436.200	8152.6	11480.5	784.00	4209.00	7.2000
87:	4	4226.70	279.400	-672.000	8726.7	11050.6	1226.80	4425.20	8.0000
88:	1	3609.50	234.600	-440.800	9994.3	9601.60	958.50	3070.80	7.0000
88:	2	3683.70	209.600	-438.100	11942.1	8993.80	921.60	4901.90	7.5000
88:	3	4235.30	216.800	-307.000	13913.9	8568.70	1063.70	4659.90	8.4000
88:	4	4718.00	213.000	-326.400	15046.3	7981.90	744.00	4927.10	9.0000
89:	1	3872.70	74.6000	-261.600	15355.6	7952.90	1075.30	3549.20	9.8100
89:	2	4233.10	.0000	-270.900	16379.2	7890.40	1235.70	5491.00	9.7800
89:	3	4838.50	.0000	-186.100	16514.6	7364.20	1219.60	5551.50	8.9300
89:	4	5305.00	.0000	-175.100	16594.1	7224.30	1401.90	6440.40	8.6200

(continued)

		FLS	FLNM	FLM	TR	GNPA	GNPAV	CG	CGV
80:	1	3081.10	11228.2	9611.9	33.0000	380.90	278.00	1667.70	1031.20
80:	2	3701.40	11637.3	9968.6	34.0000	1186.40	903.50	1672.30	1042.80
80:	3	4208.50	12282.4	11286.4	35.0000	1640.10	1154.50	1748.80	1136.50
80:	4	4132.20	12691.3	11835.1	36.0000	4449.40	3341.50	1786.50	1176.00
81:	1	4754.20	13243.1	11727.8	37.0000	399.30	329.30	1815.40	1355.60
81:	2	5078.50	13489.6	12714.4	38.0000	1121.20	1106.20	1784.20	1310.70
81:	3	4830.10	13887.7	12818.8	39.0000	1654.40	1374.10	1807.40	1398.70
81:	4	4049.90	14323.0	14451.7	40.0000	5574.80	4621.10	1860.40	1449.90
82:	1	4082.10	14398.6	14620.4	41.0000	447.30	420.60	1665.40	1446.30
82:	2	4109.00	14691.5	15150.2	42.0000	1210.50	1261.90	1721.10	1377.50
82:	3	3740.50	15213.8	15277.5	43.0000	1790.00	1523.10	1822.30	1562.80
82:	4	4053.50	15688.4	17255.6	44.0000	5953.50	4783.60	2130.20	1868.20
83:	1	4264.10	16081.2	16913.3	45.0000	509.40	638.50	1804.80	1647.20
83:	2	4438.60	16173.9	17296.3	46.0000	1287.20	1411.10	1832.10	1572.20
83:	3	4663.20	16386.5	17547.1	47.0000	2105.40	1709.20	1867.60	1718.40
83:	4	4947.00	16517.0	17566.0	48.0000	6226.50	4919.40	2085.70	1914.00
84:	1	4820.20	16747.6	17477.6	49.0000	565.70	607.40	1770.00	1680.90
84:	2	4707.20	16739.7	18625.3	50.0000	1187.40	1358.90	1840.70	1633.90
84:	3	4976.80	16992.1	18562.1	51.0000	2047.90	1982.60	1896.20	1839.50
84:	4	4189.10	17031.4	19263.4	52.0000	6176.20	5443.20	2195.20	2108.30
85:	1	4351.90	17184.3	19015.6	53.0000	611.60	611.60	1987.30	1961.60
85:	2	4111.60	17128.8	19684.7	54.0000	1356.20	1356.20	1900.60	1787.90
85:	3	3523.80	17136.3	20066.0	55.0000	2301.60	2301.60	1973.10	2021.20
85:	4	3601.60	17187.7	20616.9	56.0000	6082.40	6082.40	2274.90	2365.20
86:	1	3495.40	17331.5	20356.2	57.0000	671.50	686.30	2070.20	2176.70
86:	2	3467.20	17316.1	20320.8	58.0000	1378.30	1289.70	2071.20	2053.80
86:	3	3325.00	17470.8	19306.7	59.0000	2582.30	2248.70	2243.70	2377.20
86:	4	3209.50	17155.9	19124.0	60.0000	6197.50	6503.80	2628.60	2793.00
87:	1	3286.40	17141.3	17019.6	61.0000	571.90	649.20	2182.30	2379.70
87:	2	2890.60	16583.2	16842.6	62.0000	1413.90	1302.00	2387.50	2531.20
87:	3	2809.20	16001.3	16184.3	63.0000	2318.80	2152.40	2306.00	2632.90
87:	4	3202.50	14722.7	15159.6	64.0000	5792.90	7249.80	2760.90	3164.70
88:	1	3757.20	14407.5	9237.3	65.0000	614.70	802.70	2357.50	2766.50
88:	2	4446.70	14138.6	8289.7	66.0000	1383.20	1592.00	2365.00	2689.00
88:	3	5236.30	13461.0	7299.0	67.0000	2443.20	2479.10	2624.20	3224.80
88:	4	4538.80	12420.8	6169.8	68.0000	6461.60	8620.10	3191.30	3806.80
89:	1	4444.00	11722.7	7543.4	69.0000	675.80	916.90	2512.20	3197.10
89:	2	5234.00	11174.2	7178.3	70.0000	1430.10	1877.40	2538.20	3143.10
89:	3	5281.00	11127.1	7459.8	71.0000	2303.70	2521.50	2817.60	3761.60
89:	4	4269.60	10528.8	6583.6	72.0000	6415.80	9230.10	3497.20	4491.20

(continued)

		RD	HWN	LCB	SCB	EOBP	NTR	RTJAP	RTGER
80:	1	23.4000	50.600	319.40	893.400	-356.700	88.800	243.540	1.77340
80:	2	24.0000	52.300	557.30	620.300	-313.900	110.300	232.690	1.81050
80:	3	23.7000	51.400	685.90	507.100	-202.300	104.300	220.080	1.77560
80:	4	20.5000	52.000	293.90	-76.300	503.000	145.900	210.650	1.91120
81:	1	19.5000	50.000	987.50	622.000	-922.200	83.000	205.570	2.08660
81:	2	19.5000	53.000	267.40	324.300	-74.1000	113.100	220.000	2.27580
81:	3	19.5000	52.100	648.40	-248.400	-109.200	178.600	231.890	2.43270
81:	4	18.5000	52.500	938.60	-780.200	694.900	126.000	224.680	2.24480
82:	1	15.1000	50.600	158.80	32.200	-648.300	109.400	233.490	2.34590
82:	2	12.4000	52.500	115.90	26.900	-203.800	109.700	244.270	2.37800
82:	3	8.0000	52.900	774.50	-368.500	-110.900	152.900	258.860	2.48120
82:	4	8.0000	52.500	181.10	313.000	-332.500	127.000	259.680	2.50120
83:	1	8.0000	51.100	224.80	210.600	131.600	163.400	235.740	2.40780
83:	2	8.0000	53.000	291.00	174.500	-389.500	138.400	237.530	2.48480
83:	3	8.0000	52.500	-63.00	224.600	-639.900	145.400	242.530	2.64290
83:	4	8.0000	53.200	817.60	283.800	-44.5000	144.900	234.240	2.67760
84:	1	8.8000	51.900	580.10	-126.800	-275.500	115.300	231.010	2.70250
84:	2	9.0000	53.000	-31.50	-113.000	-115.500	139.000	229.610	2.70950
84:	3	9.0000	51.700	608.90	269.600	-181.100	126.900	234.460	2.91890
84:	4	9.6000	52.900	909.90	-787.700	-322.300	159.700	246.020	3.05290
85:	1	10.0000	50.500	275.80	162.800	-254.900	127.400	257.680	3.25630
85:	2	10.0000	52.600	-102.90	-240.300	-226.600	125.400	250.730	3.08670
85:	3	10.0000	52.300	452.00	-587.800	8.800	163.100	238.640	2.84900
85:	4	10.0000	52.700	475.90	77.800	-407.700	161.800	207.090	2.58390
86:	1	10.0000	50.800	43.60	-106.200	372.600	178.100	187.880	2.34630
86:	2	10.0000	53.100	-263.80	-28.200	-348.100	222.100	170.130	2.24640
86:	3	10.0000	52.500	-29.40	-142.200	-265.100	338.600	155.770	2.08560
86:	4	10.0000	53.400	-1732.30	-115.500	-302.900	299.800	160.290	2.00760
87:	1	10.0000	51.100	-139.50	76.900	-22.000	238.900	153.170	1.83950
87:	2	10.0000	53.700	-1526.90	-395.800	-171.600	288.600	142.670	1.80520
87:	3	10.0000	51.700	-1920.30	-81.400	486.500	277.100	146.920	1.83930
87:	4	10.0000	51.100	-2249.10	393.300	898.100	412.900	135.790	1.70550
88:	1	10.0000	50.000	78.10	554.700	189.400	481.500	128.000	1.67580
88:	2	10.0000	51.200	-687.40	689.500	38.600	358.300	125.610	1.70750
88:	3	10.0000	51.000	-583.20	789.600	-64.200	337.100	133.710	1.86610
88:	4	10.0000	52.100	-1540.30	-697.500	-752.800	271.200	125.280	1.77560
89:	1	10.0000	49.000	-1783.90	-94.800	907.800	143.900	128.450	1.84930
89:	2	10.0000	50.500	-614.20	790.000	647.500	70.300	138.070	1.93390
89:	3	10.0000	49.400	47.00	248.500	-231.700	11.000	142.290	1.92420
89:	4	10.0000	49.400	-1011.40	-883.400	-622.900	21.40	143.040	1.81280

(continued)

		RTBRI	WPIAME	WPJAP	WPIGER	WPIBRI	GNPGER	GNLPJAP	GDPBRI
80:	1	.443750	83.9000	97.500	80.000	69.200	1758.60	258857.	327.580
80:	2	.437660	85.6000	101.400	81.800	72.000	1728.20	259042.	321.790
80:	3	.419970	88.4000	101.900	82.300	73.300	1733.40	261845.	325.450
80:	4	.419180	90.4000	101.100	83.500	74.300	1722.60	264893.	320.230
81:	1	.432880	93.1000	100.500	85.500	76.300	1738.50	268573.	320.890
81:	2	.480470	95.2000	101.600	87.600	78.800	1726.40	269845.	319.650
81:	3	.544510	95.9000	102.900	89.500	79.800	1742.70	272148.	319.820
81:	4	.530870	95.8000	102.600	90.800	81.400	1735.70	272645.	320.660
82:	1	.541390	96.6000	103.000	92.300	83.500	1724.50	275248.	322.840
82:	2	.562090	96.7000	103.300	93.200	84.900	1725.90	278469.	324.300
82:	3	.579610	97.1000	104.300	94.100	85.700	1713.80	280694.	323.480
82:	4	.606170	97.2000	104.200	94.400	86.700	1712.40	282513.	327.300
83:	1	.652610	97.3000	102.200	94.200	87.900	1736.20	283769.	333.840
83:	2	.642880	97.6000	101.200	94.400	89.700	1753.00	286549.	333.460
83:	3	.662210	98.6000	101.400	95.200	90.300	1743.20	290853.	338.940
83:	4	.680180	99.1000	100.800	95.800	91.500	1744.50	292103.	339.220
84:	1	.697060	100.200	100.900	96.700	93.200	1817.50	297201.	342.550
84:	2	.715970	100.800	100.800	97.400	95.300	1777.80	301474.	339.560
84:	3	.770590	100.600	101.600	97.800	95.900	1811.90	304377.	341.920
84:	4	.822230	100.300	101.300	98.600	97.100	1829.70	308509.	345.710
85:	1	.896700	100.100	102.300	99.600	98.200	1820.30	311662.	351.320
85:	2	.795170	100.200	101.100	100.200	99.900	1832.50	316504.	355.780
85:	3	.726800	99.5000	99.700	100.200	100.500	1863.80	319466.	356.410
85:	4	.696040	100.100	96.900	100.000	101.400	1860.50	322956.	357.820
86:	1	.694250	98.6000	94.900	99.300	102.800	1847.60	320997.	362.540
86:	2	.662820	96.8000	91.400	98.000	104.200	1893.80	324499.	366.100
86:	3	.671370	96.3000	89.000	97.200	104.600	1903.20	327508.	369.120
86:	4	.699590	96.7000	88.100	95.500	105.500	1904.10	329619.	373.420
87:	1	.648640	97.8000	87.500	95.000	106.900	1891.00	333662.	376.000
87:	2	.608750	99.4000	86.800	94.700	108.000	1906.00	335093.	381.040
87:	3	.618580	100.500	87.900	95.100	108.600	1931.20	342593.	387.790
87:	4	.569900	100.900	87.600	95.400	109.800	1947.60	348555.	391.670
88:	1	.556580	101.500	86.600	95.400	111.000	1977.50	357064.	399.670
88:	2	.542620	103.300	86.300	96.000	112.600	1974.70	354049.	401.720
88:	3	.589800	104.700	87.100	96.500	113.900	1997.20	362177.	406.480
88:	4	.558530	105.200	86.400	97.000	115.200	2006.50	365253.	409.860
89:	1	.571980	107.500	86.800	98.400	116.800	2059.80	373846.	411.080
89:	2	.614210	109.400	89.100	99.200	118.300	2063.60	371021.	412.000
89:	3	.626210	109.000	89.800	99.400	119.700	2056.10	381778.	414.250
89:	4	.630760	109.400	89.600	100.100	121.200	2076.60	384955.	416.000

(continued)

		GNPANE	TXED	TXDF	STD	DCP	OL	BSDOTH	GE
80:	1	3587.40	.000	252.20	-44.600	12237.3	-2681.8	197.40	2011.2
80:	2	3502.60	.000	202.80	-17.000	13277.0	-2786.7	-81.70	1794.1
80:	3	3504.90	.000	244.80	60.600	14219.5	-3062.6	3.70	1991.8
80:	4	3549.40	.000	163.90	225.400	15501.1	-3368.2	-488.40	2386.2
81:	1	3618.10	.000	326.70	-.400	16434.0	-3697.0	379.00	2648.5
81:	2	3606.00	.000	248.80	45.600	17503.8	-3910.0	73.70	2442.0
81:	3	3622.00	.000	311.10	130.300	18641.5	-3721.6	-153.40	2483.8
81:	4	3571.40	.000	223.70	-55.300	20076.0	-3849.0	-594.50	3018.3
82:	1	3517.50	15.800	283.40	60.700	21323.1	-3887.9	142.80	2534.9
82:	2	3528.00	58.600	278.90	112.600	22668.4	-3842.4	-65.00	2383.7
82:	3	3499.80	58.200	339.80	173.600	24306.0	-3646.7	153.80	2713.3
82:	4	3505.20	65.300	286.60	79.200	24923.4	-3373.1	88.70	3470.7
83:	1	3535.40	61.200	292.30	109.200	26000.2	-3158.1	30.30	2639.6
83:	2	3615.00	64.900	339.40	135.500	27184.1	-3300.0	-145.80	2856.6
83:	3	3668.40	63.900	381.90	60.600	28392.5	-3221.0	107.50	2853.3
83:	4	3733.50	73.100	321.60	.200	29586.9	-3350.0	-312.90	3510.0
84:	1	3827.00	66.400	362.60	73.100	30535.2	-3939.0	438.40	2996.5
84:	2	3874.90	70.100	391.40	118.900	31453.4	-4384.0	138.40	2981.2
84:	3	3894.70	70.000	408.60	-26.800	32850.8	-4899.0	211.50	2974.7
84:	4	3922.20	78.300	348.60	283.700	33926.0	-5029.0	-538.70	4052.7
85:	1	3969.10	74.700	402.00	66.100	35032.2	-5397.0	401.80	3091.9
85:	2	3993.20	78.900	459.50	89.500	36801.5	-5398.0	30.00	3159.8
85:	3	4033.80	78.800	485.80	-135.700	38963.5	-5541.0	204.90	3620.2
85:	4	4063.30	88.800	347.80	125.400	40286.7	-6172.0	-547.10	4233.1
86:	1	4126.50	84.300	456.60	84.400	38478.1	-6646.0	3723.30	3534.2
86:	2	4117.90	90.900	496.90	134.900	40070.1	-6484.0	-65.90	3739.6
86:	3	4128.70	93.700	523.40	122.100	41349.1	-6934.0	318.00	3798.4
86:	4	4143.50	103.600	402.00	28.400	42882.4	-8118.0	-699.70	4941.3
87:	1	4190.10	97.100	556.50	129.300	43961.6	-9517.0	1262.80	3482.0
87:	2	4241.50	97.400	619.00	77.700	46393.5	-11092.0	115.10	4616.9
87:	3	4288.40	106.300	665.50	179.200	47969.1	-11921.0	733.00	4374.1
87:	4	4352.50	110.500	525.10	-109.400	48740.1	-13629.0	866.60	5891.6
88:	1	4404.80	114.000	718.70	416.100	48705.4	-16224.0	2362.10	4060.7
88:	2	4444.30	121.600	750.90	75.800	50894.9	-18607.0	-182.70	5207.8
88:	3	4473.50	138.900	858.10	276.100	53042.2	-19770.0	193.10	5107.4
88:	4	4503.70	137.900	650.70	-393.800	55121.9	-20697.0	-1628.00	8026.5
89:	1	4544.10	108.500	876.00	373.200	56773.6	-21392.0	1474.40	4404.0
89:	2	4562.40	103.200	940.60	215.000	60168.2	-23030.0	453.80	5714.1
89:	3	4581.80	98.600	1058.40	239.300	64070.2	-23066.0	-1005.50	6239.1
89:	4	4585.70	113.100	739.60	114.700	67800.9	-25767.0	-2088.80	12009.9

(continued)

		GLDMB	GRO	XSFSV	E	POP	PMOS	MGSO	MGSNO
80:	1	22.500	462.70	253.618	571.010	37976.0	101.107	1374.19	3272.35
80:	2	37.500	483.50	242.377	594.070	38124.0	108.876	1092.80	3664.95
80:	3	29.300	491.90	345.890	613.330	38723.0	114.055	1188.46	3596.30
80:	4	2.900	538.90	386.859	651.320	38422.0	121.824	1398.25	3792.33
81:	1	58.100	636.50	284.918	667.170	38572.0	127.416	1501.30	3216.52
81:	2	-7.400	589.80	348.079	680.950	38723.0	127.303	1140.19	4102.26
81:	3	12.400	586.60	373.949	685.890	38874.0	128.167	1070.17	4201.67
81:	4	65.800	562.10	521.469	690.100	39026.0	129.293	1268.29	4153.60
82:	1	-30.400	567.90	552.397	710.070	39178.0	125.952	1161.55	3604.97
82:	2	33.700	409.60	558.164	728.280	39331.0	124.639	1199.31	4182.21
82:	3	22.100	512.90	537.496	741.300	39486.0	120.135	1187.00	4468.50
82:	4	20.800	591.50	347.046	744.690	39641.0	122.049	1408.45	4529.50
83:	1	-17.100	438.90	315.708	753.430	39795.0	116.044	1376.28	4274.91
83:	2	41.100	447.70	290.730	769.540	39949.0	106.812	1061.03	4824.23
83:	3	-23.900	359.60	272.699	785.250	40108.0	105.085	1033.16	4905.58
83:	4	26.300	702.90	249.742	794.780	40266.0	105.348	1671.22	5095.35
84:	1	-6.600	577.80	330.902	795.730	40420.0	106.286	1396.23	4838.96
84:	2	2.800	689.50	314.192	798.170	40576.0	106.474	1277.21	5395.43
84:	3	.900	447.40	265.248	810.520	40737.0	105.573	1496.50	5246.69
84:	4	.400	673.20	349.301	819.490	40898.0	103.509	1319.98	5295.40
85:	1	7.600	535.60	371.958	838.720	40896.0	102.346	1460.64	4806.79
85:	2	-4.100	544.80	203.878	867.040	41054.0	100.769	1361.52	5218.67
85:	3	-1.400	647.30	238.535	882.950	41219.0	97.5418	1267.87	5077.94
85:	4	-7.400	657.70	204.329	891.370	41380.0	99.3432	1494.92	5762.02
86:	1	-13.900	695.20	253.794	887.080	41403.0	84.0683	1644.26	5641.23
86:	2	-24.300	831.40	287.786	887.050	41563.0	44.8865	1395.97	6493.38
86:	3	7.600	510.00	192.046	882.180	41730.0	36.5922	1508.79	6452.90
86:	4	40.100	682.00	313.178	869.500	41893.0	47.6637	1645.70	6927.86
87:	1	-107.100	729.90	457.462	855.690	41912.0	59.3357	1281.35	6898.02
87:	2	50.600	817.70	406.989	827.800	42074.0	63.6892	1461.79	8410.34
87:	3	6.100	616.10	236.150	807.540	42243.0	65.3781	1199.18	8621.93
87:	4	50.900	710.50	224.036	799.240	42408.0	64.9653	1888.39	8513.99
88:	1	-83.600	1089.70	159.987	762.830	42315.0	59.5984	1608.26	8497.50
88:	2	67.500	1289.60	230.247	733.730	42478.0	55.3950	1663.69	9096.01
88:	3	8.800	747.70	145.802	721.600	42649.0	51.6795	2058.26	9128.34
88:	4	-66.100	1399.40	174.352	691.000	42816.0	43.4603	1711.91	9451.75
89:	1	-225.500	1281.10	355.301	675.200	42723.0	51.7546	2077.69	9165.86
89:	2	217.700	2470.80	220.829	666.730	42888.0	62.9386	1963.34	10433.6
89:	3	63.600	1062.40	354.918	668.870	43061.0	60.6868	2009.66	10895.1
89:	4	-18.800	2610.80	429.122	674.630	43229.0	60.6868	2310.06	11124.7

(continued)

		PMGSNO	WPIO
80:	1	111.037	63.200
80:	2	109.816	72.100
80:	3	114.248	76.100
80:	4	110.568	85.200
81:	1	115.805	91.300
81:	2	116.053	100.400
81:	3	112.148	103.000
81:	4	113.769	105.200
82:	1	106.711	109.000
82:	2	104.901	107.300
82:	3	102.878	107.300
82:	4	100.223	107.300
83:	1	101.312	105.700
83:	2	100.576	101.500
83:	3	100.382	100.900
83:	4	103.691	101.100
84:	1	103.727	100.900
84:	2	104.527	100.200
84:	3	104.708	100.200
84:	4	102.498	100.000
85:	1	100.200	99.900
85:	2	101.691	99.900
85:	3	100.864	100.100
85:	4	97.6515	100.100
86:	1	99.2195	93.200
86:	2	103.222	78.100
86:	3	105.449	77.700
86:	4	104.760	78.000
87:	1	102.218	78.200
87:	2	106.428	78.200
87:	3	106.410	77.400
87:	4	114.002	71.200
88:	1	114.663	67.600
88:	2	121.052	61.000
88:	3	126.459	57.800
88:	4	129.257	55.400
89:	1	129.091	54.600
89:	2	122.658	54.200
89:	3	122.768	53.700
89:	4	124.708	53.800

Chapter 5

Econometric Model for Simulation of Alternative External Trade Scenarios in Indonesia

Iwan J. Azis[1]

1 Introduction

The model for Indonesia in this study is constructed for the specific purpose of policy simulation under different scenarios of trade, particularly with Indonesia's major trading partners[2]. In line with such a purpose, the trade block is disaggregated based on the basis of commodity types and countries of destination. The baseline period used (1977-1988) is designed to capture significant shifts in policies and trends during the second half of 1980.

Following the discussion of model structure and estimation results, policy simulation involving various external trade scenarios is dicussed. Although eight scenarios were examined here, they are basically classified into five. The first is a twenty percent appreciation of the Yen vis-a-vis the US dollar; the second is a ten percent increase of Japan's imports, ten percent decrease of US' imports, ten percent increase of EC's imports and a combination of those three. The third scenario is on a fifty percent increase in intra-ASEAN trade; and the fourth scenario is a high price of oil, i.e. the 1982 price level, throughout 1988. The last scenario is on a fifty percent (import) tariff reduction.

2 Model Structure and Estimation Result

The Indonesian model consists of four blocks: aggregate demand, trade, fiscal and monetary blocks. In the aggregate demand block, 13 endogenous variables are estimated, while in the trade block, which is the largest among the four, there are 21 endogenous items determined within the model. The monetary block is comprised of 8 endogenous elements representing the price level of the following items: consumers goods (CPI), gross domestic product (DEF or GDP deflator), and exports-imports (MDEF, XNOGDEF and XDEF).

Exports and imports are classified by 1-digit SITC: primary goods(SITC 0 to 4 except 3), oil and gas (SITC 3), manufactured products and the rest (SITC 5 to

[1] Inter-University Center for Economics, University of Indonesia (IUC-EC-UI)

[2] With some modifications, the model should also be suitable for a short term projection.

8 plus 9).[3] Exports are also broken down by country (or group of countries) of destination: ASEAN, Japan, USA and EC plus the rest of the world. A bottom-up approach is applied to exports, in which each category of commodity group and country of destination is independently estimated in order to yield the total values of exports.

Manufactured exports in particular are modeled as a function of exchange rates. For those destined for Japan and the U.S.A an attempt was made to use real exchange rates; but due to its statistical insignificance at this stage we are forced to keep the exchange rate at its nominal value. Nevertheless, when manufactured exports are further disaggregated by commodity, real exchange rates would be more explanatory. For example, textile exports to Japan, and, to some extent, also those bound for the US market, are significantly affected by the real exchange rates. Thus, the statistical insignificance obtained was due primarily to the broad aggregation of non-oil & gas exports in the model.

From various studies of the determinants of non-oil & gas exports it is clear that, along with demand constraints, the supply side is also a decisive factor.[4] In addition to the standard external variables, e.g. exchange rates:YENUS and ER, manufactured exports to ASEAN and the U.S.A are also affected by domestic factors, the major one being the lagged private investments. Such an assumption relates to the fact that recently most private investments in Indonesia, both domestic and foreign, have been oriented toward exports. However, to capture the environmental differences between the period of export-ledgrowth and the prior period, the use of some dummy variables is necessary to correct the estimated trend.[5]

The level of primary exports is set to be determined mainly by the estimated price level (unit-price), which is consistent with the assumption adopted by many studies on Indonesia's primary exports. In the case of oil & gas, the independent variables are the price of oil (POIL) and the domestic production level (PRODOIL). The only exception is in the estimate of oil & gas exports to ASEAN in which the level of ASEAN's investments is also included in the model.

Along with the exchange rate, the price (unit value) of manufactured imports and the nominal GDP are set to affect imports. Meanwhile, the net export of services is estimated by taking into account the magnitude of trade flows (XTOT and MTOT to capture non-factor services) and dollar values of lagged investments (as a proxy variable to reflect the trend of factor services).

---

[3] Not all items in STIC 9 are manufactured products. However, in some cases the term "industry sector" includes those items as well. See, for example, C. Moran, A Structural Model for Developing Countries' Manufactured Exports, in The World Bank Economic Review, vol.2,3, pp 321-340. 1988

[4] Among others, see Iwan J. Azis, Economic Development and Recent Adjustment in Resource-Rich Countries: The Case of Indonesia, in T. Fukuchi & M. Kagami (eds.), Perspectives on the Pacific Basin Economy:A Comparison of Asia and Latin America, Institute of Developing Economies & The Asian Club Foundation, 1990.

[5] The term "export-led growth" is to be associated in particular with the strategy of expanding exports of non-oil & gas, despite the fact that the period of the oil-boom with a strong oil export in the 70s was also characterized by high rates of economic growth.

In the monetary block, the nominal (broad) money supply and its real values are estimated independently in order to obtain values of GDP deflator (DEF). The real money supply is a function of economic activity (Y), while its nominal values are determined by the size of base money (RM). The RM is specified as a function of credit size (for the net domestic assets, NDA) and the value of exports (for the net foreign assets, NFA). The price levels of exports and imports are basically determined by the exchange rates and price commodity group (PMCON and POIL).

From a historical point of view, the CPI in Indonesia has been influenced by deliberate government policies with respect to the price of rice (RICEPR). The weight of rice prices in the Indonesian CPI has been always significant, even though it is currently lower than in the past. It is for this reason that the variable RICEPR is the most significant in explaining the movement of CPI. In addition, the effect of monetary phenomena on the CPI are reflected through a variable indicating the magnitude of credit from monetary authorities (CREDIT) in which, the special direct credit and the, gradually phased-out, liquidity credit are dominant.

A trend reversal in the fiscal block is noticeable. The share of government revenues from oil is no longer dominant. The shift began in 1986 immediately following the implementation of tax reform. The shift in the oil revenues (GRO) is set through a dummy variable D6. In the non-oil component (GDRNO) the jump has been observed since 1985, and is reflected in the dummy variable D5.

Having described the interconnection of all variables, the next step is to search for the precise specification or form of each equation. Based on the premise that some structural parameters may alter as selected independent variables change (The Lucas critique), each equation is tested to evaluate whether changing parameters are indeed the case. For that purpose a quadratic form is derived for each equation and a test on the significance of parameters in the non-linear variables is carried out.

These tests indicated that there are five equations within the trade block that need to be adjusted (to include the non-linearity case); these are the equations for XMUSA, XMJAP, XOILRE, XOILASE, XPR, MM and MPR. In the monetary block, the two equations for CPI and RM also need some adjustments, but none were indicated in the other two blocks. These adjustments and the complete set of equations are shown in the following.

2.1 Model Estimation

Aggregate Demand Block

(1) $PC = 1486.22 + 0.49224 * PC_{-1} + 0.319 * GDY$

(1.40) (3.86) (4.26)

R^2=0.9878 DW=2.8079 Estimation Period=1970-1988

(2) $PI = -4143.13 + 0.17952 * Y + 2023.13 * D6$

(-4.64) (11.96) (2.34)

R^2=0.9539 DW=1.6712 Estimation Period=1970-1988

(3) $GC = 116.38 + 0.6707 * GC_{-1} + 0.16302 * GRREAL$

(0.533) (4.703) (2.38)

R^2=0.9863 DW=2.3664 Estimation Period=1970-1988

Trade Block

(4) $XMASE = -254.708 + 0.40025 * ER + 49.6924 * PICURD_{-1}$

(-3.38) (31.68) (5.988)

R^2=0.9071 DW=1.8054 Estimation Period=1976-1988

(5) $XMUSA = -181.33 + 0.000319 * ER^2 + 23.2253 * PXMUSA$

(-6.46) (31.104) (3.55)

$+ 22.617 * PICURD_{-3}$

(6.47)

R^2=0.9946 DW=1.8474 Estimation Period=1975-1988

(6) $XMJAP = -29.224 + 50.831(\frac{ER}{YENUS}) + 3.0569(\frac{ER}{YENUS})^2$

(-0.66) (2.79) (2.43)

R^2=0.9813 DW=2.0205 Estimation Period=1975-1988

(7) $XMRE = -436.04 + 1.3612 * ER + 968.04 * D8$

(-14.19) (38.97) (15.17)

R^2=0.9957 DW=1.3937 Estimation Period=1975-1988

(8) $XOILRE = 1671.98 - 116.877 * POIL + 4.2435 * POIL^2$

(2.1) (-1.57) (2.72)

R^2=0.909 DW=2.534 Estimation Period=1975-1988

(9) $XOILUSA = -5142.63 + 98.173 * POIL + 10.3883 * PRODOIL$

$$\begin{array}{ccc}(-7.66) & (11.03) & (7.83)\end{array}$$

R^2=0.8964 DW=1.4015 Estimation Period=1975-1988

(10) $XOILASE = 235.38 + 1.0225 * POIL^2 + 0.797 * ICURASE^2 - 898.98 * D4$

$$\begin{array}{cccc}(2.01) & (3.51) & (2.71) & (-5.96)\end{array}$$

R^2=0.947 DW=1.684 Estimation Period=1975-1988

(11) $XOILJAP = 492.063 + 287.797 * POIL$

$$\begin{array}{cc}(0.94) & (11.78)\end{array}$$

R^2=0.9151 DW=1.0791 Estimation Period=1975-1988

(12) $XPR = 729.985 + 1.9316 * ER + 57255.4 * PXPR^2$

$$\begin{array}{ccc}(3.35) & (15.12) & (9.13)\end{array}$$

R^2=0.912 DW=1.944 Estimation Period=1975-1988

(13) $MM = -1554.69 + 0.43233 * MM_{-1} + 4581.56 * PMM^2 - 0.00163 * ER2$

$$\begin{array}{cccc}(-1.49) & (2.97) & (3.69) & (-3.76)\end{array}$$

R^2=0.9064 DW=1.9347 Estimation Period=1976-1988

(14) $MPR = -474.53 + 56.8587 * YCURD - 0.29401 * YCURD^2$

$$\begin{array}{ccc}(-1.07) & (3.59) & (-2.64)\end{array}$$

$- 0.6053 * ER + 730.5 * D7$

$$\begin{array}{cc}(-3.32) & (3.98)\end{array}$$

R^2=0.9117 DW=2.8108 Estimation Period=1975-1988

(15) $SER = -792.663 - 0.08389 * (XTOT + MTOT) - 179.837 * ICURD_{-1}$

$$\begin{array}{ccc}(-1.61) & (-2.61) & (-4.51)\end{array}$$

R^2=0.9233 DW=1.622 Estimation Period=1975-1988

Monetary Block

(16) $MS2 = -184.014 + 0.8059 * RM + 0.9094 * MS2_{-1} + 1152.55 * D5$

(-0.751) (2.6) (7.46) (1.54)

$+ 3511.31 * D8$

(2.6)

R^2=0.9984 DW=2.592 Estimation Period=1970-1988

(17) $MPIEL2 = -1256.13 + 0.09818 * Y + 0.59904 * MRIEL2_{-1}$

(-1.45) (2.78) (3.84)

$+ 3677.49 * D5 + 2130.6 * D8$

(3.85) (2.32)

R^2=0.9942 DW=1.7076 Estimation Period=1970-1988

(18) $RM = 258.174 + 0.989 * CREDIT - 0.0000445 * CREDIT^2$

(1.1) (4.26) (3.06)

$+ 0.0874 * XCUR$

(1.95)

R^2=0.9664 DW=1.3187 Estimation Period=1970-1988

(19) $CPI = 1.28104 + 0.9613 * RICEPR - 0.00134 * RICEPR^2$

(0.89) (15.64) (-2.72)

$+ 0.00539 * CREDIT - 0.2001 * E6CREDIT^2$

(6.92) (-3.5)

R^2=0.9989 DW=2.3234 Estimation Period=1970-1988

(20) $XDEF = -0.14889 + 0.4974 * XNOGDEF + 0.01747 * POIL$

(-2.1) (27.17) (6.59)

R^2=0.9616 DW=2.0567 Estimation Period=1970-1988

(21) $XNOGDEF = -0.43742 + 0.001646 * ER$

(-9.89) (45.04)

R^2=0.979 DW=2.249 Estimation Period=1970-1988

(22) $MDEF = -0.2406 + 0.00109 * ER + 0.00197 * PMCON - 0.3531 * D5$

(-3.84) (11.36) (3.19) (-4.04)

R^2=0.9619 DW=2.0714 Estimation Period=1970-1987

Fiscal Block

(23) $GRO = -363.347 + 0.69055 * VALOIL + 9.133 * D6$

(-1.34) (21.65) (1.86)

R^2=0.9734 DW=2.6059 Estimation Period=1970-1988

(24) $GDRNO = 180.576 + 0.01937 * YCUR + 0.717975 * GDRNO_{-1}$

(1.31) (2.33) (5.4)

$+ 1834.51 * D5$

(4.58)

R^2=0.9925 DW=2.9723 Estimation Period=1970-1988

2.2 Identities

Y	=	$PC + GC + PI + GI + X - M$
YCUR	=	$Y * DEF$
YCURD	=	$\frac{YCUR}{ER}$
GDY	=	$Y + (\frac{XDEF}{MDEF})_{-1} * X$
GI	=	$\frac{GICUR}{IDEF}$
PICURD	=	$\frac{PI*IDEF}{ER}$
ICURD	=	$\frac{(PI+GI)*IDEF}{ER}$
XTOT	=	$XOIL + XM + XPR$
XM	=	$XMUSA + XMJAP + XMASE + XMRE$
XOIL	=	$XOILUSA + XOILJAP + XOILASE + XOILRE$
XCUR	=	$XTOT * ER * ERAX$
X	=	$\frac{XCUR}{XDEF}$
XNOGUS	=	$XPR + XM$
MTOT	=	$MOIL + MM + MPR$
MCUR	=	$MTOT * ER * ERAM$
M	=	$\frac{MCUR}{MDEF}$
MNOGUS	=	$MPR + MM$
CA	=	$XTOT * ADJX - MTOT * ADJM + SER$
INFL	=	$\frac{CPI}{CPI^2_{-1}}$
DEF	=	$\frac{MS2}{MRIEL2}$
GR	=	$GRR + LOAN$
GRR	=	$GDRNO + GRO$
GRREAL	=	$\frac{GR}{DEF}$
VALOIL	=	$POIL * PRODOIL * ER$

Notes: Instrument 'Two-Stage Least Sqare':
Constant ER BANK CREDIT POIL PMM PXPR PRODOIL PXMUSA ICURASE GICUR PMCON YENUS MOIL LOAN IDEF

3 Model Simulation

The standard procedure for model simulation is conducted for the period 1977-1988. There are six indicators to reflect the quality of the model: the correlation coefficient (CC), the root mean square error (RMSE), the mean absolute error (MAE), the mean error (ME), the regression coefficient of actual on predicted values (RCAP) and the Theil Inequality Coefficient (Theil). Values of these indicators for each endogenous variable are shown in table 1.

It is clear from that table that the variations of each variable are predicted by the model in a fairly satisfactory manner with results in the trade block being the best among the four blocks. A trend in which the predicted values are larger than the actual values (RCAP > 1) is found in 6 out of 9 cases within the aggregate demand block, 8 out of 21 cases in the trade block, 1 out of 4 in the fiscal block and 2 out of 6 in the monetary block.

Table 1. Selected Indicators for Quality of the Model

Aggregate Demand Block

Variables	CC	RMS	MAE	ME	RCAP	Theil
1 Y	0.8893	6553.390	5122.460	1539.680	1.0045	0.0428
2 GDY	0.9182	6631.940	4843.930	551.770	1.0312	0.0446
3 YCUR	0.9918	5059.000	3667.710	327.995	0.9565	0.0307
4 YCURD	0.9446	5.899	4.542	0.971	0.8297	0.0378
5 PC	0.9397	4189.380	3043.950	-146.690	1.1450	0.0447
6 GC	0.9746	459.052	385.047	142.123	1.1508	0.0297
7 PI	0.8995	1564.960	1344.920	308.577	1.0946	0.0752
8 I	0.9357	1564.960	1344.920	308.577	1.0368	0.0437
9 ICURD	0.9326	1.585	1.301	0.217	0.9674	0.0429

Trade Block

Variables	CC	RMS	MAE	ME	RCAP	Theil
10 XTOT	0.9885	662.124	525.146	-59.696	0.9707	0.0175
11 XCUR	0.9956	807.609	578.650	43.688	1.0091	0.0203
12 XNOGUS	0.9895	322.122	243.550	59.877	0.9815	0.0259
13 XPR	0.9458	285.354	228.432	42.078	0.9132	0.0379
14 XM	0.9979	115.228	87.468	17.799	1.0164	0.0210
15 XMASE	0.9329	112.863	96.584	8.501	1.0283	0.0874
16 XMUSA	0.9950	35.336	31.295	0.479	1.0243	0.0361
17 XMJAP	0.9900	48.687	36.858	0.881	0.9789	0.0505
18 XMRE	0.9980	48.861	43.777	7.939	0.9853	0.0209
19 XOIL	0.9863	757.853	623.429	-119.572	0.9870	0.0284
20 XOILRE	0.9514	236.661	202.174	-18.855	1.0362	0.0700
21 XOILUSA	0.9646	226.534	186.157	-7.853	0.9707	0.0400
22 XOILASE	0.9752	180.730	132.505	26.115	0.9367	0.0629
23 XOILJAP	0.9714	587.175	451.982	-118.978	0.9989	0.0391
24 MTOT	0.9744	825.885	634.894	-165.753	1.0936	0.0344
25 MCURN	0.9862	1397.870	953.598	-267.895	0.9906	0.0381
26 MNOGUS	0.9516	825.885	634.894	-165.753	1.1086	0.0407
27 MPR	0.8566	135.078	115.535	28.633	0.9299	0.0409
28 MM	0.9492	788.420	634.932	-194.386	1.1120	0.0463
29 SER	0.9424	475.400	391.469	18.339	0.9204	0.0367
30 CA	0.9521	1090.890	888.647	213.603	0.7658	0.1603

(continued)

Fiscal Block

Variables	CC	RMS	MAE	ME	RCAP	Theil
31 GDRNO	0.9957	402.938	359.762	138.047	0.9517	0.0307
32 GRO	0.9644	804.696	655.273	6.795	1.0079	0.0512
33 GRR	0.9878	956.293	772.844	144.842	0.9745	0.0340
34 GR	0.9936	956.293	772.844	144.842	0.9791	0.0266

Monetary Block

Variables	CC	RMS	MAE	ME	RCAP	Theil
35 MS2	0.9985	766.553	613.691	-377.007	0.9991	0.0185

4 Policy Simulation

Five policy simulations are conducted by modifying the structure of the model. The baseline (simulated) values are those generated by the model under no policy changes. It is by itself a separate scenario.

A special attempt is made to evaluate cases in which the interaction among different exogenous variables (or policy) variables is taken explicitely in the model. When applied to the scenario of changing yen-US$ rate, such particular cases (hereafter WEPC or "with explicit policy change") assume that the Rp-US$ will also alter. Similarly, for the high-oil price scenario, the following exogenous variables are simultaneously changed: government investment (GICUR), foreign loan (LOAN), CREDIT and the exchange rate (ER).

To distinguish these results from the ones where there are no simultaneous changes in other exogenous variables, the scenarios under WEPC are compared with those under NEPC ("no explicit policy change").

4.1 20% Apreciation of Yen Against US Dollar (YENUS)

YENUS is the variable which is altered under the present simulation. This variable directly and indirectly affects trade variables. The direct effect is set to be on the manufactured exports to Japan (XMJAP), while the indirect effect of altering YENUS is transmitted through changes in other variables.

By 1988 the percentage deviation of manufactured exports has reached more than 39 points. The deviations for manufactured exports to USA and ASEAN are lower, i.e., 0.22% and 1.09% respectively. The resulting outcome of total manufactured exports would reflect an increase of 8.04% from the baseline scenario and the increase for non-oil & gas exports would be 4.28% .

Improvement in the current account (CA) is also observed, although a surplus remains unattainable. When the WEPC scenario is carried out, the improvement in CA is so dramatic that by the beginning of 1987 the deficit turns into surplus.[6]

[6] Despite some changes in the policy with respect to exchange rate determination, in the past years, a twenty percent appreciation of YENUS will depreciate the RP-US$ rate (ER) by 10.5%. Thus, under the WEPC scenario the twenty percent appreciation of YENUS is combined simultaneously with the 10.5% depreciation of ER.

As expected, the percentage (positive) deviation of XMJAP is substantially larger than in the preceding NEPC case, i.e., 63% versus 39%. So are the manufactured exports to the U.S.A. (XMUSA) and to the ASEAN countries (XMASE). Interestingly enough, in contrast to the NEPC scenario, total imports under the WEPC has markedly declined. The performance of total non-oil & gas exports (XNOGUS) is also dramatically improved. All these factors have contributed to the improved balance-of-payments position discussed earlier.

Under the WEPC scenario, the net-impact of a twenty percent YENUS appreciation on GDP (Y) would be very positive (more than a 23% deviation from the baseline by 1988). What is more important to note is the fact that the size of the deviation accelerates continuously from 1980. Fiscal revenues and monetary variables are also driven up under this scenario. The simulation result indicates a 5% to 8% positive deviation in government revenues (GR) and around a 4% increase in the nominal money supply, implying a soft inflationary pressure.

The percentage deviations from the baseline for selected endogenous variables are presented in table 2.

4.2 10% Increase of Japan's Imports, 10% Decrease of US Imports and 10% Increase of EC's Imports (Separate and Combined Scenario)

Historically, a one percent increase in Japan's imports has been accompanied by a 0.82 percent increase (in values) in Indonesian exports to Japan. During 1977-1988 the sectoral disaggregation of exports to Japan has averaged out 82.8% for oil & gas, 3.8% for manufactured products and 13.3% for primary exports. We assume different growth rates for individual sector in total exports to Japan. The resulting revisions assume a 6.8% increase in oil & gas exports, and 0.32% and 1.1% increases in exports of manufactured and primary exports respectively. These were inserted into the database for the simulation purpose.

The greatest effects appear to be on exports of oil & gas. It is estimated that the deviation from the baseline figures could reach as much as 4.5%. The largest gap will occur in 1986, 1988 and 1987 (listed in order). Total government revenues (GR) will also increase in a similar order. The percentage deviation of primary and manufactured exports vary from year to year.

As shown in table 2(4.2a), a ten percent increase in total import of Japan would generate a decrease in Indonesian primary exports for the first two simulation years, an increase for the next five years, and a decline in 1987 and 1988. On the other hand, a persistent increase in manufactured exports, although with decreasing rates, is evident throughout the simulation period.

The net results of those trends would be positive for total exports and therefore, an improvement in the current account balance is expected. It is important to note that in table 3 the positive percentage for CA of 1980 and 1981 and the negative percentage for the rest of the simulation period are all implying improvements in the current account since during those years the Indonesian CA was in surplus.

Following the specification of the model, the simulation of a 10 percent increase in Japan's total import would also affect the reserve money, RM, through exports (net foreign assets) and this, in turn, will generate greater (broad) money supply M2. It is simulated that the increase in money supply would be in the range of 0.7% to 0.99% (see table 2(4.2a)).

With an improvement in the balance of payments and government budget, the resulting GDP would be higher by 3% to 5.7% compared to the baseline. The percentage increase of GDP follows a pattern in which an acceleration will occur up to 1985 followed by a deceleration during 1985-1988.

From an historical perspective, a ten percent increase in US imports results in a 6.5% increase in Indonesian exports to the US. Thus, this implies a lower elasticity than in the case of Japanese imports. Indeed, the predominance of Japan as the destination of exports is the case of fact. By implementing a procedure similar to that used in the Japanese case, the implicit rates of reduction in Indonesian exports due to a ten percent decrease in US imports would be 4.8%, 0.6% and 1.07% for oil & gas, manufacturing and primary exports, respectively.

As expected, the trend observed in the previous case is reversed. Declining exports, particularly for oil & gas, would deteriorate the current account balance at an accelerating rate. By 1988 the current account deficit would have been almost 16.8% higher (US$ 0.57 billion compared to US$ 0.49 billion). Obviously, in absolute terms, the impact is softer than in the case of Japanese imports. This is also true with respect to the impact on the government budget. The percentage decline of government revenues never exceeds 0.1%, and the lowest is 0.03% for 1984. The money supply would decrease with a decelerating pace to only 0.2% lower than the baseline figure in 1988. Meanwhile, the resulting GDP would be lower by 1.29% for the same year.

Therefore, in absolute terms, the overall impact of a ten percent decrease in US imports is smaller than that of a ten percent increase in total Japanese imports.

The EC share of Indonesian exports has been lower than the Japanese and US shares, except for primary exports since 1984. It is therefore not surprising that the elasticity of increase in EC imports is even lower (0.524). In the EC case, the following rates of increase for Indonesian exports to EC were used: 0.43%, 1.33% and 3.5% for oil & gas, manufacturing and primary commodities respectively. However, one finds, unlike in the previous two cases, that the largest impact of a ten percent increase in EC imports is in primary exports. Indeed, by 1988, the EC is the second largest market after Japan for Indonesian primary exports. Yet, the percentage increase of primary exports never exceeds 0.84%.

The maximum improvement in the current account balance occurs in 1988 where there is a 9.33% decrease in the deficit. Improvement in the government budget is also minimal (it never exceeds 0.03%) as is the deviation of GDP from the baseline scenario.

It is interesting to examine the combined effects of the three hypothetical scenarios. Table 2(4.2d) presents the net results of such a combination. Notice that, due to the predominance of Japan in Indonesian exports of oil & gas, the largest overall impact is on this variable (by 1988, the increase is 3.6%). The resulting current account deficit shrinks by 52.4% in 1988. The largest increase in government revenues takes place in 1986 while the peak of the GDP improvement is estimated to occur in 1985, in which an increase of more than 4% is indicated.

4.3 50% Increase in Intra-ASEAN Trade

In our simulation, changes in intra-ASEAN trade are defined in the following way. Exports by four member countries, (ASEAN excluding Indonesia), to five countries of the Association, is what intra-ASEAN exports would mean to Indonesian imports. On the other hand, imports by four member countries from five countries is the relevant component for Indonesian exports to ASEAN countries. Given the sectoral composition of exports and imports to and from ASEAN, and considering the historical elasticities of Indonesia's trade flows with respect to ASEAN exports and imports (0.62 and 0.86 respectively) we come up with the following estimated growth rates of Indonesian imports and exports under the scenario of a fifty percent increase in intra-Asean trade: 15.2%, 10.2% and 5.6% for oil & gas, manufacturing and primary imports, respectively and 21.1%, 10.1% and 11.9% for exports of the same sector.

In table 2(4.3) displays the outcomes of the simulation. In general, the improvement in the current account will not be as extensive as in the combined case presented earlier. Reduction of the current account deficit will reach 12.3% in 1988. The largest export increase is expected to originate in manufactured exports. A smaller improvement is also indicated for the deviation of the money supply.

The largest percentage improvement in GDP occurs in 1981 (in which a 1.5% increase is indicated and it eventually reaches 0.43% in 1988. Therefore, it seems clear from the above analysis that, as far as trade altering scenarios are concerned, the case of increased Japan's imports generates the most significant impact, judging from the percentage changes of individual variables.

4.4 50% Tariff Reducation

There are at least two exogenous variables in the model that will alter, as import duties increase: the import prices of consumption goods (PMCON) and of manufactured goods (PMN). There is historical evidence that a fifty percent decrease in import duties, will reduce PMCON by 36.9% and PMN by only 2.2%. Since these two variables are exogenous, a simultaneous change is conceivable in the model. The necessary assumption would be an automatic repercussion with the same magnitude of tariff reduction and import duty upon PMCON and PMM.

As displayed in table 2(4.4), the increase in imports is only for the category of primary products. On the other hand, a significant downward trend is observed for manufactured imports. Much of the explanation rests upon the dominating price effect of PMM on manufactured imports (see the equation for MM in 2.1 Model Estimation) such that a reduction in PMM would lower the value of manufactured imports, MM, despite the increase in import volume. Since most of the raw material (primary)imports are needed for the processing of export-oriented goods, and since this is applicable for both the import-substitution and the export-oriented periods, increased primary imports may also generategrowth in manufactured exports. Such a mechanism, along with the reduction in net-exports of services, will produce a dramatic improvement in the current account balance. In fact, a surplus on current account could have been generated under this scenario. To some extent the scenario demonstrates beneficial consequences to the nation's balance of payments due to the adoption of less restrictive, or freer trade policies through the removal of tariff barriers.

It is also worth noting that such a significant improvement will not reinforce inflationary pressures through monetary expansion. The (broad) money supply is estimated to grow at a very slow rate and it even declines during the early years of the simulation period. Although not too significant in percentage terms, improvement is also indicated in government revenues from non-oil & gas taxes (GDRNO).

The welfare effect of tariff reduction is also encouraging. While the import deflator (NDEF) is reduced, the real GDP rises as much as 4.5% higher than the baseline scenario.

4.5 High Oil Price (1982-1988 = US$34.5/Barrel)

Despite the general belief that the era of high oil price is already over, the last Middle-East crisis has rejuvenated interest in such a scenario. In our study, the high price level adopted is based on the level of 1982.

The largest deviation under the NEPC scenario is in the current account, which becomes positive (surplus) from 1984 onward. By 1988, the surplus in CA reached US$ 8.5 billion, which is higher than the surplus in CA during the oil boom period of the 70s. Obviously the strongest force behind such a trend is a dramatic increase in oil & gas exports (XOIL). The deviation of this export accelerates to a peak in 1986. By 1988 the deviation from the baseline is as much as 133%.

The repercussion on government revenues of an oil tax (GRO) is not difficult to predict. Basically a pattern similar to that of XOIL applies with the peak reached in 1986.

When the WEPC scenario is used, four other exogenous variables, ER, LOAN, GICUR and CREDIT, are simultaneously altered. With the exception of ER, the magnitude of the changes is determined on the basis of a 15.23% annual increase in oil-prices during 1975-1982.[7] The resulting magnitudes of those variables in 1982 are then assumed invariant throughout 1988. As a result, LOAN and CREDIT in 1988 are only 30.6% and 40.3% of their actual respective values. On the other hand, the size of GICUR is 7% higher than its actual value.

The decreasing LOAN could have something to do with the attitudes of donors which tend to relate the size of loans to oil-prices. The fear of inflationary pressures from expanding net foreign assets (particularly from oil exports) has logically

[7] The ER, throughout 1988, is assumed to be the same as the level in 1982 (Rp 661 per US$ 1).

become the force behind the shrinking of CREDIT.[8] Meanwhile, most of the additional GICUR will be financed by domestic tax revenues.

With such a specification the resulting outcomes of high oil-price case under WEPC are different from those under the NEPC scenario. While the pattern of estimated XOIL remains the same, the balance-of-payments position is worse. The primary reason is the negative deviation of non-oil & gas exports (XNOGUS or other tradeables in general), conforming the "Dutch disease" phenomenon.

The resulting GDP under the WEPC scenario is lower than that under the NEPC scenario. Such a trend clearly depends on the assumptions being adopted with respect to changes in other exogenous variables. It would seem unrealistic to expect a decline in GDP when the price of oil is high. The effect of declining LOAN and CREDIT as well as overvalued ER has apparently been so strong that some variables including the GDP have shown negative deviations from the baseline.

Table 2. Impact of Selected Scenarios

(4.1a)20 Percent Apreciation of Yen Against US$ (Ratex NECP)

	1980	1981	1982	1983	1984	1985	1986	1987	1988
Y	0.27	0.30	0.33	0.44	0.48	0.69	1.09	1.64	2.13
XTOT	0.22	0.21	0.22	0.37	0.43	0.52	1.52	2.14	2.55
XNOGUS	0.85	1.00	1.27	1.54	1.57	1.80	3.11	4.24	4.28
XM	5.28	4.39	3.67	3.80	3.89	3.87	6.41	8.04	8.04
XMUSA	0.35	0.52	0.59	0.27	0.26	0.26	0.25	0.18	0.22
XMJAP	35.85	35.71	36.03	35.14	35.16	35.24	36.71	38.85	39.77
XMASE	0.53	0.39	0.42	0.41	0.48	0.50	0.64	0.74	1.09
MPR	0.03	0.02	-0.00	0.03	-0.01	0.13	0.28	0.49	0.40
MTOT	0.01	0.00	-0.00	0.00	-0.00	0.02	0.03	0.08	0.06
CA	1.00	3.43	-0.53	-0.77	-3.17	-2.71	-2.51	-37.02	-84.21
SER	0.18	0.16	0.17	0.21	0.27	0.31	0.56	0.87	1.21
GDRNO	0.05	0.05	0.05	0.06	0.07	0.11	0.18	0.31	0.47
GR	0.01	0.01	0.01	0.02	0.02	0.04	0.09	0.12	0.19
RM	0.10	0.08	0.06	0.12	0.12	0.15	0.35	0.71	0.87
MS2	0.09	0.08	0.08	0.09	0.10	0.11	0.15	0.25	0.33

(continued)

[8]To a large extent this scenario is almost a replica of the oil-boom situation in the 1970s. During that time credit limitations were a normal practice to control the money supply.

(4.1b) 20 Percent Apreciation of Yen Against US$ (Ratex NEPC)

	1980	1981	1982	1983	1984	1985	1986	1987	1988
Y	6.05	7.26	8.29	9.71	10.29	18.08	17.47	21.38	23.39
XTOT	1.48	1.31	1.56	2.53	2.96	3.52	7.48	8.36	9.06
XNOGUS	5.58	6.28	9.18	10.52	10.73	12.31	15.34	16.62	15.21
XM	21.37	16.87	16.53	16.95	17.71	17.77	23.31	24.31	22.79
XPR	2.56	3.15	5.30	6.16	6.01	7.54	7.82	8.02	6.59
XMUSA	19.52	15.23	22.55	15.96	16.31	18.39	20.43	20.59	24.18
XMJAP	55.62	55.43	55.89	54.74	54.86	55.04	57.74	61.45	63.03
XMASE	6.82	3.27	4.34	6.70	8.59	8.41	16.87	12.49	14.56
XMRE	21.57	21.42	20.47	16.28	15.34	14.82	14.06	13.10	8.56
MM	-2.97	-2.86	-2.34	-4.10	-5.94	-7.41	-9.56	-15.23	-16.39
MPR	-5.90	-4.38	-2.72	-5.38	-3.79	-5.04	-6.78	-5.64	-5.21
MTOT	-2.95	-2.68	-1.88	-3.17	-4.52	-6.33	-8.34	-12.29	-13.47
CA	20.80	83.64	-14.56	-17.64	-64.15	-62.33	-31.37	-346.24	-703.15
SER	-1.88	-2.57	-2.17	-2.06	-1.28	-1.38	1.46	0.72	2.37
GRO	11.09	11.00	11.07	10.99	10.91	10.92	9.68	10.00	9.92
GDRNO	2.85	3.28	3.41	3.56	3.49	3.97	4.05	4.70	5.47
GR	7.94	7.81	7.27	7.19	6.93	6.44	5.03	5.52	5.21
RM	5.50	4.33	3.46	4.27	3.86	4.11	4.34	6.60	6.99
MS2	4.11	4.26	4.07	4.18	4.13	3.96	3.90	4.31	4.30
XDEF	8.17	7.15	7.33	8.78	8.95	9.21	12.01	11.02	11.31
XNOGDEF	18.31	18.22	17.64	14.90	14.23	13.87	13.30	12.58	12.52
MDEF	11.45	10.09	10.58	11.03	10.62	14.65	12.31	13.89	13.45

(4.2a) 10 Percent Increase in Total Imports of Japan

	1980	1981	1982	1983	1984	1985	1986	1987	1988
Y	2.96	3.50	4.21	4.50	4.42	5.74	4.86	4.58	4.19
XTOT	2.75	2.92	3.32	3.15	3.13	3.31	2.69	2.43	2.01
XNOGUS	0.11	0.47	1.25	1.05	0.89	1.07	0.92	0.54	0.35
XM	1.97	2.37	2.81	2.27	2.08	2.02	1.74	1.08	0.86
XOIL	3.70	3.57	3.74	3.82	3.98	4.20	4.38	4.34	4.47
XPR	-0.25	-0.09	0.43	0.23	0.08	0.25	0.13	-0.06	-0.24
MTOT	0.07	0.04	-0.00	0.02	-0.01	0.11	0.09	0.12	0.07
MPR	0.46	0.29	-0.02	0.20	-0.07	0.85	0.71	0.75	0.47
CA	12.80	49.90	-8.73	-5.94	-21.18	-15.93	-2.70	-32.10	-49.96
SER	1.84	1.90	2.13	2.29	2.48	2.54	2.76	2.26	2.14
GRO	0.00	0.00	0.00	0.00	0.00	0.00	0.00	0.00	0.00
GDRNO	0.53	0.61	0.70	0.70	0.59	0.77	0.76	0.77	0.80
GR	0.12	0.14	0.19	0.19	0.16	0.26	0.35	0.30	0.33
MS2	0.88	0.96	0.97	0.99	0.96	0.92	0.83	0.80	0.70

(continued)

(4.2b) 10 Percent Decrease in Total Imports of USA

	1980	1981	1982	1983	1984	1985	1986	1987	1988
Y	-1.13	-1.27	-1.32	-1.36	-1.35	-1.65	-1.44	-1.38	-1.29
XTOT	-1.01	-0.97	-0.77	-0.77	-0.86	-0.79	-0.76	-0.74	-0.66
XNOGUS	-0.74	-0.66	-0.40	-0.48	-0.54	-0.45	-0.46	-0.47	-0.51
XM	-0.84	-0.96	-1.08	-0.83	-0.77	-0.72	-0.60	-0.43	-0.33
XOIL	-1.10	-1.05	-0.85	-0.86	-0.99	-0.92	-1.04	-1.01	-0.88
XPR	-0.73	-0.57	-0.04	-0.24	-0.39	-0.22	-0.33	-0.53	-0.71
MTOT	-0.02	-0.01	0.00	-0.00	0.00	-0.03	-0.03	-0.04	-0.02
MPR	-0.16	-0.09	0.00	-0.03	0.01	-0.23	-0.21	-0.23	-0.16
CA	-4.63	-16.17	1.77	1.32	5.68	3.46	0.74	9.86	16.83
SER	-0.71	-0.68	-0.67	-0.67	-0.73	-0.73	-0.79	-0.67	-0.66
GDRNO	-0.20	-0.21	-0.19	-0.16	-0.12	-0.18	-0.19	-0.21	-0.23
GR	-0.05	-0.05	-0.05	-0.04	-0.03	-0.06	-0.09	-0.08	-0.10
MS2	-0.34	-0.35	-0.31	-0.30	-0.28	-0.26	-0.23	-0.23	-0.20

(4.2c) 10 Percent Increase in Total Imports of EEC

	1980	1981	1982	1983	1984	1985	1986	1987	1988
Y	0.20	0.20	0.21	0.23	0.24	0.30	0.32	0.33	0.36
XTOT	0.17	0.13	0.11	0.14	0.16	0.17	0.27	0.26	0.30
XNOGUS	0.63	0.62	0.62	0.59	0.59	0.58	0.56	0.52	0.51
XM	0.45	0.39	0.39	0.32	0.31	0.30	0.27	0.22	0.25
XPR	0.67	0.68	0.74	0.78	0.77	0.82	0.83	0.84	0.80
MTOT	0.00	0.00	-0.00	0.00	-0.00	0.01	0.01	0.01	0.01
MPR	0.03	0.01	-0.00	0.01	-0.00	0.05	0.06	0.07	0.06
CA	0.77	2.10	-0.24	-0.26	-1.11	-0.79	-0.38	-4.00	-9.33
SER	0.13	0.11	0.10	0.11	0.13	0.13	0.17	0.17	0.19
GDRNO	0.04	0.03	0.03	0.03	0.02	0.04	0.05	0.06	0.07
GR	0.01	0.01	0.01	0.01	0.01	0.01	0.02	0.02	0.03
MS2	0.06	0.06	0.05	0.05	0.05	0.05	0.05	0.05	0.06

(4.2d) Combination of (4.2a), (4.2b) and (4.2c)

	1980	1981	1982	1983	1984	1985	1986	1987	1988
Y	2.24	2.62	3.22	3.49	3.44	4.52	3.87	3.71	3.52
XTOT	2.18	2.23	2.63	2.55	2.50	2.70	2.28	2.11	1.96
XNOGUS	0.99	1.10	1.33	1.26	1.20	1.24	1.16	0.91	0.85
XM	1.67	1.94	2.27	1.84	1.69	1.65	1.45	0.91	0.81
XOIL	2.61	2.52	2.90	2.96	3.00	3.28	3.35	3.34	3.59
XPR	0.86	0.85	0.83	0.86	0.87	0.88	0.89	0.91	0.91
MTOT	0.06	0.04	-0.00	0.02	-0.01	0.09	0.07	0.10	0.06
MPR	0.39	0.23	-0.01	0.17	-0.06	0.70	0.59	0.64	0.42
CA	10.19	38.02	-7.01	-4.88	-17.09	-13.16	-2.42	-28.91	-52.40
SER	1.41	1.44	1.63	1.78	1.94	2.00	2.21	1.84	1.81
GDRNO	0.43	0.49	0.56	0.57	0.49	0.63	0.62	0.64	0.69
GR	0.10	0.11	0.16	0.16	0.13	0.22	0.29	0.25	0.28
MS2	0.67	0.73	0.74	0.77	0.76	0.73	0.67	0.65	0.59

(continued)

(4.3) 50 Percent Increase in INTRA-ASEAN Trade

	1980	1981	1982	1983	1984	1985	1986	1987	1988
Y	1.45	1.50	1.10	0.61	0.72	0.78	0.30	0.38	0.43
XTOT	2.21	2.50	2.85	2.87	1.19	1.62	1.05	1.30	1.22
XNOGUS	1.88	2.48	3.31	2.62	2.24	2.37	1.88	1.63	1.42
XM	4.18	5.70	6.11	4.21	3.46	3.45	2.50	2.13	1.75
XOIL	2.33	2.50	2.76	2.94	1.78	1.32	0.26	0.95	0.91
XPR	1.44	1.53	1.83	1.55	1.42	1.43	1.29	1.08	1.05
MTOT	0.55	0.59	0.55	0.56	0.55	0.66	0.61	0.66	0.65
MM	0.47	0.57	0.68	0.75	0.75	0.73	0.71	0.68	0.67
MPR	1.47	1.21	0.83	0.77	0.33	0.78	0.43	0.98	0.84
CA	5.54	18.79	0.56	3.05	-0.60	-3.20	1.00	-4.85	-12.29
SER	1.40	1.49	1.71	1.64	1.03	0.83	0.71	0.56	0.58
MS2	0.69	0.79	0.81	0.84	0.76	0.67	0.55	0.48	0.42

(4.4) 50 Percent Decrease in Tariffs

	1980	1981	1982	1983	1984	1985	1986	1987	1988
Y	0.10	-0.74	-0.77	1.22	1.76	0.89	0.92	4.07	4.50
XTOT	-0.05	-0.03	-0.03	-0.03	0.03	0.06	0.08	0.07	0.16
XNOGUS	-0.17	-0.13	-0.20	-0.12	0.11	0.20	0.15	0.14	0.26
XM	-1.06	-0.55	-0.58	-0.30	0.27	0.43	0.32	0.27	0.49
MTOT	-4.28	-4.41	-3.95	-3.98	-4.66	-5.44	-5.90	-6.33	-6.70
MM	-6.40	-6.28	-5.86	-6.34	-6.78	-7.09	-7.51	-8.67	-8.78
MPR	0.59	0.04	-0.00	0.28	-0.12	0.03	0.08	1.09	0.62
CA	14.97	64.39	13.59	-11.32	-34.04	-29.74	-13.07	-97.28	-185.91
SER	-0.88	-0.56	-0.97	-0.96	-0.27	-0.03	-0.61	-0.62	0.41
GDRNO	0.47	0.32	0.23	0.54	0.61	0.32	0.22	0.59	0.80
GR	0.11	0.07	0.06	0.15	0.17	0.11	0.10	0.23	0.33
MS2	-0.02	-0.02	-0.02	-0.01	-0.01	-0.00	0.00	0.01	0.01
MDEF	-10.98	-13.98	-12.26	-7.70	-7.75	-10.83	-12.16	-4.43	-5.06

(4.5a) High Price of Oil(1982-1988 = US$ 34.5/Barrel,Ratex NEPC)

	1980	1981	1982	1983	1984	1985	1986	1987	1988
Y	0.00	0.00	0.00	4.79	7.46	14.31	32.77	39.78	46.64
PC	0.00	0.00	0.00	3.69	6.65	11.65	26.21	36.31	45.14
GC	0.00	0.00	0.00	3.58	6.77	10.10	26.34	37.04	45.39
I	0.00	0.00	0.00	3.76	5.68	10.79	22.76	29.97	34.87
PI	0.00	0.00	0.00	6.82	10.23	21.06	38.46	45.94	53.21
XTOT	0.00	0.00	0.00	14.41	14.50	18.63	82.71	53.54	55.46
XNOGUS	0.00	0.00	0.00	0.00	0.62	1.08	1.71	2.69	2.72
XM	0.00	0.00	0.00	0.00	1.55	2.32	3.52	5.10	5.11
XOIL	0.00	0.00	0.00	18.96	19.78	25.67	159.74	105.09	133.08
MM	0.00	0.00	0.00	0.00	0.00	0.00	0.00	0.00	0.00
MPR	0.00	0.00	0.00	0.79	-0.93	2.95	4.41	7.42	1.39
MTOT	0.00	0.00	0.00	0.08	-0.11	0.37	0.53	1.15	0.21
CA	0.00	0.00	0.00	-35.97	-119.59	-109.48	-148.34	-925.19	-1844.87
SER	0.00	0.00	0.00	3.17	5.37	7.24	20.94	23.60	27.59
GRO	0.00	0.00	0.00	17.64	17.52	21.78	140.54	90.38	113.89
GDRNO	0.00	0.00	0.00	1.31	2.39	3.26	6.40	8.71	10.97
GR	0.00	0.00	0.00	10.32	10.25	11.25	48.81	36.78	38.51
RM	0.00	0.00	0.00	4.61	4.05	5.30	19.10	17.86	18.85
MS2	0.00	0.00	0.00	1.30	2.11	2.77	5.82	7.98	8.95

(continued)

(4.5b) High Price of Oil(1982-1988 = US$ 34.5/Barrel,Ratex NEPC)

	1980	1981	1982	1983	1984	1985	1986	1987	1988
Y	0.00	0.00	0.00	6.80	2.53	-29.38	-7.62	-59.72	-69.92
PC	0.00	0.00	0.00	6.08	6.75	-0.03	4.94	-7.90	-22.59
GC	0.00	0.00	0.00	-0.89	-3.35	-9.38	-5.04	-16.60	-27.60
I	0.00	0.00	0.00	30.35	13.33	-7.64	5.76	-36.73	-49.84
PI	0.00	0.00	0.00	9.69	3.47	-43.23	-8.94	-68.97	-79.76
XTOT	0.00	0.00	0.00	9.11	7.79	9.73	60.17	26.88	24.23
XNOGUS	0.00	0.00	0.00	-22.08	-23.75	-30.05	-44.54	-50.27	-49.71
XM	0.00	0.00	0.00	-31.14	-28.89	-31.34	-53.69	-54.57	-60.04
XOIL	0.00	0.00	0.00	18.96	19.78	25.67	159.74	105.09	133.08
XPR	0.00	0.00	0.00	-15.94	-20.28	-28.92	-35.91	-45.46	-37.95
MM	0.00	0.00	0.00	6.31	13.58	19.93	29.65	54.58	61.09
MPR	0.00	0.00	0.00	-2.93	-25.82	21.50	-4.07	36.96	31.29
MTOT	0.00	0.00	0.00	3.68	6.21	18.02	22.84	46.64	52.01
CA	0.00	0.00	0.00	-12.67	110.94	146.34	-33.81	606.60	1025.56
SER	0.00	0.00	0.00	2.61	41.33	44.80	43.58	66.27	41.67
GRO	0.00	0.00	0.00	-15.62	-25.52	-28.96	27.96	-20.36	-12.53
GDRNO	0.00	0.00	0.00	0.99	-2.45	-8.48	-7.68	-16.30	-23.44
GR	0.00	0.00	0.00	-6.59	-17.91	-22.91	-2.01	-28.46	-33.53
RM	0.00	0.00	0.00	-1.68	-24.11	-25.31	-23.32	-33.98	-38.19
MS2	0.00	0.00	0.00	-0.48	-7.31	-11.20	-13.16	-16.81	-18.59

Table 3. Export Growth to European Countries 1986-1988

(Percent/Annum)

Country	1986	1987	1988
NIEs			
(Without Singapore)			
Hong Kong	38.5	49.5	19.7
Taipei,China	32.1	31.4	19.9
Republic Korea	32.3	53.2	20.1
ASEAN			
Indonesia	-26.9	83.8	28.2
Malaysia	-8.7	26.3	15.7
Philippines	35.5	23.9	3.5
Singapore	3.8	39.5	32.6
Thailand	40.0	31.1	16.8
People of Republic of China	76.0	-2.5	15.8
SOUTH ASIA			
Bangladesh	5.6	35.8	-51.2
India	4.4	37.9	19.9
Nepal	23.9	49.5	-
Pakistan	55.0	37.5	14.1
Sri Lanka	13.9	12.6	-

Souce : Asian Development Bank, Asian Development Outlook 1989

5 Conclusions

To evaluate alternative external situations, the Indonesian model being developed is characterized by disaggregated trade block (classified by commodities and countries of destination). The term "RATEX" is used intentionally to reflect the incorporation of "Lucas critique" and the scenarios of WEPC/NEPC ("with/no explicit policy change"). However, the nature of the adjustment indicates that the model is not RATEX in the true sense but, on the other hand, it is different from the standard model.

Although there are a few specifications unique to the Indonesian economy which might deserve some elaboration, most of the discussion in this paper omits this as it is not too relevant given the emphasis of the present study. The use of dummy variables is to be related with shifts and changes of policies or trends in the Indonesian economy, particularly during the second half of 1980.

Using the baseline period of 1977-1988 six indicators reflecting the quality of the model were evaluated. In general the model is able to predict variations of each variable in a fairly satisfactory way. The disaggregated trade block turns out to be the best among the four.

In the simulation under twenty percent Yen appreciation, the most favorably affected component is manufactured exports to Japan. The enhancement of exports results in a dramatic improvement in the current account balance and it becomes a surplus under the WEPC scenario. The net effect is also positive for GDP, in which an accelerating rate of deviation from the baseline is clearly observed. By 1988 the percentage deviation reacted as much as 23.4%.

The most affected variable under the scenario of a ten percent increase in Japanese imports was exports of oil & gas. Among the non-oil & gas exports the trend of primary products tends to be volatile while manufactured exports show a relatively stable increase. Despite the increasing deficit in net-exports of services the resulting outcome was an improvement in the current account balance. The estimated increase of GDP from the baseline scenario is estimated to be between 3% and 5.7%.

The reversed effect of a ten percent decrease in US' imports turns out to be less prevalent in that the most affected component would be exports of oil & gas. Similarly, the positive impact of a 10 percent increase in EC imports is relatively minimal compared to the case of increasing Japanese imports. The most favorably affected component was exports of primary products. This is as expected, since up to 1988 EC is the second largest market, after Japan, for Indonesian primary exports.

The effect of the combined three scenarios is an improvement of as much as 52.4% in the current account balance. Due to the dominance of Japan, the largest overall impact measured by the size of percentage changes from the baseline is expected to occur in exports of oil & gas. The GDP figure rises as much as 4.5% higher than the baseline.

A milder improvement in current account is predicted with a fifty percent increase in intra-ASEAN trade. Most of the increase comes from manufactured exports. The GDP positive deviation is likely to be less than 0.7%.

The scenario of a fifty percent tariff reduction is perhaps most interesting. The strong price effect in manufactured imports yields a positive relation between the two. Only primary imports is expected to rise. Such a trend combined with strong growth in manufactured exports generates a dramatic improvement in the current account balance and yields a surplus position. The GDP effect is also desirable, for it may be as much as 4.5% higher than the baseline scenario. Another nice feature is the predicted absence of excessive monetary expansion, implying the lack of inflationary pressures. This scenario demonstrates clearly the benefit to Indonesia of adopting freer trade policies through the reduction of tariff barriers.

The simulation results of the high oil-price under the WEPC scenario is rather unrealistic. The scenario is shown only to demonstrate the case of simultaneous variations in some exogenous variables, particularly those variables under the category of policy instruments. Under the NEPC scenario, however, the impact of a high oil-price is quite substantial. The current account surplus reaches US$ 8.5 billion in 1988 and government revenues from oil taxes also reach a peak in 1986. Nevertheless, under the WEPC and the NEPC scenario the performance of non-oil & gas exports are likely to be poor, a trend resulting from the phenomenon often termed as the "Dutch disease". Further more, inflationary pressures are greater due to a strong increase in the money supply.

References

[1] Ahmed, S. and A. Chibber (1989) "How can Indonesia Maintain Creditworthiness and Noninflationary Growth?", IMF Working Paper.

[2] Asian Development Bank(1989) *Asian Developnment Outlook.*

[3] Azis, I.J. (1990) "Economic Development and Recent Adjustment in Resource-Rich Countries: The Case of Indonesia" in Fukuchi, T. and M. Kagami eds., *Perspectives on the Pacific Basin Economy: A Comparison of Asia and Latin America*, Institute of Developing Economies & The Asian Club Foundation.

[4] Azis, I.J. & E. Ekawati (1990) "A Simulation Study of Changing External Trade Situations: Econometric Model for Indonesia," in Y.Nakamura and J.T.Yap, *Asean Link: An Econometric Study*, Longman, 1990.

[5] Azis, I.J. & S. Mangkusuwondo (1990) "Indonesia: Economic Outlook for 1990-1991", Pacific Economic Outlook Meeting, Osaka, Japan, March 27-30.

[6] Berndt, E.K., B.H. Hall, R.E. Hall and J.A. Hausmann (1974) "Estimation and Inference in Nonlinear Structural Models," Annals of Economic and Social Measurement.

[7] Central Bureau of Statistics (1985) "A Macroeconometric Model of Indonesia," in Econometric Link System for ASEAN: Final Report Vol.1, Institute of Developing Economies, Tokyo, 1985.

[8] Ezaki, M. (1983) "An Econometric Model of Indonesia with Particular Reference to the Monetary Sector: 1970-1980," Southeast Asian Studies, Vol.21, No.2, September, pp.141-63.

[9] Haas, R. D. (1989) "INDOMOD: A Simulation Model of the Indonesian Economy", IMF Working Paper.

[10] Intrilligator, M.D. (1978) *Econometric Models, Technique and Applications*, Prentice-Hall, Inc., N.J.

[11] Kobayashi, K. et al. (1989) "Indonesia Model," in S. Ichimura and M. Ezaki eds., *Econometric Models of Asian Link,* Springer-Verlag, Tokyo.

[12] Klein, L. (1985) "Economic Theory and Econometrics", in J.Marquez ed., Basil Blackwell, Oxford.

[13] Litterman, R. B. (1984) "Forecasting and Policy Analysis with Bayesian Vector Autoregression Models," Federal Reserve Bank of Minneapolis Quarterly Review, Vol. 8, No. 4.

[14] Lucas, R. E. Jr. (1976) "Econometric Policy Evaluation: A Critique," in K. Brunner and A. H. Neltzer, *The Phillips Curve and Labor Markets,* Carnegie-Rochester Conference Series on Public Policy I, Amsterdam: North Holland.

[15] Moran, C. (1988) "A structural Model for Developing Countries: Manufactured Exports," The World Bank Economic Review, Vol.2 No.3, pp. 321-340.

[16] Pindyck, R. and D. Rubinfeld (1983) *Econometric Models and Economic Forecasts,* McGraw Hill.

[17] Sims, C. A. (1980) "Macroeconomics and Reality," Econometrica, Vol.48, No.1.

[18] Takayama, A. (1971) *International Trade,* Holt, Rinehart and Winston Inc.

[19] Todd, R. M. (1984) "Improving Economic Forecasting with Bayesian-Vector Autoregression," Federal Reserve Bank of Minneapolis Quarterly Review, Vol. 8, No.4.

[20] Wallis, K. F. (1980) "Econometric Implications of the Rational Expectations Hypothesis," Econometrica, Vol. 48, No. 1.

[21] Yokoyama, H. (1985) "Models for ASEAN Countries: A Common Approach," Econometric Link System for ASEAN: Final Report, Vol. 2, Institute of Developing Economies, Tokyo.

Appendix

A The Variables

1	ADJM	Adjustment factors for imports
2	ADJX	Adjustment factors for exports
3	CA	Currant account at US$ current prices
4	CPII	Consumers' price index, 1983=100
5	CREDIT	Credit from monetary authorities
6	DEF	GDP deflator, 1983 = 100
7	DR	Deposit rate, annual average
8	ER	Exchange rate, annual average
9	ERAX	Adjustment factors for exchange rate and exports in services
10	ERAM	Adjustment factors for exchange rate and imports in services
11	GC	Government consumption at Rp. 1983 prices
12	GDRNO	Government routine revenues from Non-Oil and Gas at Rp. current prices
13	GDY	Gross domestic income at Rp. 1983 prices
14	GI	Government investment at Rp. 1983 prices
15	GICUR	Government investment at Rp. current prices
16	GR	Total government revenues (domestic and foreign) at Rp. current prices
17	GRO	Government routine revenues from Oil at Rp. current prices
18	GRR	Total government routine revenues at Rp. current prices
19	GRREAL	Real government revenues (Total government revenues deflated by GDP deflator)
20	I	Total investment at Rp.1983 prices
21	ICUR	Total investment at Rp.current prices
22	ICURASE	Total investment of ASEAN countries at US$ current prices
23	ICURD	Total investment at US$ current prices(ICUR/ER)
24	IDEF	Investment deflator, 1983=100
25	INFL	Annual inflation Rate
26	LOAN	Government foreign loan at Rp. current prices
27	M	Total imports of goods and services at Rp. 1983 prices
28	MCUR	Total imports of goods and services at Rp. current prices
29	MDEF	Import deflator, 1983=100
30	MM	Imports of manufacturing goods at US$ current prices
31	MNOGUS	Non-Oil and Gas imports at US$ current prices
32	MOIL	Imports of Oil and Gas at US$ current prices
33	MPR	Imports of primary goods at US$ current prices
34	MRIEL2	Stock of broad money (= Narrow Money + Savings + Time Deposit) in Real Terms
35	MS2	Stock of broad money (= Narrow Money + Savings + Time Deposit)

36	MTOT	Total imports at US$ current prices
37	PC	Private consumption at Rp. 1983 prices
38	PI	Private investment at Rp. 1983 prices
39	PICURD	Private investsent at US$ current prices
40	PMCON	Unit value of consumption imports
41	PMM	Unit value of manufacturing imports
42	POIL	Price of Oil (US$/barrel)
43	POP	Number of population
44	PRODOIL	Oil Production
45	PXMUSA	Unit value of manufacturing exports to USA
46	PXPR	Unit value of primary exports
47	RM	Reserve money
48	SER	Net export of services at US$ current prices
49	VALOIL	Value of Oil production (Rp.)
50	X	Total exports of goods and services at Rp.1983 prices
51	XCUR	Total exports of goods and services at Rp.1983 prices
52	XNOGDEF	The deflator for Non-Oil and Gas Exports, 1983=100
53	XDEF	Exports deflator, 1983=100
54	XNOGUS	Non-Oil and Gas exports at US$ current prices
55	XM	Exports of manufactured products at US$ current prices
56	XMRE	Exports of manufactured products to Europe and Rest of the world at US$ current prices.
57	XMASE	Exports of manufactured products to ASEAN at US$ current prices
58	XMJAP	Exports of manufactured products to Japan at US$ current prices
59	XMUSA	Exports of manufactured products to USA at US$ current prices
60	XPR	Exports of primary goods at US$ current prices
61	XOIL	Exports of Oil and Gas at US$ current prices
62	XOILASE	Exports of Oil and Gas to ASEAN at US$ current prices
63	XOILUSA	Exports of Oil and Gas to USA at US$ current pricces
64	XOILJAP	Exports of Oil and Gas to Japan at US$ current prices
65	XOILRE	Exports of Oil and Gas to Europe and the rest of the World at US$ current prices
66	XTOT	Total export at US$ current prices
67	Y	Gross domestic products at Rp. 1983 prices
68	YCUR	Gross domestic products at Rp. current prices
69	YCURD	Gross domestic products at US$ current prices $\frac{YCUR}{ER}$
70	YENUS	Exchange rate for Yen per US$, annual average

B Data

Year	ADJM	ADJX	CA	CPII	CREDIT	DR	ER	ERAX
1970	NA	NA	NA	14.56	120.00	21.00	365.00	NA
1971	NA	NA	NA	15.14	149.00	21.00	393.40	NA
1972	NA	NA	NA	16.16	170.00	15.00	415.00	NA
1973	NA	NA	NA	21.11	204.00	12.00	415.00	NA
1974	NA	NA	NA	29.77	302.00	12.00	415.00	NA
1975	1.1465	0.9698	-1108.60	35.37	548.00	12.00	415.00	0.9830
1976	1.2019	1.0080	-908.60	42.43	652.00	12.00	415.00	1.0210
1977	1.1995	0.9957	-49.49	47.09	648.00	9.00	415.00	1.0063
1978	1.2529	0.9464	-1425.29	50.95	860.00	6.00	442.00	1.0183
1979	1.2830	0.9710	968.98	61.43	1152.00	6.00	623.00	1.0299
1980	1.1628	0.9933	2856.26	72.78	1636.00	6.00	627.00	1.1766
1981	1.2512	0.9294	-589.24	81.66	2596.00	6.00	631.00	1.0182
1982	1.0589	0.8840	-5280.26	89.45	3890.00	6.00	661.00	1.0233
1983	1.0825	0.8850	-6288.66	100.00	4264.00	6.00	909.30	1.0322
1984	1.0833	0.9476	-1859.90	110.41	7045.00	16.00	1025.90	1.0243
1985	1.2402	0.9960	-1957.79	115.65	7039.00	18.00	1110.60	1.0433
1986	1.1155	0.9758	-3878.30	122.42	7747.00	15.40	1282.60	1.0538
1987	1.0590	1.0496	-1885.80	133.77	8100.00	16.78	1643.80	1.0605
1988	1.0600	0.0500	-1900.00	144.55	11711.00	17.72	1685.70	1.0700

Year	ERAM	GC	GDRNO	GDY	GI	GICUR	PRODOIL
1970	NA	2143.50	246.11	20749.24	1116.51	162.02	311.55
1971	NA	2176.70	313.90	23650.39	1317.88	201.15	325.66
1972	NA	2484.60	359.14	25491.47	1306.95	247.61	395.56
1973	NA	3171.70	559.30	29034.89	1837.57	419.23	488.54
1974	NA	2839.70	756.48	33935.06	3135.12	892.54	501.84
1975	1.4204	3700.60	911.10	34521.23	3142.02	1117.10	476.85
1976	1.4961	3971.80	1206.73	36369.66	4591.13	1811.30	550.32
1977	1.4946	4359.60	1450.63	43382.81	5519.21	2178.42	615.12
1978	1.5892	5128.00	1825.05	47532.02	4777.88	2325.26	596.70
1979	1.7363	5743.30	2320.61	54360.06	5167.08	3199.87	580.45
1980	1.4552	6874.00	3044.61	64797.02	8695.49	5863.15	577.02
1981	1.7387	7550.70	3436.34	72241.18	8061.07	6551.45	584.84
1982	1.3627	8230.30	3919.02	71914.15	8981.69	7583.22	488.17
1983	1.3200	8077.30	4811.30	77676.30	7950.70	7950.70	490.48
1984	1.3934	8353.00	4860.80	82802.39	8951.21	9851.20	516.99
1985	1.7409	8991.20	7056.10	86210.02	8365.72	9539.00	483.77
1986	1.5302	9241.30	9853.70	86426.86	8419.78	9740.50	507.23
1987	1.3748	9225.70	10738.30	91129.18	7294.82	10001.20	502.92
1988	1.3958	9954.30	12796.75	97104.71	7921.38	11562.00	480.23

(continued)

Year	PXMUSA	PXPR	RM	SER	VALOIL	X	XCUR
1970	NA	NA	207.00	-367.00	216.06	11117.10	434.00
1971	NA	NA	261.00	-453.00	283.12	11893.20	526.80
1972	NA	NA	387.00	-681.00	485.91	15157.00	762.40
1973	NA	NA	501.00	-1028.00	756.24	18063.30	1356.10
1974	NA	NA	776.00	-2033.00	2436.68	19219.30	3044.50
1975	4.6675	0.0987	1063.00	-2528.00	2533.03	18825.40	2897.30
1976	4.9319	0.1163	1330.00	-2705.00	3014.65	22025.40	3621.30
1977	5.2898	0.1430	1672.00	-3336.00	3458.97	24016.00	4512.80
1978	1.3943	0.1460	1848.00	-4062.00	3613.26	24254.90	5240.50
1979	1.0907	0.2068	2421.00	-4929.00	6635.73	24810.40	10003.30
1980	0.9804	0.2306	3277.00	-6306.00	10672.85	26182.00	16162.20
1981	1.1990	0.1932	3920.00	-7372.00	12916.19	21456.70	16167.70
1982	1.0806	0.0965	4108.00	-7167.00	11142.15	19524.10	15103.10
1983	0.7249	0.0956	5139.00	-7301.00	13170.19	19847.00	19847.00
1984	0.9156	0.1156	5701.00	-7563.00	15662.12	21144.90	22999.30
1985	0.7688	0.0472	6721.00	-7745.00	15328.45	19494.70	21533.90
1986	0.8456	0.0487	8171.00	-6369.00	8873.82	22460.30	20009.90
1987	0.8731	0.0688	9032.00	-6772.00	14616.05	25744.80	29874.30
1988	1.1056	0.1465	8381.00	-6915.00	12644.76	26015.50	34655.60

Year	XNOGDEF	XDEF	XNOGUS	XM	XMRE	XMASE	GR
1970	NA	0.0390	NA	NA	NA	NA	420.92
1971	NA	0.0443	NA	NA	NA	NA	544.72
1972	NA	0.0503	NA	NA	NA	NA	679.62
1973	NA	0.0751	NA	NA	NA	NA	1010.67
1974	NA	0.1584	NA	NA	NA	NA	1876.07
1975	0.1296	0.1539	1791.68	171.85	76.67	32.75	2328.79
1976	0.1516	0.1644	2542.22	186.46	86.50	53.55	3394.40
1977	0.2032	0.1879	3427.51	397.94	170.05	97.71	4136.32
1978	0.2637	0.2161	3656.95	506.89	218.42	145.46	4749.84
1979	0.5078	0.4032	5424.65	872.40	376.69	358.68	7140.88
1980	0.8544	0.6173	6165.74	960.21	441.89	356.72	11097.62
1981	0.6054	0.7535	4545.48	1175.62	503.69	469.50	13131.58
1982	0.6958	0.7736	3920.44	1258.64	517.56	516.06	14088.45
1983	1.0000	1.0000	4992.90	2053.64	725.18	814.27	16368.10
1984	1.4274	1.0877	5843.18	2494.39	899.70	812.33	19877.10
1985	1.3167	1.1046	5827.82	2580.34	1040.89	642.26	21011.60
1986	1.5877	0.8909	6495.45	3014.15	1323.45	616.08	22018.20
1987	2.3100	1.1604	8554.92	4583.03	1844.95	862.35	26849.70
1988	2.3160	1.3325	11495.28	6225.23	2818.79	1239.46	31486.50

(continued)

Year	GRO	GRR	GRREAL	I	ICUR	ICURASE
1970	64.27	310.38	3883.93	3134.80	454.90	4.2404
1971	97.16	411.06	4940.01	3800.60	580.10	4.6845
1972	176.83	535.97	5526.05	4523.00	856.90	5.3399
1973	276.16	835.46	6313.85	5294.90	1208.00	7.3704
1974	896.67	1653.15	7849.97	6312.10	1797.00	10.6453
1975	1079.18	1990.28	8510.93	7233.00	2571.60	11.5112
1976	1500.86	2707.59	10989.70	7667.00	3024.80	13.0777
1977	1930.87	3381.50	11900.42	9694.50	3826.40	15.4207
1978	2126.79	3951.84	11399.56	11289.10	5494.10	18.9690
1979	3205.99	5526.60	12661.86	12381.80	7667.80	24.2228
1980	6833.75	9878.36	15127.37	15646.00	10549.70	29.3586
1981	7922.20	11358.54	16016.56	17658.70	14351.70	33.4574
1982	8211.16	12130.18	16095.74	18740.30	15822.40	35.6692
1983	9093.70	13905.00	16368.10	19467.90	19467.90	37.1527
1984	11637.60	16498.40	18371.56	18296.50	20136.10	36.5287
1985	9755.90	16812.00	18431.83	19615.80	22366.90	29.7536
1986	7846.90	17700.60	19329.44	21421.70	24781.90	26.4833
1987	9137.20	19875.50	20364.26	22596.80	30980.20	30.4071
1988	9657.00	22453.75	22257.25	24136.70	35229.80	30.5000

Year	ICURD	IDEF	INFL	LOAN	M	MCUR	MDEF
1970	1.2463	0.1451	12.36	110.55	2395.20	522.70	0.2182
1971	1.4746	0.1526	4.00	133.66	2655.00	623.40	0.2348
1972	2.0648	0.1895	6.73	143.65	3611.60	778.20	0.2155
1973	2.9108	0.2281	30.63	175.21	4817.50	1330.80	0.2762
1974	4.3301	0.2847	41.03	222.92	6357.80	2318.30	0.3646
1975	6.1966	0.3555	18.83	338.51	6931.60	2811.70	0.4056
1976	7.2887	0.3945	19.96	686.81	8092.60	3522.30	0.4352
1977	9.2202	0.3947	10.98	754.82	10824.00	3864.50	0.3570
1978	12.4301	0.4867	8.19	798.00	12193.60	4699.60	0.3854
1979	12.3079	0.6193	20.57	1614.27	13546.60	7790.90	0.5751
1980	16.8257	0.6743	18.48	1219.26	14865.60	9885.60	0.6650
1981	22.7444	0.8127	12.20	1773.04	19890.10	14561.10	0.7321
1982	23.9371	0.8443	9.54	1958.27	20170.60	15185.50	0.7529
1983	21.4098	1.0000	11.80	2463.10	19625.90	19625.90	1.0000
1984	19.6277	1.1005	10.41	3388.70	18151.20	19844.70	1.0933
1985	20.1395	1.1402	4.75	4199.60	19109.10	19835.20	1.0380
1986	19.3216	1.1569	5.85	4317.60	19905.60	21036.20	1.0568
1987	18.8467	1.3710	9.27	6974.20	20999.00	27955.80	1.3313
1988	20.1445	1.4596	8.06	9032.75	20999.00	31171.40	1.4844

(continued)

Year	MM	MNOGUS	MOIL	MPR	MRIEL2	MS2	MTOT
1970	NA	NA	44.60	NA	3044.97	330.00	NA
1971	NA	NA	44.60	NA	4244.23	468.00	NA
1972	NA	NA	44.60	NA	5659.22	696.00	NA
1973	NA	NA	44.64	NA	6209.70	994.00	NA
1974	NA	NA	185.35	NA	6083.91	1454.00	NA
1975	3756.08	4513.02	256.75	756.94	7389.72	2022.00	4769.78
1976	4229.68	5232.68	440.41	1003.00	8582.88	2651.00	5673.09
1977	4281.77	5495.57	734.69	1213.80	9013.82	3133.00	6230.26
1978	4678.79	6107.90	582.52	1429.11	9172.76	3822.00	6690.42
1979	4948.43	6405.16	797.12	1456.73	9147.70	5159.00	7202.28
1980	7254.02	9080.64	1753.75	1826.62	10505.55	7707.00	10834.39
1981	9550.44	11544.94	1727.16	1994.50	11837.16	9705.00	13272.10
1982	11561.40	13308.51	3550.37	1747.11	12651.80	11074.00	16858.88
1983	10351.90	12201.89	4149.86	1849.99	14669.00	14669.00	16351.75
1984	9535.56	11176.98	2705.09	1640.42	16570.08	17937.00	13882.07
1985	7629.91	8971.42	1287.66	1341.51	20332.25	23178.00	10259.09
1986	8125.42	9611.53	1106.88	1486.11	24242.48	27615.00	10718.41
1987	9482.31	11226.32	1144.04	1744.00	25715.38	33905.00	12370.36
1988	10231.42	12289.52	958.96	2058.10	29740.65	42073.00	13248.48

Year	PC	PI	PICURD	PMCON	PMM	POIL	POP
1970	15877.40	2018.29	0.8024	52.15	NA	1.90	116.20
1971	18084.50	2482.72	0.9633	58.03	NA	2.21	119.21
1972	18557.20	3216.05	1.4682	51.93	NA	2.96	122.20
1973	20476.70	3457.33	1.9006	49.70	NA	3.73	125.40
1974	22791.70	3176.98	2.1794	73.16	NA	11.70	128.60
1975	23376.60	4090.98	3.5048	77.93	0.66	12.80	131.80
1976	24503.40	3075.87	2.9241	67.73	0.89	13.20	135.20
1977	27512.90	4175.29	3.9710	75.42	1.04	13.55	138.30
1978	29711.50	6511.22	7.1693	80.55	1.02	13.70	141.60
1979	32388.10	7214.72	7.1716	74.80	1.11	18.35	144.50
1980	32838.50	6950.51	7.4746	94.79	1.25	29.50	147.50
1981	44837.20	9597.63	12.3617	137.83	1.27	35.00	151.31
1982	45053.00	9758.61	12.4647	120.70	1.47	34.53	154.66
1983	49910.00	11517.20	12.6660	100.00	1.33	29.53	158.08
1984	53267.50	9345.29	10.0252	118.02	1.35	29.53	161.58
1985	55966.50	11250.08	11.5504	129.47	1.39	28.53	165.15
1986	56735.00	13001.92	11.7273	199.71	1.45	13.64	168.66
1987	57865.60	15301.98	12.7625	82.64	1.54	17.68	171.61
1988	60689.80	16215.32	14.0403	NA	1.63	15.62	175.22

(continued)

Year	XMJAP	XMUSA	XPR	XOIL	XOILASE	XOILUSA	XOILJAP
1970	NA	NA	NA	NA	NA	NA	NA
1971	NA	NA	NA	NA	NA	NA	NA
1972	NA	NA	NA	NA	NA	NA	NA
1973	NA	NA	NA	NA	NA	NA	NA
1974	NA	NA	NA	NA	NA	NA	NA
1975	34.63	27.79	1619.84	5310.86	386.03	1670.52	2597.68
1976	22.58	23.83	2355.76	6004.24	342.34	2097.85	2845.72
1977	87.25	42.93	3029.58	7378.57	663.27	2455.32	3505.24
1978	104.86	38.15	3150.06	7986.22	818.91	2448.07	3672.51
1979	114.61	22.43	4552.24	10165.49	1135.80	2539.96	5700.51
1980	124.68	36.92	5205.53	15743.14	1552.46	3572.03	9033.89
1981	129.36	73.07	3369.87	20619.01	2332.40	4286.94	10862.83
1982	78.30	146.72	2661.80	18407.90	2583.43	2961.09	10288.42
1983	225.63	288.56	2939.26	16152.95	2253.67	3394.83	8642.24
1984	318.09	464.28	3348.78	16044.58	1197.06	3290.89	9258.42
1985	361.81	535.38	3247.49	12757.29	965.75	2859.79	7549.40
1986	431.21	643.40	3481.30	8309.59	559.80	1605.61	5402.18
1987	927.11	948.62	3971.89	8581.86	365.71	1687.91	5519.22
1988	1176.04	990.94	5270.05	7723.22	117.40	1231.56	5383.47

Year	XOILRE	XTOT	Y	YCUR	YCURD	YENUS	DEF
1970	NA	NA	29877.60	3238.00	8.87	360.00	0.1084
1971	NA	NA	33300.00	3671.90	9.33	349.33	0.1103
1972	NA	NA	37110.20	4564.00	11.00	303.17	0.1230
1973	NA	NA	42189.10	6753.30	16.27	271.70	0.1601
1974	NA	NA	44805.00	10708.00	25.80	292.08	0.2390
1975	656.62	7102.54	46204.00	12642.50	30.46	296.79	0.2736
1976	718.32	8546.46	50075.00	15466.70	37.27	296.55	0.3089
1977	754.73	10806.07	54759.00	19033.00	45.86	268.51	0.3476
1978	1046.72	11643.17	58189.90	24245.90	54.85	210.44	0.4167
1979	789.23	15590.14	61777.00	34840.20	55.92	219.14	0.5640
1980	1584.77	21908.89	66674.90	48913.50	78.01	226.74	0.7336
1981	3136.84	25164.50	71613.20	58713.90	93.05	220.54	0.8199
1982	2574.94	22328.33	71377.10	62475.70	94.52	249.08	0.8753
1983	1862.21	21145.85	77676.30	77676.30	85.42	237.51	1.0000
1984	2298.21	21887.76	82910.70	89750.30	87.48	237.52	1.0825
1985	1382.35	18585.11	84959.10	96850.20	87.21	238.54	1.1400
1986	741.99	14805.04	89952.70	102465.30	79.95	168.52	1.1391
1987	1009.01	17136.78	94433.90	124508.40	75.76	144.64	1.3185
1988	990.79	19218.50	99767.30	141137.10	82.73	128.15	1.4147

Chapter 6

The Quest Model of the European Community

Andries Brandsma[1]

1 Introduction

This paper provides a description of features of the Quest model which are relevant for model builders wanting to attach detailed models of non-OECD members, such as the Asian newly industrializing economies or the ASEAN countries, to an existing model of the world economy. It is also intended to be of some use to international model builders that wish to cover the EC economy, either by including models for individual Member States or by constructing an aggregate model. For that purpose, the key parameters estimated for the EC countries, which are all represented in the Quest model, are summarized in the form of elasticities for the EC economy as a whole. More detailed information about the system can be found in European Economy No.47, which documents the 1990 version of the models and from which most of the material in this paper is taken.

The 1990 version of the Quest model[2] covers the economies of all EC Member States. Each country molel can be operated separately or in conjunction with the models for the other EC countries. Macroeconomic models for the United States and Japan are also included in the linked system. All country models are similar in structure, but have estimated parameters that make the magnitude and timing of their response to shocks quite different. The linkage is provided by a model of bilateral trade in goods.

In recent years there has been a real proliferation of models of the world economy, which are usually built by a single modelling team but are transferable to other institutes.[3] A common feature of these multinational models is that structural

[1] Commission of the European Communities, Directorate-General for Economic and Financial Affairs, and professor in the Economics of European Integration at Erasmus University, Rotterdam. Any views expressed in this paper represent exclusively the positions of the author and do not necessarily correspond with those of the Commission.

[2] The first version of the Quest model (1988 version) was presented in P.Bekx, A.Bucher, A.Italianer and M.Mors, Economic Papers No.75, March, 1989.

[3] The Quest model is included in a SPES project entitled Macro Analysis and Modelling of Interdependencies between European Economies. This project, which is supported by the Commission, uses three other world models:

- MIMOSA, jointly developed by the Centre d'Etudes Prospectives et d'Informations Internationales and the Observatoire Francais des Conjonctures Economiques, both in Paris
- GEM, developed by the National Institute for Economic and Social Research and now jointly maintained with the London Business School

differences between the countries are allowed for only when institutional arrangements or other information on the structure of the economy clearly point to it. The older generation, of which the LINK project is still the prime representative, uses the approach of linking existing models of national economies.

The Quest model is constructed and maintained by the Directorate-General for Economic and Financial Affairs (DGII), mainly to assist in macroeconomic forecasting and policy analysis. The Compact model[4], in which all EC countries are aggregated into a single block, served as a prototype for the Quest model. A stated aim of the work on econometric modelling at the Commission is to enhance the understanding of the different economies and their interaction on a world level.

This paper is organized as follows. Section 2 presents the general framework in which the equations are embedded: the linkage system at the international level and the sectoral income accounts for the national modules. The description of the equations of the international linkage block follows in section 3. A summary of the key parameters of the national models is given in section 4 for the economies of the EC, the United States and Japan. Section 5 concludes with a summary of the policy regimes under which the model can be operated. A complete listing of the model in its present functional form, accompanied by a list of variables, is given in European Economy No. 47. The construction of the Quest databank is laid out in the annex.

2 General Framework

A macroeconomic model describes the behaviour of economic agents at an aggregate level as they engage in activities such as production, consumption and trade. The grouping of agents and activities determines the level of aggregation of the model. In the Quest model, this is governed by the system of national accounts which identifies sectors of the economy that, as a group, generate a registered surplus or deficit. It is assumed that there is only one productive sector. Standard regression techniques have been used to estimate the parameters of the key behavioural relations. Most equations are linear with respect to the coefficients and their general form is derived within a theoretical context. Country-specific elements are introduced to a very limited extent and only when they are statistically significant. Country models which are set up in this way are called structural models in the Quest termonology. The system is organized so that they can be operated in unlinked mode.

At the international level, the country as a whole is the basic unit of aggregation.

- PRIMO, under construction at Prometeia, Bologna

The SPES project compares the results of standard simulations for Germany, France, Italy and the United Kingdom on each of these models. Simulations with the Quest model for this purpose are performed at the Deutsches Institut fur Wirtschaftsforschung in Berlin. The Central Planning Bureau in The Hague operates a world model which includes a detailed monetary sector in the form of a portfolio model. Except for Quest, none of those models contains separate submodels for all EC countries.

[4] A full description of the Compact model was given in Dramais (1986)

It is important to recognize that, at this level, the Quest model may be operated without any reference to the sectoral disaggregation of the national economies. The linkage system could be closed by any country model which links import volumes to export volumes and export prices to import prices. In fact, models which do only that are included for all countries or zones which are not modelled in a structural way. These trade-feedback models provide an echo for the structural models in linked simulations. Since the scope for linking structural country models to the system is, in the first instance, limited by the choice of countries and zones in the trade linkage block, this section begins with a general description of this part of the model. In doing so, the minimum requirements to be imposed on the structural models become clear before the more elaborate modelling of the national economies is set out in general terms.

2.1 The Trade Linkage Model

The Quest model distinguishes 26 zones, 13 of which are represented by country models in structural form. The trade linkage model[5] takes the import demand for each country or zone as given and then determines the exports of all zones from bilateral trade equations. An adding-up constraint is imposed to make sure that bilateral exports to each country sum to the total imports of that country. Apart from the well-known discrepancy, which is attributed in the model to the internal trade of the rest of the world zone, world exports are therefore constrained to add up to world imports. The bilateral shares in the imports of each country are then used to determine import prices from the export prices given by the country models. These bilateral shares are also used as the basis for calculating an index of competitors' export prices used in the export price equations of the structural models.

The basic assumption behind the setting up of the trade linkage system is that the allocation of total imports over trading partners is independent of the division of final demand into imports and domestic production[6]. This separability theorem does not generally stand up against rigorous empirical testing. The most obvious example in which it does not hold is that of energy trade between countries which produce oil and countries which do not. For such cases a special provision has been made in the Quest model which is discussed in more detail below. Non-energy goods, on the other hand, are produced and traded by all but a few countries. Therefore for this category the convenient framework of the two-stage approach is taken to apply. Total non-energy imports are first derived from the country models and, in stage two, imports are allocated to trading partners taking account of their relative export prices.

Services cannot be included in the linkage system since no data for trade in services are available on a bilateral basis and so do not feature in the trade-feedback models either. The structural models contain equations for both imports

[5] This part of the model is specified in more detail in Section 3. A full exposition is given in Italianer (1987).

[6] Cf. Italianer(1986)

and exports of services, which are needed to close the GDP identities and to properly define the balance of trade. To satisfy the adding-up constraint and in the absence of a complete trade linkage system, trade in services is assumed in principle to move in line with trade in goods. This is accomplished by establishing a direct relationship between the growth of imports and exports of services and that of goods, or at least by a close resemblance in specification between the equation for services and the aggregate equation for trade in goods.

2.2 The Treatment of Energy

Among traded goods, energy has a special role to play because it is a crucial input for many production processes and because in the short to medium term few substitutes are available for it. Moreover, while many countries are net importers of energy, some are net exporters and some almost exclusively export oil. In the Quest system five of the trade feedback countries/zones are identified as regions for which energy exports are important (Canada, Australia, Norway, the CPEs and the rest of the world zone). The United Kingdom is a net exporter of energy for which a structural model is included, while OPEC only exports oil and is treated as the swing producer. The output of energy (natural gas) in the Netherlands is similar to that of the United Kingdom expressed as a percentage of GDP. In 1985 the Netherlands also became a net exporter of energy. Finally, France is a major producer of nuclear energy which is used strategically to replace energy imports.

Provisionally, the system has been set up as follows:

1. as a net exporter of oil represented by a structural model, a supply- determined equation for energy exports has been estimated for the United Kingdom;

2. in the trade linkage block, energy exports from the United Kingdom to the other EC countries, the United States and Japan are distributed to the bilateral export equation for total goods according to these countries' proper share in the United Kingdom energy exports (taken together, they account for more than 80% of the total);

3. the same is done for the Netherlands (almost 90% of Dutch exports of energy go to the other EC countries);

4. the bilateral trade flow (consisting only of oil) from OPEC to these same countries is set equal to the difference between their imports of energy and exports from the United Kingdom and the Netherlands;

5. for bilateral exports from OPEC to the other countries/zones, the price elasticity is set equal to zero under the assumptions that OPEC only exports oil, that it only competes with other energy exporters and that the law of one price holds for energy products.

Since the relative price terms have all been redefined so as to relate to non-energy goods only, and the trade feedback models contain no separate equations for energy imports, the trade linkage model mainly serves the purpose of reflecting changes in exports of non-energy goods. Energy exports follow directly from exogenous energy production in the structural models for the United Kingdom and the Netherlands. The other energy exporters, except OPEC, are assumed to maintain their market shares in each importing country. The market shares of OPEC are only affected in so far as the imports of energy derived from the structural models change. In this respect, the performance of the linkage system will improve as more structural models are added to the system.

2.3 The Sectors of the National Economy

On the income side, the Quest model distinguishes four sectors of the economy. Their accounts are modelled in line with the tables of DGII's economic forecasts.

2.3.1 Households

Households have different sources of income:

- they supply labour to firms and to the government
- they obtain their share of the gross operating surplus of enterprises, either because they are self-employed or because they receive dividends on share ownership
- they receive interest on holdings of government bonds
- they are the beneficiaries of income transfers from the government and from abroad.

The wage bill paid by firms and by the government, including employees' social security contributions, corresponds to the first item. It follows from an estimated wage equation which is described in detail in Section 6. The next two items together constitute non-wage income. A semi-behavioural relationship has been estimated in order to determine non-wage income of households. The general form of the equation is

(2.1) $$ynw = a_0 + a_1 * lse * wr + a_2 * int + a_3 * gos$$

where			
	ynw	=	non-wage income of households
	lse	=	number of self-employed
	wr	=	wage rate
	int	=	interest payments on government debt
	gos	=	gross operating surplus

The parameter which is of greatest interest from the point of view of estimation is that determining the household share in the gross operating surplus. A typical estimate of the share is of the order of one-third. The coefficient on the income imputed to self-employed is expected to be close to one. The number of self-employed is assumed to be determined exogenously. The wage rate variable is included in the equation in order to approximate the wage element of the income of the self-employed and is assumed to be the going rate for the economy as a whole. This is quite an important equation in determining the overall simulation properties of the model because of the role it plays in determining disposable income and therefore consumption expenditure.

Income transfers from the government to households are related to unemployment by a semi-behavioural relation. The sum of all the components of income net of taxes and social security contributions paid by households is disposable income. The consumption function determines how much of it is spent on the purchase of goods and services and how much is saved.

2.3.2 Firms

Firms combine labour with capital to produce goods and services. Labour demand and investment may be derived from profit maximization under the constraint of a production function. Although this derivation is not followed rigorously in the investment function (in which an accelerator-type approach is used instead) it can be reconciled with a putty-clay decision framework in which substitution between production factors is possible before but not after capital has been installed[7]. The value added to inputs on a macro level is distributed to the two production factors.

Firms are assumed to have access to both internal and external means of financing. The internal means correspond to the part of the gross operating surplus which does not accrue to households or the government, i.e. companies' after-tax profits. The external sources are household savings, public savings and foreign savings. Profitability and interest rates may therefore both be expected to play a role in determining investment, keeping in mind that full articulation of financial flows is not included in the Quest model.

2.3.3 Government

The government receives taxes and social security payments from households and firms, and has limited income sources of its own in the form of the trading surplus and profits of public companies. Government consumption is split into an (imputed) wage component and exogenous non-wage expenditure. Wages account for between 20% and 30% of current government expenditure. The other outlays are interest payments on government debt, transfers to households, subsidies and investment expenditure. Current transfers to households in the EC countries range from 30% to almost 50% of government expenditure.

An overview of the structure of the government sector is given in table 2.1 below.

There are only three genuinely endogenous variables among those making up the government sector, namely, transfers to the household sector, interest payments on government debt and taxes on income. Government consumption and investment may be set in real or in nominal terms. The same applies to subsidies. Social

[7] Cf. Catinat et al (1987)

security contributions are determined by reference to an exogenous rate of contribution applied to the wage bill. A similar approach is used in the case of corporate taxes, the rate in this instance being applied to the level of profits. Indirect taxes have two components - value added tax and other indirect taxes. The VAT rate is exogenous and the base is assumed to be the level of consumption. Other indirect taxes are a function of total demand. The trading and investment income of the government is related to the gross operating surplus.

Table 2.1: The government account

Expenditure		
1.	Government consumption	cg
2.	Government investment	ig
3.	Net subsidies	sub
4.	Current transfers to households	tph
5.	Interest payments on public debt	int
Revenue		
6.	Income tax	tyh
7.	Corporate tax	tyc
8.	Indirect taxes	ti
9.	Employers' social security contributions	scc
10.	Employees' social security contributions	sch
11.	Other non-tax income	yg

Government deficit = cg+ig+sub+tph+int-tyh-tyc-ti-scc-sch-yg

Income taxes are behaviourally determined in the model. The tax base is the sum of the wage bill, non-wage income and net income transfers received by households. An income elasticity greater than one may be taken to be an indicator of progressivity in the tax system. Estimates range from 1.02 to 1.36 in the structural models.

In determining transfers received by households, the rate of unemployment and in some cases the population not of working age are used as explanatory variables. The range of estimates from across the models indicates that, on average, a one percentage point increase in the rate of unemployment results in an increase of 0.4 percentage points of GDP in transfer payments.

Finally, a behavioural equation for the implicit rate of interest on government bonds is estimated wherein the long-term rate of interest is the explanatory variable. Interest payments are then set equal to the product of this interest rate and government debt which in turn is the accumulation of the deficit over time.

2.3.4 The Foreign Sector and the Balance of Payments

The sectoral income accounts for each country are closed by their current transactions with the rest of the world. The balance of trade is defined in Quest so as to include trade in both goods and services. The current account of the balance of payments is then given by the sum of the balance of trade and the exogenously-set level of net international transfers.

Since data for the quarterly country models are extracted from national sources and national accounting conventions differ between countries, the uniform framework adopted for the country module had to be filled in using quite liberal assumptions on occasion.

3 The Trade Linkage Equations

3.1 The Bilateral Trade-relations

The trade linkage block contains bilateral export equations for trade in goods between 20 OECD countries and the rest of the world divided into 6 zones (the 4 most advanced newly-industrializing economies in East Asia have been separated from the other NICs in the 1990 version of Quest). The architecture of the Quest system is such that the trade linkage block can be run without recourse to the structural models. To do so, the only requirements are import volumes and export prices for the 26 countries/zones.

The bilateral export equations are all of the form

(3.1) $$lnx_{ij} = a_{ij} + lnm_j + b_{ij} * ln(\frac{x_{ij}}{m_j})_{-1} + c_{ij}(1 - b_{ij}) * ln(\frac{px_i}{pm_j})$$

where x_{ij} are the bilateral exports from country i to country j in real terms, m_j are the real imports of country j, px_i is the export price of country i and pm_j the import price of country j.

Table 3.1 summarizes the estimated long-run price elasticities for the bilateral trade flows. The importing countries have been grouped into blocks for which the range of price elasticities are given, excluding the outliers at both ends. Export price elasticities for trade with the US are given separately. Outliers are excluded because the estimates were found to be unreliable for small trade flows. No clear pattern arises regarding whether trade partners belong to the same block or not. Except for the UK, the ranges for the EC and the group of other countries overlap to a large extent. The average long-run elasticity is determined by the simulation of price shocks in the trade linkage model only, and is found to lie between -0.7 and -1.2 for all OECD countries. This range is extended to -1.5 if non-OECD zones are included. The world average is very close to -1.0. This value has been imposed on the NICs following the separation of the 4 Asian newly industrializing countries from the other countries in the NI zone.

Table 3.1 Long-term bilateral price elasticities

Exporting country/zone	Importing country/zone: EC(range)	US	Others(range)	Simulated average
EC:				
B/L	0.4 - 1.3	1.9	0.1 - 1.3	0.7
DK	0.6 - 1.3	1.6	0.8 - 1.7	1.1
D	0.6 - 1.2	1.7	0.3 - 1.4	0.8
GR	0.3 - 2.4	0.6	0.6 - 1.7	0.7
E	0.5 - 1.4	0.0	0.1 - 1.4	0.9
F	0.7 - 1.5	0.9	0.0 - 1.5	0.7
IRL	0.7 - 2.6	1.6	0.7 - 2.8	1.2
I	0.5 - 1.5	1.2	0.6 - 2.0	1.1
NL	0.6 - 1.6	1.0	0.2 - 2.2	0.8
P	0.5 - 1.7	0.9	0.6 - 2.1	1.1
UK	0.5 - 1.0	1.6	0.7 - 2.3	1.1
US	1.0 - 1.8	-	0.6 - 1.7	1.0
JA	0.5 - 2.7	1.7	0.5 - 1.9	1.1
Others:				
CA	0.1 - 2.2	0.5	0.5 - 1.4	0.7
AU	0.1 - 1.7	0.9	0.2 - 1.5	1.1
AT	0.4 - 1.5	1.1	0.1 - 1.1	0.8
FI	0.5 - 2.0	1.2	0.3 - 1.6	0.9
NO	0.6 - 2.2	2.0	0.4 - 2.4	1.2
SE	0.5 - 1.3	1.2	0.1 - 1.0	0.8
SW	0.2 - 1.3	0.7	0.4 - 1.5	0.7
RO	0.7 - 1.9	1.2	0.8 - 2.4	1.5
OP	0.4 - 1.9	2.7	0.1 - 3.0	0.9
CP	0.8 - 2.2	2.2	0.1 - 1.5	0.8
TI/NI	0.1 - 2.2	2.0	0.5 - 2.4	1.3
RW	0.8 - 1.8	1.0	0.9 - 1.8	1.4

Note: Price elasticities are of course negative in all cases.

Import prices are a trade weighted average of export prices

(3.2) $pm_j = \sum_i x_{ij} px_i \sum_i x_{ij}$

As long as relative prices remain constant, world exports are equal to world imports, since in accordance with the equations in (3.1) aggregate exports have an elasticity of one with respect to the weighted sum of imports (which corresponds to world trade). If relative prices do change, the adding-up constraint ensures that the total volume of world exports remains equal to the total volume of world imports. For this purpose, c.i.f. imports are first made compatible with exports which are expressed on a f.o.b. basis in the country models.

3.2 The Trade Feedback Equations

In order to close the model and to provide an echo for the structural models in linked simulation, reduced form equations linking the import volumes of goods to exports and the export price to the import price have been estimated for the countries and zones which are not represented by structural models (13 in the 1990 version of Quest). In general, the import equations have the following error correction form

$$(3.3) \qquad lnm_j = a + k(b * \Delta lnx_j + c * \Delta ln(\frac{pm_j}{px_j})) + (1-d)(b * ln(x_j)_{-1} + c * ln(\frac{pm_j}{px_j})_{-1} - ln(m_j)_{-1})$$

Assuming that k = 1-d, this reduces to the partial adjustment form

$$(3.4) \qquad lnm_j = a + (1-d)b * lnx_j + (1-d)c * ln(\frac{pm_j}{px_j}) + d * ln(m_j)_{-1}$$

The long-run elasticities b and c are estimated to be not greater than one for all countries. Their absolute value mostly varies between 0.50 and 1.0. Unit elasticities have been imposed for the zones covering OPEC, NICs and the LDCs (rest of the world).

The export price equation assumes the following general form

$$(3.5) \qquad lnpx_j = a + kb * ln(pm_j)_{-1/2} + (1-d)b * ln(pm_j)_{-3/2} + d * ln(px_j)_{-1}$$

In the long run, it is estimated that between 60% and 100% of the changes in the import price of non-energy goods is transmitted directly into an export price change.

Box 1. Countries and zones in the Quest model

Complete country models

1. B/L Belgium-Luxembourg Economic Union (BLEU)
2. DK Denmark
3. D Germany
4. GR Greece
5. E Spain
6. F France
7. IRL Ireland
8. I Italy
9. NL Netherlands
10. P Portugal
11. UK United Kingdom
12. US United States

13. JA	Japan	

Country trade-feedback models

14. CA	Canada	
15. AU	Australia	
16. AT	Austria	
17. FI	Finland	
18. NO	Norway	
19. SE	Sweden	
20. SW	Switzerland	

Zone trade-feedback models

21. RO	The rest of the OECD countries:	Iceland,New Zealand,Turkey
22. OP	OPEC:	Algeria,Ecuador,Gabon,Indonesia, Iran,Iraq,Kuwait,Libya,Nigeria, Qatar,Saudi Arabia,United Arab Emirates,Venezuela
23. CP	Centrally planned economies:	Albania,Bulgaria,Czechoslovakia, former German Democratic Republic, Hungary,Poland,Romania,Union of Soviet Socialist Republics
24. TI	The 4 Asian newly industrializing economies:	Hong Kong,Korea,Singapore, Taiwan
25. NI	Other newly industrializing countries:	Argentina,Brazil,Israel, Malaysia,Philippines,Thailand, South Africa,Yugoslavia
26. RW	The rest of the world:	All countries not included elsewhere including trade not specified in terms of estimation

4 The Key Parameters of the Structural Models

The country module used to build the structural models in Quest is of a moderate size. Although, in total, it consists of more than a hundred equations, only a dozen of them represent behavioural relations, not counting pseudo-definitions. The equations for income taxes, current transfers to households and non-wage income do contain parameters which are estimated, but only because more detailed information is not available or lost in the process of aggregation. The remaining behavioural relations can easily be grouped to explain

- private consumption
- private investment
- imports
- labour demand
- wages and prices.

For each of these variables, the most important elasticities have been computed by using single-equation simulation techniques. Shocks of one percent are applied to each of the explanatory variables in turn, while holding the other right-hand side variables at their baseline levels, except for the lagged dependent variable. The results are presented in this section. Computing the elasticities by simulation in this case is easier than analytical calculations, since a special feature of the Quest model is that it combines annual and quarterly models. The analytical derivation of annual effects from equations expressed in quarterly terms may become quite cumbersome. Presenting short-run and long-run elasticities on an annual basis also allows to calculate an EC average, which may be compared to the corresponding effects in the United States and Japan.

4.1 The Components of Demand

The behavioural relations for consumption, investment and imports are of a fairly conventional type. In the consumption function, the elasticity to changes in disposable income is constrained to be equal to one in the long run:

$$(4.1) \qquad ln(\frac{c}{pop}) = (1 - a_1) * ln(\frac{c}{pop})_{-1} + a_1 ln(\frac{y}{pop}) + a_2 pc + other\ terms$$

where	c	=	real private consumption
	pop	=	total population
	y	=	real disposable income
	pc	=	consumer price inflation

This constraint is far from being rejected in the estimations for the individual countries, and in most cases did not even have to be formally imposed. The income effect for the EC as a whole is the same as for the United States, and has only a slightly longer median lag of one year[8].

The second entry into table 4.1 gives the semi-elasticity to inflation in consumer prices. It represents the effect on private consumption of the devaluation of wealth which results from a permanent rise in inflation by 1% point. This real wealth effect in the EC is remarkably similar to that in the United States and Japan, and amounts to a fall in consumption of about 0.75 percent in the long run.

[8] The median lag is defined as the period which elapses before 50% of the long-run effect has taken place. It is expressed in a number of quarters, which for the annual models (Denmark, Greece, Spain, Ireland and Portugal) is determined by intrapolation.

Table 4.1 Elasticities of the consumption function

	BL	DK	D	GR	E	FR	IRL
Income elasticity							
Short run(1 Year)	0.44	0.63	0.67	0.30	0.23	0.32	0.60
Long run	1.00	1.00	1.00	1.00	1.00	1.00	1.00
Median lag (in quarter)	2	1	1	3	9	4	1
Real wealth effect (semi - elasticity)							
Short run	-0.20	-0.17	-0.18	-0.14	-0.15	-0.23	0.00
Long run	-0.46	-0.46	-0.26	-0.65	-0.98	-0.76	-0.45
Median lag	2	2	1	7	9	4	8

	I	NL	P	UK	EC	US	JA
Income elasticity							
Short run(1 Year)	0.23	0.38	0.25	0.24	0.37	0.37	0.28
Long run	1.00	1.00	1.00	1.00	1.00	1.00	1.00
Median lag (in quarter)	6	3	8	5	4	3	4
Real wealth effect (semi - elasticity)							
Short run	-0.13		-0.21	-0.40	-0.21	-0.29	-0.25
Long run	-0.60		-1.20	-1.63	-0.76	-0.81	-0.91
Median lag	6		8	5	4	3	4

The other terms[9] in the consumption function include the effect of the interest rate, which is significant in only 4 out of 5 annual models and in the Netherlands. A change in the unemployment rate only has substantial direct effects in the consumption function of the Netherlands. The coefficient is also large in the model for Japan, but historically the Japanese unemployment rate shows very little variation over time.

Private investment is disaggregated in most of the country models. The principal force driving the productive capacity of the economy is considered to be investment in equipment, which is explained by an accelerator-type relation. Investment in structures follows investment in equipment with a lag. For some countries, effects of real interest rates and profitability, which add to the ones already present in the equation for equipment, were found. The two equations can be combined into

$$lninv = a_1 * lninv_{-1} + a_2 * \Delta lnyf + a_3 * rlr + a_4 * lnpro \qquad (4.2)$$

where inv = private non-residential investment
yf = real final demand

[9] Only the effects which are present in all but a few EC countries are presented in the tables of this section. The missing, statistically in-significant, coefficients are replaced by zero in the calculation of the EC average. Their undetermined median lag assimilates the EC average.

rlr	=	real long-term interest rate
pro	=	profitability

In Table 4.2 elasticities are presented for non-residential investment only[10].

Table 4.2 Simulated elasticities of private non-residential investment

	BL	DK	D	GR	E	FR	IRL
Accelerator							
Short run(1 Year)	0.79	0.59	0.61	0.85	0.71	0.92	1.28
Long run	2.56	1.37	1.90	1.73	1.76	2.38	3.05
Median lag							
(in quarter)	3	3	3	2	2	3	2
Real wealth effect							
(semi - elasticity)							
Short run	-1.30	-0.17	-0.18	-0.14	-0.15	-0.23	0.00
Long run	-5.07	-0.46	-0.26	-0.65	-0.98	-0.76	-0.45
Median lag	4	2	1	7	9	4	8
Profitability effect							
Short run	0.07	0.11	0.29	0.65	0.61	0.12	0.26
Long run	0.21	0.14	0.57	0.80	0.76	0.75	0.81
Median lag	3	0	2	0	0	7	3

	I	NL	P	UK	EC	US	JA
Accelerator							
Short run(1 Year)	0.54	0.58	0.56	0.43	0.64	0.61	0.76
Long run	1.83	1.15	1.19	1.46	1.85	2.86	1.56
Median lag							
(in quarter)	3	2	2	4	3	5	5
Real wealth effect							
(semi - elasticity)							
Short run	-0.47	-0.34	-0.40	-0.14	-0.51	-0.43	-0.28
Long run	-1.69	-3.68	-0.50	-1.73	-2.35	-1.55	-0.74
Median lag	4	7	0	7	4	4	3
Profitability effect							
Short run	0.39	0.43	0.22	0.06	0.26	0.29	
Long run	0.91	1.93	0.30	0.38	0.69	0.71	
Median lag	2	4	1	5	3	3	

The accelerator effect corresponds to the semi-elasticity of investment to a permanent rise in the growth of final demand. A prolonged rise in the growth rate, everything else staying the same, would have substantial effects on investment, ranging from slightly above 1 percent in the Netherlands to 3 percent in Ireland.

[10] The specifications of the equations for residential investment and stock building are too diverse to be melted into an overall equation for the EC.

The average for the EC as a whole lies between the 1.6 percent for Japan and the 2.9 percent for the United States.

The two other effects belong to the theory which relates investment decisions to capital cost and profits. Real interest rates reflect the opportunity cost of productive investment and the cost of external financing. Profitability, expressed roughly as the share of the gross operating surplus in GDP, is included as an indicator of the means of internal financing. The profitability effect is equally strong in the EC and the United States. In addition, European investment appears to be highly sensitive to changes in interest rates, especially in contrast to Japan.

The national data distinguish between the imports of energy, non-energy goods and services. Bilateral exports of goods are covered by the trade linkage block, with a special proviso for energy, and import volumes together with export prices are the main input from the structural models. In turn, import prices and the total exports of goods are derived in the trade linkage block and taken as given by the country models. Equations for the trade in services, which simply mirror the trade in goods, are included in the structural models.

The distinction between energy and non-energy goods seems to be more important on the supply side than on the demand side. The equations for the imports of both types of goods have similar specifications of the form

$$\text{(4.3)} \qquad lnm = a_1 * lnm_{-1} + a_2(lnyf - a_1 * lnyf_{-1}) + a_3(1 - a_1) * lnpm + a_4(uc - a_1 * uc_{-1})$$

where	m	=	real imports
	yf	=	real final demand
	pm	=	price of imports relative to price of final demand
	uc	=	capacity utilization rate.

The final demand variable is corrected for the trend in trade integration in the equation for non-energy goods, which keeps the demand elasticity down in comparison with conventional estimates. For most countries, the long-run demand elasticity of energy imports is constrained to one. For important energy producers (France, the Netherlands and the United Kingdom) the apparent consumption of energy is modelled instead of the imports. Imports then make up for the difference between consumption and the domestic production of energy. The price and demand elasticities of the total imports of goods are presented in Table 4.3. For the EC as a whole, they are larger than in Japan, except for the long-run price elasticity, but smaller than in the United States. The capacity utilization effect, which reflects the need to meet excess demand in the domestic market by higher imports, is somewhat more prominent in the EC than in the United States.

Table 4.3 Simulated elasticities of the imports of goods

	BL	DK	D	GR	E	FR	IRL
Demand elasticity							
Short run(1 Year)	1.14	0.76	1.10	0.71	0.88	1.13	1.13
Long run	1.18	0.82	1.20	0.94	2.03	1.20	1.25
Median lag							
(in quarter)	0	0	0	0	2	0	0
Price elasticity							
Short run	-0.24	-0.43	-0.24	-0.72	-0.37	-0.33	-0.13
Long run	-0.29	-0.51	-0.37	-0.97	-0.84	-0.61	-0.34
Median lag	0	0	1	0	2	2	3
Utilization rate effect							
Short run	0.48		0.14			0.44	0.79
Long run	0.50		0.15			0.46	0.84
Median lag	0		0			0	0

	I	NL	P	UK	EC	US	JA
Demand elasticity							
Short run(1 Year)	1.21	0.98	0.90	1.16	1.10	1.61	0.89
Long run	1.21	0.99	1.12	1.23	1.26	1.61	0.95
Median lag							
(in quarter)	0	0	0	0	2	0	0
Price elasticity							
Short run	-0.26	-0.57	-0.73	-0.29	-0.32	-0.61	-0.25
Long run	-0.30	-0.84	-0.97	-0.39	-0.49	-0.96	-0.57
Median lag	0	1	0	1	1	1	3
Utilization rate effect							
Short run	0.53	0.92		0.50	0.37	0.28	
Long run	0.66	1.11		0.56	0.42	0.28	
Median lag	0	0		0	0	0	

4.2 The Supply Side

In a broad sense, the supply aspect of the model is formed by all decisions of firms regarding investment, the hiring of labour and the setting of prices. This sub-section only presents the elasticities of labour demand[11]. Investment and value-added pricing are treated in the adjacent parts of section 4. The labour demand equation is derived from a production function which would also allow for the derivation of investment, but this approach is not rigorously followed in the model. Potential output is assumed to be constrained by the capital stock, so that the capacity utilization rate refers mainly to the utilization of capital. Its

[11] Labour supply is exogenous in the country models, except that the Irish model allows for migration. The Japanese model includes a 'discouraged worker' effect, reducing the effect of changes in employment on unemployment by 95 percent.

complement on the side of labour is, of course, the unemployment rate, and both exert a significant influence on wages and prices. In the short run, labour demand reacts to the change in actual output and real wage cost, although the reaction is lagged, displaying some degree of labour hoarding. In the long run, the build-up of the stock of equipment helps to alleviate the pressure of demand. Employment follows the adjustment of output to potential output.

Table 4.4 presents the elasticities of a labour demand function of the form

$$lnleep = a_1 * lnleep_{-1} + (1 - a_1) * lny + a_2 * ln(\frac{wc}{py}) + a_3 * t \qquad (4.4)$$

where

leep	=	number of employees in the private sector
y	=	real GDP
wc	=	wage cost per employee
py	=	GDP deflator
t	=	time trend

Table 4.4 Elasticities of the labour demand function

	BL	DK	D	GR	E	FR	IRL
Demand elasticity							
Short run(1 Year	0.35	0.61	0.43	0.48	0.67	0.26	0.40
Long run	1.00	1.00	1.00	1.00	1.00	1.00	1.00
Median lag							
(in quarter)	3	2	2	2	1	5	3
Substitution elasticity							
Short run	0.17	0.35	0.21	0.45	0.71	0.13	0.15
Long run	0.50	0.89	0.49	0.86	1.06	0.49	0.38
Median lag	3	2	2	2	1	5	3

	I	NL	P	UK	EC	US	JA
Demand elasticity							
Short run(1 Year)	0.22	0.19	0.72	0.25	0.34	0.68	0.24
Long run	1.00	1.00	1.00	1.00	1.00	1.00	1.00
Median lag							
(in quarter)	6	8	1	5	4	1	6
Substitution elasticity							
Short run	0.09	0.08	0.80	0.13	0.21	0.36	0.08
Long run	0.41	0.39	1.12	0.50	0.55	0.53	0.33
Median lag	6	8	1	5	4	1	5

In order to distinguish between scale effects and the technical progress term the long-term elasticity of labour demand with respect to output is constrained to one. The substitution elasticity ($-a_2$) is centered strongly around 0.50. The last term in equation (4.4) reflects autonomous technical progress (labour-saving). Some caution is counselled, since the estimates are over different periods, but in general the annual rate of technical progress ranges from 0.5 to 3.0 for the European countries, lies in the middle of that range for Japan, and is found to be much lower for the United States.

4.3 Wages and Prices

The equations of the wage-price block are strongly interrelated. Firms are assumed to set their product prices in line with unit labour cost in the long run via the adjustment process

(4.5) $$p = a_1 * wc + a_2 * upro + a_3 * uc + error\ correction$$

where	p	=	value-added price
	wc	=	nominal wage cost per employee
	upro	=	labour productivity
	uc	=	capacity utilization rate

(all variables expressed in percentage changes)

Deflators for consumption and investment are determined by pseudo-definitions as a weighted average of value-added and import prices. Export prices adjust to competitors' prices in Germany more slowly than in other countries.

The wage rate equation can be derived from a bargaining model between employers and employees as

(4.6) $$wr = b_1 * pc + b_2 * p + b_3 * upro + Phillips\ curve$$

where	wr	=	compensation per employee
	pc	=	consumption price

(again in percentage changes)

The error ccrrection mechanism in (4.5) ensures that the labour share in income is constant in the long run. The coefficients a_2 and b_3 are constrained so that labour productivity also has no effect on nominal wages in the short run. Tables 4.5 and 4.6 contain the elasticities of the price and wage functions separately. Wages react to price changes with an elasticity of one, and vice versa. Prices receive a further upward push from higher capacity utilization in most countries, as would wages from lower unemployment. The labour productivity effect on wages is computed in single-equation mode, and would be overridden by the error correction mechanism in full simulations. The same should in the long run apply to the labour demand function, but there a constant labour share in income would conflict with a substitution elasticity which is not equal to one. Ultimately, the difference may be explained by variations in technical progress. In the mean time, the long-run behaviour of the system as a whole can best be studied if either the development of labour productivity or inflation is fixed.

Table 4.5 Elasticities of the value-added price equation

	BL	DK	D	GR	E	FR	IRL
Elasticity to							
to wage change							
Short run(1 Year)	0.88	0.80	0.69	0.77	0.76	0.86	0.89
Long run	1.00	1.00	1.00	1.00	1.00	1.00	0.89
Median lag							
(in quarter)	0	0	1	1	0	0	0
Labour productivity							
effect on price							
Short run	-0.38	-0.11	-0.27	-0.47	-0.15	-0.29	-0.41
Long run	-1.00	-1.00	-1.00	-1.00	-1.00	-1.00	-1.00
Median lag	3	35	11	3	30	10	8
Utilization rate							
effect on prices	0.29	0.09	0.15	0.42	0.10	0.12	

	I	NL	P	UK	EC	US	JA
Elasticity to							
to wage change							
Short run(1 Year)	0.70	0.70	0.64	0.73	0.75	0.79	0.72
Long run	1.00	1.00	1.00	1.00	1.00	1.00	1.00
Median lag							
(in quarter)	1	1	1	1	1	1	1
Labour productivity							
effect on price							
Short run	-0.31	-0.29	-0.15	-0.31	-0.28	-0.43	-0.70
Long run	-1.00	-1.00	-1.00	-1.00	-1.00	-1.00	-1.00
Median lag	7	5	33	4	11	2	1
Utilization rate							
effect on prices	0.19	0.48	0.15	0.07	0.15	0.04	0.25

Table 4.6 Elasticities of the wage equation

	BL	DK	D	GR	E	FR	IRL
Price elasticity							
Short run(1 Year)	0.84	0.80	0.84	0.80	0.90	0.84	0.67
Long run	1.00	1.00	1.00	1.00	0.90	1.00	1.00
Median lag							
(in quarter)	1	1	1	1	0	1	1
Labour productivity							
effect on wages							
Short run	0.18	0.08	0.20	0.37	0.12	0.22	0.25
Long run	0.21	0.08	0.23	0.37	0.12	0.27	0.25
Median lag	1	0	1	0	0	1	0
Unemployment effect							
(semi-elasticity)							
Short run	-1.14	-0.39	-1.11	-0.09	-0.28	-0.78	-0.34
Long run	-1.10	-0.39	-0.39	-0.08	-0.28	-0.54	-0.34

	I	NL	P	UK	EC	US	JA
Price elasticity							
Short run(1 Year)	0.76	0.67	0.84	0.67	0.79	0.21	0.66
Long run	1.00	1.00	1.00	1.00	1.00	1.00	1.00
Median lag							
(in quarter)	1	1	1	1	1	6	1
Labour productivity							
effect on wages							
Short run	0.26	0.07	0.11	0.18	0.20	0.35	0.59
Long run	0.35	0.11	0.11	0.27	0.25	0.45	0.71
Median lag	1	1	0	1	1	1	1
Unemployment effect							
(semi-elasticity)							
Short run	-1.30	-0.60	-2.60	-1.70	-1.08	-0.92	-3.59
Long run	-0.93	-0.27	-2.60	-0.44	-0.57	-0.87	-4.20

5 The Use of the Model

The Quest model may be simulated under different regimes for the policy instruments. Government expenditure may be fixed in real or nominal terms, and the same is possible for interest rates. More elaborate monetary regimes in which interest rates are set so as to fix the money supply are technically possible. Exchange rates may be fixed in real instead of nominal terms. In simulations which involve ex ante exchange rate shocks, the return to the baseline may be governed by interest arbitrage schemes. The implementation of a regime of forward-looking exchange rates is still in an experimental phase. Finally, the setting of any combination of instruments may be facilitated by the application of target-oriented approaches[12].

Procedures are in place for reproducing DGII's Economic Forecasts on the Quest model. These are short-term forecasts (up to 8 quarters ahead). Similar procedures may be applied to reproduce medium-term forecasts as a baseline, but in this case the hands-off projection of the model itself may be allowed to play a more prominent role. Nevertheless, the main use of the model will be in policy evaluation. It has already been deployed in background studies of German unification, in analysing the effects of the oil price shock and in the study on the costs and benefits of European Monetary Union[13].

[12] Cf. Brandsma (1989)

[13] One market, one money, European Economy, No 44, October 1990.

References

[1] Bekx, P., A. Bucher, A. Italianer and M. Mors (1989) "The Quest Model (Version 1988)," Economic Papers No 75, March

[2] Brandsma, A. (1989) "Ambition and Risk Aversion in the Design of Economic Policies," Rotterdam, World Scientific Publishing Co., forthcoming

[3] Catinat, M., R. Cawley, F. Ilzkovitz, A. Italianer and M. Mors (1987) "The Determinants of Investment," European Economy No 31, March

[4] Commission of the European Communities (1990) "One Market, One Money. An Evaluation of the Potential Benefits and Costs of Forming an Economic and Monetary Union," European Economy, No. 44, October, Brussels

[5] Commission of the European Communities (1991) "Quest. A Macroeconomic Model for the Countries of the European Community as Part of the World Economy," document prepared by A. Brandsma, J. op de Beke, L. O'Sullivan and W. Roger, European Economy, No. 47, March

[6] Dramais, A. (1986) "Compact - A Prototype Macroeconomic Model of the European Community in the World Economy," European Economy, No 27, March

[7] Italianer, A. (1987) "Estimation and Simulation of International Trade Linkages in the Quest Model," European Economy, No 31, March

[8] Italianer, A. (1986) *Theory and Practice of International Trade Linkage Models*, Martinus Nijhoff Science Publisher, Dordrecht/Boston

Appendix

The parameters of the country models have been estimated on data from the following main sources:

B	Wharton Econometric Group
DK	Danish Statistical Office
D	Deutsches Institut für Wirtschaftsforschung
GR	Eurostat
E	Organisation for Economic Cooperation and Development
F	Institut National de la Statistique et des Etudes Economiques
IRL	Department of Finance, Economic and Social Research Institute (Hermes model databank)
I	Prometeia (model databank)
NL	Central Planning Bureau (model databank)
P	Bank of Portugal
UK	Central Statistical Office
US	Bureau of Economic Analysis
JA	Dutch Central Planning Bureau (model databank).

The model for Germany is estimated on data for the former Federal Republic, and will be expanded to include Eastern Germany as soon as data for the united Germany become available. In the same way, the model estimated on Belgian data is magnified to form the Belgium-Luxembourg Economic Union.

The trade linkage data are obtained from the Direction of Trade data of the International Monetary Fund with data extracted from the United Nations Trade Statistics.

If necessary, the national datasets are completed using data from other official sources, mostly assembled by the Commission services, and brought in line with the DGII forecasts. The use of reconciliation factors for data from different sources is kept to a minimum. They correct for simplifying pseudo-definitions in the country models, for differences between the base year of price indices in the country models and the trade linkage block, and for differences between c.i.f. (including the cost of carriage, insurance and freight) and f.o.b. (free-on-board) statistics. Finally the estimation residuals are fed back into the model to make sure that the baseline reproduces the historical figures. In summary, the Quest databank is fully consistent with DGII forecast definitions, but, except for the basic national accounts data in current prices, the series are not necessarily exactly the same as the data published by the original source. The databank will be updated biannually from DGII's economic forecasts.

Appendix

Chapter 7

Hong Kong Model: The Revised 1990 Version

W.L. Chou and T.B. Lin[1]

1 Introduction

In recent years, the error correction model has gained popularity for dynamic equations in quantitative economics. It has been applied to such main stream problems as personal consumption, investment, and the demand for money.[2] As the error correction process is attractive, in that it contains both levels and differences of variables and is compatible with long-run equilibrium behavior, we have introduced the error correction mechanism to the ERC econometric forecasting model of the Hong Kong economy Constructed by Lin and Chou (1985). The major changes in the model lie in the specification of private consumption, private investment in building and construction, wages, prices, and the demand for money. From the estimation results we can conclude that the introduction of the error correction mechanism has resulted in significant improvements in the accuracy of the forecast performance for such variables as the gross domestic product (GDP) and its main components, the GDP deflator, the consumer price index, wages, and the demand for money. The purpose of this article is to present the revised 1990 version of the ERC econometric forecasting model of the Hong Kong economy and to study the properties of the model as revealed by dynamic multiplier analysis for a set of policy simulations.

The improved version of the ERC model is an aggregate annual model containing 130 variables (of which 50 are exogenous), with 24 behavior equations. It is basically of the Keynesian type, emphasizing real flows rather than monetary ones. The model is aggregated to five sectors: aggregate demand, labor, wages, prices, and money. In section 2 we describe the main equations of the ERC model. The emphasis is on the relations among economic variables represented by structural form. Section 3 discusses the model performance. The article ends with the dynamic multiplier analysis.

---

[1] Department of Economics, The Chinese University of Hong Kong.

[2] Contributions in these areas have been made by Rose(1985), Sargan(1984), Davidson, Hendry, Srba, and Yeo(1978), Dawson(1981), Hendry(1984), among others.

2 The Model

The model determines expenditure using the framework of the GDP identity. Development of the supply side in macroeconomic models is one of the major challenges in economics, as pointed out by Klein (1978). The main problem is that' potential output' is unobservable. No attempt is made in this modeling exercise to incorporate such a supply side into our model. The following section describes the main equations of the model. References are to the list of equations given in Appendix 1, where the definitions of endogenous variables and the exogenous variables are also provided.

2.1 Aggregate Demand

2.1.1 Private consumption (equation 1)

The private consumption equation is in error correction form, where the private consumption is determined in the short and long run by real GDP (GDPMP) which proxies the income level. The equation for private consumption in double-log is written as:

$$(1)\quad \Delta ln(\frac{CP}{N}) = C(\Delta ln(\frac{GDPMP}{N}), ln(\frac{GDPMP}{N})_{-1} - ln(\frac{CP}{N})_{-1})$$

where all variables are in per-capita terms, and N is population. It has a short-run real income elasticity of 0.61, and a long-run income elasticity of unity.

2.1.2 Fixed Investment (equations 2-3)

Gross domestic capital formation (CF) consists of four parts: private investment in building and construction (IPBC); investment in plant, machinery and equipment (IPPD); transfer costs of land and building and real estate developers margin (IPPL+REDM); and government investment (IG). IPBC and IPPD are endogenous variables in our model, while the remaining variables are exogenous.

The equation for building and construction investment (equation 2) has an error correction specification, in which the investment in building and construction is related to real GDP in the short and the long run. A dummy variable D83 which accounts for the effect of political uncertainties after negotiations over Hong Kong's future began in September 1982 was also included. The equation for investment in plant, machinery and equipment (equation 3) has a conventional specification, whereby the real interest rate influences investment. The demand for Hong Kong domestic exports (DEC) also affects the investment level. In addition, a dummy variable (D5) is included to account for the effect of the economic recession that occurred during the periods 1974-75, 1982-83, and 1985. The two equations can be written as:

$$(2)\quad \Delta IPBC = I_1(\Delta GDPMP, GDPMP_{-1}, IPBC_{-1}, D83)$$

$$(3)\quad IPPD = I_2(DEC, RIT, DEC, D5)$$

2.1.3 The Stochastic Equations for the Foreign Sector

There are three exports equations (equations 5,6,9). Total exports (E) in the model comprise exports of goods (EC), and exports of services (ES). Only the demand side of the export sector is considered here.

Demand for exports of goods is divided into the demand for domestic exports (DEC) by SITC and reexports (RE). The former includes four SITC categories of commodities (SITC 0-1, 2+4, 3, 5-9), namely, domestic exports under SITC 0-1 (DEC01), SITC 2+4 (DEC24), SITC 3 (DEC3), and SITC 5-9 (DEC59), with DEC24 and DEC3 treated as exogenous variables. Hong Kong's domestic exports are greatly influenced by the economic conditions in its major overseas markets and the changes in exchange rates. The determinants of DEC01 include the exchange rate (EX), and the linear spline variables T and T84. DEC59 is dependent on the lagged exchange rate variable (EX_{-1}), the lagged U.S.GNP, and the lagged value $DEC59_{-1}$. A dummy variable (D59) is used to account for the effect of the recession period. The equations are written as:

$$(4) \quad DEC01 = E_1(EX, T, T84)$$

$$(5) \quad DEC59 = E_2(EX_{-1}, USGNP_{-1}, DEC59_{-1}, D59)$$

Demand for exports of services is related to exports of goods (EC), and tourist arrivals (TA). Assuming a log-linear specification, the equation is written as:

$$(6) \quad lnES = E_3(lnEC, lnTA)$$

2.1.4 The Five Imports Equations (equations 11-14, 17)

Hong Kong's total imports (M) consist of imports of goods (MC) and imports of services (MS). Imports of goods are further divided into retained imports of goods (RM) and reexports (RE). The model includes four stochastic retained imports equations explaining separately demand for retained imports under SITC 0-1 (RM01), SITC2 (RM2), SITC 3 (RM3), and SITC 5-9 (RM59). Retained imports of SITC 4 and reexports are exogenous variables.

The demand for retained imports depends on income and relative prices. The explanatory variables used in the demand equation for RM01 include per capita income, $\frac{GDPMP}{N}$, the relative prices, $\frac{PM01}{P}$, and the lagged value $(\frac{RM01}{N})_{-1}$. The equation is of the form:

$$(7) \quad \frac{RM01}{N} = M_1(\frac{GDPMP}{N}, \frac{PM01}{P}, (\frac{RM01}{N})_{-1})$$

The equations for RM2 and RM3 are based on the error correction specification. RM2 is determined in the short and the long run by the textile production level (ITP) and the linear spline variables T, T79 and T84, whereas RM3 depends in the short and the long run on the real GDP and a dummy variable, D3. The equations are written as:

(8) $\Delta\frac{RM2}{N} = M_2(\Delta ITP, ITP_{-1}, (\frac{RM2}{N})_{-1}, T, T79, T84)$

(9) $\Delta ln(\frac{RM3}{N}) = M_3(\Delta ln\frac{GDPMP}{N}, ln(\frac{GDPMP}{N})_{-1}, ln(\frac{RM3}{N})_{-1}, D3)$

where D3 accounts for the effect of oil crisis, and the change in the demand for oil products. RM59, the largest component of retained imports of goods, is mainly composed of capital goods and manufactured goods, and it depends on private domestic demand (TDD-IG-CG), domestic exports of goods (DEC) and a dummy variable, D59. The equation for RM59 is of the form:

(10) $\frac{RM59}{N} = M_4(\frac{TDD - IG - CG}{N}, \frac{DEC}{N}, D59)$

Demand for imports of services (MS) depends on real personal disposable GDP(Y) and relative prices $\frac{PIMS}{PC}$. The equation is written as:

(11) $lnMS = M_5(lnY, ln(\frac{PIMS}{PC}))$

2.2 Labor Market and Wages (equations 23-25, 28)

It has been estimated that up to 90 percent of Hong Kong's manufacturing output is eventually exported. The output level of the manufacturing sector (XM) is explained by the foreign demand for Hong Kong's domestic exports and a dummy variable (D6). The equation for XM is:

(12) $XM = F(DEC, D6)$

Employment in the manufacturing sector (NIM) is determined mainly by the output level of manufacturing industries (KM). The employment equation is in an error correction format. It relates the employment to the manufacturing output in the long run, as a separate short-run effect could not be estimated. It is written as:

(13) $\Delta lnNIM = N(lnXM_{-1}, lnNIM_{-1}, D9)$

The model considers the determination of wages in the manufacturing (WMF) and building and construction (WBC) sectors. The equations feature an error correction structure. Wage rates in the manufacturing sector are determined in the short and the long run by domestic prices (P); and the unemployment rate (UE) is also important in the short run. The unemployment rate is expected to have a negative effect on the wage rate, reflecting the possibility that when the labor market is slack (high UE), then nominal wages will be lower, other things being constant. For the building and construction sector, only a short-run effect of domestic prices (P) on wage rates could be estimated. The equations can be written as:

(14) $\Delta WMF = W_1(\Delta P, P_{-1}, UE, WMF_{-1})$

(15) $\Delta WBC = W_2(\Delta P, WSC_{-1}, T, T84, T86)$

where T, T84 and T86 are the linear spline variables.

2.3 Prices (equations 30-32)

The equations used in the model to determine domestic as well as export price deflators are based on the error correction formulation.

The implicit GDP deflator (P) is determined in the short and the long run by prices of total domestic demand (PDM). The consumer price index (PC) is explained in the short and the long run by import prices for goods and services (PIMMS) and prices of total domestic demand (PDM). The export price deflator (PDEC) is determined in the short and the long run by prices of raw materials (PRM) and the wage rate paid by the manufacturing sector (WMF) which proxies labor cost. The price equations are written as:

(16) $\Delta P = P_1(\Delta PDM, PDM_{-1}, P_{-1})$

(17) $\Delta PC = P_2(\Delta PIMMS, PDM_{-1}, PC_{-1})$

(18) $\Delta PDEC = P_3(\Delta PRM, PRM_{-1}, \Delta WMF, PDEC_{-1})$

2.4 The Stochastic Equations for the Monetary Sector (equations 35-37)

The monetary sector consists of three behavior equations explaining the demand for currency (CUR), demand for demand deposits (DD), and demand for savings deposits (DS). Time deposits (DT) and negotiable certificates of deposit issued by banks and held outside the monetary sector (CD) are treated as exogenous. The three money demand equations in the model are in the error correction form. Also, the three types of money demand are determined in real terms. The real demand for savings deposits $\frac{DS}{P}$ is determined in the long run by real disposable GDP(Y) and interest rates (RIS). In the case of real demand for demand deposits $\frac{DD}{P}$, it relates to real disposable GDP in the short run. The real demand for currency $\frac{CUR}{P}$ is determined in the short and the long run by real total domestic demand (TDD). The equations can be written as:

(19) $\Delta(\frac{DS}{P*N}) = D_1((\frac{Y}{N})_{-1}, RIS_{-1}, (\frac{DS}{P*N})_{-1})$

(20) $\Delta(\frac{DD}{P*N}) = D_2(\Delta(\frac{Y}{N}), (\frac{DD}{P*N})_{-1}, T, T73, T81)$

(21) $\Delta(\frac{CUR}{P*N}) = D_3(\Delta(\frac{TDD}{N}), (\frac{TDD}{N})_{-1}, (\frac{CUR}{P*N})_{-1}, D85)$

3 The Model Performance

The sample estimates of the ERC model are presented in Appendix 1. All equations were solved by using Gauss-Seidel technique with annual data over the period 1967-88. The principal data sources were Estimates of Gross Domestic Product 1966 to 1989; Hong Kong Economic Prospects; Hong Kong Monthly Digest of Statistics and International Financial Statistics. A historical simulation of the model was performed over the period 1968-1988 in order to check whether it is stable; how well it tracks past turning points; and how well it fits the historical data in terms of average errors. The simulated and actual paths for a number of key variables are shown in Appendix 2. The model appears to be stable, with no tendency for the simulated paths of the variables to diverge progressively away from the actual paths. The ability of the model to track major historical turning points is quite good, suggesting the introduction of the error correction mechanism into the model has brought improvements in the model performance.

Table 1 shows the root mean squared error (RMSE)and Theil's inequality coefficient (U) of historical simulation for twelve selected endogenous variables. For the inequality coefficient, a value of one implies a no-change forecast (future values forecast as last available observed value). A U value greater than one means that the forecast is less accurate than the simple forecast of no change. The mean squared error has been decomposed into three quantities UM, UR and UD. UM arises from systematic underestimation or overestimation of the average change; UR arises from incorrect regression slope; and UD is random. For optimal forecasts, both UM and UR should not significantly differ from zero, and, hence, UD should be close to unity.

Table 1. Results of Historical Simulations of Selected Variables

Variable	RMS error	Theil's forecast error decomposition Bias (UM)	Reg. (UR)	Dist.(UD)	U
CP	0.0346	0.0150	0.0059	0.9790	0.3381
IPBC	0.0800	0.0338	0.0034	0.9628	0.6161
IPPD	0.0917	0.0360	0.1942	0.7699	0.5135
CF	0.0316	0.0000	0.0063	0.9937	0.2535
DEC	0.0686	0.0053	0.1177	0.8771	0.5189
EC	0.0510	0.0068	0.0417	0.9515	0.3124
RM	0.0510	0.0000	0.0424	0.9575	0.4153
MC	0.0387	0.0000	0.0007	0.9992	0.2513
GDPMP	0.0316	0.0000	0.1030	0.8970	0.3113
PC	0.0200	0.0018	0.0049	0.9933	0.2125
WMF	0.0520	0.4814	0.0239	0.4947	0.4331
MS2	0.0648	0.0015	0.0569	0.9416	0.2333

Variables are measured in percentage changes.

The mean value of U in Table 1 is 0.3674. With the exception of the wage rate variable, WMF, the bias proportions (UM) and regression proportions (UR) are low. The mean value of UD shows that about 90 percent of the total forecasting error is random. The modest size of the inequality coefficients suggests the results of the historical simulation are satisfactory.

4 Impact and Dynamic Multipliers

4.1 Simulation Assumptions

The purpose of this section is to perform policy simulations for the economy of Hong Kong on the basis of the estimated model. Three types of policy shocks are of interest: autonomous shifts in the level of activity; a depreciation of the Hong-Kong dollar against the U.S. dollar; and an increase in the growth rate of the U.S. economy.

The following four simulations were performed:

- an autonomous increase in real government consumption expenditure equivalent to 1 per cent of GDP;
- an autonomous increase in real government investment equivalent to 1 per cent of GDP;
- a 10 percent depreciation of the Hong Kong dollar against the U.S. dollar;
- a 1 percent increase in U.S. GNP.

Policy simulations are attempted for the period 1980-88.

4.2 Simulation Results

4.2.1 Increase in Government Consumption Expenditure

This shock involves an increase in the level of government consumption equivalent to 1 percent of real GDP. The effect on real activity is an increase in real GDP ranging between 1.02 and 1.25 percent over the simulation period (Table 2). The impact, expenditure multiplier for real GDP in the first period is 1.02, and as the time horizon progresses, the rise in GDP gets larger.

The multiplier for GDP is 1.25 in the sixth period and becomes smaller in subsequent periods. Imports of goods increase as they depend on real GDP, resulting in an increase in the visible trade deficit. The GDP deflator rises because of the increase in domestic demand. The increases in real GDP and prices have a positive effect on the demand for money, and the money supply rises throughout the whole simulation period.

4.2.2 Increase in Government Investment

The higher government investment also leads to an increase in GDP and its components. The impact multiplier for real GDP is 1.02, identical to that of the expenditure policy. However, the higher government investment over time tends to induce more imports of goods, hence a smaller dynamic effects on GDP than the boost in the government consumption expenditure. The elasticity of real GDP with respect to government investment is 0.05 in the first two periods, increases to 0.07 in the third and fourth periods and becomes smaller in subsequent periods (Table 2). The effects are smaller than those of the expenditure policy.

4.2.3 Depreciation of the Hong Kong Dollar

A shock, consisting of a permanent 10 per cent decrease in the value of the Hong Kong dollar against the U.S. dollar was imposed on our model. The exchange rate changes are passed through to the domestic price of imports, resulting in increases in the GDP deflator, total domestic demand deflator and the consumer price index. Domestic exports rise as a result of the depreciation, leading to higher real output and domestic demand. Total import of goods are also higher since merchandise imports and exports are complementary. The visible trade balance deficit widens. The elasticity of real GDP with respect to the exchange rate is 0.17 in the absolute value in the first year, grows to 0.27 in the fourth year, and becomes smaller thereafter (Table 2). The GDP deflator as well as the consumer price index rise due to the increase in the domestic demand deflator and import prices.

4.2.4 Increase in the Growth Rate of U.S. Economy

This shock involves a 1 per cent increase in U.S. GNP. Exports rise as a result of the increase, leading to higher real GDP and domestic demand. Higher total imports of goods are generated in response to increased activity, but resulting in a smaller visible trade deficit. The elasticity of real GDP is 0.34 in the first year. It fluctuates over time, but becomes smaller towards the end of the simulation period (Table 2). Over the whole simulation period, the elasticities are found to be larger than those of the exchange rate depreciation.

When we compare the elasticities of real GDP for the four policy simulations, the elasticity with respect to the increase in U.S. GNP is found to be the largest, the elasticity with respect to the exchange rate ranks the second, whereas the elasticity with respect to government investment is the smallest for the entire simulation period. These results suggest that the economy of Hong Kong responds more strongly to changes in external factors than to policy actions taken by the Hong Kong government.

Table 2. Effects of Simulation Assumptions

		1980	1981	1982	1983	1984	1985	1986	1987	1988
		Percentage deviations from the baseline								
Real GDP										
Simulation	i)	1.02	1.12	1.17	1.20	1.22	1.25	1.24	1.23	1.24
	ii)	1.02	1.10	1.15	1.18	1.19	1.22	1.21	1.21	1.21
	iii)	0.47	0.59	0.61	0.63	0.50	0.55	0.46	0.39	0.33
	iv)	0.34	0.33	0.35	0.33	0.32	0.34	0.32	0.29	0.28
Price Level										
Simulation	i)	0.00	0.09	0.08	0.14	0.13	0.13	0.12	0.12	0.11
	ii)	0.00	0.00	-0.08	-0.07	-0.07	-0.06	-0.06	-0.06	-0.05
	iii)	1.00	1.99	2.20	2.14	2.04	2.05	1.99	1.89	1.81
	iv)	-0.00	-0.00	-0.00	-0.00	-0.00	-0.00	-0.00	-0.00	-0.00
Visible Trade Balance										
Simulation	i)	2.06	2.41	2.72	3.11	9.60	24.56	10.04	-10.52	3.80
	ii)	2.01	2.30	2.64	3.07	9.49	24.45	9.97	-10.47	3.76
	iii)	27.21	25.18	25.29	24.20	76.50	177.11	69.94	-68.10	23.83
	iv)	-2.31	-1.69	-1.54	-1.44	-4.01	-10.28	-3.93	3.74	-1.27
Multipliers										
Simulation	i)	1.02	1.12	1.17	1.20	1.22	1.25	1.24	1.23	1.24
	ii)	1.02	1.10	1.15	1.18	1.19	1.22	1.21	1.21	1.21
Elasticities										
Simulation	i)	0.07	0.08	0.09	0.09	0.08	0.09	0.08	0.07	0.07
	ii)	0.05	0.05	0.07	0.07	0.06	0.05	0.04	0.04	0.03
	iii)	0.17	0.22	0.22	0.27	0.21	0.24	0.20	0.17	0.14
	iv)	0.34	0.33	0.35	0.33	0.32	0.34	0.32	0.29	0.28

Notes:

Simulation i): Increased government consumption
Simulation ii): Increased government investment
Simulation iii): Depreciation of H.K. dollar
Simulation iv): Increase in U.S. GNP

References

[1] Davidson, J. E. H., D. F. Hendry, F. Srba, and S. Yeo (1978) "Econometric Modelling of the Aggregate Time-series Relationship Between Consumers Expenditure and Income in the United Kingdom," The Economic Journal, vol.88, pp.661-692.

[2] Dawson, A. (1981) "Sargan's Wage Equation: A Theoretical and Empirical Reconstruction," Applied Economics, vol.13, pp.351-363.

[3] Hendry, D. F. (1984) "Econometric Modelling of House Prices in the United Kingdom," in D. F. Hendry and K. F. Wallis eds., *Econometrics and Quantitative Economics*, Oxford: Basil Blackwell

[4] Klein, L. R. (1978) "The Supply Side," American Economic Review, vol.68, pp.1-7.

[5] Lin, Tzong-biau and Chou, W. L. (1985) "Hong Kong Model," in S. Ichimura and M. Ezaki eds., *Econometric Models of Asian Link*, Tokyo: Springer-Verlag

[6] Rose, A. K. (1985) "An Alternative Approach to the American Demand for Money," Journal of Money, Credit, and Banking, vol.17, pp.439-455.

[7] Sargan, J. D. (1984) "Wages and Prices in the United Kingdom: A Study in Econometric Methodology," in D. F. Hendry and K. F. Wallis eds.,*Econometrics and Quantitative Economics*, Oxford: Basil Blackwell.

Appendix

A The Hong Kong Model 1990 Version

A.1 Estimated Equations

(22) $\Delta ln\frac{CP}{N} = -0.2068 + 0.6064\Delta ln\frac{GDPMP}{N}$

(-1.8448) (2.9374)

$+ 0.4589(ln(\frac{GDPMP}{N})_{-1} - ln(\frac{CP}{N})_{-1})$

(2.1245)

R^2=0.3751 adj.R^2=0.3093 SE=0.0384 DW=1.6097

(23) $\Delta IPBC = -0.5161 + 0.0206GDPMP_{-1} + 0.0403\Delta GDPMP$

(-1.4706) (2.2677) (1.5469)

$- 0.1694IPBC_{-1} - 1.8874D83$

(-1.3856) (-3.9182)

R^2=0.5207 adj.R^2=0.4080 SE=0.5507 DW=1.7828

(24) $IPPD = -0.2384 + 0.1673DEC - 0.1191RIT - 0.0063DEC * D5$

(-0.5213) (25.1870) (-2.0069) (-0.7917)

R^2=0.9736 adj.R^2=0.9692 SE=1.0536 DW=0.9697

(25) $CF = IPBC + IPPD + IPPL + REDM + IG$

(26) $DEC01 = 1.2952 + 0.0317T - 0.8122EX + 0.1969T84$

(3.8539) (4.8032) (-2.7117) (8.1630)

R^2=0.9772 adj.R^2=0.9733 SE=0.0966 DW=1.4277

(27) $DEC59 = 6.8620 - 10.5274D59 - 37.0183EX_{-1} + 0.0203USGNP_{-1}$

(0.3750) (-4.5330) (-2.4329) (2.3693)

$+ 0.6793DEC59_{-1}$

(4.1924)

R^2=0.9911 adj.R^2=0.9890 SE=3.5921 DW=2.3950

(28) $DEC = DEC01 + DEC24 + DEC3 + DEC59$

(29) $EC = DEC + RE$

(30) $lnES = 0.7468 + 0.4889 lnEC + 0.2138 lnTA$

(3.4217) (8.2641) (3.2544)

R^2=0.9953 adj.R^2=0.9948 SE=0.0355 DW=1.6593

(31) $E = EC + ES$

(32) $\frac{RM01}{N} = 1.8290 + 0.0054\frac{GDPMP}{N} + 0.5893(\frac{RM01}{N})_{-1}$

(5.1847) (1.4572) (4.5706)

$- 0.9913\frac{PM01}{P}$

(-4.3542)

R^2=0.9441 adj.R^2=0.9348 SE=0.0696 DW=2.2574

(33) $\Delta\frac{RM2}{N} = 0.2615 - 1.2154(\frac{RM2}{N})_{-1} + 0.4890 ITP_{-1}$

(1.4831) (-4.3625) (2. 3102)

$+ 0.5758\Delta ITP + 0.0019T + 0.0374T84$

(3.5800) (0.3939) (1.2014)

$- 0.0356T79$

(-1.8007)

R^2=0.8033 adj.R^2=0.7247 SE=0.550 DW=1.9296

(34) $\Delta ln\frac{RM3}{N} = -0.2026 + 0.0859 ln(\frac{GDPMP}{N})_{-1} + 0.4966\Delta ln\frac{GDPMP}{N}$

(-1.0248) (1.2000) (1.9142)

$- 0.2281 ln(\frac{RM3}{N})_{-1} - 0.0883D3$

(-2.2468) (-2.7799)

R^2=0.6379 adj.R^2=0.5527 SE=0.0471 DW=1.8516

(35) $\frac{RM59}{N} = -1.8832 + 0.3127(\frac{TDD - IG - CG}{N}) + 0.4011\frac{DEC}{N}$

(-5.3466) (4.0898) (3.5109)

$- 0.4614D59$

(-1.2827)

R^2=0.9893 adj.R^2=0.9875 SE=0.5378 DW=0.8141

(36) $RM = RM01 + RM2 + RM3 + RM4 + RM59$

(37) $MC = RM + RE$

(38) $lnMS = -3.9172 + 1.3919lnY - 0.7469ln\frac{PIMS}{PC}$

(-52.6227) (80.5892) (-8.1854)
R^2=0.9988 adj.R^2=0.9987 SE=0.0291 DW=1.5363

(39) $M = MC + MS$

(40) $GDPMP = CP + CG + CF + IIS + E - M$

(41) $NDPMP = GDPMP - DC$

(42) $GDPFC = NDPMP - \frac{NTI}{PCG}$

(43) $Y = GDPFC - \frac{NTD}{PCG}$

(44) $\Delta lnNIM = -0.2008 + 0.0590lnXM_{-1} - 0.0917D9$

(-1.3206) (1.5172) (-5.7218)

$- 0.2468lnNIM_{-1}$

(-1.9039)
R^2=0.6875 adj.R^2=0.6355 SE=0.0328 DW=1.2789

(45) $XM = 2.6470 + 0.3811DEC - 0.3876D6$

(4.0233) (41.6664) (-0.4752)
R^2=0.9892 adj.R^2=0.9881 SE=1.4748 DW=0.6921

(46) $\Delta WMF = -0.0621 + 0.2618P_{-1} - 0.1755(WMF)_{-1}$

(-2.2379) (1.419) (-1.1314)

$+ 0.8455\Delta P - 0.0061\Delta UE$

(6.2988) (-1.6379)
R^2=0.8902 adj.R^2=0.8644 SE=0.0192 DW=1.2619

(47) $NE = NIM + NEO$

(48) $UE = (1 - \frac{HE}{HC}) * 100$

(49) $\Delta WBC = -0.0025 + 1.0086\Delta P - 0.1516WBC_{-1} + 0.0105T$

(-0.1233) (3.3634) (-1.8728) (1.7411)

$- 0.0192T84 + 0.1414T86$

(-0.9350) (4.3306)

R^2=0.9157 adj.R^2=0.8894 SE=0.0343 DW=1.8775

(50) $PDM = \frac{(CP*PCP + CC*PCG + CT*PCF + IIS*PIIS)}{(CP + CG + CF + IIS)}$

(51) $\Delta P = -0.0216 + 0.8044\Delta PDM + 1.0566PDM_{-1} - 1.0225P_{-1}$

(-2.4967) (9.0606) (4.4471) (-4.4036)

R^2=0.9170 adj.R^2=0.9031 SE=0.0135 DW=2.4920

(52) $\Delta PC = -0.0021 + 0.4201\Delta PIMMS + 0.7954PDM_{-1} - 0.6922PC_{-1}$

(-0.2954) (6.1403) (7.4652) (-7.0156)

R^2=0.9213 adj.R^2=0.9082 SE=0.0149 DW=1.2468

(53) $\Delta PDEC = 0.0107 + 0.5874\Delta PRM + 0.2438PRM_{-1}$

(0.9858) (9.4608) (1.6019)

$+ 0.3193\Delta WMF - 0.2659PDEC_{-1}$

(2.3621) (-1.7419)

R^2=0.8943 adj.R^2=0.8695 SE=0.0167 DW = 1.0258

(54) $PRA = 0.0704 + 0.4013P + 0.5967PRA_{-1}$

(4.5839) (5.8736) (7.5079)

R^2=0.9984 adj.R^2=0.9982 SE=0.0178 DW=1.2338

(55) $PDEC = PDEC_{-1} + \Delta PDEC$

(56) $\Delta(\frac{DS}{P*N}) = -2.5769 + 0.3974\frac{Y}{N}_{-1} + 0.1278RIS_{-1}$

(-1.7272) (2.3473) (1.5446)

$- 0.5454(\frac{DS}{P*N})_{-1}$

(-2.1576)

R^2=0.2686 adj.R^2=0. 1467 SE=1.2653 DW= 1.8771

(57) $$\Delta(\frac{DD}{P*N}) = 0.8014 + 0.2226\Delta\frac{Y}{N} - 0.4606(\frac{DD}{P*N})_{-1}$$

(1.3344) (1.5881) (-2.5719)

$$+ 0.1032T - 0.1699T73 + 0.2578T81$$

(0.9266) (-1.1314) (2.3551)

$R^2 = 0.4356$ adj.R^2=0.2592 SE=0.5537 DW= 2.3405

(58) $$\Delta(\frac{CUR}{P*N}) = 0.3490 + 0.0157\Delta\frac{TDD}{N} + 0.0061(\frac{TDD}{N})_{-1}$$

(1.6789) (0.5994) (1.0233)

$$- 0.2966(\frac{CUR}{P*N})_{-1} + 0.3783D85$$

(-1.7191) (3.4569)

R^2=0.5294 adj.R^2=0.4187 SE=0.1281 DW=1.6991

(59) $MS1 = CUR + DD$

(60) $MS2 = MS1 + DT + DS + CD$

(61) $NTI = -0.5013 + 0.0480GDPMP * P$

(-1.6192) (27.6925)

R^2=0.9746 adj.R^2=0.9733 SE=0.9886 DW=0.3698

(62) $NY = GDPMP * P - NTI$

(63) $NTD = -0.9515 + 0.0768NY_{-1}$

(-3.3086) (39.0493)

R^2= 0.9871 adj.R^2=0.9864 SE= 0.9190 DW = 0.8971

(64) $$KPBC = \sum_{i=0}^{I9}(1 - \sum_{j=0}^{i} DR_j) * IPBC_{-i}$$

(65) $$KPPD = \sum_{i=0}^{I5}(1 - \sum_{j=0}^{i} d_j) * IPPD_{-i}$$

(66) $$DC = \sum_{i=0}^{I5} d_i * IPPD_{-1} + \sum_{j=0}^{I9} DR_j * IPBC_{-j}$$

(67) $TB = EC * PEC - MC * PIM$

(68) $TDD = CP + CG + CF + IIS$

(69) $K = KPBC + KPPD$

(70) $$TX = \frac{NTI + NTD}{PCG}$$

Note:Estimation period: 1967 to 1988

A.2 Variables[3]

Endogenous Variables

CP	Private consumption expenditure, in constant (1980) dollars.
IPBC	Private sector investment in building and construction, in constant (1980) dollars.
IPPD	Private sector investment in plant, machinery and equipment, in constant (1980) dollars.
CF	Gross domestic fixed capitai formation, in constant (1980) dollars.
DEC01	Domestic exports of goods under SITC 0 and 1, in constant (1980) dollars
DEC09	Domestic exports of goods under SITC 5 to 9, in constant (1980) dollars.
DEC	Domestic exports of goods, in constant (1980) dollars.
EC	Total exports of goods, in constant (1980) dollars.
ES	Exports of services, in constant (1980) dollars.
E	Total exports of goods and services, in constant (1980) dollars.
RM01	Retained imports of goods under SITC 0 and 1, in constant (1980) dollars.
RM2	Retained imports of goods under SITC 2, in constant (1980) dollars.
RM3	Retained imports of goods under SITC 3, in constant (1980) dollars.
M59	Retained impots of goods under SITC 5 to 9, in constant (19810) dollars.
RM	Retained imports, in constant (1980) dollars.
MC	Imports of goods, in constant (1980) dollars.
MS	Imports of services, in constant (1980) dollars.
M	Total imports of goods and services, in constant (1980) dollars.
GDPMP	Gross domestic products at market prices, in constant (1980) dollars.
NDPMP	Net domestic products at market prices, in constant (1980) dollars.
GDPFC	Gross domestic products at factor cost, in constant (1980) dollars.
Y	Personal disposable income, in constant (1980) dollars.
NIM	Persons engaged in manufacturing sector, million persons.
XM	Value added in manufacturing sector, in constant (1980) dollars.
WMF	Nominal wage rate index (including fringe benefits) for manufacturing workers, 1980=100.
NE	Total employed persons, million persons.
UE	Unemployment rate (%).
WBC	Wage rate index in building and construction sector, 1980=100.
PDM	Implicit price deflator of domestic demand,1980 = 100.

[3]Notes:

1. All variables, unless otherwise specified, are expressed in billions of Hong Kong dollars.
2. $RIS = IS - 100 * \frac{PC-PC_{-1}}{PC_{-1}}$

$RIT = IT - 100 * \frac{PC-PC_{-1}}{PC_{-1}}$

where the latter term appearing in the right hand side of both equations is the inflation rate expressed in % per annum.

P	GDP deflator, 1980 = 100.
PC	Consumer Prig index (A), 1980 = 100.
Δ PDEC	Change in implicit price deflator for domestic exports.
PRA	Rent index, 1980=100.
PDEC	Implicit price deflator for domestic exports, 1980=100.
DS	Savings deposits with licensed banks, in current dollars.
DD	Demand deposits with licensed banks, in current dollars.
CUR	Currency (in hands of public), in current dollars.
MS1	honey supply definition 1, in current dollars.
MS2	honey supply definition 2, in current dollars.
NTI	Indirect tax in current dollars, including government subsidies.
NY	Nominal income, in current dollars
NTD	Direct tax, in current dollars.
KPBC	Capital stock in building and construction in private sector, in constant (1980) dollars.
KPPD	Capital stock in plant, machinery and equipment in private sector, in constant (1980) dollars.
DC	Depreciation, private investment in plant, machinery and equipment, and in building and construction, in constant (1980) dollars.
TB	Visible trade balance, in current dollars.
TDD	Total domestic demand, in constant (1980) dollars.
K	Total stock of capital, in constant (1980) dollars.
TX	Total tax receipts, in constant (1980) dollars.

Exogenous Variables

CD	Negotiable certificates issued by licensed banks and held outside the monetary sector.
CG	Government consumption expenditure,in constant (1980) dollars.
DEC24	Domestic exports of goods under SITC 2 and 4, in constant (1980) dollars.
DEC3	Domestic exports of goods under SITC 3, in constant (1980) dollars.
DT	Time deposits with licensed banks, in current dollars.
d_i	Depreciation rate for plant, machinery and equipment, i=0,...,15
DR_i	Depreciation rate for building and construction, i=0,...,19.
EX	Trade-weighted effective exchange rate index,Dec.18.1971=100.
IG	Government sector investment, in constant (1980) dollars.
IIS	Increase in stocks, in constant (1980) dollars.
IPPL	Transfer costs of land and buildings,in constant (1980) dollars.
IS	Savings deposits rate paid by principal banks, % per annum, end of period figure.
IT	12 month time deposits rate paid by principal banks, % per annum, end of period figure.
ITP	Index of textile production, 1980=100.
N	Population, million persons.

NC	Total labour force, million persons.
NEO	Persons engaged in all sectors except the manufacturing sector, million persons.
PCF	Deflator of gross domestic fixed capital formation,1980=100.
PCG	Price deflator of government consumption expenditure,1980 = 100.
PCP	Price deflator of private consumption expenditure,1980 = 100.
PEC	Deflator of total exports of goods, 1980 = 100.
PIIS	Deflator of changes in stocks, 1980 = 100.
PIM	Implicit price deflator of imports of goods, 1980 = 100.
PIMS	Implicit price deflator of imports of services,1980 = 100.
PIMMS	Implicit price deflator of imports of goods and services, 1980 = 100.
PM01	Unit value index for imported goods under SITC 0 & 1,1980=100.
PRM	Unit value index of raw materials and semi-manufactures, 1980=100.
RE	Re-exports of goods, in constant (1980) dollars.
REDM	Real estate developers' margin,in constant (1980) dollars.
RIS[2]	Savings deposits rate paid by principal banks, % per annum, in real terms, end of period figure.
RIT[2]	12-month time deposits rate paid by principal banks, % per annum, in real terms, end of period figure.
RM4	Retained imports of goods under SITC 4, in constant (1980) dollars.
USGNP	Gross National Product of the United States, in constant (1980) US dollars.
T	Time trend.
T73	Linear spline time dimension variable, max (T-6, 0).
T79	Linear spline time dimension variable, max (T-12, 0).
T81	Linear spline time dimension variable, max (T-14, 0).
T84	Linear spline time dimension variable, max (T-17, 0).
T86	Linear spline time dimension variable, max (T-19, 0).
TA	Tourist arrivals, million persons.
D3	Dummy variable, with 1 assigned to 1975, 1985, 1987 and 1988 to account for low demand for oil imports.
D5	Dummy variable, with 1 assigned to 1974, 1975, 1982, 1983 and 1985 to account for oil crises and political disturbances.
D6	Dummy variable, with 1 assigned to 1974, 1975, 1982 and 1985 to account for recession.
D9	Dummy variable, with 1 assigned to 1972-74, 1977, 1982, 1985, 1987 and 1988 to account for low activities in the manufacturing sector.
D59	Dummy variable, with 1 assigned to 1974, 1982, and 1985.
D83	Dummy variable, with 1 assigned to 1983 - 1988.
D85	Dummy variable, with 1 assigned to 1985 - 1988.

B Simulation Results for Selected Variables

Private Consumption Expenditure

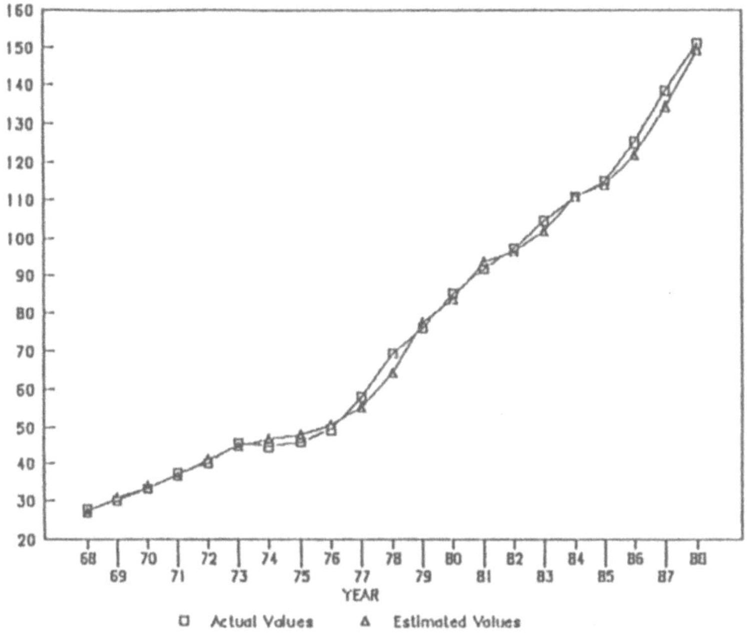

Gross Domestic Fixed Capital Formation

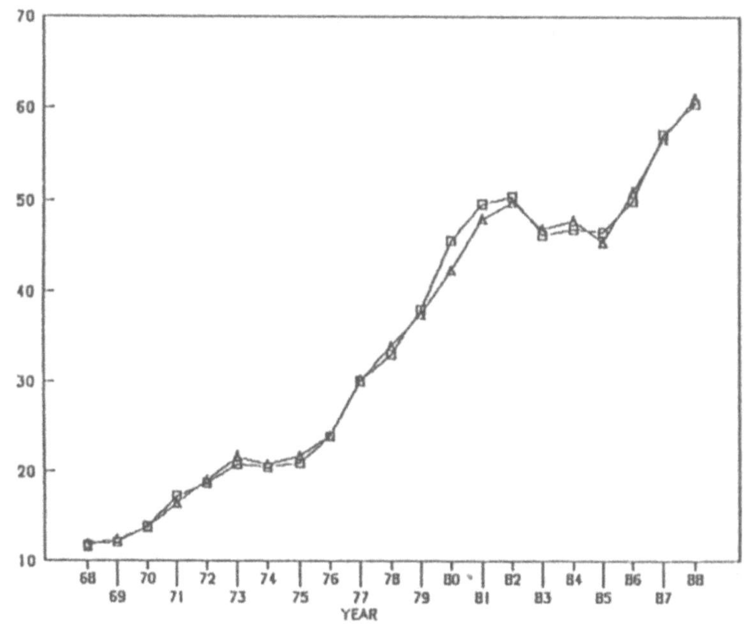

Private Investment in Building and Construction

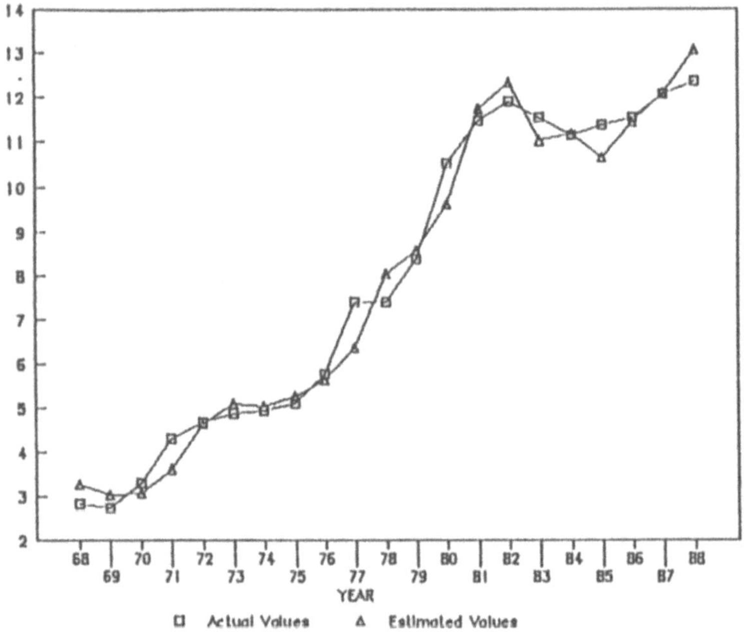

Private Investment in Plant, Machinery and Equipment

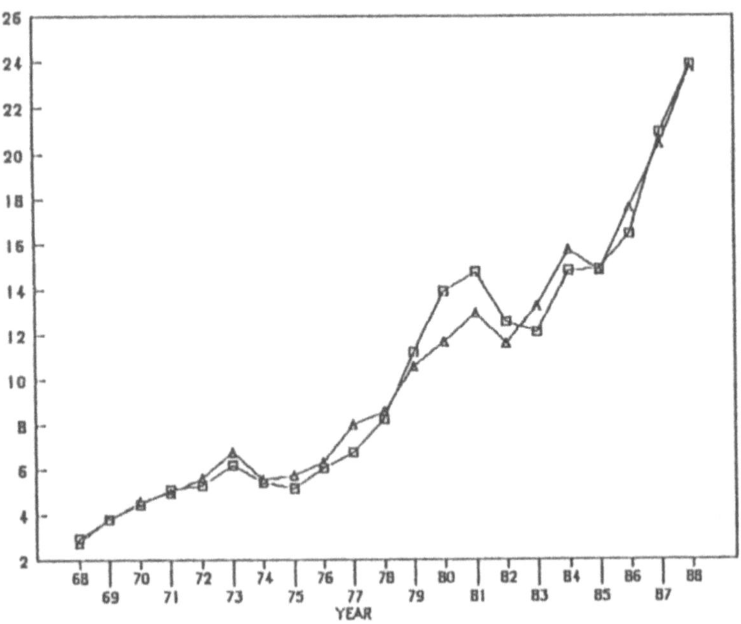

Domestic Exports of Goods

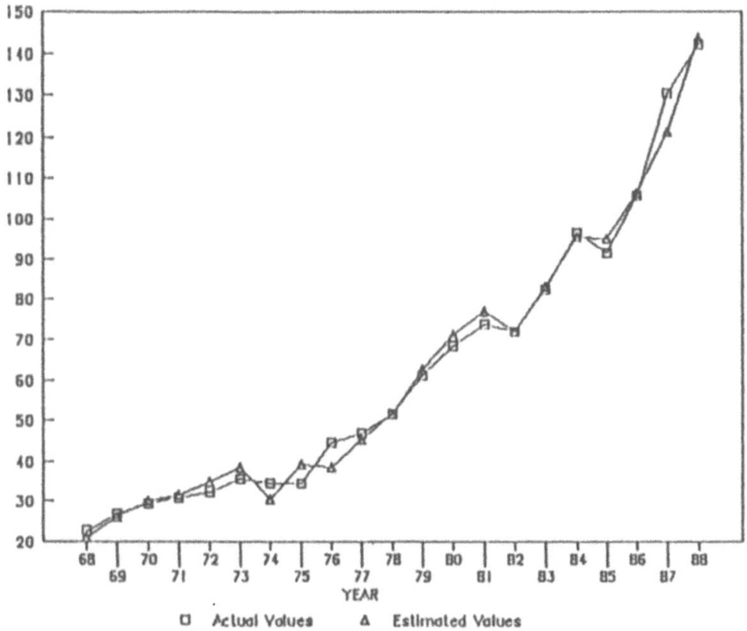

Total Exports of Goods

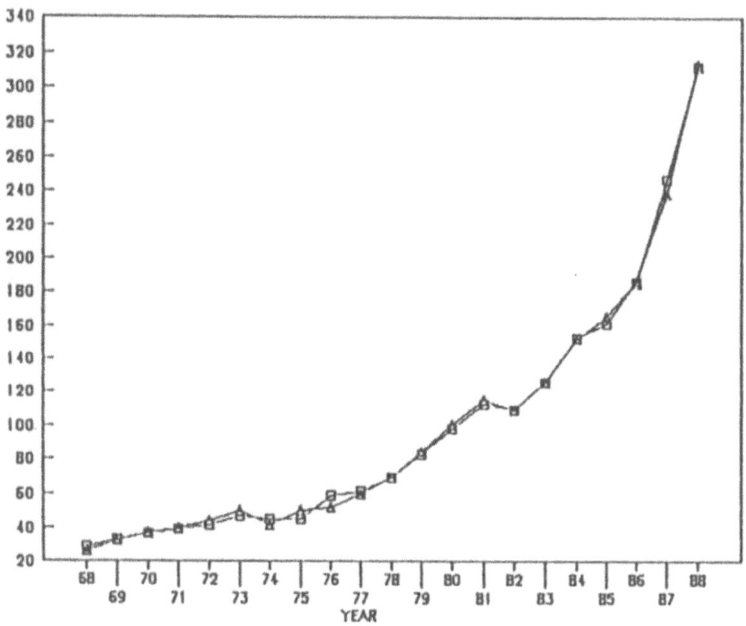

Retained Imports of Goods

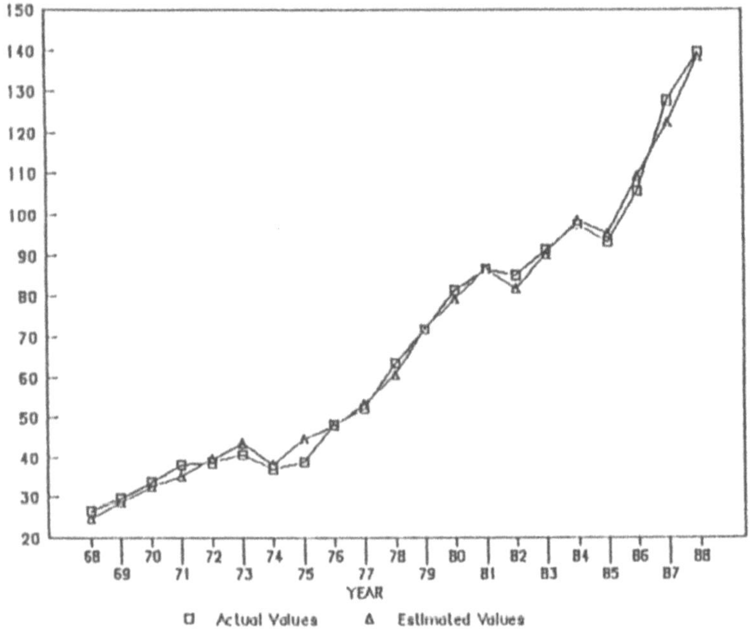

Total Imports of Goods

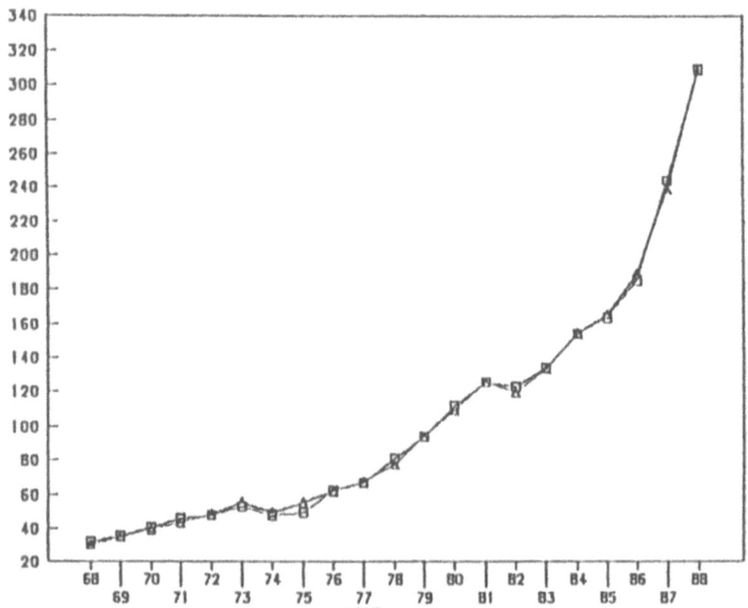

Gross Domestic Product at Market Price

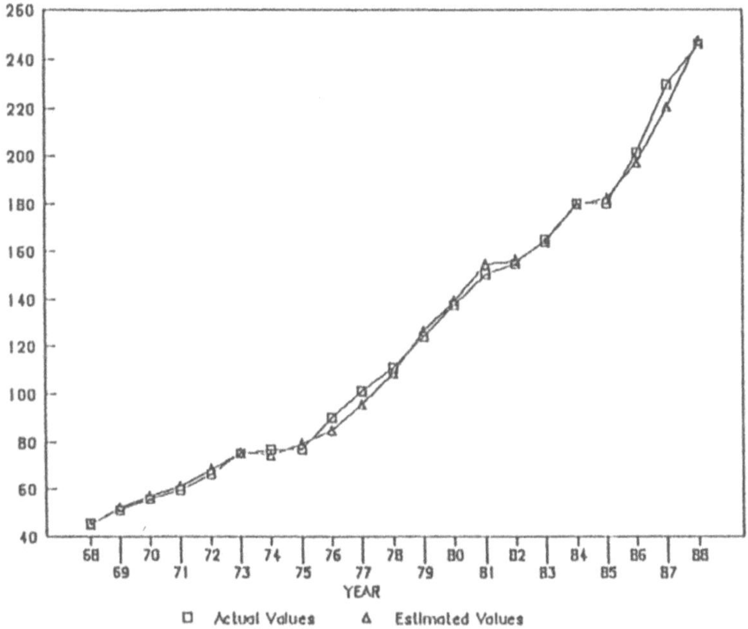

Money Supply Definition 2

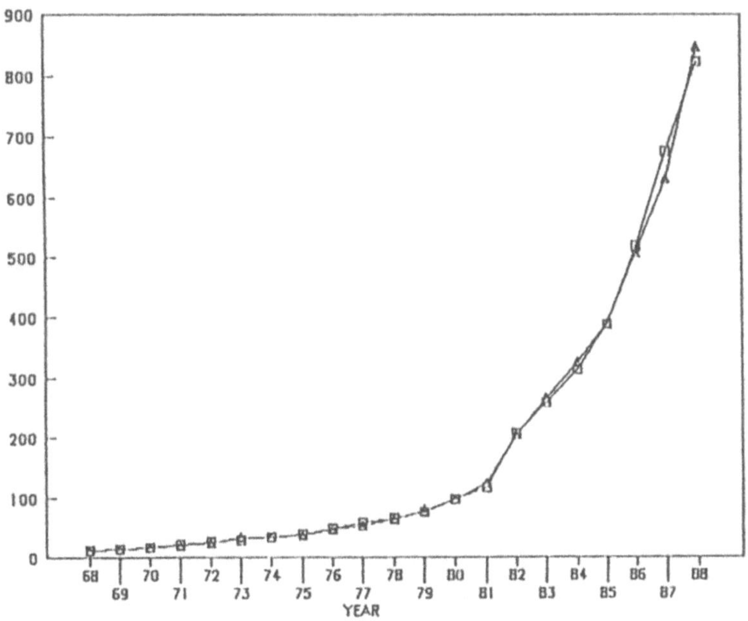

Consumer Price Index (A)

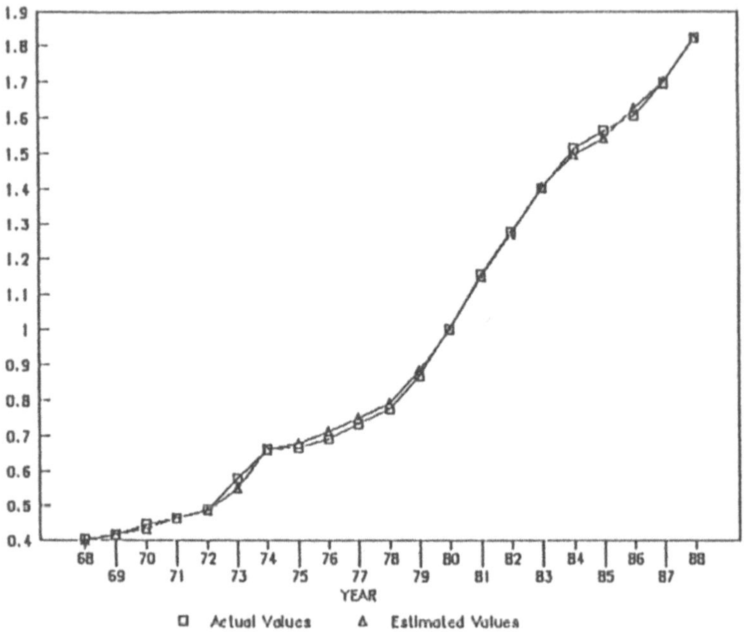

Nominal Wage Rate Index for Manufacturing Workers

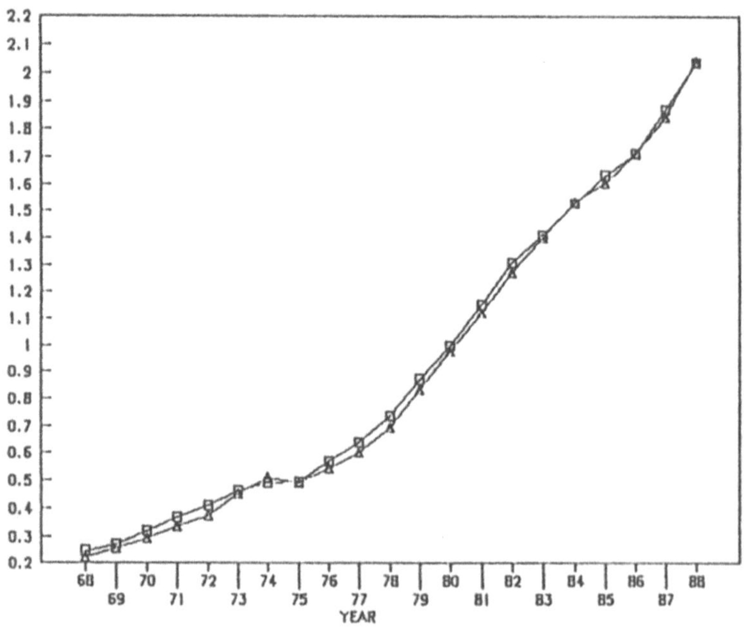

C Data for Hong Kong Model

Year	CP	IPBC	IPPD	CF	ES	E	RM01
1967	25.185	3.399	2.799	12.890	8.674	33.386	5.7905
1968	27.763	2.824	2.984	11.727	9.703	38.026	5.8630
1969	30.109	2.739	3.790	12.178	11.054	44.352	6.2308
1970	33.167	3.307	4.461	13.904	12.828	49.049	6.6570
1971	37.499	4.282	5.111	17.223	12.422	51.126	7.6129
1972	40.110	4.647	5.299	18.715	13.948	55.590	7.7678
1973	45.502	4.848	6.180	20.867	14.341	61.512	8.4964
1974	44.619	4.922	5.409	20.563	13.729	58.960	8.0355
1975	46.002	5.111	5.150	20.969	13.799	59.244	8.3733
1976	49.277	5.747	6.079	23.894	17.374	75.906	8.5614
1977	58.090	7.390	6.795	30.068	17.774	78.811	9.0990
1978	69.215	7.405	8.250	33.065	20.141	88.971	10.0089
1979	75.650	8.355	11.197	38.038	22.236	104.973	10.4667
1980	85.262	10.526	13.919	45.548	22.162	120.404	11.4326
1981	91.723	11.488	14.785	49.591	24.758	137.072	11.3052
1982	96.993	11.906	12.594	50.414	25.687	134.992	11.5261
1983	104.658	11.558	12.092	46.197	28.354	153.658	11.6157
1984	110.620	11.147	14.795	46.928	31.273	183.967	11.3184
1985	115.076	11.375	14.917	46.536	32.408	193.821	11.5822
1986	125.267	11.556	16.419	49.910	37.509	223.433	11.8303
1987	138.489	12.083	20.927	57.172	44.359	291.523	13.6039
1988	150.951	12.385	23.917	60.625	50.182	362.561	15.0217

Year	RM2	RM3	RM59	RM	MC	MS	M
1967	1.9861	2.7234	11.480	22.149	27.908	3.092	31.00
1968	2.6195	2.9629	15.076	26.693	32.324	3.496	35.820
1969	2.2568	3.4972	17.445	29.605	36.059	3.860	39.919
1970	2.5121	3.6880	20.807	33.860	40.605	4.287	44.892
1971	2.7100	4.0933	23.370	38.030	45.888	4.766	50.654
1972	2.3248	4.5393	23.800	38.647	47.758	5.266	53.024
1973	2.6927	4.8316	24.602	40.827	52.474	6.085	58.559
1974	2.2099	5.1613	21.543	37.188	47.943	6.134	54.077
1975	2.8669	4.7273	22.554	38.810	49.635	6.480	56.115
1976	3.1802	5.6885	30.559	48.250	62.092	7.567	69.659
1977	2.9226	6.1307	33.725	52.157	66.449	8.523	74.972
1978	3.2219	6.2905	43.711	63.535	80.777	9.960	90.737
1979	2.9569	6.9474	51.101	71.822	93.717	13.227	106.904
1980	2.8938	7.5500	59.515	81.722	111.794	14.912	126.702
1981	2.0545	8.1023	64.956	86.738	125.336	17.649	142.985
1982	2.1170	8.4478	62.783	85.144	122.579	17.844	140.463
1983	2.7073	7.7954	68.739	91.174	134.334	20.840	155.174
1984	2.5272	7.6650	75.839	97.681	154.025	23.663	177.688
1985	2.1055	7.1596	72.069	93.298	163.566	25.493	189.059
1986	2.7366	8.0186	82.884	105.751	185.854	29.128	214.982
1987	3.7517	8.3564	101.763	127.753	244.623	33.353	277.976
1988	2.8407	8.1606	113.028	139.366	309.691	38.679	348.370

(continued)

Year	GDPMP	NDPMP	GDPFC	Y	NIM	XM	WMF
1967	44.242	41.422	39.247	37.864	0.6069	9.0707	0.2330
1968	45.658	42.377	40.059	38.594	0.6224	9.4276	0.2468
1969	51.046	47.241	44.626	42.969	0.6518	10.7560	0.2717
1970	55.844	51.459	48.801	46.945	0.6695	14.1155	0.3187
1971	59.921	54.928	52.075	49.919	0.6775	14.4796	0.3693
1972	66.512	60.929	57.693	55.422	0.6520	15.8856	0.4071
1973	74.959	68.828	65.574	62.901	0.6264	16.4502	0.4641
1974	76.608	69.989	67.294	63.981	0.6001	13.6749	0.4880
1975	76.761	69.704	66.561	63.040	0.6789	15.0750	0.4952
1976	89.887	82.407	78.705	74.905	0.7737	18.0756	0.5722
1977	101.124	93.203	89.110	84.577	0.7551	21.0998	0.6419
1978	110.725	102.344	97.590	92.304	0.8167	23.6265	0.7380
1979	123.642	114.770	109.895	104.064	0.8709	27.8572	0.8726
1980	137.081	127.679	122.483	115.344	0.9075	30.5490	1.0000
1981	149.987	139.972	134.649	126.908	0.9059	33.0422	1.1548
1982	154.512	143.724	138.965	129.612	0.8472	31.4983	1.3097
1983	164.550	152.732	146.919	138.759	0.8554	34.7286	1.4129
1984	180.149	166.957	160.290	151.926	0.8989	38.7923	1.5290
1985	179.946	165.325	157.554	147.880	0.8476	37.2428	1.6323
1986	201.350	184.563	176.003	165.336	0.8656	43.1441	1.7162
1987	229.421	210.667	200.619	188.771	0.8679	50.5545	1.8710
1988	245.919	225.351	214.913	201.343	0.8371	54.9207	2.0387

Year	WBC	PDM	P	PC	Δ PDEC	PRA	PDEC
1967	0.1005	0.349	0.333	0.3917	0.0276	0.5075	0.3535
1968	0.9940	0.357	0.343	0.4016	0.0506	0.5075	0.3714
1969	0.1587	0.376	0.360	0.4160	0.0549	0.5075	0.3914
1970	0.2090	0.408	0.392	0.4456	0.0692	0.5274	0.4189
1971	0.3169	0.425	0.420	0.4607	0.0642	0.5408	0.4458
1972	0.3742	0.457	0.457	0.4889	0.0511	0.5721	0.4686
1973	0.4331	0.530	0.522	0.5777	0.1669	0.6184	0.5482
1974	0.4827	0.617	0.582	0.6608	0.2121	0.6667	0.6645
1975	0.4705	0.624	0.605	0.6685	0.0063	0.7254	0.6603
1976	0.5046	0.661	0.660	0.6915	0.1057	0.7588	0.7301
1977	0.5987	0.692	0.681	0.7320	0.0249	0.8145	0.7483
1978	0.7080	0.747	0.733	0.7755	0.0547	0.8539	0.7892
1979	0.8742	0.877	0.866	0.8657	0.1643	0.9345	0.9189
1980	1.0000	1.000	1.000	1.0000	0.0883	1.0000	1.0000
1981	1.1401	1.117	1.100	1.1536	0.0910	1.1265	1.0910
1982	1.2757	1.207	1.206	1.2749	0.0589	1.2372	1.1553
1983	1.3269	1.257	1.261	1.4011	0.1001	1.3479	1.2710
1984	1.3610	1.370	1.381	1.5156	0.1264	1.4398	1.4316
1985	1.4160	1.406	1.452	1.5635	0.0046	1.5337	1.4250
1986	1.5088	1.487	1.494	1.6075	0.0211	1.5820	1.4551
1987	1.8251	1.605	1.610	1.6959	0.0435	1.6558	1.4986
1988	2.2591	1.767	1.755	1.8215	0.0337	1.7131	1.5323

(continued)

Year	DS	DD	CUR	MS1	MS2	NTI	NY
1967	2.180	2.658	1.974	4.632	10.136	0.772	13.961
1968	2.791	3.144	1.821	4.965	12.188	0.844	14.817
1969	3.367	3.714	1.928	5.642	14.225	0.952	17.425
1970	4.222	4.326	2.222	6.548	17.177	1.055	20.836
1971	6.074	4.089	2.574	6.663	21.360	1.184	23.983
1972	8.306	6.729	2.912	9.641	27.526	1.505	28.891
1973	7.610	5.924	3.138	9.062	29.329	1.629	37.437
1974	8.637	6.078	3.209	9.287	34.207	1.590	42.996
1975	12.803	7.760	3.652	11.412	39.995	1.923	44.517
1976	15.940	9.667	4.383	14.050	48.413	2.425	56.900
1977	20.753	12.650	5.431	18.081	58.450	2.861	66.004
1978	24.850	13.567	6.543	20.110	66.472	3.523	77.638
1979	33.258	13.566	7.285	20.851	75.270	4.061	103.013
1980	42.808	15.831	8.367	24.198	96.240	5.196	131.885
1981	52.852	15.367	9.827	25.194	116.756	6.117	158.869
1982	69.590	16.043	11.442	27.485	206.688	6.230	180.111
1983	71.156	18.182	12.714	30.896	257.685	8.103	199.395
1984	81.150	23.518	13.273	36.791	314.081	9.894	238.892
1985	98.765	28.409	16.857	45.266	390.239	12.333	248.949
1986	125.476	36.799	19.295	56.094	518.131	14.750	286.067
1987	181.109	57.138	24.764	81.902	677.042	18.649	530.719
1988	175.529	58.958	29.877	88.834	824.648	21.451	410.137

Year	NTD	KPBC	KPPD	DC	DEC58	TB	TDD
1967	0.491	28.564	17.459	2.8202	18.059	-1.730	41.856
1968	0.533	29.960	18.590	3.2805	21.715	-1.990	43.542
1969	0.603	30.920	20.354	3.8049	25.757	-1.882	46.613
1970	0.737	32.043	22.614	4.3854	28.329	-2.450	51.687
1971	0.895	33.708	25.349	4.9927	29.828	-3.028	59.449
1972	1.056	35.328	28.092	5.5826	31.496	-2.264	63.946
1973	1.390	36.800	31.517	6.1311	34.420	-3.211	72.006
1974	1.955	38.103	33.927	6.6187	33.350	-4.079	71.725
1975	2.155	39.463	35.768	7.0574	33.678	-3.546	73.632
1976	2.493	41.411	38.163	7.4850	43.465	-0.792	83.640
1977	3.169	44.994	40.044	7.9205	45.352	-3.077	97.285
1978	3.917	48.566	44.547	8.3807	50.724	-8.923	112.491
1979	4.857	52.994	50.798	8.8720	59.080	-10.283	125.809
1980	7.139	59.418	59.418	9.4020	66.038	-13.552	143.383
1981	8.894	66.538	68.556	10.0146	71.607	-16.714	155.900
1982	12.243	73.727	75.080	10.7876	69.888	-17.505	159.983
1983	11.375	80.145	80.494	11.8177	79.143	-17.253	166.066
1984	12.412	85.649	87.745	13.1919	93.367	-6.280	173.870
1985	15.353	90.790	94.002	14.6209	88.053	-2.577	175.184
1986	18.379	95.449	100.511	16.7866	102.746	-6.942	192.899
1987	21.991	99.902	110.313	18.7535	126.495	7.413	215.874
1988	27.886	103.890	122.061	20.5676	137.550	-22.422	231.728

(continued)

Year	K	TX	DECO1	UE	DEC	EC	T75	SKIPPD
1967	46.022	3.5577	0.5318	3.4	18.953	24.712	0	14.6624
1968	48.550	3.7830	0.5897	5.1	22.692	28.323	0	15.6091
1969	51.274	4.2720	0.6330	3.9	26.844	33.298	0	16.5678
1970	54.657	4.5139	0.5801	3.1	29.476	36.221	0	18.1574
1971	59.057	5.0096	0.6449	3.1	30.846	38.704	0	20.2431
1972	63.420	5.5075	0.6161	2.7	32.531	41.460	0	22.7986
1973	68.317	5.9269	0.6078	1.0	35.524	41.171	0	25.3432
1974	72.029	6.0085	0.5207	3.6	34.476	45.231	0	28.5233
1975	75.233	6.6634	0.6106	7.8	34.620	45.445	1	30.6248
1976	79.574	7.4970	0.8159	5.1	44.690	58.532	2	32.0899
1977	85.838	8.6266	0.9115	4.2	46.775	61.067	3	34.0560
1978	93.113	10.0405	0.9708	2.8	51.588	68.830	4	36.3053
1979	103.793	10.7059	0.9978	2.9	60.846	82.737	5	39.6127
1980	118.836	12.3350	0.9269	3.8	68.171	98.242	6	45.5126
1981	135.094	13.0644	1.1077	3.9	73.716	112.314	7	53.7856
1982	148.807	14.1123	1.1606	3.6	71.870	109.305	8	62.4985
1983	160.639	13.9727	1.3878	4.5	82.144	125.304	9	68.4142
1984	173.394	15.0310	1.4165	3.9	96.350	152.694	10	72.9645
1985	184.793	17.4455	1.7274	3.2	91.145	161.413	11	79.1003
1986	195.961	19.2275	1.9014	2.8	105.821	185.924	12	84.1009
1987	210.422	21.8966	2.1760	1.7	130.294	247.164	13	89.4073
1988	226.157	24.0082	2.6772	1.4	142.054	312.379	14	98.1675

Year	IPPL	PEC	SDIPPD	D6	T79	IG	CG	IT
1967	0.445	0.355	1.6774	0	0	1.857	3.392	6.250
1968	0.511	0.373	1.8595	0	0	1.760	3.560	6.250
1969	0.585	0.396	2.0223	0	0	1.536	3.878	6.250
1970	0.600	0.421	2.1966	0	0	1.267	4.125	6.250.
1971	0.661	0.433	2.3708	0	0	1.645	4.199	4.875
1972	1.010	0.466	2.5503	0	0	1.765	4.535	4.875
1973	1.204	0.551	2.7491	0	0	2.383	4.975	8.000
1974	0.665	0.664	2.9937	1	0	3.215	5.419	7.500
1975	0.761	0.656	3.3020	1	0	3.354	5.760	5.500
1976	0.869	0.710	3.6798	0	0	3.775	6.136	5.000
1977	1.004	0.734	4.1067	0	0	5.339	6.757	3.000
1978	1.221	0.783	4.5389	0	0	6.773	7.496	6.750
1979	1.066	0.918	4.9343	0	1	6.743	8.199	11.500
1980	1.110	1.000	5.2859	0	2	6.723	8.828	14.500
1981	1.568	1.088	5.6321	0	3	7.337	10.790	12.000
1982	1.517	1.165	6.0573	1	4	9.439	11.391	8.000
1983	1.433	1.282	6.6657	0	5	9.729	11.994	8.500
1984	1.429	1.450	7.6733	0	6	8.657	12.323	7.000
1985	2.046	1.457	8.7776	1	7	6.799	12.346	4.000
1986	2.621	1.487	9.8935	0	8	6.421	13.328	4.000
1987	3.649	1.529	11.1037	0	9	6.996	13.889	2.750
1988	3.396	1.578	12.1459	0	10	7.026	14.600	7.500

(continued)

Year	D5	IIS	PIMS	N	T	T84	$USGNP_{-1}$	D85	PCP
1967	0	0.389	0.390	3.7228	1	0	1892.9	0	0.410
1968	0	0.402	0.404	3.8027	2	0	1946.9	0	0.413
1969	0	0.448	0.427	3.8639	3	0	2027.7	0	0.430
1970	0	0.491	0.447	3.9590	4	0	2077.1	0	0.446
1971	0	0.528	0.460	4.0453	5	0	2071.1	0	0.454
1972	0	0.586	0.479	4.1157	6	0	2129.9	0	0.489
1973	0	0.662	0.539	4.2126	7	0	2235.9	0	0.575
1974	1	1.124	0.663	4.3196	8	0	2352.1	0	0.667
1975	1	0.901	0.693	4.3958	9	0	2339.5	0	0.678
1976	0	4.313	0.739	4.5180	10	0	2310.1	0	0.717
1977	0	2.370	0.788	4.5837	11	0	2422.9	0	0.746
1978	0	2.724	0.831	4.6675	12	0	2536.1	0	0.782
1979	0	3.722	0.905	4.9297	13	0	2670.2	0	0.884
1980	0	3.745	1.000	5.0631	14	0	2736.3	0	1.000
1981	0	3.796	1.094	5.1834	15	0	2732.0	0	1.117
1982	1	1.185	1.174	5.2645	16	0	2784.8	0	1.226
1983	1	3.217	1.211	5.3451	17	0	2713.8	0	1.326
1984	1	3.999	1.269	5.3979	18	0	2810.7	0	1.434
1985	1	1.026	1.316	5.4562	19	1	2971.8	1	1.476
1986	1	4.394	1.348	5.5326	20	2	3100.3	1	1.530
1987	1	6.324	1.384	5.6134	21	3	3188.2	1	1.601
1988	1	5.552	1.427	5.6813	22	4	3296.9	1	1.703

Year	TA	RM4	PM01	RE	SDIPBC	CD	D3	$PIMMS_{-1}$
1967	0.5274	0.1685	0.3987	5.759	1.1356	0.000	0	0.3721
1968	0.6184	0.1717	0.4153	5.631	1.4243	0.000	0	0.3766
1969	0.7652	0.1756	0.4402	6.454	1.7752	0.000	0	0.3884
1970	0.9273	0.1959	0.4568	6.745	2.1800	0.000	0	0.4155
1971	0.9073	0.2382	0.4651	7.858	2.6112	0.000	0	0.4355
1972	1.0923	0.2150	0.4817	9.111	3.0210	0.000	0	0.4437
1973	1.2920	0.2045	0.5814	11.647	3.3695	0.000	0	0.4584
1974	1.2955	0.2381	0.7558	10.755	3.6132	0.000	0	0.5520
1975	1.3008	0.2884	0.7267	10.825	3.7436	0.000	1	0.7065
1976	1.5600	0.2607	0.7442	13.842	3.7916	0.000	0	0.6776
1977	1.7557	0.2796	0.7733	14.292	3.7974	0.000	0	0.7050
1978	2.0547	0.3024	0.8198	17.242	3.8239	0.000	0	0.7405
1979	2.2132	0.3495	0.9070	21.891	3.9156	0.000	0	0.7884
1980	2.3015	0.3302	1.0000	30.072	4.0885	1.120	0	0.9193
1981	2.5352	0.3194	1.1802	38.598	4.3528	2.471	0	1.0000
1982	2.6091	0.2703	1.3095	37.435	4.7022	4.987	0	1.1089
1983	2.7750	0.3165	1.4762	43.160	5.1249	5.098	0	1.1730
1984	3.1517	0.3313	1.6071	56.344	5.6330	4.703	0	1.3005
1985	3.4432	0.3804	1.5119	70.268	5.8136	6.158	1	1.4342
1986	3.7885	0.2816	1.5476	80.103	6.8617	7.483	0	1.4078
1987	4.5657	0.2775	1.5714	116.870	7.6132	10.592	1	1.4735
1988	5.6928	0.3154	1.6071	170.325	8.3817	15.782	1	1.5330

(continued)

Year	SKIPBC	ITP_{-1}	REDM	PCG	PCF	PIIS	ITP	D9	D83
1967	25.1691	0.9131	4.390	0.355	0.231	0.296	0.9459	0	0
1968	27.1394	0.9459	3.648	0.364	0.223	0.303	1.0166	0	0
1969	28.1846	1.0166	3.528	0.364	0.248	0.319	0.9932	0	0
1970	28.7400	0.9932	4.269	0.397	0.325	0.348	1.0235	0	0
1971	29.4316	1.0235	5.524	0.415	0.363	0.373	0.9616	0	0
1972	30.6870	0.9616	5.994	0.465	0.387	0.403	0.7946	0	0
1973	31.9585	0.7946	6.252	0.520	0.435	0.458	0.9259	1	0
1974	33.1870	0.9259	6.352	0.590	0.518	0.603	0.8796	1	0
1975	34.3590	0.8796	6.593	0.612	0.502	0.811	0.9722	0	0
1976	35.6718	0.9722	7.424	0.656	0.541	0.691	1.1667	0	0
1977	37.6139	1.1667	9.540	0.699	0.584	0.718	1.0185	1	0
1978	41.1704	1.0185	9.407	0.741	0.674	0.759	1.0278	0	0
1979	44.6503	1.0278	10.677	0.833	0.872	0.875	1.0926	0	0
1980	48.9059	1.0926	13.270	1.000	1.000	1.000	1.0000	0	0
1981	55.0654	1.0000	14.413	1.149	1.117	1.041	0.8704	0	0
1982	61.8363	1.1000	14.958	1.309	1.148	1.184	0.7778	1	0
1983	68.6019	1.2060	11.385	1.394	1.123	1.346	0.8519	0	1
1984	74.5164	1.2610	10.900	1.484	1.184	1.451	0.8175	0	1
1985	79.4303	1.3810	11.399	1.587	1.184	1.432	0.8089	1	1
1986	83.9084	1.4520	12.893	1.723	1.321	1.407	0.9810	0	1
1987	87.8362	1.4940	13.518	1.856	1.561	1.541	1.1610	1	1
1988	91.5028	1.6100	13.901	2.055	1.863	1.718	1.1015	1	1

Year	DEC3	DEC24	NC	PIMMS	EX	EX_{-1}	T81	T86
1967	0.0000	0.3624	1.4050	0.3766	1.0438	1.0692	0	0
1968	0.0000	0.3875	1.4548	0.3884	1.0185	1.0438	0	0
1969	0.0000	0.4551	1.4934	0.4155	1.0094	1.0185	0	0
1970	0.0000	0.5693	1.5542	0.4355	1.0116	1.0094	0	0
1971	0.0000	0.3733	1.6102	0.4437	0.9910	1.0116	0	0
1972	0.0000	0.4200	1.6565	0.4584	0.9810	0.9910	0	0
1973	0.0000	0.4964	1.7210	0.5520	1.0290	0.9810	0	0
1974	0.0000	0.6050	1.7933	0.7065	1.0510	1.0290	0	0
1975	0.0000	0.3329	1.9470	0.6776	1.0630	1.0510	0	0
1976	0.0000	0.4093	1.8953	0.7050	1.1240	1.0630	0	0
1977	0.0000	0.5114	1.9267	0.7405	1.0560	1.1240	0	0
1978	0.0000	0.5265	2.0213	0.7884	0.9270	1.0560	0	0
1979	0.0540	0.7130	2.1410	0.9193	0.9150	0.9270	0	0
1980	0.0889	1.1179	2.3234	1.0000	0.8760	0.9150	0	0
1981	0.0918	0.9102	2.4895	1.1089	0.8520	0.8760	1	0
1982	0.0919	0.7292	2.4981	1.1730	0.7950	0.8520	2	0
1983	0.1258	1.4876	2.5405	1.3005	0.6830	0.7950	3	0
1984	0.2169	1.3484	2.6062	1.4342	0.7590	0.6830	4	0
1985	0.3110	1.0537	2.6269	1.4078	0.7060	0.7590	5	0
1986	0.3159	0.8555	2.7015	1.4735	0.6480	0.7060	6	1
1987	0.3350	1.2881	2.7360	1.5330	0.5540	0.6480	7	2
1988	0.3399	1.4868	2.7786	1.5971	0.5640	0.5540	8	3

(continued)

NAME	PRM	PRM_{-1}	IS_{-1}	D59	N_{-1}	DT	IS	PIM	NEO
1967	0.4046	0.4004	3.00	0	3.6299	3.324	3.00	0.375	0.7517
1968	0.4171	0.4046	3.00	0	3.7228	4.432	3.50	0.387	0.7458
1969	0.4343	0.4171	3.50	0	3.8027	5.126	3.50	0.414	0.7704
1970	0.4514	0.4343	3.50	0	3.8639	6.407	3.50	0.434	0.8018
1971	0.4515	0.4514	3.50	0	3.9590	8.623	3.50	0.442	0.8326
1972	0.4686	0.4514	3.50	0	4.0453	9.579	3.50	0.456	0.9244
1973	0.5714	0.4686	3.50	0	4.1157	12.657	4.00	0.554	1.0431
1974	0.7692	0.5714	4.00	1	4.2126	16.283	5.00	0.712	1.0897
1975	0.6703	0.7692	5.00	0	4.3196	15.780	2.50	0.676	1.0022
1976	0.7033	0.6703	2.50	0	4.3958	18.423	2.00	0.701	1.0264
1977	0.7363	0.7033	2.00	0	4.5180	19.616	1.75	0.734	1.0905
1978	0.7582	0.7363	1.75	0	4.5837	21.512	4.50	0.783	1.1475
1979	0.9121	0.7582	4.50	0	4.6675	21.161	9.25	0.921	1.2090
1980	1.0000	0.9121	9.25	0	4.9297	28.114	11.00	1.000	1.3286
1981	1.0989	1.0000	11.00	0	5.0631	36.239	10.00	1.111	1.4872
1982	1.1538	1.0989	10.00	1	5.1834	104.626	4.75	1.173	1.5598
1983	1.2857	1.1538	4.75	0	5.2645	150.535	8.00	1.314	1.5712
1984	1.4725	1.2857	8.00	0	5.3451	191.436	5.50	1.460	1.6063
1985	1.4066	1.4725	5.50	1	5.3979	240.050	2.25	1.422	1.6957
1986	1.4505	1.4066	2.25	0	2.4562	329.078	2.00	1.493	1.7596
1987	1.5054	1.4505	2.00	0	5.5326	403.439	1.50	1.553	1.8206
1988	1.5762	1.5054	1.50	0	5.6134	544.502	5.25	1.681	1.9036

Chapter 8

The Effectiveness of Monetary and Fiscal Policies in Thailand

Kitti Limskul[1]

1 Introduction

Short-term economic fluctuations are familiar phenomena in Thailand at present. This is perhaps due to the industrialization process and to the openness of the Thai economy. Since the end of 1985, it seems that the Thai economy has finally entered a new epoch of economic development. The manufacturing sector's share to the total value-added rose to 22 percent in 1985, thus exceeded for the first time that of agriculture, and has been rapidly increasing since then.

The economic expansion during 1986-1990, as well as other factor such as the need for investment funds to finance development projects both by the central government and by private and public enterprises demand a move to deregulation of the money and of capital markets. Inherently, deregulation implies reduced control by the central bank of these markets. Proposals such as those to replace the business tax with a value-added tax and to reform the income tax and tariff structure seem to imply that fiscal policy is still a prominent government policy instrument whereas central bank rate policy and other instrumets of monetary policy are becoming relatively less powerful.

The objective of this paper is to test the relative effectivenes of fiscal and monetary policies in Thailand. The period examined was from the first quarter of 1975 to the fourth quarter of 1984. This is a period which we consider to have involved no abrupt structural change in the economy. Moreover, we think that this is a period where conventional fiscal and monetary policies have been used as important instruments. There have been some earlier studies of the relative effectiveness of fiscal and monetary policies in Thailand. One of these is a macroeconometric model simulation done by Chenbhanich (1983). Her study is an extension of the studies done by Arya (1976), Chantakul (1977), and Saowalak (1979).

Arya's study is based on a macro model which concentrates mainly on the foreign sector while Chantakul's study deals with the effectiveness of fiscal and monetary policies but has no explicit details on aggregate supply function and response. Saowalak's study uses a single-equation approach which cannot separate the truly exogenous variables from its endogenously determined features. Chenbhanich's study adds the importance of aggregate supply but does not include the production

[1]Economic Modelling and Forecasting Program, Chulalongkorn University, Bangkok, Thailand

function directly. All these studies, quantitatively show the relative effectiveness of fiscal over monetary policy.

Limskul (1985) has extended the detail of this line of study by adding a production function and capital stock formation function explicitly into his model. Both Chenbhanich and Limskul use quarterly data from 1971:1-1979:4. However, they differ in the means of determining domestic price levels. The latter treats price adjustment as a reflection of disequilibrium in the product market. In other words, in Limskul (1985), the model is closed by adjustment in inventory investment. This model cannot reject the hypothesis that fiscal policy is more effective than monetary policy. Areephasert (1988) has also concluded that fiscal policy is more effective than the monetary policy.

This paper will first discuss the model structure and then discuss the results of model validation procedures. Finally, the model will be used to test the relative effectiveness of fiscal and monetary policy.

2 Model Structure and Data Base

The model used in our study is basically a quarterly model (1970:1-1984:4). Real and monetary sectors comprise its main blocks. The data base for the monetary sector is derived from monthly data published in the Bank of Thailand's monthly bulletins. Quarterly data for the real sector is interpolated from annual data series by means of a splicing procedure. We applied a generalized least squares procedure to approximate a quadratic loss function such that the latter is minimized. The method has been applied to annual data of Thailand by K. Meesook and P. Saisonkrala (1980) following earlier pioneering work by the International Monetary Fund (1978). In order to validate the data series, we also compare them with the cyclical indicators of Thailand constructed by Limskul (1987).

The quarterly model used here is more comprehensive than Limskul's model (1985). The base data for the real sector is partly derived from Areephasert (1988) and Limskul (1989). Limskul estimated quarterly data series by applying cyclical indicators to validate the series. While the NESDB (1989) has also estimated quarterly data for internal use, the Limskul series is used here as our data base.

In our study, production and supply in both the agriculture and non-agriculture are explicitly determined. Nevertheless, given the supply of labor in both sectors, equilibrium is reached in the non-agriculture labor market with employment in agriculture determined as residual.

Demand components are determined as follows. Private consumption and investment are endogenously determined whereas government expenditure in current prices is exogenously given. Imports are determined solely by domestic demand and purchasing ability both income and price effects. Exports, on the other hand, are determined by world income and relative prices, or the competitiveness of Thai exports.

The quilibrium in the real sector is reached through price and quantity adjustment. The latter implies that when aggregate demand is not equilibrated with supply, adjustment will be made through the build-up of an excess demand/supply of inventory investment. On the financial side, the deficits in the government budget and the balance of payments, hypothetically, put pressure on the expansion of the money supply. This is reflected through the building up of the monetary base. Balance in the demand and supply of money is restored through adjustment of the average commercial loan rate.

2.1 Real Sector

2.1.1 Production and Supply

Determination of Cultivated Area

(1) $A = EXP(10.74017 + 0.07301016 \log PN1 + 0.08038165 \log T$

(332.93) (3.96) (6.88)

$- 0.04180617DLA1 + 0.04225208DLA2$

(-8.039) (7.504)

R^2=0.96 F(92,54)=451.580 DW=1.68 N=57:OLSQ

Production in Agricultural Sector

(2) $YR1 = -6634.597 + 0.1897217K1 + 0.08055805N1 + 0.2994421A$
$-2100.072DYR11 + 3351.840DYR12$

Production in Non-Agricultural Sector

(3) $YR2 = EXP(6329111 + 1.229185 \log K2_{-1} + 0.2716303 \log N2$

(-14.228) (4.5504) (5.666)

$- 0.05244669DLYR21 + 0.06725795DLYR22)$

R^2=0.99 F(2,55)=2486.87 DW=1.99 N=58:OLSQ

Demand for Labor and Wage in Non-Agricultural Sector

(4) $N2 = 851.0159 + 0.02564820K2 - 15.06042\frac{W2_{-1}}{PN2_{-1}} + 40.69827T$

(1.661) (5.690) (-2.286)

$- 395.8579ZN21 + 375.0049ZN22$

R^2=0.99 F(3,54)=1385.24 DW=1.35 N=58:2SLS

(5) $W2 = -10.67301 + 1.847805\frac{YR2_{-1}}{N2_{-1}} + 24.31026PD_{-1}$

(-3.216) (3.864) (44.321)

$- 5.230375DW21 + 3.281753DW22$

(-8.479) (5.738)

R^2=0.9878 F(2,55)=1073.68 DW=1.54 N=58:OLSQ

Employment in Agricultural Sector

(6) $N1 = N - N2$

Aggregate Supply

(7) $YSR = YR1 + YR2$

(8) $Y1 = YR1 * PD1$

(9) $Y2 = YR2 * PD2$

(10) $YS = Y1 + Y2$

2.1.2 Aggregate Demand Determination

Private Consumption Expenditure

(11) $PCER = -2398.851 + 0.7097989\frac{YD_{-1}}{PD_{-1}} - 15862.38(PD - PD_{-1})$

(1.501) (5.175) (-2.234)

$+ 0.3477216PCER_{-1} - 3621.405DPCER1$

$+ 3323.798DPCER2$

(2.774)

R^2=0.95 F(3,52) DW=1.95 N=56:2SLS

(12) $PCE = PCER * PD$

Government Current Expenditure

(13) $GCER = \frac{GCEV}{PD}$

Private Investment Expenditure

Agricultural Sector

(14) $KPR1 = 0.4941354YR1_{-1} + 1757.262PN1_{-2} + 0.2089508KPR1_{-1}$

(5.434) (1.972) (2.038)

$- 4031.992DKPR11 + 2968.647DKPR12$

R^2=0.83 F(2,55)=40.3447 DW=2.06 N=58:OLSQ

(15) $IPR1 = KPR1 - (1 - D1) * KPR1_{-1}$

Non-Agricultural Sector

(16) $IPR2 = 0.0622139YR2_{-1} + 9079.110\frac{PN2}{PD2} - 14.20035RR_{-1}$

(1.499) (3.765) (-1.592)

$- 1154.942ZIPR21 + 507.0354ZIPR22$

R^2=0.83 F(2,51)=65.992 DW=1.86 N=54:2SLS

(17) $KPR2 = IPR2 + (1 - S2)KPR2_{-1}$

Government Investment Expenditure

(18) $IGR = \frac{IGV1 + IGV2}{PD}$

(19) $IPG = IPR1 + IPR2 + IGR$

(20) $KGR1 = IGR1 + (1 - G1)KGR1_{-1}$

(21) $KGR2 = IGR2 + (1 - G2)KGR2_{-1}$

(22) $K1 = KPR1 + KGR1$

(23) $K2 = KPRS + KGR2$

(24) $K = K1 + K2$

(25) $GE = GCEV + IGV1 + IGV2$

Determination of Stock of Inventory

$$(26)\quad KIV = 6044.328 + 0.1958155 YSR_{-1}\frac{YSR_{-1}}{YSR_{-2}}$$

(2.956) (25.035)

$$+\ 43811.33PD_{-1} - 0.3926041INV_{-1}$$

(5.152) (-7.576)

$$-\ 4187.762DKIV1 + 5673.140DKIV2$$

R^2=0.97 F(3,50)=429.934 DW=1.98 N=54:2SLS

Demand for Imports of Goods and Services

Raw Materials

$$(27)\quad MRMR = EXP(-6.905914 + 1.017704 \log YR2 - 0.4721954 \log PTMRM$$

(-8.931) (11.122) (-10.570)

$$+\ 5559669 \log MRMR_{-1} - .1523497ZLMRM1$$

(12.246)

$$+\ 0.2169082ZLMRM2)$$

R^2=0.93 F(3,52)=151.882 DW=1.99 N=57:2SLS

Capital Goods

$$(28)\quad MKR = -378.3668 + 0.1384724IPG - 1021.086PTMK$$

(-2.572) (6.800) (-5.702)

$$+\ 1684.907PD_1 + 0.4958786MKR_{-1} - 519.3413DMKR1$$

(6.387) (10.215)

$$+\ 631.4900DMKR2$$

R^2=0.93 F(4,53)=136.183 DW=1.7 N=58:2SLS

Consumer Goods

$$(29)\quad MCR = 389.3439 + 0.007648682PCER - 191.6751PTMC$$

(5.898) (2.818) (-6.126)

$$+\ 555.4142PD + .2703968MCR_{-1} - 193.4275DMCR1$$

(8.308) (4.402)

$$+\ 245.4129DMCR2$$

R^2=0.93 F(4,53)=136.183 DW=1.7 N=58:25L5

Services

$$(30)\quad MSR = -345.2723 + 0.03192822YSR - 170.1769\frac{PTMS}{PWI}$$

(-5.329) (10.731) (-8.340)

$$+\ 0.3842286MCR_{-1} - 215.3864DMSR1$$

(6.923)

$$+\ 257.3777DMCR2$$

R^2=0.98 F(3,54)=904.069 DW=1.98 N=58:OLS

$$(31)\quad MGSR = MRMR + MKR + MCR + MSR$$

$$(32)\quad MRMV = MRMR * PMRM$$

$$(33)\quad MKV = MKR * PMK$$

$$(34)\quad MCV = MCR * PMC$$

$$(35)\quad MSV = MSR * PMS$$

$$(36)\quad MGSV = MRMV + MKV + MCV + MSV$$

Demand for Exports of Goods and Services

Agricultural Goods

$$(37)\quad XGR1 = EXP(8.287914 + 0.5517766\log YW - 0.9474241\log\frac{PX1D}{PXWD}$$

(179.716) (10.581) (-9.303)

$$-\ 0.1914339DLXG11 + 0.1712419DLXG12)$$

R^2=0.92 F(2,55)=178.87 DW=1.89 N=58:AR1

Non-Agricultural Goods

$$(38)\quad XGR2 = EXP(7.246752 + 1.037966\log YW - 1.009892\log\frac{PX2D}{PXWD}$$

(77.795) (8.253) (-8.546)

$$-\ 0.08353318DLXG21 + 0.05140095DLXG22)$$

R^2=0.81 F(2,55)=61.206 DW=1.87 N=58:AR1

Services

(39) $XSR = EXP(7.610032 + 0.6013536 \log YW - 0.7673165 \log \frac{PXSD}{PWID}$

(28.503) (2.12) (-6.574)

$- 0.04676293DLXSR1 + 0.05710732DLXSR2)$

R^2=0.82 F(2,55)=24.97 DW=1.60 N=58:AR1

(40) $XGSR = XGR1 + XGR2 + XSR$

(41) $XGV1 = XGR1 * PX1$

(42) $XGV2 = XGR2 * PX2$

(43) $XSV = XSR * PXS$

(44) $XGSV = XGV1 + XGV2 + XSV$

Price Determination

General Price Level

(45) $PD = 0.3152289 + 0.4473159PM + 0.05235483\frac{M2}{YSR}$

(20.925) (3.992) (5.069)

$+ 0.9523596\frac{KIVKIV_{-1}}{YSR} - 0.04196359DPD1$

(2.989)

$+ 0.08596767DPD2$

R^2=0.99 F(3,55)=2771.00 DW=2.08 N=59:OLSQ

(46) $PG = 100\frac{PD - PD_{-1}}{PD_{-1}}$

Agricultural Sector

(47) $PD1 = EXP(0.02085795 + 0.9200452 \log PX1 + 0.6701168 \log \frac{PD}{PX1}$

(.7527) (2.808) (3.807)

$- 0.03435623DLPD11 + 0.03418464DLPD12)$

R^2=0.94 F(2,55)=235.849 DW=2.06 N=58:2SLS

Non-Agricultural Sector

(48) $PD2 = -0.1433047 + 1.049802PD - 0.02201243DPD21 + 0.009743253DPD22$

(-2.768) (4.706)

R^2=0.96 F(1,55)=565.508 DW=1.66 N=57:2SLS

Export Price of Non-Agriculture

(49) $PX2 = 0.8680990PD2 + 0.5231247\frac{PM}{PD2} - 0.2726214ZPX21 + 0.2215577ZPX22$

(7.720) (4.285)

R^2=0.93 F(1,56)=290.733 DW=1.79 N=58:AR1

Export Price of Agriculture

(50) $PX1 = PX1D\frac{ZEX}{20.98}$

(51) $PX2D = \frac{PX2}{\frac{ZEX}{20.98}}$

Export price of Services

(52) $PXS = PXSD\frac{ZEX}{20.98}$

Net Value-Added Price

(53) $PN1 = PD1 - TAX12 - TAX10$

(54) $PN2 = PD2 - TAX22 - TAX21$

Import Prices in Local Currency

(55) $PM = \frac{MGSV}{MGSR}$

(56) $PMRM = PMRMD\frac{ZEX}{20.98}$

(57) $PMK = PMKD\frac{ZEX}{20.98}$

(58) $PMC = PMCD\frac{ZEX}{20.98}$

(59) $PMS = PMSD\frac{ZEX}{20.98}$

(60) $PTMRM = PMRM * (1 + ZTMRM)$

(61) $PTMK = PMFF * (1 + ZTMK)$

(62) $PTMC = PMC * (1 + ZTMC)$

(63) $PTMS = PMS * (1 + ZTMS)$

Equilibrium of Aqgregate Demand and Supply for Goods and Services

(64) $INV = YSR + MGSR - PCER - GCER - IPR1 - IPR2 - IGR - XGSR$

2.1.3 Determination of Income

Wage Income in the Non-Agriculture

(65) $YL2 = N2 * W2$

Tax Income

Direct Tax on Income

(66) $TDH = YL2 * ZTDH$

Tax on Imports of Goods and Services

(67) $TMRMR = ZTMRM * MRMR$

(68) $TMCR = ZTMC * MCR$

(69) $TMKR = ZTMK * MKR$

(70) $TMSR = ZTMS * MSR$

(71) $TMR = TMRMR + TMCR + TMKR + TMSR$

Tax on local production and Sales

(72) $TOIAG = TAX12 * Y1$

(73) $TOINA = TAX22 * Y2$

Tax on Exports

(74) $TAX11 = TAX10 * X1$

(75) $TAX21 = \frac{TMR}{YSR}$

(76) $TR = TAX21 * MGSR + TDC + TDH + TOINA + TOIAG + TAX11 + TOT$

Disposable Income

(77) $YD = YS - TAX11 - TOIAG - TAX21 * MGSR - TOINA - TDH - TDC$

$- NPKY - NGKY$

Government Deficit

(78) $DEF = TR - GE$

2.2 Financial Sector

2.2.1 Commercial Bank's Credit to Private and Government Sector

(79) $DCB = 7669.852 + 0.8073725QM + 3.107482CCBBT + 0.9885566FLCB$

(2.572) (16.823) (5.116) (3.426)

$- 30111.64DDCB1 + 16218.37DDCB2$

R^2=0.99 F(3,55)=1245.44 DW=2.17 N=58:OLSQ

2.2.2 Commercial Bank's Credit to Private Sector

(80) $CPCB = DCB - NDCGCB^*$

(81) $DCP = CPCB + DCG^*$

2.2.3 Domestic Credit to Government Sector

(82) $NDCG = 48106.30 - 3.866219DEF_{-1} - 2.839667DEF_{-2}$

(11.628) (-6.957) (-4.923)

$- 32676.01DNDCG1 + 66301.05DNDCG2$

R^2=0.82 F(2,52)=64.676 DW=1.72 N=55:OLSQ

2.2.4 Total Domestic Credit

(83) $NDC = NDCG + DCP + OT2$

2.2.5 Net Private Capital Movement

(84) $NPKY = -15033.62 + 0.1281204MGSV + 2002.813BR_{-1}$

(-8.238) (4.137) (7.563)

$- 532.4025RFY - 3910.870DNPKY1$

(-4.279)

$+ 4724.815DNPKY2$

R^2=0.89 F(3,52)=97.247 DW=2.31 N=56:OLSQ

2.2.6 Balance of Payments

(85) $BP = XGSV - MGSV + NGKY + NPKY + NTRAN + OT1$

2.2.7 Net Flow of Foreign Asset

(86) $NFA = NFA_{-1} + BP + ADJ$

2.2.8 Monetary Base

(87) $B = NFA + NDC$

2.2.9 Quasi Monetary

(88) $QM = M2 - M1$

2.2.10 Determination of Interest Rate (Average Loan Rate)

(89) $$RLCB = 4.255199 - 0.000006136351B_{-1} + 0.00001881934YS_{-1}$$

$$- 0.037911112 * PG_{-1} + 5.253220PD$$

$$- 1.150447DRLCB1 + 1.680342DRLCB2$$

Note: This equation is a result of equating demand with supply of money (M2) equations and solving to obtain RLCB as an endogenous variable.

2.2.11 Real Interest Rate

(90) $$RR = \frac{RLCB - PG + RLCB_{-1} - PG_{-1}}{2}$$

3 Model Evaluation

We applied Theil's inequality coefficient to test the validity of model.

$$U = \frac{RMSE}{\sqrt{\frac{1}{T}\sum_{t=1}^{T}(Ys_t)^2} + \sqrt{(1-T)\sum_{t=1}^{T}(Ya_t)^2}}$$

where

Ya_t = actual value of variable Y at period t-th

Ys_t = forecasted value of variable Y at period t-th

T=number of period under simulation

and

$$RMSE = \sqrt{\sum_{t=1}^{T}(Ys_t - Ya_t)^2}$$

Testing of Model's Validity

Variable	Theil's Inequality Index
YR1	0.01733
YR2	0.00375
PCER	0.01307
IPR1	0.00148
IPR2	0.01442
XGR1	0.00060
XGR2	0.01172
XSR	0.00015
MRMR	0.01494
MKR	0.01580
MCR	0.00420
MSR	0.00569
RLCB	0.00374

Note: See list of variables and descriptions in the appendix.

According to Theil (1961), the value of the inequality index "in" is between zero and one. Most of the selected list of variables above, show a rather low value of "in". This may indicate that the model is validated for further use.

4 Model Simulation Experiment

The monetary policy simulation increases the central bank rate (BR) by 1 percent in the base period 1975:1. The multiplier effect of monetary policy is allowed to spread throughout 1975:1-1984:4. The objective of this experiment is to measure the magnitude of the impact of monetary policy on the economy. At present, in 1991, the average deposit rate in Thailand has been liberalized although there is still a ceiling for the loan rate. During the sample period of 1975:1-1984:4, both deposit and loan rates were regulated and managed by the Bank of Thailand. The fiscal policy instrument in this study is the tax rate in the non-agriculture sector (Tax22). It is designed to represent the average tax rate, on ad varolem basis, levied on activities in the non-agriculture sector. It is a replica of what is generally known as a "business tax" such as is often charged on both specific and ad varolem bases. As a simulation of monetary policy, a one-time (1975:1) increase of 1 percent in the central bank rate as a monetary policy instrument,gives the following results. Investment in agriculture responds by decreasing. There is an even clearer decline in private consumption expenditure (PCER). It decreases by 1,000 million baht in 1975:3 and by 109.23, 29.07, 24.54 and 12.42 million baht during the following four quarters (1975:4-1986:3). It increases thereafter, however, up to the end of 1984:4. Since the increase in the nominal interest rate gives rise to a general price increase, it thus causes the real interest rate to decline. This perhaps has a positive effect on private investment in the non-agriculture sector.

However, the shock initially seems also to have negative effects on disposable income (YD) and production (YSR). Later these variables become positive again. This reflects the long-run positive impact on the economy even where there is an increase of the interest rate at the base period. Nevertheless, a negative response of much larger magnitude will result if a once and for all increase of interest rate policy is pursued.

Table 1. Economic Response After Using Monetary Policy: 1 percent increase of the Central Bank Rate (BR)

(Million Baht)

Year	Quarter	IPR1	PCER	IPR2	YSR	YD
1975	1	0.00	0.00	0.00	0.00	0.00
	2	0.00	0.00	0.00	0.00	-2002.81
	3	0.00	-1000.00	1.35	1.47	83.50
	4	0.69	-109.24	-1.09	-0.91	-171.84
1976	1	0.49	-29.08	1.86	-0.54	256.32
	2	-4.02	-24.55	6.34	13.25	457.56
	3	11.25	-12.43	9.59	14.76	325.31
	4	8.02	2.42	1.84	12.11	108.81
1977	1	-0.81	-9.36	-2.59	7.44	34.10
	2	-5.30	5.88	-1.39	6.76	30.25
	3	-4.10	0.14	2.10	5.26	12.92
	4	1.67	-2.07	3.66	5.46	17.96
1978	1	3.49	0.62	2.95	3.59	10.45
	2	1.02	3.15	1.14	2.63	9.35
	3	-0.59	3.67	0.59	1.89	5.21
	4	0.59	2.87	0.79	1.69	1.58
1979	1	-1.05	1.03	0.45	1.22	1.54
	2	0.32	0.87	0.36	1.19	1.51
	3	1.16	1.60	0.29	1.02	1.48
	4	1.34	2.08	0.24	1.09	1.36
1980	1	-0.52	2.35	0.20	1.05	1.29
	2	-0.52	2.24	0.10	1.09	1.34
	3	-1.51	2.31	0.09	1.06	1.38
	4	1.58	2.10	0.09	1.06	1.36
1981	1	-1.45	1.97	0.09	1.10	1.30
	2	0.24	1.22	0.08	1.02	1.30
	3	-0.07	1.40	0.08	1.10	1.30
	4	3.09	1.40	0.08	1.01	1.31
1982	1	-1.52	1.66	0.10	1.08	1.26
	2	-1.50	1.54	0.09	1.06	1.22
	3	-0.43	1.43	0.08	1.06	1.19
	4	-2.60	1.48	0.06	1.06	1.18

(continued)

Year	Quarter	IPR1	PCER	IPR2	YSR	YD
1983	1	1.41	1.60	0.07	1.01	1.14
	2	-0.30	1.13	0.08	1.00	1.22
	3	-0.26	0.93	0.08	0.98	1.19
	4	2.03	1.00	0.05	1.01	1.19
1984	1	-0.11	1.09	0.06	0.99	1.11
	2	-1.28	1.13	0.05	0.91	1.06
	3	-0.42	1.07	0.04	0.90	1.09
	4	0.17	0.83	0.05	0.86	1.08

Table 2. Economic Response after using Fiscal Policy: 1 percent increase of the Average Tax Rate on the Non-Agriculture Sector (Tax22)

(Million Baht)

Year	Quarter	YR2	PCER	IPR2	PD	YSR
1975	1	-5.31	-5.39	-44.13	0.00	-18.01
	2	-12.21	-20.97	-22.48	-0.00	-44.77
	3	-8.47	-11.45	-11.89	-0.00	-38.25
	4	-8.56	-10.51	-16.33	0.00	-38.25
1976	1	-7.72	-4.88	-4.53	-0.00	-8.24
	2	-6.81	-12.67	-8.28	0.00	-12.28
	3	-6.33	26.48	-1.27	-0.00	-6.79
	4	-6.31	-5.18	-2.44	-0.00	-6.94
1977	1	-4.73	-15.00	-2.05	-0.00	-5.58
	2	-4.38	-15.72	-1.13	-0.00	-5.29
	3	-4.02	-11.80	-0.75	-0.00	-4.88
	4	-4.54	-4.26	-0.74	0.00	-5.31
1978	1	-3.82	-3.86	-1.13	-0.00	-4.61
	2	-3.90	-3.91	-1.11	-0.00	-4.75
	3	-3.49	-5.92	-1.06	-0.00	-4.34
	4	-2.67	-4.35	-0.88	-0.00	-3.55
1979	1	-3.17	-3.58	-0.69	0.00	-4.02
	2	-2.89	-2.49	-0.84	0.00	-3.75
	3	-2.57	-1.49	-0.83	-0.00	-3.46
	4	-2.23	-1.69	-0.77	-0.00	-3.14
1980	1	-2.26	-0.66	-0.68	-0.00	-3.16
	2	-2.05	-0.70	-0.67	-0.00	-2.97
	3	-1.91	-0.67	-0.63	-0.00	-2.83
	4	-1.83	-0.80	-0.60	-0.00	-2.77
1981	1	-1.46	-0.82	-0.57	-0.00	-2.40
	2	-1.62	-0.78	-0.48	-0.00	-2.56
	3	-1.35	-0.31	-0.53	-0.00	-2.29
	4	-1.41	-0.45	-0.48	-0.00	-2.36

(continued)

Year	Quarter	YR2	PCER	IPR2	PD	YSR
1982	1	-1.09	-0.34	-0.49	-0.00	-2.05
	2	-0.98	-0.26	-0.43	-0.00	-1.95
	3	-0.92	-0.02	-0.40	-0.00	-1.89
	4	-0.85	-0.03	-0.38	-0.00	-1.80
1983	1	-0.77	-0.03	-0.37	0.00	-1.74
	2	-0.68	-0.00	-0.34	0.00	-1.64
	3	-0.59	-0.00	-0.33	-0.00	-1.56
	4	-0.59	-0.00	-0.32	-0.00	-1.58
1984	1	-0.49	0.00	-0.31	-0.00	-1.46
	2	-0.30	0.00	-0.30	-0.00	-1.29
	3	-0.23	-0.00	-0.25	0.00	-1.21
	4	-0.33	0.00	-0.23	-0.00	-1.29

The tax rate (Tax22) being increased by 1 percent has a much more negative effect on the real sector. Non-agriculture production (YR2) declines with a magnitude of 5.31 and 12.21 million baht in1975:1 and 1975:2. It declines thereafter with smaller magnitudes. Private investment, consumption, and income decline as results of this fiscal policy.

The elasticities of fiscal policy instruments seem to be larger than those of monetary policy. The elasticity of indirect tax policy on the general price level is 3.086 whereas the elasticity of bank rate policy is 2.136. In addition, the elasticity of fiscal policy on private consumption expenditure is -2.039 while it is 1.411 on the central bank rate. The elasticities of fiscal and monetary policies on private investment are somewhat smaller. They are -0.752 and 0.486, respectively. On the production and supply side, the tax elasticity on gross domestic product is -2.621 and 1.813 according to the fiscal and monetary policies, respectively.

Table 3. Elasticity of Fiscal and Monetary Policy Instrument: Central Bank Rate (BR) and Indirect Tax Rate on Non-Agriculture Sector (Tax22)

	(4-period)		(20-period)	
	BR	Tax22	BR	Tax22
PD	0.046	-0.047	2.136	-3.086
YSR	-0.479	-0.492	1.813	-2.621
IPR	0.596	-0.678	0.486	-0.752
PCER	-0.687	-0.734	1.411	-2.039

Note: Elasticity is defined as a percentage change of the target variable as affected by 1 percent change of the instrument variable.

First, it should be noted that the above elasticity has a somewhat medium-term effect after 20 quarters. Secondly, the signs for monetary and fiscal policies are opposite. The former is positive while the latter is negative after the hypothetical increase of the rate by 1 percent each.

The increase (decrease) of indirect tax rate has a strong impact on the contraction (expansion) of the Thai economy. This may provide a rationale for the Ministry of Finance proposal to introduce the value added tax as a substitute for the business tax. In other words, a cascade effect makes the impact of this tax too strong. In general, tax rate deduction is not usually practiced. In general, tax deductions are not allowed and, thus, any tax increase may make a contraction stronger than targeted. If, as a result, the government collects insufficient tax revenues and has to rely on an increase in the indirect tax rate, the policy may give rise to undesirable effects.

The opposite signs after 20 quarters imply that monetary policy as no effectiveness in the medium-term. Rather, some though not all of the policy instruments are effective in the short term, i.e., after 4 quarters. Thus, we are not totally convinced by the claim that an increase in the interest rate ceiling or in the central bank rate would really curb inflation.

Moreover, the policy has adverse effect in the sense that the general price level seems to be induced to increase. Production or the supply of goods and services (GDP), although decreasing in the short run, increases in the medium run. Similarly, private consumption expenditure decreases in the short run and increases in the medium run as a result of an increase in income. The interest rate increase has no immediate impact on private investment owing to its lagged impact on investment decisions. However, it still induces an increase in investment in the medium run.

With a one percent increase in either policy instrument, fiscal policy is more effective than monetary policy. There is, however, a threshold of effectiveness issue; it may be the case that the bank rate has to be increased by more than just 1 percent. This, in fact, has been practiced by the Ministry of Finance during the latter part of 1990. The interest rate ceiling for loans was increased in increments of 0.5% to 1.0% each from 16.3% to 19.0%. As expected, inflationary pressure measured in terms of the consumer price index and private consumption expenditure decreased. Nevertheless, the policy also caused a contraction of the economy as our model simulation would predict. However, this contraction seems to have also been a policy goal, i.e., to cool down the "overheated economy" of 1990. According to our simulation exercise, fiscal policy, despite its effectiveness, should not be judged considered the best policy instrument because the indirect tax rate cannot be easily decreased. In practice, it has only been increased, and quite often.

5 Conclusions

In our study, a quarterly model of the Thai economy is constructed based on a two-sector framework. We use the model to experiment with the relative magnitude of fiscal and monetary policies in the 1975:1 - 1984:4 sample period. The financial sector is basically affected by external influences, such as short term financial capital movements and the government deficit/surplus. This makes the money supply increase/decrease. Although, the financial sector is assumed to attain equilibrium through adjustment in the average loan rate, the real sector has been modeled so as to have an explicit disequilibrium feature.

Fiscal policy action seems to have a stronger impact on the real economy and income as compared with interest rate policy. However, fiscal policy instruments such as the indirect tax rate, seem to be too effective, relative to monetary policy instruments, such as the interest rate. Though it appears that the effectiveness threshold of the magnitude of the latter instrument may be somehere above 1 percentage point, and beyond this it may be as effective as fiscal policy. In the short run, within four quarters, the exercise of monetary policy through an interest rate increase seems to be effective in slowing down private consumption expenditure and the growth of gross domestic products but not private investment expenditure or the general price level. In the medium run, interest rate policy soon loses effectiveness. Fiscal policy, on the contrary, has stronger impact in the medium run, with a clear direction of impact, as revealed in the signs of elasticity.

References

[1] Arya, G. (1976) *A Structural Model of the Thai Balance of Payments: 1956-1973,* Ph.D. Dissertation, Faculty of Arts and Science, University of Pittsburgh

[2] Areephasert, P. (1988) *A Quarterly Simulation Model of Fiscal and Monetary Policy for the Thai Economy: 1970:1-1984:4,* M.A. Thesis, Faculty of Economics, Chulalongkorn University, Bangkok, Thailand

[3] Chantakul, P. (1977) "Empirical Evidence of Fiscal and Monetary Policies in Thai Economy," Economic Pager No.2001, Department of Economics and Business Administration, Kasetsart University, Bangkok, Thailand

[4] Chenbhanich, C. (1983) *The Relative Influence of Fiscal and Monetary Policies on Economic Activities in Thailand,* M.A. Thesis, Department of Economics, Thammasat University, Bangkok Thailand

[5] International Monetary Fund(1978) *Alternative Approaches to the Estimation of Short-Term Economic Indicators,* IMF

[6] Limskul, K. (1985) "The Effectiveness of Fiscal Policy under Budget Constraint: A Case Study of Thailand," The Economic Science, Vol.32-4, Department of Economics, Nagoya University, Nagoya, Japan

[7] Limskul, K. and Kantigaroon (1987) "A Construction of Business Cycle Indicators for Thailand," Discussion Paper No.10, Socio-Economic Policy and Forecasting Unit, Social Research Institute, Chulalongkorn University, Bangkok, Thailand (in Thai)

[8] Limskul, K. (1989) "Cyclical Pattern of Imports and Economic Activities in Thailand," in H. Osada and D. Hiratsuka eds., *Business Cycles in Five ASEAN Countries, India and Korea (II),* The Institute of Developing Economies, Tokyo, Japan

[9] Limskul, K. and T. Kantigaroon (1989) "The Compilation of International Trade Indices for Thailand-Japan and Thailand-ASEAN," Discussion Pager No.5, Economic Policy Modelling and Forecasting Program, Faculty of Economics, Chulalongkorn University, Bangkok, Thailand (in Thai)

[10] Limskul, K. (1989) "Estimation of Quarterly National Accounts Data by Using Leading, Coincidence Lagging Indicators," Discussion Paper No.2, Economic Policy Modelling and Forecasting Program, Faculty of Economics, Chulalongkorn University, Bangkok, Thailand

[11] Limskul, K. and T. Kantigaroon (1990) "Diffusion Indices for the Construction Industry in Thailand," Discussion Paper No.10, Economic Modelling and Forecasting Program, Faculty of Economics, Chulalongkorn University, Bangkok, Thailand (in Thai)

[12] Meesook, K. and P. Saisongkrala (1980) *Monthly and Quarterly Estimation of the National Account Data,* The Bank of Thailand

[13] The National Accounts Division (1989) *Report on the Estimation of Quarterly National Accounts Statistics: Production Side,* The National Economic and Social Development Board, Bangkok, Thailand

[14] Saowalak, T. (1979) *The Relative Contribution of Monetary and Fiscal Changes to Economic Growth: 1961-1977,* M.A. Thesis, Department of Economics, Thammasat University, Bangkok, Thailand

[15] Theil, H. (1961) *Economic Forecasts and Policy,* Amsterdam, North-Holland

Appendix

List of Variables and Notations

A	Aggregate cultivated area
ADJ	Adjusting factor in change of net foreign asset in the balance of payments
B	Monetary base
BP	Balance of payments
BR	Average standard rate of interest
CCBBT	Credit from Bank of Thailand to commercial banks
CPCB	Commercial banks' credit to private sector
D1	Depreciation rate of capital stock
DCB	Total credit from commercial banks to private and government sectors
DCG	Government saving bank's credit to private sector
DCP	Total credit to private sector
DEF	Budget deficit
FLCB	Commercial banks' loan from abroad
GCER	Government's current expenditure in real terms
GCEV	Government's current expenditure in nominal terms
GE	Total government expenditure
GRV	Total government revenue
ICR	Government investment in real terms
IGV2	Government investment: non-agriculture, in nominal terms
IGV1	Government investment: agriculture, in nominal terms
INV	Investment in inventory
IPG	Total investment
IPR1	Private investment: agriculture, in real terms
IPR2	Private investment: non-agriculture, in real terms
K	Total fixed capital stock
K1	Total fixed private capital stock: agriculture
K2	Total fixed private capital stock: non-agriculture
KGR1	Fixed government capital stock: agriculture
KGR2	Fixed government capital stock: non-agriculture
KIV	Stock of inventory
KPR1	Fixed private capital stock: agriculture
KPR2	Fixed private capital stock: non-agriculture
M1	Money supply
M2	Money supply
MCR	Import of consumer goods in real terms
MCV	Import of consumer goods in nominal terms
MGSR	Total import of goods and services in real terms
MGSV	Total import of goods and services in nominal terms
MKR	Import of capital goods in real terms

MKV	Import of capital goods in nominal terms
MRMR	Import of raw materials in real terms
MRMV	Import of raw materials in nominal terms
MSR	Import of services in real terms
MSV	Import of services in nominal terms
N	Total labor supply
N1	Employment in agriculture
N2	Employment in non-agriculture
NDC	Total domestic credits
NDCG	Total domestic credits to government
NDCGCB	Total net credit from commercial banks to government
NFA	Net foreign asset
NGKY	Net government capital movement
NPKY	Net private capital movement
NTRAN	Net transfer from abroad
OT1	Other factors in monetary survey account
OT2	Other factors in balance of payments account
PCE	Private consumption expenditure in nominal terms
PCER	Private consumption expenditure in real terms
PD	General price level
PD1	Price level in agriculture
PD2	Price level in non-agriculture
PG	Percentage change of general price level
PM	Total import price
PMC	Import price of consumer goods in local currency
PMCD	Import price of consumer goods in foreign currency
PMK	Import price of capital goods in local currency
PMKD	Import price of capital goods in foreign currency
PMRM	Import price of raw materials in local currency
PMRMD	Import price of raw materials in foreign currency
PMS	Import price of services in local currency
PMSD	Import price of services in foreign currency
PN1	Net value added price in agriculture
PN2	Net value added price in non-agriculture
PTMC	Import price of consumer goods including import tax
PTMK	Import price of capital goods including import tax
PTMRM	Import price of raw material including import tax
PTMS	Import price of services including import tax
PWI	World price index in local currency
PWID	World price index in foreign currency
PX1	Export price of agriculture in local currency
PX1D	Export price of agriculture in foreign currency
PX2	Export price of non-agriculture in local currency
PX2D	Export price of non-agriculture in foreign currency
PXS	Export price of services in local currency

PXSD	Export price of services in foreign currency
PXWD	World export price index in foreign currency
QM	Quasi Money
RFY	Average foreign loan rate of interest
RLCB	Average loan rate of commercial bank
RR	Real interest rate
S	Rate of depreciation of non-agriculture
T	Time trend
TAX10	Specific tax rate on agriculture
TAX11	Tax revenue accrued from specific tax of agriculture
TAX12	Ad varolem tax rate on agriculture
TAX21	Effective import tax rate
TAX22	Ad varolem tax rate on non-agriculture
TDC	Direct tax on corporate income
TDH	Direct tax on personal income
TMC	Import tax revenue from consumer goods
TMR	Total import tax revenue
TMRM	Import tax revenue from raw materials
TMS	Import tax revenue from services
TOIAG	Total indirect tax from agriculture
TOINA	Total indirect tax from non-agriculture
TOT	Other government revenues
TR	Total tax revenue
W2	Wage rate in non-agriculture
XGR1	Export: agriculture, in real terms
XGR2	Export: non-agriculture, in real terms
XGSR	Total export in real terms
XGSV	Total export in nominal terms
XGV1	Export: agriculture, in nominal terms
XGV2	Export: non-agriculture, in nominal terms
XSR	Export: services, in real terms
XSV	Export: services, in nominal terms
Y1	GDP: agriculture, in nominal terms
Y2	GDP: non-agriculture, in nominal terms
YD	Disposable income
YL2	Wage income of non-agriculture
YR1	GDP: agriculture, in real terms
YR2	GDP: non-agriculture, in real terms
YS	Total GDP in nominal terms
YSR	Total GDP in real terms
YW	Index of world income
ZEX	Exchange rate Baht/U.S. dollar
ZTDH	Tax rate on wage income
ZTMC	Import tax on consumer goods
ZTMK	Import tax on capital goods

ZTMRM	Import tax on raw materials
ZTMS	Import tax on services

Chapter 9
Treasury Macroeconomic (TRYM) Model of the Australian Economy

Bruce Taplin, Paddy Jilek, Lawrence Antioch, Andrew Johnson, Priya Parameswaran and Craig Louis[1]

1 Introduction

The Treasury Macroeconomic (TRYM) model of the Australian economy has been developed and is used within the Commonwealth Treasury of Australia[2]. For over 20 years, Treasury has developed and maintained models of the Australian macroeconomy. This research effort has previously been documented by Higgins and FitzGerald (1973), in the 1981 documentation of the NIF-10 model of the Australian economy, and in the 1988 documentation of the NIF-88 model. The TRYM model incorporates the best features of the NIF-88 model but it is more focussed than its predecessors on developing a framework for policy analysis. The model can be used for a wide range of different policy simulations including fiscal and monetary policies, wages, productivity improvements, international linkages between Australia and its major trading partners, and the impact of higher efficiency on the macroeconomy. In addition, the TRYM model can also be used to analyse recent economic developments and as an input into macroeconomic forecasting.

2 The Structure of the TRYM Model

The TRYM model has a core of key macroeconomic relationships that are estimated using historical data wherever possible. These are linked together by a larger number of accounting identities. In particular, there are 23 estimated equations, 3 financial market identities, 2 default response functions for monetary and fiscal policy and about 100 identities linking these key variables. A key feature of the TRYM model is its focus on the main macroeconomic linkages in the Australian economy. Wherever possible, the behaviour of economic variables has been analysed in aggregate rather than in terms of individual components, with the result that the TRYM model is smaller than its predecessors. This has a number of advantages. A smaller model is easier to understand and is more transparent, which is important when it is being used for policy analysis. A smaller model is

[1]The authors would like to acknowledge the substantial contributions in developing the model from Mark Upcher and Brett Ryder. We are also grateful to Barry Gray, Michael Kouparitsas and Melvino Mangolini for their assistance.

[2]A full set of the documentation can be obtained by wirting to the Treasury, Modelling Section.

also easier to maintain, and has greater flexibility in policy and simulation analysis because assumptions can be changed easily and quickly. Finally, by making the TRYM model smaller, it has been easier to maintain a balance between the results implied by the data and the underlying economic theory.

Effort has been directed to making the TRYM model as internally consistent as possible, with many equations being jointly specified and estimated. Separate demand and supply curves have been identified, where possible. Equations are estimated for the key components of the expenditure side of the National Accounts, namely consumption, business and dwelling investment, farm and non-farm stockbuilding, commodity and non-commodity exports, and imports. Relative price equations for these components are estimated, with the exception of stockbuilding. Other important equations are for wage inflation, producer prices, private employment and labour supply. Accompanying attachments provide a listing of the behavioural equations and their estimated results, as well as the mnemonics.

Diagram 1 below summarises the key linkages in the real economy in the TRYM mode.

Diagram 1. The Linkages in the TRYM Model

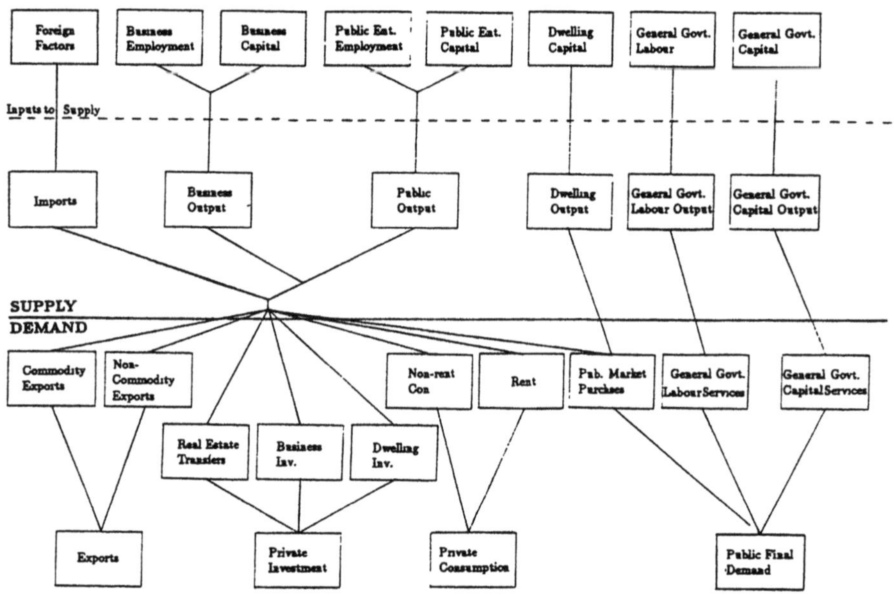

3 Sectoral Overview

There are six sectors of the economy identified in the TRYM model. They are the private business sector, the household sector, the public sector, the international sector, the financial sector, and the stock building sector.

The Private Business sector is specified as including all private, non-dwelling production. The main focus in this sector is to ensure a consistent approach is taken in analysing the factors influencing supply. Three are jointly specified and estimated: the demand for labour by private businesses; business fixed investment; and the price of non-commodities (the domestic price of commodities is determined by international commodity markets). A representative firm is assumed to maximise profits by producing goods and services using a specified technology, capital and labour as the only inputs into a CES production process. Imported goods and service are assumed to be 'final goods' and are therefore not included as inputs into the production process.

The production process determines the key factors influencing labour demand, investment and prices in long run equilibrium. In the short to medium term, however, these key aggregates are assumed to adjust toward their equilibrium in accordance with adjustment costs, expectations and the extent of any aggregate demand-supply imbalances. For example, an aggregate demand shock will affect labour demand relatively quickly, with prices adjusting with more delay and business capital adjusting only gradually.

Labour demand is affected by average hours worked as well as the number of people employed. This measure of labour demand captures the dominant sectoral trend decline in average hours worked over the 1970s and 1980s, arising partly from a shift to part time work. In both the short and long run, labour demanded by private sector firms is a function of the demand for business output, real wages and the underlying efficiency of labour. An increase in the demand for output increases the level of labour demanded, while an increase in real wages results in a fall in labour demand.

The price equation in the private business sector only relates to non-commodity prices. The price of commodities is determined by the price Australian exporters of commodities receive on world markets and is determined as part of the international sector. This distinction was made because non-commodity prices are sticky, while commodity prices are assumed to be flexible and to clear the market for commodities. In this way, the features of the 'Neo-classical' commodity sector are combined with a more 'Keynesian' non-commodity sector.

Non-commodity prices have considerable inertia. The growth in non-commodity prices will move in response to changes in demand and supply. Excess demand will increase inflation and excess supply will reduce it. Hence supply is measured as a function of capital, wages and efficiency. Changes in wage inflation have a large effect on price inflation through this channel. Changes in import prices also affect non-commodity prices in the short run.

In the long run, business investment ensures that capital grows in line with adult population and underlying productivity. In the short run, investment is affected by a range of other factors. First, it is assumed that the relationship between demand and supply (which may be interpreted as capacity utilisation) impacts on investment decisions. The relationship between the expected rate of return on an investment and the cost of borrowing funds for investment (the Q ratio) is assumed to impact on investment decisions. In this way, the level of real wages, inflationary expectations, long term interest rates and efficiency all affect the decision to invest. However, investment may be constrained by insufficient demand and spare capacity in the short run, even if it is expected to be profitable over the longer term.

The Household Sector The household sector in the TRYM model can be divided into two subsectors: household decisions about consumption, savings and labour supply; and the dwellings sector.

Consumption, Wages and Labour Supply Household decisions concerning consumption also affect savings. Households choose their level of consumption and their level of participation in the workforce. To quantify these decisions, factors determining the behaviour of wages, total private consumption and labour supply are examined in detail.

Total private consumption is driven in the long run by real after tax income and real private wealth. The inclusion of wealth provides a channel through which fluctuations in the property and financial markets can influence consumption behaviour. For example, a real increase in the value of dwellings or business assets, which together account for about 80 per cent of wealth, will increase the level of consumption. The measure of income includes labour income (wages) and government transfers. In the short run, changes in the unemployment rate also affect consumption, capturing the impacts that labour market conditions have on consumer confidence. The data determines that the adjustment of consumption toward its long run equilibrium is slow. This sluggish adjustment is expected given the general tendency of households to smooth consumption patterns and consumer uncertainty about whether changes in conditions will be permanent.

Labour supply is analysed by relating the participation rate to the level of employment (capturing the so-called encouraged worker effect), real wages and average hours worked. Also captured by the analysis is the general trend in the participation rate due to a combination of social and demographic factors in the 1970s and 1980s. These factors include demographic changes, increases in the female participation rate, falling male participation rates on account of earlier retirement and longer periods spent in higher education and the increasing availability of part time work. The small positive income effect on the participation rate was also found. However, movements in the participation rate appear to be dominated by the encouraged worker effect, with a 1 per cent increase in the employment to population ratio quickly leading to about a 1/2 per cent increase in the participation rate.

As with many macroeconometric models, an expectations augmented Phillips Curve is used to explain the behaviour of wages in equilibrium; the difference between the actual rate of unemployment and the non accelerating inflation rate of unemployment (NAIRU) therefore determines the long run level of wages. The NAIRU used in the model has been estimated from historical data commencing in the early 1970s, and an exogenous upward shift in the NAIRU in 1974 is suggested[3]. In the short to medium term, wage inflation is closely tied to price inflation and the acceleration of business output. An attempt is also made to incorporate some of the effects that varying degrees of centralisation of the wages system have had on wages growth since the early 1970s.

The Dwellings Sector The dwellings sector produces rental services from dwelling capital. Consistent with the current practice in the National Accounts, vacancy rates are ignored so that the consumption of rental services is equal to their production. The supply of rental services is essentially fixed in the short run because the supply of dwellings is fixed in the short run.

Once households have decided their total level of consumption, they choose between the consumption of rental services and 'other' consumption. In the short run, given that the supply of rental services is fixed, these preferences by households drive the relationship for the price of rents. If the demand for rental services increases relative to 'other' consumption, the price of rents will rise relative to the price of non-rent consumption. Changes in population growth rates are also assumed to impact on this relationship by affecting the demand for land in the short run.

Consistent with the deregulated financial sector, it has been assumed that the rate of return on investing in housing relative to the cost of borrowing funds (the Q ratio) is a key determinant of dwelling investment. The rate of return is assumed to be driven by the price received for rental services relative to the price of investment, while the cost of funds is calculated as a weighted average of short term and long term interest rates, adjusted for inflationary expectations.

The incentive to invest in housing, based on the rate of return and the cost of obtaining funds, affects investment with lags of up to one year or more. Both short term interest rates and long term rates determine the cost of funds for housing investment. The state of the labour market also affects dwelling investment.

The Public Sector The public sector is broken down into two subsectors: the government enterprise sector (which consists of government business enterprises and government financial enterprises); and the general government sector (aggregated across all tiers of government).

---

[3] While general developments in the economy can have an impact on the NAIRU, indeed there can be differences between its short and long run levels, sensitivity analysis with the TRYM model is usually conducted by exogenously maintaining the NAIRU at its historically estimated level. This practice reflects an emphasis on macroeconomic issues, but should not be taken to infer that policies, particularly of a more microeconomic nature, will not have an influence on the future level of the NAIRU.

Government Enterprises Government Enterprises (GEs) are treated separately from private sector firms because they have had different objectives and behaviour over most of the historical period. Despite these differences, GEs are assumed to have the same underlying production process as private sector firms. GE's labour demand is largely determined by the available capital stock. Output is determined by demand in the short run, but is constrained by supply in the long run. Prices charged by GEs are assumed to move in line with prices charged by the private business sector.

General Government Sector The general government (GG) sector consists of three areas: expenditure, revenue and the public sector borrowing requirement (PSBR). The former two are analysed explicitly, with the PSBR being determined as a residual. The stock of public debt is determined, in turn, by the PSBR.

Real general government expenditure, with the exception of transfer payments, is usually set exogenously. Transfers payments include expenditure on unemployment benefits, other personal payments, net interest payments, transfers to non profit institutions for consumption purposes, and transfers overseas. Indirect tax rates are fixed, so that this source of revenue only fluctuates with changes in the tax base. The incidence of the indirect taxes is consistent with Treasury's microeconomic model, PRISMOD.

Once the expenditure and revenue decisions have been determined, the PSBR is derived. It is split into debt issued domestically, overseas in Australian dollars and overseas in foreign currencies, and revenue from overseas reserve assets.

The International Sector

Exports In the TRYM model exports are separated into commodity exports (consisting primarily of mining and agricultural products) and non-commodity exports (consisting primarily of manufactured goods and services).

Foreign demand for our exports depends on our external competitiveness - the price of Australian exports relative to the price of substitutes on world markets. Demand rises as our export prices fall relative to world prices or, more specifically, as our export prices fall relative to the price of goods and services produced by other countries that are competing with Australia on world markets.

The supply of exports is driven by internal competitiveness, or the ability of the traded sector to attract resources from the non-traded sector. Domestic (internal) producers move resources into the production of exports when there is an increase in the domestic prices of traded goods relative to non-traded goods.

To capture the impacts of the two different types of cost competitiveness, exports are examined using a simple demand and supply framework. This framework recognises that the demand and supply elasticities for exports of commodities and non-commodities differ substantially.

For commodity exports, Australia is a small open economy where commodity export prices are determined by world prices. Exporters of Australian commodities are price takers in the international market place. This implies that the demand curve for Australian commodity exports is infinitely elastic and therefore the volume of commodities exported is supply determined. Attention is also given to links between the growth of Australia's major trading partners and the price and volume of our exports. Among other things, this linkage gives the TRYM model the capacity to examine the relationship between Australia's growth and that of its major trading partners.

Many domestic producers of non-commodities export only a small proportion of their total output. Therefore, foreigners can change their demand for Australia's exports without affecting the price. This implies that the supply curve for Australian non-commodity exports is infinitely elastic. The volume of non-commodity exports is demand determined with external competitiveness being the major factor.

Imports Imports of goods and services is also modelled using a demand and supply framework, with the demand equation determining the quantity of goods imported and the supply equation determining import prices.

The primary factors determining the demand for imports are changes in the level and composition of domestic activity and the price competitiveness of imports.

The supply of imports is infinitely elastic in the long run, since Australia is a small economy that cannot influence world prices. This treatment of import supply is consistent with the treatment of non-commodity exports supply. The price of imports is modelled as a function of world prices, the exchange rate, and the world price of oil.

The Financial Sector The financial sector, which includes relationships for interest rates, the yield curve, inflationary expectations and the exchange rate, is one of the most difficult areas to model satisfactorily. This is due to the combination of a number of difficulties. There is little consensus on the best way to represent these relationships at the theoretical level, although there are various working hypotheses. The expectations variables that are thought to be important are not measured with series like the expectations of inflation being measured for the household sector rather than the financial sector. The changes in these relationships - especially flowing from financial market deregulation - mean that, even if theory and data were available, they may only be relevant to the environment of recent years.

Given these difficulties and the desirability of keeping the TRYM model as simple and transparent as possible, the specification of the financial sector is largely based on theoretical considerations.

Interest Rates Short term interest rates are determined by the money supply and transactions demand within the economy. This relationship effectively acts as a default monetary policy response mechanism and does not necessarily represent our view of how monetary policy actually works, but is merely a simple, transparent and stable way of allowing interest rates to respond to changes in the economy.

Long term interest rates can be simulated using either model consistent or backward looking expectations. In the equation using backward looking expectations, long term interest rates are determined by short term interest rates, world long term interest rates and expectations of inflation in a way that gives plausible simulation results.

Exchange Rate and Expectations of Inflation Empirically, it has been difficult for the economics profession to obtain satisfactory explanations for the behaviour of the exchange rate. Theory suggests that expected exchange rate movements should be related to the difference between domestic and overseas interest rates using an interest parity condition. The main problem is determining the expected exchange rate.

There is an equilibrium exchange rate implicit in the TRYM model that is calculated numerically using a steady state analogue of TRYM. This exchange rate achieves internal balance and a stable ratio of net external liabilities to GDP when the economy is in equilibrium. Using the interest parity condition, the current value of the exchange rate is determined by its equilibrium value and the difference between real long term bond rates in Australia and overseas. Under this framework, a whole range of factors can influence the current exchange rate through the equilibrium exchange rate. Fluctuations in the terms of trade today, for example, will impact on the equilibrium exchange rate and therefore the current exchange rate.

Inflationary expectations are measured in history by the difference between the yield on non-indexed and indexed 10 year Treasury bonds. To be consistent with the behaviour of the exchange rate, it has been assumed that the equilibrium price level used to determine the equilibrium exchange rate is known and expectations of inflation are determined by the difference between this future price level and prices today.

Stockbuilding and the Relative Price Block

Stockbuilding The analysis of farm and non-farm stocks is undertaken separately. Both are examined relative to sales. Particular attention is given to the trend decline in the non-farm stocks to sales ratio over the past fifteen years, which appears to have occurred at least partly in response to the introduction of computer technology and better stock management techniques. Higher or lower than average growth in imports is also found to have had an impact on the non-farm stocks to sales ratio. Farm stocks are analysed as part of exportable commodity production, so that fluctuations in commodity output have an impact on the stocks to sales ratio. Weather conditions also affect farm stockbuilding.

The Determination of Relative Prices Particular effort has been made to determine the relative prices of the major expenditure aggregates. These respond differently to a variety of factors, particularly changes in import prices, partly reflecting the different import penetration ratios for the various expenditure aggregates. Linking changes in relative domestic prices to changes in import prices ensures that there is a link between changes in relative expenditure prices and changes in the exchange rate.

The estimated results show that of the major expenditure categories, the order of import penetration ratios from highest to lowest is business investment; government purchases; private consumption and dwelling investment. This implicit ranking in the price data is the same as that found in the Treasury's microeconomic model, PRISMOD.

4 Overview of the TRYM Model Properties

TRYM is a small aggregate quarterly econometric model of the Australian macroeconomy. Its specification of estimated equations are based on theoretical and data considerations. Overall, the TRYM model can be described as having a mixture of 'Neo-Classical' and 'Keynesian' properties. 'Keynesian' properties are exhibited in the short run, with output being demand determined and prices relatively sticky. More 'Neo-Classical' properties are exhibited in the long run as markets clear and firms optimise.

In the short run, production in the economy is largely demand driven, with any disequilibrium between demand and supply affecting the rate of inflation. The labour market does not necessarily clear in the short run, but any gap between labour supply and demand affects real wages. Households and firms generally make decisions based on current and past information in a way that is consistent with macroeconomic theory. Adjustment toward any level of price or quantity desired by households or firms is usually accomplished only over some period of time. One key exception is that financial markets exhibit some forward looking behaviour. In particular, financial markets are assumed to anticipate the effects of known developments in the economy, such as fluctuations in the terms of trade, on the future equilibrium exchange rate. They use this information in determining the current exchange rate.

In the long run, production is determined by the supply of inputs, with firms setting prices that equate demand and supply for any given level of employment and capital. The supply of factors is influenced by factor incomes, the cost of funds and the 'natural' rate of unemployment. Similarly, households make 'optimal' decisions given income and relative prices. Both flows (such as consumption) and stocks (such as private sector wealth) are at their desired levels in the long run. Perfect capital mobility is assumed in the long run, ensuring that domestic interest rates are determined by world interest rates and any difference between world and domestic inflation. In the long run the economy grows along a balanced, stable path determined by the growth of factor inputs and productivity. The adjustment path from the short run to the long run is characterised by a series of damped oscillations. These oscillations reflect the business cycles observed in the economy. The TRYM model also has a steady-state representation of the long run behaviour of the economy. This shows what the structure of the economy would be if adjustment to equilibrium was simultaneous and instantaneous in all sectors of the economy.

5 Model Simulation of a Productivity Shock

Nature of the Simulation The simulation experiment reported here consists of a one off, one percent increase in the growth rate of Harrod neutral technical efficiency. This permanent increase in the level of labour efficiency is broadly based, affecting all sectors of the economy except the general government sector. Fiscal policy operates to maintain a constant public debt to GDP ratio, while monetary policy targets a constant level of transactions demand.

The increase in labour efficiency is assumed to be accompanied by a simultaneous 0.5 per cent increase in nominal wages. The shock is completely unanticipated. Once it has occurred however, the financial markets calculate the effects that it will have on the economy and adjust their long run values for the exchange rate and the price level accordingly.

Short Run Effects A rise in labour efficiency increases aggregate supply increase while demand remains largely unchanged. Lower prices also reduce nominal transactions demand, enabling interest rates and the exchange rate to fall causing an improvement in international competitiveness.

Medium to Long Run Effects Lower interest rates, higher real incomes and lower real unit labour costs stimulate activity, particularly investment. The increase in demand cause prices to stop falling after the third year of the simulation. The higher level of transactions demand increases interest rates, that serves to slow the economy as it begins to accelerate. The current account and net foreign liabilities are broadly unchanged. Ten years after the shock the economy is still a long way from its long run equilibrium, due to the slow rate of adjustment of the capital stock.

The long run gains from the higher level of underlying productivity are considerable. They include higher GDP and incomes. If households respond to the higher wages by increasing their willingness to work, as in this simulation, then higher employment will also result. The simulation also shows that the community generally enjoys lower prices, lower inflation and lower tax rates. Australia's trading partners also benefit from a higher level of underlying productivity through a lower relative price of Australia's export.

The following table and charts summarise the results of the simulation.

Table 1. Effects of Higher Efficiency under Slow Adjustment Assumptions

Deviations from Control (per cent)

Number of Years after Initial Efficiency Rise	1	2	3	4	6	8	10	Long Run
Consumption	0.1	0.2	0.6	0.9	1.1	0.9	0.9	1.3
Bus. Invest.	-1.3	-0.5	1.7	2.6	0.8	0.3	0.6	1.1
Dwelling Invest.	0.1	1.6	3.4	2.7	-0.1	-0.2	0.3	1.4
Public Demand	0.0	0.0	0.0	0.0	0.0	0.0	0.0	0.0
GNE	-0.1	0.3	0.9	1.2	0.7	0.6	0.6	1.1
Exports	0.2	0.5	0.9	1.2	1.2	1.2	1.1	1.1
Imports	-0.6	-0.3	0.5	0.9	0.6	0.5	0.5	0.8
GDP	0.0	0.4	1.0	1.2	0.9	0.7	0.7	1.2
Employment	-0.2	-0.3	0.1	0.4	0.3	0.1	0.1	0.2
Labour Supply	-0.1	-0.1	0.0	0.3	0.3	0.1	0.1	0.2
Unemployment	0.1	0.2	0.0	-0.2	-0.1	0.0	0.0	0.0
Productivity (L)	0.3	0.7	0.9	0.7	0.5	0.6	0.7	1.0
Nominal Wages	0.1	-0.7	-1.0	-0.7	0.0	0.1	-0.1	-0.2
Cons. Deflator	-0.4	-1.0	-1.3	-1.2	-0.6	-0.5	-0.6	-1.1
GDP Deflator	-0.3	-1.0	-1.4	-1.2	-0.6	-0.5	-0.7	-1.1
Terms of Trade	-0.4	-0.8	-0.9	-0.6	-0.1	-0.1	-0.2	-0.2
90 day bill rate	-0.3	-0.5	-0.2	0.1	0.1	0.0	0.0	0.0
10 year bond	-0.1	-0.1	0.0	0.0	0.0	0.0	0.0	0.0
Exchange Rate	-0.4	-0.3	0.4	0.8	0.5	0.4	0.4	0.8
Private Wealth	0.8	0.9	0.2	-0.4	0.1	0.4	0.5	0.2
CAD	-0.2	-0.2	0.0	0.1	-0.1	-0.1	-0.1	0.0

Note: Productivity (L) refers to labour productivity.
Interest rates and unemployment rate are expressed in percentage point deviations.

Chart 1: GDP(A)
(Deviation from Baseline)

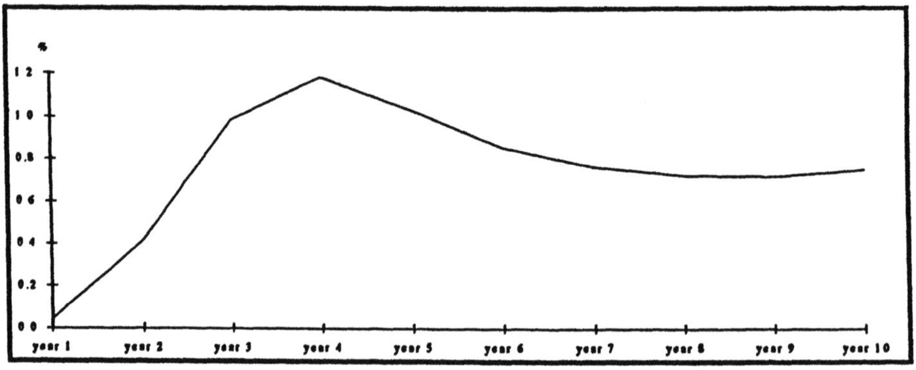

Chart 2: Business Investment
(Deviation from Baseline)

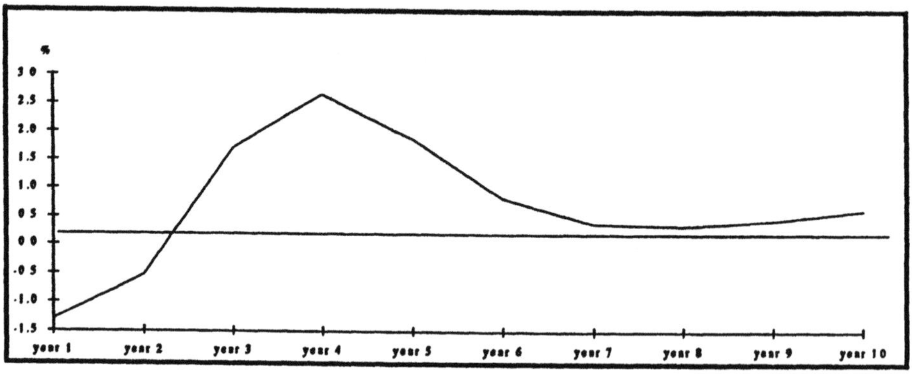

Chart 3: Employment
(Deviation from Baseline)

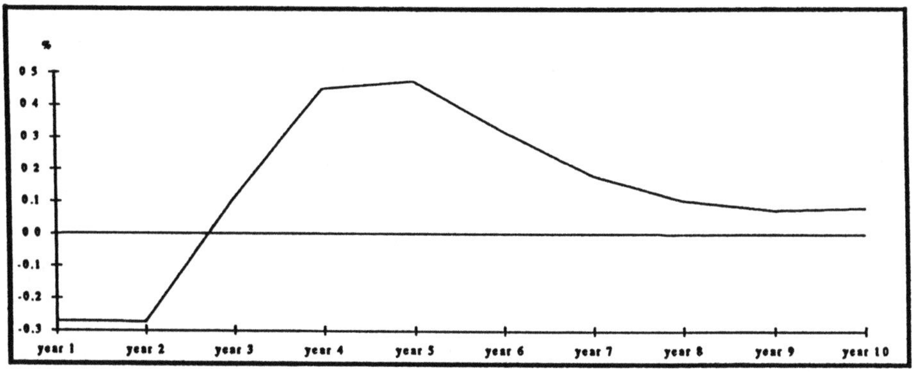

6 Conclusion

The new Treasury Macroeconomic (TRYM) Model of the Australian economy was released at a public conference in late June 1993. The model documentation is based upon research and development work undertaken in recent years in the Modelling Section of the Treasury. It has been released in the interests of evaluating the research results embodied within the model and to encourage public discussion. We feel the TRYM model in its current state is a useful resource for the Treasury and the economics profession more generally. However, there is still room for further development and refinement which will continue as part of the on-going research effort within the Treasury.

References

[1] Treasury (1981) "The NIF-10 Model of the Australian Economy," AGPS.

[2] Simes, R. M., P. M. Horn and M. Kouparitsas (1988) "Equation Listing for the NIF88 Model," mimeo. Background Paper No.2 for the Conference of the Australian Macroeconomy and the NIF88 Model, 14-15 March 1988, CEPR, ANU.

[3] Dixon, P. B., B. R. Parmenter, J. Sutton and D. P. Vincent (1982) "ORANI: A Multisectoral Model of the Australian Economy," North Holland, Amsterdam.

[4] Henry, K. R. and J. S. Wright (1992) "PRISMOD - Development, Database and Methodology," Paper presented for the Australasian Economic Modelling Conference, September 2-5.

[5] Higgins, C. I. and V. W. FitzGerald (1973) "An Econometric Model of the Australian Economy," Journal of Econometrics, 1:229-265.

[6] McKibbin, W. J. and J. D. Sachs (1991) "Global Linkages - Macroeconomic Interdependence and Cooperation in the World Economy," The Brookings Institution, Washington D.C.

[7] Murphy, C. W. (1992) "Access Economics Murphy Model - The Model in Detail (version 2.1)," Access Economics Murphy Model - User's Guide.

[8] Murphy, C. W., I. A. Bright, R. J. Brooker, W. D. Geeves and B. K. Taplin (1986) "A Macroeconomic Model of the Australian Economy for Medium-Term Policy Analysis," Office of the Economic Planning Advisory Council.

[9] Taplin, B., P. Jilek, L. Antioch, A. Johnson, P. Parameswaran and C. Louis (1993) "An Introduction to the Treasury Macroeconomic (TRYM) Model of the Australian Economy," (TRYM Paper No.1), Treasury Conference on TRYM Model of the Australian Economy

[10] Taplin, B., P. Jilek, L. Antioch, A. Johnson, P. Parameswaran and C. Louis (1993) "Documentation of the Treasury Macroeconomic (TRYM) Model of the Australian Economy," (TRYM Paper No.2, Treasury Conference on TRYM Model of the Australian Economy

[11] Taplin, B. and P. Parameswaran (1993) "Employment, Investment Inflation and Productivity: Decisions by the Firm," (TRYM Paper No.3), Treasury Conference on TRYM Model of the Australian Economy

[12] Jilek, P., A. Johnson and B. Taplin (1993) "Exports, Imports and the Trade Balance," (TRYM Paper No.4), Treasury Conference on TRYM Model of the Australian Economy

[13] Antioch, L., and B. Taplin (1993) "Savings, Dwelling Investment and the Labour Market: Decisions by Households", (TRYM Paper No.5), Treasury Conference on TRYM Model of the Australian Economy

[14] Ryder, B., A. Johnson, B. Taplin and P. Jilek (1993) "Australia's Trade Linkages with the World," (TRYM Paper No.6), Treasury Conference on TRYM Model of the Australian Economy

[15] Taplin, B., and C. Louis (1993) "The Macroeconomic Effects of Higher Productivity," (TRYM Paper No.7), Treasury Conference on TRYM Model of the Australian Economy

Appendix

A Equations of TRYM Model

The Private Business Sector

Labour Demand

(1) $$\Delta\log NB = \Delta_8\frac{\log NAP}{8} - A2LD * CSIG * (\Delta\log\frac{WBH * RTPRB}{PGB}$$

$$-\frac{CLAM}{4}) + A3LD * \Delta\log\frac{GBA}{KB_{-1}} - (1 - A5LD) * \Delta\log NH_{-1}$$

$$- A0LD * (\frac{\log NB_{-1}}{GBA_{-1}} + \log NH - CSIG * \log CLAB$$

$$+ CSIG * (\log(WBH_{-1} * \frac{RTPRB_{-1}}{PGB_{-1}}) - CLAM * QTIME_{-1})$$

$$+ CLAM * QTIME_{-1})$$

Results

Sample: 70(2)-92(4) SE = 0.54% DW = 1.84

Parameter	Estimate	t-Statistic
A2LD	0.147	3.12
CSIG	0.755	19.24
CLAM	0.011	8.35
A5LD	0.706	3.90
A3LD	0.130	3.60
A0LD	0.245	10.94

Non-Commodity Prices

(2) $$\Delta\log PNC = A0PNC * \Delta\log PSTAR + (1 - A0PNC - A2PNC$$

$$- A3PNC - A4PNC - A5PNC) * \Delta\log PSTAR_{-1}$$

$$+ A2PNC * \Delta\log PSTAR_{-2} + A3PNC * \Delta\log PSTAR_{-3}$$

$$+ A4PNC * \Delta\log PSTAR_{-4} + A5PNC * \Delta\log PSTAR_{-5}$$

$$- A6PNC * \Delta\log PMGS + A6PNC * \Delta\log PMGS_{-1}$$

$$+ C0PNC * (\log PSTAR_{-6} - \log PNC_{-6})$$

Results

Sample: 70(2)-92(4) SE = 1.3% DW = 1.92

Parameter	Estimate	t-Statistic
A0PNC	0.323	6.06
A2PNC	-0.057	-1.05
A3PNC	0.109	1.99
A4PNC	0.189	3.59
A5PNC	0.169	3.19
C0PNC	0.036	2.10
A6PNC	0.143	4.06
CKAP	0.404	9.52

Investment

$$(3) \quad \frac{IB}{KB_{-1}} = RDKB + GR + C0IB * (\frac{IB_{-1}}{KB_{-2}} - RDKB_{-1} - GR_{-1})$$

$$+ C01IB * (\frac{IB_{-2}}{KB_{-3}} - RDKB{-2} - GR_{-2})$$

$$+ C02IB * (\frac{IB_{-3}}{KB_{-4}} - RDKB_{-3} - GR_{-3})$$

$$+ C5IB * (QRAT_{-2} + (XRITC_{-2} - 1))$$

$$+ C3IB * \log \frac{GBA}{YSTAR} + C4IB * DMIN$$

Results

Sample: 70(2)-92(4) SE = 0.17% DW = 1.79

Parameter	Estimate	t-Statistic
C0IB	0.544	5.48
C01IB	0.365	3.19
C02IB	-0.179	-1.77
RISK	2.119	0.75
C5IB	0.004	2.85
C3IB	0.0465	4.92
C4IB	0.001	1.84
CLAB	0.353	6.21

The Household Sector

Labour Supply

$$(4)\quad \Delta \log \frac{NLF * NHLR}{NAP} = A1LS * \Delta \log \frac{NT}{NAP} - A2LS * \Delta \log \frac{NT_{-2}}{NAP_{-2}}$$

$$- A3LS * (\log(NLF_{-1} * \frac{NHLR_{-1}}{NAP_{-1}}) + C1LS$$

$$- C2LS * \log(NT_{-1} * \frac{NHLR_{-1}}{NAP_{-1}})$$

$$- C3LS * (\log((1 - RTN_{-1}) * \frac{WT_{-1}}{NH_{-1}} * PCON_{-1})$$

$$- CLAM * QTIME_{-1})$$

$$- C4LS * D80_{-1} * (QTIMF_{-1} + 10.725)$$

$$- C5LS * QTIMF_{-1})$$

Results
Sample 76(1)-92(4) SE = 0.26% DW = 1.84

Parameter	Estimate	t-Statistic
A1LS	0.552	10.02
A2LS	0.158	2.70
A3LS	0.384	5.59
C1LS	0.369	7.29
C2LS	0.528	13.32
C3LS	0.0741	3.21
C4LS	0.00693	7.18
C5LS	0.00326	4.27

Wages

$$(5)\quad \Delta \log \frac{WT}{NH} = \frac{CLAM}{4} + (1 - A1WT) * \Delta \log PCON$$

$$+ A1WT * \Delta \log PCON_{-1}$$

$$+ A2WT * (\Delta \log GBA - \Delta \log GBA_{-1})$$

$$- (A3WT * DCC) * \Delta RNU_{-1} - A4WT * (DCC - DCC_{-4})$$

$$+ A5WT * \frac{1}{RNU} * (NAIRU * (1 - QS741)$$

$$+ NAIRU0 * QS741 - RNU)$$

Results

Sample: 70(1)-92(4) SE = 1.2% DW = 2.17

Parameter	Estimate	t-Statistic
A1WT	0.405	2.47
A2WT	0.108	1.88
A3WT	0.123	2.22
A4WT	0.0157	2.55
A5WT	0.0128	3.51
NAIRU	7.032	8.70
NAIRU0	3.111	5.34

Private Final Consumption

(6) $$\log CON = (1 - A0CON) * \log CON_{-1}$$

$$+ A0CON * (\log C0CON + \log(\frac{YLZ}{PCON}$$

$$+ C1CON * \frac{WMZ_{-1}}{PCON})) + A2CON * (RNU - RNU_{-4})$$

Results

Sample: 80(1)-92(4) SE = 0.69% DW = 2.22

Parameter	Estimate	t-Statistic
AOCON	0.209	3.71
A2CON	-0.002	-2.74
C0CON	0.812	15.96
C1CON	0.0132	3.80

The Demand for Rental Services

(7) $$\Delta \log \frac{PCRE}{PCNR} = A2PCR * \Delta \log \frac{CNR}{CRE} - A0PCR * (log \frac{PCRE_{-1}}{PCNR_{-1}}$$

$$- C0PCR - \frac{1}{CDWSIG} * \log \frac{CNR_{-1}}{CRE_{-1}})$$

Results

Sample 82(3)-92(2) SE = 0.49% DW = 1.83

Parameter	Estimate	t-Statistic
A0PCR	0.111	2.74
A2PCR	0.439	4.24
C0PCR	-1.700	-1.50
CDWSIG	0.886	1.49

Dwelling Investment

$$(8)\quad \frac{IDW}{KDW_{-1}} = (\exp GR - 1 + RDKDW) * (1 - A1DW - A2DW - A3DW$$

$$- A4DW) + A1DW * \frac{IDW_{-1}}{KDW_{-2}} + A2DW * \frac{IDW_{-2}}{KDW_{-3}}$$

$$+ A3DW * \frac{IDW_{-3}}{KDW_{-4}} + A4DW * \frac{IDW_{-4}}{KDW_{-5}}$$

$$+ A0DW * QRATH + A0DW * QRATH_{-1}$$

$$+ A0DW * QRATH_{-2} + A0DW * QRATH_{-3}$$

$$+ A0DW * QRATH_{-4} + A5DW * (RNU - NAIRU)$$

Results

Sample: 86(1)-92(4) SE = 0.26% DW = 1.69

Parameter	Estimate	t-Statistic
A0DW	0.000339	3.28
A1DW	0.417	2.39
A2DW	0.521	3.17
A3DW	-0.0314	-0.22
A4DW	-0.256	-2.11
A5DW	-0.0000959	-2.41
C1DW	0.351	3.04

Public Sector

Government Enterprise Labour Demand

$$(9)\quad \Delta\log(NGE * \frac{NH}{KGE_{-1}}) = -C2NG * \Delta QTIME - \frac{CLAM}{4}$$

$$+ A1NG * (\Delta\log(NGE_{-1} * \frac{NH_{-1}}{KGE_{-2}})$$

$$+ C2NG * (\Delta QTIME + \frac{CLAM}{4})$$

$$+ A2NG * (C1NG - C2NG * QTIME_{-1}$$

$$- CLAM * QTIME_{-1}$$

$$- log(NGE_{-1} * \frac{NH_{-1}}{KGE_{-2}}))$$

Results
Sample: 70(1)-92(4) SE = 0.83% DW = 1.99

Parameter	Estimate	t-Statistic
A1NG	0.385	3.91
A2NG	0.140	3.22
C1NG	-6.15	648.8
C2NG	0.024	25.84

Government Enterprise Output

(10) $\Delta \log GGE = GR + C00LG$

$$+ A1LG * (\log \frac{GB + GGE}{GB_{-1} + GGE_{-1} * \exp C00LG} - GR)$$

$$+ A2LG * (\log \frac{GB_{-1} + GGE_{-1}}{GB_{-2} + GGE_{-2} * \exp C00LG} - GR_{-1}$$

$$- C00LG) + A3LG * (\log GGE_{-1} - \log GGE_{-2} - GR_{-1}$$

$$- C00LG) + A0LG * (\log(C0LG + C00LG * QTIME)$$

$$+ \frac{CSIG}{CSIG - 1} * \log(CLAB * (NGE_{-1} * NH_{-1}$$

$$* \exp(CLAM * QTIME_{-1}))^{1-\frac{1}{CSIG}} + CKAP * KGE_{-2}^{1-\frac{1}{CSIG}})$$

$$- \log GGE_{-1})$$

Results
Sample: 70(1)-92(4) SE = 1.4% DW = 1.98

Parameter	Estimate	t-Statistic
A1LG	0.765	7.78
A2LG	-0.235	-1.90
A3LG	0.283	2.71
A0LG	0.145	2.75
C0LG	3.132	10.43
C00LG	0.053	8.72

The Default Fiscal Policy Response Mechanism

$$(11)\quad Deficit\,to\,GDP\,ratio = \frac{1}{GTMAZ} * (WDGOAZ + WDGOFZ$$

$$+ WDGPZ - WDOGFZ$$

$$(12)\quad \Delta RTN = 0.12 * \frac{1}{GTMAZ} * (WDGOAZ + WDGOFZ + WDGPZ$$

$$- WDOGFZ) - XRWDGT - \frac{1}{GTMAZ_{-1}} * (WDGOAZ_{-1}$$

$$+ WDGOFZ_{-1} + WDGPZ_{-1} - WDOGFZ_{-1}) - XRWDGT_{-1}$$

$$- XRUBR * 0.01 * (RNU - NAIRU) * NLF * \frac{PCON}{GTMAZ}$$

$$- RTN_{-1} * 0.01 * (RNU - NAIRU) * NLF * \frac{1}{GTMAZ}$$

$$* (WT + QTCB * XRUBR * PCON) + 0.007 * \frac{1}{GTMAZ}$$

$$* (WDGOAZ + WDGOFZ + WDGPZ$$

$$- WDOGFZ) - XRWDGT)$$

The International Sector

Commodity Export Demand

$$(13)\quad \Delta\log(PXC * \frac{RTWI}{WPGTM}) = A0PXC * (\Delta\log WGTM - GR$$

$$+ \Delta\log WGTM_{-1} - GR_{-1} + \Delta\log WGTM_{-2}$$

$$- GR_{-2} + \Delta\log WGTM_{-3} - GR_{-3})$$

$$+ A1PXC * \Delta\log\frac{WPMPE}{WPGTM}$$

$$+ A2PXC * \Delta\log(RTWI * \frac{PGTMA}{WPGTM})$$

$$+ A3PXC * (\log(PXC_{-1} * \frac{RTWI_{-1}}{WPGTM_{-1}})$$

$$- C0PXC - C1PXC * QTIME_{-1})$$

Results (from joint estimation of commodity demand and supply equations)

Sample: 75(1)-92(4) SE = 3.06% DW = 1.5

Parameter	Estimate	t-Statistic
A0PXC	0.710	2.44
A1PXC	0.158	5.80
A2PXC	0.250	constrained
A3PXC	-0.063	-2.35
C0PXC	1.418	4.84
C1PXC	-0.051	-4.20

Commodity Export Supply

(14) $\Delta \log(XC + SFM - QRAIN)$

$$= GR + \frac{C2XC}{4} * (1 - A2XC)$$

$$+ A1XC * \Delta \log(XC_{-1} + SFM_{-1} - QRAIN_{-1})$$

$$+ A2XC * (\log \frac{XC_{-1} + SFM_{-1} - QRAIN_{-1}}{YSTAR_{-1} - XC_{-1} - SFM_{-1} + QRAIN_{-1}} - C0XC$$

$$- C1XC * log(PXC_{-1} * \frac{1 - RTXC_{-1}}{PNC_{-1}} - C2XC * QTIME_{-1})$$

Results (from joint estimation of commodity demand and supply equations)
Sample: 75(1)-92(4) SE = 5.5% DW = 2.0

Parameter	Estimate	t-Statistic
A1XC	-0.293	-2.59
A2XC	-0.175	-4.04
C0XC	-1.548	-76.23
C1XC	0.516	6.04
C2XC	0.035	constrained

Non-Commodity Export Demand

(15) $\log \frac{XNC}{WGTM} = (1 - A0XNC - A1XNC) * \log \frac{XNC_{-1}}{WGTM_{-1}}$

$$+ A1XNC * \log \frac{XNC_{-3}}{WGTM_{-3}} + A0XNC$$

$$* (C0XNC - C1XNC * \log(PXNC * \frac{RTWI}{WPGTM}))$$

Results
Sample: 75(1)-92(4)

Parameter	Estimate	t-Statistic
A0XNC	0.081	2.38
A1XNC	0.238	2.79
C0XNC	6.962	5.28
C1XNC	1.748	2.96

Import Demand

$$(16)\ \Delta \log MGS = (GR + C2MGS * \Delta QTIME) * (1 - A3MGS - A4MGS)$$

$$+ A1MGS * (\Delta \log DDMGS - GR)$$

$$- A5MGS * C1MGS * \Delta \log(PMGS * \frac{1 + RTMGS}{PDDMGS})$$

$$+ A3MGS * \Delta \log MGS_{-2} + A4MGS * \Delta \log MGS_{-3}$$

$$- A5MGS * (\log \frac{MGS_{-1}}{DDMGS_{-1}} - C0MGS$$

$$+ C1MGS * \log(PMGS{-1} * \frac{1 + RTMGS_{-1}}{PDDMGS{-1}})$$

$$- C2MGS * QTIME_{-1})$$

Import Supply

$$(17)\ \log(PMGS * \frac{RTWI}{WPGTM})$$

$$= A1PM * \log(PMGS_{-1} * \frac{RTWI_{-1}}{WPGTM_{-1}})$$

$$+ (1 - A1PM) * (A0PM + A2PM * \log \frac{WPMPE}{WPGTM}$$

$$+\log XRWPXGS) + A3PM * \Delta_2 \frac{\log \frac{WPMPE}{WPGTM}}{2}$$

$$+ A4PM * \Delta \log(RTWI * \frac{PDDMGS}{WPGTM})$$

Joint Estimation Results

Sample: 78(1)-92(4) SE = 2.14% DW = 1.93

Parameter	Estimate	t-Statistic
A1MGS	1.698	8.67
A3MGS	0.247	3.41
A4MGS	0.200	2.59
A5MGS	0.515	6.77
C0MGS	0.0542	2.73
C1MGS	0.622	5.90
C2MGS	0.00571	3.42
A0PM	1.787	22.0
A1PM	0.879	23.9
A2PM	0.167	5.13
A3PM	0.047	2.54
A4PM	0.529	13.5

The Financial Sector

Money Demand

$$(18) \quad \Delta \log \frac{MTAZ}{PGNEA} = A1MD * (\Delta \log GNEA - GR)$$

$$+ A2MD * (\log(\frac{MTAZ_{-1}}{GNEAZ_{-1}}$$

$$- (-C0MD - C2MD * R90_{-1} + C3MD * D813_{-1}))$$

Results

Sample: 75(3)-92(4) SE = 1.96% DW = 1.97

Parameter	Estimate	t-Statistic
A1MD	0.747	3.85
A2MD	0.376	4.63
C0MD	0.833	17.6
C2MD	0.0124	3.88
C3MD	0.077	4.15

The Default Monetary Policy Response Mechanism

$$(19) \quad R90X = \frac{1}{C2MD} * (-\log \frac{MTAZ}{GNEAZ} - C0MD + C3MD * D813)$$

Exchange Rate Identity

$$(20)\quad RTWI = RTWIX(+40) * \exp(10 * \log(\frac{RGL - WRGL}{100} + 1))$$

Inflationary Expectations Identity

$$(21)\quad INFEXP = \exp\frac{\log\frac{PGNEAX(+40)}{\frac{GNEAZ}{GNEA}}}{10} * 100 - 100$$

Stocks and Relative Prices

Non-Farm Stockbuilding

$$(22)\quad \Delta\log KSN = GR + ADJ + A1KSN * (\log KSN_{-1} - logKSN_{-2}$$

$$- (GR_{-1} + ADJ_{-1})) + A2KSN * (\log\frac{MGS}{MGS_{-1}} - GR)$$

$$- A3KSN * (C0KSN + (\frac{C1KSN}{1 + \exp(-\frac{QTIME_{-1} - C2KSN}{C3KSN})}$$

$$- \log\frac{KSN_{-1}}{DDSNN_{-1}})$$

Results

Sample: 74(3)-92(4) SE = 0.75% DW = 2.23

Parameter	Estimate	t-Statistic
A1KSN	0.553	7.28
A2KSN	0.076	3.64
A3KSN	-0.200	-4.59
C0KSN	-0.278	-7.64
C1KSN	0.343	6.86
C2KSN	-4.662	-7.22
C3KSN	-2.920	-4.12

Farm Stockbuilding

$$(23)\quad \Delta\log KSFM = GR + \frac{C1SAG}{4} + A0SAG * (\Delta\log KSFM_{-1}$$

$$- (GR_{-1} + \frac{C1SAG}{4})) + A2SAG * (\Delta\log(XC + SFM)$$

$$- GR_{-1}) + A3SAG * RAIN_{-4} - A1SAG * (\log \frac{KSFM_{-2}}{XC_{-1}}$$

$$- C0SAG - C1SAG * QTIME_{-1})$$

Results
Sample: 74(3)-92(4) SE = 1.39% DW = 2.20

Parameter	Estimate	t-Statistic
C0SAG	0.756	22.63
C1SAG	-0.026	-5.91
A0SAG	0.710	7.97
A1SAG	0.071	2.94
A2SAG	0.210	7.99
A3SAG	-0.006	-3.59

Relative Prices

(24) $$\log \frac{PCNR}{PT} = \frac{A1 + A2 * QTIME + A3 * log(PMGS_{-1} * \frac{1+RTMGS_{-1}}{PD_{-1}})}{1 - RTCNR_{-1}}$$

(25) $$\log \frac{PIDW}{PT} = \frac{B1 + B2 * QTIME + B3 * \log(PMGS * \frac{1+RTMGS}{PD})}{1 - RTIDW}$$

$$+ B4 * \log \frac{PMGS_{-1} * \frac{1+RTMGS_{-1}}{PD_{-1}}}{1 - RTIDW_{-1}}$$

(26) $$\log \frac{PIRET}{PT} = C1 + C2 * QTIME + C3 * \log(PMGS * \frac{1 + RTMGS}{PD})$$

$$+ C4 * \log(PMGS_{-1} * \frac{1 + RTMGS_{-1}}{PD_{-1}})$$

(27) $$\log \frac{PIB}{PT} = \frac{D1 + D2 * QTIME + D3 * \log(PMGS_{-1} * \frac{1+RTMGS_{-1}}{PD_{-1}})}{1 - RTIB_{-1}}$$

(28) $$\log \frac{PGMD}{PT} = E1 + E2 * QTIME + E3 * \log(PMGS * \frac{1 + RTMGS}{PD})$$

Results
Sample: 80(1)-92(4) SE = 0.55% DW = 0.41

Parameter	Estimate	t-Statistic
A1	0.016	7.04
A2	-0.0006	-2.06
A3	-0.049	-5.52
B1	0.032	3.01
B2	0.002	1.85
B3	-0.110	-1.90
B4	-0.267	-4.54
C1	-0.208	-3.97
C2	0.043	6.69
C3	-0.528	-1.80
C4	0.702	2.50
D1	-0.048	-8.05
D2	-0.002	-2.43
D3	0.241	9.99
E1	-0.013	-1.68
E2	-0.006	-5.43
E3	0.110	3.41

Scaling Factor Equation

(29) sf

$$= \frac{pt(cnr + idw + ib + gmd + iret)}{pcnrf * cnr + pibf * ib + pidwf * idw + piretf * iret + pgmdf * gmd}$$

Scaled Price Equations

(30) $pcnr = pcnrf * sf$

(31) $pidw = pidwf * sf$

(32) $pib = pibf * sf$

(33) $piret = piretf * sf$

(34) $pgmd = pgmdf * sf$

Non-Commodity Stockbuilding

$$(35)\quad ksn = \exp(\log ksn_{-1} + gr + \frac{c1ksn}{1+\exp(-\frac{qtimf - c2ksn}{c3ksn})}$$

$$- \frac{c1ksn}{1+\exp(-\frac{qtimf_{-1} - c2ksn}{c3ksn})} + a1ksn * (\log \frac{ksn_{-1}}{ksn_{-2}} - (gr_{-1}$$

$$+ \frac{c1ksn}{1+\exp(-\frac{qtimf_{-1} - c2ksn}{c3ksn})} - \frac{c1ksn}{1+\exp(-\frac{qtimf_{-2} - c2ksn}{c3ksn})}))$$

$$+ a2ksn * (\log \frac{mgs}{mgs_{-1}} - gr) - a3ksn * (\log \frac{ksn_{-1}}{ddsnn_{-1}} - c0ksn$$

$$- \frac{c1ksn}{1+exp(-\frac{qtimf_{-1} - c2ksn}{c3ksn})}) + u_k sn)$$

Long-Term Interest Rate

$$(36)\quad rgl = rgl_{-1} + infexp - infexp_{-1}$$

$$+ a0rgl * ((\frac{mtaz}{mtaz_{-1} * \exp gr})^4 * 100 - 100 - infexp)$$

$$+ a1rgl * (r90x - infexp - (r90x_{-1} - infexp_{-1}))$$

$$- a2rgl * (r90x_{-1} - infexp_{-1} - (r90x_{-2} - infexp_{-2}))$$

$$+ a3rgl * (c1rgl * r90x_{-1} + (1 - c1rgl)$$

$$* (wrgl_{-1} - winfexp_{-1} + infexp_{-1}) - rgl(-1)) + u\_rgl$$

Short Run Supply of Output Identity

$$(37)\quad ystar = (clab * ((nb * nh) * \exp eff)^{-\frac{1-csig}{csig}} + ckap * kb_{-1}^{-\frac{1-csig}{csig}})^{-\frac{csig}{1-csig}}$$

$$(38)\quad ystwk = kb_{-1} * (\frac{1 - clab^{csig} * (wbh * \frac{\frac{rtprb}{pgb}}{\exp eff})^{1-csig}}{ckap})^{\frac{csig}{1-csig}}$$

Business Capital Stock Identity

$$(39)\quad kb = kb_{-1} * (1 - rdkb) + ib$$

Dwelling Capital Stock Identity

$$(40)\quad kdw = kdw_{-1} * (1 - rdkdw) + idw$$

Government Enterprise Capital Stock Identity

$$(41)\quad kge = kge_{-1} * (1 - rdkge) + ige$$

General Government Capital Stock

$$(42)\quad kgg = kgg_{-1} * (1 - rdkgg) + igg$$

Hourly Business Wage Identity

$$(43)\quad wbh = \frac{wt * (nb + nge + ngg + ndf)}{nh * (nb + xrwg * (nge + ngg + ndf))}$$

Unemployment Rate

$$(44)\quad rnu = 100 * \frac{nlf - (nb + nge + ngg)}{nlf}$$

Long-run Inflationary Expectations Identity

$$(45)\quad \inf\exp = (\exp \frac{\log \frac{pgneax(+40)\frac{gneax}{}}{gnea}}{10}) * 100 - 100$$

Agricultural Stocks Identity

$$(46)\quad sfm = ksfm - ksfm_{-1}$$

Non-commodity Stocks Identity

$$(47)\quad snn = ksn - ksn_{-1}$$

Production of Rent

$$(48)\quad cre = xrcre * kdw_{-1}$$

Business Sector Output at Factor Cost

$$(49)\quad gb = (con + ib + idw + iret + gfd + disa + snn + sfm + xnc + xc$$

$$- mgs) - xrgdw * cre - gge - (ngg + ndf) * \exp \frac{clam * qtime}{xrngg} - ggk$$

Stocks Generating Demand Identity

(50) $ddsnn = con + ib + idw + gmd + disa - xrcre * kdw_{-1}$

Labour Income Identity

(51) $ylz = (1 - rtn) * wt * (nb + nge + ngg + ndf) + xrocb * npop * pcon$

$+ xrubr * 0.01 * rnu * nlf * pcon$

Price of Consumption Identity

(52) $pcon = \dfrac{pcnr * (con - cre) + pcre * cre}{con}$

Government Market Demand Identity

(53) $gfd = (ngg + ndf) * \exp \dfrac{clam * qtime}{xrngg} + ggk + gmd$

Price of Stocks Generating Demand Identity

(54) $pddsnn = \dfrac{1}{ddsnn}(con * pcon - xrcre * kdw_{-1} * pcre + ib * pib$

(55) $+ idw * pidw + gmd * pgmd + disaz)$

Price of Non-commodity Stockbuilding Identity

(56) $psnn = xrpsnn * pddsnn$

Government Capital Production Identity

(57) $ggk = xrggk * rdkgg * kgg_{-1}$

Private Wealth at Market Value

(58) $wmz = xrwmz * (xrmtaz_{-1} * mtaz_{-1} + pib * kb_{-1} * qrat - wepoz_{-1}$

$- wdpoaz_{-1} - wdpofz_{-1} + pidw * kdw_{-1} * qrath + wdgpz_{-1} * rval$

$+ weopz_{-1} + ksn_{-1} * xrpksn * pddsnn + ksfm_{-1} * xrpksfm * pxc)$

Dwelling Sector Q-ratio

$$(59)\quad qrath = pcre * (1 - rtcre) * \frac{xrcre}{\frac{pidw}{\frac{rgl-infexp}{400}+rdkdw}}$$

Business Sector Q-ratio

$$(60)\quad qrat = \frac{1}{\frac{rgl-infexp+risk}{400}+rdkb}(ckap^{1+\frac{1}{csig-1}} * \frac{pgb}{pib} * (1 - clab^{csig}$$

$$* (wbh * \frac{rtprb}{\frac{pgb}{\exp eff}})^{1-csig})^{\frac{1}{1-csig}})$$

NPSBR Identity

$$(61)\quad npsbr = gmd * pgmd + (ngg + ndf) * wbh * nh * xrwg$$

$$+ xrocb * npop * pcon + xrubr * 0.01 * rnu * nlf * pcon$$

$$+ xrspe * sfm * pxc * xrsfmz + \frac{ydgpz}{1 - rpfe}$$

$$+ ydgoz + xryotdz * gtmaz - (rtk * ykz_{-4} + rtmgs * mgs * pmgs$$

$$+ rtn * (wt * (nb + nge + ngg + ndf)) + (rtprb - 1) * nb * nh * wbh$$

$$+ (rtprg - 1) * nge * wbh * nh * xrwg + rtcnr * cnr * pcnr$$

$$+ rtib * ib * pib + rtidw * idw * pidw + rtgmd * gmd * pgmd$$

$$+ rtcre * cre * pcre + rtxc * xc * pxc + rtxnc * xnc * pxnc)$$

$$- xryge * (gge * pgge - nge * rtprg * wbh * nh * xrwg + ydogz$$

$$+ rpfe * (\frac{ydgpz}{1 - rpfe} + ydgoz)) + xrgrnec * gtmaz$$

Capital Income

$$(62)\quad ykz = gb * pgb.25 * (xrcre * kdw_{-1} * pcre * (1 - rtcre)$$

$$- rdkdw * pidw * kdw_{-1}) + yeopz + ydgpz + ydgoz - yepoz - ydpoz$$

$$- wbh * nb * nh * rtprb - rdkb * kb_{-1} * pib$$

Valuation Ratio for Government Securities

$$(63) \quad rval = \frac{1}{0.2 * r90 + 0.8 * (rgl - rmarg)} * (0.2 * r90_{-1} + \frac{0.8}{40}$$

$$* (rgl_{-1} - rmarg_{-1} + rgl_{-2} - rmarg_{-2} + rgl_{-3} - rmarg_{-3}$$

$$+ rgl_{-4} - rmarg_{-4} + rgl_{-5} - rmarg_{-5} + rgl_{-6} - rmarg_{-6}$$

$$+ rgl_{-7} - rmarg_{-7} + rgl_{-8} - rmarg_{-8} + rgl_{-9} - rmarg_{-9}$$

$$+ rgl_{-10} - rmarg_{-10} + rgl_{-11} - rmarg_{-11} + rgl_{-12} - rmarg_{-12}$$

$$+ rgl_{-13} - rmarg_{-13} + rgl_{-14} - rmarg_{-14} + rgl_{-15} - rmarg_{-15}$$

$$+ rgl_{-16} - rmarg_{-16} + rgl_{-17} - rmarg_{-17} + rgl_{-18} - rmarg_{-18}$$

$$+ rgl_{-19} - rmarg_{-19} + rgl_{-20} - rmarg_{-20} + rgl_{-21} - rmarg_{-21}$$

$$+ rgl_{-22} - rmarg_{-22} + rgl_{-23} - rmarg_{-23} + rgl_{-24} - rmarg_{-24}$$

$$+ rgl_{-25} - rmarg_{-25} + rgl_{-26} - rmarg_{-26} + rgl_{-27} - rmarg_{-27}$$

$$+ rgl_{-28} - rmarg_{-28} + rgl_{-29} - rmarg_{-29} + rgl_{-30} - rmarg_{-30}$$

$$+ rgl_{-31} - rmarg_{-31} + rgl_{-32} - rmarg_{-32} + rgl_{-33} - rmarg_{-33}$$

$$+ rgl_{-34} - rmarg_{-34} + rgl_{-35} - rmarg_{-35} + rgl_{-36} - rmarg_{-36}$$

$$+ rgl_{-37} - rmarg_{-37} + rgl_{-38} - rmarg_{-38} + rgl_{-39} - rmarg_{-39}$$

$$+ rgl_{-40} - rmarg_{-40}))$$

Interest Received on Official Reserve Assets

$$(64) \quad ydogz = wdogfz_{-1} * (\frac{wr90_{-1}}{400} + u\_dog)$$

Balance on Current Account

$$(65) \quad cab = xnc * pxnc + xc * pxc - mgs * pmgs + yeopz - yepoz + ydogz$$

$$- ydpoz - ydgoz + xrymtcz * nim * wgtm * \frac{wpgtm}{\frac{wnpop}{rtwi}}$$

$$+ xrytocz * wgtm * \frac{wpgtm}{rtwi} - xryotdz * gtmaz - xrytodz * gtmaz$$

Dividends and Remitted Profits Paid to Overseas

$$(66)\quad yepoz = wepoz_{-1} * ((1 - rtk_{-1}) * \frac{1}{pib_{-1} * kb_{-1} * qrat_{-1}} * (pgb_{-1} * gb_{-1}$$

$$- rtprb_{-1} * wbh_{-1} * nb_{-1} * nh_{-1} - ydpoz_{-1}) + u\_epo)$$

Dividends and Remitted Profits Received from Overseas

$$(67)\quad yeopz = weopz_{-1} * \frac{wrgl_{-1} + 2.5 - winfexp_{-1} + u\_eop}{400}$$

Private Interest Payments on Overseas Debt

$$(68)\quad frml\, ydpozeq\, ydpoz = wdpoaz_{-1} * (\frac{r90_{-1}}{400} + u\_dpo)$$

$$+ wdpofz_{-1} * (\frac{wrgl_{-1}}{400} + u\_dpo)$$

Interest Payments by Government to Private Sector

$$(69)\quad ydgpz = wdgpz_{-1} * ((0.8 * rgl_{-1} + 0.2 * r90_{-1}) * \frac{rval_{-1}}{400} + u\_dgp)$$

Government Interest Payments on Overseas Debt

$$(70)\quad ydgoz = wdgoaz_{-1} * (\frac{rgl_{-1}}{400} + u\_dgo) + wdgofz_{-1} * (\frac{wr90_{-1}}{400} + u\_dgo)$$

Overseas Holding of Australian Equity

$$(71)\quad wepoz = wepoz_{-1} * (1 + \log \frac{qrat}{qrat_{-1}} + \log \frac{pib}{pib_{-1}} + u\_epo) + bepoz$$

Australian Holding of Overseas Equity

$$(72)\quad weopz = weopz_{-1} * (1 - \log \frac{rtwi}{rtwi_{-1}} + \log \frac{wpgtm}{wpgtm_{-1}} + u\_eop) + beopz$$

Official Reserve Assets

$$(73)\quad wdogfz = wdogfz_{-1} * (1 - \log \frac{rtwi}{rtwi_{-1}} + u\_dogf) + bdogfz$$

Private Sector $A Debt

$$(74)\quad wdpoaz = wdpoaz_{-1} * (1 + u\_dpoa) + bdpoaz$$

Private Sector Foreign Currency Debt

(75) $$wdpofz = wdpofz_{-1} * (1 - \log \frac{rtwi}{rtwi_{-1}} + u\_dpof) + bdpofz$$

Government Debt held by Private Sector

(76) $$wdgpz = wdgpz_{-1} * (1 + u\_dgp) + bdgpz$$

Government $A Debt held by Overseas Sector

(77) $$frml\, wdgoazeq\, wdgoaz = wdgoaz_{-1} * (1 + u\_dgoa) + bdgoaz$$

Government Foreign Currency Debt held by Overseas Sector

(78) $$wdgofz = wdgofz_{-1} * (1 - \log \frac{rtwi}{rtwi_{-1}} + u\_dgof) + bdgofz$$

$$+ alpha * (xreop_{-1} * pib_{-1} * kb_{-2} - weopz_{-1})$$

$$+ gamma * (xreop * pib * kb_{-1} - weopz$$

$$- (xreop_{-1} * pib_{-1} * kb_{-2} - weopz_{-1})) + u\_eop$$

Change in Official Reserve Assets

(79) $$bdogfz = wdogfz * (\frac{bdogfz_{-1}}{wdogfz_{-1}}$$

$$+ alpha * (xrdogf_{-1} * gtmaz_{-1} - wdogfz_{-1})$$

$$+ gamma * (xrdogf * gtmaz - wdogfz$$

$$- (xrdogf_{-1} * gtmaz_{-1} - wdogfz_{-1})) + u\_dogf)$$

Government Foreign Currency Borrowing from Overseas

(80) $$bdgofz = wdgofz * (\frac{bdgofz_{-1}}{wdgofz_{-1}}$$

$$+ alpha * (xrdgof_{-1} * gtmaz_{-1} - wdgofz_{-1})$$

$$+ gamma * (xrdgof * gtmaz - wdgofz$$

$$- (xrdgof_{-1} * gtmaz_{-1} - wdgofz_{-1})) + u\_dgof)$$

Government Borrowing from Private Sector

$$(81)\quad bdgpz = wdgpz * (\frac{bdgpz_{-1}}{wdgpz_{-1}}$$

$$+ alpha * (xrdgp_{-1} * wmz_{-2} - wdgpz_{-1})$$

$$+ gamma * (xrdgp * wmz_{-1} - wdgpz$$

$$- (xrdgp_{-1} * wmz_{-2} - wdgpz_{-1})) + u\_dgp)$$

Government $A Borrowing from Overseas

$$(82) frml\, bdgoazeq\, bdgoaz = npsbr - (mtaz * xrmtaz - mtaz_{-1} * xrmtaz_{-1})$$

$$- bdgofz - bdgpz + bdogfz + rfi$$

Private Foreign Currency Borrowing from Overseas

$$(83)\quad bdpofz = wdpofz * (\frac{bdpofz_{-1}}{wdpofz_{-1}}$$

$$+ alpha * (xrdpof_{-1} * gtmaz_{-1} - wdpofz_{-1})$$

$$+ gamma * (xrdpof * gtmaz - wdpofz$$

$$- (xrdpof_{-1} * gtmaz_{-1} - wdpofz_{-1})) + u\_dpof)$$

Private $A Borrowing from Overseas

$$(84)\quad bdpoaz = -cab + rbiz * gtmaz$$

$$- (bepoz + bdgofz + bdgoaz + bdpofz - beopz - bdogfz)$$

Real GDP

$$(85)\quad gtma = con + ib + iret + idw + gfd + snn + sfm + disa$$

$$+xnc + xc - mgs$$

Nominal GDP

(86) $gtmaz = con * pcon + ib * pib + idw * pidw + iret * piret$

(87) $+ ggk * pgmd * xrpggk + (ngg + ndf) * wbh * nh * xrwg$

$+ gmd * pgmd + snn * psnn + xrsfmz * sfm * pxc + disaz + xc * pxc$

$+ xnc * pxnc - mgs * pmgs$

Real Estate Transfer Expenses

(88) $iret = xriret * idw$

Real Statistical Discrepancy

(89) $disa = xrdisa * gtma$

Exchange Rate Equation

(90) $rtwi = rtwix(+40) * \exp(10 * \log(\frac{rgl - wrgl}{100} + 1))$

Rate of Tax on Labour Income

(91) $rtn = rtn_{-1} + 0.01 * (\frac{wdgoaz + wdgofz + wdgpz - wdogfz}{gtmaz} - xrwdgt)$

$+ 0.2 * (\frac{wdgoaz + wdgofz + wdgpz - wdogfz}{gtmaz} - xrwdgt$

$- (\frac{wdgoaz_{-1} + wdgofz_{-1} + wdgpz_{-1} - wdogfz_{-1}}{gtmaz_{-1}} - xrwdgt_{-1})$

$- xrubr * 0.01 * (rnu - nairu) * nlf * \frac{pcon}{gtmaz}$

$- rtn_{-1} * 0.01 * (rnu - nairu) * nlf * \frac{wt}{gtmaz})$

GNEA Price Deflator

(92) $pgnea = \frac{gneaz}{gnea}$

Import Generating Demand

$$(93)\quad ddmgs = 0.17 * cnr + 0.03 * cre + 0.29 * ib + 0.13 * idw + 0.25 * xnc$$
$$+ 0.10 * xc + 0.33 * gmd + 0.20 * disa$$

Import Genrating Demand Deflator

$$(94)\quad pddmgs = \frac{1}{ddmgs}(0.17 * cnr * pcnr * (1 - rtcnr)$$
$$+ 0.03 * cre * pcre * (1 - rtcre) + 0.29 * ib * pib * (1 - rtib)$$
$$+ 0.13 * idw * pidw * (1 - rtidw) + 0.25 * xnc * pxnc * (1 - rtxn$$
$$+ 0.10 * xc * pxc * (1 - rtxc)$$
$$+ 0.33 * gmd * pgmd * (1 - rtgmd) + 0.20 * disaz)$$

Non-Rent Consumption

$$(95)\quad cnr = con - cre$$

Rain Adjusted Business Output

$$(96)\quad gba = gb - qrain$$

Price of Non-Commodity Exports

$$(97)\quad pxnc = pnc * xrpxnc$$

GDP(A) Deflator

$$(98)\quad pgtma = \frac{gtmaz}{gtma}$$

B List of Mnemonics

Variables ending in Z are the nominal values of the corresponding real variables. EN stands for endogenous, and EX stands for exogenous.

Mnemonic	Status	Description
BDGOAZ	EN	Government borrowing from overseas in $A
BDGOFZ	EN	Government foreign currency borrowing from overseas
BDGPZ	EN	Government borrowing from private sector
BDOGFZ	EN	Change in official reserve assets
BDPOAZ	EN	Private $A borrowing from overseas
BDPOFZ	EN	Private foreign currency borrowing from overseas
BEOPZ	EN	Private equity financing overseas
BEPOZ	EN	Private equity financing from overseas
BIZ		Balancing item
CAB	EN	Balance on current account
CNR	EN	Consumption of non-rent
CON	EN	Private consumption
CRE	EN	Consumption of rental services
DCC	EX	Dummy variable for centralised wage fixing systems
DDMGS	EN	Weighted demand for imports
DDSNN	EN	Weighted demand for non-farm stock
DISA	EN	Statistical discrepancy
DMIN	EX	Dummy variable for mining investment booms
GB	EN	Business output (at factor cost)
GBA	EN	Rain adjusted private output
GFD	EN	Government final demand
GGE	EN	Public enterprise output (at factor cost)
GGK	EN	Government capital production
GMD	EN	Government market demand
GNEA	EN	Gross national expenditure (Average levels)
GTMA	EN	Gross domestic product (Average levels)
IB	EN	Business investment
IDW	EN	Dwelling investment
IGE	EX	Government enterprise investment
IGG	EX	General government investment
INFEXP	EN	Long-run inflationary expectations (ten years ahead)
IRET	EN	Real estate transfer expenses
KB	EN	Private business capital stock
KDW	EN	Dwelling capital stock
KGE	EN	Government enterprise capital stock
KGG	EN	General government capital stock
KSFM	EN	Farm and public authority stocks
KSN	EN	Stock of inventories
MGS	EN	Imports of goods and services

Mnemonic	Status	Description
MTAZ	EX	Weighted M1 money supply measure
NAP	EX	Adult population
NB	EN	Number of people employed
NBH	EN	Number of hours worked in private business sector
NDF	EX	Defence personnel
NFLZ	EN	Net foreign liabilities
NGE	EN	Public enterprise employment
NGG	EX	General government employment
NH	EX	Number of hours worked per employee
NIM	EX	Immigration
NLF	EN	Civilian labour force
NPOP	EX	Population
NPSBR	EN	Net public sector borrowing requirement
NT	EN	Total employment (civilian)
PCNR	EN	Price of non-rent consumption
PCNRF	EN	Indicator level for PCNR
PCON	EN	Price of private consumption
PCRE	EN	Price of rent consumption
PCREX	EN	Underlying price of rents
PD	EN	Price of the domestic supply component of expenditure
PDDMGS	EN	Price of weighted demand for imports
PDDSNN	EN	Price of weighted demand for non-farm stocks
PGB	EN	Price of domestic output
PGGE	EN	Price of public enterprise output
PGMD	EN	Price of government market demand
PGMDF	EN	Indicator level for PGMD
PGNEA	EN	Gross National Expenditure Deflator (A)
PIB	EN	Price of business investment
PIBF	EN	Indicator level for PIB
PIDW	EN	Price of dwelling investment
PIDWF	EN	Indicator level for PIDW
PIRET	EN	Price of real estate transfer expenses
PIRETF	EN	Indicator level for PIRET
PMGS	EN	Price of imports
PNC	EN	Price of non-commodity private product
PSNN	EN	Price of non-commodity stock-building
PT	EN	Price of certain major items of expenditure
PXC	EN	Price of commodity exports
PXGS	EN	Price of exports
PXNC	EN	Non-commodity exports
Q833	EX	Dummy variable for outlier in price of mining exports equation
Q864	EX	Dummy variable fore outlier in price of imports equation

Mnemonic	Status	Description
QRAIN	EX	Output affected by rain
QRAT	EN	Business sector Q-ratio
QRATH	EN	Dwelling sector Q-ratio
QS	EX	Dummy variable for shift in natural rate in wages equation
QSM	EX	Dummy variable for the March quarter
QTIME	EX	Time trend
QTIMF	EX	Time trend (fixed in forecast period)
R90	EN	Rate on 90-day bills
RAIN	EN	Rainfall index
RDKB	EX	Rate of depreciation on business capital stock
RDKDW	EX	Rate of depreciation on dwelling capital stock
RDKGE	EX	Rate of depreciation on government enterprise capital stock
RDKGG	EX	Rate of depreciation on general government capital stock
RFI	EX	Residual finance item
RGL	EN	Rate on 10-year Treasury bonds
RMARG	EX	Fixed interest margin
RNU	EN	Unemployment rate
RPIRET	EN	$\ln \frac{PIRET}{PT}$
RPCNR	EN	$\ln \frac{PCNR}{PT}$
RPIDW	EN	$\ln \frac{PIDW}{PT}$
RPIB	EN	$\ln \frac{PIB}{PT}$
RPFE	EX	Ratio of public financial enterprise holdings of govt debt / total govt debt
RPGEK	EX	$\frac{PGEK}{PIB}$
RPGMD	EN	$\ln \frac{PGMD}{PT}$
RTCNR	EX	Indirect tax rates on CNR
RTCRE	EX	Indirect tax rates on CRE
RTFB	EX	Fringe benefit tax rate
RTGMD	EX	Indirect tax rates on government market demand
RTIB	EX	Indirect tax rates on business investment
RTIDW	EX	Indirect tax rates on dwelling investment
RTK	EX	Rate of tax on capital income
RTMGS	EX	Rate of customs duty
RTN	EN	Rate of tax on labour income
RTWI	EN	Exchange rate (Trade weighted index)
RTXC	EX	Indirect tax rates on commodity exports
RTXNC	EX	Indirect tax rates on non-commodity exports
RVAL	EN	Government securities V-ratio
RWDGT	EN	Public debt / GDP ratio

Mnemonic	Status	Description
SF	EN	Scaling factor for the relative price bloc
SFM	EN	Farm stock-building
7SNN	EN	Non-farm stock-building
KSN	EN	Non-farm stocks
WBH	EN	Hourly business wage
WDGOAZ	EN	Government $A debt held by overseas sector
WDGOFZ	EN	Government foreign currency debt held by overseas sector
WDGPZ	EN	Government debt held by private sector
WDOGFZ	EN	Official reserve assets
WDPOAZ	EN	Private sector $A debt
WDPOFZ	EN	Private sector foreign currency debt
WEOPZ	EN	Australian holding of overseas equity
WEPOZ	EN	Overseas holding of Australian equity
WGTM	EX	Major trading partners GDP
WINFEXP	EX	World Inflationary Expectations
WMZ	EN	Private wealth at market value
WNPOP	EX	Major trading partners population
WPGTM	EX	Major trading partners GDP reflector
WPMPE	EX	World price of petroleum products
WR90	EX	Major trading partners short term interest rates
WRGL	EX	Major trading partners long term interest rates
WT	EN	Average earnings (National Account Basis)
XGS	EN	Exports of goods and services
XC	EN	Exports of commodities
XNC	EN	Non-commodity exports
XRCRE	EX	$\frac{CRE}{KDW_{-1}}$
XRDGP	EX	$\frac{WDGPZ}{GTMZ}$
XRDISA	EX	$\frac{DISA}{GTMA}$
XRDISAZ	EX	$\frac{DISAZ}{GTMAZ}$
XRDOGF	EX	$\frac{WDOGFZ}{GTMZ}$
XRDPOF	EX	$\frac{WDPOFZ}{PIB*KB}$
XREOP	EX	$\frac{WEOPZ}{PIB*KB}$
XREPO	EX	$\frac{WEPOZ}{PIB*KB}$
XRGRNEC	EX	Govt revenue not elsewhere classified (ratio of GDP)
XRITC	EX	Investment tax credits
XRMTAZ	EX	Ratio of MTAZ to money base
XROCB	EX	Non-unemployment pensions rate
XRPGGE	EX	$\frac{PGGE}{PGB}$
XRPKSN	EX	$\frac{\frac{KSNZ}{KSN}}{PDDSNN}$
XRPXNC	EX	$\frac{PXNC}{PNC}$
XRRTK	EX	$\frac{RTK}{RTN}$
XRSFMZ	EX	$\frac{\frac{SFMZ}{SFM}}{PXC}$
XRUBR	EX	Unemployment benefit rate

Mnemonic	Status	Description
XRWDGT	EX	Ratio of Govt debt to GDP
XRWG	EX	$\frac{WG}{WB}$
XRYMTCZ	EX	Migrant transfer credits
XRYOTDZ	EX	$\frac{YOTDZ}{GTMAZ}$
YDGOZ	EN	Government interest payments on overseas debt
YDGPZ	EN	Interest payments by government to private sector
YDOGZ	EN	Interest received on official reserve assets
YEOPZ	EN	Dividends and remitted profits received from overseas
YEPOZ	EN	Dividends and remitted profits paid to overseas
YKZ	EN	Capital income
YLZ	EN	Labour income
YSTAR	EN	Short-run supply of output
YSTWK	EN	Desired output based on wages and capital

Chapter 10

The FOCUS Model of The Canadian Economy

Gregory Jump and Peter Dungan[1]

1 Introduction

FOCUS is a quarterly macro-econometric model of the Canadian economy, developed and maintained at the Institute for Policy Analysis, University of Toronto. It is an acronym for Forecasting and User Simulation mode. It is a direct descendent of the now-retired University of Toronto Quarterly Model. However, unlike its predecessor which was used primarily for short-term forecasting, FOCUS is designed for policy analysis and trend projection over the medium and the long term.

In size, FOCUS is a medium-scale model consisting of some 300+ behavioural equations and identities. Its orientation is Keynesian as opposed to monetarist or Neoclassical, though the model can (at least theoretically) depict full-employment or long-run equilibria in addition to the familiar under-employment equilibria of the Keynesian short run. Some care has been taken in developing the model's structural equations to ensure that they embody desirable long-run properties as well as plausible short-run dynamics. The equations of the model are ordered by sector and described individually in the body of the manual of the model.[2]

2 Overview of FOCUS Model

The simplest way to describe FOCUS is to use the familiar IS-LM textbook presentation of the macroeconomic system. At a given price/wage level, real output and the real rate of interest are found at the intersection of the IS and LM curves. Varying the price level and re-solving the IS-LM system will sketch out a downward sloping aggregate demand (AD) curve for the economy. Meanwhile, rigidities

[1] Gregory Jump is the model's chief archtect and designer; most of the original FOCUS model was entirely his work. Peter Dungan is the current model custodian. Thomas Wilson has made important contributions to the model from its earliest versions. FOCUS benefited from the works of France St-Hilaire, Mary MacGregor, Andre Plourde, Joan Head, Samuel Rea Jr., Dan Markovich and Nanda Choudhry and from the services of a dedicated group of research assistants, including Hohn Wooders, West Suhanic, Evelyn Forget, Barry Ma and Valerie Bencivenga. Steve Murphy reestimated the FOCUS equations using the 1986-based national income accounts.

[2] (Editor's Note) There is a detailed manual of the model produced by the group about FOCUS model. This article is a summary of that manual. The interested reader may obtain the manual directly from the Institute for Policy Analysis, University of Toronto.

in the labour market which prevent instantaneous achievement of full employment will yield an upward-sloping aggregate supply curve (AS). Equating AD and AS (and IS and LM) determines real output, price, employment and the real interest rate fro a temporary equilibrium which will typically be a point of Keynesian under- (or over-) employment.

2.1 IS Curve, LM Curve and the External Balance (BP) Curve

Many equations can be grouped into blocks corresponding to the IS, LM, AD and AS curves. A solution of the model may be regarded as simultaneously determining endogenous variables as described above. For example, the IS curve is represented by all of the equations in FOCUS which determine components of real aggregate demand. These include consumption, investment, government expenditure, exports and imports equations. The equations which determine various components of national income, taxes and personal and disposable incomes also belong to this block, since income shares are part of the circular flow of spending which give rise to the multiplier behaviour exhibited by real aggregate demand. This block of equations representing the IS curve accounts for a large fraction (probably over 60 percent) of the total equations. The attention given here reflects the orientation of the model builders, who would describe themselves as neo-Keynesians. If, as Keynes asserted, wage/price rigidities of one form or another are prevalent in the economy, then the main sources of period-to-period variations in output and employment are traceable to shifts in aggregate demand; namely, shifts in the IS curve. To understand such variations requires a detailed understanding of the factors underlying the IS curve, and care has been taken to model of those factors in a manner consistent with the present state of economic theory.

A more compact block of equations (some 10 percent of the total) comprises the model's representation of the LM curve. Included in this block are equations determining interest rates and/or the money supply. A liquidity preference approach has been used here so that a number of financial markets, most notably the bond market, do not appear explicitly in the model. This accounts for the small size of this block relative to that of the IS curve. However, size should not be taken as an indication that financial variables are unimportant to the working of FOCUS or that monetary policy is deemed to be ineffective. Quite the contrary, the model shows relatively strong responses to variation in financial variables and monetary policy. In the jargon of economics, the LM curve in FOCUS is relatively interest-inelastic, while the IS curve is relatively interest-elastic.

Another small group of equations determines international capital flows and so gives the model a 'BP' curve sketching points of external balance. If the exchange rate is permitted to float, FOCUS solutions will always lie along the (short-run) BP curve. If the exchange rate is held fixed, the balance of payments deficit or surplus at equilibrium can be determined.

2.2 The Labour Market and Aggregate Supply

The labour market and aggregate supply are represented by equations determining wage rates, employment and the labour force and by the production function. The key wage variable is determined by an extended Phillips curve, with wage inflation being a function of productivity, the actual and 'full employment' unemployment rates, and both past and anticipated inflation. The rigidity which characterizes wage determination occurs partly via a gradual adjustment of the labour market to differences between actual and full employment and partly via the price inflation terms. Theoretically, if employers and employees were always able to fully anticipate the rate of price inflation, money wage rates would reflect this, and the economy would find itself always at the full employment unemployment rate. In reality at least two factors operate to prevent this: 1. future rates of price inflation cannot always be accurately predicted in advance; and 2. a substantial portion of wage settlements are based on past actual rates of inflation rather than on expected future rates of inflation (e.g., COLA clauses). FOCUS incorporates both factors via its key wage equation with the result that solutions to the model produce unemployment rates which can, usually do, deviate from the full employment rate. The Phillips curve nature of the wage equation shows a short-run trade off between unemployment and wage inflation.

The natural rate of unemployment is not an absolute barrier within the model. Solutions with a measured rate of unemployment less than the natural rate are not only feasible but fully consistent with the existence of a downward-sloping short-run Phillips curve. Rather than a barrier, the natural rate acts as a magnet towards which the model's solutions for the measured unemployment are drawn in longer term simulations. This is in keeping with current theoretical literature which posits the long-run Phillips curve to be a vertical line passing through the natural rate of unemployment. The key employment equation in FOCUS is based on cost minimization and derived from an explicit aggregate production function. All else equal, a higher real wage will lower employment for any given level of output; the model in effect causes capital and other inputs to be used more intensively in place of some labour.

A small block of six equations determines labour force participation rates for six age/sex categories. The overall labour force is computed by multiplying each participation rate by the corresponding)exogenous) source population and summing up. Participation is found to vary primarily with the level of unemployment (the 'discouraged worker effect') and not with real wages.

Aggregate Supply in FOCUS is relatively well integrated both in itself and with the rest of the model structure. Factor demand equations for labour and machinery and equipment capital are derived from a common production function so that labour/capital ratios are responsive to relative prices. In itself, this is not unique to the FOCUS model, but the nature of the production function is. The private sector of the economy is viewed as consisting of N nearly-identical plants. There is assumed to be an optimal plant size, and production within any given plant is constrained to follow a Cobb-Douglas production function with factor inputs of production labour and machinery and equipment. The production function exhibits strictly decreasing returns. Investment in new non-residential structures is identified with the time rate of change in N. Positive net investment occurs whenever the rate of return on structures and the real, after-tax rate of interest on government bonds. This internal rate of return is determined endogenously as the ratio of corporation profits after-tax to the replacement cost of the capital stock. When the profits/replacement cost ratio is high, structures investment increases and the number of firms expands. The profit rate also determined the level at which the existing stock of plant capacity is utilized. Labour and machinery and equipment stock are viewed partly as "overhead' to plants and partly as variable inputs into the production process. Because of the production function constraint they are substitute factors of production: a rise in wage rates relative to the service price of machinery and equipment will reduce the demand for the former and increase the demand for the latter. When relative prices are stable, both factors are complementary to structures investment; i.e. an increase in N will normally lead to increased demand for both labour and machinery equipment. The workings of this sector approximate the textbook description of a competitive industry. When profits are high, the number of firms entering the industry increases, driving down prices, thereby reducing profitability and moderating the incentives for further entry. Thus the specifications here bridge the short run and the long run.

2.3 Price Determination; Equating Aggregate Demand and Supply

The key price variable is designated PGDPP and represents the implicit price index for privately-produced GDP. In the textbook discussion the aggregate price level is usually determined by equating aggregate demand and aggregate supply. That is, prices adjust instantly to changes in either demand or supply conditions, and all 'rigidity' stems from wages and the labour market. An alternative, more Keynesian, view sees prices set in the short run as rule-of-thumb mark-ups on costs. Prices as well as wages are, therefore, 'sluggish' in their response to changed conditions of demand and supply. Interestingly most macroeconometric models of Canada or other industrialized market economies have customarily used mark-up equations for the price level. FOCUS however offers users a choice. They may specify a cost 'mark-up' regime in which PGNPP is determined by a behavioural equation with unit-labour costs, import prices, indirect taxes and inventory interest charges as explanatory variables. Alternatively, they may specify a more neoclassical 'market-clearing' regime in which PGNPP equates supply and demand for aggregate output with the model. The latter specification produces a 'perfectly flexible' price level and PGNPP responds not only to changes in unit labour costs and capital goods prices, which are 'supply-side' variables, but also to variations in aggregate demand.

2.4 Special Features of FOCUS: Inflation Expectation and Policy Levers and Switches

Inflation expectations play an important role in FOCUS and are modeled in an unusual and interesting fashion. It uses synthetic expectations series to represent expected rates of price inflation, 90 days, one year and two years into the future. These series are constructed by regressing actual future rates of price inflation on a set of explanatory variables that we believe comes closer to the kinds of variables on which market participants base expectations than the usual distributed lags of past rates of changes in prices. For example, 90-day expectations are specified to depend upon recent observations of money supply growth, unemployment rates, foreign prices and the exchange rate in addition to the actual past rates of price inflation. These additional variables add credibility as well as explanatory power to the specifications.

The use of synthetic expectations series permits the model to explicitly identify and predict expectations in an internally consistent manner. Variations in expectations will simultaneously alter both interest rates and wage settlements. The model also makes some allowance for errors in expectations. The wage equation contains a term for 'catch up' which is activated whenever past inflation expectations turn out to have been faulty. This means that FOCUS is able to simulate the impacts of shifts in inflation expectations as a matter of course in much the say way as sit might be used to simulate shifts in government policies.

An experimental version of FOCUS makes use of 'consistent' expectations (CE), defined as expectations determined by the equations and future exogenous values of the model itself. Under CE for example, inflation one year into the future in 89:1 is that actually generated by the model solution in 90:1. In the CE version expectations of this type can be invoked for inflation, short-term interest rates, the exchange rate, corporate after-tax profits and personal disposable income. The method requires a more elaborate solution method than the standard versions of FOCUS and so must be used with greater care.

FOCUS offers a wide range of policy levers embedded throughout its structure and a number of useful switches for selecting alternative monetary, price or exchange-rate regimes. It will suffice here to simply list a number of fiscal and monetary policy actions which may readily be simulated with the model by changing the value of an exogenous variable or parameter. The following list does not include some of the more obvious policy levers (e.g., changes in government expenditures or the application of surcharges on personal income taxes), nor does it include some of the more esoteric options. It does, however, provide an indication of the rich variety possible with the model.

3 Glossary

FOCUS behavioral equations and identities are presented in detail in the following sections. An index of model variables is given in the following. This note will assist in reading and interpreting the behavioral equations.

Methods of estimation are generally either ordinary least squares (OLS) or maximum likelihood for equations with first-order autocorrelation (AR1), as outlined by Beach and MacKinnon. Note that when regressions containing both autocorrelated errors and a lagged dependent variable are estimated using the latter method of estimation,m the computed standard errors, and hence the t-statistics, on the estimated coefficients are biased. Although methods for "correcting" these biased standard errors are available, the t-statistics are presented here without adjustment.

'Dependent variable' indicates the transformation, if any, applied to the endogenous variable before estimation. All statistics etc. reported are for the transformed left-handed-side variable. This should be kept in mind when interpreting R2 and other goodness-of-fit criteria. The equation written out here, however, has been renormalized to isolate the endogenous variable on the lefthand side.

In the equations, variables entirely in capitals are FOCUS variables; variables in lower case or mixed upper/lower case are not distinct variables in FOCUS but are defined only to simplify presentation. The following appear in equation descriptions* -—, etc: a 2-quarter lag, J4A, etc.: a four-quater moving average, J8W: an eight-quarter weighted moving average (with weights given in the description), DOT( ): the proportional rate of change, DIFF( ): the first difference, DTIME: time trend (=1 in 50:1 etc.), DSQ_i: seasonal dummies, $\sum a < i >$: a polynomially distributed lag (Almon lag); also given are the DEG (degree) and any constraints (e.g., FAR).

MNEMONIC	DESCRIPTION	UNIT	SOURCE
AFDIJ	Value of federal debt recorded by inflation	$ mill	
ANPDF	Net public debt (dep't of finance def'n)	$ mill	
ARRCB	Chartered bank (repuired) cash reserves	$ mill	nsa
AW1	Wealth estimate (1): capital stock + fed debt - for'n debt	$ mill	
BPC	Current account balance	$ mill	saar
BPCN	BP: balance on current account	$ mill	ar,nsa
BPCNSF	BP: seasonal factors (current account)	$ mill	ar
BPDIA	Canadian direct investment abroad	$ mill	ar,nsa
BPDIL	BP: foreign direct investment in Canada	$ mill	ar,nsa
BPLCBS	BP: trade in outstanding bonds & stocks	$ mill	ar,nsa
BPLCN	New issues of corporate bonds abroad	$ mill	ar,nsa
BPLCR	Retirements of foreign held corporate bonds	$ mill	ar,nsa
BPLGCN	BP: new issues (federal gov't bonds)	$ mill	ar,nsa
BPLGCR	BP: retirements (federal gov't bonds)	$ mill	ar,nsa
BPLN	BP: net capital movements in long-term forms	$ mill	ar,nsa
BPLOTH	BP: long-term capital (all other flows)	$ mill	ar,nsa
BPLPMN	BP: net new issues prov'l and mun'l bonds	$ mill	ar,nsa
BPME	BP: net inheritances and migrants funds	$ mill	saar
BPOS	BP: official settlements balance	$ mill	ar,nsa
BPRES	BP: balance of payments (change in reserves)	$ mill	ar,nsa
BPRESX	BP: exogenous value of BPRES for float rate; set to history		
BPSDR	BP: allocation of special drawing rights	$ mill	ar,nsa
BPSN	Net capital movement in short-term forms		
C	Consumption (total goods and services)	$ 86 mill	saar
CCA	Capital consumption allowances	$ mill	saar
CCAC	Capital consumption allowances (corp'tions)	$ mill	saar
CCAG	Capital consumption allowances (governments)	$ mill	saar
CCAGB	Capital consumption allow's (gov't bus ent)	$ mill	saar
CCAGF	Capital consumption allowances (federal)	$ mill	saar
CCAGH	Capital consumption allowances (hospitals)	$ mill	saar

MNEMONIC	DESCRIPTION	UNIT	SOURCE
CCAGL	Capital consumption allowances (local)	$ mill	saar
CCAGP	Capital consumption allowances (provinsial)	$ mill	saar
CCAPU	Capital consumption allow's (persons & uninc)	$ mill	saar
CCOST	Capital cons cost allow of corp (tax purpos)	$ mill	saar
CD	Consumption: durables	$ 86 mill	saar
CDA	Consumption: autos, parts and repairs	$ 86 mill	saar
CDAV	Consumption: autos, parts and repairs	$ mill	saar
CDO	Consumption: other durables	$ 86 mill	saar
CDOV	Consumption: other durables	$ mill	saar
CDV	Consumption: durables	$ mill	saar
CND	Consumption: non-durables	$ 86 mill	saar
CNDV	Consumption: non-durables	$ mill	saar
CPI	Consumer price index	(86 = 1.0)	
CPIA	Cpi for automobile purchases	(86 = 1.0)	
CPIG	Cpi for gasoline	(86 = 1.0)	
CS	Consumption: services	$ 86 mill	saar
CSD	Consumption: semi-durables	$ 86 mill	saar
CSDV	Consumption: semi-durables	$ mill	saar
CSV	Consumption: services	$ mill	saar
CV	Consumption: total goods and services	$ mill	saar
DCCAHY	Dummy for half-year CCA deduction; 1.0 for 82:1-on		
DCCIME	Switch: ratio of new m&e indexed for tax depreciation		
DCCINR	Switch: ratio of new non-residential structure indexed for tax depreciation		
DFX	Dummy lever for fix(=0) float(=1) exchange rate		
DFX12	Dummy: flexible exchange rate regime, used in BPLPMN		
DFXIR	Lever for exchange rate intervention rule; intervention coefficient		
DFXIRC	Level for exchange intervention; 0 for no intervention (stnd)		
DFXIRM	Lever for exchange intervention rule; max intervention		
DFXRCO	Lever for key rate-of-response coefficient in exchange rate equation		
DG	Switch for bov curr & cap; 0=real, 1=nominal		
DGTRF	Real per-capita growth rate for federal trans to pers (ex ui)	%	
DGTRL	Real per-capita growth rate for local trans to pers (trgpl)	%	
DGTRP	Real per-capita growth rate for provincial trans to pers (trgpp)	%	
DGTRPE	Real per-capita growth rate for pension trans to pers (trgppe)	%	
DHYDRO	Dummy for hydro borrowings; in 75q4 thru 77q3		
DIFM	Dummy variable for 2 year write offs for m&e by manuf & proc		
DINVAL	Dummy for inventory on allowance on corporate taxes		
DLINK	Lever: project link (0-no link; 1-link; 2-link + int rt & infl)		
DM	Switch for monetary policy (set to 1 thru 7)		
DMPRX	Damp factor for exchange-rate equation (std = 1)		
DMRX	Adj. coeff. (damp) for money rule no.6, etc.		
DP	Switch for key price determination (set to 0 or 1)		
DP2	Switch for detail prices (0=estimated eqns;1=grow as PGDPPF etc)		
DPH2	Switch: gst switch: 0=gst in 91; 1=no gst-keep mst *tune*		
DPROD	Dummy for shift in productivity growth (0 thru 73; rises to 1.0)		
DQUE	Dummy: Quebec elect. and expectations (direct investment)		
DRL	Switch: 0 - normal eqns; 1- immed pass thru; 2 - ch as rmf		

MNEMONIC	DESCRIPTION	UNIT	SOURCE
DSQ1	Seasonal dummy=1.0 in q1 and zero otherwise		
DSQ2	Seasonal dummy=1.0 in q2 and zero otherwise		
DSQ3	Seasonal dummy=1.0 in q3 and zero othrewise		
DSQ4	Seasonal dummy=1.0 in q4 and zero otherwise		
DSTER	Dmy var.=fraction of off res. changes sterilized by b.o		
DTAX	Dummy variable for 1972 tax reform		
DTFP	Change in total factor productivity growth (p.c. per ann)		
DTIME	Time trend		
DUIC	Dummy variable for 1971 uic act, =1. prior to 72q1, 0 elesewhere		
DUM1	Dummy variable no.1 (for special simulations)		
DUM2	Dummy variable no.2 (for special simulations)		
DUM3	Dummy variable no.3 (for special simulations)		
FDBTF	Debt outstanding (estimate) (federal government)	$ mill	
FDBTL	Debt outstanding (estimate) (local gpvernment)	$ mill	
FDBTP	Debt outstanding (estimate) (provincial government)	$ mill	
FDGCCB	Government of Canada deposits at chartered banks	$ mill	
FNBIL	Net new bond issues (local governments)	$ mill	
FNBIP	Net new bond issues (provinces)	$ mill	
G	Government current & capital expenditure	$ 86 mill	saar
GBAL	Government surplus (+), deficit (-) (total)	$ mill	saar
GBALF	Government surplus (+), deficit (-) (federal)	$ mill	saar
GBALFJ	Federal surplus (+) or deficit (-); inflation-adjusted		
GBALH	Government surplus (+), deficit (-) (hospitals)	$ mill	saar
GBALL	Government surplus (+), deficit (-) (local)	$ mill	saar
GBALP	Government surplus (+), deficit (-) (provincial)	$ mill	saar
GBALPE	Govt surplus (+), deficit (-) (can/que pensions)	$ mill	saar
GBALUI	Balance on unemployment insurance	$ mill	saar
GBFRF	Federal financial requirements	$ mill	
GBPAF	Federal budjet surplus/deficit, public accounts definition	$ mill	
GC	Government current expenditure, goods & services	$ 86 mill	saar
GCF	Government current expenditure, goods & services (federal)	$ 86 mill	saar
GCFV	Government current expenditure, goods & services (federal)	$ mill	saar
GCH	Government current expenditure, goods & services (hospitals)	$ 86 mill	saar
GCHV	Government current expenditure, goods & services (hospital)	$ mill	saar
GCL	Government current expenditure, goods & services (local)	$ 86 mill	saar
GCLV	Government current expenditure, goods & services (local)	$ mill	saar
GCP	Government current expenditure, goods & services (plovincial)	$ 86 mill	saar
GCPE	Government current expenditure, goods & services (pension plans)	$ 86 mill	saar
GCPEV	Government current expenditure, goods & services (pension plans)	$ mill	saar
GCPV	Government current expenditure, goods & services (provincial)	$ mill	saar
GCV	Government current expenditure, goods & services	$ mill	saar
GDP	Gross domestic product	$ 86 mill	saar
GDPF	Gross domestic product at factor cost	$ 86 mill	saar
GDPFV	Gross domestic product at factor cost	$ mill	saar
GDPGAP	Potential GDP 'gap'	%	
GDPOTL	Potential GDP	$ 86 mill	
GDPP	GDP originating in the private sector	$ 86 mill	saar
GDPPF	Real private GDP at factor cost	$ 86 mill	saar
GDPPFS	Real pvivate GDP at factor cost (supply measure)	$ 86 mill	saar
GDPPFV	Private GDP at factor cost	$ mill	saar
GDPPV	GDP originating in the private sector	$ mill	saar

MNEMONIC	DESCRIPTION	UNIT	SOURCE
GDPV	Gross domestic product	$ mill	saar
GEXP	Government expenditure (total)	$ mill	saar
GEXPF	Government expenditure (federal)	$ mill	saar
GEXPH	Government expenditure (hospital)	$ mill	saar
GEXPL	Government expenditure (local)	$ mill	saar
GEXPP	Government expenditure (provincial)	$ mill	saar
GEXPPE	Government expenditure (pension plans)	$ mill	saar
GI	Government capital and inventory expenditure	$ 86 mill	saar
GIF	Government gross capital formation (federal)	$ 86 mill	saar
GIFV	Government gross capital formation (federal)	$ mill	saar
GIH	Government gross capital formation (hospitals)	$ 86 mill	saar
GIHV	Government gross capital formation (hospitals)	$ mill	saar
GIL	Government gross capital formation (local)	$ 86 mill	saar
GILV	Government gross capital formation (local)	$ mill	saar
GIP	Government gross capital formation (provincial)	$ 86 mill	saar
GIPV	Government gross capital formation (provincial)	$ mill	saar
GIV	Government capital and inventory expenditure	$ mill	saar
GNP	Gross national product	$ 86 mill	saar
GNPG	Gnp originating in the government sector	$ 86 mill	saar
GNPGV	Gnp originating in the government sector	$ mill	saar
GNPV	Gross national product	$ mill	saar
GREV	Government revenue (total)	$ mill	saar
GREVF	Government revenue (federal)	$ mill	saar
GREVH	Government revenue (hospitals)	$ mill	saar
GREVL	Government revenue (local)	$ mill	saar
GREVP	Government revenue (provincial)	$ mill	saar
GREVPE	Government revenue (pension plans)	$ mill	saar
GV	Government current & capital expenditure	$ mill	saar
HCM	Housing completions (multiples, all Canada)	'000	ar,nsa
HCS	Housing completions (singles, all Canada)	'000	ar,nsa
HS	Housing starts (all Canada)	'000	ar,nsa
HSM	Housing starts (multiples, all Canada)	'000	ar,nsa
HSS	Housing starts (singles, all Canada)	'000	ar,nsa
IFB	Business investment (fixed capital)	$ 86 mill	saar
IFBV	Business investment (fixed capital)	$ mill	saar
IFHB	Business residential construction	$ 86 mill	saar
IFHBV	Business residential construction	$ mill	saar
IFMB	Business investment (machinery & equipment)	$ 86 mill	saar
IFMBV	Business investment (machinery & epuipment)	$ mill	saar
IFNB	Business non-residential construction	$ mill	saar
IFNBV	Business non-residential construcution	$ mill	saar
IIB	Change in total business inventories	$ 86 mill	saar
IIBV	Change in total business inventories	$ mill	
IIF	Change in inventories (farm & grain)	$ 86 mill	saar
IINF	Change in inventories (non-farm)	$ 86 mill	saar
J4LCA	Wage plus uic and cpp/qpp costs per employee, 4 quarters moving average	$ '000	
JCAPG	Capacity utilization rate (goods excl. ag & fish)		sa
JCAPGN	'Natural' capacity utilization rate (goods producing)		
JCCHCM	Undepreciated capital costs, m&e (historical cost)	$ mill	
JCCHCN	Undepreciated capital costs, structures (historical cost)	$ mill	
JCCIFM	Undepreciated capital costs, private mach & eq	$ mill	
JCCIFN	Undepreciated capital costs, private structure	$ mill	
JCOLDM	Undeprec cap costs, m&e, stock pre-tax reform	$ mill	
JCOL2M	Undaprec cap costs, m&e, stock pre-1992 buddget	$ mill	
JCOLDN	Undeprec cap costs, non-res, stock, pre-tax reform	$ mill	
JFMNEW	'Effectiveness' of new capital stock (m&e)	dflt=1.0	
JFNNEW	'Effectiveness' of new capital stock (non-res)	dflt=1.0	
JGDPPF	Ratio: real private GDP at factor cost /real private GDP at market prices		
JLPRIV	'Effectiveness' of labour (for experiments)	default=1.0	
JMGY	Import share: W.Germany		
JMJA	Import share: Japan		
JMUK	Import share: U.K.		

MNEMONIC	DESCRIPTION	UNIT	SOURCE
JMUS	Import share: U.S.		
JNPROD	Trend productivity: output/employee, 5 year moving average	$ '000	
JUCA	Index of the user cost of car ownership, 1986=1.0 (constructed)		
JUCIFM	Index of user cost of new machinery & equipment		
JULCN	Unit labour costs	$/$ 86	
JUTXN	Unit indirect taxes	$/$ 86	
JXGY	Export share: W.Germany		
JXJA	Export share: Japan		
JXUK	Export share: U.K.		
JXUS	Export share: U.S.		
KBBC	Bp: stock of corp bonds outstanding abroad	US$ mill	
KBBPL	Bp: stock of prov and mun bonds outstanding abroad	US$ mill	
KBDIAR	Bp: accum stock of real cdndir invest abroad	US$ 82 mill	
KBDILR	Bp: accum stock of real dir invest in Canada	$ 86 mill	
KBS	Bp: stock of cdn short-term liabs(+)/assets abroad	US$ mill	
KBXRU	Bp: stock of off'l int'l reserves	US$ mill	
KCARS	Stock of pssenger cars, start of quarter		
KFHB	Stock of private residential structures	$ 86 mill	
KFMB	Stock of machinery & equipment	$ 86 mill	
KFMNEW	'New' capital stock (m&e) (for sim experiments only)		
KFNB	Stock of non-residential structures	$ 86 mill	
KFNNEW	'New' capital stock (non-res) (for sim experiments only)		
KH	Housing stock (total)	'000 units	
KHM	Housing stock (multiples, based on completions)	'000 units	
KHS	Housing stock (singles, based on completions)	'000 units	
KINF	Beginning of quarter stock of bus non-farm inventories	$ 86 mill	
LE	Employed both sexes 15 years & over	'000	sa
LF	Labour force	'000	sa
JGC	Government civilian employment	'000	sa
LGM	Canadian armed forces	'000	
LPNAT	'Natural' employment level in private sector	'000	
LPRIV	Employed in the private sector	'000	
LU	Unemployed	'000	sa
M	Imports of goods and services	$ 86 mill	saar
M01G	Imports: SITC 0.1 (food, beverage)	$ 86 mill	
M24G	Imports: SITC 2.4 (crude material)	$ 86 mill	
M3G	Imports: SITC 3 (fuel & lubricant)	$ 86 mill	
M59G	Imports: SITC 5-9 (manufacturing)	$ 86 mill	
MG	Imports: merchandise	$ 86 mill	saar
MGAUS	Imports: autos and parts from US	$ 86 mill	ar,nsa
MGAUSV	Imports: autos and parts from US	$ mill	ar,nsa
MGO	Imports of goods excluding US-autos & petroleum	$ 86 mill	ar,nsa
MGOV	Imports of goods excluding US-autos & petroleum	$ mill	ar,nsa
MGPT	Imports of petroleum	$ 86 mill	ar,nsa
MGPTV	Imports of petroleum	$ mill	ar,nsa
MGV	Imports (merchandise)	$ 86 mill	saar
MONCUR	Currency outside banks	$ mill	nsa
MONM1	Narrowly defined money supply (ml)	$ mill	nsa
MONM2A	Broadly defined money supply (m2 variant)	$ mill	nsa
MS	Imports (services)	$ 86 mill	saar
MSCAPV	Capital service payments	$ mill	saar
MSV	Imports (services)	$ mill	saar
MV	Imports of goods and services	$ mill	saar
N	Total Canadian population	'000	
N15	Source population aged 15 years & over	'000	
N16	Source population aged 16 years & over	'000	
NCARSL	New passenger car sales	'000 units	saar
NF15	Population: female 15-24 years	'000	
NF25	Population: female 25-54 years	'000	
NF55	Population: female 55 years & over	'000	
NHH	Number of households (proxied by occupied dwelling stock)	'000	

MNEMONIC	DESCRIPTION	UNIT	SOURCE
NM15	Population: male 15-24 years	'000	
NM25	Population: male 25-54 years	'000	
NM55	Population: male 55 years & over	'000	
NMWUIB	Number of weeks of U.I. benefits paid in quarter	'000	nsa
NTXF	Total tax filers	'000	
ODBPCI	*Energy sims* change from control in energy corp new iss abroad		
ODBPDI	*Energy sims* change from contrl in foreign direct investment for energy		
ODCPAF	*Energy sims* change from control in cap assist (federal)		
ODCPAP	*Energy sims* change from control in cap assist (provincial)		
ODCRAT	*Energy sims* change from control in corporate revenue after tax		
ODCRP	*Energy sims* change from control in corp revenues		
ODECC	*Energy sims* change from control in exrta porfits;energy sector		
ODECCA	*Energy sims* change from contrl in energy corp cap cons allow		
ODEE	*Energy sims* change from control in energy sector employment		
ODEP	*Energy sims* change from control in energy RDP	$ 86 mill	
ODEWC	*Energy sims* change from control in wage bill - energy and supply sector		
ODIM	*Energy sims* change from control in real m&e invstment		
ODIN	*Energy sims* change from control in real non-residential invstment		
ODMP	*Energy sims* change from control in net petroleum & natural gas imports	$ mill	
ODROYP	*Energy sims* change from control in provincial royalties		
ODSBF	*Energy sims* change from control in fed subsidies		
ODTXF	*Energy sims* change from control in fed ind taxes		
PC	Deflator: consumption	86=1.0	
PCD	Deflator: consumption (durables)	86=1.0	
PCDA	Deflator: consumption (autos, parts & repairs)	86=1.0	
PCDO	Deflator: consumption (other durables)	86=1.0	
PCND	Deflator: consumption (non-durables)	86=1.0	
PCS	Deflator: consumption (services)	86=1.0	
PCSD	Deflator: consumption (semi-durables)	86=1.0	
PGC	Deflator: government current expenditure on goods & services	86=1.0	
PGDP	Deflator: gross domestic product	86=1.0	
PGDPF	Deflator: GDP at factor cost	86=1.0	
PGDPP	Deflator: private-sector GDP	86=1.0	
PGDPPF	Deflator: private GDP at factor cost	86=1.0	
PGI	Deflator: government capital formation & inventories	86=1.0	
PGNP	Deflator: gross national product	86=1.0	
PIFHB	Deflator: business residential construction	86=1.0	
PIFMB	Deflator: business investment in machinry & equipment	86=1.0	
PIFMBJ	After-tax cost of new machinery & equipment		
PIFNB	Deflator: business non-residential structures		
PIFNBJ	After-tax cost of new non-residential strucutures		
PIIB	Deflator: change in business inventories	86=1.0	
PM	Deflator: imports of goods & services	86=1.0	
PM01G	Import deflator: SITC 0, 1 (food, beverage)	86=1.0	nsa
PM24G	Import deflator: SITC 2, 4 (crude material)	86=1.0	nsa
PM3G	Import deflator: SITC 3 (fuel & lubricant)	86=1.0	
PM59G	Import deflator: SITC 5-9 (manufacturing)	86=1.0	
PMG	Deflator: imports of merchandise	86=1.0	
PMGAUS	Import deflator: autos and parts from US	86=1.0	
PMGO	Import deflator: goods excluding US-autos, petroleum	86=1.0	nsa

MNEMONIC	DESCRIPTION	UNIT	SOURCE
PMGPT	Import deflator: petroleum	86=1.0	nsa
PMS	Import deflator: services	86=1.0	
POIL	Refinery feedstock price of crude oil (Toronto)	$/bbl.	
PTTG	Terms of trade: merchandise (PXG/PMG)	86=1.0	
PTTR	Terms of trade: (PX/PM)	86=1.0	
PTTS	Terms of trade: services (PXS/PMS)	86=1.0	
PWG	Deflator: government wages	86=1.0	
PX	Deflator: exports of goods & services	86=1.0	
PX01G	Export deflator: SITC 0, 1 (food, beverage)	86=1.0	
PX24G	Export deflator: SITC 2, 4 (crude material)	86=1.0	nsa
PX3G	Export deflator: SITC 3 (fuel & lubricant)	86=1.0	
PX59G	Export deflator: SITC 5-9 (manufacturing)	86=1.0	nsa
PXG	Export deflator: merchandise	86=1.0	
PXGAUS	Export deflator: autos and parts to US	86=1.0	
PXGO	Export deflator: goods excluding US-autos, petroleum & natural gas	86=1.0	nsa
PXGPN	Export deflator: petroleum and gas	86=1.0	nsa
PXS	Export deflator: services	86=1.0	
RCDIFM	Rate of investment tax credit on machinery & equipment		
RCDIFN	Rate of investment tax credit on non-residential structures		
RDEPM	Rate of depreciation allowed for taxes (mach. & equip.)		
RDEPN	Rate of depreciation allowed for taxes (non-res. structures)		
RDFUL	Canada-US interest rate differential (long)		
RDFUS	Canada-US interest rate differential (short)		
RDGU	Canada-US GNP growth-rate differential	%	
RDIS	Adjustment ratio for 'key' price reconsiliation (NRML=1)		
RDIU	Canada-US inflation rate differential (GNP deflator)	%	
RECP90	Expected rate of CPI infalation 90 days ahead	%	ar
RECPI1	Expected rate of CPI inflation 1 year ahead	%	ar
RECPI2	Expected rate of CPI inflation 2 years ahead	%	
RERX5	Expected change in exchange rate 5 years ahead	%	
RERX90	Expected change in exchange rate 1 quarter ahead	%	ar
RESALL	Resource allowance reduction rate		
RFDBTF	Ratio of federal debt to nominal GNP	%	
RGGNP	Rate of growth of real GNP (year-over-year)	%	
RGPFL	Productivity growth: private sector, factor cost	%	
RGPRD5	Growth rate of labour productivity (private sector, 5 year moving average)	%	
RIFYC	Ratio: business non-residential investment / profits + CCA		
RINFC	Inflation rate (CPI), year-over-year	%	
RINFG	Inflation rate (PGDP), year-over-year	%	
RMBC	Bank of Canada bank rate	%	
RMBG1	Yield on 1 to 3 year government of Canada bonds	%	
RMBG10	Yield on 10 year & over government of Canada bonds	%	
RMCBP	Chartered banks prime lending rate	%	
RMF	Yield on 90-day prime corporate paper	%	
RMMTG	Convential mortgage yield	%	
RMMYWI	Mcleod young weir yield on 10 industrial bonds	%	
RMMYWM	Mcleod young weir yield on 10 municipal bonds	%	
RMMYWP	Mcleod young weir yield on 10 provincial bonds	%	
RMRL1	Real rate of interest on 1-3 year government bonds	%	
RMRLF	Real rate of interest on 90-day finance company paper	%	
RP	Participation rate (total economy)	%	sa
RPF15	Participation rate (female 15-24 years)	%	sa
RPF25	Participation rate (female 25-54 years)	%	sa
RPF55	Participation rate (female 55 years & over)	%	sa
RPM15	Participation rate (male 15-24 years)	%	sa
RPM25	Participation rate (male 25-54 years)	%	sa

MNEMONIC	DESCRIPTION	UNIT	SOURCE
RPM55	Participation rate (male 55 years & over)	%	sa
RPRDG	Output per employee, (GDPF/LE)	$ 86 '000	
RRDD	Legal reserve ratio on chartered bank demand deposits		
RRDIF	Difference in internal and external after-tax rates of return		
RRIFN	After-tax real rate of return on new non-residential structures		
RRTD	Legal res. ratio on chartered bank time & notice deposits		
RSP	Personal saving rate as percent of disposable income		
RSPJ	Inflation-adjusted personal saving rate	%	
RTCFCR	Ratio: federal corporate tax investment tax credits/total investment		
RTCPP	Statutory rate for contributions to Canada pension plan		
RTCUI	Statutory rate for contributions to unemployment insurance		
RTDPOP	Average tax rate: 'other' provincial personal taxes		
RTFBAV	Average basic federal tax rate of average taxfiler (rate)		
RTIATF	Average rate for federal alcoh & tob excise duties and taxes		
RTIFMS	Federal manuf. sales tax rate, expressed as a decimal		
RTIFTA	Federal rate of taxation for alcohol and tobacco		
RTIGSF	Average rate for federal gasoline tax (constructed)		
RTIGSP	Average tax rate (provincial gasoline taxes, rate of CNDV)		
RTILCP	Average tax rate (provincial liquor commissions, rate of CNDV)		
RTIMO	Tax rate (import duties, calculated on MGOV)		
RTIPO	Average tax rate (provincial other indirect taxes, rate of GDPPV)		
RTIRSP	Average tax rate (provincial retail sales taxes, rate)		
RTPDXJ	'Floor' to personal tax indexation rate (3.0 for 1985 -)		
RTPIDX	Personal tax indexation factor (growth rate)	%	
RTX16	Income tax exemption/credit (children 16 and over)	$ '000	
RTX16U	Income tax exemption/credit (children under 16)	$ '000	
RTX65	Income tax exemption/credit (65 and over)	$ '000	
RTXCDV	Rate of dividend tax credits on VAVGY		
RTXEX	Tax exemption/credit (basic personal)	$ '000	
RTXEXS	Income tax exemption/credit (married or equivalent)	$ '000	
RTXINT	Rate of interest income deductions applied to VAVGY		
RTXRPP	Rate of registered pension plan deductions applied to VAVGY		
RTXRSP	Rate of RRSP deductions applied to VAVGY		
RTYCEF	Effective rate of tax-corp. income- sum of fed, oas & prov rates		
RTYCFH	Tax rate: corp. income, federal high rate (on inc ¿ YCMAXL)		
RTYCFL	Tax rate: corp. income, federal low rate (appl. to 1st YCMAXL)		
RTYCOA	Rate of tax-old age security: applied to corp. income 1952-71		
RTYCP	Tax rate: corporate income, weighted average of provincial rates		
RTYPS	Average rate of surtax on federal basic tax		
RTYPWQ	Weighted average provincial personal tax rates on federal basic tax		

MNEMONIC	DESCRIPTION	UNIT	SOURCE
RU	Unemployment rate	%	sa
RUNAT	Natural rate of unemployment		
RWPAA	Wage inflation (private sector, 4-quarter percent change in WPAA)		
RWPAAR	Real wage (growth rate)	%	
RWSUB	Rate of wage subsidy (Zero historical rate)		
RXEX90	Expected level of spot exchange rate 1 quarter in future	CDN$/US$	
RXUS	Exchange rate	CDN$/US$	noon
RXUSX	Exch rate exogenized (for exog exch rate sims)		
RXWM	Foreign (weighted (imports) exchange rate index)	c$/wrld (86=1)	
RXWX	Foreign (weighted (exports) exchange rate index)	c$/wrld (86=1)	
RYCG	Ratio: profits of government bus enterprises to corporate profits		
RYCGDP	Ratio: corporate profit & CCA's/GDP Personal saving	$ mill	saar
SU	Government subsidies (total)	$ mill	saar
SUF	Government subsidies (federal)	$ mill	saar
SUL	Government subsidies (local)	$ mill	saar
SUP	Government subsidies (provincial)	$ mill	saar
TDCF	Direct taxes (corporate and government enterprises, federal)	$ mill	saar
TDCFGE	Corporate taxes (federal, government bus enterprises)	$ mill	saar
TDCP	Direct taxes (corporate and governmentt enterprises, provincial)	$ mill	saar
TDNF	Federal direct tax (withholding) on non-residential	$ mill	saar
TDP	Current transfer & direct taxes (personal to government)	$ mill	saar
TDPENF	Direct taxes (federal contribution to public services, pension)	$ mill	saar
TDPENP	Direct taxes (provincial contribution to public services)	$ mill	saar
TDPF	Direct taxes and transfers from persons (federal)	$ mill	saar
TDPH	Ohter current transfers from persons (hospital)	$ mill	saar
TDPL	Other current transfers from persons (local)	$ mill	saar
TDPOF	Direct taxes (others, federal)	$ mill	saar
TDPOP	Direct taxes (others, provincial)	$ mill	saar
TDPP	Direct taxes and transfers from persons, provincial	$ mill	saar
TDPPE	Employer & employee contribution (Canada & Quebec pension plan	$ mill	saar
TDPY	Personal income taxes, federal & provincial	$ mill	saar
TDPYF	Personal income taxes, federal	$ mill	saar
TDPYFB	Basic federal tax of average taxfiler	$ '000	
TDPYP	Personal income taxes, provincial	$ mill	saar
TDUNF	Direct taxes(unemployment insurance contributions, federal)	$ mill	saar
TDWCP	Direct taxes (contributions to workmens compensation, provincial)	$ mill	saar
TI	Indirect taxes (total)	$ mill	saar
TIATF	Federal excise duties & taxes on alcohol & tobacco	$ mill	saar
TIENRF	Federal indirect taxes on energy production/sales	$ mill	saar
TIF	Indirect taxes (federal)	$ mill	saar
TIFO	Indirect taxes (others, federal)	$ mill	saar
TIGSF	Federal indirect taxes(gasoline tax)	$ mill	saar
TIGSP	Indirect taxes (gasoline tax, provincial)	$ mill	saar
TIL	Indirect taxes (local)	$ mill	saar
TILCP	Indirect taxes (profits on liquor commissions, provincial)	$ mill	saar
TIM	Indirect tax (import duties, federal)	$ mill	saar
TIP	Indirect taxes (provincial)	$ mill	saar
TIPO	Indirect taxes (all other indirect taxes, provincial)	$ mill	saar
TIPROP	Indirect taxes (property taxes, local)	$ mill	saar

MNEMONIC	DESCRIPTION	UNIT	SOURCE
TIRSP	Indirect taxes (retail sales tax, provincial)	$ mill	saar
TISF	Indirect taxes (manufacturers' sales tax, federal)	$ mill	saar
TRCP	Current transfers from corporations to persons	$ mill	saar
TRGC	Government capital assistance (tatal)	$ mill	saar
TRGCAP	Current transfers from government (capital assistance)	$ mill	saar
TRGCF	Government capital assistance (federal)	$ mill	saar
TRGCP	Government capital assistance (provincial)	$ mill	saar
TRGID	Interest on the public debt (total)	$ mill	saar
TRGIDF	Interest on the public debt (federal)	$ mill	saar
TRGIDH	Interest on the public debt (hospitals)	$ mill	saar
TRGIDL	Interest on the public debt (local)	$ mill	saar
TRGIDP	Interest on the public debt (provincial)	$ mill	saar
TRGN	Government transfers to non-residents (total)	$ mill	saar
TRGNF	Corrent government transfers to non-residents (federal)	$ mill	saar
TRGNPE	Current government transfers to non-residents (CPP & QPP)	$ mill	saar
TRGP	Current transfers from government to persons	$ mill	saar
TRGPF	Transfers to persons (federal)	$ mill	saar
TRGPFO	Transfers to persons (federal, except UI)	$ mill	saar
TRGPL	Transfers to persons (local)	$ mill	saar
TRGPP	Transfers to persons (provincial)	$ mill	saar
TRGPPE	Transfers to persons (CPP & QPP)	$ mill	saar
TRGUI	Federal: total unemployment benefits paid	$ mill	saar
TRNETF	Net transfer from (+) or to (-) other government (federal)	$ mill	saar
TRNETH	Net transfer from (+) or to (-) other government (hospital)	$ mill	saar
TRNETL	Net transfer from (+) or to (-) other government (local)	$ mill	saar
TRNETP	Net transfer from (+) or to (-) other government (provincial)	$ mill	saar
TRNP	Current transfers from non-residents to persons	$ mill	saar
TRPC	Current transfers from persons to corporations	$ mill	saar
TRPIP	Petroleum incentives payments grants		
TRPN	Current transfers from persons to non-residents	$ mill	saar
TXPGRT	Petroleum and gas revenue tax + IORT (federal corporate tax)	$ mill	saar
UGYQIN	W. Germany: Index of Industrial Production	86=1.0	
UGYWPI	W. Germany: Wholesale Price Index	86=1.0	
UJAQIN	Japan: Index of Industrial Production	86=1.0	
UJAWPI	Japan: Wholesale Price Index	86=1.0	nsa
UPMGPT	Import deflator: petroleum (CDN$, 86=1.0)	US$	
UPXGPN	Export deflator: petroleum and gas (CDN$, 86=1.0)	US$	
USCDA	US consumption: motor vehicles & parts	$ 82 bill	
USCPI	US consumer price index	67=1.00	
USDRTF	US: change in tariff rates on 'XGO'; used in UWWPIX	%	
USGNP	US: gross national product	$ 82 bill	
USGNPV	US: gross national product	$ bill	
USPCDA	US: deflator, consumption of motor vehecle & parts	82=1.0	
USPGNP	US: GNP deflator	82=1.0	
USQIND	US: industrial production index	86=1.0	
USRMAA	US: yield on Moodys AAA industrial bonds	%	
USRMTB	US: average market yield on 3-Month T-bills		
USRU	US: unemployment rate	%	
USRXGY	W. Germany: exchange rate	US$/DM	
USRXJA	Japan: exchange rate	US$/Yen	
USRXUK	UK: exchange rate	US$/Sterling	
USWPI	US: wholesale price index	86=1.0	
USWRPW	US: index of hourly earnings production workers	67=1.00	
UUKQIN	UK: index of industrial production	86=1.0	
UUKWPI	UK: wholesale price index	86=1.0	
UWQIND	Foreign: weighted (exports) index of industrial production	86=1.0	

MNEMONIC	DESCRIPTION	UNIT	SOURCE
UWWPIM	Foreign: weighted (imports) index of WPI's	86=1.0	
UWWPIX	Foreign: weighted (exports) index of WPI's	86=1.0	
VAVGY	Gross income reported by average taxfiler	$ '000	
VELM1	Velocity of narrowly-defined money (GDPV/MONM1)		
VELM2	Velocity of broadly-defined money (GDPV/MONM2A)		
VRBATE	Rate of abatement of corporate tax income from federal government to province		
VRBATW	weighted average abatement rate for personal income taxes (rate)		
VTCFCR	Federal investment tax credits	$ mill	saar
VTDCPP	CPP/QPP deductions/credits of average taxfiler	$ '000	
VTDEMP	Employment expense deductions of average taxfiler	$ '000	
VTDINT	Interest income deductions of average taxfiler	$ '000	
VTDOTH	Residual deductions of average taxfiler	$ '000	
VTDRPP	Registered pension plan deductions of average taxfiler	$ '000	
VTDRSP	RRSP deductions of average taxfiler	$ '000	
VTDUIC	UIC deductions/credits of average taxfiler	$ '000	
VTXCDV	Dividend tax credits of average taxfiler	$ '000	
VTXCOT	Other tax credits of average taxfiler(diff post reform)	$ '000	
VTXCST	Federal sales tax credits of average taxfiler	$ '000	
VTXCTC	Child tax credits of average taxfiler	$ '000	
VTXDED	Total deductions of average taxfiler	$ '000	
VTXPEX	Total personal exemptions/credits of average taxfiler	$ '000	
VTXRED	Average federal tax reduction per avg taxfiler	$ '000	
VTXYP	Taxable income of average taxfiler	$ '000	
VTXYPZ	Other adjustments to taxable income of average taxfiler	$ '000	
VWBUIM	Maximum weekly unemployment insurance benefit payable	$	
VWTDM	Import demand based on Input-Output weights	$ 86 Mill	saar
VYWCPP	Maximum wage earnings subject to Canada pension plan contributions		
VYWUIN	Maximum annual earnings subject to unemployment insurance contributions	$ '000	
WPAA	Average annual wage of employees in the private sector	$ '000	
X	Exports of goods and services	$ 86 mill	saar
X01G	Exports: SITC 0, 1 (food, beverage)	$ 86 mill	saar
X24G	Exports: SITC 2, 4 (crude material)	$ 86 mill	saar
X3G	Exports: SITC 3 (fuel & lubricant)	$ 86 mill	
X59G	Exports: SITC 5-9 (manufacturing)	$ 86 mill	
XG	Exports: merchandise	$ 86 mill	saar
XGAUS	Exports: autos and parts to US	$ 86 mill	ar,nsa
XGAUSV	Exports: autos and parts to US	$ mill	ar,nsa
XGO	Exports of goods excluding US-autos, petroleum & natural gas	$ 86 mill	ar,nsa
XGOV	Exports of goods excluding US-autos, petroleum & natural gas	$ mill	ar,nsa
XGPN	Exports: petroleum & natural gas	$ 86 mill	ar,nsa
XGPNV	Exports: petroleum & natural gas	$ mill	ar,nsa
XGV	Exports: merchandise	$ mill	saar
XS	Exports: services	$ 86 mill	saar
XSCAPV	Capital service receipts	$ mill	saar
XSV	Exports: services	$ mill	saar
XV	Exports of goods and services	$ mill	saar
Y	Net domestic income at factor cost	$ mill	saar
YC	Corporation profits before taxes	$ mill	saar
YCAT	Corporation profits after taxes	$ mill	saar
YCBDCH	Corporate bad debts and charitable contributions	$ mill	saar
YCG	Pre-tax profits of government enterprises	$ mill	saar
YCMAXL	Maximum corporate taxable income subject to low rate	$ '000	
YCU	Undistributed corporation profits	$ mill	saar
YCWT	Corporate withholding taxes paid to non-residents	$ mill	saar

MNEMONIC	DESCRIPTION	UNIT	SOURCE
YDN	Dividends paid to non-residents	$ mill	saar
YDRES	Dividends paid to Canadian residents	$ mill	saar
YGI	Government investment income (total)	$ mill	saar
YGIF	Government investment income (federal)	$ mill	saar
YGIH	Government investment income (hospitals)	$ mill	saar
YGIL	Government investment income (local)	$ mill	saar
YGIOP	Government non-royalty investment income (provincial)	$ mill	
YGIP	Government investment income (provincial)	$ mill	saar
YGIPE	Government investment income (CPP & QPP)	$ mill	saar
YICNR	Corporate interest and miscellanious paid to non-residents	$ mill	saar
YIND	Interest, dividends and miscellanious investment income	$ mill	saar
YINMIS	Interest and miscellanious investment income	$ mill	saar
YINRC	Corporate interest and dividends from non-resident	$ mill	saar
YIVA	Inventory valuation adjustment	$ mill	saar
YN	Net national income at factor cost	$ mill	saar
YNRENT	Net rental income (unincorporate business)	$ mill	saar
YP	Personal income	$ mill	saar
YPD	Personal disposable income	$ mill	saar
YPINM	Interest & miscellanious investment income of persons	$ mill	saar
YPPMHR	Real permanent income per household	$ 86 '000	saar
YPTRHR	Real transitory income per household	$ 86 '000	saar
YROYP	Government royaties (provincial)	$ mill	
YUAF	Accrued net income of farm operators from farm production	$ mill	saar
YUAFAD	Adjustment on grain transactions	$ mill	saar
YUNFRT	Net income of non-farm unincorporate bus., including rent	$ mill	saar
YURF	Net income received by farm operators from farm production	$ mill	saar
YW	Wages, salaries and supplementary labor income	$ mill	saar
YWG	Wages, salaries and supplementary labor income (government)	$ mill	saar
YWP	Wages, salaries and supplementary labor income (private)	$ mill	saar
ZC	Adjusting entry (consumption)	$ 86 mill	saar
ZGBFRF	Difference between PA financial required & NA surplus/deficit	$ mill	
ZGBPAF	Difference between public & national accounts surplus/deficit	$ mill	
ZGDP	Adjusting entry (GDP)	$ 86 mill	saar
ZIFB	Adjusting entry (business investment)	$ 86 mill	saar
ZM	Adjusting entry (imports)	$ 86 mill	saar
ZMTISF	Rate of advantage manufacturing sales tax gives imports (0.2 of tax rate)		
ZPCHK	Check on 'key' price reconciliation (diff in GDPP calcs)		
ZSD	Statistical discrepancy	$ 86 mill	saar
ZSDV	Statistical discrepancy	$ mill	saar
ZX	Adjusting entry (exports)	$ 86 mill	saar
ZYIND	Adjustment (interest, div & misc inv of persons)	$ mill	saar

4 The FOCUS Model Equations

4.1 Auto and Consumer Spending

$$YPPMHR = \frac{nlag-1}{nlag} * YPPMHR + \frac{1}{nlag^{nlag}} * \frac{YPD}{\frac{PC}{NHH}}$$

$$YPTRHR = \frac{YPD}{\frac{PC}{NHH}} - YPPMHR$$

$$AW1 = FDBTF + MONM1 + (KFNB + KFMB + KFHB) * PC$$

$$-(KBBC + KBBPL) * RXUS - KBDILR * Pkb$$

$$+KBDILR * USPGNP * RXUS$$

$$AFDIJ = J12A * FDBTF * \frac{RINFG}{100}$$

$$JUCA = 9.67014 * CPIA * (0.8333 + \frac{RMF - RECPII}{400} - \frac{\frac{CPIA}{CPIA|8} - 1}{8}$$

$$+0.222808 * CPIG$$

$$CDA = YPPMHR * NHH * (0.1797441 + 0.008692256 * \frac{YPTRHR}{YPPMHR}$$

(3.6) (0.41)

$$+0.02571205 * \frac{N16}{NHH} - \frac{0.09637693KCARS}{NHH} - 0.01204968 * \frac{JUCA}{PC}$$

(2.1) (2.9) (2.0)

$$-0.12390980 * \frac{PCDA}{PC} - 0.003002015 * (RU - RUNAT) - 0.4344678$$

(9.5) (10.4) (5.1)

$$* \frac{\frac{AFDIJ}{\frac{PC}{NHH}}}{YPPMHR} + 0.01735384 * \frac{\frac{AW1}{\frac{PC}{NHH}}}{YPPMHR}$$

(5.2)

$$NCARSL = -353.2489 + 0.1669059 * CDA - 0.0007217037 * CDA * DTIME$$

$$(7.1) \qquad (20.8) \qquad (13.9)$$

$$CDO = YPPMHR * MHH * (0.06353099 + 0.01579680 * \frac{YPTRHR}{YPPMHR}$$

$$(4.6) \qquad (1.6)$$

$$+0.01671279 * \frac{HCS}{NHH} - 0.02380637 * \frac{PCDO}{PC} - 0.001051306 * RU$$

$$(0.54) \qquad (6.0) \qquad (3.4)$$

$$-RUNAT - 0.1264560 * \frac{\frac{\frac{AFDIJ}{PC}}{NHH}}{YPPMHR} + 0.007259062 * \frac{\frac{\frac{AW1}{PC}}{NHH}}{YPPMHR}$$

$$(1.0) \qquad (2.0)$$

$$CSD = YPPMHR * NHH * (0.08019116 + 0.02709282 * \frac{YPTRHR}{YPPMHR}$$

$$(9.4) \qquad (2.3)$$

$$+0.008161273 * \frac{N}{NHH} - 0.02541081 * \frac{PCSD}{PC} - 0.0005787084 * (RU - RUNAT)$$

$$(1.8) \qquad (1.3) \qquad (2.3)$$

$$-0.3650955 * \frac{\frac{\frac{AFDIJ}{PC}}{NHH}}{YPPMHR} + 0.006072079 * \frac{\frac{\frac{AW1}{PC}}{NHH}}{YPPMHR}$$

$$(5.7) \qquad (5.9)$$

$$CND = YPPMHR * NHH * (0.1754502 + 0.08625385 * \frac{N}{NHH} - 0.2648446 * \frac{PCND}{PC}$$

$$(2.9) \qquad (10.2) \qquad (5.3)$$

$$-0.00001074256 * (RU - RUNAT) - 0.4310440 * \frac{\frac{\frac{AFDIJ}{PC}}{NHH}}{YPPMHR}$$

$$(0.01) \qquad (1.5)$$

$$+0.02984222 * \frac{\frac{\frac{AW1}{PC}}{NHH}}{YPPMHR}$$

$$(5.5)$$

$$CS = YPPMHR * NHH * (0.2350314 - 0.0007125589 * DTCS + 0.01625966 * \frac{N}{NHH}$$

$$(1.0) \qquad (0.62) \qquad (0.5)$$

$$-0.5655446 * \frac{\frac{\frac{AFDIJ}{PC}}{NHH}}{YPPMHR} + 0.06466136 * \frac{\frac{\frac{AW1}{PC}}{NHH}}{YPPMHR}$$

$$(1.6) \qquad (4.8)$$

Definitions and Identities

$$CD = CDA + CDO$$

$$C = CD + CSD + CND + CS + ZC$$

$$CDAV = PCDA * CDA$$

$$CDOV = CDV - CDAV$$

$$CSDV = PCSD * CSD$$

$$CNDV = PCND * CND$$

$$CSV = PCS * CS$$

$$CDV = PCD * CD$$

$$CV = CDV + CSDV + CNDV + CSV$$

4.2 Public Finance / Government Expenditure

Government current and capital expenditure may be specified to be exogenous in real terms (DG(424)=0, default) or in nominal terms (DG=1). Under the first option, the exogenous items are real expenditures by level of government. In the data bank, each of these series is simply the appropriate nominal expenditure deflated by the aggregate expenditure deflator. Under the second option, it is the nominal expenditures by level of government that are exogenous, while real expenditure are calculated endogenously with the aggregate deflator.

Real Spending Exogenous (DG=0) GCF, GTCP, GCL, GCH, GCPE (Federal, Provincial, Local, Hospitals, Pension Plans) are exogenous. $GC_iV = GC_i * PGC$ for i=F, P, L, H, PE and GIF, GIP, GIL, GIH are exogenous. $GI_iV = GI_i * PGI$ for i=F, P, L, H.

Nominal Spending Exogenous (DG=1) GCFV, GCPV, GCLV, GCHV, GCPEV (Current Expenditure) are exogenous. $GC_i = \frac{GC_iV}{PGC}$ for i = F, P, L, H, PE. GIFV, GIPV, GILV, GIHV (Capital Expenditure) are exogenous. $GI_i = \frac{GI_iV}{PGC}$ for i = F, P, L, H.

Identities

$$BC = BCF + GCP + GCL + GCH + GCPE$$

$$GI = GIF + GIP + GIL + GIH$$

$$GCV = GCFV + GCPV + GCLV + GCPEV$$

$$GIV = GIFV + GIPV + GILV + GIHV$$

$$G = GC + GI$$

$$GV = GCV + GIV$$

4.3 Investment and Inventories

$$RRIFN = 400 * (\frac{(1 - RTYCEF) * \frac{YC_{-1} + YIVA_{-1} + CCAC_{-1}}{(0.7530 - \frac{2.5312}{DTIME}) * KFNB} - 0.0125 * PIFNBJ}{(1 - 0..125) * PIFNBJ + (1 - 0.0357) * \frac{JFNB}{KFNB} * PIFMBJ}$$

$$+ \frac{0.0357 * \frac{KFMB}{KFNB} * PIFMBJ}{(1 - 0..125) * PIFNBJ + (1 - 0.0357) * \frac{JFNB}{KFNB} * PIFMBJ})$$

$$PIFNBJ = PIFNB * (1 - (RCDIFN + RTYCEF * (1 - RCDOFM) * RDEPN$$

$$*(DCCAHY * (0.5 + (1 - \frac{RDEPN}{2}) * (1 + \frac{RMBG1}{100} + RDEPN)))$$

$$+(1 - DCCAHY) * (\frac{1 + \frac{RMBG1}{100}}{\frac{RMBG1}{100} + RDEPN})))$$

$$PIFMBJ = PIFMB * (1 - (RCDIFM + RTYCEF * (1 - RCDIFM) * RDEPM$$

$$*(1 + \frac{RMBG1}{100}) * (1 + \frac{RMBG1}{100} + RDEPM)$$

$$*(1 + DCCIMR * 0.5 * (\frac{\frac{RECPI1}{100}}{\frac{RMRL1}{100}} + RDEPM))$$

$$+(1 - DCCAHY) * \frac{1 + \frac{RMBG1}{100}}{\frac{RMBG1}{100} + RDEPM}))$$

$$RTYCEF = RTYCFH + RTYCOA + RTYCP - VRBATE$$

$$KFNB = (1.0 - 0.0125) * KFNB_{-1} + \frac{IFNB_{-1}}{4}$$

$$IFNB = 0.0125 * KFNB + KFNB * (0.05627872 + 0.001478874 * (0.3679086 * RRDIF$$

(6.2) (2.63) (2.0)

$$+(1 - 0.36779086) * J8W(RRDIF)|1)) + 974.6860 * D75$$

(2.0) (1.77)

$$IFNBV = PIFNB * IFNB$$

$$JUCIFM = PIFMBJ * \frac{\frac{0.1429 + J6A(RMRL)1}{100}}{1 - RTYCEF}$$

$$KFMB = (1 - 0.0357) * KFMB_{-1} + \frac{IFMB_{-1}}{4}$$

$$IFMB = kpoh < t + 1 > + kpprod < t + 1 > - KFMB + 0.0357 * KFMB$$

where

kpoh$< t+1 >$	:	overhead machinery and equipment capital stock (at the end of period) $= 0.1 * (0.9875 * KFNB + IFNB)$
kpprod$< t+1 >$	:	production (variable) machinery and equipment stock (at the end of current period, actual) $= 0.1 * kpprod * + (1 - 0.1) * lpprod < t >$
kpprod$< t >$	:	production (variable) machinery and equipment stock (at end of previous period) $= KFMB - (0.1 * (0.9875 * KFNB\|1 + IFNB\|1))$
kpprod*	:	desired (cost-minimizing) stock of production (variable) machinery and equipment $= 0.1549715 * (0.2354911 * kpoc + (1.2354911) * J8W(kpoc)\|1)$
kpoc	:	'output/cost' expression $= \frac{GDPPFV}{JUCIFM}$

$$IFMBV = PIFMN * IFMN$$

$$IFB = IFHB + IFNB + IFMB + ZIFB$$

$$IFBV = IFHBV + IFNBV + IFMNV$$

$$RIFYC = \frac{IFNBV + IFMBV}{YC + CCAC}$$

$$KINF = KINF_{-1} + \frac{IINF_{-1}}{4.}$$

$$IINF = \underset{(0.94)}{22516.65} + \underset{(2.31)}{0.1425119} * \frac{sales + sales|1}{2} - \underset{(0.43)}{6.243757}$$

$$* \frac{\frac{Sales + Sales|1}{2}}{DTIME} - \underset{(2.63)}{0.4735543} * KINF - \underset{(4.76)}{49812.85}$$

$$* \frac{Sales + Sales|1}{Sales|1}$$

$$IIB = IINF + IIF$$

$$IIBV = PIIB * IIB.$$

4.4 Housing and Residential Investment

$$HSS = NHH * (\underset{(6.8)}{0.2379572} - \underset{(19.9)}{0.0064020} * (DSQ1 - DSQ4) + \underset{(8.8)}{0.002836237} * (DSQ2$$

$$-DSQ4)) + \underset{(8.3)}{0.002644279} * (DSQ3 - DSQ4) + \underset{(3.9)}{0.0006393063} * {}_{J}8A(RINFC)$$

$$+\frac{2.357065}{DTIME} - 0.001480092 * (RU - RUNAT) - 0.001575017$$

(4.9) (5.8) (7.5)

$$*J2A(RMMTG) - 0.3694633 * \frac{KHS}{NHH} + 0.003839528 * Chosp$$

(5.9) (2.4)

where Chosp is a dummy for Canadian Home Ownership Stimulation Program (CHOSP) 1 for 82.2 - 83.2

$$HSM = NHH * (0.0715841 - 0.004704620 * (DSQ1 - DSQ4) + 0.001218166 * (DSQ2$$

(1.1) (10.6) (2.8)

$$-DSQ4) + 0.001436924 * (DSQ3 - DSQ4) - \frac{0.9571025}{DTIME} - 0.001271726$$

(3.3) (1.0) (2.4)

$$*(RU - RUNAT) - 0.0006976166 * J2A(RMMYWI) - 0.0936899 * \frac{KHM}{NHH}$$

(1.2) (0.7)

$$IFHB = 546.6918 + 0.002858013 * (DSQ1 - DSQ4) * KFHB + 0.002038372 * (DSQ2$$

(0.7) (9.2) (1.0)

$$-DSQ4) * KFHB - 0.001467505 * (DSQ3 - DSQ4) * KFHB + 0.03577875$$

(5.9) (12.0)

$$*KFHB + \sum_{i=0}^{3} a < i > *HSS * \frac{DTIME}{146.5(i)} + \sum_{i=0}^{3} b < i > *HSM * \frac{DTIME}{146.5_{-i}}$$

where

a0 = 9.6551(9.9), Sum = 96.551; b0 = 11.8566(3.4), b1 = 8.8924(3.4),
b2 = 5.9283(3.4), b3 = 2.9641(3.4), Sum= 29.641, DEG 1
FAR.

$$HCS = \sum_{i=0}^{3} a < i > *HSS_{-i}$$

where

a0 = 0.3588(16.6), a1 = 0.3720(45.6) a2 = 0.2525(17.3), Sum = 0.9833
DEG2, FAR

$$HCM = \sum_{i=0}^{3} a < i > *HSM_{-i}$$

where

a0 = 0.1505(6.6), a1 = 0.1433(10.4), a2 = 0.1344(21.7), a3 = 0.1237(83.4),
a4 = 0.1113(22.7), a5 = 0.0971(12.4), a6 = 0.0812(8.7), a7 = 0.0635(6.8),
a8 = 0.0441(5.7), a9 = 0.0229(5.0), Sum=0.97218, DEG 2,
FAR

4.5 Foreign Trade

$$XGO = \exp(11.31997 + (Dummies for 673, 703, 713, 721, 742, 744, 763, 793)$$

$$+ \sum a < i > * \log UWQIND_{-i} + SUMb < i > * \log(PXGO$$

$$* \frac{1 + RTFUS}{RXWX})_{-i} + \sum c < i > \log UWWPIX_{-i}$$

where

a0 = 0.4797 (12.0),	b0 = -0.1696 (2.4),	c0 = 0.2876 (4.0)
a1 = 0.3598 (12.0),	b1 = -0.2185 (3.0),	c1 = 0.3921 (4.3)
a2 = 0.2399 (12.0),	b2 = -0.1852 (5.0),	c2 = 0.3611 (5.0)
a3 = 0.1199 (12.0),	b3 = -0.1082 (4.0),	c3 = 0.2423 (7.4)
	b4 = -0.0260 (0.4),	c4 = 0.0834 (4.0)
	b5 = +0.0229 (0.4),	c5 =-0.0680 (1.1)
		c6 =-0.1641 (2.0)
		c7 =-0.1574 (2.4)
Sum = 1.1993	Sum = -0.684557	Sum = 0.9770
DEG 1, FAR	DEG 2, FAR	DEG 2, FAR

$$UWQIND = JXUS * USQIND + JXJA * UJAQIN + JXUK * UUKQIN$$

$$+ JXGY * UGYQIN$$

$$JXUS = 1.0 - (JXJA + JXUK + JXGY)$$

$$JMUS = 1.0 - (JAJA + JMUK + JMGY)$$

$$UWWPIX = JXUS * \frac{USWPI}{1.0 + USDRTR * 0.01} + JXJA * UJAWPI$$

$$+ JXUK * UUKWPI + JXGY * UGYWPI$$

$$RXWX = RXUS * \frac{JXUS + JXJA * \frac{USRXJA}{0.46275}}{1.38988}$$

PXGO : Deflator-Exports of merchandise excluding petroleum and natural gas and automobile trade with the US, 1986=1.0

1) version 0 (AA(PXGO,1)=0.0): Price-Maker (Growth Rate)

$PXGO = Pxgtmp * (0.05 + 0.95 * \frac{PXGO\_1}{Pxgtmp\_1}$

where $Pxgtmp = ((1 - 0.23010) * PGDPPF + 0.23010 * PMGO$
$*(1 + RTIMO)) * (1 + (1.7 * 0.043) * RTIFMS)$
$*(1 + (1.7 * 0.051) * RTIRSP)$

Note: as of 91:1, RTIFMS term disappears, reflecting GST.

2) version 1 (AA(PXGO,1)=1.0): Price-Taker (Growth Rate)

$PXGO = Pftmp * (0.05 + 0.95 * \frac{PVGO\_1}{Pftmp\_1})$

where $Pftmp = UWWPIX * RXWX$

3) version 2 (AA(XGO,1)=2.0): Mixed Price Maker-Taker

$PXGO = (0.25 * Pxgtmp + 0.75 * Pftmp) * (0.05$
$+0.95 * \frac{PXGO\_1}{(0.25*Pxgtmp+0.75*Pftmp)\_1})$

4) version 3 (AA(PXGO,1)=3.0): Price-Maker (change from base)

$PXGO = BasePXGO * \frac{Pxgtmp}{BasePxgtmp}$

5) version 4 (AA(PXGO,1)=4.0): Price-Taker (change from base)

$PXGO = BasePXGO * \frac{Pftmp}{BasePftmp}$

6) version 5 (AA(PXGO,1)=5.0): Mixed Maker-Taker (Change from Base)

$PXGO = BasePXGO * \frac{0.25*Pxgytmp+0.75Pftmp}{Base(0.25*Pxgrmp+0.75*Pftmp)}$

$$XGAUS = \exp(3.776463 + 0.8360 * \log USCDA + 0.4180 * \log USCDA|1$$

(7.3) (11.1) (PDL-DEG2,FAR)

$$+0.5458 * \log RXUS + 0.2729 * \log RXUS|1)$$

(3.2)

PXGAUS : Deflator-Exports of Autos and Parts to the US, 1986=1.0

1) version 0 (Default) (AA(146,1) =0.0)

$PXGAUS = (BasevalueofPXGAUS) * (1 + 0.6002934$
$*(\frac{USPCDA}{BaseUSPCDA} - 1)$
$+0.6216833 * (\frac{RXUS}{BaseRXUS} - 1))$

2) version 1 (AA(146,1)=1.0): SEE/MDV=41%, RB2 = 0.767, DW = 0.65

$PXGAUS = PXGAUS|4 * (1.0 + 0.3028526 * (\frac{PGDPPF}{PFDPPF|4} - 1)$

(5.02)

$+0.6002934 * (\frac{USPCDA}{USPCDA|4} - 1) + 0.6216383 * (\frac{RXUS}{RXUS|4} - 1)$

(6.90) (10.66)

$$XS = \exp(2.269587 + 0.2716536 * \log \frac{USGNP}{\frac{PXS}{RSUS}}$$

(2.93) (1.67)

$$+\sum_{i=0}^{3} a < I > * \log USGNP_{-I} + \sum_{i=0}^{5} B < I > * \log USRMTB_{-i})$$

a0 = 0.3523 (9.2)	a1 = 0.2642 (9.2)	a2 = 0.1762 (9.2)	a3 = 0.0881 (9.2)
Sum= 0.88076	DEG 1, FAR;		
b0 = 0.0205 (1.74)	b1 = 0.0171 (1.74)	b2 = 0.0137 (1.74)	b3 = 0.0102 (1.74)
b4 = 0.0068 (1.74)	b5 = 0.0034 (1.74)	Sum= 0.071696	DEG 1, FAR

PXS : Deflator-Exports of Services, 1986 = 1.0

1) version 0 (default) (AA(501,1)=0.0); coefficient(3)=1, (4)=0

2) version 1 (AA(501,1)=1.0)

$$PXS = PXS|4 * (\underset{(41.7)}{\overset{(3)}{1.190933}} * \frac{CPI}{CPI|4} - \underset{(4.4)}{\overset{(4)}{0.03060813}} * \frac{USRMTB}{USRMTB|4})$$

XSCAPV : Exports-Capital service receipts

$$XSCAPV = \exp(\underset{(1.6)}{0.2799979} + \underset{(30.6)}{0.7617416} * \log(KBDIAR * USPGNP * RXUS) + \underset{(1.3)}{0.1173981} * \log USRMTB + \sum a < i > * \log \frac{USRMTB}{USRMTB|1})$$

where

a0 = -0.1610(1.35), a1 = -0.1207(1.35), a2 = -0.0805(1.35),
a3 = -0.0402(1.35), Sum = -0.40243, DEG 1, FAR

MGO : Imports of merchandise (excluding petroleum & autos to the US) \$ 86 mill, SAAR

$$MGO = \exp(-\underset{(3.0)}{1.16670} + \underset{(6.9)}{0.887231} \log JCAPG + (Dummies743, 762) + \sum_{i=0}^{5} a < i > * \log VWTDM_{-i} + \sum_{i=0}^{4} b < i > * \log(PGDPPF * \frac{1 + ZMTISF * RTIFMS}{PMGO * (1 + RTIMO)})$$

a0 = 0.3144 (29.3)	a1 = 0.2620 (")	a2 = 0.2096 (")
a3 = 0.1572 (")	a4 = 0.1048 (")	a5 = 0.0524 (")
Sum = 1.1004	DEG 1, FAR;	
b0 = 0.8701 (7.9)	b1 = 0.3415 (13.4)	b2 = -0.0098 (0.29)
b3 = -0.1838 (3.4)	b4 = -0.1805 (4.1)	Sum = 0.8375
DEG 2, FAR		

Supplementary Equations:

$$VWTDM = (0.31277 * CDO + 0.246228 * CDA + 0.29239 * CSD + 0.13184 * CND + 0.03590 * CS + 0.14249 * IFNB + 0.11763 * IFHB + 0.52405 * IFMB + 0.05069 * GC + 0.22277 * GI + 0.30000 * XGO)$$

PMGO : Deflator: Imports of merchandise excluding petroleum and automobile trade with the US, 1986=1.0

version 0 (Default) (AA(516,1)=0) Coefficent (3) below =1;

$$PMGO = PMGO|1 * \frac{UWWPIM * RXWM}{UWWPIM|1 * RXWM|1}$$

$$UWWPIM = JMUS * ISWPI + JMJA * WJAWPI + JMUK * IILW@O + JMGY * UGYWPI$$

$$RXWM = RXUS * \frac{1}{1.38980} * (JMUS + JMJA * \frac{USRXJA}{0.00597246} + JMUK * \frac{USRXUK}{1.46703} + JMGY * \frac{USRXGY}{0.46275})$$

MGAUS : Imports of automobiles from the US, \$86 mill, saar

$$MGAUS = \exp(-\underset{(1.0)}{0.07617724} + \sum_{i=0}^{3} a < i > * \log CDA_{-1} + \sum_{i=0}^{3} b(i) * \log(\frac{PCDA}{PMGAUS})_{-1})$$

a0 = 0.4376 (13.6) a1 = 0.3282 (") a2 = 0.2188 (")
a3 = 0.1094 (") Sum = 1.0941 DEG 1, FAR;
b0 = 0.1214 (1.44) b1 = 0.0911 (") b2 = 0.0607 (")
b3 = 0.0304 (") Sum = 0.0304 (") DEG 1, FAR

PMGAUS : Deflator-Imports of Autos and Parts from the US, 1986=1.0
1) version 0 (default) (AA(149,1)=0; coeffic. below (2)=1, (3)=0.85
2) version 1 (AA(149,1)=1.0)

$$PMGAUS = PMGAUS\_4 * (1.0 + \underset{(17.7)}{\overset{(2)}{1.270952}} * (\frac{USPCDA}{USPCDA\_4} - 1)$$
$$+ \underset{(8.7)}{\overset{(3)}{0.8021449}} * (\frac{RXUS}{TXUS\_4} - 1.0))$$

MS : Imports of services, $86 mill, saar

$$MS = \exp(-4.588520 + 0.006643723 * \log MG$$
$$+ \sum_{i=0}^{5} a<i> * \log(\frac{PGDPPF}{PMS})_{-1}$$
$$+ \sum_{i=0}^{3} b<i> * \log GDPP_{-1})$$

a0 = 0.5023 (4.0) a1 = 0.3118 (6.2) a2 = 0.1641 (4.5)
a3 = 0.0590 (1.0) a4 = 0.0033 (0.05) Sum = 1.0108
DEG 2, FAR;
b0 = 0.6341 (2.6) b1 = 0.3360 (7.0) b2 = 0.1310 (1.2)
b3 = 0.0189 (0.18) a5 = 0.0230 (0.53) Sum = 1.1200
DEG 2, FAR

PMS : Deflator-Imports of Services, 1986=1.0
1) version 0 (default) (AA(513,1)=0.0: Coefficient (2) below =1.0
2) version 1 (AA(513,1)=1.0)

$$PMS = PMS\_4 * (1.0 + \underset{(40.2)}{\overset{(2)}{1.075939}} * (\frac{USPGNP}{USPGNP\_4} - 1.0)$$
$$+ \underset{(22.4)}{\overset{(3)}{0.9370981}} * (\frac{RXUS}{RXUS\_4} - 1))$$

MSCAPV : Imports-Capital service payments, $ mill, saar

$$MSCAPV = \exp(-3.567092 + 1.037633 * \log(KBBC + KBBPL)$$
$$+ \sum a<i> * \log USRMAA_{-1} + 1.0 * \log RXUS)$$
$$+ YDN$$

where
a0 = 0.2462 (9.1), a1 = 0.1847 ("), a2 = 0.1231 (")
a3 = 0.0616 ("), Sum = 0.61560, DEG 1, FAR

Definitions and Identities

$$XGOV = XGO * PXGO$$

$$XGAUSV = XGAUS * PXGAUS$$

$$PXGPN = UPXGPN * RXUS$$

$$XGPNV = XGPN * PXGPN$$

$$XGV = XGOV + XGAUSV + XGPNV$$

$$XG = XGO + XVAUS + XGPN$$

$$PCG = \frac{XGV}{XG}$$

$$XSV = XS * PXS$$

$$X = XG + XS + ZX$$

$$XV = XGV + XSV$$

$$PX = \frac{XV}{X}$$

$$MGOV = MGO * PMGO$$

$$MGAUSV = MGAUS * PMGAUS$$

$$PMGPT = UPMGPT * RXUS$$

$$MGV = MBOV + MGAUSV + MGPTV$$

$$MG = MGO + MGAUS + MGAUSV + MGPT$$

$$PMG = \frac{MGV}{MG}$$

$$MSV = MS * PMS$$

$$PXG = \frac{XGV}{XG}$$

$$XGV = XS * PXS$$

$$X = XG + XS + ZX$$

$$XV = XGV + XSV$$

$$PS = \frac{XV}{X}$$

$$M = MG + MS + ZM$$

$$MV = MGV + MSV$$

$$PM = \frac{MV}{M}$$

$$PTTR = \frac{PX}{PM}$$

$$PTTG = \frac{PXG}{PMG}$$

$$PTTS = \frac{PXS}{PMS}$$

$$USGNPV = USGNP * USPGNP$$

$$RDGU = (\frac{GNP}{GNP\_4} - 1.0 - (\frac{USGNP}{USGNP\_4} - 1.0)) * 100$$

$$RDIU = (\frac{PGNP}{PGNP\_4} - 1.0 - (\frac{USGNP}{USGNP\_4} - 1.0)) * 100$$

$$RDFUS = RMF - USRMTB$$

$$RDFUL = RMMYWI - USRMAA$$

4.6 Capital Flows and the Balance of Payments

The Current Account

$$BPME = PGDP * (4281.665 - \frac{175286.5}{DTIME})$$

(2.2) (1.7)

$$BPC = XV + XSCAPV - MV - MSCAPV + TRNP + TDNF + BPME$$
$$-TRGN - TRPN - YCWT$$

$$BPCN = BPC + BPCNSF$$

$$BPDIL = J8A(IFNBV + IFMBV) * (0.04381887 - 0.04933314 * DQUE$$

(4.8) (5.0)

$$+(Dummies for 784, 794, 812, 851, 853) - 0.003210146 * (\frac{RXUS}{RXUS|4} - 1) * 100$$

(3.2)

$$+0.01225957 * (RMMYW1 - USRMAA))$$

(1.5)

$$BPDIA = 930.0959 + (Dummines for 663, 713, 734, 743, 821) - 1.178069 * USGNPV$$

(3.3) (14.0)

$$*RVS$$

$$BPLPMN = 561.6051 + 3411.637 * DOLYM + 8655.594 * D814$$

(2.7) (3.5) (4.6)

$$-0.2800868 * (GBALP + GBALL + BBALH + GBALPE)$$

(3.6)

$$+0.04048286 * ((RMMYWP + RMMYWM|2$$

(3.0)

$$(Change from base in RECPI2) - USRMAA) * KBBPL$$

$$+0.001932474 * (\frac{RXUS}{RSUS|4} - 1) * 100 * KBBPL + 0.3846865 * BPLPMN|1$$

(1.7) (4.0)

$$BPLCN = 2243.019 + 1212.077 * DHYDRO + 6787.207 * D814 - 36.83237 * DTIME$$

(2.1) (3.3) (6.1) (2.2)

$$+2406.588 * (D812, 823) + 4578.066 * (D852, 854) + 0.01038802$$

(3.5) (8.6) (3.1)

$$*J4A(GDPV) + 0.002591664 * (RMMYWI - (Ch. from base in RECOI2)$$

(3.9)

$$-USRMAA) * J4A(GDPV)$$

$$BPLCR = 20.03882 - 0.03143775 * KBBC + 0.5841784 * BPLCR|1$$

(0.4) (3.9) (5.5)

$$BPLCBS = KBBC * (-0.2549989 + 0.03415299 * (RMMYWI$$

(4.1) (1.6)

$$-Ch.frombaseRECPI2 - USRMAA) + 0.002474184 * DTIME)$$

(5.1)

$$BPLN = BPDIA + BPDIL + BPLPMN + BPLCN + BPLCR$$

$$+BPLCBS(Endogenous\,items) + BPLGCN + BPLGCR$$

$$+BPLOTH(Exogenous\,items)$$

$$BPSN = 367.7667 + 0.009081690 * (DSQ1 - DSQ4) * GDPV$$

(0.23) (3.2)

$$+0.002501845 * (DSQ2 - DSQ4) * GDPV$$

(0.82)

$$-0.009580504 * (DSQ3 - DSQ4) * GDPV + (Dummies\,for\ 783,\ 822,\ 842)$$

(3.4)

$$+0.0005219277 * (RND - YAENRV) * (GDPV + 1000 * USGNPV)$$

(3.6)

$$-0.003374321 * GDPV + 1000 * USGNPV)$$

(5.5)

$$-0.7765537 * BPLN + \sum_{i=1}^{15} a < i > *BPLN|i + 0.02 * GDPV$$

(9.2)

$$*(1 + RXU - RXEX90|1)$$

a1 = 0.0173, a2 = 0.0324, a3 = 0.0451, a4 = 0.0555, a5 = 0.0636,
a6 = 0.0694, a7 = 0.0729, a8=0.0741, a9 = 0.0729, a10 = 0.0694,
a11 = 0.0636, a12 = 0.0555, a13 = 0.0451, a15 = 0.0173,
Sum = 0.78750 (2.9)

Balance of Payments Identities

$$BPOS = BPCN + BPLM + BPSN(Current a/c + Long - Term\, B.$$

$$+ Short - term\, B. and\, errors)$$

$$BPRES = BPOS + BPSDR(Official\, Settlement\, B. + New\, Allocations\, of\, SDR)$$

RXUS : Exchange rate, Canadian dollars per US dollar

The Balance of Payments with Fixed or Floating Exchange Rate DFX (Variable 418) is the lever which determines whether FOCUS is solved with the exchange rate freely floating (DFX=1.0) or 'fixed'(DFX=0.0).

The Solution of the Model with 'Fixed' Exchange Rate RXUS is set equal to an exogenous target value – RXUSXG –, which may be altered from history or base for simulation purposes. Equations are solved in the form and in the order given above. The sum of the current account (BPC), long-term capital account (BPLN) and short-term capital account (BPSN) – each in part determined by the exogenous exchange rate – equals the "Official Settlements" balance (BPOS) which is also (unless there is a new allocation of SDR) the change in official reserves in dollars (BPRES). Note that the last variable is therefore endogenous. The managers of the Exchange Rate Account are assumed to intervene just sufficiently to cause the foreign exchange market to clear at the exogenous exchange rate. Naturally should model solutions begin to show excessive levels of intervention it becomes necessary to re-think the plausibility of the simulation.

It is important to note that the current version of FOCUS includes no automatic reaction function relating payments imbalances or exchange rate changes to changes in monetary policy. Nor have we embedded an implicit reaction function in the model by including foreign interest rates in the domestic interest-rate equations. Because Canadian interest rates have typically been kept in line with those abroad, inclusion of foreign interest rates in the domestic interest-rate equations makes impossible an accurate estimate of the contribution of domestic explanatory terms. We prefer to keep more 'visible' the avenue by which the balance of payments affects monetary policy – but at the cost, in the present model, of making it exogenous. The user who develops a simulation with unacceptable payments imbalances must alter the exogenous monetary policy targets so as to produce a more reasonable scenario or select Money rule No.6, which uses monetary policy to achieve a target exchange rate. Alternatively, a more automatic reaction by the Bank of Canada can be invoked in rough fashion by specifying less-than-complete sterilization, although the correct value of DSTER to use will remain a matter of judgment.

Solution of the Model with the Exchange Rate Floating When the exchange rate is endogenous and floating, FOCUS uses the same equations for the current account and capital flows listed above and hence the same behaviour. But with the exchange rate endogenous, the change in official reserves (BPRES) becomes exogenous – or it may be determined by an intervention rule (see below). Solution of the foreign sub-model proceeds as follows: The official Settlements Balance must equal the change in reserves (given) less any new allocations of SDR: $BPOS = BPRES - BPSDR$. FOCUS then solves for the current account balances (BPCN,BPLN) as before, as well as for short-term flows (BPSN). A 'tatononnment' rule is then invoked to search iteratively for the exchange rate which will equalize the sum of these three balances and the official-settlements balance: Find RXUS such that $BPOS = BPC + BPLN + BPSN$.

Behaviour of the Model with an Endogenous Exchange Rate The major problem in devising an endogenous floating rate for FOCUS is that the model's basic balance (BPCN+BPLN) exhibits a J-curve response to exchange-rate changes. The current-quarter reaction of the basic balance to an exchange-rate shock is 'perverse'; a depreciation, for example, will cause the basic balance to decline, not increase. The cause of the J-curve is, of course, the fact that trade volumes respond only slowly to exchange-rate market. Dealers in short-term funds are assumed to 'know' that the J-curve exists and to move their funds in anticipation of the eventual 'correct' response to exchange-rate changes. In terms of the short-term flows equation , this means that there must be a positive coefficient (a 'correct' response) on exchange-rate changes which is also sufficiently large to more than outweigh the 'perverse' response of the basic balance.

$$KBDIAR = KBDIAR|1 - \frac{\frac{BPDIA}{4.0}}{\frac{USPGNP|1}{RXUS|1}}$$

$$KBBPL = KBBPL|1 + \frac{\frac{BPLPMN|1}{4.0}}{RXUS}$$

$$KBBC = KBBC|1 + \frac{\frac{BPLCN|1+BPLCR|1+BPLCBS|1}{4.0}}{RXUS}$$

$$KBS = KBS|1 + \frac{\frac{BPSN|1}{4.0}}{RXUS|1}$$

$$KBXRU = KBXRU|1 + \frac{\frac{BPRES|1}{4.0}}{RXUS|1}$$

4.7 GNP/GDP and Production – Potential GDP

$$GNPG = \frac{YWG}{PWG} + \frac{CCAG}{PGI}$$

$$GNPGV = YWG + CCAG$$

$$JCAPG = JCAPB|1 * (1.0 - 0.004146174 + 0.9359531 * RGdppfa$$

(3.5) (9.8)

$$+0.1407084 * RGdppfa|1)$$

(1.3)

where

$$RGdoofa = Dot(GDPPF) - 0.1180388 * Dot(KFNB)$$
$$-(1.1180388 - 0.3252374) * Dot(KFNB)$$

Private Demand and Supply

$$GDPP = GDP - GNPG$$

$$GDPPF = JGDPPF * GDPP$$

$$GDPPFS = \exp(0.3091117 + 0.009803563 * DTIME + 0.7154515 * DPROD$$

(0.79) (2.78) (2.20)

a) $- 0.007198892 * DPROD * DTIME)$

(2.19) (Ebeta) (Mbeta)

b) $* (KFNB * JCAPG)^{1.0-0.32525-0.15497}$

(Eoh) (Mbeta)

c) $* (LPRIV - 0.015 * KFNB)^{0.32525}$

(Kpoh) (Mbeta)

d) $* ((KFMB - 0.10 * KFNB) * JCAPG)^{0.15497}$

where
Eoh : overhead employment – see LPRIV in Section 4.14
Kpoh : overhead stock of machinery and equipment

While based on the Cobb-Douglas approach, the production function above and its associated factor-demand equation embody a somewhat different view of the world than is customarily encountered. FOCUS assumes that all private production is carried out in a number of plants; the number of plants is not known but is assumed proportional to the stock of non-residential structures (KFNB). Each plant requires overhead labour and machinery and equipment (m&e). 'Overhead' factor demand is estimated as part of the factor demand equations and is assumed proportional to the structures capital stock. Overhead turns out to be important, with estimation showing values of 30% - 40% of total m&e stock or employment (or higher still for m&e is not constrained).

Overhead labour and m&e make their contribution to output through the maintenance of plant. Thus they are subtracted from total labour and m&e in the production function (see c) and d) above). Overhead employment was found to be insensitive to the capacity utilization rate, for the most part the overhead employees associated with the structures stock continue to be employed no matter what the utilization level of the stock. On the other hand, we assume that m&e is more directly 'tied' to plants and that when plant is not utilized its associated overhead m&e is also not utilized – thus the Kpoh term in the production function above. In the absence of information, we much assume that m&e is fully utilized (or utilized at a constant rate) in plants which are utilized.

Production Function Plant, multiplied by thc utilization rate (JCAPG) – expression b in the equation – is combined with 'production' (non-overhead) labour (c) and m&e (d) to produce output. The Cobb-Douglas elasticity coefficient for production labour (Ebeta) is 0.325 while that of 'production' m&e is 0.155. This leaves the coefficient on plant as 0.52 (= 1 - 0.325 - 0.155) since overall constant returns to scale are assumed. However, there are (severely) diminishing returns with respect to 'production' (variable) m&e and labour. Thus in FOCUS the importance of plan-in-place – with all its associated overhead – is emphasized relative tot he usual two or three factor Cobb-Douglas formulations.

Another noteworthy result of the FOCUS production function and factor-demand equations is that while production labour and m&e continue to be gross substitutes (with demand depending on relative costs), labour and m&e are complements with respect to plant (the structures stock). New plant investment requires both overhead labour and m&e and also some additional 'production' inputs – although the weight given to production labour and m&e will depend upon their relative cost.

Expression a) in the equation is the usual 'constant plus time trend' – the latter to capture growth in total factor productivity usually attributed to 'technical change'. The coefficient on DTIME says that total factor productivity grew, through 1973, at a rate of 0.98 per cent per quarter – or approximately 3.9 percent per year. This figure seems high – especially when it is recalled that the equation is measuring labour input in terms of person, not hours. The figure thus also incorporates the negative effect of declining hours-per-week over the period. The second and third terms in a) attempt to capture the effects – but not the cause – of the commonly-credited productivity slowdown in the mid to late 1970s. DPROD is zero through 1973:3 and then rises by 0.1 per quarter to a value of 1.0 which is then maintained. The dummy was constricted to allow for a gradual productivity shift due, primarily to the oil-price shock of late 1973. DPROD alone is included to capture any one-time productivity shifts but also to allow for a changing 'intercept' with the shift in time trend. The shift in time-trend after the presumed shock is quite pronounce. Annual total-factor-productivity growth in the equation is about 3.9% per year before the shock, and only about 1.0% per year thereafter.

It is often useful to be able to alter the rate of total factor productivity growth for simulation analysis. A variable DTFP exists for this purpose. The default value is zero. A value greater than zero is an addition to TFP growth above base case. Thus, entering DTFP adjustment applied both to the production function for GDPPFS above when under the 'flexible-price' mode, and to the production function inverted as an alternate employment equation under the 'mark-up' price (see Section 4.14).[3]

$$GDP = C + G + IFB + IIB + X - M + ZSD + ZGDP$$

where

ZSD	:	statistical discrepancy
ZGDP	:	adjusting entry

$$GNP = GDP + \frac{XSCAPV - MSCAPV}{PGDP}$$

$$GDPV = CV + GCV + GIV + IFBV + XV - MV + ZSDV$$

$$GNPV = GDPV + XSCAPV - MSCAPV$$

$$GDPPV = GDPV - GNPGV$$

$$GDPPFC = GDPPF * PGDPPF$$

$$ZSDV = ZSD * PGDP$$

[3]In the current model version the equations for production and for factor demands are estimated separately. Thus, the beta coefficients above are as estimated from the demands for KFMB and for LPRIV. Ideally the system can and should be estimated simultaneously and this improvement will be attempted in subsequent versions.

Gross Domestic Product =

$$GDPFV = GDPPFV + GNPGV$$

$$GDPF = GDPPF + GNPG$$

$$PGDPF = \frac{GDPFV}{GDPF}$$

$$RPRDG = \frac{GDPF}{LE}$$

$$RGPFL = 100 * \frac{\frac{GDPPF}{LPRIV}}{\frac{GDPPF|_4}{LPRIV|_4}}$$

Potential GDP In order to calculate potential GNP we must have some notion of 'full employment'. Exogenous to FOCUS is the variable RUNAT, an estimate of the non-accelerating inflation rate of unemployment (or 'full employment' or 'natural' rate). The RUNAT estimate used is from Dungan and Wilson, "Potential GNP – Performance and Prospects," Institute Report Series, 1983) is based on earlier work by Jump. In brief, the RUNAT series in FOCUS tries to take into account two major factors which are thought to have altered the level of unemployment insurance availability and payments in 1971 and after. At the foundation of the measure is an assumed constant natural unemployment rate for 'prime-age' (25-54) makes (aside from unemployment insurance effects). In the RUNAT currently used by FOCUS, a 'base' prime-age natural rate of 3.5% is assumed. LPNAT is that level of private-sector employment which would yield RUNAT (assuming government employment remains unchanged). The expression is somewhat complicated in that participation rates in FOCUS are themselves determined by the level of employment, reflecting the 'discouraged worker' effect. The equation for LPNAT takes into account this secondary reaction of the labour force in moving to potential employment.

$$LPNAT = \frac{(1.0 - RUNAT * 0.01) * (LF - wpop * LE)}{1.0 - (1.0 - RUNAT * 0.01) * wpop} - LGC$$

where

$$wpop = 0.01 * \frac{1}{N15} * (44.622 * NM15 + 4.9696 * NM15 + 38.457 * NM55$$
$$+82.056 * NF15 + 47.845 * NF25 + 49.569 * NF55)$$

$$GDPOTL = (\exp(0.3091117 + 0.009803563 * DTIME + 0.7154515 * DPROD$$

$$a) \quad - 0.007191929 * DPROD * DTIME)$$

$$b) \quad * (KFNB * JCAPGN)^{1.0-0.32525-0.15497}$$

$$c) \quad * (LPNAT - 0.015 * KFNB)^{0.32525}$$

$$d) \quad * \frac{((KFMB - 0.1 * KFNB) * JCAPGN)^{0.15497}}{JGDPPF}$$

$$e) \quad + GNPG$$

$$GDPGAP = \frac{GDPOTL - GDP}{GNPOTL} * 100$$

The potential GNP is based directly on the production function in FOCUS. In converting from actual to potential GNP, the following features should be noted.

1. Trend total factor productivity growth and the break in such growth after 1973 a) are assumed to be maintained at potential.

2. the actual rate of capacity utilization is replaced with a judgmental natural rate, JCAPGN – set presently at 0.93 through 73:4, declining by 0.001 per quarter through 81:4 and set at 0.90 for 82:1 on.

3. Total private-sector employment, LPRIV c) is replaced by the level corresponding to the natural unemployment rate, LPNAT, as described above.

4. Capital stocks in the calculation may be held exogenous (the usual case with potential GNP calculations), or a long-run 'sustained' potential path may be generated in which capital stocks are altered over time (relative to history or a control simulation). In normal operation, capital stock remain endogenous in FOCUS, therefore, the potential routinely generated is that based on actual stocks.

5. Expression e) included the various terms necessary to go from the production function (real private domestic demand and supply at factor cost) to total real GDP at market prices, the real-GNP concept. The variable JGDPPF is used to translate between real private GDP at market prices and at factor cost. It is assumed that GNP (or GDP) generated in the government sector is in effect always at potential.

4.8 National Income

$$YWP = WPAA * LPRIV + 0.5 * TDCQPP$$

$$+TDUNF * (0.5 * DUIC + \frac{1.4}{2.4} * (1.0 - DUIC))$$

$$YWG = PWG * (LGM + LGC) * 74.218$$

$$YW = YWP + YWG$$

$$YPINM = \exp(-8.104676 + 1.5 * \log J4AMONM1 + 0.7101235 * \log J4ARMF$$
$$\qquad (13.4) \qquad\qquad\qquad (3.8)$$
$$+21.57750 * \frac{1.0}{DTIME})$$
$$(0.9)$$

$$YINMIS = YGI + YPINM$$

$$YUAF = YUAF|4 * (1.0 + (\frac{PGDP}{PGDP|4} - 1.0) + 0.75 * (\frac{GDP}{GDP|4} - 1.1)$$

$$YUNFRT = \exp(-0.8402983 + 0.8669216 * \log CV + \frac{9.999744}{DTIME})$$
$$(0.78) \qquad (10.6) \qquad (0.77)$$

$$YNRENT = \exp(-6.642821 + 1.507026 * \log YYBFRT + \frac{67.72375}{DTIME})$$
$$(4.5) \qquad (10.8) \qquad (3.2)$$

$$YIVA = 1059.039 - 0.1085561 * (Psales - Psales|4) * (C - CS + 0.35 * G$$
$$(1.5) \qquad (2.7)$$
$$+IFB + XG) + 3418.945 * D(824)$$
$$(10.0)$$

where
Psales : Price of Final sales = $\frac{GDPPV+MV}{GDPP+M}$

$$CCAGB = \exp(3.362917 + 0.4944066 * \log CCAC - \frac{63.75605}{DTIME})$$
$$(3.8) \qquad (6.3) \qquad (4.5)$$

$$CCAPU = 226.9655 + 0.01020253 * (IFNBV + IFHBV) + 0.9711844 * CCAPU|1$$

(2.8) (2.7) (67.1)

$$- \frac{11991.16}{DTIME}$$

(2.3)

$$CCA = CCAC + CCAG + CCAGB + CCAPU$$

$$Y = YW + YINMIS + YC + YUNFRT + YUAF + YIVA$$

$$YN = Y + XSCAPV - MSCAPV$$

4.9 Corporation Profits

$$YC = GDPV + ZSDV - CCA - TI + SY - (YW + YINMIS + YIAF + YUNFRT)$$

$$RYCGDP = \frac{YC + CCAC}{GDPV}$$

$$YCAT = YC - (TDCF - TDCFGE) - TDCP + YINRC - YICNR$$

$$YCU = YCAT - (YDN + YCWT + YDRES + YCBDCH)$$

$$YINRC = \exp(11.29876 + 0.1353561 * \log USRMAA - \frac{472.7815}{DTIME})$$

(14.7) (0.6) (8.6)

$$YICNR = \exp(-2.490394 + 0.7984390 * \log KBBE + 1.323057 * \log USRMAA)$$

(6.2) (18.6) (8.9)

$$TDCFGE = YCG * (-0.04049127 + 1.080454 * \frac{TDCF}{YC} - \frac{19.66.35}{DTIME}$$

(1.9) (11.0) (10.2)

$$-0.02559794 * (YCG - J4A(YCG)|1)YCG)$$

(3.1)

$$YCG = RYCG * YC$$

$$YDN = YCAT * (0.1483724 + \frac{3.998145}{DTIME} + 0.1294097 * \frac{YIVA}{YC} - 0.1730144$$

$$*(YCAT - \frac{J4A(YCAT|1)}{YCAT}))$$

$$YCWT = 55.47512 + 0.005689002 * (YDN + YICNR)$$

$$YDRES = YCAT * (0.1991862 - 0.41022450 * \frac{YIVA}{YC}$$

(6.1) (2.8)

$$-0.3752131 * (YCAT - \frac{J4A(YCAT|1)}{YCAT}))$$

(8.5)

$$YCBDCH = YC * (0.01521600 - 0.01214643 * \frac{YC - J4A(YC)|1}{YC})$$

(8.0) (7.8)

$$CCAC = 0.03544380 * (0.753 - \frac{2.5312}{DTIME}) * (IFNBV + IFMBV)$$

(5.1)

$$+0.9656307 * CCAC|1$$

(87.3)

$$CCOST = \exp(0.927124 + 1.0 * \log(0.753 - \frac{2.5312}{DTIME}) * (\frac{RDEPN}{4} * (JCCIFN$$

$$+(1 - RCDIFN) * \frac{IFNBV}{4}) + \frac{RDEPM}{4} * (JCCIFM + (1 - RCDIFM)$$

$$*\frac{IFMBV}{4})) + \frac{0.05}{4} * JCOLDN + \frac{0.45}{4} * JCOLDM))$$

$$JCCIFN = (1 - \frac{RDEPN|1}{4}) * (JCCIFN|1 + (1 - RCDIFN|1) * \frac{IFNBV|1}{4})$$

$$+(1 - \frac{RDEPN|1}{4}) * (JCCIFN|1 - JCCHCN|1) * (\frac{PGDPP}{PGDPP|1} - 1)$$

$$JCCHCN = (1 - \frac{RDEPN|1}{4}) * (JCCHCN|1 + (1 - RCDIFN|1) * IFNBV|1$$

$$*(1 - DCCINR))$$

$$JCOLDN = (1.0 - \frac{0.05}{4}) * JCOLDN|1$$

$$JCCIFM = (1 - \frac{RDEPM|1}{4}) * (JCCIFM|1 + (1 - RCDIFM|1) * \frac{IFMBV|1}{4}$$

$$-((1 - DIFM) * \frac{0.05}{0.1125} * 25522.0 * (1 - 0.05)^{DTIME-94})$$

$$+((1 - DIFM) * \frac{0.05}{0.1125} * 25522.0 * (1 - 0.05)^{DTIME-93}))$$

$$+\frac{1 - RDEPN|1}{4} * (JCCIFM)|1 - JCCHCM|1) * (\frac{PGDPP}{PGDPP|1} - 1)$$

$$JCCHCM = \frac{1 - RDEPM|1}{4} * (JCCHCM|1 * IFMBV|1) * (1 - DCCIME|1)$$

$$-((1 - DIFM) * \frac{0.05}{0.075} * 25522.0 * (1 - 0.05)^{DTIME-94}) + ((1 - DIGM)$$

$$*\frac{0.05}{0.75} * 99620.0 * (1 - 0.05)^{DTIME-93})$$

$$JCOLDM = (1.0 - \frac{0.45}{4}) * JCOLDM|1$$

4.10 Taxes and Transfers

Direct Taxes – Corporations

$$TDCF = 0.8186578 * TaxCalc - 0.1387528 * Taxcalc * DTAX - 1.051171 * CarryFwd$$

(66.0) (3.9) (10.9)

$$-VTCFCR + TXPGRT$$

$$VICFCR = RTCFCR * (IFNBV + IFMBV)$$

where

TaxCalc	=	Initial Tax Calculation (rate * base)
	=	$TaxProfits * ((1 - SmallBus.Ratio)$ $*(RTYCFH - VRBATE)$ $+SmallBus.Ratio * (RTYCFL - URBATE))$
TaxProfits	=	Taxable Profits of Corps and Gov. Bus. Ent.
	=	$YC + YCG + CCAC - CCOST + YROYP$ $*(1 - RESALL) - KINF * PGDP * 0.03 * DINVAL$
Small Bus. Ratio	=	Ratio of Small Business Deduction to Taxable Profits
	=	$0.015 + 0.022356 * \frac{YCMAXL}{\frac{TaxProfits}{NumTaxFirms}}$
NumTaxFirms	=	Number of Taxable Firms
	=	$37545 * (1.062866^{\frac{DTIME-1}{4}} - 3.0)$
CarryFwd	=	Effect of loss carryforwards-ratio of current taxable profits to wighted moveing average of past taxable profits
	=	$TaxCalc * \frac{J4A(YC)}{0.5 * J4A(YC) + 0.25 * J4A(YC\|4) + 0.10 * J4A(YC\|12)}$
TDCP	=	$\exp(1.405022 + 0.7851901 * \log TaxCalc)$

where

TaxCalc = RTYCP * (YC + CCAC - CCOST)

Direct Taxes – Personal Income Taxes The determination of personal income taxes in FOCUS begins with a calculation of the basic federal tax of the average taxfiler (TDPYFB). The total number of tax filers is also estimated. Total federal and provincial personal tax collections are then related to the basic federal tax as adjusted for sur-taxes, tax credits and rates of abatement, and to the number of filers.

$$VAVGY = \exp(1.0 * \log \frac{YP}{NTXF} - 0.3005246)$$

$$NTXF = 2195.252 + 0.7006337 * N15 + 0.4380336 * N78 - 8911.095 * D78$$

(1.7) (10.1) (5.5) (6.2)

$$-552.1073 * D72$$

(4.8)

RTPIDX	=	Index Factor for Personal Taxation,	Growth Rate(%)
	=	0.0	for 1973 and before
	=	$(\frac{J4ACPI\|2}{J4ACPI\|6} - 1.0) * 100$ (Q1 only)	for 1974-82
	=	6.0	for 1983
	=	5.0	for 1984
	=	$(\frac{J4ACPI\|2}{J4ACPI\|6} - 1.0) * 100 - RTPDXJ$	for 1985

$$RTXEX = RTXEX|1 * RTPIDX + Statutory\ adjustment\ (Q1\ only)$$

$$RTXES = RTEXS|1 * RTPIDX + Statutory\ adjustment\ (Q1\ only)$$

$$RTX65 = RTX65|1 * RTPIDX + Statutory\ adjustment\ (Q1\ only)$$

$$RTX16 = TRX16|1 * RTPIDX + Statutory\ adjustment\ (Q1\ only)$$

$$RTX16U = RTXEX|1 * Statutory\ adjustment\ (Q1\ only)$$

$$VTXPEX = RTXEX + 1.053214 * WtdExempt + 0.09421233 * D78$$

where

WtSpouse	=	Weight for 'Married and Equivalent' Exemption
	=	$\frac{NF25*(1-0.01*RPF25)+NF55*(1-0.01RPF55)}{N15}$
Wt16U	=	Weight for Children under 16
	=	$\frac{N-N15}{N15}$
Wt16	=	Weight for Children 16 +
	=	$\frac{NF15*(1-0.01*RPF15)+NM15*(1-0.01RPM15)}{N15}$
Wt65	=	Weight for Age Exemption
	=	$0.5 * \frac{NF55*(1-0.01*RPF55)+NM55*(1-0.01RPM55)}{N15}$
WtdExempt	=	$RTXEXS * WtSpouse + RTX16U * Wt16U + RTX16 * Wt16$ $+RTX65 * Wt65$
VTXDED	=	$VTDCPP + VTDRSP + VTDUIC + VTDRPP + VTDINT$ $+VTDEMP + VTDOTH$
	=	$VTDCPP + VTDUIC + VTDOTH$ (post reform)
VTDCPP	=	CPP/QPP Deductions = $0.5 + RTCPP$ $+MIN(VYWCPP, VAVGY)$ (Post reform: tax credit at above * 0.17)
VTDRSP	=	RRSP Deductions = $RTXRSP * VAVGY$
VTDUIC	=	UIC Deductions = $0.5 * PTCUI * MIN(VYWUIN, VAVGY)$ (Post reform: Tax credit at above * 0.17)
VTDRPP	=	Pension Contribution Deductions = $RTXRPP * VAVGY$
VTDINT	=	Interest Deduction = $RTXINT * VAVGY$
VTDEMP	=	Employment Deduction = Exogenous
VTDOTH	=	All Other Deductions = Exogenous
VTXYP	=	$VAVGY - VTXPEX - VTXDED - VTXYPZ$ (Post reform = $VAVGY - VTXDED$)

Tax Credits: VTXCTCM, VTXCST, VTXCOT: Exogenous

$$VTXCDV = RTXCDV * VAVGY$$

TDPYFB : Basic Federal Tax of the Average taxfiler

$$TDPYFB = (RTFBAV * VTXYP) - VTXCDV \qquad (Pre-reform)$$

$$= (RTFBAV * VTSYP) - VTXCDV - VTXPEC - VTDCPP$$

$$-VTDUIC - VTXCOT \qquad (Post-reform)$$

$$TDPYF = \exp(\underset{(640)}{1.006114} * \log((TDPYFB * (1 - VRBATW + RTYPS)$$

$$-(VTXRED + VTXCTC + VTXCST + VTXCOT)) * NTXF)$$

$$+\underset{(13.4)}{0.2924092} * DTAX)$$

$$TDPYP = \exp(0.08482273 + 0.07693225 * DTAX - 0.07036067 * D78$$

$$+0.9896614 * \log(TDPYFB * RTYPWQ * MTXF))$$

Direct Taxes – Other Personal Taxes; Totals

$$TDNF = \underset{(4.6)}{100.1569} + \underset{(33.4)}{0.09287592} * (YDN + YICNR)$$

$$TDUNF = (0.89 * (RTCUI + (1.4 - 0.4 * DUIC) * RTCUI) * VYWUIN * LE)$$

$$*(1 - \underset{(85.3)}{0.3371670} * \frac{VYWUIN}{W})$$

where RTCUI is exogenous.

$$VYWUIN = VYWUIN|1 * (DSQ2 + DSQ3 + DSQ4) * DSQ1 * VYWUIN|4$$

$$* \frac{\sum_{i=2}^{5} W|I}{\sum_{i=6}^{9} W|i}$$

$$TDPENF = 2293.931 + 0.02707653 * (j4AGCFV) - \frac{160546.9}{DTIME}$$

(4.0) (2.5) (3.3)

$$TDPENP = -208.7935 + 0.02830266 * (GCPV + GCLV + GCHV)$$

(3.2) (24.1)

$$TDWCP = -609.4353 + 0.01455963 * YW$$

$$TDPPO = RTDPPO * YP$$

$$TDPPE = (2 * RTCPP * VYWCPP * LE) * (1 - 0.3543093 * \frac{VYWCPP}{W})$$

(56.4)

$$VYWCPP = VYWCPP|1 * (DSQ2 + DSQ3 + DSQ4)$$

$$+DSQ1 * VYWCPP|4 * \frac{\sum_{i=2}^{5} CPI|i}{\sum_{i=6}^{9} CPI|i}$$

$$TDPF = TDPYF + TDUNF + TDPENF + TDPOF$$

$$TDPP = PDPYP + PDPENP + TDWCP + TDPOP$$

$$TDP = TDPF + TDPP + TDPL + TDPH + TDPPE$$

Indirect Taxes

$$TISF = -844.1237 + 1.101973 * TaxCalc$$

(8.7) (85.4)

where

$$
\begin{aligned}
\text{TaxCalc} &= \text{Initial Sales Tax Calculation (Rate * Base)}\\
&= RTUFNS * (0.573 * \frac{CDV}{(1+0.887*RTIRSP)*(1+0.573*RTIFMS)}\\
&\quad +0.219 * CSDV * \frac{DumSD}{(1+0.595*RTIRSP)*(1+0.219*RTIFMS)}\\
&\quad +\frac{0.219}{0.43} * CSDV * \frac{1-DumSD}{(1+0.595*RTIRSP)*(1+\frac{0.219}{0.43FMS})}\\
&\quad +0.174 * \frac{CNDV-TILCP-0.5*TIGSP}{1+0.722*RTIRSP} * (1+0.174 * RTIFMS))\\
&\quad +0.040 * \frac{CSV}{1+0.212*RTIRSP} * (1+0.040 * RTIFMS))\\
&\quad +0.201 * \frac{IFNBV+IFHBV}{(1+0.365*RTIRSP)*(1+0.201*RTIFMS)}\\
&\quad +0.0401 * \frac{IFMBV}{(1+0.387*RTIRSP)*(1+0.401*RTIFMS)}\\
&\quad +(0.12 * 0.713 + 0.88 * 0.214)\\
&\quad * \frac{GIV}{(1+(0.12*0.427+0.88*0.391)*RTIRSP)*(0.12*0.713+0.88*0.214)*RTIFMS})\\
&\quad +0.069 * \frac{GCV}{(1+0.077*RTIRSP)*(1+0.069*RTIFMS)}\\
&\quad +0.043 * \frac{XV}{(1+0.051*RTIRSP)*(1+0.043*RTIFMS)})\\
&\quad +RTIFTA * 0.069CNDV
\end{aligned}
$$

where

$$
\begin{aligned}
\text{DumSD} &= \text{Dummy for Clothing Exemption from MST}\\
&= 0.0 \text{ for } 54{:}1 - 74{:}2;\\
&= 1.0 \text{ for } 74{:}3 -
\end{aligned}
$$

$$TISF = -844.1237 + 1.101973 * TaxCalc$$

$$
\begin{aligned}
\text{TaxCalc} &= \text{Initial Sales Tax Calculation (Rate * Base)}\\
&= RTIFMS * 1.0 * \frac{CDV}{1+0.965*RTIRSP+RTIFMS}\\
\text{(A)} &\quad +1.0 * \frac{CSDV}{1+0.790*RTIRSP+RTIFMS}\\
&\quad +0.407 * \frac{CNDV-0.5*TIGSP}{1+0.459*RTIRSP+RTIFMS}\\
&\quad +0.531 * \frac{CSV}{1+0.227*RTIRSP+0.531*RTIFMS}\\
\text{(B)} &\quad +75 * \frac{IFHBV}{1+0.460*RTIRSP+0.75RTIFMS}\\
\text{(C)} &\quad +(1.2 * 0.75 + 0.88 * 0.50) * \frac{GIV}{1+0.414*RTIRSP}\\
&\quad +(1.2 * 0.75 + 0.88 * 0.50) * RTIFMS))\\
&\quad +(0.13 * \frac{GCV}{1+0.095*RTIRSP+0.13*RTIFMS}\\
\text{(D)} &\quad +RTIFTA * 0.069 * CNDV
\end{aligned}
$$

An initial tax calculation term, TaxCalc above, is constructed by weighting each major component of demand by a coefficient extracted from the 1984 Input-Output tables. The coefficient includes not only direct taxation but the cumulative effect of taxation of business inputs in the production chain. Thus, while exports are technically exempt from direct taxation, 4.3% of their (pre-tax) final value is indirectly taxed through levies on intermediate inputs. The TaxCalc term looks complex because the National Accounts final expenditure components are values after both federal and provincial taxes.

To calculate the appropriate base, the expenditure term must be divided by the term $(1+wf*rf)*(1+wp*rp)$ where rf and rp are the federal and provincial sales tax rates and wf and wp are the proportions of the base expenditure subject to tax. The provincial tax must be included in the calculation because it is applied on top of the federal sales tax. For non-durables (CNDV) the base also omits the profits of provincial liquor commissions (TILCP) and half of provincial gasoline taxes (the other half falls on business inputs). TaxCalc includes an additional term for that portion of non-durables (estimated at 6.9% of total non-durables expenditure) taxed at the rate (RTIFTA) for alcohol and tobacco. The coefficient of 1.11 on TaxCalc indicates that the constructed term slightly underpredicts TISF revenue growth over time. Once the adjustment coefficient is added, the fit is generally quite good. Finally, it should be noted that no explicit attempt has been made to model the Telecommunications. Services Tax (TST). In effect, revenue from this tax becomes an 'add factor' to TISF and is assumed not to vary under shocks.

$$TIM = RTIMO * MGOV$$

$$TIGSF = RTIGSF * CNDV$$

$$TIATF = RTIATF * CNDV$$

$$TIF = TISF + TIM + TIGSF + TIATF + TIENRF + TIFO$$

$$TIRSP = RTIRSP * (0.965 * \frac{CDV}{1 + 0.965 * RTIRSP + RTIFMS}$$

$$+0.790 * \frac{CSDV}{1 + 0.790 * RTIRSP + RTIFMS}$$

$$+0.459 * \frac{CNDV}{1 + 0.459 * RTIRSP + 0.407 * RTIFMS}$$

$$+0.227 * \frac{CSV}{1 + 0.227 * RTIRSP + 0.531 * RTIFMS}$$

$$+0.460 * \frac{IFHBV}{1 + 0.460 * RTIRSP + 0.75 * RTIFMS}$$

$$+0.370 * \frac{IFNBV}{1 + 0.370 * RTIRSP}$$

$$+0.541 * \frac{IFMBV}{1 + 0.541 * RTIRSP}$$

$$+0.414 * \frac{GIV}{1 + 0.414 * RTIRSP + (0.12 * 0.75 + 0.88 * 0.50) * RTIFMS}$$

$$+0.095 * \frac{GCV}{1 + 0.095 * RTIRSP + 0.13 * RTIFMS}$$

$$+0.051 * \frac{XV}{1 + 0.051 * RTIRSP})$$

$$TIGSP = RTIGSP * CNDV$$

$$TILCP = RTILCP * CNDV$$

$$TIPO = RTIPO * GDPV$$

$$TIP = TIRSP + TIGSP + TILCP + TIPO$$

$$TIL = DSQ1 * (N * \exp(0.1384675 - \frac{72.97679}{DTIME} + 0.8661748 * \log J4APC|1)$$

$$\quad (3.4) \qquad (12.1) \qquad (29.6)$$

$$+(DSQ2 + DSQ3 + DSQ4) * TIL|1$$

$$TIPROP = 0.88 * TIL * DSQ1 + TIPROP|1 * (DSQ2 + DSQ3 + DSQ4)$$

$$TI = TIF + TIP + TIL$$

4.11 Personal Income

$$YURF = YUAF - YUAFAD$$

$$YIND = YPINM + TRGID + YDRES + TRPC + XSCAPV$$

$$-(MSCAPV - YDN) + ZYIND$$

$$TRPC = 0.6875536 + TRPC|1 * \frac{J6A(RMF)}{J6A(RMF)|1} + 0.3707562 * \frac{\frac{RMF*CDV+GMF|1*CDV|1}{2}}{100}$$

$$TRGCAP = 18.89918 + 0.006633322 * (IFNBV + IFMBV)$$

$$\quad (0.1) \qquad (2.2)$$

$$TRCP = PGDP * (815.7852 - \frac{25189.70}{DTIME})$$

(18.0) (6.8)

$$NMWUIB = -1139.630 + 11.62901 * \frac{LU + LU|1}{2} + 3952.005 * DSQ1$$

(2.4) (20.2) (42.3)

$$+1910.281 * DSQ2 - 329.4464 * DSQ3$$

(17.9) (3.6)

$$VWBUIM = 0.66667 * (1000 * VYWUIN|1)$$

$$(\textit{through}\ 1978);\ 0.60(1000 * VYWUIN|1)$$

$$\frac{TRGUI}{MDV} = \exp(-0.3265845 - 0.4597508 * DSQ1 - 0.2947777 * DSQ2$$

(17.3) (29.3) (15.9)

$$+0.06243279 * DSQ3 + 0.8284720 * \log(VWBUIM * NMWUIB)$$

(1.9) (28.5)

$$-0.5539194 * DUIC)$$

(7.1)

$$TRGPFO = \exp(\frac{-18.91967}{DTIME} + LOG(N) + J4ACPI|2)$$

where

J4ACPI—2	:	4-quarter moving average of CPI, lagged two quaters.
(Alternate:)	=	$TRGPFO|4 * (\frac{N}{N|4} + \frac{CPI|1}{CPI|4} + \frac{DGTRF}{100} - 1)$

$$TRGPF = TRGPFO + TRGUI$$

$$TRGPP = \exp(0.8281380 - \frac{143.8620}{DTIME} + \log N + \log J4ACPI|2)$$

$$(\text{Alternate:}) \quad = \quad TRGPP|4 * (\frac{N}{N|4} + \frac{CPI|1}{CPI|4} + \frac{DGTRF}{100} - 1)$$

$$TRGPL = \exp(-2.799749 - \frac{64.6284}{DTIME} + \log N + \log J3ACPI|2)$$

$$(\text{Alternate:}) \quad = \quad TRGPL|4 * (\frac{N}{N|4} + \frac{CPI|1}{CPI|4} + \frac{DGTRL}{100} - 1)$$

$$TRGPPE = \exp(3.207401 - \frac{396.5577}{DTIME} + \log(NM55 + NF55) + \log(J4ACPI|2)$$

(18.1) (17.2)

$$+0.007717848 * DSQ1 * \log TRGPPE|1 + 0.005125988 * DSQ2$$

(12.0) (7.1)

$$* \log TRGPPE|1 + 0.002737479 * DSQ3 * \log TRGPPE|1)$$

(4.4)

$$\text{(Alternate:)} \quad = \quad TRGPPE|4 * (\frac{NF55+NM55}{NM55|4+NF55|4} + \frac{CPI|1}{CPI|4} + \frac{GTRPE}{100} - 1)$$

$$TRGP = TRGPF + TRGPP + TRGPL + TRGPPE$$

$$TRNP = PGDP * (879.2600 - \frac{29640.57}{DTIME})$$

$$YP = YW + YURF + YUNFRT + YIND + TRGP + TRGCAP + TRCP + TRNP$$

$$YPD = YP - TDP$$

4.12 Government Surplus or Deficit

This section presents the surplus and deficit identities by level of government and also various items of transfers and receipts which are not required for the calculation of national expenditure or income.

Capital Assistance

$$TRGCF = -31.73414 + 0.02414775 * (IFNBV + IFMBV) + TRPIP$$

(0.13) (3.8)

$$TRGCP = -62.08730 + 0.01127520 * (IFNBV + IFMBV) + 532.6873 * D824834$$

(0.9) (6.3) (7.7)

$$TRGC = TRGCF + IRGCP$$

Transfers to Non-Residents

$$TRGNF = \exp(8.479248 - \frac{146.2916}{DTIME} + \log J4ACPI|2)$$

(32.5) (14.0)

Subsidies (Impact Mode)

$$SUF = SUF < base > * \frac{PGDP}{PGDP}base[+RWSUB * LE * WPAA]$$

$$SUP = SUP|base * \frac{PGDP}{PGDP|base}$$

$$SU = SUF + SUP + SUL$$

In impact mode, SUF and SUP is held exogenous in real terms. In projection mode, they are exogenous in nominal form. Note that RWSUB (wage subsidy rate) is normally zero. If non-zero, the subsidy is assumed to be federal. In this case, SUF is adjusted as above.

Interest Payments on the Debt

$$TRGIDF = TRGIDF|1 + \frac{RFed}{100} * (FDBTF - FDBTF|1) + 82.94163$$

(1.4)

$$-448.3547 * D831 + 0.1797748 * \frac{RFed - RFed|4}{100} * FDBTF|4$$

(0.8) (5.0)

$$TRGIDP = TRGIDP|1 + \frac{RFed}{100} * (FDBTP - FDBTP|1) - 861.3845 * D831$$

(3.2)

$$TRGIDH = \exp(5.789312 - \frac{292.8148}{DTIME} + 0.5004379 * \log J16ARMBG10)$$

(10.7) (13.7) (3.0)

$$TRGID = TRGIDF + TRGIDP + TRGIDL + TRGIDH$$

Government Investment Income

$$YGIF = \exp(-5.204327 + 1.081249 * \log GDPV - 0.7829121 * D824)$$

(19.0) (49.6) (12.1)

$$YGIOP = \exp(-0.5120326 + 1.216418 * \log GREVP + 0.3493830 * \log J2ARMBG1)$$

(22.7) (38.3) (4.4)

$$YROYP = YROYP|1 * 1.0 < AA(196,2) > * \frac{GDPV}{GDPV|1}$$

$$YGIP = YGIOP + YROYP$$

$$YGIL = \exp(-9.303674 + 1.159147 * \log GDPV + 0.5205910 * \log J2ARMBG1)$$

(11.6) (15.0) (3.4)

$$YGIH = \exp(5.744687 + 0.9445109 * \log J2ARMBG1 - \frac{479.2749}{DTIME})$$

(5.43) (3.0) (7.4)

$$YGIPE = YGIPE|1 + 1.032336 * GBALPE * \frac{RMBG1}{400}$$

(19.8)

Capital Consumption Allowances

$$CCAGF = CCAGF|1 + 0.01 * GIFV + 4.404884 - \frac{225.3528}{DTIME}$$

(1.2) (0.7)

$$CCAGP = 0.9700768 * CCAGP\_1 + 0.02379100 * GIPV$$

(72.4) (3.4)

$$CCAGL = 0.9940931 * CCAGL\_1 + 0.01243463 * GILV$$

(93.7) (2.4)

$$CCAGH = CCAGH|1 + 0.01769468 * GIHV$$

(17.5)

$$CCAG = CCAGF + CCAGP + CCAGL + CCAGH$$

Intergovernmental Transfers

$$TRNETF = TRBETF(base) * \frac{PWG}{PWG(base)}$$

$$TRNETP = -(TRNETF + TRNETL + TRNETH)$$

TRNETL : exogenous; new default; or if GBALL or GBALH is exogenous,
$$= GBALL + GEXPL - CCAGL - TIL - TDPL - YGIL$$

$$TRNETH = GBALH + GEXPH - CCAGH - TDPH - YGIH$$

Net transfers to (-) or receipts from (+) other levels of government – local or hospitals – are normally exogenous. If the balance of the local governments GBALL or hospitals' balance GBALH is set exogenous, then TRNETL or TRNETH is calculated so as to make the local sector balance at the exogenously fixed level. Barring a change in federal transfers, this in effect passes any potential change in local balances through to the provincial sector.

Government Surplus or Deficit

$$GBALF = GREVF - GEXPF + CCAGF$$

$$GREVF = TIF + TDCF + TDPF + TDNF + YGIF + TRNETF$$

$$GEXPF = GCFV + TRGPF + TRGPF + SUF + TRGCF + TRGNF + TRFIDF$$

$$GBALFJ = GBALF + 0.01 * RINFG * FDBTF$$

$$GBPAF = GBALF + ZGBPAF$$

$$GBFRF = GBALF + ZGBFRF$$

$$GBALP = GREVP - GEXPP + CCAGP$$

$$GREVP = TIP + TDCP + TDPP + YFIP + TRNETP$$

$$GEXPP = GDPV + GIPV + TRGPP + SUP + TRGCP + TRGIDP$$

$$GBALL = GREVL - GEXPL + CCAGL$$

$$GREVL = TIL + TDPL + YGIL + TRNETL$$

$$GEXPL = GCLV + GILV + SUL + TRGPL + TRGIDL$$

$$GBALH = GREVH - GEXPH + CCAGH$$

$$GREVH = TDPH + GIHV + TRNETH$$

$$GEXPH = GCHV + GIHV + TRGIDH$$

$$GBALPE = GREVPE - GEXPPE$$

$$GREVPE = TDPPE + YGIPE$$

$$GEXPPE = GDPEV + TRGPPE + TRGNPE$$

$$GBAL = GBALF + GBALP + GBALL + GBALH + GBALPE$$

$$GEXP = GEXPF + GEXPP + GEXPL + GEXPH + GEXPPE$$

$$GREV = GREVF + GREVP + GREVL + GREVH + GREVPE$$

$$GBALUI = TDUNF - TRGUI$$

Debt and Bond Levels

$$FDBTF = FDBTF|1 - < coeff. > *(\frac{GBALF|1}{4} + DIFF(ARRCB|1 + MONCUR|1))$$

where

$< coeff. >$ = -1.8 (through 1980)

= 1.2 (for 1981 and later)

$$RFDBTF = \frac{FDBTF}{GDPV} * 100$$

$$ANPDF = ANPDF_{-1} + GBPAF$$

$$FNBIP = \exp(2.266675 + 0.6312377 * \log GEXPP - 1.791255 * D793)$$

(3.11) (9.1) (4.2)

This simple equation relates provincial bond issues to expenditures. No term representing the relative deficit or surplus position of the provinces was significant when included. A switch has been added to allow FNBIP to move with changes from base provincial deficit or surplus. AA(FNBIP,1)=1.0; changes from base FNBIP are modelled as changes from base in GBALP:

$$FNBIP = FNBIP(base) - (GBALP - GBALP(base))$$

$$FDBTP = FDBTP|1 + FNBIP|4$$

$$FNBIL = 822.0168 + 0.1 * J4AGILV$$

(5.8)

$$FDBTL = FDBTL|1 + FNBIL|4$$

4.13 Gross Saving

$$SP = YPD - CV - TRPC - TRPN$$

$$RSP = \frac{SP}{YPD} * 100$$

$$RSPJ = \frac{SP - FDBTF * \frac{RINFG}{100}}{YPD} * 100$$

$$TRPN = PGDP * (644.8044 - \frac{12151.50}{DTIME} + 15.23295 * DSQ1 + 10.27626 * DSQ2$$

(6.6) (1.09) (4.1) (2.4)

$$+11.10679 * DSQ3)$$

(3.0)

4.14 Labor Force and Employment

Employment

$$LPRIV = eoh + eprod$$

where

eoh (actural overhead employment) = 0.01 * KFNB, and

eprod (actual production employment) = $1.0 * eprod'' + (1.0 - 1.0) * eprod|1$

EPROD" = (desired 'cost minimizing' production employment)

$= 0.390412 * (0.444575 * EOW + (1.0 - 0.444575) * \jmath 8W(EOW)|1)$

(10.4) (6.9)

$$EOW = \frac{GDPPFV}{WPAA*(1.0+RTCUI*(1.4-0.4*DUIC)+RTCPP-RWSUB)}$$

The first form of employment is derived from the production function for the private sector as was discussed in Section F. In addition to production workers a number of overhead workers are associated with each plant. Total employment is the sum of eoh and eprod employment. Since, however, data are not available at the aggregate level to distinguish the two, we should ideally determine the breakdown as part of the estimation exercise. Unfortunately in the current equation the coefficient relating LPRIV to KFNB proved unstable and the value of .01 was imposed; this yields a value for eoh which averages about 30% of total LPRIV -which is in line with estimates of non-production workers in the manufacturing sector.

Actual production employment(eprod) is hypothesized to be a combination of desired, cost-minimizing, production employment (EPROD") and actual production employment in the previous quarter (eprod—1). In estimation the coefficient on EPROD" was slightly greater than 1.0, so that a value of exactly 1.0 has been imposed. This would indicate quite rapid adjustment to 'desired' levels of production employment, but note that the desired employment term itself contains lags, so that adjustment to changes in wages and output is still much less than instantaneous.

EPROD" itself is obtained from cost minimization subject to the assumed production function. The simplest formulation would be: Ebeta*EOW, where Ebeta is the elasticity of output with respect to production labour in the Cobb-Douglas function and where EOW is the ratio of nominal private domestic output to total wage costs per employee. However, to allow for lags in perception and the formulation of expectations, a weighted average of current and past values of EOW is specified – with a weight of just under 45% assigned to the current quarter. In the EOW expression itself, note that the basic wage rate is adjusted for employer contribution rates to unemployment insurance RTCUI and the Canada Pension Plan RTCPP. Allowance is also made for a possible wage subsidy rate RWSUB, normally zero in base cases.

The estimated employment function in FOCUS differs from that in many other Canadian macro-models in that employment is a function not only of output but also of real wages. This specification is most appropriate for market-clearing pricing; under markup pricing an 'inverted production function' specification may be preferable. Therefore, a switch has been provided. AA(LPRIV, 1)=0: estimated employment function above, and AA(LPRIV,1)=1: production function 'inverted' and lags entered as is shown below. Simply inverting the production function would give instantaneous adjustment of labour demand; lagged adjustment has been imposed as $0.5*(invertedproductionfunction)+0.5*(weightedaverageofpastemployment)$.

$$LPRIVV = \exp(-0.528901 + 8.57495 * \frac{1}{DTIME} - 0.124662 * (KFNB + KFMB)$$

(1.0) (2.2) (3.1)

$$+ \sum_{i=0}^{8} a<i> *REALW|i + \sum_{i=0}^{12} b<i> *GDPPF|i)$$

where
a0 = -0.11720 (4.5), a1 = -0.09608 (6.2), a2 = -0.07697 (8.1),
a3 = -0.05989 (6.1), a4 = -0.04483 (3.6), a5 = -0.03181 (2.2),
a6 = -0.02081 (1.5), a7 = -0.01185 (1.0), a8 = -0.00491 (0.7),
Sum = -0.4644 (2.2);
b0 = 0.1979 (11.4), b1 = 0.1699 (13.4), b2 = 0.1440 (15.3),
b3 = 0.1202 (12.5), b4 = 0.0986 (12.5), b5 = 0.0791 (9.1),
b6 = 0.0617 (6.5), b7= 0.0465 (4.6), b8 = 0.0334 (3.3),
b9 = 0.0224 (2.4), b10 = 0.0136 (1.7), b11 = 0.0069 (1.1)
b12 = 0.0024 (0.7), Sum=0.9966 (3.6),
second degree; constrained FAR for both ai and bi,
where

$$REALW = WPAA * \frac{1.0+TRCUI*(1.4-0.4*DUIC)+RTCPP-RWSUB}{PGDPPF}$$

$$LE = LPRIV + LGC$$

Population and Participation Rates

$$N15 = NM15 + NM25 + NM55 + NF15 + NF25 + NF55$$

$$N16 = N15 - 0.10 * (NM15 + NF15)$$

$$RPM15 = 0.4284569 + 122.4123 * \frac{LE}{N15} - \frac{166.1233}{DTIME} - 0.4497643 * DUIC$$

(0.04) (7.9) (0.9) (0.7)

$$RPM25 = 87.66043 + 26.93644 * \frac{LE}{N15} + \frac{422.5588}{DTIME} + 0.6742843 * \frac{VWBUIM}{\frac{WPAA}{52}}$$

(55.8) (9.8) (20.5) (0.7)

$$-23.97078 * \frac{NM25 + NF25}{N15}$$

(8.7)

$$RPM55 = 12.34757 + \frac{178.0925}{DTIME} - 34.44868 * \frac{NM55 + NF55}{N15} + 0.8704326 * RPM44|1$$

(3.4) (5.3) (10.3) (1.8)

$$RPF25 = -1.367099 + 5.276797 * \frac{LE}{N15} - \frac{531.4415}{DTIME} - 3.953123 * \frac{VWBUIM}{\frac{WPAA}{52}}$$

(0.5) (1.3) (3.0) (1.9)

$$+22.80862 * \frac{NM25 + NF25}{N15} + 0.8707814 * RPF25|1$$

(2.1) (20.1)

$$RPF55 = 6.886728 - 1.820716 * \frac{LE}{N15} + \frac{30.79391}{DTIME} + 0.6613448 * RPF55|1$$

Unemployment

$$LU = LF - LE$$

$$RU = 100 * \frac{LU}{LF}$$

4.15 Wages and Prices

FOCUS uses a 'key series' approach to the determination of wages rates and implicit price indexes. Detailed behavioral specifications are made for one wage series and one price series. The remaining wage and prices variables are then determined by one or the other of these two key series.

Key Wages Equation

$$RWPAA = RGPRD5 + 3.830093 * J4A(\frac{RUNAT}{RU} - 1.0) - 2.055671 * DAIB1$$

(1.6) (2.0)

$$-2.347599 * DAOB2 - 1.632080 * D6 \quad 5 + 0.3900700 * RECPI1$$

(2.3) (1.8) (2.5)

$$+0.2271304 * (RINFC - (RWPAA|4 - RPRDG5)) + \sum_{i=0}^{11} a < i > *RINFC|i$$

(2.4)

where

a0 = 0.0212,	a1 = 0.0390,	a2 = 0.0531,	a3 = 0.0637,
a4 = 0.0708,	a5 = 0.0744,	a6 = 0.0744,	a7 = 0.0708,
a8 = 0.0637,	a9 = 0.0531,	a10 = 0.0390,	a11 = 0.0212,

Sum= 0.64447(3.5)

second degree; Constrained Near/FAR;

DAIB1	:	AIB dummy 1, =1 in 77:1-78:2
DAIB2	:	AIB dummy 2, =1 in 78:3-79:2
D6&5	:	dummy for '6&5' program, =1 in 83:1-84:2
RECPI1	:	expected inflation, 1 year ahead (synthetic expectations)
RINFC	:	four quarter inflation in CPI
RGPRD5	:	5 year moving average of labour productivity growth, private sector (GDPP/LPRIV)

$$WPAA = (1.0 + \frac{RWPAA}{100}) * WPAA|4$$

$$RGPRD5 = J20A(100 * (\frac{\frac{GDPP}{LPRIV}}{GDPP|4} - 1.0))$$

$$RWPAAR = RWPAA - RINFC$$

The key wage equation is driven by three principal explanatory variables.

1) Productivity (RGPRD5): Any change in labor productivity is passed through to wages using a five year moving average. This assures that secular shifts in productivity will be captured and that policy shocks having a long-term effect on labour productivity will have the appropriate impact on wages. A five year moving average was marginally superior in estimation to a shorter lag.

2) Unemployment 'Gap'(RUNAT/RU) Labour market conditions enter the equation through the ratio of NAIRU to the actual rate. The NAIRU estimate used assumes a constant full employment rate for prime age males through the estimation period, but allows for demographic shifts, greater participation by women in the labour force, and the effects of various alterations in the unemployment insurance system. The actual unemployment rate enters in a non-linear form with this

specification. Thus, with a RUNAT of 6.0, a fall in unemployment from 5% to 4% would yield 1.6% additional wage inflation, while a fall from 12% to 11% will give only 0.24% additional wage inflation. A 'linear' specification for RU fits effectively as well as the non-linear version and may actually reduce errors for 1982-83 when the unemployment rate climbed out of its previous range. A linear specification for RU has been included as an alternate below. Attempts to enter additional terms on RU – such as squared deviations or changes in the unemployment rate – were not successful.

3) Inflation (RECPI1 and following) Three terms together capture the impact of inflation on private wages. RECPI1 is a 'synthetic' expectation term for inflation expected one year in the future (see Section P). The term $(RINFC-(RWPAA|4-RGPRD5))$ represents catch-up between past wage and current inflation. Note that by this specification catch-up pressures do not vary directly with labour-market conditions, as perhaps they should. The final term is an Almon lag on past inflation, reaching back over three years (since the lags are on four-quarter CPI changes). The zero constraint at the 'near' end is somewhat suspicious and must be reviewed in future work – especially in light of COLA effects. Previous versions of the equation also included the difference between output prices and the CPI to reflect the different inflationary concerns of workers and management. The term was not significant in the present version.

Long-run Properties As a dynamic Phillips Curve specification, the equation is designed to settle at the full-employment rate at a constant rate. As can be seen, if RU=RUNAT, if there is no further catch-up, if expected inflation equalled actural inflation and with the sum of the price-term coefficients near unity (it is in fact 1.03). real wages would simply grow at the rate of long-term roductivity growth, and all would be well.

Alternate: Linear RU version

$$RWPAA = RGPRD5 - 0.5850259 * J4A(RU - RUNAT) - 2.062947 * DAIB1$$

$$\qquad\qquad (2.2) \qquad\qquad\qquad (2.1)$$

$$-2.319579 * DAIB2 - 1.337445 * D6 \quad 5 + 0.3426615 * RECPI1$$

$$(2.3) \qquad\qquad (1.4) \qquad\qquad (2.2)$$

$$+0.2376347 * (RINFC - (RWPAA|4 - RPRODG5))$$

$$(2.5)$$

$$+\sum_{i=0}^{11} a<i> *RINFC|i$$

where

a0 = 0.0241,	a1 = 0.0443,	a2 = 0.0604,	a3 = 0.0724,
a4 = 0.0805,	a5 = 0.0804,	a6 = 0.0845,	a7 = 0.0805,
a9 = 0.0604,	a10 = 0.0443,	a11 = 0.0241,	Sum=0.73245 (3.9)
2nd Degree,	Constrained	near FAR	

Key Price Determination The key price in FOCUS is PGDPPF, the implicit deflator for privately produced GDP at factor cost. It is determined in one of two methods, as governed by the lever DP: (a) 'market-clearing' price (DP=0): it is determined so as to equate the demand and supply for real private domestic output at factor cost, or (b) 'mark-up' price (DP=1): it is determined by a behavioral equation based on a cost mark-up of unit labour costs and (depending on the option chosen) on unit import costs and inventory carrying costs. Supply is presumed to equal whatever demand is forthcoming at the price set.

(a) Market-Clearing Option: In this option there is no price equation as such. The solution routine searches for a value of PGDPPF which equalizes demand and supply for GDPPF and GDPPFS. See Section F, too. Since an iterative solution method is used, demand and supply will not be exactly equal at convergence, however experience has shown 'residual' excess demand to be generally only several million 1986 dollars.

(b) Mark-Up Option: There are several alternative versions for this option.

version 0:

$$PGDPPF = PGDPPF|1 * (1.0 + \underset{(14.8)}{0.9623472} * DOT(Ulcn) + \underset{(4.1)}{0.4257833} * (Rulcan)$$
$$+ \underset{(2.7)}{0.02136522} * DOT(CostInv))$$

version 1:

$$PGDPPF = PGDPPF|1 * (1.0 + \underset{(7.8)}{0.7032488} * DOT(Ulcn) + \underset{(3.9)}{0.3378443}$$
$$* DOT(J4APMAdj) + \underset{(3.9)}{0.3787893} * (Rulcan) + \underset{(2.6)}{0.01894070} * DOT(CostInv))$$

version 2:

$$PGDPPF = PGDPPF|1 * (1.0 + \underset{(15.8)}{1.011757} * DOT(Ulcn) + \underset{(4.2)}{0.4444907} * (Rulcan)$$

version 3:

$$PGDPPF = PGDPPF|1 * (1.0 + \underset{(7.9)}{0.7322754} * DOT(Ulcn)$$
$$+ \underset{(4.0)}{0.3566680} * DOT(J4APMAdj) + \underset{(3.9)}{0.3926321} * (Rulcan)$$

where

Ulcn	=	$\frac{JNPROD}{J4LCA}$
	:	nominal unit labour costs
J4LCA	=	$J4A(WPAA*(1+RTCUI*(1.4-0.4*DUIC)+RTCPP))\|1$
	:	labour cost adjusted for employer contributions
PMAdj	=	$PM*(1+\frac{TIM}{MV})$
	:	import deflator adjusted for tariffs
Rulcan	=	$\frac{Ulca}{Ulca\|1}-\frac{Ulcn}{Ulcn\|1}$
	:	Difference: changes in actual vs. normal unit labour costs
Ulca	=	$JNPROD*(WPAA*(1+RTCUI*(1.4-0.4*DUIC)$ $+RTCPP))$
	:	unit labor costs
CostInv	=	$(KINF*PGDPP)*0.01*RMF$
	:	interest cost of inventory holdings.

The price equations above view changes in output prices as primarily mark-ups on long-run or 'noirmal' unit labour costs. As can be sen, the estimated coefficients are of from 0.7 to just over 1, depending on whether import costs are also included in the equation. Labour costs include the employer contributions to unemployment insurance and the public pension plans as well as basic wages. Import costs also appear in some versions. These will capture the pass-through of costs of imported intermediate inputs and raw materials and also perhaps may reflect oligopolistic pricing practices by domestic producers.

The translation of PGDPPF to PGDPP – deflator at market prices – is done by the following identity.

$$PGDPP = \frac{PGDPPF*GDPPF+(TI-SU)}{GDPP}$$

Other Wages and Prices

Government Sector Wages and Salaries

$$PWG = \exp(-0.7472959+0.2567479*\log WPAA+(1-0.2567479)*PG(PWG)|1)$$

(4.5) (4.7)

Consumption Deflators

$$PCDA = Pgmtmp*(0.07256239+0.9158220)*\frac{PCDA|1}{Pgmtmp|1})$$

where

Pgmtmp	=	$(1.4*PGDPPF+0.3*PMGAUS$ $+0.1*PMGO*(1+RTIMO))*RTax$	

where

RTax	=	$(1+0.573*RTIFMS)*(1+0.965*RTIRSP)$	before 91:1
	=	$(1+1.0*RTIFMS)+0.965*RTIRSP)$	after 91:2

$$PCDO = Pgmtmp * (0.1071361 + 0.7606896 * \frac{PCDO|1}{Pgmtmp|1} + \frac{14.33747}{DTIME})$$

(3.6) (10.7) (2.6)

$$Pgmtmp = ((1 - 0.30525) * PGDPPF + 0.30525 * PMGO * (1 + RTIMO)) * RTax$$

$$PCSD = Pgmtmp * (0.1442950 + 0.872725 * PCSD|1 - \frac{3.742944}{DTIME})$$

(2.8) (17.2) (2.4)

where

Pgmtmp	=	$((1 - 0.27622) * PGDPPF + 0.27622 * PMGO * (1 + RTIMO))$ $*RTax$
RTax	=	$(1 + (0.219 * RTIFMS * Dsd + \frac{0.219}{0.43} * RTIMFMS$ $*(1 - Dsd))) * (1 + 0.790 * RTIRSP)$ (before 91:1)
	=	$(1 + 1.0 * RTIFMS + 0.790 * RTIRSP)$ (after 91:2)
Dsd	=	Dummy for change in coverage of manufacturers' tax
	=	0 prior to 74:3 and =1 later

$$PCND = Pgmtmp * (0.09493166 + 0.9242579 * \frac{PCND|1}{Pgmtmp|1} - \frac{4.446396}{DTIME})$$

(2.4) (27.3) (2.3)

where

Pgmtmp	=	$((1 - 0.13232) * pgdppf + 0.13232 * pmgo * (1 + rtimo)) * RTax$
where		
RTax	=	$(1 + 0.174 * RTIFMS + 0.069 * RTIFTA + RTIGSF + RTIATF)$ $*(1 + 0.722 * RTIRSP + RTILCP + 0.5 * RTIGSP)$ (before 91:2)
	=	$1 + 0.407 * RTIFMS + 0.069 * RTIFTA + RTIGSF + RTIATF$ $+0.459 * RTIRSP + RTIATF + 0.459 * RTIRSP + RTILCP$ $+0.5 * RTIGSP)$ (after 91:2)

$$PCS = Pgmtmp * (0.01865189 + 0.9803939 * \frac{PCS|1}{Pgmtmp|1})$$

where

Pgmtmp	=	$((1 - 0.03530 * PGDPPF + 0.03530 * PMGO * (1 + RTIMO))$ $*RTax$
where		
RTax	=	$(1 + 0.040 * RTIFMS) * (1 + 0.227 * RTIRSP)$ (before 91:2)
	=	$(1 + 0.531 * RTIFMS + 0.227 * RTIRSP)$ (after 91:2)

$$CPI = \exp(-0.002482109 + 1.055912 * \log(0.07 * CPIG + 0.363 * PCND$$

$$+0.053 * PCDA + 0.091 * PCDO + 0.125 * PCSD + 0.298 * PCS))$$

$$CPIA = CPIA|1 * \frac{PCDA}{PCDA|1}$$

$$PCD = \frac{CDV}{CD}$$

$$PC = \frac{CV}{C}$$

$$PGC = Pgmtmp * (0.2109240 + 0.8052810 * \frac{PGC|1}{Pgmtmp|1} - \frac{2.701031}{DTIME})$$

(2.8) (11.6) (2.1)

where

Pgmtmp	=	$0.7 * PWG + ((0.3 - 0.03673) * PGDPPF + 0.03673 * PMGO$ $*(1 + RTIMO)) * RTax$	
RTax	=	$(1 + 0.069 * RTIFMS) * (1 + 0.077 * RTIRSP)$	(before 91:1)
	=	$(1 + 0.13 * RTIFMS + 0.095 * RTIRSP)$	(after 91:2)

$$PGI = Pgmtmp * (0.1373525 + 0.8535921 * \frac{PGI|1}{Pgmtmp|1})$$

(2.6) (15.1)

Pgmtmp	=	$(1 + 0.18508) * PGDPPF + 0.18508 * PMGO * (1 + RTIMO))$ $*RTax$	
where			
RTax	=	$(1 + (0.12 * 0.713 + 0.88 * 0.214) * RTIFMS)$ $*(1 + (0.12 * 0.427 + 0.88 * 0.391) * RTIRSP)$	(before 91:1)
	=	$+(0.12 * 0.75 + 0.88 * 0.50) * RTIFMS + 0.414 * RTIRSP)$	(after 91:2)

$$PIFHB = Pgmtmp * (0.0915384 + 0.8063913 * PIFHB|1 - \frac{5.080298}{DTIME}$$

(2.0) (14.9) (3.0)

$$+1.873776 * \frac{IFHB}{GDPP})$$

(4.3)

Pgmtmp	=	$((1 - 0.12072) * PGDPPF + 0.12072 * PMGO * (1 + RTIMO))$ $*RTax$	
where			
RTax	=	$(1 + 0.201 * RTIFMS) * (1 + 0.370 * RTIRSP)$	(before 91:1)
	=	$(1 + 0.75 * RTIFMS + 0.460 * RTIRSP)$	(after 91:2)

$$PIFNB = Pgmtmp * (0.3019925 + 0.6869754 * \frac{PIFHB|1}{Pgmtmp|1} - \frac{5.572730}{DTIME}$$

(3.6) (8.2) (3.0)

$$+0.5519473 * \frac{IFNB}{GDPP})$$

(2.1)

$$\begin{aligned}\text{Pgmtmp} &= ((1-0.14518)*PGDPPF+0.14518*PMGO*(1+RTIMO)) \\ &\quad *RTax \\ \text{RTax} &= (1+0.201*RTIFMS)*(1+0.370*RTIRSP) \qquad \text{(before 91:1)} \\ &= (1+0.0*RTIFMS+0.370*RTIRSP) \qquad \text{(after 91:2)}\end{aligned}$$

$$PIFMB = Pgmtmp*(0.0340033+0.9620246*\frac{PIFMB|1}{Pgmtmp|1})$$

$$\begin{aligned} & \qquad\qquad (1.0) \qquad\qquad (30.2) \\ \text{Pgmtmp} &= ((1-0.43414)*PGDPPF+0.43414*PMGO*(1+RTIMO)) \\ \text{where} & \\ \text{RTax} &= (1+0.401*RTIFMS)*(1+0.541*RTIRSP) \qquad \text{(before 91:1)} \\ &= (1+0.0*RTIFMS+0.541*RTIRSP) \qquad \text{(after 91:2)}\end{aligned}$$

$$PIIB = PIIB|1*\frac{PGDPP}{PGDPP|1}$$

$$PGDP = \frac{GDPV}{GDP}$$

$$PINFG = 100*(\frac{PGDP}{PGDP|4}-1)$$

$$PGNP = \frac{GNPV}{GNP}$$

Reconciling Component Deflators with the Key Price PGDPP The key price approach requires some method of reconciling the estimate of nominal GDP obtained from the key price ($GDPPV = PGDPP*GDPP$) with the estimate which would be obtained from adding up the components of private GDP, each calculated with their own deflators (i.e., $GDPPV = PC*C+PIFHB*IFHB+PIFNB*IFBN...$). In FOCUS an adjustment is made every iteration to each of the non-trade final-demand deflators. If the value of GDPPV obtained by adding up individual components is different from PGDPP*GDPP, then each final-demand deflator is raised or lowered the same proportional amount. The adjustment variable RDIS. As a check, the difference is calculated:

$$ZPCHK = (PGDPP*GDPP)-GDPPV$$

4.16 Financial: Money Stock and Related Assets

The main channel by which financial variables influence real quantities and prices in FOCUS is via real interest rates. Capital spending is especially sensitive to variations in real rates. Capital spending is especially sensitive to variations in real rates, which in turn depend critically on monetary policy. The model uses a liquidity preference approach to the determination of its key nominal rate: RMF, the rate of interest on 90-day finance company paper. This rate equates the demand and supply of money within the model and longer-term rates are derived from it through term-structure or other assumed relationships. Ex-ante real rates for the 90-day paper rate (RMRLF) or for 1-3 year government bonds (RMRL1) are calculated by subtracting estimates of expected future inflations from the corresponding nominal rates. It s the latter real rate that is especially important for driving capital spending.

$$ARRCB = (0.9738968 + 0.0467625 * (DSQ1 - DSQ4) - 0.004345452 * (DSQ2 - DSQ4)$$

(5.4) (9.4) (0.88)

$$-0.02894313 * (DSQ3 - DSQ4)) * (RRDD * (0.667 * (MONM1$$

(5.9)

$$-MONCUR - FDGCCB) + 0.333 * (MONM1|1 - MONCUR|1$$

$$-FDGCCB|1) + RRTD * (0.667 * (MONM2A - MONM1A)$$

$$+0.333 * (MONM2A|1 - MONM1A|1)))$$

$$MONCUR = \exp(0.0727476 - 0.003008878 * (DSQ1 - DSQ4) * \log CV$$

(0.3) (43.7)

$$+0.0008658775 * (DSQ2 - DSQ4) * \log CV$$

(12.8)

$$+0.002028231 * (DSQ3 - DSQ4) * \log CV + 1.0003564 * \log MONCUR|1$$

(29.8)

$$-0.008565777 * \log RMF$$

$$FDGCCB = \exp(0.2718505 + 0.00282459 * (DSQ1 - DSQ4) * \log GREVF$$

(0.6) (0.4)

$$-0.02626845 * (DSQ2 - DSQ4) * \log GREVF$$

(4.2)

$$-0.01875224 * (DSQ3 - DSQ4) * PG(GREVF) + 0.8292599$$

(3.0) (6.3)

$$* \log FDGCCB|1 - 0.009507156 * \log RM + 0.09951859 * \log GREVF)$$

(0.6) (1.4)

$$VELM1 = \frac{GDPV}{MONM1}$$

$$VELM2 = \frac{GDPV}{MONM2A}$$

4.17 Internal Rates and Price Expectations

Interest rate formation in FOCUS proceeds in three stages:

A. 'Synthetic' expectations for prices 1 quarter, 1 year and 2 years into the future are calculated based on simple reduced-form forecasting equations for inflations. These expectation terms are used here and elswhere in the model in place of more customary distributed lags.

B. The key short-term nominal rate of interest (RMF) is determined based on one or other specification of Bank of Canada policy. The key short-term real rate is then computed as the nominal rate less expected inflation.

C. Additional long and short rates are related to the key rate and sometimes to inflation and to other variables. A number of options are available for specifying the 'term structure'.

$$RECP90 = -0.2463269 + 0.6504693 * (\frac{CPI}{CPI|1} - 1) * 100 + 0.1400150 * (DSQ1 - DSQ4)$$

(0.68) (6.7) (3.3)

$$*(\frac{CPI}{CPI|1} - 1) * 400 + 0.09126645 * (DSQ2 - DSQ4) * (\frac{CPI}{CPI|1} - 1) * 400$$

(2.4)

$$+0.1356940 * (DSQ3 - DSQ4) * (\frac{CPI}{CPI|1} - 1) * 400$$

(3.5)

$$-0.4325042 * (RU - J8A(RU|1))$$

(2.6)

$$+0.1629630 * \frac{\frac{MONM1}{MONM1|12} - 1}{3} * 100 + 0.06780406$$

(3.1) (2.1)

$$*((\frac{RXUS}{RXUS|1} - 1) * 400 - \frac{\frac{RXUS}{RXUS|8} - 1}{2} * 100)$$

$$+0.1794045 * ((USCPI.USCPI|4) - 1) * 100$$

(2.0)

$$RECPI1 = -0.3480406 + 0.4898068 * (\frac{CPI}{CPI|4} - 1) * 100 - 0.4904272$$

(1.2) (6.5) (3.7)

$$*(RU - J8A(RU|1)) + 0.2467254 * (\frac{MONM1}{MONM|12} - 1) * 3 * 100$$

(6.0)

$$+0.03289229 * ((\frac{RXUS}{RXUS|1} - 1) * 400 - \frac{\frac{RXUS}{RXUS|8} - 1}{2} * 100)$$

(1.3)

$$+0.2883752 * (\frac{USCPI}{USCPI|4} - 1) * 100$$

(4.2)

$$RECCPI2 = -1.283684 + 0.2367207 * \frac{\frac{CPI}{CPI|24} - 1}{6} * 100$$

(3.8) (4.9)

$$-0.5475887 * (RU - J8A(RU|1)) + 0.5097778 * \frac{\frac{MONM1}{MONM1|12} - 1}{2} * 100$$

(4.0) (12.3)

$$+0.3669574 * \frac{\frac{USCPI}{USCPI|8} - 1}{2} * 100$$

(6.0)

$$RMF = \exp(-7.829918 - 0.002907293 * (DSQ1 - DSQ4) * \log GDP - 0.001370543$$

$$*(DSQ2 - DSQ4) * \log GDP + 0.002034548 * (DSQ3 - DSQ4) * \log GDP$$

$$+1.604356 * \log GDP + 0.0001894666 * DPost * \log GDP - 0.01474533$$

$$*DTIME79 - 1.054353 * \log \frac{MONM1}{PGDP} + 0.2248711 * \log RMF|1)$$

Here is presented only Monetary Rule 1 which is one of the rules to solve the FOCUS model for monetary policy. The equation for RMF used when MONM1 is controlled is a simple re-normalized demand for money function. The postal dummy is based on the work of A.W.Gregory and J.G.MacKinnon (CJE 13:4, Nov.1980) but is entered in the equation in a different fashion. It is significant. The time trend DTime79 is an inelegant but necessary means of capturing structural and technical changes in recent years that permit economizing on cash balances. Time trends starting in each year from 1977 through 1082 were tried in the equation. Each was significant but the trend starting in 1979 fit best. The long-run elasticity with respect to real GDP is over 2.0, and with respect to the real money supply it is 1.36. Still, by far the greatest effect occurs in the current quarter.

Chapter 11
Malaysia Model II

Shigeyuki Abe[1]

1 Introduction

Malaysia Model II is an updated version of the model presented in the Conference on Econometric Models of Asian LINKS. Data have been updated to 1989 and the model structure has been expanded to clarify government and external sectors. Various minor changes can be found in this new model. Interest and exchange rates are treated explicitly and the generalized least squares method is used to correct serious serial correlation. The basic structure of the model, however, remains the same as before. Basic policy simulations are performed to demonstrate the model's performance.

Although the model performs relatively well in terms of RMSE (root mean square errors), the defective nature of the data cannot be avoided. For Malaysia it is still a very difficult task to obtain consistent time series of some key economic variables. Every year a summary table of economic statistics is appended to the Economic Report. We find revised estimations of many variables and, normally, serious gaps for some period of time. In this regard our model estimation itself should be redone in a few years when more accurate data will likely be available. For the moment our model can serve as a concise model to simulate some key aspects of the Malaysian economy.

2 Overview of the Malaysian Economy

The Malaysian economy is a small open economy, easily influenced by external business conditions. Spectacular growth in the 1970's was led by the export sector's performance but featured the positive participation of government. In the first half of the 1970's Malaysia's GDP recorded an 8 percent growth rate and, in the second half an 8.6 percent. The Malaysian economy experienced a turbulence in the 1980s in the face of external shocks. During the early 1980's public expenditure rose markedly as government began a number of infrastructural and heavy industrial projects, which resulted in imbalances in the balance of payments, and increasing external indebtedness. Eventually, it became necessary to correct the imbalances by cutting public expenditures. Efforts were also made to encourage the role of the private sector through privatisation, tax incentives and deregulation. The economy rebounded until 1985 when the Malaysian economy faced difficulties due

[1] Kobe University

to a drastic decline in major commodity prices and a world wide slump. In 1986 the economy overcame the trough and in 1987 the economy continued to expand at a rate of about 5.2 percent. By 1988 the economy had fully recovered from the trough of 1985 and recorded a growth rate of 8.7 percent. Manufacturing production and exports spurted during this period.

A model of this economy, thus, should highlight the performance of each sector in terms of production and exports, the latter being very important in the case of Malaysia. Government performance should be duly evaluated in contrast with private sector performance. The role of external loans and foreign capital cannot be neglected. World trade and economic fluctuations also directly affect the economy of Malaysia. All these features are included in our model.

3 Specification of the Model

The Malaysian Model II consists of production, demand, prices, employment, government budget, balance of payments, and money blocks as was the case for the earlier version of the model. Basically, GDP in constant prices is determined by the supply side. The gap between supply and demand is filled in by changes in stocks, or inventory investment. Money in circulation plays a role of determining investment, consumption and prices.

Production is broken down into four sectors: agriculture, mining, manufacturing, and "other." In each, production is a function of capital and labor. The agriculture sector is assumed to absorb redundant labor while employment in the mining sector is exogenously given. Employment in manufacturing and other sectors is determined to fill the demand for labor in these sectors, a proxy of which is being the growth of production. The total level of employment or unemployment is determined by the Phillips' curve relationship. Since capital stock figures are not available, accumulated investments for the past five years with a 5

Aggregate demand components take the usual forms. Private consumption is a function of real disposable income and wealth, a proxy for which is money balances. Private investment is determined by the level of GDP, real interest rate, and money balances. Nominal government consumption and nominal public investment are exogenously given. Imports of goods and services is a function of relative prices and disposable income. Exports, usually treated as exogenous, is endogenous and treated as a function of world business conditions, relative prices, and domestic production levels; this reflects a reduced form treatment of the demand and supply of export goods. To bridge the gap between GDP on the production side and GDP on the demand side changes of stocks are treated as a residual so that demand is equal to supply at all times.

The money supply is considered as a function of monetary policy. The monetary base is affected by the government budget and the balance of payments. The money equation is a reduced form of the money supply and money demand equations.

In the following section the model is shown in detail together with regression results.

3.1 Malaysia Model II

3.1.1 Production Block

Production: Agriculture, Forestry and Fishery

$$(1)\quad \log\frac{Y1}{LW1} = -2.72699 + 0.14285\log\frac{\Sigma 0.95^t IG_{-t}}{LW1}$$

(0.512) (1.304)

[GLS] Range=1970 to 1989 RHO=0.98221 (11.189)
$\overline{R}^2$=0.9568 SE=0.0474 DW=2.5085 F=200.4391

Production: Mining and Quarrying

$$(2)\quad \log\frac{Y2}{LW2} = 0.38670 + 0.67943\log\frac{\Sigma 0.95^t IG_{-t}}{LW2} + 0.17125\log(1-\frac{S}{GDP})$$

(0.366) (3.978) (1.212)

[GLS] Range=1970 to 1989 RHO1=0.4944 (1.7474)
$\overline{R}^2$=0.9790 SE=0.0956 DW=1.4735 F=280.9580

Production: Manufacturing

$$(3)\quad \log\frac{Y3}{LW3} = 2.8750 + 0.3140\log\frac{\Sigma 0.95^t (IP_{-t}+IG_{-t})}{LW3}$$

(0.142) (1.783)

[GLS] Range = 1970 to 1989 RHO1=0.9868 (5.9819)
$\overline{R}^2$=0.8502 SE=0.0602 DW=2.0689 F=52.11035

Production: Others

$$(4)\quad \log\frac{YO}{LWO} = 1.6972 + 0.1693\log\frac{\Sigma 0.95^t (IP_{-t}+IG_{-t})}{LWO}$$

(3.9665) (1.2879)

[GLS] Range=1970 to 1989 RHO1=1.0756 (4.2244)
RHO2=-0.4505 (-1.7280)
$\overline{R}^2$=0.6808 SE=0.0261 DW=2.0212 F=13.0904

Production: GDP Identity

$$(5)\quad GDP = Y1 + Y2 + Y3 + YO$$

3.1.2 Employment Block

Employment: Labor Force

(6) $LF = -883.9533 + 0.54451 NPOP$

(-1.9410) (14.3531)

[GLS] Range=1970 to 1989 RHO1=1.3686 (6.4947)
RHO2=-0.5742 (-2.6713)
$\overline{R}^2$=0.9971 SE=50.2608 DW= 2.2662 F=1954.959

Employment: Unemployment Rate Definition

(7) $$U = \frac{LF - LW}{LF}$$

Employment: Unemployment Rate

(8) $$U = 0.01870 - 0.0302 \frac{PCP - PCP_{-1}}{PCP_{-1}}$$

(2.0427) (-1.2996)

$$- 0.1410 \frac{GDP - GDP_{-1}}{GDP_{-1}} + 0.8812 U_{-1}$$

(-3.1440) (6.4503)

[OLS] Range=1970 to 1989
$\overline{R}^2$=0.7217 SE=0.0050 DW=1.7573 F=16.55981

Employment: Agriculture, Forestry and Fishery

(9) $LW1 = LW - LW2 - LW3 - LWO$

Employment: Manufacturing

(10) $LW3 = 49.2659 + 0.9343 LW3_{-1} + 0.0447(Y3 - Y3_{-1})$

(1.9881) (23.3024) (3.1676)

[OLS] Range=1970 to 1989
$\overline{R}^2$=0.9778 SE=34.5715 DW=1.8277 F=398.9604

Employment: Others

(11) $LWO = 23.0584 + 1.0132 LWO_{-1} + 0.0516(YO - YO_{-1})$

(0.5220) (56.0281) (3.6939)

[OLS] Range=1971 to 1989
$\overline{R}^2$=0.9942 SE=54.6669 DW=1.8886 F=1569.678

3.1.3 Aggregate Demand Block

Aggregate Demand: Private Consumption

$$(12)\quad CP = -896.5517 + 0.3400\frac{GDPV - TY}{PGDP} + 0.4549\frac{M2}{PGDP}$$

(-0.1042) (1.2043) (4.9152)

[GLS] Range=1970 to 1989 RHO1=1.0141 (3.8857)
RHO2=-0.5759 (-2.1875)
$\overline{R}^2$=0.9273 SE=1878.898 DW=1.8162 F=55.2885

Aggregate Demand: Government Consumption

$$(13)\quad CG = \frac{CGV}{PCG}$$

Aggregate Demand: Private Investment

$$(14)\quad IP = 5078.4929 + 0.05540GDP_{-1} - 63.4905\frac{R - 100(PGDP - PGDP_{-1})}{PGDP_{-1}}$$

(2.9532) (1.2648) (-3.1467)

[GLS] Range=1970 to 1989 RHO1=1.2730 (4.5562)
RHO2=-1.1386 (-3.7667)
$\overline{R}^2$=0.9423 SE=616.2503 DW=1.9661 F=70.5002

Aggregate Demand: Government Investment

$$(15)\quad IG = \frac{IGV}{PIG}$$

Aggregate Demand: Import of SITC 0,4

$$(16)\quad \frac{MF}{PM} = 1576.8339 + 0.0413\frac{GDPV - TY}{PGDP} - 931.6311\frac{PM(1 + TMR)}{PCP}$$

(2.2650) (8.1245) (-1.4275)

[GLS] Range=1971 to 1989 RHO=0.3597 (1.2812)
$\overline{R}^2$=0.9001 SE=174.4404 DW=1.4809 F=55.1174

Aggregate Demand: Import of SITC 2,3,5

$$(17)\quad \frac{MR}{PM} = 2533.8191 + 0.1232GDP - 1494.6089EXRATE$$

(1.2300) (6.2071) (-1.6735)

[GLS] Range=1971 to 1989 RHO=0.5595 (2.7710)
$\overline{R}^2$=0.9287 SE=469.3376 DW=1.6350 F=79.2153

Aggregate Demand: Import of SITC 6,8

$$(18)\quad \frac{MM}{PM} = -17975.770 + 0.2934\frac{GDPV - TY}{PGDP} - 1968.6535\frac{PM(1+TMR)}{PCP}$$

(-1.0898) (6.2086) (-1.4234)

[GLS] Range=1971 to 1989 RHO=0.9726 (21.6295)
$\bar{R}^2$=0.9672 SE=338.4371 DW=2.2024 F=178.0826

Aggregate Demand: Import of SITC 7

$$(19)\quad \frac{MI}{PM} = -24769.460 + 0.6543\frac{GDPV - TY}{PGDP} - 2253.0318\frac{PM(1+TMR)}{PCP}$$

(-1.3393) (4.3895) (-0.5235)

[GLS] Range=1971 to 1989 RHO=0.9243 (11.7922)
$\bar{R}^2$=0.9538 SE=1032.083 DW=1.73278428 F=125.0792

Aggregate Demand: Import of Services and Other Goods

$$(20)\quad \frac{MO}{PMO} = -2835.0945 + 0.1801\frac{GDPV - TY}{PCP}$$

(-2.2326) (6.8092)

[GLS] Range=1971 to 1989 RHO1=0.6588 (3.5067)
$\bar{R}^2$=0.9458 SE=589.1661 DW=1.6353 F(2/10)=158.0958

Aggregate Demand: Total Real Import of Goods and Services Definition

$$(21)\quad MGS = \frac{MI}{PMI} + \frac{MR}{PMR} + \frac{MM}{PMM} + \frac{MF}{PMF} + \frac{MO}{PMO}$$

Aggregate Demand: Total Nominal Import of Goods and Services Definition

$$(22)\quad MGSV = MGSPM$$

Aggregate Demand: Export of SITC 2,3,5

$$(23)\quad \frac{XR}{PX} = -1082.3645 + 2.6284Y2$$

(-1.2156) (14.427)

[GLS] Range=1971 to 1989 RHO=0.2610 (1.1103)
$\bar{R}^2$=0.9501 SE=890.8664 DW=1.9414 F=182.0287

Aggregate Demand: Export of SITC 6,8

$$(24)\quad \frac{XM}{PM} = \underset{(1.9401)}{1998.5849} + \underset{(4.9937)}{.3212Y3} - \underset{(-1.2911)}{1414.3813}(2.21\frac{PGDP}{EXRATE})$$

[GLS] Range=1971 to 1989 RHO=0.6622 (3.2638)
$\overline{R}^2$=0.8737 SE=413.2588 DW=2.0645 F=42.5396

Aggregate Demand: Export of Services and Other Goods

$$(25)\quad \frac{XO}{PX} = \underset{(1.5471)}{3406.0142} + \underset{(2.6151)}{0.7439YO} - \underset{(-7.3715)}{30410.237}(2.21\frac{PGDP}{EXRATE})$$
$$+ \underset{(3.5165)}{4924.1601WLDB}$$

[OLS] Range=1970 to 1989
$\overline{R}^2$=0.9454 SE=1765.362 DW=1.6764 F=110.6974

Aggregate Demand: Total Real Export of Goods and Services

$$(26)\quad XGS = \frac{XR}{PX} + \frac{XM}{PX} + \frac{XO}{PX}$$

Aggregate Demand: Total Nominal Export of Goods and Services

$$(27)\quad XGSV = XGSPX$$

Aggregate Demand: Changes of Real Stock

$$(28)\quad S = GDP - IG - CG - IP - CP - XGS + MGS$$

Aggregate Demand: Total Nominal Aggregate Demand

$$(29)\quad GDPV = IGV + CGV + IPPIP + CPPCP + XGSV$$
$$- MGSV + SPGDP + GDPVADJ$$

3.1.4 Price Block

Price: Private Consumption

$$(30)\quad PCP = \underset{(5.3919)}{0.4667} + \underset{(3.2688)}{0.3786PM} + \underset{(4.9481)}{0.000008005M2}$$

[GLS] Range=1970 to 1989 RHO=0.4314 (1.9102)
$\overline{R}^2$=0.9791 SE=0.0395 DW=1.6639 F=297.8967

Price: Government Consumption

(31) $PCG = 0.6478 + 0.2139PM + 0.000006098M2$

(2.6479) (1.4538) (1.6341)

[GLS] Range=1970 to 1989 RHO=0.8534 (3.8209)
$\overline{R}^2$=0.9801 SE=0.0325 DW=1.9588 F=313.1778

Price: Private Investment

(32) $PIP = 0.0350467 + 0.8156PM + 0.000004146M2$

(0.2698) (4.9881) (1.9274)

[GLS] Range=1970 to 1989 RHO=0.5242 (2.2597)
$\overline{R}^2$=0.9803 SE=0.0469 DW=1.5932 F=316.2624

Price: Government Investment

(33) $PIG = 0.1826 + 0.8786PIP$

(3.9074) (19.9758)

[OLS] Range=1970 to 1989
$\overline{R}^2$=0.9544 SE=0.0641 DW=1.9714 F=399.0346

Price: GDP

(34) $PGDP = \frac{GDPV}{GDP}$

3.1.5 Government Budget

Government Budget: Income Tax

(35) $TY = TYRGDPV$

Government Budget: Export Tax

(36) $TX = TXRXGSV$

Government Budget: Import Tax

(37) $TM = TMRMGSV$

Government Budget: Indirect Taxes

(38) $TI = TIRGDPV$

Government Budget: Total Governmnet Revenue

(39) $GRN = TY + TX + TM + TI + TOH$

Government Budget: Government Budget Surplus

(40) $GB = GRN - IGV - CGV - GEO + ADJGB$

Government Budget: Net Borrowing from Abroad

(41) $GBNBF = -GB - GBNBD - GBNBF - GBOF$

3.1.6 Balance of Payments Block

Balance of Payments: Overall Balance

(42) $BOP = XGSV - MGSV + GBNBF + BOPADJ$

Balance of Payments: Foreign Debt

(43) $FDEBT = FDEBT_{-1} + GBNBF + ADJFD$

3.1.7 Money Supply Block

Money Supply: Changes of M1

(44) $M2 = -1541.9057 + 0.2250GDPV + 0.5887(BOP + GBNBD) + 0.6459M2_{-1}$

(-0.8485) (2.6136) (2.2654) (4.738)

[OLS] Range=1970 to 1989
$\overline{R}^2$=0.9942 SE=1419.318 DW=2.4599 F=861.9128

3.2 List of Variables

3.2.1 Endogenous Variables

CG	Public consumption (constant price)
CP	Private consumption (constant price)
GB	Government overall surplus (current price)
GDP	Gross Domestic Product (constant price)
GDPV	Gross Domestic Product (current price)
GRN	Government revenue (current price)
IG	Public investment (constant price)
IP	Private investment (constant price)
LF	Labor force
LW	Total employment
LW1	Employment in agriculture,forestry and fishing sector

LW3	Employment in manufacturing sector
LWO	Employment in other sector
M2	Money supply broadly defined (current price)
MF	Import of goods, SITC0 + SITC 4 (constant price)
MGS	Total import of goods and services (constant price)
MGSV	Total import of goods and services (current price)
MM	Import of goods, SITC 6 + SITC 8 (constant price)
MR	Import of goods, SITC 2 + SITC 3 + SITC 5(constant price)
MI	Import of goods, SITC 7
MO	Import of other goods
NPOP	Mid year population
PCG	Public consumption deflator, 1970=1.0
PCP	Private consumption deflator, 1970=1.0
PGDP	General price level, or GDP deflator, 1970=1.0
PIG	Public investment deflator, 1970=1.0
PIP	Private investment deflator, 1970=1.0
S	Changes in stock (constant price)
TI	Indirect taxes (current price)
TM	Import tax (current price)
TX	Export tax (current price)
TY	Income tax (current price)
XGS	Total export of goods and services (constant price)
XGSV	Total export of goods and services (current price)
XM	Export of goods, SITC 6 + SITC 8 (constant price)
XO	Export of other goods (constant price)
XR	Export of goods, SITC 2 + SITC 3 + SITC 5(constant price)
Y1	Production of agriculture, forestry and fishing(constant price)
Y2	Production of mining and quarrying (constant price)
Y3	Production of manufacturing (constant price)
YO	Production of others (constant price)

3.2.2 Exogenous Variables

GDVADJ	Adjustment factor for GDPV identity
CGV	Public consumption (current price)
GEO	other government expenditure
IGV	Public investment (current price)
LW2	Employment in mining and quarrying sector
PM	Import price index, 1970=1.0
PX	Export price index, 1970=1.0
TIR	Indirect tax rate (average)
TMR	Import tax rate (average)
TOH	Other government revenue
REND	Time trend, 1963=1.

TXR	Export tax rate (average)
TYR	Income tax rate (average)
WLDB	Index of GNP of Japan and USA, 1970=1.0

4 Model Performance

The final test compares actual values with the solutions of the simultaneous equations when the lagged endogenous variables are calculated ones. This test gives dynamic solutions of the system. The following table shows final test results in terms of RMSE and mean percentage error. In those cases where variables take both positive and negative values, such as the government budget and the balance of payments, RMSE normally will not represent goodness of simulation performance. Dynamic simulation has been carried out for the period from 1980 to 1989. Errors, for most of the vaiables, are successfully below 10 percent. Errors related to inventory investment are large as expected due to the fluctuating nature of this variable. Unemployment figures also result in a very large RMSE. On the whole, however, model performance indicates a good representation of the workings of the Malaysian economy.

Model Performance

	RMSPE	MPE		RMSPE	MPE
BOP	62.794	-20.802	MMR	0.163	0.045
CG	0.054	0.046	MOR	0.139	-0.039
CP	0.174	0.078	MRR	0.142	-0.011
GB	1.469	-1.370	PCG	0.050	-0.043
GDP	0.042	-0.008	PCP	0.045	-0.041
GDPV	0.057	-0.035	PGDP	0.030	-0.027
GRN	0.042	-0.011	PIG	0.059	-0.020
IG	0.072	0.024	PIP	0.026	-0.024
IP	0.202	-0.143	S	15.376	3.903
LF	0.004	0.001	U	0.198	0.151
LW	0.014	-0.009	XGS	0.117	0.057
LW1	0.124	0.115	XGSV	0.117	0.057
LW3	0.076	0.025	XMR	0.294	0.160
LWO	0.104	-0.098	XOR	0.127	-0.040
M2	0.214	-0.152	XRR	0.166	0.119
MFR	0.092	-0.010	Y1	0.088	0.082
MGS	0.136	0.007	Y2	0.206	0.141
MGSV	0.136	0.007	Y3	0.107	0.012
MIR	0.168	0.042	YO	0.095	-0.082

5 Policy Simulations

Based upon the model presented, various policy simulations have been carried out for the years 1989 through 1995. First we should establish a baseline forecast for this period. Some of the exogenous variables were extrapolated directly, some were set at the level of the most current year, and some were determined arbitrarily. Most of the data are available up to 1990, and, thus, only the data from 1991 to 1995 were extrapolated. Policy simulation results are to be compared with this baseline simulation result. For policy simulations we specified the following four type of policy simulations. They are:

1. An increase in government consumption equal to 1 % of GDP, financed by foreign loans
2. An increase in government investment equal to 1 % of GDP, financed by foreign loans
3. A 10 % increase in the money supply
4. A 1 % increase in the interest rate.

For the first and second simulations we increased nominal government consumption and nominal government investment respectively by the equivalent of 1 % of real GDP. In the model real government consumption and investment are both endogenous. The money supply is also endogenous in the model. Thus, in the third simulation, a 10% increase of the money supply is modelled by increasing the adjustment factor of money supply (M2ADJ) by the equibalent of 10% of M2. For the fourth and last policy simulation we simply set the domestic interest rate 1 point above the baseline.

For the fiscal policy experiments the impact of GDP is strongest in case of government investment with monetary sterilization. Toward the end of the simulation period, however, the impact tends to be negative. The impact on PGDP is mixed. In the case of sterilization the impact is negative due to monetary contraction. In the case of nonsterilization the impact turns out to be positive. Toward the end to the period these impacts become very substantial. In all cases the current balance of payments suffers from a deficit.

The monetary shock policy simulation produces a negative impact on real GDP and a positive impact on nominal GDP. As a matter of course, the impact on PGDP is positive and the balance of payments deteriorates. The last policy has a negative impact on GDP.

6 Conclusions

The model can simulate a standard set of policy simulations with outcomes encouragingly consistent with those one would anticipate. By expanding the model to include the impact of foreign debt, interest repayment, foreign direct investment, exchange rate manipulation, and ASEAN economic cooperation, we can meaningfully discuss the most current economic issues in the framework of macro econometric models. The author is planning to incorporate these issues in Malaysia Model III.

References

[1] Abe, S. (1985) "Malaysia Model," in S. Ichimura and M. Ezaki eds., *Econometric Models of Asian Link*, Springer-Verlag, Tokyo

[2] Cheong, K. C. (1976) "A Macroeconomic Model for West Malaysia, 1948-68," The Developing Economies, vol.14, No.1, March

[3] Ministry of Finance of Malaysia, *Economic Reports,* various issues

[4] Semudram, M. (1982) "A Macromodel of the Malaysian Economy: 1959-77," The Developing Economies, vol.20, No.2, June

Appendix Data

	BOP	BOPADJ	CG	CGV	CP	CPV	EXRATE	FDEBT
1970			2928	2062	10863	7151	3.08	
1971			3219	2170	11414	7911	2.89	
1972			3763	2738	12531	8613	2.82	
1973			3935	2919	13660	10450	2.45	
1974	452	1603	4522	3516	13532	12776	2.31	
1975	171	1236	4829	3924	14359	13086	2.59	3424
1976	2048	406	5239	4301	15854	14594	2.54	2806
1977	755	-397	5754	5388	17420	16812	2.36	3349
1978	625	272	6090	6090	19584	19584	2.21	3859
1979	1789	-261	6195	6475	21698	22406	2.19	4538
1980	1002	1622	7750	8815	24445	26946	2.22	4860
1981	-1093	4540	8784	10425	25686	30594	2.24	8278
1982	3209	4731	9417	11844	29242	40283	2.42	23070
1983	312	4229	9500	11741	29142	39594	2.42	20848
1984	4345	4661	9536	12127	26315	36499	2.60	28310
1985	-614	7795	9552	11469	26531	33226	2.32	13158
1986	2893	-3561	9676	12239	26857	37685	2.49	27629
1987	-55	8062	9989	12156	27376	35998	2.34	17728
1988	-1104	-5824	10149	12997	31189	44856	2.71	25946
1989	1505	1282	10920	14180	35643	52930	2.70	25272

	FDEBTAD	GB	GBADJ	GBNBD	GBNBF	GBOF	GDE	GDEECON
1970		-432	-1386	308	3	121	451	725
1971		-1068	-1622	676	344	48	703	1085
1972		-1550	-2324	826	306	418	836	1242
1973		-1147	-2406	877	68	202	786	1128
1974	-226	-1440	-3288	826	226	388	1313	1878
1975	2512	-2459	-4220	1209	912	338	1398	2151
1976	-987	-1998	-5010	1660	369	-31	1550	2378
1977	8	-3011	-6156	1910	535	566	2129	3217
1978	-31	-3483	-6838	1299	541	1643	2529	3782
1979	0	-8112	-8270	2547	679	4886	2250	4282
1980	13	-12112	-12402	2331	309	9472	4833	7463
1981	509	-12480	-18586	4091	2909	5480	6813	11358
1982	1266	-5708	-21708	3591	956	1161	4303	7142
1983	27	-7075	-24092	3156	3093	826	5061	8407
1984	3892	-7506	-17219	4930	1348	1228	4538	7559
1985	107	-10726	-22756	5909	4773	44	5967	11485
1986	1757	-6153	-14757	8693	-2438	-102	3255	4741
1987	167	-7813	-23901	4315	4403	-905	5779	9669
1988	1412	-3890	-16886	7857	-3095	-872	3587	5231
1989	0	-5244	-21908	3655	-674	2263	4119	7696

	GDP	GDPV	GDPVADJ	GEA	GEO	GRN	IG	IGV
1970	20851	12253	90	198	-538	2861	1496	693
1971	22149	12955	-529	228	-1027	2940	1287	811
1972	24228	14220	-528	300	-1106	3456	1734	1162
1973	27063	18622	-282	334	-1125	4100	1695	1203
1974	29315	22858	-1335	436	-1833	5553	2000	1644
1975	29550	22332	-749	506	-2354	5929	2460	2110
1976	32967	28085	188	514	-2552	7360	2768	2505
1977	35522	32340	-670	591	-3659	9114	3238	3078
1978	37866	37866	0	716	-2815	8841	3419	3419
1979	41428	46424	721	877	-8007	10505	3651	4135
1980	44512	53308	-1144	1138	-11020	13926	4252	6203
1981	47602	57613	1	1481	-8568	15806	7364	9293
1982	57093	77470	-45	1287	-4124	21114	8396	10854
1983	57741	79550	-6	1122	-4093	20805	9375	12046
1984	57751	71594	1	1144	-6258	19518	6686	8639
1985	50430	62579	-0	1550	-4569	16690	8888	11378
1986	60683	79625	330	924	-4786	18143	5550	7271
1987	53582	69941	-309	1187	-1744	18608	9531	12521
1988	66298	90861	-14	1010	-4914	21967	5830	7946
1989	72134	101536	10	1140	-3830	23863	7782	11097

	INDEX4	IP	IPV	LF	LW	LW1	LW2	LW3	LWO
1970	1.00	2993	1181	3610	3278	1776	87	301	1113
1971	1.22	3522	1890	3720	3402	1803	87	326	1186
1972	1.49	3591	2049	3840	3532	1830	87	353	1262
1973	1.88	4810	2908	3960	3665	1857	87	382	1339
1974	2.26	5939	4151	4090	3805	1885	88	414	1418
1975	2.35	4783	3492	4320	3945	1915	88	448	1495
1976	2.69	4804	3701	4470	4104	1945	89	498	1572
1977	3.28	5428	4387	4765	4393	1941	88	663	1700
1978	4.15	5962	5962	5056	4670	2026	89	710	1846
1979	4.39	7400	8115	5216	4833	2056	90	755	1932
1980	5.17	8725	10394	5377	4980	1961	90	802	2128
1981	5.23	9086	11466	5512	5190	1934	76	787	2394
1982	5.73	9492	12270	6039	5625	1760	44	855	2965
1983	5.56	10386	13345	5907	5565	1724	47	879	2915
1984	5.89	7915	10226	6222	5707	1807	37	861	3002
1985	5.21	8879	11367	5643	5317	1929	69	799	2519
1986	6.07	8404	11009	6409	5881	1876	37	921	3048
1987	5.31	9662	12692	5764	5429	1925	66	815	2624
1988	6.46	10254	13976	6622	6088	1908	37	1013	3129
1989	6.85	13430	19151	6834	6351	1935	38	1090	3288

	M2	MER	MF	MFR	MGS	MGSV	MI	MIR	MM
1970	4122	1954	904	1675	8906	4807	1197	2218	970
1971	4668	2157	850	1513	8997	5056	1343	2390	976
1972	5762	2545	917	1503	8871	5412	1373	2251	1053
1973	7552	3122	1203	1825	10179	6711	1787	2711	1584
1974	8714	3586	1744	2210	13928	10989	3207	4065	2425
1975	9982	3931	1547	1774	11547	10071	2774	3180	1854
1976	12748	6071	1578	1641	12086	11620	3180	3308	2112
1977	14819	6565	1815	1922	14598	13788	3761	3982	2369
1978	17467	7189	2193	2193	16477	16477	4950	4950	2988
1979	21616	8976	2268	2057	19844	21884	6374	5780	3750
1980	27652	10304	2696	2197	23914	29342	9105	7421	4824
1981	32370	9794	3232	2420	25251	33717	9884	7402	5354
1982	48396	12457	3374	2631	30067	38561	13262	10341	6093
1983	45888	9630	3560	2850	33347	41653	15129	12112	6802
1984	53767	16539	3191	2497	28122	35941	12579	9842	5739
1985	37648	9332	3283	2528	28724	37300	11548	8893	6270
1986	56459	19432	3363	2591	30505	39592	14400	11095	6906
1987	41193	9443	3291	2576	31310	39996	13171	10311	6278
1988	60360	18328	4314	3161	37984	51835	19359	14186	9817
1989	60949	17497	5117	3582	49440	70622	29180	20428	12484

	MMR	MO	MOR	MR	MRR	NPOP	PCG	PCP	PCPG
1970	1797	583	1080	1153	2136	10395	0.70	0.66	-0.03
1971	1736	699	1243	1189	2115	10700	0.67	0.69	0.05
1972	1725	1007	1651	1062	1740	11003	0.73	0.69	-0.01
1973	2403	845	1282	1292	1960	11310	0.74	0.76	0.11
1974	3073	1187	1504	2426	3075	11608	0.78	0.94	0.23
1975	2126	1608	1844	2288	2623	11922	0.81	0.91	-0.03
1976	2197	1983	2063	2767	2878	12236	0.82	0.92	0.01
1977	2508	2704	2863	3139	3323	12574	0.94	0.97	0.05
1978	2988	2926	2926	3420	3420	12903	1.00	1.00	0.04
1979	3400	4813	4364	4679	4243	13275	1.05	1.03	0.03
1980	3932	6088	4962	6629	5403	13745	1.14	1.10	0.07
1981	4010	7381	5528	7866	5891	14128	1.19	1.19	0.08
1982	4751	8434	6576	7398	5768	15681	1.26	1.38	0.01
1983	5446	9036	7234	7126	5705	15270	1.24	1.36	0.03
1984	4490	8341	6526	6091	4766	16110	1.27	1.39	0.01
1985	4828	8532	6570	7667	5904	14507	1.20	1.25	0.05
1986	5321	7975	6145	6948	5353	16530	1.26	1.40	0.01
1987	4915	9402	7360	7854	6148	14888	1.22	1.31	0.05
1988	7194	9338	6843	9007	6600	16940	1.28	1.44	0.02
1989	8740	13024	9118	10817	7573	17400	1.30	1.49	0.03

	PCPI	PGDP	PIG	PIP	PM	PX	R	RUSA	S
1970	0.61	0.59	0.46	0.39	0.54	0.51	5.13	4.83	877
1971	0.62	0.58	0.63	0.54	0.56	0.48	4.79	3.73	882
1972	0.64	0.59	0.67	0.57	0.61	0.48	3.85	5.11	458
1973	0.65	0.69	0.71	0.60	0.66	0.62	3.73	7.41	534
1974	0.85	0.78	0.82	0.70	0.79	0.76	4.56	7.11	2632
1975	0.89	0.76	0.86	0.73	0.87	0.72	4.77	5.21	488
1976	0.91	0.85	0.90	0.77	0.96	0.88	4.38	4.30	-162
1977	0.96	0.91	0.95	0.81	0.94	0.94	3.56	6.14	1007
1978	1.00	1.00	1.00	1.00	1.00	1.00	4.21	9.34	703
1979	1.04	1.12	1.13	1.10	1.10	1.19	4.04	12.23	404
1980	1.11	1.20	1.46	1.19	1.23	1.36	4.45	14.99	635
1981	1.22	1.21	1.26	1.26	1.34	1.34	4.50	14.11	-498
1982	1.39	1.36	1.29	1.29	1.28	1.33	4.12	7.60	-1262
1983	1.39	1.38	1.28	1.28	1.25	1.36	5.06	8.13	952
1984	1.39	1.24	1.29	1.29	1.28	1.13	3.88	5.74	-211
1985	1.29	1.24	1.28	1.28	1.30	1.28	5.12	8.50	478
1986	1.40	1.31	1.31	1.31	1.30	1.25	3.22	5.84	-118
1987	1.33	1.31	1.31	1.31	1.28	1.30	5.19	9.38	445
1988	1.44	1.37	1.36	1.36	1.36	1.34	4.26	8.22	1223
1989	1.48	1.41	1.43	1.43	1.43	1.39	4.89	7.77	-130

	TI	TM	TOH	TX	TY	U	XGS	XM	XO
1970	484	557	905	258	657	0.092	10600	1226	961
1971	555	582	885	231	687	0.085	10823	1161	1148
1972	772	589	1122	232	741	0.080	11023	1290	1424
1973	973	746	1106	437	838	0.074	12609	1544	1627
1974	1091	893	1404	943	1222	0.070	14617	2362	3252
1975	1129	801	1448	625	1926	0.087	14179	2153	3741
1976	1336	978	1970	1010	2066	0.082	16549	2742	4157
1977	1594	1140	2199	1390	2791	0.078	17274	2869	5183
1978	1896	1325	996	1463	3161	0.076	18585	3317	6458
1979	2169	1512	1211	1939	3674	0.073	21924	3916	8589
1980	2503	2061	1555	2567	5240	0.074	22619	4429	10072
1981	2621	2245	2896	2225	5819	0.058	22431	3981	11124
1982	3084	2518	4874	1839	8799	0.069	31875	4486	18324
1983	4206	2697	3815	2090	7997	0.058	31733	3751	19437
1984	2822	2066	5210	1141	8279	0.083	35632	4378	19850
1985	2858	2315	3749	1720	6048	0.058	24826	3379	12667
1986	2805	1934	6009	1267	6128	0.082	40819	6328	24194
1987	3951	2591	2912	1892	7262	0.058	27889	3937	14504
1988	3398	2406	7635	1395	7133	0.081	45637	8334	30507
1989	4394	2899	7690	1588	7292	0.071	53929	8990	41110

	XR	Y1	Y2	Y3	YO
1970	3180	6639	2850	2930	8432
1971	2933	6532	3095	3273	9249
1972	2615	7030	3300	3606	10292
1973	4596	7858	3162	4418	11625
1974	5429	8401	2954	4876	13084
1975	4278	8146	2940	5021	13443
1976	7655	9143	3545	5949	14330
1977	8164	9359	3589	6579	15995
1978	8810	9513	3912	7189	17252
1979	13499	10060	4586	8004	18778
1980	16175	10189	4487	8742	21094
1981	15049	10689	4289	9155	23469
1982	19727	11854	5985	11263	27991
1983	19983	11623	6073	11711	28334
1984	16077	12348	6368	12111	26924
1985	15800	11375	4617	9668	24770
1986	20316	13216	6409	13734	27324
1987	17857	11302	5342	10429	26509
1988	22418	13928	6803	16151	29416
1989	24873	14737	7385	18089	31923

Source: Various issues of Economic Report, Ministry of Finance, Malaysia.

Chapter 12

A Structural Model of Singapore for Asian Link

Toh Mun Heng and Eric D. Ramstetter[1]

1 Introduction

This paper presents a basic econometric model of the Singaporean economy.[2] The model is designed for incorporation in a multi-country model such as the ASIAN LINK (Ichimura and Ezaki, 1985). The paper begins with a brief overview of the Singaporean ecomomy (section 2). Model specification is then described (section 3) and seven historical simulation experiments are presented to illustrate how the Singaporean economy responds to various shocks, both external and internal (section 4). In the concluding section, a summary of remaining tasks for integration of this model into a system such as ASIAN LINK is presented.

2 Overview of the Singaporean Economy[3]

Singapore is an extremely open economy. Trade has always been quite an essential activity in the country. Moreover, trade has played an increasingly important role in the economy during the 1972-1989 period. The ratio of the sum of real merchandise exports and imports to real gross domestic expenditure (GDE) rose from 181 percent in 1972 to 274 percent in 1980,then stagnated in the 253-267 percent range in 1981-1985 before climbing to 284-297 percent in 1986-1987 and 347-349 percent in 1988-1989. The ratio of service trade to real GDE was relatively constant at 61-68 percent in 1972-1979 before rising to 75-95 percent in 1980-1987 and 104-108 percent in 1988-1989. Thus, both merchandise and service trade have come to exceed real GDE and activities have been expanding rapidly relative to GDE in recent years.[4]

---

[1]National University Singapore, Singapore, and Kansai University, Osaka, Japan, respectively. The authors wish to thank Shinichi Ichimura and other participants of the Workshop on Asia-Pacific Modeling (Bandung, Indonesia, August 24, 1990) for comments and suggestions on an earlier version of this model.

[2]Previous models of the Singaporean economy are summarised in Lim, et al. (1988, Ch. 16) and Toh (1990).

[3]See Lim et al. (1988) for a comprehensive treatment of Singapore's economic development since 1965 and additional references.

[4]Merchandise trade figures (fob) are taken from the balance of payments and GDE from the national accounts since exports and imports are not separately available in the national accounts. Ratios are calculated from data in Appendices A and B.

Merchandise trade is especially large and trade in manufactures (the sum of SITC sections 5 through 9) has come to dominate this trade.[5] In the 1970s the share of imports of manufactures to the total merchandise import actually fell in real terms from 55 percent in 1972-1973 to 38-45 percent in 1974-1979 before increasing to 49-56 percent in 1980-1988 and 60 percent in 1989. On the export side, the share of manufactures increased much more steadily than that of imports from 40-43 percent in 1972-1975 to 46-54 percent in 1976-1979,57-60 percent in 1980-1986, and 65-68 percent in 1987-1989. Thus by 1989, trade in manufactures accounted for a little under two-thirds of all trade measured in real terms.

Of course a large portion of this trade is entrepot trade. Nonetheless, entrepot exports accounted for only 21-31 percent of the real merchandise exports in the 1972-1989 period. Manufactures have also accounted for a large and increasing share of real entrepot exports in 1972-1989 (60-84 percent) but the share of entrepot exports in the total exports of manufactures has been relatively constant at 34-41 percent over this period. On the other hand, food and beverages (SITC section 0 and 1) accounted for only 9-27 percent of all entrepot exports but these same entrepot exports accounted for 65-81 percent of total food and beverage exports. In other words, while exports of manufactures accounted for a relatively large share of entrepot exports, entrepot exports accounted for a smaller share of total exports in the case of manufactures than in the case of food and beverages.

The growth of Singapore's manufacturing sector has been a key element of Singapore's overall economic growth since independence in 1965. Foreign investments have played an especially important role in the manufacturing sector with wholly foreign-owned firms accounted for 49 percent of employment, 62 percent of value added, 67 percent of capital expenditures, and 73 percent of direct exports by all manufacturing firms Singapore in 1988 (EDB 1990). In addition to manufacturing, the service sector has also played an extremely important role. By 1989, the share of financial and business services in real GDE (30 percent) exceeded that of manufacturing (29 percent). Moreover, commerce (18 percent),transport and communications (14 percent),and other services (10 percent) also accounted for large shares of real GDE (DOS 1988, various years).

In short, since independence in 1965, Singapore has been transformed from an entrepot with a smattering of labour intensive industries to an economy with an increasingly sophisticated manufacturing base and a vibrant service sector which has become the engine of economic growth in recent years. One result of these changes in the economic structure has been a high GDE (growth domestic expenditure) growth rate, averaging 7.0 percent annually during 1972-1989 period. During the same period population grew an average of only 1.2 percent annually, implying an average annual increase in per capita GDE of 5.8 percent (DOS, 1983,

[5]The figures below refer to merchandise exports and imports as compiled in Singapore's external trade statistics. Note that the totals reported in these statistics are often substantially different from those in the balance of payments. Note also the data here have been adjusted to compensate for adding up problems in published data (e.g., Department of Statistics, various years) and are thus somewhat different than published data. See Appendices A and B for the original data used in this study.

1988, various years).

By the beginning of the period studied here (1972), the labour market was characterized by excess demand, which in turn led to rising wages. However, even with rapidly rising wages it was impossible to meet the demand for labour in Singapore; thus, workers from neighbouring countries were admitted to alleviate the labour shortage problem. The large number of foreign workers, estimated to be almost 200,000 or 15 percent of the labour force, has moderated wage growth in a very tight labour market. Also the pool of foreign workers has provided Singapore with a buffer against disruptive unemployment among local workers when the econmy suffers downturns.

On the other hand, the government has used instruments such as the foreign worker levy and work permits to limit the number of foreign workers, especially foreign workers with few skills. The goals of these policies include (1) inducing firms to upgrade their production techniques and (2) minimizing the social and political costs of hosting guest workers. Social stability has also been partially due to effective use of the Central Provident Fund (CPF), a social security fund that has also been used to facilitate the private ownership of dwellings. Moreover, close management of the labour market by the government through measures such as the Employment Act of 1968 and the establishment of the National Wages Council in 1972 has also helped to nurture a disciplined labour force and facilitate orderly settlement of wage disputes during this period of rapid growth and structural change.

Finally, prudent management of the exchange rate, coupled with a policy of importing whatever is needed for consumption and production from the cheapest foreign sources, has enabled the economy to enjoy a relatively low inflation rate, with the GDE deflator inreasing at an average of 3.9 percent annually during 1972-1989. It may be argued that the extreme degree of openness to trade in Singapore has made the economy susceptible to external shocks, but it is also true that the same openness has helped avoid price distortions and thereby has facilitated rapid and efficient adjustment to changes in the world economy that would inevitably affect a small economy like Singapore.

3 Model Specification

The model constructed for this exercise consists of 22 behavioural equations and 10 identities which, along with variable definitions, are presented in Table 1. Income and prices are basically demand determined and the model is very Keynesian in nature. The model can be partitioned into four major blocks, domestic final demand, the labour market, money and prices, and international trade.

In the domestic final demand block, behavioural equations are estimated for private consumption expenditure (equation 1), private investment in machinery and equipment (equation 2), private investment in transport equipment (equation 3), and taxes on income (equation 4). The private consumption equation is specified in the standard form with disposable income and lagged consumption as explanatory variables. A dummy variable for the years 1985 and 1986 is included to capture the effects of a recession in these years. As is often the case, private investment behaviour proved to be one of the most difficult aspects of the economy to model and in the end, private investment in construction and works had to be taken as exogenous.[6] Private investment in machinery and equipment is a function of real GDE, the real interest rate, lagged investment, and a dummy for 1985. The dummies reflect the unusual slowdown of machinery investment before and during the 1985-1986 recession. Private investment in transport equipment is also related to real GDE and lagged investment but was unresponsive to interest rate changes. Due to the lumpiness of this investment, much of it undertaken by the national airline, several dummies had to be used to track the dependent variable in year when investment was unusually low (1975, 1981,and 1983-1988). Taxes on income are then estimated as a logarithmic function of the lagged profit to GDE ratio (in nominal terms), lagged nominal GDE, and a lagged dependent variable. Dummy variables to account for the unpredicted growth in taxes in 1980-1984 and 1986 are also included. It should also be noted that taxes on income play an important role in the determination of disposable income and, thus, consumption.

The labour market consists of three behaviourial equations. The nominal weekly wage level (equation 5) is basically an increasing function of nominal labour productivity and the consumer price index, the former reflecting demand-pull forces and the latter representing the cost-push forces in wage inflation. The lag structure in this equation is somewhat complex with both contemporaneous and lagged productivity as well as a lagged dependent variable affecting wages. Aggregate employment is postulated to be equal to labour demand with real GDE, the real wage, and a lagged dependent variable as the explanatory variables (equation 6); there is also a dummy to account for an exceptional slowdown in 1974-1975. The other equation in the labour block describes the gross contribution to the CPF (in nominal terms) made by both employees and the employers as a logarithmic function of the employment level, the nominal wage level, the average rate of contribution, and a lagged dependent variable (equation 7). As is the case with taxes on income, the contribution to the CPF is deducted from GDE to derive disposable income and, thus, affects private consumption.

In the money and price block, there are also three behavioural equations. For the money market, it is also assumed that equilibrium values equal demand and the demand for money (M1; equation 8) is estimated as a function of real GDE, the nominal interest rate, and a dummy variable for 1984-1985 reflecting an unusual decrease before and during the 1985-1986 recession. Note that the openness of asset markets in Singapore provides a rationale for taking both the money supply and the real interest rate as exogenous. The consumer price index (CPI, equation 9) and the GDE deflator (equation 10) are both functions of the import price of oil, the import price of manufactures, the nominal wage rate, and the nominal velocity of money. These equations thus account for imported cost-push inflation, domestic cost-push inflation, and domestic demand-pull inflation, and provide two

[6] Investment in construction and works accounted for 39 percent of total private investment in 1972 and 26 percent in both 1980 and 1989.

important measures of inflation in the economy.

The final 12 behavioural equations relate to the trade sector. There are four different categories of traded goods, food and beverages (SITC sections 0 and 1), non-fuel raw materials (SITC sections 2 and 4), mineral fuels (SITC section 3), and manufactures (SITC sections 5 through 9). In view of the importance of entrepot trade in Singapore, a distinction is also made between domestic trade and entrepot trade. Due to the lack of data on entrepot imports, we are forced to assume that entrepot exports and entrepot imports are equal in this study. Note that this assumption would be valid if both imports and exports were valued on the same basis and entrepot trade took place instantaneously (that is no inventories were accumulated or depleted during a year).

In reality, of course, there are differences in valuation and changes in inventories that make this assumption invalid in the strict sense but it is likely that the assumption is a close approximation of reality.[7]

The demand for domestic imports of food and beverages (equation 11) is a simple function of disposable income in quadratic form and import prices; a quadratic functional form is chosen to reflect the decreasing income elasticity of demand for foods as income rises. For other categories of domestic imports, export prices are added to import prices and an income variable (either disposable income or real GDE) to reflect the positive impact of higher export prices on the demand for imports of intermediate goods in these categories.[8]In the case of domestic imports of non-fuel raw materials(equation 12), real GDE and the two price variables are the only explanatory variables. The mineral fuel function (equation 13) also uses the same arguments and, in addition, a dummy variable for 1973. Domestic imports of manufactures are somewhat different in that imports of capital goods, particularly machinery, are also an important component, in addition to intermediate goods and final consumption goods. This is reflected by the fact that the domestic imports of manufactures (equation 14) increase much more rapidly in response to the increase in private investment in machinery and equipment and in transport equipment (a proxy for capital goods demand) than in response to the increase in other disposable income (a proxy for final goods demand). Note, however, that both of these elements are highly significant determinants of these imports. The export and import price variables also have the anticipated effects and a dummy variable for the unusual increase in 1988 is also included as an independent variable. Total real imports of services are then a more standard function of real GDE, the price of total imports, and a dummy for 1984-1985 (equation 15).

Domestic exports are basically determined by external demand factors, real gross national product (GNP) in the OECD countries, real gross domestic prod-

[7]Note also that the trade data used here differ from published data (e.g., DOS various years). Assuming that entrepot exports and entrepot imports are equal, published figures yield negative domestic imports for SITC section 2 for many years (in either nominal or real terms); hence the data had to be adjusted for use in this model.

[8]In 1989, for example, the ratio of domestic exports to domestic imports was 1.2 for non-fuel raw materials, 1.1 for manufactures,0.8 for mineral fuels, and 0.5 for food and beverages, indicating that the share of intermediate goods in domestic imports of the first three categories of goods were higher than the corresponding share for food and beverages.

uct (GDP) in the ASEAN-4 countries (Indonesia, Malaysia, the Philippines, and Thailand), and the trade-weighted real price of exports in foreign currency. For food and beverages, a dummy for the primary product boom in 1975 is added to these arguments (equation 16) and for non-fuel raw materials, only the basic income and price variables are used (equation 17); one also notes that the effects of prices are not instantaneous but lagged one year. For mineral fuels, GNP in the OECD was the only significant argument, though the significant dummies for 1973 and 1986 are clearly related to the large discrete changes in oil prices in those years (equation 18). Interestingly, the rise in 1973 discouraged exports and the fall in 1986 stimulated them, presumably by affecting profit margins in petroleum refining. For domestic exports of manufactures, the ratio of cumulative direct foreign investment to cumulative private investment since 1972 is added as an explanatory variable to the two foreign income arguments, a lagged price variable, and a dummy variable for 1975-1977 (equation 19). As explained earlier, the expansion of foreign firms has greatly contributed to increased export capacity in manufacturing and services. The direct foreign investment variable is thus a proxy for the positive impact such investment has had on the supply of manufactured exports.

In contrast to domestic exports, entrepot exports were not found to be responsive to prices. Entrepot exports of food and beverages are a function of GNP in the OECD and GDP of the ASEAN-4 (equation 20) while entrepot exports of manufactures are not responsive to ASEAN-4 GDP and are thus a function of GNP in the OECD, a lagged dependent variable, and a dummy for 1984-1986 (equation 21). Entrepot exports of non-fuel raw materials and of mineral fuels could not be modelled satisfactorily and are taken as exogenous here.[9] The total export of services is a function of GNP in the OECD, GNP in the ASEAN-4, the ratio of cumulative direct foreign investment to total private investment since 1972, and a lagged dependent variable (equation 22) in a function similar to that used for domestic exports of manufactures. To complete the model, there are 10 identities which calculate nominal GDE, real GDE, cumulative direct foreign investment, cumulative private investment, total real merchandise imports and exports, the nominal interest rate, the nominal rate of profit, the nominal velocity of money, the total real wage cost, and disposable income. The first two of these identities, nominal and real GDEs, serve to close the model.

[9] These two categories account for a relatively small portion of entrepot exports, their combined share of total real entrepot exports being 12-16 percent in 1972-1975 and 10 percent or less since 1976.

Table 1. The Model (OLS Estimation) and Variable Definitions

Equation 1: Private Consumption (CPR), 1973-1989

variable	coefficient	std. error	t-test	2-tail sig.
C	1803.6721	358.44143	5.0319857	0.0002
YDR	0.3164184	0.0381523	8.2935647	0.0000
CPR_{-1}	0.3828530	0.0895506	4.2752709	0.0009
D8586	-502.38077	161.46270	-3.1114354	0.0083

Adj. R^2 =0.998008; F=2673.647; DW=2.165205

Equation 2: Private Investment in Machinery & Equipment (IMERP), 1973-1989

variable	coefficient	std. error	t-test	2-tail sig.
C	-1141.5779	175.15492	-6.5175327	0.0000
GDER	0.0902710	0.0138464	6.5194497	0.0000
MLRR	-92.792649	17.599922	-5.2723331	0.0003
$IMERP_{-1}$	0.7712831	0.0991271	7.7807467	0.0000
D8284	-596.85023	151.08360	-3.9504634	0.0023
D85	-1436.7050	226.94217	-6.3307098	0.0001

Adj. R^2 =0.987280; F=249.3693; DW=1.982975

Equation 3: Private Investment in Transport Equipment (ITERP), 1973-1989

variable	coefficient	std. error	t-test	2-tail sig.
C	92.340689	89.360868	1.0333459	0.3236
GDER	0.0260025	0.0025770	10.090225	0.0000
$ITERP_{-1}$	0.7682427	0.0428171	17.942442	0.0000
D75	-599.63707	86.528069	-6.9299717	0.0000
D81	-512.32620	95.145457	-5.3846628	0.0002
D8388	-860.03118	55.007748	-15.634728	0.0000

Adj. R^2=0.979252; F=152.0281; DW=2.533589

Equation 4: Taxes on Income ($\log TY$), 1973-1989

variable	coefficient	std. error	t-test	2-tail sig.
C	-0.5488012	0.2735768	-2.0060228	0.0701
$\log RATP_{-1}$	3.2432953	0.6166879	5.2592171	0.0003
$\log GDEN_{-1}$	0.6766434	0.0699486	9.6734315	0.0000
D8084	0.2239788	0.0276176	8.1100145	0.0000
D86	-0.1888143	0.0489430	-3.8578381	0.0027
$\log TY_{-1}$	0.3593982	0.0591190	6.0792330	0.0001

Adj. R^2=0.994457; F=575.1141; DW=1.872817

Equation 5: Nominal Weekly Wage (W), 1973-1989

variable	coefficient	std. error	t-test	2-tail sig.
C	-32.780401	7.6276827	-4.2975570	0.0010
$\frac{GDEN}{LE}$	0.0024783	0.0005822	4.2565912	0.0011
$(\frac{GDEN}{LE})_{-1}$	0.0026765	0.0011286	2.3713998	0.0353
CPI	51.247173	15.256316	3.3590792	0.0057
W_{-1}	0.2735885	0.1015609	2.6938366	0.0195

Adj. R^2=0.998718; F=3117.335; DW=1.908016

Equation 6: Employment ($\log LE$), 1973-1989

variable	coefficient	std. error	t-test	2-tail sig.
C	-2.0332268	0.4437693	-4.5817198	0.0006
log GDER	0.3705134	0.0650165	5.6987634	0.0001
$\log \frac{W}{P}$	-0.3279612	0.0679151	-4.8289884	0.0004
D7475	-0.0362542	0.0102186	-3.5478634	0.0040
$\log LE_{-1}$	0.5784396	0.0827402	6.9910327	0.0000

Adj. R^2=0.994371; F=707.5719; DW=2.152210

Equation 7: Nominal Total Contribution to the CPF ($\log GCPF$), 1973-1989

variable	coefficient	std. error	t-test	2-tail sig.
C	3.3043754	0.5404942	6.1136185	0.0001
log LE	1.0333350	0.2736022	3.7767781	0.0026
log W	0.6109196	0.2030200	3.0091592	0.0109
log AROC	0.9050003	0.1003847	9.0153217	0.0000
$\log GCPF_{-1}$	0.2861351	0.0824639	3.4698230	0.0046

Adj. R^2=0.998152; F=2160.990; DW=2.278853

Equation 8: Money Demand M1 (MS1R), 1973-1989

variable	coefficient	std. error	t-test	2-tail sig.
C	1243.0252	507.55721	2.4490347	0.0293
GDER	0.2345065	0.0085801	27.331327	0.0000
MLR_{-1}	-79.862018	43.461631	-1.8375292	0.0891
D8485	-939.98097	278.55570	-3.3744811	0.0050

Adj. R^2=0.981266; F=280.3534;DW=1.733173

Equation 9: Consumer Price Index ($\log CPI$), 1973-1989

variable	coefficient	std. error	t-test	2-tail sig.
C	-1.7980566	0.1118861	-16.070421	0.0000
log PM3	0.0462783	0.0132597	3.4901448	0.0045
log PM59	0.2922468	0.0569720	5.1296536	0.0002
log W	0.2648462	0.0223972	11.824962	0.0000
log VELN	0.2182020	0.0679162	3.2128118	0.0075

Adj. R^2=0.992935; F=563.1431; DW=1.942961

Equation 10: Gross Domestic Expenditure Deflator ($\log P$), 1973-1989

variable	coefficient	std. error	t-test	2-tail sig.
C	-1.9696057	0.0877529	-22.444910	0.0000
log PM3	0.0654225	0.0103997	6.2908300	0.0000
log PM59	0.1579388	0.0446835	3.5346128	0.0041
log W	0.3043130	0.0175663	17.323721	0.0000
log VELN	0.2013503	0.0532670	3.7800165	0.0026

Adj. R^2=0.995637; F=913.8391; DW=1.803807

Equation 11: Domestic Retained Imports of Foods & Beverages (MR01R), 1973-1989

variable	coefficient	std. error	t-test	2-tail sig.
C	1133.2023	307.70452	3.6827612	0.0028
YDR	0.1144342	0.0389828	2.9355036	0.0116
YDR^2	-9.562E-07	5.997E-07	-1.5943219	0.1349
PM01	-1650.0159	490.74000	-3.3623016	0.0051

Adj. R^2=0.904363; F=51.43329; DW=2.300005

Equation 12: Domestic Retained Imports of Non-fuel Raw Materials (MR24R), 1973-1989

variable	coefficient	std. error	t-test	2-tail sig.
C	528.50831	436.17617	1.2116854	0.2472
GDER	0.0438264	0.0054119	8.0981492	0.0000
PM24	-2709.9839	1601.0982	-1.6925782	0.1143
PX24	3198.2641	1694.4102	1.8875383	0.0816

Adj. R^2=0.806962; F=23.29503; DW=1.441864

Equation 13: Domestic Retained Imports of Mineral Fuels (MR3R), 1973-1989

variable	coefficient	std. error	t-test	2-tail sig.
C	5013.5759	1947.5963	2.5742378	0.0244
GDER	0.3431267	0.0466893	7.3491497	0.0000
PM3	-19184.288	9544.7077	-2.0099398	0.0675
PX3	17431.939	9085.8224	1.9185868	0.0791
D73	-6110.3958	1294.6042	-4.7198948	0.0005

Adj. R^2=0.925696; F=50.83318; DW=2.434650

Equation 14: Domestic Retained Imports of Manufactures (MR59R), 1973-1989

variable	coefficient	std. error	t-test	2-tail sig.
C	-4793.4520	1288.0078	-3.7216016	0.0034
YDR-IMERP-ITERP	0.6225796	0.0357524	17.413640	0.0000
IMERP+ITERP	2.3927554	0.0997667	23.983499	0.0000
PM59	-10610.949	1959.2728	-5.4157590	0.0002
PX59	9181.2286	2291.7388	4.0062282	0.0021
D88	2247.3277	465.25352	4.8303293	0.0005

Adj. R^2=0.997703; F=1390.756; DW=6.777300

Equation 15: Total Imports of Services (MSVR), 1973-1989

variable	coefficient	std. error	t-test	2-tail sig.
C	-3937.1328	656.74718	-5.9948987	0.0000
GDER	0.6156324	0.0125175	49.181869	0.0000
PM_{-1}	-5766.9829	841.60381	-6.8523727	0.0000
D8385	-2611.5311	313.51258	-8.3299084	0.0000

Adj. R^2=0.994477; F=961.3229; DW=2.482553

Equation 16: Domestic Exports of Food & Beverages (X01DR), 1973-1989

variable	coefficient	std. error	t-test	2-tail sig.
C	-2881.8060	269.30772	-10.700793	0.0000
OECD85	0.0004254	2.614E-05	16.277394	0.0000
ASEAN4	0.0040105	0.0006265	6.4011998	0.0000
$(\frac{PX01}{REEXCH})_{-1}$	-973.70580	145.73667	-6.6812682	0.0000
D75	410.25238	75.466674	5.4362059	0.0002

Adj. R^2=0.963130; F=105.4900; DW=2.109112

Equation 17: Domestic Exports of Non-fuel Raw Materials (X24DR), 1973-1989

variable	coefficient	std. error	t-test	2-tail sig.
C	-3434.0351	843.22125	-4.0725197	0.0013
OECD85	0.0006691	7.021E-05	9.5306370	0.0000
ASEAN4	0.0086415	0.0022659	3.8136588	0.0022
$(\frac{PX24}{REEXCH})_{-1}$	-633.72418	363.17667	-1.7449474	0.1046

Adj. R^2=0.874382; F=38.12352; DW=1.500822

Equation 18: Domestic Exports of Mineral Fuels (X3DR), 1973-1989

variable	coefficient	std. error	t-test	2-tail sig.
C	-14136.286	929.37551	-15.210522	0.0000
OECD85	0.0031082	0.0001144	27.180544	0.0000
D73	-3078.3026	502.23675	-6.1291863	0.0000
D86	2443.2326	491.94914	4.9664334	0.0003

Adj. R^2=0.985985; F=376.1984; DW=2.259324

Equation 19: Domestic Exports of Manufactures (X59DR), 1973-1989

variable	coefficient	std. error	t-test	2-tail sig.
C	-91086.645	9162.7539	-9.9409682	0.0000
OECD85	0.0107633	0.0006720	16.015702	0.0000
ASEAN4	0.0391330	0.0165617	2.3628536	0.0376
$(\frac{PX59}{REEXCH})_{-1}$	-16450.596	3937.7662	-4.1776466	0.0015
$KRFKRP_{-1}$	101112.21	21866.417	4.6240868	0.0007
D7577	4827.5836	1528.2006	3.1589986	0.0091

Adj. R^2=0.975957; F=130.8972; DW=2.212269

Equation 20: Entrepot Exports of Food & Beverages (X01RR), 1973-1989

variable	coefficient	std. error	t-test	2-tail sig.
C	-4262.7005	653.46879	-6.5231891	0.0000
OECD85	0.0006365	4.944E-05	12.874532	0.0000
ASEAN4	0.0032921	0.0014210	2.3166970	0.0375
D84	757.37376	174.75114	4.3340134	0.0008

Adj. R^2=0.940439; F=85.21133; DW=1.618360

Equation 21: Entrepot Exports of Manufactures (X59RR), 1973-1989

variable	coefficient	std. error	t-test	2-tail sig.
C	-19343.605	4603.3770	-4.2020468	0.0010
OECD85	0.0029997	0.0007133	4.2052652	0.0010
$X59RR_{-1}$	0.6441347	0.1395787	4.6148504	0.0005
D8486	-2688.5142	559.48546	-4.8053334	0.0003

Adj. R^2=0.984884; F=348.4837; DW=2.063899

Equation 22: Total Exports of Services (XSVR), 1973-1989

variable	coefficient	std. error	t-test	2-tail sig.
C	-43572.898	7294.8980	-5.9730647	0.0001
OECD85	0.0029796	0.0007242	4.1144491	0.0014
ASEAN4	0.0430096	0.0101294	4.2460047	0.0011
KRFKRP	68015.106	13885.734	4.8982004	0.0004
$XSVR_{-1}$	0.5972034	0.1168044	5.1128488	0.0003

Adj. R^2=0.982528; F=225.9395; DW=2.059408

Equation 23: Nominal Gross Domestic Expenditure (=Gross Domestic Product)
$GDEN = GDER * P$

Equation 24: Real Gross Domestic Expenditure (=Gross Domestic Product)
$$GDER = CPR + CGR + ICWRP + IERP + SDRIP + IRG + SDRI + JR \\ +XFOBR + XSVR - MFOBR - MSVR + SDRT + SDR$$

Equation 25: Cumulative Real Direct Foreign Investment Since 1972
$KRF = KRFKRP * KRP$

Equation 26: Cumulative Real Private Investment Since 1972
$KRP = KRP_{-1} + IMERP + ITERP + ICWRP + SDRIP$

Equation 27: Real Merchandise Import
$$MFOBR = MR01R + MR24R + MR3R + MR59R + X01RR + X24RR + X3RR \\ +X59RR + ERRMR$$

Equation 28: Nominal Interest Rate
$MLR = MLRR + 100\frac{P-P_{-1}}{P_{-1}}$

Equation 29: Rate of Profit
$RATP = \frac{GDEN - W*LE*50}{GDEN}$

Equation 30: Nominal Velocity
$VELN = \frac{GDEN}{MS1R*P}$

Equation 31: Real Merchandise Exports

$$XFOBR = X01DR + X24DR + X3DR + X59DR + X01RR + X24RR + X3RR + X59RR + ERRXR$$

Equation 32: Real Disposable Income

$$YDR = \frac{GDEN - TY - GCPF}{P}$$

Variable Definitions

AROC	Actual rate of contribution to CPF for employers & employees, ratio
ASEAN4	Combined GDP of ASEAN-4 countries: Malaysia, Indonesia, Philippines and Thailand, real, US$ millions
C	A constant term
CGR	Government consumption expenditure, real
CPI	Consumer price index
CPR	Private consumption expenditure, real
D73	Dummy variable, 1973=1
D7475	Dummy variable, 1974=1, 1975=1
D75	Dummy variable, 1975=1
D7577	Dummy variable, 1975=1, 1976=1, 1977=1
D8084	Dummy variable, 1980=1, 1981=1, 1982=1, 1983=1, 1984=1
D81	Dummy variable, 1981=1
D8284	Dummy variable, 1982=1, 1983=1, 1984=1
D8385	Dummy variable, 1983=1, 1984=1, 1985=1
D8388	Dummy variable, 1983=1, 1984=1, 1985=1, 1986=1, 1987=1, 1988=1
D84	Dummy variable, 1984=1
D8485	Dummy variable, 1984=1, 1985=1
D8486	Dummy variable, 1984=1, 1985=1, 1986=1
D85	Dummy variable, 1985=1
D8586	Dummy variable, 1985=1, 1986=1
D86	Dummy variable, 1986=1
D88	Dummy variable, 1988=1
ERRMR	Merchandise import statistical discrepancy, real
ERRXR	Merchandise export statistical discrepancy, real
GCPF	Total amount contributed to CPF, nominal
GDEN	Gross domestic expenditure, nominal
GDER	Gross domestic expenditure, real
ICWRP	Private investment in construction and works, real
IMERP	Private investment in machinery and equipment, real
IRG	Total public investment (construction & works, machinery, and transport equipment), real
ITERP	Private investment in transport equipment, real
JR	Inventory investment, real
KRF	Cumulative direct foreign investment since 1972, real
KRFKRP	Ratio of KRF to KRP
KRP	Cumulative total private investment since 1972, real

LE	Employment, millions
MFOBR	Total merchandise imports, real
MLR	Minimum lending rate, nominal
MLRR	Minimum lending rate, real
MR01R	Domestic imports, food and beverages, real
MR24R	Domestic imports, non-fuel raw materials, real
MR3R	Domestic imports, mineral fuels, real
MR59R	Domestic imports, manufactures, real
MS1R	Money Supply M1, real
MSVR	Total import of services, real
OECD85	Real OECD GNP in 1985 prices (billion US$)
P	Gross domestic expenditure deflator
PM	Import price deflator, goods and services
PM01	Import price deflator, foods & beverages
PM24	Import price deflator, non-oil raw materials
PM3	Import price deflator, mineral fuels
PM59	Import price deflator, manufactures
PX	Export price deflator, goods and services
PX01	Export price deflator, foods & beverages
PX24	Export price deflator, non-oil raw materials
PX3	Export price deflator, mineral fuels
PX59	Export price deflator, manufactures
RATP	Rate of profit, nominal ratio
REEXCH	Real effective exchange rate index, S$ per foreign currency
SDR	Gross domestic expenditure statistical discrepancy, real
SDRI	Total investment statistical discrepancy, real
SDRIP	Private investment statistical discrepancy, real
SDRT	Trade statistical discrepancy, real
TY	Taxes on income, nominal
VELN	Velocity, nominal
W	Average national weekly wage rate, nominal
X01DR	Domestic exports, food & beverages, real
X01RR	Entrepot exports, food & beverages, real
X24DR	Domestic exports, non-oil raw materials, real
X24RR	Entrepot exports, non-oil raw materials, real
X3DR	Domestic exports, mineral fuels, real
X3RR	Entrepot exports, mineral fuels, real
X59DR	Domestic exports, manufactures, real
X59RR	Entrepot exports, manufactures, real
XFOBR	Total merchandise exports, real
XSVR	Total service exports, real
YDR	Disposable income, real

All nominal and real values in million Singapore dollars except as noted; all real values take 1985 as the base year; all deflators and indices equal to 1 in 1985.

4 Simulation Experiments

The simulation experiments cover the period 1980-1989 and the base case simulation is shown in Table 2. As can be seen from the table, for 1980-1989 the model tracks most of the variables rather well with average percentage root mean square errors of 12.6 percent or less for all dependent variables in the model. Moreover, errors for 24 of the 32 endogenous variables average 5 percent or less for the 10 year period. In individual years there are somewhat larger errors for some variables but, in general, the model predicts past performance rather well. Moreover, the model tracks recent performance relatively well, indicating that it is suitable for analysis of policy issues affecting Singapore in the next few years.

Table 2. Base Case Solution (percentage root mean square errors)

Equation/ Variable	1980	1981	1982	1983	1984	1985	1986	1987	1988	1989	1990
1. CPR	1.1	1.8	1.9	2.1	0.9	2.8	2.2	2.7	1.9	2.4	2.1
2. IMERP	6.5	3.8	1.4	3.0	2.3	1.4	10.4	8.3	0.9	0.2	5.0
3. ITERP	1.6	0.5	2.8	5.0	2.6	1.2	5.2	0.4	4.2	0.1	3.0
4. TY	2.5	2.0	1.1	1.8	2.8	5.6	12.2	4.8	2.9	7.1	5.3
5. W	0.6	2.7	0.1	1.4	2.8	0.2	0.0	0.6	1.6	1.6	1.5
6. LE	0.9	0.6	0.0	0.4	0.7	3.5	2.6	0.8	0.3	0.3	1.5
7. GCPF	0.8	0.9	0.9	1.8	0.4	1.9	4.8	0.5	6.4	4.3	3.0
8. MS1R	1.8	2.3	0.1	8.3	2.2	1.5	2.3	2.3	0.8	1.7	3.1
9. CPI	2.0	0.9	1.0	2.1	0.1	0.5	2.0	0.6	1.1	0.6	1.3
10.P	0.2	1.1	0.8	3.9	0.1	2.8	0.3	2.0	0.9	1.0	1.8
11.MR01R	3.1	2.8	7.5	7.8	3.5	2.6	1.8	2.8	2.7	0.7	4.2
12.MR24R	5.9	7.3	6.2	1.4	6.6	13.0	1.8	2.0	0.7	4.8	6.1
13.MR3R	10.1	4.1	3.0	0.7	2.7	4.1	4.1	2.0	6.0	4.9	4.8
14.MR59R	4.6	0.6	0.8	1.1	2.4	7.2	3.7	2.6	0.5	1.5	3.2
15.MSVR	5.5	5.9	5.7	4.1	1.4	9.6	4.5	4.1	4.8	4.4	5.4
16.X01DR	5.1	4.6	6.8	10.2	6.1	15.0	0.0	0.2	0.3	5.4	7.0
17.X24DR	8.3	3.4	6.6	2.3	5.0	0.4	2.1	6.1	3.5	4.3	4.8
18.X3DR	3.2	2.1	5.7	0.6	0.7	2.6	0.0	4.5	3.6	0.3	3.0
19.X59DR	5.0	4.7	5.8	0.2	5.1	12.2	6.4	2.1	4.3	2.0	5.7
20.X01RR	9.8	0.6	21.4	5.6	0.0	6.7	5.2	3.8	3.5	3.0	8.3
21.X59RR	3.4	13.2	15.3	9.9	0.1	0.4	5.7	7.4	4.8	2.3	7.9
22.XSVR	5.2	0.9	0.1	1.7	4.1	9.7	1.6	0.8	3.3	1.2	4.0
23.GDEN	0.9	3.6	1.3	2.2	1.8	6.5	2.7	2.7	2.6	3.6	3.2
24.GDER	1.1	2.5	2.1	1.7	1.8	3.6	3.0	0.7	1.7	2.6	2.2
25.KRF	0.5	0.7	0.4	0.1	0.2	0.1	0.3	0.6	0.7	0.6	0.5
26.KRP	0.5	0.7	0.4	0.1	0.2	0.1	0.3	0.6	0.7	0.6	0.5
27.MFOBR	0.4	1.0	1.2	1.7	0.2	5.0	1.2	3.7	3.1	0.3	2.3
28.MLR	12.2	4.9	7.9	18.2	12.3	11.0	6.1	19.2	17.3	7.3	12.6
29.RATP	0.3	0.2	0.8	0.2	0.2	1.7	0.1	0.8	2.2	1.0	1.0
30.VELN	2.8	4.9	2.1	6.1	0.4	2.1	0.7	3.1	2.5	0.9	3.1
31.XFOBR	2.4	4.1	3.8	2.2	2.6	6.0	3.7	4.4	4.0	1.8	3.7
32.YDR	1.4	3.4	2.4	1.0	2.6	4.6	2.0	0.8	1.6	3.2	2.6

In order to illustrate the characteristics of the Singaporean economy, seven historical simulation experiments have been conducted. In these experiments five external shocks and two internal shocks are examined. The first experiment investigates the effects of a simultaneous and continuous 50 percent increase in import and export prices of mineral fuels (Table 3). The effects of this shock are seen to be quite small, with real GDE being higher than the base case in some years and smaller in others. In only two years (1980 = -1.2; 1985 = 1.8) are the deviations from the base case more than 1 percent in absolute value; interestingly, the results indicate that higher oil prices would have lowered real GDE at the peak of the business cycle (1980) and increased it at the trough (1985). However, in general, the effects are relatively small and this is not surprising as Singapore is both heavily dependent on imported oil and a significant exporter of refined oil products. Since prices do not directly affect exports of mineral fuels in the model, the effects are concentrated on domestic imports of mineral fuels, which fluctuate somewhat but are generally lower than in the base case. Also, reflecting the relatively low elasticity of the general price level with respect to the import price of mineral fuels, both the CPI and the GDE deflator change very little from the base case (0.3 percent or less in absolute value).

Table 3. The Effects of a Continuous 50 Percent Increase in Import and Export Prices of Mineral Fuels (percentage change from base case)

Equation/ Variable	1980	1981	1982	1983	1984	1985	1986	1987	1988	1989
1. CPR	-0.7	0.3	-0.1	0.0	0.6	1.3	0.3	1.0	0.5	0.5
2. IMERP	-1.0	-0.1	-0.2	-0.1	0.7	2.4	1.6	1.9	1.4	1.2
3. ITERP	-0.3	-0.0	-0.1	-0.1	0.4	1.3	1.1	1.8	1.6	1.1
4. TY	0.0	-1.9	1.0	-0.2	0.2	1.5	3.1	-0.2	1.9	0.5
5. W	-0.4	-0.3	0.1	-0.0	0.3	0.8	0.8	0.6	0.7	0.5
6. LE	-0.4	0.1	-0.0	0.0	0.3	0.6	0.2	0.5	0.3	0.3
7. GCPF	-0.6	-0.2	-0.1	-0.0	0.4	1.3	1.1	1.2	1.1	0.9
8. MS1R	-1.1	0.9	-0.2	-0.0	1.0	1.9	-0.1	1.3	0.5	0.6
9. CPI	-0.1	-0.1	0.0	0.0	0.1	0.2	0.2	0.2	0.2	0.1
10.P	-0.1	-0.1	0.0	0.0	0.1	0.2	0.3	0.2	0.2	0.2
11.MR01R	-1.4	1.0	-0.4	0.1	0.9	1.6	-0.2	1.0	0.2	0.3
12.MR24R	-0.6	0.4	-0.1	0.0	0.6	1.2	0.0	0.9	0.3	0.4
13.MR3R	4.7	-3.6	1.2	-0.3	-4.2	-8.8	0.2	-7.0	-2.0	-3.0
14.MR59R	-1.5	0.8	-0.4	0.1	1.2	2.6	0.4	2.1	0.9	1.0
15.MSVR	-2.7	1.5	-0.4	0.2	1.9	3.6	0.0	2.1	0.7	0.9
16.X01DR	0.0	0.0	0.0	0.0	0.0	0.0	0.0	0.0	0.0	0.0
17.X24DR	0.0	0.0	0.0	0.0	0.0	0.0	0.0	0.0	0.0	0.0
18.X3DR	0.0	0.0	0.0	0.0	0.0	0.0	0.0	0.0	0.0	0.0
19.X59DR	0.0	0.0	0.0	0.0	0.0	0.0	0.0	0.0	0.0	0.0
20.X01RR	0.0	0.0	0.0	0.0	0.0	0.0	0.0	0.0	0.0	0.0
21.X59RR	0.0	0.0	0.0	0.0	0.0	0.0	0.0	0.0	0.0	0.0
22.XSVR	0.0	0.0	0.0	0.0	0.0	0.0	0.0	0.0	0.0	0.0
23.GDEN	-1.3	0.6	-0.2	0.1	1.0	2.1	0.3	1.6	0.7	0.8
24.GDER	-1.2	0.7	-0.2	0.1	0.9	1.8	0.0	1.4	0.5	0.6
25.KRF	-0.1	-0.1	-0.1	-0.1	-0.0	0.1	0.2	0.3	0.3	0.4
26.KRP	-0.1	-0.1	-0.1	-0.1	-0.0	0.1	0.2	0.3	0.3	0.4
27.MFOBR	0.9	-0.7	0.2	-0.1	-0.8	-1.5	0.2	-0.9	-0.1	-0.3
28.MLR	-1.0	0.3	1.5	-0.0	0.5	2.6	0.4	-0.7	-0.2	-1.0
29.RATP	-0.3	0.4	-0.1	0.1	0.2	0.4	-0.5	0.3	-0.2	-0.0
30.VELN	-0.1	-0.2	0.0	0.1	-0.1	-0.1	0.1	0.1	-0.0	0.0
31.XFOBR	0.0	0.0	0.0	0.0	0.0	0.0	0.0	0.0	0.0	0.0
32.YDR	-1.4	1.1	-0.4	0.1	1.1	2.0	-0.3	1.6	0.3	0.6

The second experiment involves a continuous 10 percent increase in the real exchange rate or a depreciation of the Singapore dollar (Table 4). In this model, the exchange rate directly affects only direct exports since entrepot and service exports are not responsive to prices and import prices are measured in Singapore dollars. Domestic exports of food and beverages increase the most in percentage terms but there is also a significant increase in manufactures through 1986. It is to be noted that non-fuel raw materials are not affected much and that the impact of the shock becomes relatively smaller over time, despite the fact it is continuous. However, despite the relatively large impact on total merchandise exports early in the experiment (3.8-4.2 percent increase in 1981-1983), the impact on real GDE is relatively small (1.8-2.0 percent increase in 1981-1983). The impacts on the CPI and the GDE deflator are also small (0.5 percent or less) but the increase of the nominal wage is somewhat larger and the employment increase is much smaller than the real GDE increase.

Table 4. The Effects of a Continuous 10 Percent Increase in the Real Effective Exchange Rate (percentage change from base case)

Equation/ Variable	1980	1981	1982	1983	1984	1985	1986	1987	1988	1989
1. CPR	0.0	1.2	1.5	1.5	1.5	1.4	1.4	1.2	1.1	1.0
2. IMERP	0.0	1.4	2.8	4.0	4.4	5.3	4.9	3.8	3.0	2.5
3. ITERP	0.0	0.6	1.0	1.7	2.4	3.0	3.5	3.6	3.5	2.2
4. TY	0.0	0.0	2.9	3.5	3.1	2.5	2.2	2.1	1.7	1.4
5. W	0.0	0.6	1.3	1.5	1.5	1.4	1.3	1.2	1.0	0.9
6. LE	0.0	0.6	0.8	0.8	0.8	0.8	0.8	0.7	0.6	0.5
7. GCPF	0.0	0.9	1.9	2.4	2.4	2.4	2.3	2.1	1.8	1.6
8. MS1R	0.0	1.8	1.8	1.6	1.9	1.9	1.6	1.2	1.1	1.1
9. CPI	0.0	0.1	0.4	0.5	0.4	0.3	0.4	0.3	0.3	0.2
10. P	0.0	0.2	0.4	0.5	0.5	0.4	0.4	0.4	0.3	0.3
11. MR01R	0.0	2.1	1.9	1.5	1.4	1.3	1.2	0.9	0.7	0.6
12. MR24R	0.0	1.0	1.2	1.1	1.2	1.1	1.0	0.8	0.7	0.7
13. MR3R	0.0	1.3	1.4	1.4	1.4	1.4	1.2	1.1	0.9	0.9
14. MR59R	0.0	2.3	2.7	2.9	3.1	3.3	3.3	2.7	2.2	2.0
15. MSVR	0.0	3.8	4.0	4.4	3.9	3.4	2.7	2.0	1.8	1.6
16. X01DR	0.0	11.5	12.8	15.1	13.1	13.0	12.3	8.9	6.7	5.5
17. X24DR	0.0	2.2	1.9	1.7	1.9	2.0	1.6	1.2	1.2	1.3
18. X3DR	0.0	0.0	0.0	0.0	0.0	0.0	0.0	0.0	0.0	0.0
19. X59DR	0.0	8.8	10.1	9.8	8.5	7.4	6.7	4.6	3.5	3.0
20. X01RR	0.0	0.0	0.0	0.0	0.0	0.0	0.0	0.0	0.0	0.0
21. X59RR	0.0	0.0	0.0	0.0	0.0	0.0	0.0	0.0	0.0	0.0
22. XSVR	0.0	0.0	0.0	0.0	0.0	0.0	0.0	0.0	0.0	0.0
23. GDEN	0.0	2.0	2.5	2.5	2.3	2.1	2.0	1.7	1.5	1.4
24. GDER	0.0	1.8	2.0	1.9	1.8	1.7	1.6	1.3	1.2	1.1
25. KRF	0.0	0.1	0.3	0.5	0.7	0.8	1.0	1.2	1.3	1.3
26. KRP	0.0	0.1	0.3	0.5	0.7	0.8	1.0	1.2	1.3	1.3
27. MFOBR	0.0	1.6	1.8	1.8	1.8	1.9	1.8	1.5	1.2	1.1
28. MLR	0.0	1.6	3.2	0.9	-0.9	-1.1	0.4	-0.4	-1.2	-0.8
29. RATP	0.0	0.5	0.2	0.0	0.0	-0.0	-0.0	-0.1	-0.1	-0.0
30. VELN	0.0	0.0	0.3	0.3	-0.0	-0.2	0.1	0.1	0.0	0.0
31. XFOBR	0.0	3.8	4.2	4.1	3.6	3.3	2.9	2.3	1.8	1.6
32. YDR	0.0	2.2	2.1	1.8	1.7	1.6	1.6	1.3	1.1	1.1

The third external shock involves a continuous 1 percent increase in the real GNP of the OECD countries (Table 5). All endogenous exports are positively affected by this shock with domestic exports of manufactures and food and beverages registering the largest increase. However, here again the shock's effects are largest in the early years of the experiment. For example, the increase in real merchandise exports declines from 4.1-4.5 percent in 1980-1985 to under 3 percent in 1988-1989; the increase in real GDE declines less and at a much slower rate, from 2.0 percent in 1980-1986 to 1.8 percent in 1988-1989. As in the previous experiment, wages rise significantly more than prices in response to increased aggregate demand and the resulting increase in the real wage keeps the rise in employment under 1 percent throughout the experiment. Finally, merchandise import growth is somewhat slower than merchandise export growth but service imports increase relatively more than service exports.

Table 5. The Effects of a Continuous 1 Percent Increase in Real GNP in the OECD Countriese (percentage change from base case)

Equation/ Variable	1980	1981	1982	1983	1984	1985	1986	1987	1988	1998
1.CPR	1.2	1.5	1.6	1.6	1.6	1.6	1.7	1.7	1.6	1.5
2.IMERP	1.6	2.5	3.7	4.8	5.1	6.2	5.8	4.7	4.0	3.5
3.ITERP	0.5	1.1	1.4	2.0	2.8	3.4	4.1	4.4	4.6	3.1
4.TY	0.0	3.2	3.4	3.2	2.8	2.6	2.6	2.7	2.6	2.4
5.W	0.6	1.4	1.6	1.7	1.6	1.5	1.5	1.5	1.4	1.4
6.LE	0.6	0.8	0.9	0.9	0.9	0.9	0.9	0.9	0.9	0.8
7.GCPF	1.0	2.0	2.5	2.6	2.6	2.6	2.6	2.6	2.5	2.4
8.MS1R	1.8	1.8	1.7	1.8	2.1	2.2	1.9	1.7	1.7	1.7
9.CPI	0.2	0.4	0.5	0.5	0.4	0.4	0.4	0.4	0.4	0.4
10.P	0.2	0.5	0.6	0.5	0.4	0.4	0.5	0.5	0.5	0.4
11.MR01R	2.3	1.9	1.8	1.6	1.6	1.5	1.5	1.3	1.1	0.9
12.MR24R	1.0	1.1	1.2	1.2	1.3	1.2	1.2	1.2	1.1	1.2
13.MR3R	1.2	1.5	1.4	1.4	1.5	1.6	1.5	1.6	1.4	1.4
14.MR59R	2.5	2.7	2.9	3.3	3.5	3.9	4.0	3.6	3.1	2.9
15.MSVR	4.4	4.2	4.0	4.6	4.2	3.9	3.2	2.9	2.7	2.5
16.X01DR	5.0	4.8	5.2	6.2	5.7	5.6	5.4	4.4	3.6	3.2
17.X24DR	1.6	1.5	1.5	1.6	1.7	1.8	1.7	1.7	1.6	1.6
18.X3DR	2.4	2.4	2.4	2.3	2.1	2.1	1.7	1.9	1.9	1.8
19.X59DR	6.5	5.7	5.8	5.6	5.1	4.7	4.4	3.5	2.9	2.6
20.X01RR	3.1	3.0	3.0	3.1	2.1	2.8	2.8	2.6	2.4	2.3
21.X59RR	2.7	3.9	4.5	4.6	5.4	5.6	5.5	4.3	3.6	3.3
22.XSVR	1.6	2.1	2.2	2.5	2.8	3.0	3.0	2.7	2.4	2.1
23.GDER	2.2	2.5	2.6	2.5	2.4	2.4	2.5	2.4	2.3	2.2
24.GDER	2.0	2.0	2.0	2.0	2.0	2.0	2.0	1.9	1.8	1.8
25.KRF	0.1	0.3	0.5	0.7	0.9	1.1	1.3	1.5	1.6	1.7
26.KRP	0.1	0.3	0.5	0.7	0.9	1.1	1.3	1.5	1.6	1.7
27.MFOBR	2.3	2.7	2.9	3.1	3.2	3.5	3.5	3.1	2.7	2.5
28.MLR	1.6	2.4	1.0	-0.2	-0.9	-0.5	0.9	0.1	-0.6	-0.5
29.RATP	0.5	0.2	0.1	-0.0	-0.0	0.0	0.0	0.0	-0.0	-0.0
30.VELN	0.1	0.3	0.3	0.2	-0.0	-0.2	0.1	0.2	0.1	0.1
31.XFOBR	4.2	4.2	4.5	4.5	4.2	4.1	3.8	3.4	2.9	2.7
32.YDR	2.3	2.1	2.0	1.9	1.9	1.9	2.0	1.9	1.8	1.7

The fourth external shock experiment assumes a 1 percent increase in real GDP in the ASEAN-4 (Table 6). This experiment has the same basic character as the previous one involving real GNP in the OECD but it is so small as to have little if any effect. This is despite the fact that, per US dollar, the effects of an increase in real GDP in the ASEAN-4 are several times larger than the effects of an increase in GNP in the OECD (c.f., Table 1, equations 16, 17, 19, 20, and 22). On the other hand, real GDP in the ASEAN-4 was only 2-4 percent of real GNP in the OECD, with the result that the effects of shocks of equal relative size are much larger for real GNP in the OECD.

Table 6. The Effects of a Continuous 1 percent Increase in Real GNP in the ASEAN-4 Countries (percentage change from base case)

Equation/ Variable	1980	1981	1982	1983	1984	1985	1986	1987	1988	1989
1.CPR	0.2	0.3	0.3	0.3	0.3	0.3	0.3	0.2	0.2	0.2
2.IMERP	0.3	0.5	0.8	1.0	1.0	1.1	1.0	0.8	0.6	0.5
3.ITERP	0.1	0.2	0.3	0.4	0.5	0.6	0.7	0.7	0.7	0.5
4.TY	0.0	0.6	0.7	0.7	0.5	0.4	0.4	0.4	0.3	0.3
5.W	0.1	0.3	0.3	0.4	0.3	0.3	0.2	0.2	0.2	0.2
6.LE	0.1	0.2	0.2	0.2	0.2	0.1	0.1	0.1	0.1	0.1
7.GCPF	0.2	0.4	0.5	0.6	0.5	0.5	0.4	0.4	0.4	0.3
8.MS1R	0.3	0.4	0.4	0.3	0.4	0.4	0.3	0.2	0.2	0.2
9.CPI	0.0	0.1	0.1	0.1	0.1	0.1	0.1	0.1	0.1	0.0
10.P	0.0	0.1	0.1	0.1	0.1	0.1	0.1	0.1	0.1	0.1
11.MR01R	0.4	0.4	0.4	0.3	0.3	0.2	0.2	0.2	0.2	0.1
12.MR24R	0.2	0.2	0.3	0.2	0.2	0.2	0.2	0.2	0.2	0.2
13.MR3R	0.2	0.3	0.3	0.3	0.3	0.3	0.2	0.2	0.2	0.2
14.MR59R	0.5	0.6	0.6	0.7	0.7	0.6	0.7	0.5	0.5	0.4
15.MSVR	0.8	0.9	0.9	0.9	0.8	0.6	0.5	0.4	0.4	0.3
16.X01DR	1.6	1.6	1.7	1.6	1.3	1.1	1.0	0.8	0.6	0.6
17.X24DR	0.7	0.7	0.7	0.6	0.5	0.5	0.4	0.4	0.4	0.4
18.X3DR	0.0	0.0	0.0	0.0	0.0	0.0	0.0	0.0	0.0	0.0
19.X59DR	0.8	0.7	0.7	0.6	0.4	0.4	0.3	0.2	0.2	0.2
20.X01RR	0.6	0.5	0.5	0.5	0.3	0.3	0.3	0.2	0.2	0.2
21.X59RR	0.0	0.0	0.0	0.0	0.0	0.0	0.0	0.0	0.0	0.0
22.XSVR	0.8	1.0	1.1	1.1	1.1	1.1	1.0	0.8	0.7	0.6
23.GDER	0.4	0.5	0.6	0.5	0.4	0.4	0.4	0.3	0.3	0.3
24.GDER	0.4	0.4	0.5	0.4	0.4	0.3	0.3	0.3	0.2	0.2
25.KRF	0.0	0.1	0.1	0.2	0.2	0.2	0.3	0.3	0.3	0.3
26.KRP	0.0	0.1	0.1	0.2	0.2	0.2	0.3	0.3	0.3	0.3
27.MFOBR	0.3	0.4	0.4	0.4	0.4	0.4	0.4	0.3	0.3	0.2
28.MLR	0.3	0.5	0.3	-0.0	-0.3	-0.3	0.1	-0.1	-0.2	-0.1
29.RATP	0.1	0.0	0.0	-0.0	-0.0	-0.0	-0.0	-0.0	-0.0	-0.0
30.VELN	0.0	0.0	0.1	0.0	-0.0	-0.0	0.0	0.0	0.0	0.0
31.XFOBR	0.4	0.4	0.4	0.3	0.2	0.2	0.2	0.1	0.1	0.1
32.YDR	0.4	0.5	0.4	0.3	0.3	0.3	0.3	0.2	0.2	0.2

The final external shock involves a continuous 1 percentage point increase in the ratio of cumulative direct foreign investment to cumulative private investment (Table 7; if the actual ratio was 0.20, for example, the shock involves increasing the ratio to 0.21).

Table 7. The Effects of a Continuous 1 percentage Point Increase in the Ratio of Cumulative Direct Foreign Investment to Cumulative Private Investment (percentage change from the base case)

Equation/ Variable	1980	1981	1982	1983	1984	1985	1986	1987	1988	1989
1.CPR	0.6	0.8	2.2	2.2	2.2	2.3	2.3	2.2	2.0	1.9
2.IMERP	0.8	2.5	4.4	6.2	6.7	8.2	7.7	6.2	5.2	4.4
3.ITERP	0.3	1.1	1.6	2.6	3.7	4.6	5.4	5.9	6.0	3.9
4.TY	0.0	1.6	4.4	4.9	4.4	3.9	3.5	3.9	3.3	2.9
5.W	0.3	1.2	2.0	2.3	2.2	2.1	2.1	2.0	1.9	1.7
6.LE	0.3	0.9	1.2	1.2	1.2	1.2	1.2	1.2	1.1	1.0
7.GCPF	0.5	1.8	3.0	3.5	3.7	3.6	3.6	3.5	3.3	3.1
8.MS1R	0.9	2.6	2.5	2.4	2.9	3.0	2.5	2.3	2.2	2.0
9.CPI	0.1	0.3	0.6	0.7	0.6	0.5	0.6	0.6	0.5	0.5
10.P	0.1	0.4	0.7	0.8	0.7	0.6	0.6	0.6	0.6	0.5
11.MR01R	1.1	2.8	2.7	2.3	2.2	2.0	1.9	1.6	1.3	1.1
12.MR24R	0.5	1.5	1.7	1.7	1.8	1.7	1.6	1.5	1.4	1.4
13.MR3R	0.6	1.9	2.0	2.0	2.1	2.2	1.9	2.0	1.8	1.7
14.MR59R	1.2	3.4	3.9	4.5	4.8	5.2	5.3	4.8	4.0	3.6
15.MSVR	2.2	5.6	5.8	6.6	5.9	5.4	4.3	3.7	3.4	3.0
16.X01DR	0.0	0.0	0.0	0.0	0.0	0.0	0.0	0.0	0.0	0.0
17.X24DR	0.0	0.0	0.0	0.0	0.0	0.0	0.0	0.0	0.0	0.0
18.X3DR	0.0	0.0	0.0	0.0	0.0	0.0	0.0	0.0	0.0	0.0
19.X59DR	0.0	6.8	6.9	6.5	5.6	5.0	4.5	3.5	2.8	2.4
20.X01RR	0.0	0.0	0.0	0.0	0.0	0.0	0.0	0.0	0.0	0.0
21.X59RR	0.0	0.0	0.0	0.0	0.0	0.0	0.0	0.0	0.0	0.0
22.XSVR	4.7	5.9	6.4	7.2	7.8	8.1	7.8	6.9	5.9	5.0
23.GDER	1.1	3.1	3.6	3.6	3.5	3.3	3.3	3.1	2.9	2.7
24.GDER	1.0	2.7	2.9	2.8	2.8	2.7	2.7	2.5	2.3	2.1
25.KRF	4.2	4.1	4.3	4.7	5.1	5.4	5.5	5.3	5.4	5.3
26.KRP	0.1	0.3	1.5	1.8	1.1	1.3	1.6	1.9	2.0	2.2
27.MFOBR	0.8	2.3	2.6	2.7	2.8	3.0	3.0	2.6	2.2	2.0
28.MLR	0.8	2.7	3.5	0.9	-1.1	-1.2	0.9	-0.1	-1.1	-1.0
29.RATP	0.3	0.5	0.2	0.1	-0.0	-0.0	0.0	-0.0	-0.1	-0.0
30.VELN	0.1	0.1	0.4	0.4	-0.1	-0.3	0.1	0.2	0.1	0.1
31.XFOBR	0.0	2.6	2.6	2.5	2.2	2.0	1.8	1.6	1.3	1.2
32.YDR	1.1	3.0	2.9	2.7	2.6	2.6	2.6	2.4	2.2	2.1

It should be stressed here that it is the ratio which is the exogenous variable (direct foreign investment is assumed to increase or decrease with total private investment). The shock is thus equivalent to a 4.1-5.5 percent increase in cumulative direct foreign investment. This shock works through domestic exports of manufactures and service exports to producing a 6.9 percent increase in domestic exports of manufactures by 1982 and as much as a 8.1 percent increase in service exports in 1985; the effects dissipate somewhat after these years. Here again real wage and employment increases are 1.2 percent or less. In contrast, the increase in real GDE reaches 2.9 percent in 1982 and stays at 2.7-2.8 percent for 1983-1986. It should be reiterated that this shock simply illustrates the effects of increasing direct foreign investment when such investment is assumed to (1) increase or decrease with total private investment and (2)stimulate aggregate demand by increasing export capacity. Thus, this is a far from rigorous treatment of the effects imparted by direct foreign investment and the results of this simulation should therefore be treated with caution.[9]

The first of the domestic shocks explored here, a continuous 10 percent increase in government consumption, illustrates the importance of fiscal policy in an open economy like Singapore (Table 8). As expected, the impact on real GDE is positive but the effect is very small, with the increase in real GDE never exceeding 0.6 percent. The effect on prices is also minimal (0.1 percent at most) but as with other demand shocks, the effect on wages is relatively large and increasing (0.4 percent in 1982-1989). Here again the increase in the real wage keeps the increase in employment far below that of GDE.

Table 8. The Effects of a Continuous 10 percent Increase in Real Government Consumption (Percentage change from base case)

Equation/ Variable	1980	1981	1982	1983	1984	1985	1986	1987	1988	1989
1.CPR	0.3	0.3	0.4	0.4	0.4	0.5	0.5	0.5	0.4	0.4
2.IMERP	0.4	0.6	0.9	1.1	1.2	1.6	1.5	1.2	1.0	0.9
3.ITERP	0.1	0.3	0.3	0.5	0.7	0.9	1.1	1.2	1.2	0.8
4.TY	0.0	0.7	0.8	0.8	0.6	0.6	0.8	0.8	0.7	0.6
5.W	0.1	0.3	0.4	0.4	0.4	0.4	0.4	0.4	0.4	0.4
6.LE	0.1	0.2	0.2	0.2	0.2	0.2	0.3	0.3	0.2	0.2
7.GCPF	0.2	0.4	0.6	0.6	0.6	0.7	0.7	0.7	0.7	0.6
8.MS1R	0.4	0.4	0.4	0.4	0.5	0.6	0.5	0.5	0.4	0.4
9.CPI	0.0	0.1	0.1	0.1	0.1	0.1	0.1	0.1	0.1	0.1
10.P	0.0	0.1	0.1	0.1	0.1	0.1	0.1	0.1	0.1	0.1
11.MR01R	0.5	0.4	0.5	0.3	0.4	0.5	0.4	0.3	0.3	0.2
12.MR24R	0.2	0.3	0.3	0.3	0.3	0.4	0.3	0.3	0.3	0.3
13.MR3R	0.3	0.3	0.3	0.3	0.4	0.5	0.4	0.4	0.4	0.4
14.MR59R	0.6	0.6	0.7	0.8	0.8	1.1	1.1	1.0	0.8	0.7
15.MSVR	1.0	0.9	1.0	1.1	1.0	1.1	0.9	0.8	0.7	0.6
16.X01DR	0.0	0.0	0.0	0.0	0.0	0.0	0.0	0.0	0.0	0.0
17.X24DR	0.0	0.0	0.0	0.0	0.0	0.0	0.0	0.0	0.0	0.0
18.X3DR	0.0	0.0	0.0	0.0	0.0	0.0	0.0	0.0	0.0	0.0
19.X59DR	0.0	0.0	0.0	0.0	0.0	0.0	0.0	0.0	0.0	0.0
20.X01RR	0.0	0.0	0.0	0.0	0.0	0.0	0.0	0.0	0.0	0.0
21.X59RR	0.0	0.0	0.0	0.0	0.0	0.0	0.0	0.0	0.0	0.0
22.XSVR	0.0	0.0	0.0	0.0	0.0	0.0	0.0	0.0	0.0	0.0
23.GDER	0.5	0.6	0.6	0.6	0.6	0.7	0.7	0.7	0.6	0.6
24.GDER	0.5	0.4	0.5	0.5	0.5	0.6	0.6	0.5	0.5	0.5
25.KRF	0.0	0.1	0.1	0.2	0.2	0.3	0.3	0.4	0.4	0.4
26.KRP	0.0	0.1	0.1	0.2	0.2	0.3	0.3	0.4	0.4	0.4
27.MFOBR	0.4	0.4	0.4	0.5	0.5	0.6	0.6	0.5	0.4	0.4
28.MLR	0.4	0.6	0.2	0.0	-0.2	-0.0	0.4	0.1	-0.3	-0.2
29.RATP	0.1	0.0	0.0	-0.0	0.0	0.0	0.0	-0.0	-0.0	-0.0
30.VELN	0.0	0.1	0.1	0.0	-0.0	-0.1	0.0	0.1	0.0	0.0
31.XFOBR	0.0	0.0	0.0	0.0	0.0	0.0	0.0	0.0	0.0	0.0
32.YDR	0.5	0.4	0.5	0.4	0.5	0.6	0.5	0.5	0.4	0.4

[9] In general, the theoretical literature stresses the role of intangible assets such as production technology, management know-how, and marketing know-how in multinationals, suggesting that the most important effects of direct investment may come from the supply side; for a detailed and more rigorous attempt to model the effects of direct foreign investment in Singaporean manufacturing, see Ramstetter (1991).

The final experiment examines another domestic shock with the autonomous nominal wage level increased by 10 percent (i.e., the constant in the wage equation is increased from -32.7804 to -29.5024)(Table 9). As expected, real GDE declines, but by very little (less than 0.1 percent in absolute value). Prices rise 0.7 to 2.1 percent and the shock translates into a wage increase of as much as 7.0 percent in 1988-1989. The higher real wage and the decline in real GDE then combine to produce a decline in employment of as much as 3.5 percent (in absolute value) in 1989.

Table 9. The Effects of a Continuous 10 Percent Increase in the Autonomous Nominal Wage (percentage change from base case)

Equation/ Variable	1980	1981	1982	1983	1984	1985	1986	1987	1988	1989
1.CPR	0.0	0.1	0.3	0.4	0.4	0.4	0.4	0.4	0.4	0.4
2.IMERP	-0.0	-0.0	-0.1	-0.1	-0.1	-0.1	-0.1	-0.1	-0.1	-0.1
3.ITERP	-0.0	-0.0	-0.0	-0.0	-0.1	-0.1	-0.1	-0.1	-0.1	-0.1
4.TY	0.0	-1.6	-2.1	-2.5	-2.6	-2.5	-2.2	-2.2	-1.9	-1.7
5.W	2.7	4.1	4.9	5.5	5.8	6.2	6.5	6.8	7.0	7.0
6.LE	-0.6	-1.2	-1.8	-2.2	-2.6	-2.8	-3.1	-3.3	-3.4	-3.5
7.GCPF	1.0	1.5	1.5	1.4	1.2	1.0	0.9	0.9	0.8	0.7
8.MS1R	-0.0	-1.1	-0.7	-0.2	-0.1	-0.1	-0.1	-0.1	-0.1	-0.0
9.CPI	0.7	1.3	1.4	1.5	1.5	1.6	1.7	1.8	1.8	1.8
10.P	0.8	1.4	1.6	1.7	1.8	1.9	2.0	2.0	2.1	2.1
11.MR01R	0.0	0.3	0.4	0.4	0.4	0.4	0.3	0.3	0.2	0.2
12.MR24R	-0.0	-0.0	-0.0	-0.0	-0.0	-0.0	-0.0	-0.0	-0.0	-0.0
13.MR3R	-0.0	-0.0	-0.0	-0.0	-0.0	-0.0	-0.0	-0.0	-0.0	-0.0
14.MR59R	0.0	0.2	0.3	0.4	0.4	0.4	0.3	0.3	0.3	0.3
15.MSVR	-0.0	-0.1	-0.1	-0.1	-0.1	-0.1	-0.1	-0.0	-0.0	-0.0
16.X01DR	0.0	0.0	0.0	0.0	0.0	0.0	0.0	0.0	0.0	0.0
17.X24DR	0.0	0.0	0.0	0.0	0.0	0.0	0.0	0.0	0.0	0.0
18.X3DR	0.0	0.0	0.0	0.0	0.0	0.0	0.0	0.0	0.0	0.0
19.X59DR	0.0	0.0	0.0	0.0	0.0	0.0	0.0	0.0	0.0	0.0
20.X01RR	0.0	0.0	0.0	0.0	0.0	0.0	0.0	0.0	0.0	0.0
21.X59RR	0.0	0.0	0.0	0.0	0.0	0.0	0.0	0.0	0.0	0.0
22.XSVR	0.0	0.0	0.0	0.0	0.0	0.0	0.0	0.0	0.0	0.0
23.GDER	0.8	1.4	1.5	1.6	1.7	1.8	1.9	2.0	2.1	2.1
24.GDER	-0.0	-0.0	-0.0	-0.0	-0.0	-0.0	-0.0	-0.0	-0.0	-0.0
25.KRF	-0.0	-0.0	-0.0	-0.0	-0.0	-0.0	-0.0	-0.0	-0.0	-0.0
26.KRP	-0.0	-0.0	-0.0	-0.0	-0.0	-0.0	-0.0	-0.0	-0.0	-0.0
27.MFOBR	0.0	0.1	0.1	0.2	0.2	0.2	0.1	0.1	0.1	0.1
28.MLR	6.0	5.8	2.0	0.6	0.9	1.5	1.6	1.2	0.8	0.2
29.RATP	-0.7	-0.8	-0.9	-0.9	-0.8	-0.8	-0.8	-0.8	-0.7	-0.7
30.VELN	-0.0	1.0	0.6	0.1	0.1	0.1	0.1	0.1	0.1	0.0
31.XFOBR	0.0	0.0	0.0	0.0	0.0	0.0	0.0	0.0	0.0	0.0
32.YDR	0.0	0.3	0.4	0.5	0.5	0.5	0.4	0.4	0.4	0.4

5 Conclusions

In this paper we have presented an econometric model of the Singaporean economy. The specification reflects the salient features of the Singaporean economy and the set of trade equations in the model highlight the important distinction between entrepot trade and domestic trade in the economy. More importantly, these trade equations are key relationships for establishing the link among country models in a multicountry project such as ASIAN LINK. Seven simulation experiments were conducted to illustrate the characteristics of the Singaporean economy, with particular focus on the role of external shocks. These experiments generally revealed that trade flows were most affected by the shocks with real GDE responding to a smaller degree. Prices were generally unresponsive while wages were more sensitive to shocks; as a result, employment tended to decrease more or increase less than real GDE.

To integrate a model of Singapore into an international system like ASIAN LINK is a challenging task for a number of reasons. First, there will be inconsistencies in the data, especially in the trade data, which will mandate the use of bridge equations or some other method to relate one set of data to another. Second, the model would of course have to be modified to be consistent with the trade linking mechanism to be used; the addition of bilateral trade equations would be one potential extension in this regard. Third, a fuller treatment of the financial sector would be mandated if financial links were to be introduced. As indicated above, this would be a particularly challenging task in the case of Singapore because asset markets are so open that domestic markets often mimic international markets, making it difficult to distinguish Singaporean markets from external ones. Another problem with a financial link would be the lack of data on bilateral financial flows to and from Singapore.

Thus, in the final analysis, several important tasks remain before this model could be successfully integrated into a system such as ASIAN LINK. Nonetheless, it is believed that the model presented above illustrates the major characteristics of the Singaporean economy and could be the core of a useful component of an international link model such as ASIAN LINK.

References

[1] ADB (Asian Development Bank) (various years) *Key Indicators of Developing Member Countries of ADB,* various issues, Manila: ADB

[2] DOS (Department of Statistics) (1983) *Economic & Social Statistics Singapore 1960-1982,* Singapore: Singapore National Printers Ltd.

[3] DOS (1988) *Singapore National Accounts 1987,* Singapore: Singapore National Printers Ltd.

[4] DOS (various years) *Yearbook of Statistics Singapore,* various issues, Singapore: Singapore National Printers Ltd.

[5] EDB (Economic Development Board) (1990) *Report on the Census of Industrial Production, 1988,* Singapore: Singapore National Printers Ltd.

[6] ESU (Econometric Studies Unit) (1991) *Data Bank,* Econometric Studies Unit, Department of Economics and Statistics, Singapore National University

[7] Ichimura, S. and M. Ezaki eds. (1985) *Econometric Models of Asian Link,* Tokyo: Springer-Verlag.

[8] IMF (International Monetary Fund) (various years) *Balance of Payments Statistics Yearbook,* various issues, Washington, D.C.: IMF

[9] Lim, C. Y. et al. (1988) *Policy Options for the Singapore Economy,* Singapore: McGraw-Hill.

[10] MTI (Ministry of Trade and Industry) (1988, 1989) *Economic Survey of Singapore,* Singapore: Singapore National Printers.

[11] OECD (Organization for Economic Cooperation and Development) (various years) *Quarterly Bulletin of National Accounts,* various issues, Paris:OECD

[12] Ramstetter, E. D. (1991) "The Macroeconomic Effects of Direct Foreign Investment in Singaporean Manufacturing: A Macroeconometric Study," in M. Toida ed., *ASEAN, Ajia NIEs no Keizai Yosoku to Bunseki (III) - Heisei Ninendo ELSA Hokokusho - [Economic Forecasts and Analyses for ASEAN and the Asia NIEs (III) - 1990 ELSA Annual Report -],* Tokyo: Institute of Developing Economies, pp.49-138.

[13] Toh, M. H. (1990) "Econometric Modelling in Singapore," Singapore Journal of Statistics, vol.1, Oct.

Appendix

A Data (see Table 1 for definitions)

Variable	1972	1973	1974	1975	1976	1977
AROC	0.220	0.250	0.280	0.300	0.300	0.305
ASEAN4	18915	210262	224568	231650	246757	267686
CGR	2145.2	2262.9	2265.3	2327.4	2443.9	2669.2
CPI	0.473	0.567	0. 639	0.711	0.698	0.719
CPR	9126.2	10031.8	10785.4	11109.0	11697.8	12341.2
ERRMR	-4742.3	-4817.6	-8900.0	-8357.7	-9508.6	-9402.2
ERRXR	-820.3	-275.7	-1731.9	-2531.8	-3204.3	-3750.3
GCPF	330.8	474.7	686.7	886.6	1008.0	1114.7
GDEN	8195.0	10256.9	12610.1	13443.0	14650.9	16039.0
GDER	15526.2	17273.6	18441.2	19171.4	20548.5	22143.3
ICWRP	1631.8	1536.5	1425.3	1414.3	1320.5	1236.0
IMERP	1874.6	2071.3	2425.2	2250.5	1902.4	1683.7
IRF	952.0	1584.9	1159.6	923.0	710.4	861.9
IRG	1447.7	1274.0	1523.7	1918.4	2391.7	2582.9
ITERP	819.7	1243.7	1416.6	1079.5	1474.4	1756.2
JR	695.7	680.2	1336.6	949.3	1096.8	665.3
KRF	952	2537	3697	4620	5330	6192
KRP	421	9020	14323	19072	23755	28412
LE	0.7250	0.7996	0.8243	0.8335	0.8740	0.9030
MFOBR	17013.7	19856.0	23214.5	21588.1	23675.6	25797.1
MLR	7.500	9.00	10.250	7.080	6.780	7.020
MLRR	1.799	-5.682	-0.874	5.268	3.380	5.425
MR01R	1449.6	1683.2	1469.4	1621.4	1662.1	1480.6
MR24R	1396.4	2178.2	1822.3	1608.5	2254.2	2294.9
MR3R	5481.5	5624.8	12562.3	11250.1	13674.5	13580.6
MR59R	10010.1	11516.3	12703.5	11326.6	10690.7	12025.6
MS1R	4518.2	4433.7	4180.8	4951.8	5610.2	6091.3
MSVR	3335.6	3870.8	3828.7	3767.8	4105.0	4646.7
OECD85	6307329	6717305	6677001	6590200	6905300	7170800
P	0.528	0.594	0.684	0.701	0.713	0.724
PM	0.517	0.586	0.815	0.825	0.881	0.920
PM01	0.488	0.553	0.769	0.750	0.797	0.910
PM24	0.619	0.701	0.975	0.806	0.936	1.059
PM3	0.242	0.275	0.382	0.405	0.440	0.470
PM59	0.498	0.565	0.785	0.802	0.839	0.861
PX	0.666	0.677	0.681	0.656	0.653	0.926
PX01	1.112	0.991	0.889	0.933	1.011	1.000
PX24	463.6	-171.0	-73.1	30.8	-90.3	1.114

(continued)

Variable	1972	1973	1974	1975	1976	1977
PX3	95.4	169.0	168.2	62.0	-19.3	0.588
PX59	-109.8	-47.8	35.6	5.2	-14.3	0.908
RATP	41.7	381.5	420.2	-151.1	64.8	0.650
REEXCH	402.7	562.7	846.7	1126.7	1150.2	1.051
SDR	3.436	3.896	4.411	3.872	3.663	-64.2
SDRI	75.60	82.90	97.60	111.10	116.30	-52.2
SDRIP	257.7	308.9	326.7	353.4	258.2	-19.3
SDRT	939.2	805.8	702.0	758.9	838.7	202.1
TY	1727.6	2867.0	2383.4	2002.9	2662.5	1275.9
VELN	173.8	171.0	269.7	216.7	182.3	3.635
W	3569.2	3664.1	7260.2	6305.0	6591.3	124.30
X01DR	238.6	269.8	265.7	425.3	275.1	340.2
X01RR	939.2	805.8	702.0	758.9	838.7	1115.0
X24DR	1727.6	2867.0	2383.4	2002.9	2662.5	2952.4
X24RR	173.8	171.0	269.7	216.7	182.3	309.9
X3DR	3569.2	3664.1	7260.2	6305.0	6591.3	7983.7
X3RR	238.6	269.8	265.7	425.3	275.1	300.7
X59DR	2947.9	4130.5	4550.1	4260.7	6051.7	7060.3
X59RR	2066.8	2424.5	2319.4	2738.2	3606.6	4091.9
XFOBR	11100.4	14365.9	16345.5	14529.4	17262.0	20403.8
XSVR	6543.3	7202.4	7409.9	9002.6	8798.7	9182.4
YDRR	14136.5	15526.5	16198.7	16300.2	17521.5	18842.9

(continued)

Variable	1978	1979	1980	1981	1982	1983
AROC	0.320	0.350	0.375	0.405	0.438	0.455
ASEAN4	279713	253386	270158	277981	271554	228092
CGR	2976.3	2961.9	3241.5	3411.6	3863.8	4235.9
CPI	0.755	0.786	0.852	0.923	0.958	0.970
CPR	13168.1	13971.4	14809.7	15491.3	16087.0	-6073.6
ERRMR	-10801.4	-8566.0	-5579.9	-4904.1	-6187.0	-6073.6
ERRXR	-5713.5	-4621.4	-3448.9	-3524.8	-4385.0	-4216.0
GCPF	1352.0	1753.1	2296.0	3007.2	3901.4	4491.0
GDEN	17830.4	20523.0	25090.7	29339.4	32669.9	36732.8
GDER	24046.0	26284.7	28832.5	31603.1	33772.3	36537.2
ICWRP	1410.8	1808.2	2199.1	3101.6	4365.7	5427.0
IMERP	2065.8	2692.1	3394.7	4052.9	3739.0	3510.2
IRF	818.2	2185.9	2596.8	3507.9	3396.0	2310.6
IRG	2678.3	2307.0	2772.7	3133.6	4463.1	5806.7
ITERP	2045.0	2450.4	2760.1	2522.2	2837.9	2323.8
JR	931.0	1596.7	1516.1	730.7	144.0	242.2
KRF	7010	9196	11793	15301	18697	21007
KRP	33933	40884	49238	58915	69557	81118
LE	0.9399	1.0211	1.0771	1.1128	1.1416	1.1677
MFOBR	29248.7	35843.7	43406.4	47869.8	50278.7	52431.1
MLR	7.650	9.480	13.600	11.830	9.330	8.980
MLRR	4.106	1.811	3.605	3.556	6.346	9.978
MR01R	1317.2	1563.8	1684.3	1731.2	1692.7	2160.7
MR24R	2353.8	2488.0	2702.5	2738.1	2795.9	2767.8
MR3R	15618.7	15238.0	14211.8	16148.9	17588.5	17832.0
MR59R	13469.5	15939.3	19099.6	21036.0	21968.5	22132.2
MS1R	6643.0	7308.1	7049.5	7800.9	8432.0	8561.9
MSVR	5083.0	6317.6	8321.0	9093.4	10136.0	10330.4
OECD85	7436700	7729800	7819700	7915300	7906300	8131100
P	0.742	0.781	0.870	0.928	0.967	1.005
PM	0.940	0.998	1.105	1.138	1.115	1.058
PM01	0.914	0.957	1.015	1.035	1.035	0.999
PM24	1.121	1.340	1.378	0.151	0.962	1.096
PM3	0.448	0.624	1.026	0.208	1.125	1.004
PM59	0.904	0.951	1.026	1.050	1.047	1.019
PX	0.926	0.944	0.995	1.132	1.129	1.075
PX01	0.926	0.962	1.001	0.968	0.955	0.937
PX24	1.195	1.398	1.408	1.160	0.998	1.107

(continued)

Variable	1978	1979	1980	1981	1982	1983
PX3	0.554	0.759	1.178	1.293	1.251	1.101
PX59	0.855	0.890	0.951	1.014	1.019	1.013
RATP	0.654	0.645	0.654	0.651	0.629	0.632
REEXCH	1.067	1.087	1.089	1.027	0.997	0.987
SDR	-110.0	-184.5	-366.2	247.8	317.3	-191.1
SDRP	0.0	-0.0	-0.0	-0.0	0.0	-0.0
SDRIP	0.0	0.0	0.0	0.0	-0.0	0.0
SDRT	22.6	86.0	834.8	1066.8	772.3	100.1
TY	1283.0	1398.0	1898.4	2634.3	3248.0	3523.3
VELN	3.620	3.597	4.090	4.051	4.005	4.267
W	131.30	142.80	161.40	184.10	212.30	231.30
X01DR	451.8	599.6	702.9	674.4	611.2	623.3
X01RR	1263.3	1318.7	1461.3	1700.5	2117.1	1763.0
X24DR	3058.4	3322.1	3617.3	3565.6	3270.7	3423.3
X24RR	286.9	449.6	498.4	301.5	298.3	204.4
X3DR	9430.9	9505.7	9857.6	10695.7	11068.3	11074.2
X3RR	188.3	263.1	300.1	267.6	615.6	705.5
X59DR	8574.3	11340.0	13609.3	14164.8	13853.0	15639.5
X59RR	5552.4	7149.2	9023.3	8850.1	9389.2	10939.1
XFOBR	23092.8	29286.4	35621.2	36695.5	36838.4	40156.3
XSVR	10097.0	11470.4	13776.2	18112.3	20759.0	20835.5
YDR	20492.5	22248.8	24012.6	25526.3	26381.7	28565.6

(continued)

Variable	1984	1985	1986	1987	1988	1989
AROC	0.480	0.500	0.387	0.350	0.355	0.370
ASEAN4	203197	186800	178053	170655	181167	188955
CGR	4457.2	5548.5	5606.8	5666.5	5407.3	5683.8
CPI	0.995	1.000	0.986	0.991	1.007	1.031
CPR	17711.6	17552.9	18287.7	20052.5	22747.9	24550.3
ERRMR	-3721.1	-4217.7	-4754.7	-3287.2	-3785.6	-2987.7
ERRXR	-3158.6	-2802.5	-3059.1	-4309.6	-5101.2	-6575.0
GCPF	5385.2	5993.4	4777.9	4446.7	4985.1	5054.9
GDEN	40047.9	38923.5	38653.5	42609.3	49365.3	5510.1
GDER	39572.5	38923.5	39641.4	43387.4	48223.7	52678.7
ICWRP	6097.1	4937.8	2849.9	2588.8	3375.6	4097.0
IMERP	4110.9	3663.7	3903.1	5292.8	7138.2	8758.8
IRF	2687.4	2303.6	3763.3	5972.4	5187.5	7302.4
IRG	6295.1	5939.5	6188.8	5470.6	4039.1	3490.7
ITERP	2174.3	1883.8	1672.7	1712.9	1714.4	2796.6
JR	273.0	126.4	637.4	1478.0	547.7	-994.3
KRF	23695	25998	29762	35734	40921	48224
KRP	93501	103986	112412	122006	134234	149887
LE	1.1748	1.1543	1.1491	1.1929	1.2385	1.2773
MFOBR	56404.6	53599.8	58839.5	67082.5	86175.6	93745.5
MLR	9.400	7.200	6.100	6.100	6.130	6.250
MLRR	5.886	4.767	11.838	4.253	3.850	3.290
MR01R	1964.2	2184.0	2177.2	2319.4	2525.8	2593.5
MR24R	2497.7	2463.0	2829.2	3016.0	3337.8	3629.5
MR3R	17040.9	16418.9	19868.7	18147.6	22114.1	20818.0
MR59R	23508.9	21658.3	23555.8	27959.1	35219.3	39915.7
MS1R	8761.0	8785.0	10072.3	11231.9	11681.2	13089.4
MSVR	11130.1	11349.6	14764.3	17251.2	20814.9	23231.2
OECD85	8541300	8834600	9069600	9388100	9778000	10071340
P	1.012	1.000	0.975	0.982	1.024	1.050
PM	1.011	1.000	0.975	0.982	1.024	1.050
PM01	1.012	1.000	1.004	1.008	1.043	1.037
PM24	1.216	1.000	0.856	0.956	0.954	1.103
PM3	0.971	1.000	0.536	0.665	0.518	0.590
PM59	1.022	1.000	1.053	1.102	1.161	1.147
PX	1.015	1.000	0.864	0.931	0.933	0.948
PX01	0.969	1.000	1.010	1.002	1.003	0.955
PX24	1.165	1.000	0.902	1.006	1.170	0.996

(continued)

Variable	1984	1985	1986	1987	1988	1989
PX3	1.020	1.000	0.592	0.646	0.542	0.605
PX59	0.990	1.000	0.984	0.990	0.997	0.990
RATP	0.629	0.614	0.607	0.623	0.645	0.640
REEXCH	0.986	1.000	1.108	1.146	1.192	1.132
SDR	-115.3	216.6	220.0	25.2	-181.1	-396.9
SDRI	0.0	0.0	-74.3	-37.1	-0.1	-0.0
SDRIP	-0.0	0.0	0.0	-0.0	0.1	0.0
SDRT	-824.6	-1406.9	-1085.1	-622.9	-1011.2	-1152.8
TY	3568.3	3006.7	2231.8	2356.6	2839.7	3618.8
VELN	4.517	4.431	3.936	3.863	4.128	4.025
W	252.70	260.30	264.50	269.30	283.00	312.10
X01DR	605.3	581.5	716.8	906.7	1150.5	1417.6
X01RR	2600.6	1852.4	2211.9	2191.4	2649.4	2688.9
X24DR	3502.6	3329.4	3466.0	3586.1	3979.0	4507.9
X24RR	747.1	905.5	237.0	189.3	234.9	248.6
X3DR	12499.5	12982.1	16497.0	14399.7	16854.4	17213.2
X3RR	427.0	612.1	643.4	688.1	1867.0	1906.8
X59DR	19063.7	18192.5	20986.5	28184.8	38301.8	42613.7
X59RR	11339.3	11723.3	12071.0	15858.9	22012.9	24932.2
XFOBR	47626.5	47376.3	53770.5	61695.5	81948.7	88953.9
XSVR	19301.4	18034.3	21267.7	23968.7	29487.6	33868.4
YDR	30725.3	29923.4	32452.5	36459.9	40579.9	44417.7

B Sources of Variables

Variable	Sources
AROC	DOS(1983,various years);ESU(1991)
ASEAN4	ADB(various years)
CGR	DOS(1988,various years)
CPI	DOS(1983,various years)
CPR	DOS(1988,various years)
ERRMR	CALULATED
ERRXR	CALCULATED
GCPF	DOS(1983,various years),ESU(1991)
GDEN	DOS(1988,various years)
GDER	DOS(1988,various years)
ICWRP	DOS(1988);MTI(various years)
IMERP	DOS(1988);MTI(various years)
IRF	IMF(various years)
IRG	DOS(1988);MTI(various years)
ITERP	DOS(1988);MTI(various years)
JR	DOS(1988,various years)
KRF	CALCULATED
KRP	CALCULATED
LE	DOS(1983,various years)
MFOBR	DOS(1988,various years)
MLR	DOS(1983,various years)
MLRR	CALCULATED
MR01R	ESU(1991)
MR24R	ESU(1991)
MR3R	ESU(1991)
MR59R	ESU(1991)
MS1R	CALCULATED (nominal figure from DOS (1983,various years); ESU(1991))
MSVR	DOS(1988,various years)
OECD85	OECD(various years)
P	DOS(1988,various years)
PM	DOS(1988,various years)
PM01	ESU(1991)
PM24	ESU(1991)
PM3	ESU(1991)
PM59	ESU(1991)
PX	DOS(1988,various years)
PX01	ESU(1991)
PX24	ESU(1991)

(continued)

Variable	Sources
PX3	ESU(1991)
PX59	ESU(1991)
RATP	CALCULATED
REEXCH	ESU(1991)
SDR	DOS(1988,various years)
SDRI	ESU(1991)
SDRIP	ESU(1991)
SDRT	ESU(1991)
TY	DOS(1983,various years),ESU(1991)
VELN	CALCULATED
W	DOS(1983,various years),ESU(1991)
X01DR	ESU(1991)
X01RR	ESU(1991)
X24DR	ESU(1991)
X24RR	ESU(1991)
X3DR	ESU(1991)
X3RR	ESU(1991)
X59DR	ESU(1991)
X59RR	ESU(1991)
XFOBR	DOS(1988,various years)
XSVR	DOS(1988,various years)
YDR	CALCULATED

Chapter 13

An Annual Philippine Macroeconometric Model for Policy Analysis

Roberto S. Mariano[1] and Winnie M. Constantino[2]

1 Introduction

Since the pioneering effort of Encarnacion, Mariano and Bautista (1971), various quantitative models of the Philippine economy have been developed over the past twenty years. Because of the diversity in their objectives, these models naturally differ among themselves in terms of philosophy, orientation, level of aggregation, and time horizon.

Macroeconometric models in the tradition of Tinbergen and Klein kave been constructed – with adaptations to institutional realities in the Philippines. Other versions of this type have incorporated demographic factors for long-term analysis. For sectoral studies, linkage with an input-output structure has also been attempted. Since the mid-1980s, computable general equilibrium models of more recent vintage have also been constructed for the Philippines – for example, to analyze tax policies and trade distortions.

Bautista (1988) provides an overview of these various models. Most of the published articles, as well as some working papers describing these models, are listed in this paper's bibliography.

This paper describes an annual macroeconometric model of the Philippines (code name: MRM-93) that is being maintained at the University of Pennsylvania. Variations of this model reside at the National Economic and Development Authority (NEDA), the Philippine Institute for Development Studies (PIDS), and the Asian Development Bank (ADB) – all in the Philippines.

All these four versions are modifications and improvements of the PIDS-NEDA annual macroeconometric model initially developed at PIDS in 1984-1985 in a research project headed by Roberto Mariano – with substantial contributions from Winnie Constantino, Clarence Dingcong, Mario Lamberte, Manuel Montes, Celia Reyes, Glenn Sipin, and Josef Yap. Initial funding for this effort came from UNDP and US-AID grants to PIDS. After 1985, subsequent grants from UN-ESCAP to PIDS provided partial support to the maintenance and revision of the model under

[1]University of Pennsylvania
[2]San Miguel Corporation

the supervision of Josef Yap and Winnie Constantino. Currently, Celia Reyes and Josef Yap are in charge of maintaining the PIDS model in the Philippines.

The main objective of the PIDS modelling project was to provide government economic planners at NEDA with a coordinated framework for the formulation of the country's medium-term economic developemnt program. The model was also meant to serve as a quantitative tool for the impact assessment of economic policy options and changes in the external environment.

When this modelling effort began, economic planners were heavily preoccupied with the country's foreign debt and an economic stabilization/recovery program fraught with tight restrictions on the governemnt budget deficit, the current account deficit, and money supply. Thus, the initial version of the PIDS-NEDA model was designed specifically for the analysis of alternative stabilization measures and scenarios for debt servicing and restructuring.

Since 1985, the initial PIDS-NEDA model, consisting of about seventy-three equations, has undergone a series of revisions aimed at rectifying observed deficiencies and enhancing capabilities for policy analysis.

Stronger and more direct linkages between the production and expenditure sides of the economy were established in the modification of the initial model. This meant a much more disaggregate treatment of the production subsectors and a finer decomposition of exports and imports.

Another revision improved the modeling of the financial sector with an endogenous determination of the money multiplier and interest rate. To achieve further logical consistency, the price determination structure was modified in the model to reflect a direct connection between sectoral prices and aggregate price indicators.

The various versions of the PIDS econometric model are discussed in Mariano and Constantino (1987 a,b); Mariano, Constantino, and Yap (1989); and Constatino et. al (1990). The MRM-93 model, which is discussed in this paper, is a compact model with very similar features to the PIDS-Version 89 model described in te last two references mentioned above. However, MRM-93 has a more explicit determination of the aggregate price level in terms of sectoral prices. An earlier version of MRM-93 with a disaggregated treatment of government operating expenditures as well as output of government services also has been used to study the macroeconomic effects of increased defense expenditures in the Philippines – as reported in Mariano, Adams, and Park (1991).

Subsequent sections of this paper discuss the basic structure of MRM-93, its observed properties based on historical simulations, and results of selected simulations for a sensitivity analysis of the model. The paper concludes with some general observations about future work on the model. A listing of the equations comprising the model, variable definitions, and data documentation is in the Appendix.

2 Structure of MRM-93

MRM-93 consists of fifty seven equations: 30 are statistically estimated; the rest are identities. Ordinary least squares was used to estimate the equations, covering periods ending in 1991.

This simultaneous system consists of four major blocks – Real, Fiscal, Financial and Externa Sectors. The flowchart in figure 1 provides a broad overview of the linkages among the various sectors and the key variables in each of them. A detailed list of the equations comprising the model, together with a documentation of the exogenous and endogenous variables in the system, is presented in the appendix.

The model combines classical, Keynesian, structuralist, and monetarist approachs to macroeconomic modeling. The core of the model is the Real Sector Block which determines domestic output, its production and expenditure components, prices, employment and wages. Domestic output is determined within the model with simultaneous feedback between the supply and demand sides in the real sector block. Supply and demand equations are estimated for production subsectors within agriculture, industry and services. As described in Constantino et. al (1990), it is assumed that sectoral prices clear the markets in agriculture. On the other hand, this market-clearing assumption is modified for the industrial sector. This sector is often characterized by excess capacity and adjustments to increases in demand consequently take place on the quantity side.

GDP is built up from the production side and GNP is then calculated with the addition of net factor income from abroad. This is reconciled with the expenditure side by taking the statistical discrepancy as a residual component of GNP from the expenditure side. In simulation exercises, especially for multiplier analysis, one must take care that the statistical discrepancy does not absorb the effects of a shock in the system. To ensure this in our model simulations, adjustments are made to maintain the same level for the statistical discrepancy when alternative simulations are being run for sensitivity analysis.

The expenditure side of the real sector is disaggregated into traditional components in the nation income accounts. The linkage from the expenditure side to the production sectors comes in two major ways. One is in the form of aggregate expenditure categories appearing as arguments in the demand functions in the production sectors. Secondly, appropriate investment expenditure variables also apper as explanatory variables in some of the supply functions in the production sectors. Feedback from production to the expenditure sector is reflected in the use of real output as an activity variable in the equations for some of the expenditure components.

Through the treatment of supply and demand for output in each production sector, sectoral prices are determined separately in MRM-93. An average of these prices, weighted by sectoral output shares, yields the implicit price deflator for GDP. Nominal GDP is calculated through these sectoral prices and real sectoral output. Nominal net factor income from abroad is added to nominal GDP to obtain nominal GNP and the GNP price deflator is then calculated as the ratio of nominal to real GNP. More details on how this price determination filters to the other components of the model, including employment and wages, can be extracted from the detailed list of equations comprising the model.

Figure 1. Flow Chart of the Model

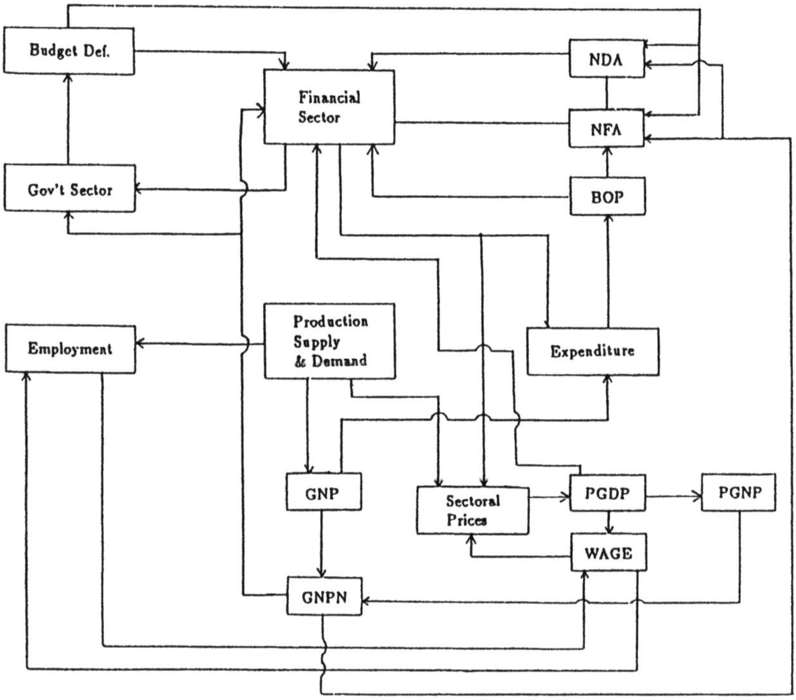

For the fiscal sector, government expenditures at the budget level are exogenous in the model and are decomposed into operating expenditures and capital outlays. These two variables then feed directly into estimated equations for national income accounts data on government consumption expenditures and government construction, respectively. Government spending for operating expenses and capital outlays affect the system differently – the former through goverment and private consumption in the expendiutre side of the model; the latter through the invesment equations in the expenditure side and the supply equations in the production side.

Goverment operating expenditures can also affect economic activity in the public-sector directly, through increases in goverment employment and/or through wage increases to public employees. To deal with these possibilities, Mariano, Adams, and Park (1991) augmented the production side of the PIDS model by treating the goverment sector as another production node and by recognizing the goverment wage rate in the goverment sector deflator. With these additional features, changes in public sector employment then affect value added produced in the goverment sector while changes in public sector wage rates affect the government sector deflator. More details about this aspect of the model and the simulation analysis of this modification are given in Mariano, Adams, and Park (1991).

The financial sector of MRM-93 contains further changes beyond the refinements done Constantino and Yap on the PIDS model as described in Constantino et. al (1990). The treatment is at a fairly disaggregated level which endogenizes base money, reserve money, net domestic assets, net foreign assets,liquidity, money supply, and T-bill interest rates. The main monetary exogenous variables are the reserve requirements on commercial banks and deposit interest rates.

The financial sector has strong linkages with the other three main blocks of MRM-93. It is affected by the fiscal sector through the goverment budget deficit and the financing requirements for it. External sector effects show through the balance of payments and net foreign assets. Nominal GNP, determeined in the real sector, affect components of liquidity in the system.

In the treatment of the external sector trade receipts and payments are calculated from real exports and imports. These, in turn, feed into the calcutlation of the current account balance in the BOP. Exchange rates, exogenous in MRM-93, are utilized for currency conversion. The exogenous treatment of exchange rates requires careful attention in simulations of the model– in terms of internal cosistencies of assumptions about exchange rates relative to the endogenous solutions for domestic inflation and interest rates.

All components of the capital account balance are exogenous; hence, for all intents and purposes, the capital account balance is exogenous in MRM-93. For the current account balance, in addition to import and export receipts, inflows and outflows of non-merchandise trade and freight and merchandise insurance are treated endogenously as well. Other impotant components of non-merchandise trade flows – such as income remittances and interest payments on foreign debt – are exogenous in the system.

3 Validation and Sensitivity Analysis of MRM-93

For partial validation, we performed dynamic and static simulations of MRM-93 over the period 1977 - 1990. The results of these historical simulations are summerized in Table 1. The results indicate some deterioration from the static simulation to the dynamic simulation. For example, the mean absolute percent error (MAPE) for GDP goes up from 2% in the static simulation to 12% in the dynamic simulation. Considering the individual components of GDP in the model, we see that the MAPEs for agriculture (VAC), industry (VIR), and services(VSER) are all below 3% in the static simulation but range between 7% and 19% in the dynamic simulation. The table also shows a poor tracking performance relative to the monetary sector; big errors in the simulation of net foreign assets (FA) due to errors in gross foreign liabilities (GFL) lead to a 25% MAPE for the treasury bill rate and a 35% MAPE for total liquidity. This poor performance in the monetary sector affects, in turn, the other sectors of the model – especially in the dynamic simulations of investment expenditures in private construction (CONDPR) and in durable equipment (IDER). Undoubtedly, these error statistics require further modifications of the model along the lines indicated above. To develop a better understanding of the dynamic behavior of the model and, in the process, identify further directions for improvement of the model, a sensitivity analysis of the model was also performed, relative to a one-time shock, introduced in 1977, reflecting

1. A 10% increase in government operating expenditures (OPEXP)
2. A 10% increases in government capital outlays (CAPUTO)
3. A 10% devaluation of the Philippine peso (ER)
4. A 10% increase in world oil prices (PMFDOL)

The results are summarized in Table 2. Increased government expenditures are expansionary and inflationary – with operating expenditures (compared to capital outlays) showing larger effects on GNP and prices. The major effect on growth is instantaneous, with considerably smaller delayed effects which are practically zero by 1990. The effects on prices show a different pattern – with maximum effects registering in either the second year (for OPEXP) or the third year (for CAPUTO). Growth implications of a devaluation reveal an unusual pattern: a positive contemporaneous growth elasticity, followed by a high contradictionary effect in the second year which tapers off to almost zero by 1990. The positive impact multiplier is the net result of a substantial increase in output in services (VSER) offsetting contractions in agriculture (VAG) and industry (VIR). Beyond the first year, tapering contradictionary effects show up on all three sectors. Changes in world oil prices are reflected in MRM-93 through the dollar import price index for fuel products (PMFDOL). A ten percent increase in this index reduce GNP by one-twentieth of a percent and increases the deflator by one-tenth of a percent. Beyond the first year, the inflationary effects of this one-time increase in oil prices are negligible. On the other hand, delayed effects on GNP, especially on industrial production, change in direction – another feature of the dynamics of the model which must be investigated in further modifications of the model.

Table 1. Summary: Error Statistics for Historical Simulations of the Model (1977-1990)

	Static		Dynamic	
	MAPE	RMSPE	MAPE	RMSPE
CET	1.73	1.95	3.17	3.55
CG	3.93	4.92	11.38	12.12
CGN	4.97	6.55	4.97	6.55
CGOVN	14.66	18.76	13.83	19.35
CONSGO	15.98	20.10	18.35	22.25
CONSPR	12.10	15.82	58.65	65.06
CP	0.88	1.05	7.70	8.75
CPI	5.51	5.33	7.12	9.36
EXPN	5.24	6.44	6.57	8.79
EXPORT	8.44	10.18	15.30	17.48
GDCF	8.60	12.06	35.79	39.80
GDP	2.12	2.80	11.66	12.83
GFL	27.99	56.39	58.25	83.88
GNP	2.15	2.86	11.77	12.94
GNPN	2.66	4.15	6.82	7.51
IDER	11.94	16.90	46.87	55.68
IMPORT	5.25	6.58	18.41	21.09
K46	0.52	0.64	10.29	11.67
KCAR	2.79	3.36	24.43	28.00
M1FUEL	7.13	8.98	11.43	13.90
MB	34.51	42.51	75.59	88.50
MGDS	6.21	7.42	20.96	24.08
MNF	7.37	8.42	24.78	28.06
MSV	6.67	8.07	12.36	15.50
NDA	4.43	7.55	7.67	11.36
NFA	64.32	132.69	207.92	409.18
PCG	3.27	5.50	11.66	12.36
PCGOV	6.59	10.00	13.60	20.51
PGDP	4.12	6.27	8.77	10.62
PGNP	4.17	6.38	8.88	10.72
PM	0.44	0.59	0.72	0.90
PMFUEL	0.00	0.00	0.00	0.00
PMNF	0.00	0.00	0.00	0.00
PNFIA	5.19	6.62	5.86	8.16
PSER	5.02	7.58	7.88	8.71
PVIR	6.76	10.42	22.00	24.58
REVN	3.10	3.56	6.03	6.92
TBILL	25.11	31.93	58.27	67.65
TL	34.51	42.51	75.59	88.50

(continued)

	Static		Dynamic	
	MAPE	RMSPE	MAPE	RMSPE
TOTTAX	3.20	3.62	6.31	7.22
TRADET	10.68	12.38	21.35	24.83
VERA	16.43	19.27	28.31	31.23
VAG	1.84	2.06	8.06	9.08
VIR	3.10	4.36	19.23	20.72
VSER	2.62	3.15	7.35	8.38
WAGE	6.15	7.27	13.51	15.96
WPI	5.82	7.98	13.57	17.84
XGDS	9.90	12.82	16.93	19.31
XSV	7.44	9.96	13.56	15.72

4 Concluding Remarks

We have presented an econometric model in progress for the Philippine economy. The diagnostics we have reported here indicate that further revisions are required before the model can be used for any practical application. In the past, alternative estimation methods, such as modified two-stage least squares, have produced equation estimates which are not too different from those obtained by ordinary least squares. We will check this again as we go through further modificatons of the model. It will also be useful to apply stochastic simulations on the model to assess the precision of forecasts and multipliers that are estimated through the model. Further simulation analysis will also be done, beyond those described in the previous section, for a deeper investigation of the dynamic properties of the model – a necessary step toward making the model more meaningfull for economic policy analysis.

Table 2. Dynamic Elasticities with Respect to the Four Exogenous Variables in the Sensitivity Analysis of the Model

OPEXP (Unit: %*100)

	CF	GDP	GNP	PGNP	VAG	VIR	VSIR
1977	2.90	7.74	7.80	1.85	-0.45	10.55	10.44
1978	-0.07	-0.67	-0.68	3.32	-0.44	-0.30	-1.21
1979	-0.27	-1.12	-1.12	2.31	-0.54	-1.57	-1.08
1980	-0.53	-1.26	-1.27	1.52	-0.81	-1.97	-0.89
1981	-0.92	-1.46	-1.47	0.74	-1.07	-2.39	-0.85
1982	-0.94	-1.41	-1.43	0.08	-1.08	-2.50	-0.65
1993	-0.70	-1.09	-1.11	-0.42	-0.88	-2.09	-0.34
1984	-0.39	-0.70	-0.72	-0.68	-0.55	-0.55	-0.08
1985	-0.13	-0.36	-0.37	-0.70	-0.20	-1.03	0.11
1986	0.04	-0.07	-0.07	-0.69	0.07	-0.51	0.23
1987	0.14	0.10	0.10	-0.60	0.25	-0.17	0.27
1988	0.19	0.21	0.22	-0.55	0.36	0.05	0.29
1989	0.23	0.29	0.29	-0.49	0.42	0.20	0.30
1990	0.22	0.32	0.32	-0.43	0.44	0.30	0.27

CAPUTO (Unit: %*100)

	CF	GDP	GNP	PGNP	VAG	VIR	VSIR
1977	0.64	1.69	1.70	0.55	3.10	2.20	0.19
1978	0.37	0.87	0.87	1.06	1.84	1.21	-0.14
1979	0.15	0.27	0.26	1.14	0.99	0.32	-0.29
1980	-0.06	-0.17	-0.17	1.02	0.39	-0.35	-0.35
1981	-0.29	-0.48	-0.48	0.75	-0.07	-0.84	-0.39
1982	-0.41	-0.64	-0.64	0.45	-0.31	-1.16	-0.38
1993	-0.40	-0.64	-0.65	0.18	-0.40	-1.21	-0.29
1984	-0.32	-0.54	-0.56	-0.04	-0.36	-1.10	-0.19
1985	-0.20	-0.41	-0.42	-0.14	-0.25	-0.91	-0.09
1986	-0.11	-0.26	-0.26	-0.22	-0.13	-0.63	-0.01
1987	-0.04	-0.15	-0.15	-0.20	-0.02	-0.43	0.04
1988	0.00	-0.08	-0.08	-0.20	0.06	-0.30	0.05
1989	0.04	-0.01	-0.01	-0.18	0.12	-0.19	0.08
1990	0.06	0.03	0.03	-0.17	0.17	-0.11	0.09

(continued)

ER (Unit: %*100)

	CF	GDP	GNP	PGNP	VAG	VIR	VSIR
1977	0.74	1.39	1.40	18.74	-9.78	-9.18	20.04
1978	-1.09	-3.41	-3.42	-1.75	-4.17	-4.84	-1.46
1979	-0.23	-1.07	-1.07	0.35	-0.05	-1.80	-1.08
1980	-0.53	-1.08	-1.08	1.58	0.33	-1.98	-1.14
1981	-1.37	-1.77	-1.78	1.56	-0.27	-3.12	-1.48
1982	-1.30	-1.92	-1.95	1.10	-0.68	-3.56	-1.25
1993	-1.02	-1.73	-1.76	0.62	-0.80	-3.33	-0.91
1984	-0.66	-1.32	-1.34	0.05	-0.72	-2.71	-0.57
1985	-0.43	-1.10	-1.12	0.21	-0.47	-2.42	-0.38
1986	-0.33	-0.90	-0.92	0.24	-0.29	-1.98	-0.30
1987	-0.27	-0.75	-0.76	0.25	-0.14	-1.64	-0.26
1988	-0.21	-0.65	-0.66	0.26	-0.02	-1.45	-0.23
1989	-0.17	-0.58	-0.59	0.31	0.09	-1.32	-0.20
1990							

PMFDOL (Unit: %*100)

	CF	GDP	GNP	PGNP	VAG	VIR	VSIR
1977	-0.54	-0.49	-0.49	1.18	0.57	-1.18	-0.50
1978	0.48	0.38	0.39	-0.29	0.28	0.79	0.06
1979	0.96	1.08	1.08	-0.32	0.77	2.06	0.36
1980	0.98	1.14	1.14	0.14	0.81	2.18	0.37
1981	0.41	0.70	0.70	0.43	0.52	1.52	0.05
1982	0.08	0.33	0.34	0.46	0.13	0.96	-0.11
1993	-0.11	0.06	0.06	0.37	-0.17	0.48	-0.17
1984	-0.21	-0.08	-0.09	0.14	-0.34	0.21	-0.17
1985	-0.16	-0.09	-0.09	-0.05	-0.37	0.13	-0.10
1986	-0.10	-0.03	-0.03	-0.22	-0.31	0.14	-0.02
1987	-0.03	0.03	0.03	-0.28	-0.23	0.17	0.05
1988	0.01	0.08	0.09	-0.32	-0.13	0.22	0.09
1989	0.04	0.13	0.13	-0.35	-0.09	0.27	0.13
1990	0.07	0.18	0.18	-0.36	-0.03	0.32	0.15

References

[1] Bautista, R. M. (1986) "Effects of Increasing Agricultural Productivity in a Multisectoral Model for the Philippines," Agricultural Economics 1, 67-85

[2] Bautista, R. M. (1988) "Macroeconomic Models for East Asian Developing Countries," Asian-Pacific Economic Literature 2, 1-25

[3] Bautista, R. M. and J. Encarnacion (1972) "A Foreign Trade Submodel of the Philippine Economy, 1950-1969," Philippine Economic Journal 11, 231-248

[4] Canlas, D. B., J. Encarnacion and T. Jayme-Ho (1976) "Sectoral Employment, Income Distribution and Consumption: A Macromodel with an Input-Output Structure," Philippine Economic Journal 15, 411-437

[5] Clarete, R. L. (1984) "The Cost and Consequences of Trade Distortions in a Small Open Economy: A General Equilibrium Model for the Philippines," Ph.D. dissertation, University of Hawaii

[6] Constantino, W. M., R. S. Mariano, and J. T. Yap (1989) "The PIDS-NEDA Annual Macroeconometric Model Version 1989: A Summary," PIDS Working Paper, Manila, Philippines, December

[7] Constantino, W. M., J. T. Yap, A. S. de la Paz and R. Q. Butiong (1990) "An Annual Macroeconometric Model for the Philippines," PIDS Working Paper, Manila, Philippines

[8] Danao, R. A. and Montes, M. F. (1985) "A Semestral Macroeconomic Model of the Philippine Economy, Model 1984C," Philippine Institute for Development Studies Discussion Paper

[9] Encarnacion, J., R. S. Mariano and R. M. Bautista (1971) "A Macroeconomic Model of the Philippines, 1950-1969," Philippines Economic Journal 10, 131-157

[10] Encarnacion, J. and A. A. Castro (1972) "A Monetary Submodel of the Philippine Economy," Philippine Economic Journal 11, 214-230

[11] Encarnacion, J., R. M. Bautista, M. Mangahas and G. M. Jurado (1972) "An Econometric Model of the Philippines with Projections through 1976," Philippine Economic Journal 11, 289-332

[12] Encarnacion, J., M. Mangahas, V. B. Paqueo, and P. C. Smith(1974) "An Economic Demographic Model of the Philippines," in A. Kintanar et.al eds., *Studies in Philippine Economic-Demographic Relationship,* University of the Philippines-Institute of Economic Development and Research, 50-117

[13] Habito, C. F. (1984) "Equity and Efficiency Tradeoffs in Philippine Tax Policy Analysis; A General Equilibirium Approach," Ph.D. dissertation, Harvard University

[14] Habito, C. F. (1987) "Equity and Efficiency Tradeoffs in Philippine Tax Policy Reforms," Journal of Philippine Development 24, 57-88

[15] Ichimura, S. and M. Ezaki eds., (1985) *Econometric Models of Asia Link,* Springer-Verlag

[16] Institute of Developing Economies (1985) *Econometric Link System for ASEAN,* Tokosha C., Ltd.

[17] Ito, S. (1987) "A CGE Analysis of the Philippine Economy," in M. Ezaki ed., *Development Planning and Policies in ASEAN Countries,* Centre for Southeast Asian Studies, Kyoto University, 249-292

[18] Jurado, G. M. and J. Encarnacion (1972) "A Government Submodel of the Philippine Economy," Philippine Economic Journal 11, 278-288

[19] Mangahas, M. and J. Encarnacion (1972) "A Production Submodel of the Philippine Economy," Philippine Economic Journal 11, 249-277

[20] Mariano, R. S., F. G. Adams and I. Park (1991) "Defense Expenditures and Economic Growth in the Philippines: A Macrosimulation Analysis," Forthcoming

[21] Mariano, R. S. and W. M. Constantino (1987a) "An Annual Econometric Model for Macro-Policy Analysis in the Philippines," Presented at the Conference on the Performance of Econometric Models of NICA and Developing Countries, Taipei, May 25-27, 1987

[22] Mariano, R. S. and W. M. Constantino (1987b) "The PIDS-NEDA Macroeconometric Model for the Philippines: Recent Implications and Experience on its Use for Policy Analysis," Presented at the ESCAP Regional Seminar on an interlinked Country Model System, Bangkok, November 17-20, 1987.

[23] Montes, V. F. (1984) "Optimal Macroeconomic Policy Responses to an Incipient External Debt Crisis; The Case of the Philippines," Ph.D. dissertation, University of Pennsylvania

[24] Narasimhan, G. V. L. and L. E. Shabater (1974) "An Econometric Model of the Philippines," Philippine Economic Journal 13, 12-26

[25] Villanueva, D. P. (1977) "A Semiannual Macroeconometric Model of the Philippines, 1967-1976," IMF Departmental Memoranda Series 77/89

[26] Yap, J. T. (1985) "Integrating the Real and Financial Sectors: A Monetary Model of the Philippine Economy, 1967-1982," Ph.D. dissertation, University of the Philippines

[27] Yap, J. T. and Y. Nakamura eds., (1990) *ASEAN LINK – An Econometric Study,* Singapore: Longman Singapore Publishers (Pte) Ltd.

[28] Zialcita, E. P. and F. R. Alfiler (1977) "A Framework for Monetary Policy Formulation in the Philippines," in Proceedings of the Third Pacific Basin Central Bank Conference on Econometric Modelling, Wellington, Federal Reserve Bank, New Zealand

Appendix

A List of Equations

A.1 Identities

(1) $bop = (pxgds * xgds - pmgds) * \frac{er}{100} + othbop$

(2) $cg = \frac{cgn}{\frac{pcg}{100}}$

(3) $consgo = \frac{cgovn}{\frac{pcgov}{100}}$

(4) $defg = expn - revn$

(5) $export = xgds + xsv$

(6) $gdcf = consgo + conspr + ider + ogdcf$

(7) $gdp = vag + vir + vser$

(8) $gnp = gdp + nfia$

(9) $gnpn = gnp * \frac{pgnp}{100}$

(10) $import = mgds + msv$

(11) $infl = 100 * \frac{cpi - cpi.1}{cpi.1}$

(12) $k46 = k46.1 + gdcf - kcar$

(13) $mb = nda + nfa$

(14) $mgds = m1fuel + mnf$

(15) $nda = dnda + nda.1$

(16) $nfa = gfa - fg1$

(17) $$pgdp = \frac{pvag * vag + pvir * vir + pser * vser}{gdp}$$

(18) $$pgnp = \frac{pgdp * gdp + pnfia * nfia}{gnp}$$

(19) $$pm = \frac{m1fuel * pmfuel + mnf * pmnf + msv * pmsv}{import}$$

(20) $$pmfuel = pmfdol * \frac{er}{18.60730}$$

(21) $$pmnf = pmnfdol * \frac{er}{18.60730}$$

(22) $$pvag = \frac{cpi}{174.666 * 100} * (0.17904 * (cp + xag) + 82374.8 - vag$$
$$- 0.79499 * (-174.666 * \frac{pvag.1}{cpi.1} * 100 + 0.17904 * (cp.1 + xag.1)$$
$$+ 82374.8 - vag.1))$$

(23) $$revn = tottax + ntaxre$$

(24) $$statd = gdp - (cp + cg + gdcf + export - import)$$

(25) $$tl = mult * mb$$

(26) $$tottaz = dtax + tradet + othtax$$

(27) $$uera = 100 * \frac{lf - cet}{lf}$$

A.2 Estimated Equations

(28) $$cet = 0.95340 * cet_{-1} + 5215.65 * \frac{gnp}{gnp.1} - 7.60151 * \frac{wage}{\frac{pgnp}{100}} - 3084.34$$

(21.2318) (2.12117) (2.50750) (0.57945)

(29) $$cgn = 0.99046 * opexp - intpay + 619.034$$

(50.5650) (0.57945)

(30) $cgovn = 0.66067 * cgovn_{-1} + 0.45017 * caputo + 752.209$

$$(5.01173) \qquad (3.35805) \qquad (0.49302)$$

(31) $conspr = 0.98238 * conspr_{-1} + 0.01799 * gnp - 941.856 * (tbill - infl)$

$$(6.59904) \qquad (1.14661) \qquad (3.98704)$$

$$-1076.41 * infl + 6985.97$$

$$(5.44540) \qquad (1.26920)$$

(32) $cp = 0.27423 * gnp - \frac{tottax}{\frac{pgnp}{100}} + 256.193 * \frac{pop15}{pop} * 1000 + 0.11048 * \frac{tl.1}{\frac{cpi.1}{100}}$

$$(5.73556) \qquad (1.45338) \qquad (2.06915)$$

$$+11322.0 * time - 101867$$

$$(2.43075) \qquad (0.61273)$$

$$AR\_0 = +0.89988 * AR\_1$$

$$(8.32843)$$

(33) $cpi = 0.81646 * pgnp + 0.15359 * pm - 0.17383$

$$(18.6327) \qquad (3.05507) \qquad (0.40512)$$

(34) $dnda = 0.48950 * defg - 0.89297 * dnfa + 1152.45$

$$(6.78903) \qquad (24.2588) \qquad (1.03479)$$

(35) $dtax = 676.764 * pgnp + 0.12134 * gnp - 90994.4$

$$(7.17479) \qquad (2.85826) \qquad (3.01993)$$

$$AR\_0 = +0.77498 * AR\_1$$

$$(5.24485)$$

(36) $expn = 0.58956 * expn_{-1} + 0.05257 * gnpn + 0.09986$

$$(2.18888) \qquad (1.71250) \qquad (1.79855)$$

$$* \frac{domd + ford + domd.1 + ford.1 + domd.2 + ford.2}{3} + 1183.07$$

$$(0.33798)$$

(37) $gfa = 0.53179 * hop * er - 35521.3 * \frac{er.1}{er.2} + 0.21662$

(3.19158) (2.43759) (9.36570)

$* \frac{3 * import * pm + 2 * import.1 * pm.1 + import.2 * pm.2}{\frac{6}{100}}$

$+41617.1$

(2.53560)

(38) $gfl = 0.53936 * gfl_{-1} + 3.10349 * \frac{defg + defg.1 + defg.2}{3} + 9956.84$

(2.16617) (2.38849) (0.61573)

$AR\_0 = +0.62085 * AR\_1$

(1.83056)

(39) $ider = 0.81295 * ider_{-1} + 0.13163 * iltlon * \frac{er}{\frac{pgnp}{100}}$

(2.31781) (0.91687)

$-771.983 * (tbill - infle) - 860.737 * infl + 19027.5$

(1.40406) (2.06767) (1.00460)

$AR\_0 = +0.52114 * AR\_1$

(1.05414)

(40) $kcar = 0.04766 * k46 - 3773.52 * time + 26462.8$

(4.29413) (1.22762) (0.24432)

$AR\_0 = +0.92602 * AR\_1$

(8.10062)

(41) $m1fuel = 0.51082 * m1fuel_{-1} - 72.7554 * \frac{pmfuel}{pgnp} * 100$

(3.10650) (2.96858)

$+0.02868 * gnp + 7686.79$

(3.22146) (2.22065)

$$(42)\quad mnf = 0.19360 * mnf_{-1} - 229.937 * \frac{pmnf}{pvir} * 100$$

$$(1.40645) \qquad (1.73975)$$

$$+0.49975 * cp + cg + gdcf - 0.35189 * vir - 114115$$

$$(3.79395) \qquad (1.31525) \qquad (2.31529)$$

$$AR\_0 = +0.87186 * AR\_1$$

$$(9.6642)$$

$$(43)\quad msv = 0.75946 * msv_{-1} - 85.6029 * \frac{pmsv}{pser} * 100$$

$$(5.39781) \qquad (2.02514)$$

$$+0.02024 * gnp + 2317.07$$

$$(2.49405) \qquad (0.81195)$$

$$(44)\quad pcg = 0.82228 * pcg_{-1} + 0.33267 * wage - 4.72882$$

$$(8.53269) \qquad (3.45560) \qquad (3.13451)$$

$$(45)\quad pcgov = 1.02647 * wpi + 0.63221$$

$$(66.5757) \qquad (0.51545)$$

$$AR\_0 = +0.37012 * AR\_1$$

$$(1.81454)$$

$$(46)\quad pnfia = 0.05167 * pgnpw * er + 2.14098$$

$$(40.7591) \qquad (1.12609)$$

$$AR\_0 = +0.33070 * AR\_1$$

$$(1.54459)$$

$$(47)\quad pser = 0.30926 * pser_{-1} + 0.66005 * wage - 1.76563$$

$$(1.77637) \qquad (6.31995) \qquad (0.14830)$$

$$AR\_0 = +0.85782 * AR\_1$$

$$(5.02209)$$

(48) $pvir = 29.2254 * wage * \frac{cei}{vir} + 0.04503 * tbill * \frac{k46}{vir}$

$(2.21887) \quad (2.06834)$

$+0.20297 * pm * \frac{import}{vir} + 58.7232$

$(1.21125) \quad (0.57523)$

$AR\_0 = +0.94452 * AR\_1$

(9.6729)

(49) $tbill = 0.39978 * tbill_{-1} - 0.06393 * \frac{tl}{\frac{\frac{pgnp}{100}}{1000}} + 0.03579 * \frac{gnp}{1000}$

$(2.96930) \quad (1.35263) \quad (1.83609)$

$+25.2798 * \frac{er}{er.1} - 28.3436$

$(3.97679) \quad (4.16267)$

(50) $tradet = 0.25666 * pmfuel * \frac{m1fuel}{100} + 0.14663 * pmnf * \frac{mnf}{100}$

$(1.97399) \quad (6.83810)$

$+362.496$

(0.24101)

(51) $vag = 0.62324 * vag_{-1} - 1.65115 * \frac{pfert}{pvag} * 100 - 562.584 * tbill - infl$

$(4.33681) \quad (2.35838) \quad (2.15514)$

$-428.339 * infl + 17.4529 * \frac{caputo}{pcgov} + 1236.42 * time + 41985.6$

$(2.43346) \quad (2.03425) \quad (2.55345) \quad (3.49981)$

(52) $vir = 0.10538 * vir_{-1} - 175.028 * \frac{pvir}{pmnf} * 100 + 0.36881 * cp$

$(1.08440) \quad (1.43464) \quad (9.34550)$

$+cg + gdcf + xnag1 - 169214$

(0.34878)

$AR\_0 = +0.98038 * AR\_1$

(15.1352)

(53) $vser = -314.581 * \frac{pser}{pgnp} * 100 + 0.35791 * cp + cg + export + 41995.7$

(1.18671) (55.5347) (1.56406)

(54) $wage = 0.85090 * wage_{-1} + 0.35799 * cpi - 1.21008 * uera + 7.47607$

(6.40576) (2.62746) (1.70933) (1.34133)

(55) $wpi = 046216 * wpi_{-1} + 0.16147 * wage + 0.46816 * pm + 0.38736 * tbill$

(3.04734) (2.14785) (3.23509) (1.40630)

-10.3060

(4.55178)

(56) $xgds = -7403.28 * \frac{pxgds}{pxw * er} * 100 + 1.04249 * \frac{pgnpw}{pgnp} + 94562.0$

(2.61401) (2.15432) (2.68465)

$AR\_0 = +0.79955 * AR\_1$

(4.68680)

(57) $xsv = 0.36449 * xsv_{-1} - 107.321 * \frac{pxsv}{pgnpw * er} * 100$

(2.12896) (0.07110)

$+0.04750 * xgds + mgds + 0.51585 * gnpw * er * \frac{pgnpw}{pgnp} - 7342.03$

(1.87748) (3.84085) (0.92271)

B Data Base

B.1 List of Variables

Name	Description	Unit	Period	Source
BCURR	Balance of Payments (current account, real)	Mill P.	'67-'91	
BOP	Balance of Payments (overall balance)	Mill $	'67-'91	
CAPOUT	Capital Outlays (cash basis)	Mill P.	'75-'91	
CAPUTO	Capital Outlays (obligation basis)	Mill P.	'69-'91	
CEA	Employment in Agricultural Sector	1000	'67-'90	
CEI	Employment in Industrial Sector	1000	'67-'90	
CES	Employment in Service Sector	1000	'67-'90	
CET	Total Employment ($= CEA + CEI + CES$)	1000	'67-'91	
CG	Government Consumption Expenditures (real)	Mill P.	'67-'91	
CGN	Government Consumption Expenditures	Mill P.	'67-'91	
CGOVN	Government Construction Expenditures	Mill P.	'67-'91	
CGOVN	Government Construction Expenditures	Mill P.	'67-'91	
CGOVN	Government Construction Expenditures	Mill P.	'67-'91	
ONSGO	Government Construction Expenditures (real)	Mill P.	'67-'91	
CONSPR	Private Construction Expenditures (real)	Mill P.	'67-'91	
CONSTOT	Total Construction Expenditures (real) $= CONSGO + CONSPR$	Mill P.	'67-'91	
CONTM	Number of Acceptors of Contraceptive Methods (modern		'67-'88	
CONTO	Number of Acceptors of Contraceptive Methods (old)		'67-'88	
CP	Private Consumption Expenditures (real)	Mill P.	'67-'91	
CPI	Consumer Price Index	'85=100	'67-'91	
CPIJAP	CPI of Japan	'85=100	'67-'91	
CPIUS	CPI of U.S.	'85=100	'67-'91	
D8491	Dummy Variable ('84-'91=1, otherwise=0)		'67-'91	
DEFG	Government Deficit (cash basis) $= EXPN - REVN$	Mill P.	'67-'91	
DOMD	Outstanding Debt of Government from Domestic Sources	Mill P.	'70-'90	
DTAX	Revenues to Direct Taxes	Mill P.	'75-'91	
ER	Nominal Exchange Rate	P/$	'67-'91	
ESCH	Number of Students enrolled in	1000	'70-'87	
ESCH	Number of Students enrolled in Elementary Schools	1000	'70-'87	
EXPN	Government Expenditures	Mill P.	'67-'91	
EXPORT	Exports of Goods & Services (real)	Mill P.	'67-'91	
FERL15	Fertility Rate, Female Age ¡ 15	/1000	'67-'88	NSO
FER1519	Fertility Rate, Female Age 15-19	/1000	'67-'88	NSO
FER2024	Fertility Rate, Female Age 20-24	/1000	'67-'88	NSO
FER2529	Fertility Rate, Female Age 25-29	/1000	'67-'88	NSO
FER3034	Fertility Rate, Female Age 30-34	/1000	'67-'88	NSO
FER3539	Fertility Rate, Female Age 35-39	/1000	'67-'88	NSO
FER4044	Fertility Rate, Female Age 40-44	/1000	'67-'88	NSO
FERG45	Fertility Rate, Female Age 45-	/1000	'67-'88	NSO
FERALL	Fertility Rate, Female All Ages	/1000	'67-'88	NSO
FM	Number of Person Migrating to Other Nations	1000	'67-'98	
FORD	Outstanding Debt of Government from Foreign Sources	Mill P.	'70-'90	

Name	Description	Unit	Period	Source
FTEMPA	Employment in Agricultural Sector (full-time equivalent)	1000	'67-'90	
FTEMPI	Employment in Industrial Sector (full-time equivalent)	1000	'67-'90	
FTEMPS	Employment in Service Sector (full-time equivalent)	1000	'67-'90	
FTEMPT	Total Employment (full-time equivalent)	1000	'67-'90	
GDCF	Gross Domestic Capital Formation (real)	Mill P.	'67-'91	
GDP	Gross Domestic Product (real)	Mill P.	'67-'91	
GDPRUR	Gross Regional Product (Rural Area, real)	Mill P.	'75-'91	
GDPURB	Gross Regional Product (Urban Area, real)	Mill P.	'75-'91	
GEXED	Government Expenditures on Education (real)	Mill P.	'67-'88	
GEXH	Government Expenditures on Health (real)	Mill P.	'67-'90	
GEXHN	Government Expenditures on Health	Mill P.	'67-'90	
GEXO	Other Government Expenditures (real)	Mill P.	'67-'88	
GFA	Gross Foreign Assets (Monetary Authorities)	Mill P.	'70-'91	
GFL	Gross Foreign Liabilities (Monetary Authorities)	Mill P.	'70-'91	
GNP	Gross National Product (real)	Mill P.	'67-'91	
GNPN	Gross National Product	Mill P.	'67-'91	
GNPW	Weighted Average of GNP of U.S. & Japan (real, weights are Philippine's relative export shares to each country) $GNPW = \frac{GNPUS*XUS+GNPJAP*xJAP}{XUS+XJAP}$	Mill $	'67-'91	
GTT	Gains from Terms of Trade (real)	Mill P.	'67-'91	
GTT	Gains from Terms of Trade (real) =EXPORT*(PX/PM-1)	Mill P.	'67-'91	
HFL15	Female Population, Age ; 15	1000	'67-'90	NSO
HF1519	Female Population, Age 15-19	1000	'67-'90	NSO
HF2024	Female Population, Age 20-24	1000	'67-'90	NSO
HF2529	Female Population, AGE 25-29	1000	'67-'90	NSO
HF3034	Female Population, Age 30-34	1000	'67-'90	NSO
HF3539	Female Population, Age 34-39	1000	'67-'90	NSO
HF4044	Female Population, Age 40-44	1000	'67-'90	NSO
HFG45	Female Population, Age 45-	1000	'67-'90	NSO
HFALL	Female Population, All Ages	1000	'67-'90	NSO
HTL1	Population, Age ; 1	1000	'67-'90	NSO
HT14	Population, Age 1-4	1000	'67-'90	NSO
HT59	Population, Age 5-9	1000	'67-'90	NSO
HT1014	Population, Age 10-14	1000	'67-'90	NSO
HT1519	Population, Age 15-19	1000	'67-'90	NSO
HT2024	Population, Age 20-24	1000	'67-'90	NSO
HT2529	Population, Age 25-29	1000	'67-'90	NSO
HT3034	Population, Age 30-34	1000	'67-'90	NSO
HT3539	Population, Age 35-39	1000	'67-'90	NSO
HT4044	Population, Age 40-44	1000	'67-'90	NSO
HT4549	Population, Age 45-49	1000	'67-'90	NSO
HTG50	Population, Age 50-	1000	'67-'90	NSO
HTALL	Total Population, All Ages	1000	'67-'90	NSO
HTG15	Population, Age 15-	1000	'67-'90	NSO
HTRUR	Total Population in Rural Area	1000	'67-'90	NSO
HTURB	Total Population in Urban Area	1000	'67-'90	NSO
IDER	Investment in Durable Equipment (real)	Mill P.	'67-'90	
IG	Government Investment (real)	Mill P.	'75-'91	

Name	Description	Unit	Period	Source
ILTLON	Inflow of Medium- & Long-Term Loan	Mill $	'70-'91	
IMOTHR	Other components of Imports (real)	Mill P.	'70-'91	
IMPORT	Imports of Goods & Services (real)	Mill P.	'67-'91	
INFL	Inflation Rate	%	'67-'91	
INFMORT	Infant Mortality	/1000	'67-'90	NSO
INTPAY	Interest Payments on Government Debt	Mill P.	'75-'91	
IP	Private Investments (real)	Mill P.	'75-'91	
K45	Capital Stock (real)	Mill P.	'67-'91	
KCAR	Capital Consumption Allowance (real)	Mill P.	'67-'91	
LF	Labor Force	1000	'67-'91	
LIBO	London Interbank Offer Rates on US Dollar Deposits (three month)	%/year	'67-'91	
LIF1014	Female Literacy Rate, Age 10-14	/1000	'67-'90	
LIF1519	Female Literacy Rate, Age 15-19	/1000	'67-'90	
LIF2024	Female Literacy Rate, Age 20-24	/1000	'67-'90	
LIF2529	Female Literacy Rate, Age 25-29	/1000	'67-'90	
LIF3034	Female Literacy Rate, Age 30-34	/1000	'67-'90	
LIF3539	Female Literacy Rate, Age 35-39	/1000	'67-'90	
LIF4044	Female Literacy Rate, Age 40-44	/1000	'67-'90	
LIFG45	Female Literacy Rate, Age 45-	/1000	'67-'90	
LIFG15	Female Literacy Rate, Age 15-	/1000	'67-'90	
LIT1014	Literacy Rate, Age 10-14	/1000	'67-'90	
LIT1519	Literacy Rate, Age 15-19	/1000	'67-'90	
LIT2024	Literacy Rate, Age 20-24	/1000	'67-'90	
LIT2529	Literacy Rate, Age 25-29	/1000	'67-'90	
LIT3034	Literacy Rate, Age 30-34	/1000	'67-'90	
LIT3539	Literacy Rate, Age 35-39	/1000	'67-'90	
LIT4044	Literacy Rate, Age 40-44	/1000	'67-'90	
LIT4549	Literacy Rate, Age 45-49	/1000	'67-'90	
LITG50	Literacy Rate, Age 50-	/1000	'67-'90	
LITG15	Literacy Rate, Age 15-	/1000	'67-'90	
LRUR	Total Employed Rural Labor Force	1000	'67-'90	
LURB	Total Employed Urban Labor Force	1000	'67-'90	
M1Fuel	Imports of Fuel Products (real)	Mill P.	'67-'91	
M2MACH	Imports of Electrical Supplies Machinery & Transport Equip. (real	Mill P.	'67-'91	
M3BM	Imports of Basic Metals (real)	Mill P.	'67-'91	
M4CD	Imports of Cereals (real)	Mill P.	'67-'91	
M5CHEM	Imports of Chemicals (real)	Mill P.	'67-'91	
M7TEXT	Imports of Textile Yarns (real)	Mill P.	'67-'91	
METCR		Mill P.	'67-'91	
MB	Monetary Base ($= NDA + NFA$)	Mill P.	'70-'91	
MB1	Monetary Base ($= NDA + NFA1$)	Mill P.	'70-'91	
MGDA	Imports of Goods (real)	Mill P.	'67-'91	
MNF	Imports of Non-Fuel Products (real)	Mill P.	'67-'91	
MSV	Imports of Services (real)	Mill P.	'67-'91	
MULT	Money Multiplier ($= \frac{TL}{MB}$)		'70-'91	
MULT1	Money Multiplier ($= \frac{TL}{MB1}$)		'70-'91	
MORT01	Mortality Rate, Age ¡ 1	/1000	'67-'90	NSO
MORT14	Mortality Rate, Age 1-4	/1000	'67-'90	NSO
MORT59	Mortality Rate, Age 5-9	/1000	'67-'90	NSO
MORT1014	Mortality Rate, Age 10-14	/1000	'67-'90	NSO
MORT1519	Mortality Rate, Age 15-19	/1000	'67-'90	NSO
MORT2024	Mortality Rate, Age 20-24	/1000	'67-'90	NSO

Name	Description	Unit	Period	Source
MORT2529	Mortality Rate, Age 25-29	/1000	'67-'90	NSO
MORT3034	Mortality Rate, Age 30-34	/1000	'67-'90	NSO
MORT3539	Mortality Rate, Age 35-39	/1000	'67-'90	NSO
MORT4044	Mortality Rate, Age 40-44	/1000	'67-'90	NSO
MORT4549	Mortality Rate, Age 45-49	/1000	'67-'90	NSO
MORTG50	Mortality Rate, Age 50-	/1000	'67-'90	NSO
MORTALL	Mortality Rate, All Ages	/1000	'67-'90	NSO
NDA	Net Domestic Asset	Mill P.	'70-'91	
NETLEN	Government's Net Lending to Other Sectors	Mill P.	'70-'91	
NFA	Net Foreign Asset (constructed)	Mill P.	'70-'91	
	$= GFA + GFL$			
	$= GFA + GFL$			
NFA1	Net Foreign Asset	Mill P.	'70-'91	
NFIA	Net Factor Income from Abroad	Mill P.	'67-'91	
NTAXRE	Non-Tax Revenue	Mill P.	'67-'91	
OGDCF	Other Components of GDCF	Mill P.	'67-'91	
OPEXP	Government's Operational Expenditures	Mill P.	'75-'91	
OTHBOP	Other Components of BOP	Mill $	'67-'91	
OTHNDA	Other Components of NDA	Mill P.	'70-'91	
PCG	Implicit Price Deflator (IPD) for CG	'85=100	'67-'91	
PCGOV	IPD for CGOVN	'85=100	'67-'91	
PFERT	Weighted Average of Fertilizer Price	P./Kg	'70-'91	
PGDCF	IPD for GDCF	'85=100	'67-'91	
PGDP	IPD for GDP	'85=100	'67-'91	
PGNP	IPD for GNP	'85=100	'67-'91	
PGNPW	IPD for GNPW	'85=100	'67-'91	
	$= \frac{PGNPUS*XUS+PGNPJAP*XJAP}{XUS+XJAP}$			
PM	IPD for Imports of Goods & Services	'85=100	'67-'91	
PMFUEL	IPD for M1FUEL	'85=100	'67-'91	
PMMACH	IPD for M2MACH	'85=100	'67-'91	
PMBM	IPD for M3BM	'85=100	'67-'91	
PMCD	IPD for M4CD	'85=100	'67-'91	
PMCHEM	IPD for M5CHEM	'85=100	'67-'91	
PMTEXT	IPD for M7TEXT	'85=100	'67-'91	
PMETC	IPD for METCR	'85=100	'67-'91	
PMOTHER	IPD for IMOTHR	'85=100	'67-'91	
PMDOL	Implicit Dollar Prices for IMPORT	$ CA/P NIA	'67-'91	
PMFDOL	Implicit Dollar Price Index for M1FUEL	PMFUEL/ER	'67-'91	
PMNFDOL	Implicit Dollar Price Index for MNF	PMNF/ER	'67-'91	
PMGDS	IPD for MGDS	'85=100	'67-'91	
PMNF	IPD for MNF	'85=100	'67-'91	
PMSV	IPD for MSV	'85=100	'67-'91	
PNFIA	IPD for NFIA	'85=100	'67-'91	
POP	Total Population	1000	'67-'91	
POP15	Population Age 15 and over	1000	'67-'91	
PSER	Price Index for VSER	'85=100	'67-'91	
PVAG	Price Index for VAG	'85=100	'67-'91	
PVIR	Price Index for VIR	'85=100	'67-'91	
PX	IPD for EXPORT	'85=100	'67-'91	
PXAG	IPD for XAG	'85=100	'67-'91	
PXDOL	Implicit Dollar Price Index for EXPORT	$ CA/P NIA	'67-'91	
PXGDS	IPD for XGDS	'85=100	'67-'91	
PXNAG	IPD for XNAG	'85=100	'67-'91	

Name	Description	Unit	Period	Source
PXNAG1	IPD for XNAG1	'85=100	'67-'91	
PXOGDS	IPD for XOGDS	'85=100	'67-'91	
PXSV	IPD for XSV	'85=100	'67-'91	
PXW	Weighted Average of Imports Price Index of U.S. & Japan (weights are relative exports shares of Philippines to each country) shares of Philippines to each country) $= \frac{PMUS*XUS+PMJAP*XJAP}{XUS+XJAP}$	'85=100	'67-'91	
REVN	Total Revenues	Mill P.	'67-'91	
SP	Private Savings (real)	Mill P.	'67-'91	
STATD	Statistical Discrepancies in GNP	Mill P.	'67-'91	
TBILL	Average Interest Rates (91-day Treasury Bill)	%	'67-'91	
TIME	Time Trend Variable		'67-'91	
TL	Total Liquidity (end of the year)	Mill P.	'67-'91	
TOTTAX	Total Taxes	Mill P.	'67-'91	
TRADET	Taxes on International Trade and Related Activities	Mill P.	'75-'91	
UERA	Unemployment Rate	%	'67-'91	
USUEMP	Unemployment Rate of U.S.	%	'67-'91	
USWAGN	Wage Rate of U.S.		'67-'91	
USWAGRX	Wage Rate Index of U.S. (real, deflated by CPIUS)	'85=100	'67-'91	
VAG	Gross Value Added (GVA) in Agricultural Sector (real)	Mill P.	'67-'91	
VIR	GVA in Industrial Sector (real)	Mill P.	'67-'91	
VSER	GVA in Service Sector (real)	Mill P.	'67-'91	
WAGE	Wage Rate Index of Unskilled Labor	'85=100	'67-'91	
WAGER	Wage Rate Index (real, deflated by CPI)	'85=100	'67-'91	
WPI	Wholesale Price Index	'85=100	'67-'91	
XAG	Exports of Agricultural Products (real)	Mill P.	'67-'91	
XGDS	Exports of Goods (real)	Mill P.	'67-'91	
XGDS	Exports of Goods (real)	Mill P.	'67-'91	
XNAG	Exports of Non-Agricultural Products (real)	Mill P.	'67-'91	
XNAG1	Exports of Non-Agricultural Products (real) $= XNAG + XOGDS$	Mill P.	'67-'91	
XOGDS	Exports of Other Goods	Mill P.	'67-'91	
XSV	Exports of Services (real)	Mill P.	'67-'91	
TD	Disposable Income (real)	Mill P.	'67-'91	

B.2 Data

year	BCURR	BOP	CAPOUT	CAPUTO	CEA	CEI	CES	CET
1967	-20320	-56	0	0	6567	1673	3122	11362
1968	-32401	-101	0	0	6459	1648	3088	11195
1969	-36873	-76	0	579	6171	1678	3110	10959
1970	-25176	23	0	699	5371	1765	3133	10269
1971	-20344	6	0	772	5768	1887	3942	11597
1972	-14466	84	0	1010	6590	1831	3674	12095
1973	-4561	674	0	1745	6880	1829	3798	12507
1974	-24548	108	0	3915	7266	1806	3980	13052
1975	-30919	-519	3441	6760	7361	2002	4728	13641
1976	-25890	-158	4540	6606	7392	2076	4424	13892
1977	-18104	137	5047	6625	6881	2165	4712	13758
1978	-25298	-91	6772	8622	7582	2239	4902	14723
1979	-37585	-578	8351	11358	8318	2438	5062	15818
1980	-25897	-353	12927	12478	8358	2500	5325	16813
1981	-11020	-547	20760	18975	8447	2364	5646	16457
1982	-38206	-1671	18646	14934	8699	2390	5727	16816
1983	-28823	-2118	16148	15479	8692	2463	5901	17056
1984	-229	243	19630	16655	8760	2640	6241	17641
1985	-3984	2301	23149	15758	8797	2542	6501	17840
1986	10184	1242	28428	22039	9382	2566	6904	18852
1987	-17621	264	17327	20261	9600	2876	7437	19913
1988	-22530	650	18485	18238	9835	3343	7991	21169
1989	-36299	451	25526	27363	9869	3457	8478	21804
1990	-47790	-185	36255	38235	10152	3454	8926	22532
1991	-22434	1405	44900	54600	0	0	0	22181

year	CG	CGN	CGOVN	CONSGO	CONSPR	CONSTOT	CONTM
1967	21301	2669	479	6598	24525	31123	0.2
1968	22796	2969	542	6810	21378	28188	2.0
1969	24151	3256	838	9841	20633	30504	3.8
1970	25712	3664	409	4405	20232	24637	5.6
1971	28150	4456	562	5576	18935	24511	7.4
1972	31822	5486	994	9183	19255	28438	9.2
1973	35567	6498	1277	10505	18955	29460	11.0
1974	40800	9298	2443	13393	18533	31926	11.7
1975	43940	11591	3836	20372	28706	49078	12.4
1976	44865	13729	7385	35902	33247	69149	13.1
1977	45283	14962	8587	38028	35414	73442	13.8
1978	46644	16820	9193	39136	36140	75276	14.5
1979	48368	19042	12256	44518	39622	84140	15.2
1980	50177	22098	11254	29813	49944	79757	15.9
1981	48675	24659	17616	40385	50736	91121	16.6
1982	52328	28927	20151	41117	51761	92878	17.3
1983	49854	30551	29016	51539	59130	110669	18.0
1984	43971	36878	42825	49241	41243	90484	18.6
1985	43520	43520	27985	27985	28907	56892	19.2
1986	43669	48429	22965	22114	30263	52377	19.8
1987	45792	57332	22390	19248	36000	55248	20.4
1988	49943	72183	25619	20182	39072	59254	21.0
1989	52755	85373	32366	24334	45430	69764	0.0
1990	57640	107331	37327	24504	41992	66496	0.0
1991	54148	116911	48928	28002	29715	57717	0.0

(continued)

year	CONTO	CP	CPI	CPIJAP	CPIUS	D8491	DEFG	DOMD	DTAX
1967	14.2	224264	8.580	30.940	31.020	0	236	0	0
1968	14.0	234656	8.760	32.600	32.330	0	262	0	0
1969	13.8	243961	8.870	34.310	34.080	0	996	0	0
1970	13.6	251195	10.190	36.940	36.090	0	-59	3861	0
1971	13.4	259689	12.420	39.280	37.620	0	183	4131	0
1972	13.2	268257	13.440	40.210	38.870	0	1101	5608	0
1973	13.0	283704	15.660	45.990	41.280	0	843	7294	0
1974	13.1	297568	21.010	56.660	45.840	0	-445	9396	0
1975	13.2	311848	22.430	63.320	50.130	0	1403	10991	6891
1976	13.3	327436	24.500	69.260	52.900	0	2349	12816	9156
1977	13.4	344706	26.930	74.910	56.330	0	2853	14784	10672
1978	13.5	362676	28.900	78.060	60.630	0	2167	15571	12610
1979	13.6	380263	33.670	80.970	67.470	0	342	16191	16477
1980	13.7	397404	39.600	87.230	76.580	0	3387	18534	18942
1981	13.8	407958	44.500	91.550	84.480	0	12146	23227	20292
1982	13.9	422067	49.040	94.060	89.680	0	14404	31772	21704
1983	14.0	424634	54.030	95.830	92.570	0	7431	42639	23360
1984	14.2	425767	81.230	98.000	96.560	1	10065	61350	32933
1985	14.4	420832	100.000	100.000	100.000	1	11141	79940	44471
1986	14.6	434815	100.750	100.620	101.860	1	31252	116236	47995
1987	14.8	452386	104.570	100.650	105.670	1	16693	224697	59931
1988	15.0	480562	113.730	101.400	109.910	1	23206	260359	65338
1989	0.0	504619	125.790	103.720	115.210	1	19568	284073	84087
1990	0.0	531772	141.730	106.940	121.430	1	37194	293821	105752
1991	0.0	543719	166.800	110.400	126.600	1	26331	0	117000

year	ER	ESCH	EXPN	EXPORT	FERL15	FER1519	FER2024	FER2529
1967	3.915800	0	3812	60123	0.030	42.078	143.029	196.458
1968	3.915800	0	4318	53344	0.033	36.076	157.118	203.118
1969	3.919100	0	5506	51012	0.037	38.934	155.332	194.902
1970	6.024600	6856	4790	61526	0.051	39.568	152.215	178.841
1971	6.431700	6969	6052	63626	0.158	41.063	151.591	169.644
1972	6.674799	7002	8073	71572	0.256	42.028	153.125	161.788
1973	6.756299	7015	10342	83058	0.081	41.415	158.566	173.216
1974	6.787899	7269	11712	73581	0.039	42.112	162.868	179.755
1975	7.247900	7453	18259	76181	0.088	45.396	174.793	209.876
1976	7.440299	7682	20438	85954	0.075	46.983	184.598	216.733
1977	7.402800	7719	22811	100062	0.097	45.945	181.567	218.353
1978	7.365799	7893	26420	106121	0.059	47.000	182.327	218.451
1979	7.377600	8179	29812	110678	0.059	45.912	181.673	224.087
1980	7.511400	8227	38118	154748	0.095	44.484	189.134	213.339
1981	7.899700	8290	48079	169354	0.097	45.700	225.201	207.626
1982	8.539999	8518	52610	151489	0.038	45.055	179.249	202.340
1983	11.11270	8591	53063	158252	0.040	44.972	178.145	198.309
1984	16.69869	8717	66926	164327	0.052	43.432	168.215	187.872
1985	18.60729	8794	80102	137030	0.039	43.595	160.465	203.594
1986	20.38570	8897	110497	160453	0.040	44.159	165.639	181.993
1987	20.56769	9230	119907	170889	0.048	45.706	170.199	186.710
1988	21.09700	0	136067	195997	0.039	42.605	163.887	181.709
1989	21.71999	0	171978	216980	0.000	0.000	0.000	0.000
1990	24.29000	0	218035	219703	0.000	0.000	0.000	0.000
1991	27.76000	0	247118	229822	0.000	0.000	0.000	0.000

(continued)

year	FER3034	FER3539	FER4044	FERG45	FERAIL	FM	FORD	FTEMPA
1967	170.404	140.928	53.325	2.956	48.923	20	0	5862
1968	175.787	143.185	58.819	3.070	50.524	24	0	5178
1969	173.879	143.706	59.730	2.915	52.326	28	0	5043
1970	169.703	136.240	62.134	2.783	52.536	32	1105	4932
1971	157.508	127.504	56.335	2.754	50.713	36	1388	5187
1972	147.844	119.605	52.868	2.756	49.392	40	1755	5754
1973	155.427	125.966	53.932	3.002	52.040	52	1999	6088
1974	155.123	124.631	51.234	2.701	52.036	64	2640	6530
1975	168.796	140.204	53.958	3.504	57.519	76	5928	6544
1976	171.781	140.733	56.971	3.301	60.097	88	6053	6784
1977	170.463	140.225	56.464	3.144	60.407	100	8510	4901
1978	172.859	136.173	55.604	4.015	61.270	98	12266	5560
1979	176.303	134.388	54.657	3.156	62.082	96	20829	5573
1980	175.747	121.079	56.088	3.224	60.323	94	22569	5640
1981	167.336	113.651	52.777	3.015	60.293	92	29992	5681
1982	163.177	109.923	52.345	2.713	58.273	90	40118	5854
1983	160.053	108.875	51.207	2.875	58.073	90	41784	5978
1984	151.418	103.434	47.993	2.917	55.847	90	97996	5687
1985	137.447	100.110	41.522	3.431	55.063	90	107992	5637
1986	138.535	98.064	39.988	2.559	53.662	90	123540	8208
1987	142.523	101.392	41.198	2.507	55.389	90	155308	8679
1988	136.761	96.885	40.767	2.226	53.548	108	165539	8772
1989	0.000	0.000	0.000	0.000	0.000	126	176037	8804
1990	0.000	0.000	0.000	0.000	0.000	144	258820	10027
1991	0.000	0.000	0.000	0.000	0.000	0	0	0

year	FTEMPI	FTEMPS	FTEMPT	GDCF	GDP	GDPRUR	GDPURB	GEXED
1967	1538	3128	10528	66554	301106	0	0	7046
1968	1453	2980	9611	67130	316000	0	0	7508
1969	1403	2840	9286	70486	330707	0	0	8029
1970	1560	2900	9392	67205	343163	0	0	8022
1971	1749	3974	10910	71218	361792	0	0	7722
1972	1645	3764	11163	73777	381499	0	0	8144
1973	1671	3919	11678	81960	415525	0	0	7651
1974	1673	4019	12222	98526	430313	0	0	6411
1975	1833	4254	12631	121931	454264	254388	199876	7567
1976	1975	4369	13128	144607	494262	270856	223406	8087
1977	2003	4430	11334	145890	521952	279767	242185	8092
1978	2126	4787	12473	156850	548947	287648	261299	9691
1979	2130	4525	12228	174156	579910	296914	282996	9379
1980	2034	4758	12432	161070	609768	304885	304883	9645
1981	2057	5114	12852	165659	630642	307751	322891	10882
1982	2074	5198	13126	179574	653467	311049	342418	15116
1983	2123	5326	13427	190243	665717	308893	356824	9764
1984	2275	5513	13475	127564	616962	278865	338097	7970
1985	2144	5600	13381	87697	571883	251627	320256	8269
1986	2249	6024	16499	94925	591423	260227	331196	11346
1987	2457	6622	17758	111588	619707	272670	347037	14464
1988	2874	7108	18754	124504	658463	288750	369713	15805
1989	3110	7493	19407	153887	698382	304130	394252	0
1990	3732	8723	22482	162645	715152	313952	401200	0
1991	0	0	0	139913	707858	311458	396400	0

(continued)

year	GEXH	GEXHN	GEXO	GFA	GFL	GNP	GNPN	GNPW
1967	1291	114	12964	0	0	297955	26305	1564.206
1968	1526	143	13762	0	0	312431	29279	1672.320
1969	1840	182	14282	0	0	327802	32418	1652.280
1970	1978	226	15712	1180	1810	336797	38472	1598.684
1971	1727	226	18701	1780	2130	357699	46803	1716.940
1972	2017	281	21661	2770	1770	377715	52633	1874.820
1973	2192	358	25724	7050	1980	414602	67725	1911.361
1974	2173	473	32216	10630	3400	432048	94048	1980.804
1975	2795	665	51852	10210	6990	453094	107815	1707.788
1976	3219	829	55630	12540	8650	490074	126228	2173.635
1977	3439	957	56104	11860	5670	518440	144282	2323.985
1978	3149	962	62633	14570	9620	546777	167036	2498.968
1979	3443	1214	65880	18680	15810	58171	205087	2438.275
1980	3467	1398	71309	23610	24670	608600	245388	2375.879
1981	3859	1746	91527	21120	31190	628325	284267	2628.183
1982	4279	2095	70979	15690	42800	646186	316351	2518.563
1983	4200	2341	64572	12110	72990	655483	365346	2786.190
1984	2717	2321	55855	17690	105350	598340	511056	3004.899
1985	2741	2741	55659	20650	138690	556074	556074	3094.105
1986	3179	3270	56518	51420	184710	579175	595737	3403.639
1987	3641	4020	42583	41880	174130	608729	672032	3660.261
1988	4487	5447	44213	45040	166620	652293	791939	3880.215
1989	4730	6227	0	53230	161460	689693	915326	3942.907
1990	5066	7646	0	57610	198160	716807	1081803	3985.149
1991	0	0	0	122430	190980	716455	1261383	4067.561

year	GTT	HFL15	HF1519	HF2024	HF2529	HF3034	HF3539	HF4044
1967	14692	7974	1802	1472	1208	996	822	689
1968	17826	8268	1868	1528	1249	1029	849	708
1969	19339	7975	1905	1659	1351	1078	889	720
1970	20750	7681	1941	1790	1452	1126	928	731
1971	16322	7945	1977	1821	1516	1186	965	767
1972	11496	8208	2013	1852	1579	1246	1002	803
1973	24788	8462	2167	1930	1590	1251	1019	851
1974	16331	8715	2320	2009	1602	1255	1036	898
1975	5865	8969	2474	2087	1613	1260	1053	946
1976	-3609	9152	2515	2156	1695	1320	1088	963
1977	-44	9213	2585	2237	1742	1349	1100	993
1978	930	9275	2655	2317	1789	1379	1111	1023
1979	10728	9336	2725	2398	1836	1408	1123	1053
1980	-6236	9903	2762	2389	1944	1485	1197	1046
1981	-13291	10061	2745	2013	2034	1561	1236	1063
1982	-9540	10227	2786	2519	2121	1645	1280	1092
1983	-22114	10399	2825	2575	2205	1734	1332	1111
1984	-23741	10465	2864	2626	2284	1825	1391	1138
1985	0	10754	2906	2674	2108	1915	1458	1171
1986	1844	10933	2951	2717	2426	2004	1534	1209
1987	9777	11110	3001	2758	2487	2091	1617	1253
1988	27343	11284	3055	2797	2543	2173	1705	1304
1989	13328	11465	3109	2838	2604	2265	1800	1355
1990	4848	11649	3164	2880	2667	2360	1900	1408
1991	21874	0	0	0	0	0	0	0

(continued)

year	HFG45	HFALL	HTL1	HT14	HT59	HT1014	HT1519	HT2024
1967	2213	17176	772	5867	5198	4379	3668	2984
1967	2213	17176	772	5867	5198	4379	3668	2984
1968	2286	17785	807	6078	5422	4498	3804	3100
1969	2520	18094	859	5639	5413	4399	3739	3232
1970	2753	18402	896	5215	5404	4299	3674	3364
1971	2828	19004	906	5413	5507	4512	3798	3427
1972	2903	19606	903	5625	5601	4725	3922	3490
1973	2894	20163	937	5692	5750	4986	4285	3678
1974	2884	20720	993	5737	5890	5248	4649	3866
1975	2875	21277	1087	5744	6030	5509	5012	4054
1976	2990	21879	1199	5819	6147	5601	5101	4221
1977	3044	22263	1254	5618	6205	5816	5646	4394
1978	3098	22647	1291	5436	6263	6031	5391	4567
1979	3152	23031	1336	5246	6321	6246	5536	4740
1980	3425	24151	1375	6245	6635	5977	5280	4609
1981	3522	24235	1394	6372	6791	6095	5408	4733
1982	3633	25303	1405	6218	6965	6208	5540	3830
1983	3758	25939	1427	6439	7154	6334	5674	4973
1984	3876	26469	1432	6437	7253	6448	5804	5094
1985	3114	26100	1402	6528	7537	6586	5929	5218
1986	4067	27841	1412	6649	7698	6753	6047	5346
1987	4253	28570	1437	6696	7669	6919	6161	5478
1988	4372	29233	1525	6717	7717	7105	6276	5612
1989	4536	29972	1548	6842	7750	7305	6401	5742
1990	4706	30735	1592	6879	7480	7489	6451	5867
1991	0	0	0	0	0	0	0	0

year	HT2529	HT3034	HT3539	HT4044	HT4549	HTG50	HTALL	HTG15
1967	2434	2000	1648	1376	1165	3165	34656	18440
1968	2520	2067	1702	1415	1194	3276	35883	19078
1969	2696	2174	1801	1456	1236	3593	36237	19927
1970	2872	2281	1900	1497	1278	3910	36590	20776
1971	2966	2391	1972	1549	1306	4070	37816	21477
1972	3060	2500	2043	1601	1333	4229	39041	22178
1973	3081	2478	2044	1690	1372	4205	40200	22834
1974	3102	2457	2045	1779	1412	4182	41358	23491
1975	3123	2435	2046	1868	1451	4158	42517	24147
1976	3283	2551	2111	1894	1518	4306	43751	24985
1977	3397	2640	2155	1969	1556	4443	44694	25800
1978	3512	2728	2200	2043	1594	4581	45637	26616
1979	3626	2817	2244	2118	1632	4718	46580	27431
1980	3872	3012	2430	2087	1668	5046	48236	28004
1981	4020	3159	2511	2145	1731	5178	49537	28885
1982	4159	3320	2602	2197	1804	5312	49560	28764
1983	4290	3487	2706	2247	1880	5454	52065	30711
1984	4418	3652	2854	2304	1956	5605	53257	31687
1985	4543	3809	2955	2372	2021	5769	54669	32616
1986	4667	3956	3000	2452	2128	5946	56054	33542
1987	4787	4095	3259	2546	2129	6136	57359	34591
1988	4908	4226	3424	2646	2662	6136	58954	35890
1989	5028	4353	3588	2761	2235	6541	60094	36649
1990	5152	4458	3744	2891	2303	6750	61146	37706
1991	0	0	0	0	0	7001	62870	39109

(continued)

year	HTRUR	HTURB	IDER	IG	ILTLON	IMOTHR	IMPORT	INFL
1967	23971	10685	23278	0	0	9701	77292	7.654
1967	23971	10685	23278	0	0	9701	77292	7.654
1968	24690	11193	26511	0	0	7908	82176	2.098
1969	24802	11434	26283	0	0	6828	84980	1.256
1970	24912	11678	26909	0	401	2300	80336	14.882
1971	25610	12206	31270	0	285	4258	79877	21.884
1972	26439	12602	29309	0	372	3834	82254	8.213
1973	27079	13121	30271	0	380	6087	86696	16.518
1974	27744	13614	38175	0	450	8171	99864	34.164
1975	28470	14047	45636	18374	677	12549	105930	6.759
1976	28878	14873	44264	22071	1407	10246	107656	9.229
1977	29075	15619	43183	22352	1242	13176	114654	9.918
1978	29234	16403	49659	28829	1850	17712	129249	7.315
1979	29354	17226	55473	30334	2110	28562	150065	16.505
1980	30214	18022	60077	34244	1579	43136	179477	17.612
1981	30857	18680	66704	47593	2072	51426	178057	12.374
1982	30130	19430	73793	38045	2533	47432	182414	10.202
1983	31862	20203	71108	28682	2336	41466	176841	10.175
1984	32256	21001	45043	22571	1259	39168	145934	50.342
1985	32847	21822	33261	23149	3962	30923	125205	23.107
1986	33389	22665	37827	27374	2545	37701	138021	0.750
1987	33829	23530	40124	14896	2437	49375	177532	3.792
1988	34538	24416	49635	14562	2412	62299	212357	8.760
1989	34772	25322	65760	19191	2824	60933	244590	10.604
1990	34900	26246	76976	23800	4398	72100	269148	12.672
1991	0	0	70047	25697	3440	90067	260853	17.689

year	INFMORT	INTPAY	IP	K46	KCAR	LF	LIBO	LIF1014
1967	72.240	0	0	718186	10783	12344	5.46	84.79
1968	70.986	0	0	773318	11998	12142	6.36	86.16
1969	67.303	0	0	830455	13349	11747	9.76	87.53
1970	59.963	0	0	882807	14853	11126	8.52	88.90
1971	61.977	0	0	937499	16526	12231	6.58	88.21
1972	67.865	0	0	992888	18388	12913	5.37	87.52
1973	74.223	0	0	1054388	20460	13137	9.42	86.83
1974	58.887	0	0	1130149	22765	13604	10.90	86.14
1975	53.327	624	103657	1226751	25329	14194	6.95	85.45
1976	56.882	743	122536	1343175	28183	14826	5.57	84.76
1977	56.758	898	123538	1457707	31538	15135	6.05	84.07
1978	53.071	1136	128021	1579667	34890	16255	8.85	83.38
1979	50.197	1841	143822	1715002	38821	17027	12.09	82.69
1980	45.097	2296	126826	1832878	43194	17572	14.19	82.00
1981	44.084	2429	118066	1950477	48060	18075	16.87	82.69
1982	41.821	3560	141529	2078647	51404	18562	13.29	83.38
1983	42.664	4996	161561	2212638	56252	19035	9.72	84.07
1984	38.491	10409	104993	2279748	60454	19690	10.94	84.75
1985	38.001	14652	64548	2310771	56674	20481	8.40	85.44
1986	34.982	20953	67551	2347239	58457	21368	6.86	86.13
1987	32.104	36929	96692	2401039	57788	22594	7.18	86.82
1988	30.144	44443	109942	2469700	55843	23449	7.98	87.51
1989	26.786	54700	134696	2569098	54489	24120	9.28	88.20
1990	24.074	72800	138845	2677592	54151	25290	8.31	88.88
1991	0.000	74900	114822	2761871	55633	25211	5.99	0.00

(continued)

year	LIF1519	LIF2024	LIF2529	LIF3034	LIF3539	LIF4044	LIFG45	LIFG15
1967	91.22	88.41	85.20	81.32	76.75	72.19	53.24	76.90
1968	91.88	89.34	86.38	82.70	78.29	73.88	54.63	77.98
1969	92.54	90.27	87.56	84.07	79.82	75.56	56.02	79.06
1970	93.20	91.20	88.73	85.45	81.35	77.25	57.41	80.14
1971	93.17	91.27	88.87	85.67	81.66	77.65	57.95	80.43
1972	93.14	91.34	89.01	85.88	81.96	78.04	58.49	80.71
1973	93.11	91.41	89.14	86.10	82.27	78.44	59.03	81.00
1974	93.08	91.48	89.28	86.31	82.57	78.83	59.58	81.28
1975	93.05	91.55	89.42	86.53	82.88	79.23	60.12	81.57
1976	93.02	91.62	89.55	86.74	83.18	79.62	60.66	81.85
1977	92.99	91.69	89.69	86.96	83.49	80.02	61.20	82.14
1978	92.96	91.76	89.83	87.17	83.79	80.41	61.74	82.43
1979	92.93	91.83	89.96	87.39	84.10	80.81	62.29	82.71
1980	92.90	91.90	90.10	87.60	84.40	81.20	62.83	83.00
1981	93.10	92.15	90.49	88.19	85.15	81.93	64.31	83.65
1982	93.29	92.41	90.89	88.79	85.89	82.65	65.79	84.30
1983	93.49	92.66	91.28	89.38	86.64	83.38	67.27	84.95
1984	93.69	92.92	91.67	89.98	87.39	84.10	68.75	85.60
1985	93.89	93.17	92.07	90.57	88.14	84.83	70.23	86.25
1986	94.08	93.43	92.46	91.17	88.88	85.55	71.70	86.90
1987	94.28	93.68	92.85	91.76	89.63	86.28	73.18	87.55
1988	94.48	93.93	93.25	92.36	90.38	87.00	74.66	88.20
1989	94.68	94.19	93.64	92.95	91.12	87.73	76.14	88.85
1990	94.87	94.44	94.03	93.55	91.87	88.45	77.62	89.50
1991	0.00	0.00	0.00	0.00	0.00	0.00	0.00	0.00

Year	LIT1014	LIT1519	LIT2024	LIT2529	LIT3034	LIT3539	LIT4044	LIT4549
1967	82.98	90.48	89.43	86.28	82.81	79.00	74.96	70.69
1968	84.42	91.22	90.12	87.27	84.03	80.41	76.40	72.00
1969	85.86	91.96	90.81	88.25	85.25	81.82	77.84	73.31
1970	87.30	92.70	91.50	89.23	86.48	83.23	79.28	74.63
1971	86.56	92.64	91.49	89.29	86.55	83.28	79.36	74.81
1972	85.82	92.58	91.48	89.35	86.63	83.33	79.45	74.99
1973	85.08	92.52	91.47	89.40	86.71	83.38	79.54	75.17
1974	84.34	92.46	91.46	89.46	86.79	83.44	79.63	75.36
1975	83.60	92.40	91.45	89.52	86.86	83.49	79.71	75.54
1976	82.86	92.34	91.44	89.57	86.94	83.54	79.80	75.72
1977	82.12	92.28	91.43	89.63	87.02	83.59	79.89	75.90
1978	81.38	92.22	91.42	89.69	87.10	83.65	79.98	76.09
1979	80.64	92.16	91.41	89.74	87.17	83.70	80.06	76.27
1980	79.90	92.10	91.40	89.80	87.25	83.75	80.15	76.45
1981	0.00	92.36	91.70	90.18	87.81	84.49	80.94	77.38
1982	0.00	92.61	91.99	90.56	88.36	85.24	81.73	78.31
1983	0.00	92.87	92.29	90.94	88.92	85.98	82.51	79.24
1984	0.00	93.13	92.58	91.32	89.47	86.73	83.30	80.17
1985	0.00	93.39	92.88	91.70	90.03	87.47	84.09	81.10
1986	0.00	93.64	93.17	92.08	90.58	88.22	84.88	82.03
1987	0.00	93.90	93.47	92.46	91.14	88.96	85.67	82.96
1988	0.00	94.16	93.77	92.84	91.69	89.70	86.46	83.89
1989	0.00	94.42	94.06	93.22	92.25	90.45	87.24	84.82
1990	0.00	94.67	94.36	93.60	92.81	91.19	88.03	85.03
1991	0.00	0.00	0.00	0.00	0.00	0.00	0.00	0.00

(continued)

year	LITG50	LITG15	LRUR	LURB	MIFUEL	M2MACH	M3BM	M4CD
1967	56.77	79.40	7608	3587	22677	16956	5861	2876
1968	58.41	80.45	7488	3471	27920	18635	6087	1566
1969	60.04	81.51	7208	3061	28666	20074	6459	1474
1970	61.68	82.56	6415	5182	32265	17804	6419	1214
1971	61.83	82.64	7082	5013	31860	16383	4507	2423
1972	61.99	82.73	7815	4692	31700	18219	5563	3093
1973	62.14	82.81	8146	4906	32111	14916	5304	2546
1974	62.29	82.89	8593	5048	32765	22443	6923	1749
1975	62.45	82.98	8787	5105	32711	28690	4872	2394
1976	62.60	83.06	8867	4891	34920	26121	6598	2466
1977	62.76	83.14	8452	6271	35825	24643	7786	2389
1978	62.91	83.23	9216	6602	36384	30357	8132	2717
1979	63.07	83.31	10005	6178	37901	33514	9824	3059
1980	63.22	83.39	10133	6324	42204	33589	8803	7083
1981	64.60	84.02	10329	6487	39049	31407	7026	4726
1982	65.98	84.66	10608	6448	34450	35182	10558	4852
1983	67.37	85.29	10659	6982	38580	34805	10139	4940
1984	68.75	85.92	10840	7000	31855	20657	4767	4746
1985	70.13	86.55	10964	7888	28515	14407	3637	5932
1986	71.51	87.18	11683	8230	30127	15633	5558	4229
1987	72.89	87.81	12079	9090	39487	23532	8951	3919
1988	74.27	88.44	12499	9305	41299	36759	10619	6241
1989	75.66	89.07	12695	9837	45910	57407	14323	8140
1990	77.04	89.70	13492	8689	47933	63832	12099	15592
1991	0.00	0.00	0	0	47597	53890	12155	6009

year	M5CHEM	M7TEXT	METCR	MB	MB1	MGDS	MNF	MSV
1967	2363	1303	4167	0	0	65904	43227	11388
1968	2079	1781	6075	0	0	72051	44131	10125
1969	2144	1386	6257	0	0	73288	44622	11692
1970	2344	984	5755	2972	3220	69085	36820	11251
1971	2663	1136	7286	2827	3546	70516	38656	9361
1972	3077	1247	6326	4392	4423	73059	41359	9195
1973	3316	1691	5557	5886	4993	71528	39417	15168
1974	5806	1718	7412	7105	6147	86987	54222	12877
1975	4360	2210	5071	8362	7004	92857	60146	13073
1976	4247	1538	5314	9657	7948	91450	56530	16206
1977	4539	2301	6252	11553	9814	96911	61086	17743
1978	4985	2120	7777	14018	12195	110184	73800	19065
1979	5448	2335	9299	16361	14817	129942	92041	20123
1980	6828	2693	11111	18081	16392	155447	113243	24030
1981	6214	2742	8309	21271	17983	150899	111850	27158
1982	6785	2508	9979	25959	19043	151746	117296	30668
1983	6289	3281	9098	28193	27958	148598	110018	28243
1984	4996	2789	7155	33630	33632	116133	84278	29801
1985	4618	2745	7773	38440	38447	98550	70035	26655
1986	6503	4563	10470	51026	51029	114784	84657	23237
1987	7227	6107	12864	57740	57738	151462	111975	26070
1988	7508	6849	14318	67283	67282	185892	144593	26465
1989	7906	9280	13370	92882	92876	217269	171359	27321
1990	8801	10018	15187	108717	108721	245562	197629	23586
1991	7526	8871	13898	129362	129363	240013	192416	20840

(continued)

year	MULT	MULT1	MORT01	MORT14	MORT59	MORT1014	MORT1519
1967	0.000000	0.000000	79.148	6.872	2.060	1.065	1.248
1968	0.000000	0.000000	79.544	6.686	1.585	1.147	1.388
1969	0.000000	0.000000	79.917	6.806	1.972	1.103	1.373
1970	3.158815	2.915527	65.223	6.343	1.524	1.064	1.411
1971	3.712062	2.959390	66.451	7.320	1.842	1.010	1.405
1972	2.703096	2.684151	73.318	8.579	2.244	1.171	1.592
1973	3.068977	3.617865	83.781	7.848	2.101	1.071	1.416
1974	3.411963	3.943712	64.512	7.165	1.967	0.981	1.268
1975	3.458861	4.129497	60.407	6.364	1.720	0.905	1.293
1976	3.726830	4.528183	62.701	6.818	1.875	0.950	1.354
1977	3.809832	4.484919	61.161	6.773	1.801	0.940	1.329
1978	3.706948	4.261090	57.298	6.703	1.728	0.932	1.306
1979	3.520444	3.887291	54.051	7.800	1.683	0.905	1.337
1980	3.775952	4.165019	47.796	5.769	1.422	0.880	1.333
1981	3.880400	4.589890	46.210	6.105	1.397	0.855	1.284
1982	3.701144	5.045318	43.896	6.317	1.410	0.856	1.295
1983	4.051041	4.085091	45.022	6.883	1.490	0.893	1.295
1984	3.640559	3.640342	39.741	6.110	1.380	0.871	1.240
1985	3.489594	3.488958	38.956	6.512	1.447	0.856	1.365
1986	2.989691	2.989515	37.010	5.494	1.327	0.826	1.283
1987	2.942137	2.942239	34.172	6.342	1.572	0.818	1.243
1988	3.108452	3.108498	30.944	4.832	1.422	0.804	1.242
1989	2.833929	2.834112	28.048	4.121	1.266	0.765	1.155
1990	2.875116	2.875010	24.896	3.479	1.156	0.729	1.069
1991	3.441226	3.441200	0.000	0.000	0.000	0.000	0.000

year	MORT2024	MORT2529	MORT3034	MORT3539	MORT4044	MORT4549
1967	1.846	2.676	3.178	4.431	4.797	6.242
1968	2.118	2.814	3.546	5.133	5.681	7.363
1969	1.935	2.461	3.034	4.090	4.815	6.216
1970	1.941	2.296	2.985	3.962	4.875	6.035
1971	2.109	2.348	2.999	4.067	4.936	5.997
1972	2.219	2.282	3.146	4.324	5.136	6.677
1973	2.117	2.277	3.088	4.323	5.060	6.700
1974	2.207	2.273	3.033	4.326	4.996	6.728
1975	1.926	2.348	2.859	4.212	4.533	6.377
1976	1.914	2.361	3.025	4.295	4.952	6.521
1977	1.944	2.422	2.971	4.125	4.794	6.379
1978	1.973	2.480	2.921	3.961	4.647	6.244
1979	1.923	2.496	2.946	3.981	4.593	6.256
1980	1.961	2.380	2.893	3.659	4.827	6.247
1981	1.895	2.337	2.835	3.519	4.639	6.190
1982	2.445	2.318	2.812	3.354	4.888	6.279
1983	1.980	2.429	2.825	3.571	4.816	6.269
1984	1.960	2.311	2.793	3.406	4.649	6.018
1985	2.068	2.597	2.864	3.741	4.704	6.331
1986	2.005	2.500	2.870	3.809	4,412	6.033
1987	1.924	2.373	2.756	3.609	4.328	6.001
1988	1.853	2.349	2.650	3.449	4.245	4.863
1989	1.778	2.226	2.580	3.242	4.152	5.791
1990	1.707	2.108	2.525	3.060	4.045	5.620
1991	0.000	0.000	0.000	0.000	0.000	0.000

(continued)

year	MORTG50	MORTALL	NDA	NETLEN	NFA	NFA1	NFIA	NTAXRE
1967	25.028	6.929	0	0	0	0	-3151	646
1968	27.920	7.299	0	0	0	0	-3569	737
1969	21.360	6.669	0	0	0	0	-2905	947
1970	20.987	6.396	3602	0	-630	-382	-6366	185
1971	20.984	6.615	3177	0	-350	369	-4093	491
1972	23.257	7.320	3392	566	1000	1031	-3784	883
1973	24.359	7.417	816	282	5070	4177	-923	276
1974	25.494	6.866	-125	1744	7230	6272	1735	-602
1975	23.727	6.377	5142	122	3220	1862	-1170	1602
1976	25.394	6.854	5767	100	3890	2181	-4188	1837
1977	24.600	6.725	5363	45	6190	4451	-3512	1257
1978	23.857	6.509	9068	238	4950	3127	-2170	937
1979	24.220	6.579	13491	853	2870	1326	1802	-321
1980	23.423	6.178	19141	675	-1060	-2749	-1168	300
1981	23.047	6.079	31341	929	-10070	-13358	-2317	628
1982	23.790	6.230	53069	2218	-27110	-34026	-7281	-367
1983	24.316	6.286	89073	2393	-60880	-61115	-10234	585
1984	23.498	5.884	121290	4423	-87660	-87658	-18622	-2117
1985	25.029	6.122	156480	1678	-118040	-118033	-15809	547
1986	24.484	5.829	184316	15148	-133290	-133287	-12248	5103
1987	24.098	5.845	189990	7077	-132250	-132257	-10978	8048
1988	24.750	5.514	188863	5415	-121580	-121581	-6170	19838
1989	23.915	5.317	201112	3666	-108230	-108236	-8689	28825
1990	23.852	5.133	249267	3787	-140550	-140546	1655	25149
1991	0.000	0.000	197912	5700	-68550	-68549	8597	39135

year	OGDCF	OPEXP	OTHBOP	OTHNDA	PCG	PCGOV	PFERT	PGDCF
1967	12153	0	5002	0	12.53	7.26	0.000	9.450
1968	12431	0	5877	0	12.98	7.96	0.000	10.040
1969	13699	0	5671	0	13.48	8.52	0.000	10.500
1970	15659	0	4675	499	14.25	9.28	289.180	12.550
1971	15437	0	7849	586	15.83	10.07	295.860	14.060
1972	16030	0	12144	919	17.24	10.82	393.590	15.050
1973	22229	0	-6030	1460	18.27	12.16	641.840	18.130
1974	28425	0	34326	845	22.79	18.24	2145.010	25.580
1975	27218	14696	75172	3857	26.38	18.83	1435.080	27.320
1976	31194	15798	75667	4433	30.60	20.57	833.300	28.910
1977	29265	17719	59689	4845	33.04	22.58	940.160	30.540
1978	31915	19230	89138	6447	36.06	23.49	1068.040	32.670
1979	34543	20608	107638	7730	39.37	27.53	1077.130	38.630
1980	21236	24516	132431	5380	44.04	37.75	1667.530	44.020
1981	7834	26390	139541	7868	50.66	43.62	1714.240	46.680
1982	12903	31746	215500	17556	55.28	49.01	1357.860	49.240
1983	8466	34522	343549	44073	61.28	56.30	1377.680	57.410
1984	-7963	42873	249582	79315	83.87	86.97	2855.480	89.600
1985	-2456	55275	198236	117761	100.00	100.00	2530.960	100.000
1986	4721	66921	107025	150664	110.90	103.85	2208.600	102.650
1987	16216	95503	438934	177121	125.20	116.32	2426.990	110.390
1988	15615	112267	475241	191152	144.53	126.94	3195.000	118.480
1989	18363	142786	1377658	215661	161.83	133.01	3969.000	131.340
1990	19173	177993	2712265	261937	186.21	152.33	4050.000	148.380
1991	12149	196500	2719789	306892	215.91	174.73	3896.000	176.960

(continued)

year	PGDP	PGNP	PGNPW	PM	PMUFEL	PMMACH	PMBM	PMCD
1967	8.831	8.828	34.023	7.129	1.981	10.12	7.99	12.39
1968	9.373	9.371	35.742	7.085	1.821	10.04	7.94	12.02
1969	9.890	9.889	37.738	6.291	1.751	9.33	7.84	11.68
1970	11.417	11.423	40.209	10.360	2.372	14.37	14.72	18.13
1971	13.081	13.084	42.318	12.189	3.512	18.79	14.47	20.04
1972	13.934	13.934	44.475	12.680	3.763	16.60	15.09	20.78
1973	16.334	16.335	49.127	15.642	4.953	23.10	20.97	34.71
1974	21.771	21.768	55.778	25.640	14.810	25.47	31.75	52.01
1975	23.794	23.795	62.526	27.655	18.283	30.65	39.11	59.45
1976	25.753	25.757	64.095	29.857	20.254	33.46	30.81	54.01
1977	27.830	27.830	68.175	30.626	21.785	33.36	32.46	44.20
1978	30.548	30.549	72.893	32.287	22.246	34.61	37.76	39.30
1979	35.255	35.256	77.887	36.035	28.810	40.23	44.54	42.00
1980	40.321	40.320	83.541	38.688	42.350	44.26	46.17	27.85
1981	45.243	45.242	88.265	42.991	52.167	48.15	49.83	46.02
1982	48.967	48.957	92.115	45.458	54.718	43.55	47.21	50.64
1983	55.753	55.737	94.521	58.628	63.955	56.85	54.87	62.66
1984	85.427	85.412	97.605	90.133	89.843	92.38	93.51	99.60
1985	100.000	100.000	100.000	100.000	100.000	100.00	100.00	100.00
1986	102.862	102.860	102.267	98.699	61.943	109.66	101.95	94.22
1987	110.370	110.399	104.510	100.837	68.958	105.65	107.01	82.72
1988	121.389	121.408	106.769	101.385	59.772	99.36	128.70	94.12
1989	132.684	132.715	110.368	114.579	71.490	101.29	151.81	105.19
1990	150.951	150.920	114.201	133.251	101.001	128.98	164.70	84.42
1991	176.058	176.059	118.370	148.628	117.172	166.25	179.44	121.04

year	PMCHEM	PMTEXT	PMETC	PMOTHR	PMDOL	PMFDOL	PMNFDOL
1967	5.05	10.22	11.06	10.23	0.0161	9.415	46.671
1968	7.47	10.17	8.84	14.76	0.0160	8.654	49.335
1969	7.43	10.04	8.90	16.43	0.0154	8.315	48.198
1970	11.03	15.16	14.10	68.50	0.0158	8.252	54.674
1971	11.40	14.10	14.81	44.79	0.0168	10.162	57.366
1972	12.34	14.45	18.07	52.27	0.0168	10.489	55.356
1973	18.03	20.24	23.25	39.45	0.0223	13.642	70.398
1974	29.27	28.90	35.56	59.17	0.0361	40.599	93.478
1975	29.00	23.51	38.66	39.37	0.0373	46.937	88.809
1976	29.59	25.91	33.29	60.35	0.0397	50.653	96.051
1977	29.78	27.32	38.16	53.62	0.0404	54.758	95.606
1978	34.18	32.49	32.68	53.02	0.0429	56.196	99.169
1979	37.68	38.88	36.06	41.31	0.0473	72.663	102.090
1980	32.38	42.46	38.69	34.06	0.0497	104.909	94.612
1981	42.26	48.04	53.25	31.88	0.0527	122.875	95.944
1982	37.71	53.37	54.27	40.12	0.0505	119.222	94.934
1983	53.84	66.09	64.12	55.58	0.0504	107.097	95.698
1984	91.60	99.75	102.62	87.39	0.0523	100.112	102.071
1985	100.00	100.00	100.00	100.00	0.0519	100.000	100.000
1986	95.26	95.73	110.30	102.83	0.0439	56.540	94.529
1987	104.54	97.05	100.22	104.50	0.0445	62.386	93.442
1988	112.58	103.23	114.52	100.27	0.0439	52.718	91.772
1989	123.68	109.74	141.10	127.04	0.0480	61.245	102.332
1990	132.96	137.74	151.40	137.04	0.0497	77.371	101.836
1991	175.12	173.42	173.73	131.58	0.0502	78.539	100.987

(continued)

year	PMGDS	PMNF	PMSV	PNFIA	POP	POP15	PSER	PVAG
1967	7.124	9.822	7.157	9.045	33702	18312	9.362	8.499
1968	7.065	10.382	7.230	9.498	34721	18864	10.088	9.411
1969	6.866	10.151	7.270	9.914	35771	19431	10.543	10.225
1970	10.683	17.702	8.381	11.090	36852	20029	11.656	11.991
1971	12.457	19.829	10.170	12.778	37876	20718	12.975	14.319
1972	12.874	19.857	11.136	13.874	38928	21440	13.899	14.834
1973	16.310	25.561	12.493	15.818	40010	21165	15.922	18.295
1974	26.835	37.100	17.574	21.095	41121	22924	20.227	26.427
1975	28.847	34.593	19.185	23.162	42259	23711	22.297	29.234
1976	31.475	38.407	20.727	25.310	43406	24521	24.793	30.201
1977	32.029	38.036	22.961	27.790	44584	25357	27.020	32.473
1978	33.639	39.256	24.469	30.323	45794	26222	29.782	35.405
1979	37.074	40.478	29.320	35.516	47037	27113	34.427	40.577
1980	39.322	38.193	34.586	41.010	48317	28003	40.099	42.885
1981	43.692	40.733	39.097	45.447	49526	28884	45.250	47.268
1982	46.102	43.571	42.275	49.897	50783	29787	50.219	49.582
1983	58.919	57.153	57.097	56.762	52055	29882	56.213	57.058
1984	91.119	91.601	86.095	85.898	53351	31655	83.097	90.584
1985	100.000	100.000	100.000	100.000	54668	32615	100.000	100.000
1986	103.564	103.564	128.631	102.964	56004	33469	104.927	99.994
1987	103.287	103.287	138.604	108.745	57356	34462	112.044	108.932
1988	104.051	104.051	151.759	119.287	58720	35600	123.343	117.974
1989	119.451	119.451	156.430	130.257	60100	36916	135.090	131.329
1990	132.937	132.937	201.420	137.591	61480	37636	154.632	146.268
1991	150.661	150.661	201.700	176.130	62870	39109	184.480	160.901

year	PVIR	PX	PXAG	PXDOL	PXGDS	PXNAG	PXAGI	PXOGDS
1967	8.248	8.871	7.338	0.0238	9.880	15.095	15.095	0.000
1968	8.524	9.453	7.836	0.0254	10.520	16.558	16.558	0.000
1969	8.848	9.545	7.437	0.0251	10.470	16.910	16.910	0.000
1970	10.666	13.854	11.712	0.0265	16.470	36.668	27.390	3.280
1971	12.194	15.316	14.037	0.0263	17.500	32.541	24.432	1.840
1972	13.253	14.716	12.772	0.0239	16.390	22.220	21.594	6.190
1973	15.263	20.310	18.767	0.0367	24.650	32.581	32.581	0.000
1974	20.107	31.331	40.005	0.0585	39.320	38.535	38.535	0.000
1975	21.737	29.784	35.034	0.0506	36.030	37.051	37.051	0.000
1976	23.798	28.604	29.307	0.0435	31.410	33.122	33.122	0.000
1977	25.676	30.612	31.461	0.0456	33.300	34.755	34.755	0.000
1978	28.278	32.570	34.764	0.0497	36.210	37.389	37.070	23.520
1979	32.868	39.527	45.760	0.0599	43.620	42.842	42.733	35.790
1980	39.032	37.129	45.997	0.0488	36.600	33.461	34.032	75.160
1981	44.074	39.617	46.481	0.0449	37.790	34.597	35.883	60.290
1982	47.491	42.595	43.038	0.0452	40.120	38.584	39.335	53.210
1983	54.620	50.435	59.844	0.0434	48.940	45.657	46.415	74.180
1984	84.631	77.094	106.622	0.0443	74.750	67.583	68.469	99.790
1985	100.000	100.000	100.000	0.0526	100.000	100.000	100.000	100.000
1986	102.478	99.833	85.114	0.0477	99.690	102.721	103.624	117.720
1987	109.410	106.606	93.585	0.0506	107.500	108.351	110.390	145.740
1988	121.795	115.529	120.892	0.0554	119.570	117.958	119.352	153.690
1989	130.803	121.617	111.497	0.0554	123.390	124.832	125.218	134.860
1990	149.597	136.191	106.233	0.0557	135.820	141.168	140.593	120.210
1991	175.806	162.774	134.246	0.0581	162.741	166.925	166.811	162.740

(continued)

year	PXSV	PXW	REVN	SP	STATD	TBILL	TIME	TL
1967	7.517	26.646	3576	40501	6156	0.000	1	7546
1968	7.596	26.702	4056	42357	25250	0.000	2	7899
1969	7.689	27.608	4510	47811	26077	0.000	3	8947
1970	8.951	29.242	4849	44772	17861	13.135	4	9388
1971	10.687	29.811	5869	56906	18986	11.948	5	10494
1972	11.638	30.158	6972	65759	18325	11.918	6	11872
1973	13.282	36.293	9499	74436	17932	9.425	7	18064
1974	17.578	56.927	12157	75886	19702	10.047	8	24242
1975	20.591	62.911	16856	77140	6294	10.342	9	28923
1976	22.395	63.481	18089	99541	-944	10.186	10	35990
1977	24.626	64.921	19959	106533	655	10.901	11	44015
1978	25.829	62.991	24073	108367	5905	10.888	12	51964
1979	30.243	76.877	29470	116950	16510	12.254	13	57598
1980	38.870	103.118	34731	125802	25846	12.141	14	68273
1981	45.188	106.759	35933	142331	17053	12.606	15	82540
1982	49.379	109.297	38206	145329	30423	13.811	16	96078
1983	54.457	102.678	45632	150028	19575	14.173	17	114211
1984	83.762	102.566	56861	103522	1267	30.534	18	122432
1985	100.000	100.000	68961	66828	8009	26.806	19	134140
1986	100.080	85.826	79245	72280	-4418	14.433	20	152552
1987	104.859	89.188	103214	70141	16584	11.390	21	169879
1988	107.981	89.715	112861	95111	19814	14.670	22	209146
1989	118.320	93.901	152410	91953	14731	18.640	23	263221
1990	136.940	98.439	180841	83973	12540	23.672	24	312574
1991	162.840	95.966	220787	0	1109	21.478	25	445164

year	TOTTAX	TRADET	UERA	USUEMP	USWAGN	USWAGREX	VAG
1967	2930	0	7.954	3.8	2.68	100.81	87006
1968	3319	0	7.802	3.6	2.85	102.86	92700
1969	3563	0	6.707	3.5	3.04	104.09	96269
1970	4664	0	7.703	4.9	3.23	104.43	96700
1971	5378	0	5.181	5.9	3.45	107.01	100606
1972	6089	0	6.331	5.6	3.7	111.07	106012
1973	9223	0	4.793	4.9	3.94	111.37	113901
1974	12759	0	4.055	5.6	4.24	107.93	110265
1975	15254	6862	3.893	8.5	4.53	105.65	112091
1976	16252	6171	6.302	7.7	4.86	107.20	123324
1977	18702	6283	9.100	7.1	5.25	108.75	128717
1978	23136	7831	9.423	6.1	5.69	109.51	133503
1979	29791	9479	7.102	5.8	6.16	106.53	137733
1980	34431	11591	7.903	7.1	6.66	101.48	143295
1981	35305	11131	8.952	7.6	7.25	100.14	148479
1982	38573	12096	9.404	9.7	7.68	99.93	149641
1983	45047	16488	10.398	9.6	8.02	101.09	144586
1984	58978	17185	10.404	7.5	8.32	100.54	143247
1985	68414	16782	12.895	7.2	8.57	100.00	140554
1986	74142	17496	11.775	7.0	8.76	100.35	145725
1987	95166	25992	11.866	6.2	8.98	99.16	150414
1988	93023	25014	9.723	5.5	9.28	98.52	155292
1989	125851	38375	9.602	5.3	9.66	97.84	159964
1990	155692	45948	8.430	5.5	10.01	96.19	160577
1991	181652	64200	12.019	6.7	10.33	95.21	161710

(continued)

year	VIR	VSER	WAGE	WAGER	WPI	XAG	XGDS	XNAG
1967	100022	114077	21.880	255.01	6.052	23160	34447	11287
1968	104407	118892	24.340	277.85	6.217	23449	33874	10425
1969	109376	125062	25.490	287.37	6.302	23151	34053	10902
1970	115661	130802	28.270	277.43	7.790	27943	40120	8793
1971	124068	137118	30.190	243.08	9.001	28826	43227	10597
1972	132894	142593	31.980	237.95	9.922	27346	46361	18272
1973	150492	151132	32.810	209.51	12.355	29485	51353	21868
1974	160720	159328	35.440	168.68	19.092	24857	46545	21688
1975	174355	167818	38.410	171.24	19.644	22954	45361	22407
1976	193505	177433	40.360	164.73	21.696	26559	59194	32635
1977	207816	185419	42.500	157.82	23.308	30500	69054	38554
1978	219412	196032	44.270	153.18	24.432	25699	68907	42213
1979	235391	206786	46.630	138.49	29.074	22513	76816	53462
1980	247059	219414	48.450	122.35	34.400	25477	118707	91954
1981	258545	223618	54.090	121.55	39.360	22948	127538	99352
1982	264957	238869	55.740	113.66	43.734	23533	110986	82961
1983	268987	252144	60.010	111.07	50.818	21685	115356	91181
1984	238038	235677	84.910	104.53	84.656	20017	121588	98777
1985	200548	230781	100.000	100.00	100.000	16182	88020	67733
1986	205164	240534	103.020	102.25	98.436	21600	101461	75052
1987	216173	253120	111.910	107.02	107.378	19449	113076	88520
1988	232500	270671	125.120	110.01	121.793	18076	127657	105305
1989	251581	286837	154.830	123.09	134.866	18799	141100	117600
1990	256136	298439	180.380	127.27	148.531	20401	146860	122986
1991	247701	298447	210.150	125.99	168.400	19027	152231	129587

year	XNAG1	XOGDS	XSV	YD
1967	11287	0	25676	264765
1968	10425	0	19470	277013
1969	10902	0	16959	291772
1970	12177	3384	21406	295967
1971	14401	3804	20399	316595
1972	19015	743	25211	334016
1973	21868	0	31705	358140
1974	21688	0	27036	373434
1975	22407	0	30820	388988
1976	32635	0	26760	426977
1977	38554	0	31008	451239
1978	43208	995	37214	471043
1979	54303	841	33862	497213
1980	93230	1276	36041	523206
1981	104590	5238	41816	550289
1982	87453	4492	40503	567396
1983	93671	2490	42896	574662
1984	101571	2794	42739	529289
1985	71838	4105	49010	487660
1986	79861	4809	58992	507095
1987	93627	5107	57813	522527
1988	109581	4276	68340	575673
1989	122301	4701	75880	596572
1990	126459	3473	72843	613645
1991	133204	3617	77591	613278

Chapter 14

A Linked International Model for the Pacific Basin Economy

Soshichi Kinoshita[1]

1 Introduction

This paper describes the structure, properties and use of a linked international model estimated from annual data. The structure of the model is designed to quantify the main macroeconomic relationships and the trade linkages among major industrial and industrializing economies, focusing on the Pacific basin economies. The model contains a separate equation block for each of the three developed countries (Japan, the US and Canada); the 12 EC countries as a group; the Asian NIES (Korea, Hong Kong and Taiwan) as a group; and the ASEAN countries(Indonesia, Malaysia, the Philippines, Singapore, and Thailand) as a group. These six equation blocks are linked together with each other through trade volume and trade price relationships. The sample period for the estimation of the model covers the years between 1975 up to 1987.

2 Structure of the Linked Model

In this section we first present the structure of the model describing the macro economic behavior in each country or economy as a group. Then we explain the features of the trade linkage method used in our modeling.

In modeling macroeconomic relationships we apply basically the same structure to each of the individual countries and to the three country groups (the 12 EC countries, the three Asian NIEs and the five ASEAN countries) which are respectively treated as though they were a single aggregate economy.

We specify the main sectors of macroeconomy based on the conventional Keynesian model, and summarize this in Table 1.

The demand and output sector includes five behavioral equations including private consumption, fixed investment, export and import. Private consumption is specified using a permanent income approach with a distributed lag of income variable. The interest and inflation factors, if significant, are also included as

[1]This paper was presented at the Workshop on Econometric Models in Asia and the Pacific at the second Convention of the East Asian Economic Association which was held in Bandung, Indonesia, August, 26-28 1990. I thank Mitsuo Yamada of Mie University for computational assistance.

additional variables. Investment components are based on the stock adjustment principle, which relates investment to output and to existing capital stock. The interest rate is included when appropriate. Total export is directly related to the commodity exports, which are determined in the trade linkage sector. Total import is a function of real GNP(GDP) and relative price with a lagged response.

Table 1. Simplified Model

Demand and Output				
(1)	C	=	$C(Y, G(PC), R, C_{-1})$	Consumption
(2)	IH	=	$IH(Y, R, G(PIH), KH_{-1})$	Housing investment
(3)	IF	=	$IF(GNP, R, KF_{-1}, IF_{-1})$	Business investment
(4)	E	=	$E(FE)$	Exports
(5)	M	=	$M(GNP, \frac{PM}{PGNP}, M_{-1})$	Imports
(6)	GNP	=	$C + IH + IF + J + G + E - M$	GNP(GDP)
Wage and Price				
(7)	$G(W)$	=	$W(G(PC), \frac{U}{LF}, \frac{PM}{PGNP}, G(W))$	Wage
(8)	PP	=	$PP(PM, \frac{YW}{GNP})$	Producer price index
(9)	PC	=	$PC(PP, WAGE or \frac{YW}{GNP})$	Consumption deflator
(10)	PIH	=	$PIH(PP, \frac{YW}{GNP})$	Housing investment deflator
(11)	PIF	=	$PIF(PP, \frac{YW}{GNP})$	Business investment deflator
(12)	PE	=	$PE(PFE, EX)$	Export deflator
(13)	PM	=	$PM(PFI, EX)$	Import deflator
(14)	$PGNP$	=	$\frac{GNPV}{GNP}$	GNP deflator
Employment andIncome				
(15)	LW	=	$LW(GNP, \frac{WAGE}{PGNP}, LW_{-1})$	Employment
(16)	U	=	$LF - LW - LS$	Unemployed
(17)	YW	=	Wage $* LW$	Labor income
(18)	Y	=	$\frac{GNPV}{PC}$	Income
(19)	$GNPV$	=	$C * PC + IH * PIH + IF * PIF$ $+ J * PP + E * PE - M * PM$	Nominal GNP

$G(x)$ = percentage change of x.

The wage-price sector explains several price variables and wage earnings as a cost component of them. The wage equation is based on an extended Phillips curve. It includes unemployment rate, rate of inflation and real input price as an indicator of ability to pay. Producer's price index, which is the key price variable in this sector, is related to import price and unit labor cost under the markup pricing principle. Demand deflators are explained by producer's price and wage variable. Export deflator is a function of producer's price and exchange rate if significant. Import deflator is related to the export price of the countries or regions as trade partners. GNP deflator is given as the ratio of nominal GNP and real GNP.

The employment and income sector explains employment, unemployment and labor income. Optimal employment is derived from profit maximization under the CES production function. Actual employment is determined by a partial adjustment to optimal employment. Unemployment is defined by the difference between labor force and employment including self-employed. Labor income is the product of wage earnings and employment. Income variable in the consumption equation is given by deflating nominal GNP with a consumption deflator, a proxy for real disposable income.

A linkage of country and regional models is realized through both trade volume and trade price relationships. As for the price relationship, the import price of each country and region is a weighted average of the export prices of trading partners converted to domestic currency unit, using 1980 import share weights:

$$PFI = \frac{\sum(w_i * PFE_i * EX_i)}{EX}$$

where w_i is the share of i-th country (region) in the import in the home country.

The volume of commodity exports is specified as a function of the activity variable determined by the import volumes of each country(region)'s trading partners and a price competitiveness variable which reflects the relative price of home country exports in foreign markets. The activity variable is constructed as the weighted sum of the import volumes of other countries by using the 1980's share of the home country in each of the foreign import markets. Price competitveness is defined as a ratio of the export price of the home country to the export price of rival countries in foreign import markets.

$$FE = FE(XFE, \frac{PFE}{PWM})$$

where XFE is the weighted sum of import volumes of trade partners, and PWM is the export price of rivals in foreign market.

Estimated parameters of consumption, import and export are shown in Tables 2 to 4. The whole structure of the model is given in the Appendix.

Table 2. Consumption Function

$$C = a + b * Y + c * G(PC) + d * C_{-1}$$

country	b	c	d	R2	s	DW	mpc.1
JA	0.2059	−77.645	0.5373	0.997	9.44	2.55	0.445
	(3.002)	(−3.227)	(5.133)				
US	0.2991	−11.773	0.5642	0.998	10.85	2.30	0.671
	(4.393)	(−7.650)	(6.464)				
EC	0.3310	−3.283	0.4847	0.999	3.69	1.86	0.642
	(11.26)	(−4.346)	(13.12)				
CA	0.2939	−	0.6207	0.962	3.53	1.87	0.775
	(2.064)		(2.878)				
AN	0.1837	−10.349	0.6674	0.998	0.98	1.60	0.550
	(4.836)	(−1.812)	(8.542)				
AS	0.3358	−0.1752	0.5006	0.993	1.68	1.57	0.673
	(4.648)	(−1.252)	(4.766)				

note: mpc.l=long−run marginal propensity to consume.

Table 3. Import Function

$$lnM = a + b * lnGNP + c * ln\frac{PM}{PGNP} + d * lnM_{-1}$$

country	b	c	d	R2	s	DW	eta(GNP)
JA	0.8611	−0.1935	−	0.929	0.042	2.45	0.861
	(11.859)	(−2.874)					
US	2.1124	−0.4794	−	0.991	0.020	2.77	2.112
	(29.330)	(−6.956)					
EC	1.6117	−0.1740	−	0.981	0.016	1.97	1.612
	(17.454)	(−2.370)					
CA	1.9418	−	−	0.976	0.032	1.67	1.942
	(21.373)						
AN	0.8665	−	0.2684	0.981	0.046	1.40	1.184
	(4.3223)		(1.672)				
AS	1.5235	−	−	0.957	0.056	0.74	1.524
	(15.737)						

note: eta(GNP)=long−run demand elasticity of imports.

Table 4. Commodity export function

$$ln(FE - FE_o) = a + b * lnXFE + c * ln\frac{PFE}{PWM}$$

country	b	c	R2	S	DW
JA	1.4260	-0.4667	0.973	0.059	1.18
	(20.386)	(-2.249)			
US	0.8590	-0.8772	0.969	0.023	1.56
	(18.642)	(-7.785)			
EC	1.2590	-0.1406	0.990	0.020	1.06
	(33.771)	(-3.043)			
CA	1.1491	-0.1365	0.981	0.033	1.03
	(15.862)	(-0.761)			
AN	2.1497	-0.8285	0.989	0.057	1.14
	(17.975)	(-4.480)			
AS	1.3164	-0.1765	0.980	0.040	1.84
	(16.896)	(-1.760)			

note: FE_o=exports to the rest of the world

3 Simulation with the Linked System

Since we obtained the satisfactory explanatory performance of the linked model for the sample period, we proceeded to conduct two types of simulation experiments to quantify the inter–dependence among industrial and developing economies. One simulated a fiscal shock and the other an exchange rate adjustment. The fiscal shock is an increase in real government expenditure equal to 1% of baseline real GNP.

First, we compare the multiplier effects of Japan, the US and EC separately. Then, we simulate the combined effects of fiscal expansion of both Japan and EC and fiscal contraction of the US. The exchange rate adjustment depreciates the US dollar against the Japanese Yen and European currencies by 10%. The results of fiscal shock are shown in Tables 5 to 8, and Table 9 shows the results of the exchange rate adjustment simulation.

The fiscal shock simulation shows US fiscal expansion to have a greater impact on trade partners than do Japanese and EC fiscal expansion. Individually the largest impact of the US is on Asian NIEs, and the smallest is on the EC. The impact on Japan by US fiscal change is more than twice as large as that by EC fiscal change. This is due to the fact that Japan's export to the US amounts to more than 30% of the total export, and that the export dependency on the US market is higher in Japan than in EC. Canada is affected heavily by the US fiscal expansion as can be expected.

Second, the EC fiscal expansion also affects trade partners greatly, its size being comparable to that of the US. The largest impact is on the Asian NIEs. The EC impact on the US is a little less than the US impact on the EC. Japan is less affected by fiscal expansion in the EC than by that in the US.

Third, Japan's fiscal expansion has a smaller impact on trade partner countries. This is explained by the inelastic nature of Japan's imports with respect to real GNP.

Comparing the individual impacts of the industrial countries on the Asian economies, the US and EC show quite a large GDP multiplier, while Japan's impact are less than one third as large. Judging from the simulation results the ASEAN countries are not as sensitive to the fiscal shock in the industrial countries as are the Asian NIEs. Also the impact of Japan's shock on the Asian economies are less than those of the US and the EC, partly reflecting the difference in the size of the respective domestic markets.

It is interesting to simulate the combined effects of US fiscal contraction and an offsetting fiscal expansion in Japan and the EC. As shown in Table 8, the negative US impact on the Asian economies are largely offset by the positive Japanese and EC impacts. This implies that policy coordination is indispensable among Japan, the US and EC in order for the US to resolve her fiscal deficit with a minimum shock.

Table 9 indicates that a 10% depreciation of the US dollar against the Japanese Yen and European currencies has a favorable impact on the Asian NIEs. Favorable effects on the US economy are decreasing and become nagative after the fourth year. As far as export markets are concerned, the impacts are positive for the US, Asian NIEs and ASEAN, reflecting the changing price competitiveness in the world export markets.

Table 5. Effects of Fiscal Expansion in JAPAN

(% multiplier)

	JAGNP	UGNP	ECGDP	CAGDP	ANGDP	ASGDP
77	1.562	0.033	0.011	0.038	0.121	0.205
78	2.063	0.058	0.022	0.067	0.179	0.290
79	2.302	0.081	0.031	0.086	0.215	0.338
80	2.453	0.095	0.045	0.100	0.245	0.343
81	2.460	0.092	0.049	0.102	0.238	0.296
82	2.475	0.093	0.052	0.113	0.224	0.282
83	2.375	0.079	0.051	0.109	0.215	0.254
84	2.038	0.061	0.048	0.095	0.191	0.221
85	1.638	0.044	0.043	0.075	0.154	0.173
86	1.270	0.027	0.034	0.049	0.086	0.120
87	0.914	0.016	0.034	0.026	0.040	0.094

(% multiplier)

	JAE	UE	ECE	CAE	ANE	ASE
77	0.254	0.149	0.038	0.169	0.299	0.488
78	0.372	0.213	0.065	0.260	0.457	0.613
79	0.419	0.257	0.081	0.317	0.564	0.685
80	0.401	0.277	0.112	0.348	0.612	0.677
81	0.338	0.255	0.109	0.339	0.569	0.606
82	0.311	0.259	0.113	0.343	0.508	0.577
83	0.238	0.248	0.104	0.312	0.512	0.506
84	0.116	0.216	0.093	0.243	0.433	0.401
85	-0.011	0.177	0.080	0.170	0.332	0.304
86	-0.193	0.138	0.060	0.080	0.192	0.188
87	-0.094	0.102	0.068	0.016	0.097	0.149

(% multiplier)

	JAM	UM	ECM	CAM	ANM	ASM
77	1.287	0.124	0.022	0.069	0.100	0.308
78	1.719	0.206	0.044	0.125	0.177	0.436
79	1.941	0.250	0.055	0.163	0.228	0.509
80	2.092	0.268	0.084	0.195	0.274	0.524
81	2.111	0.248	0.086	0.195	0.275	0.448
82	2.146	0.237	0.090	0.216	0.264	0.427
83	2.092	0.192	0.084	0.206	0.253	0.384
84	1.846	0.121	0.074	0.180	0.231	0.333
85	1.545	0.044	0.060	0.146	0.195	0.262
86	1.270	-0.013	0.039	0.097	0.130	0.184
87	0.985	-0.112	0.039	0.054	0.076	0.148

Table 6. Fiscal Expansion of the U.S.A.

(% multiplier)

	UGNP	JAGNP	ECGDP	CAGDP	ANGDP	ASGDP
77	2.030	0.511	0.165	0.650	0.906	0.519
78	2.111	0.763	0.237	0.892	1.097	0.650
79	2.211	0.956	0.291	1.033	1.253	0.718
80	2.286	1.117	0.336	1.134	1.404	0.721
81	2.248	1.205	0.371	1.184	1.495	0.663
82	2.345	1.289	0.396	1.333	1.454	0.650
83	2.248	1.323	0.417	0.398	1.592	0.656
84	1.953	1.292	0.441	1.408	1.715	0.678
85	1.816	1.216	0.459	1.411	1.822	0.676
86	1.645	1.117	0.473	1.406	1.928	0.693
87	1.486	1.041	0.498	1.377	1.972	0.757

(% multiplier)

	UE	JAE	ECE	CAE	ANE	ASE
77	0.371	2.455	0.551	2.942	2.497	1.281
78	0.477	2.909	0.687	3.391	3.028	1.397
79	0.539	3.227	0.778	3.701	3.364	1.449
80	0.570	3.071	0.834	3.836	3.454	1.415
81	0.562	2.943	0.870	3.928	3.461	1.381
82	0.580	3.101	0.918	4.128	3.182	1.365
83	0.604	3.210	0.960	4.251	3.661	1.389
84	0.591	3.113	0.998	4.030	3.734	1.352
85	0.583	3.023	1.031	3.928	3.743	1.361
86	0.595	3.157	1.071	3.763	3.864	1.292
87	0.598	3.217	1.142	3.567	3.835	1.410

(% multiplier)

	UM	JAM	ECM	CAM	ANM	ASM
77	4.258	0.422	0.272	1.266	0.784	0.789
78	4.548	0.650	0.389	1.738	1.161	0.990
79	4.845	0.817	0.472	2.014	1.398	1.094
80	5.070	0.958	0.549	2.218	1.598	1.106
81	5.057	1.028	0.599	2.312	1.718	1.013
82	5.348	1.107	0.635	2.606	1.724	0.993
83	5.223	1.138	0.664	2.732	1.845	1.002
84	4.646	1.114	0.692	2.750	1.981	1.034
85	4.400	1.052	0.715	2.758	2.114	1.033
86	4.071	0.964	0.736	2.751	2.244	1.059
87	3.757	0.900	0.782	2.695	2.319	1.161

Table 7. Fiscal Expansion of EC

(% multiplier)

	ECGNP	JAGNP	UGNP	CAGDP	ANGDP	ASGDP
77	1.709	0.177	0.134	0.167	0.370	0.230
78	2.115	0.292	0.181	0.258	0.504	0.315
79	2.406	0.403	0.227	0.328	0.636	0.380
80	2.598	0.526	0.275	0.397	0.794	0.425
81	2.723	0.597	0.280	0.431	0.856	0.404
82	2.835	0.662	0.292	0.498	0.852	0.403
83	2.891	0.687	0.275	0.525	0.922	0.404
84	2.895	0.666	0.238	0.525	0.968	0.405
85	2.880	0.621	0.221	0.523	1.016	0.395
86	2.833	0.566	0.208	0.521	1.071	0.401
87	2.798	0.529	0.202	0.515	1.100	0.440

(% multiplier)

	ECE	JAE	VE	CAE	ANE	ASE
77	1.836	0.869	0.710	0.758	1.026	0.572
78	2.307	1.170	0.851	0.993	1.396	0.689
79	2.680	1.447	0.953	1.206	1.724	0.785
80	2.921	1.553	1.038	1.404	1.967	0.867
81	3.026	1.526	1.027	1.483	2.010	0.864
82	3.192	1.634	1.081	1.591	1.877	0.865
83	3.272	1.669	1.133	1.627	2.129	0.860
84	3.261	1.575	1.088	1.512	2.108	0.799
85	3.273	1.510	1.068	1.458	2.084	0.786
86	3.283	1.570	1.092	1.393	2.138	0.741
87	3.329	1.619	1.082	1.338	2.138	0.818

(% multiplier)

	ECM	JAM	VM	CAM	ANM	ASM
77	2.763	0.144	0.279	0.321	0.316	0.344
78	3.426	0.240	0.388	0.496	0.517	0.474
79	3.900	0.336	0.493	0.632	0.684	0.572
80	4.223	0.466	0.608	0.774	0.873	0.650
81	4.424	0.504	0.626	0.836	0.973	0.613
82	4.607	0.564	0.662	0.967	0.998	0.612
83	4.696	0.589	0.632	1.019	1.065	0.612
84	4.699	0.577	0.552	1.018	1.122	0.613
85	4.673	0.546	0.514	1.018	1.182	0.602
86	4.594	0.502	0.482	1.013	1.242	0.607
87	4.547	0.477	0.468	1.006	1.293	0.676

Table 8. Combined fiscal shock of Japan, the US and EC

(% multiplier)

	JAGNP	UGNP	ECHDP	CAHDP	ANGDP	ASHDP
77	1.244	-1.877	1.562	-0.432	-0.385	-0.069
78	1.621	-1.886	1.912	-0.548	-0.373	-0.022
79	1.786	-1.918	2.159	-0.596	-0.358	0.027
80	1.904	-1.931	2.321	-0.612	-0.317	0.075
81	1.895	-1.892	2.416	-0.625	-0.342	0.063
82	1.892	-1.979	2.507	-0.694	-0.330	0.062
83	1.782	-1.913	2.540	-0.736	-0.404	0.028
84	1.444	-1.672	2.514	-0.764	-0.508	-0.029
85	1.065	-1.568	2.472	-0.791	-0.607	-0.088
86	0.733	-1.424	2.400	-0.818	-0.728	-0.155
87	0.410	-1.280	2.338	-0.822	-0.791	-0.209

(% multiplier)

	JAE	UE	ECE	CAE	ANE	ASE
77	-1.263	0.501	1.340	-1.956	-1.091	-0.188
78	-1.278	0.608	1.711	-2.058	-1.068	-0.049
79	-1.264	0.694	2.007	-2.088	-0.979	0.074
80	-1.027	0.769	2.220	-1.991	-0.761	0.182
81	-1.000	0.745	2.285	-2.013	-0.769	0.139
82	-1.068	0.787	2.408	-2.095	-0.693	0.132
83	-1.211	0.806	2.437	-2.213	-0.900	0.033
84	-1.349	0.737	2.371	-2.195	-1.088	-0.106
85	-1.465	0.681	2.328	-2.234	-1.233	-0.233
86	-1.725	0.650	2.270	-2.234	-1.443	-0.335
87	-1.888	0.600	2.251	-2.166	-1.517	-0.418

(% multiplier)

	JAN	UM	EDM	CAM	ANM	ASM
77	1.025	-3.798	2.526	-0.843	-0.338	-0.112
78	1.336	-3.886	3.102	-1.065	-0.419	-0.040
79	1.495	-4.023	3.505	-1.159	-0.428	0.034
80	1.619	-4.111	3.778	-1.184	-0.390	0.114
81	1.627	-4.102	3.932	-1.214	-0.407	0.091
82	1.646	-4.362	4.082	-1.347	-0.400	0.098
83	1.584	-4.319	4,136	-1.429	-0.463	0.037
84	1.341	-3.915	4.093	-1.482	-0.572	-0.052
85	1.060	-3.793	4.022	-1.535	-0.685	-0.140
86	0.821	-3.587	3.896	-1.586	-0.819	-0.242
87	0.570	-3.363	3.798	-1.587	-0.900	-0.315

Table 9. Depreciation of Dollar against Yen and European Currency (% multiplier)

	JAGNP	UGNP	ECGDP	CAGDP	ANGDP	ASGDP
77	0.108	0.212	-0.122	-0.041	-0.011	-0.211
78	-0.210	0.135	-0.080	-0.134	0.061	-0.008
79	-0.528	0.007	-0.068	-0.213	0.102	-0.032
80	-0.833	-0.091	-0.021	-0.229	0.187	-0.051
81	-1.252	-0.139	0.055	-0.220	0.198	-0.077
82	-1.798	-0.158	0.125	-0.224	0.207	-0.146
83	-2.471	-0.144	0.151	-0.239	0.142	-0.258
84	-2.996	-0.130	0.147	-0.262	0.087	-0.344
85	-3.252	-0.131	0.118	-0.292	0.062	-0.397
86	-3.636	-0.079	0.021	-0.405	-0.128	-0.503
87	-3.906	-0.088	-0.094	-0.550	-0.299	-0.629

(% multiplier)

	JAE	UE	ECE	CAE	ANE	ASE
77	-1.203	1.510	-0.492	-0.143	0.646	0.194
78	-1.491	1.494	-0.473	-0.475	0.849	0.646
79	-1.675	1.240	-0.472	-0.734	0.688	0.401
80	-1.497	1.009	-0.340	-0.695	0.563	0.285
81	-1.572	0.768	-0.197	-0.615	0.385	0.215
82	-1.672	0.709	-0.110	-0.543	0.282	0.113
83	-1.999	0.691	-0.115	-0.599	0.117	-0.046
84	-2.194	0.530	-0.143	-0.667	-0.029	-0.197
85	-2.285	0.447	-0.211	-0.763	-0.100	-0.277
86	-2.979	0.656	-0.464	-1.148	-0.401	-0.349
87	-3.480	0.544	-0.679	-1.589	-0.688	-0.641

(% multiplier)

	JAPFE$	USPFE$	ECPFE$	CAPFE$	ANPFE$	ASPFE$
77	6.662	1.125	8.745	2.612	1.750	0.170
78	7.521	1.872	9.087	3.612	2.233	0.337
79	7.661	2.399	9.078	4.235	2.396	0.401
80	7.488	2.590	8.745	4.390	2.422	0.351
81	7.839	2.693	8.291	4.408	2.534	0.335
82	8.126	2.717	8.159	4.418	2.612	0.343
83	9.105	2.895	8.276	4.821	3.003	0.409
84	9.556	3.154	8.245	5.232	3.139	0.446
85	9.854	3.408	8.372	5.658	3.257	0.490
86	11.848	3.948	9.311	6.870	4.332	0.775
87	12.878	4.760	9.798	8.552	4.930	1.079

4 Conclusions

There remain some possibilities for further development of the linked international model described here. The most important one is to extend the models for the EC, the Asian NIEs and ASEAN to the same size as those of Japan and the US. This needs a consistent data base of the aggregate variables in each economy as a group.

Another equally important opportunity is to develop the supply side of the model, with consistent treatment of capital stock, employment and output in the production technology.

The international linkages among industrial and developing economies must, of course, include both investment and trade linkages.

References

[1] Kinoshita, S. (1989) "An Econometric Analysis of the Transmission Mechanism of Business Fluctuation within the Pacific Basin Economy," IEC Discussion Paper No.42, Economic Research Center, Nagoya University.

[2] Kinoshita, S. and J. Nemoto (1990) "The Changing Pattern of International Specialization and Economic Interdependence among the Asia-Pacific, the US and the EC economies," IEC Discussion Paper No.46, Economic Research Center, Nagoya University.

Appendix

A List of Variables of the Linked International Model

Variable	Definition
C	: Private Consumption
IH	: Housing Investmnet
IF	: Business Investment
GDI	: Gross Investment
INV	: Gross Fixed Investment
J	: Inventory Investment
G	: Government Expenditure
GC	: Government Consumption
G	: Government Investment
E	: Exports of Goods and Services
M	: Imports of Goods and Services
GNP	: GNP
GDP	: Gross Domestic Product
KH	: Housing Stock
KF	: Fixed Business Capital Stock
PC	: Deflator for C
PIH	: do for IH
PIF	: do for IF
PG	: do for G
PGC	: do for GC
PPI	: Producer Price Index (WPI)
PE	: Deflator for E
PM	: do for M
PGNP	: do for GNP
PGDP	: do for GDP
W	: Wage Earning
YW	: Labor Income
GDPV	: Nominal GNP
GDPV	: Nominal GDP
LW	: Employee
LS	: Self-Employed
U	: Unemployed
LF	: Labor Force
R	: Interest Rate
FE	: Commodity Exports
XFE	: Export Activity
PFE	: Export Unit Value

PM$: Import Unit Value
PMBOJ$: Import Price Index (Bank of Japan)
PFI : Import Unit Value (excl. Import from Row)
PWM : Rivals' Export Price Indices in the World Market
OPPFE$: OPEC Export Price
TIME : Time Trend

			Country/Region Name			
Variable	US	JA	EC	CA	AN	AS
C	UC	JAC	ECC	CAC	ANC	ASC
IH	UIH	JAIH	-	-	-	-
IF	UIF	JAIF	-	-	-	-
GDI	-	-	-	CAGDI	-	-
INV	-	-	ECINV	-	ANINV	ASINV
J	UJ	JAJ	ECZ	-	ANZ	ASZ
G	UG	JAG	-	-	-	-
GC	UGC	JAGC	ECGC	CAGC	ANGC	ASGC
G	UGI	JAGI	-	-	-	-
E	UE	JAE	ECE	CAE	ANE	ASE
M	UM	JAM	ECM	CAM	ANM	ASM
GNP	UGNP	JAGNP	-	-	-	-
GDP	-	-	ECGDP	CAGDP	ANGDP	ASGDP
KH	UKH	JAKH	-	-	-	-
KF	UKF	JAKF	-	-	-	-
PC	UPC	JAPC	ECPC	CAPC	ANPC	ASPC
PIH	UPIH	JAPIH	-	-	-	-
PIF	UPIF	JAPIF	-	-	-	-
PG	UPG	JAPG	-	-	-	-
PGC	-	-	ECPGC	CAPGC	ANPGC	ASPGC
PPI	UPPI	JAWPI	-	-	-	-
PE	UPE	JAPE	ECPE	CAPE	ANPE	ASPE
PM	UPM	JAPM	ECPM	CAPM	ANPM	ASPM
PGNP	UPGNP	JAPGNP	-	-	-	
PGDP	-	-	ECPGDP	CAPGDP	ANPGDP	ASPGDP
W	UW	JAW	-	-	-	-
YW	UYW	JAYW	-	-	-	-
GDPV	UGNPV	JAGNPV	-	-	-	-
GDPV	-	-	ECGDPV	CAGDPV	ANGDPV	ASGDPV
LW	ULW	JALW	-	-	-	-
LS	ULS	JALS	-	-	-	-
U	UU	JAU	-	-	-	-
LF	ULF	JALF	-	-	-	-
R	URCB	JARS	-	-	-	-
FE	UFE	JAFE	ECFE	CAFE	ANFE	ASFE
XFE	UXFE	JAXFE	ECXFE	CAXFE	ANXFE	ASXFE
PFE	UPFE	JAPFE	ECPFE	CAPFE	ANPFE	ASPFE
PM$	UPM	JAPM$	ECPM$	CAPM$	ANPM$	ASPM$
PMBOJ$	-	JPMBOJ$	-	-	-	-
PFI	UPFI	JAPFI	ECPFI	CAPFI	ANPFI	ASPFI
PWM	USPWM	JAPWM	ECPWM	CAPWM	ANPWM	ASPWM
OPPFE$						
TIME						

B Data Source

USA:	National Income and Product Account Table	Dept. of Commerce
	Fixed Reproducible Tangible Wealth in the United States, 1925-85	do
	Business Statistics	do
Japan:	Annual Report on National Accounts	EPA
	Gross Capital Stock of Private Business	do
	Annual Report on Labor Force Survey	Somucho
EC & Canada:	National Accounts, vol. 1,11	OECD
Asia NIEs & ASEAN:	World Table 1988–89 Edition	World Bank
Taiwan:	Quarterly National Economic Trends, Taiwan Area	
Foreign Trade:	Direction of Trade Statistics	IMF
	International Financial Statistics	do
	Taiwan Statistical Data Book	

C The Structure of the Linked International Model

C.1 Japan Model

(1) $$JAC = 21684 + 0.20593 * \frac{JAGNPV}{JAPC} + 0.53727 * JAC_{-1} - 77645 * (\frac{JAPC}{JAPC_{-1}})_{-1}$$

(3.0016) (5.1329) (3.2274)

0.997/943/2.56

(2) $$JAIH = 14078 + 0.0387 * JAGNP - 0.08384 * JAKH_{-1} - 824.2 * JARS$$

(2.0475) (-3.1136) (-2.8604)

$$+ 0.94981 * JAIH_{-1} - 5872 * \frac{JAPLH}{JAPLH_{-1}}$$

(0.94981) (-1.9388)

0.806/808/2.10

(3) $JAIF = -3912 + 0.13099 * (JAGNP + JAGNP_{-1}) + 0.01030 * JAKF_{-1}$

(3.2338) (0.2416)

$+ 2835 * D85 + 3193 * D86 + 4491 * D87 - 43425 * \frac{JAYW}{JAGNP}$

(1.865) (1.247) (1.384) (-5.007)

0.988/1062/1.40

(4) $JAE = -7091 + 334.135 * JAFE$

(26.628)

0.985/1360/1.42

(5) $JAM = EXP(-0.1581 + 0.86115 * \log JAGNP - 0.19350 * \log \frac{JAPM}{JAPGNP}$

(11.879) (-2.874)

$+ 0.26326 * \log \frac{JAPM}{JAPM_{-1}})$

(2.9589)

0.929/0.042/2.45

(6) $JAWPI = 19.635 + 0.43896 * JAPM + 66.441 * \frac{JAYW}{JAGNP}$

(20.131) (15.003)

0.993/1.29/2.05

(7) $JAPC = 2.669 + 0.1057 * JAWPI + 53.264 * \frac{JAYW}{JAGNP} + 0.6091 * JAPC_{-1}$

(2.6923) (3.9787) (12.458)

0.998/0.96/1.61

(8) $JAPIH = 4.157 + 0.167 * JAWPI + 52.742 * \frac{JAYW}{JAGNP} + 0.5058 * JAPIH_{-1}$

(1.425) (1.1895) (2.3926)

0.974/3.10/1.59

$$(9)\quad JAPIF = 23.344 + 0.5057 * JAWPI + 44.785 * \frac{JAYW}{JAGNP}$$

(5.9154) (3.5880)

0.969/2.26/0.46

$$(10)\quad JAYW = JAW * JALW$$

$$(11)\quad JAW = (0.36402 + 0.84765 * \frac{JAPC}{JAPC_{-1}} - 0.06270 * \frac{JAPM}{JAPGNP}$$

(8.797) (-2.931)

$$- 3.9341 * \frac{JAU}{JALW} - 0.03682 * D80) * JAW_{-1}$$

(4.7279) (-2.8802)

0.973/0.11/1.53

$$(12)\quad JAW = 1.719 + 0.6335 * JAW_{-1} + 0.19015 * JAPC - 3.6421 * \frac{JAPM}{JAWPI}$$

(5.1144) (2.8752) (-1.948)

$$- 120.2 * \frac{JAU}{JALW}$$

(2.1809)

0.929/0.42/2.45

$$(13)\quad JALW = EXP(1.60485 + 0.32721 * \log(JAGNP + JAGNP_{-1})$$

(4.6745)

$$+ 0.28382 * \log JALW_{-1} - 0.05814 * \log \frac{JAW}{JAPGNP}$$

(1.692) (-1.2078)

0.994/0.006/1.97

(14) $JAU = EXP(-2.652 + 0.7114 * \log JALF - 2.5483 * \log \frac{JAGNP}{JAGNP_{-1}}$

(0.6007) (-2.7226)

$+ 0.33826 * \log JAU_{-1} - 2.4693 * \log \frac{JAW}{JAW_{-1}})$

(1.3312) (−3.120)

0.942/0.072/1.65

(15) $JAPE = 67.172 + 76.95 * JAPFE - 0.57092 * TIME$

(17.684) (-4.947)

0.967/1.37/1.19

(16) $JAKF = -354 + 0.95185 * JAKF_{-1} + JAIF + 25078 * D85 + 4291 * D86$

(276.04) (17.394) (2.8343)

$+ 10997 * D87$

(7.0037)

(17) $JAKH = 380.8 + 0.91733 * JAKH_{-1} + JAIH$

(18) $JAPM = 1.613 + 82.666 * JPMBOJ\$ * JAEX + 0.13235 * JAPGNP$

(35.081) (2.322)

0.992/1.53/1.57

(19) $JAPGNP = JAC + JAIH + JAIF + JAJ + JAG + JAE - JAM$

(20) $JAGNPV = JAC * JAPC + JAIH * JAPIH + JAIF * JAPIF$

$+ JAG * JAPG + JAE * JAPE - JAM * JAPM$

$+ JAJ * JAWPI$

(21) $JAPGNP = \frac{JAGNPV}{JAGNP}$

C.2 USA Model

(22) $UC = 75.521 + 0.27167 * \frac{UGNPV}{UPC} - 2.5027 * URCB - 1136.4 * (\frac{UPC}{UPC_{-1}})_{-1}$

(4.2826) (-1.6923) (-8.077)

$+ 0.6045 * UC_{-1}$

(7.3534)

0.998/9.77/2.85

(23) $UIF = -220.4 + 0.2325 * UGNP - 0.040 * UKF_{-1} + 63.857 * \frac{UPM}{UPGNP}$

(6.0941) (-2.2163) (1.8893)

0.958/13.47/1.32

(24) $UIH = 34.795 + 0.2084 * \frac{UGNPV}{UPC} - 0.11596 * UKH_{-1} - 4.7289 * URCB$

(6.3566) (-4.548) (-3.2277)

0.910/8.35/1.40

(25) $UE = 589.7 + 1.6331 * USFE + 7.7582 * TIME$

(13.752) (12.562)

0.982/6.64/1.53

(26) $UM = EXP(-11.07 + 2.0969 * \log UGNP - 0.4783 * \log \frac{UPM}{UPGNP})$

(34.491) (-7.2366)

0.994/0.019/2.87

(27) $UGNP = UC + UIF + UIH + UJ + UG + UE - UM$

(28) $UPPI = EXP(0.1183 + 0.4365 * \log UPM + 0.17824 * \log \frac{UYW}{UGNP}$

(10.586) (2.3082)

$+ 0.3 * \log UPPI_{-1}$

(3.5277)

0.998/0.015/2.12

(29) $UPC = 13.295 + 0.2088 * UPPI + 4.3077 * UW - 363.2 * \frac{UGNP}{ULW}$

(13.390) (36.429) (-1.607)

0.999/0.25/2.87

(30) $UPIF = 6.9497 + 0.8904 * UPPI$

(35.960)

0.988/2.31/1.52

(31) $UPIH = -10.637 + 0.4136 * UPPI + 0.1422 * \frac{UYW}{UGNP}$

(4.6265) (8.277)

0.995/1.93/0.68

(32) $UPE = 9.4928 + 0.863 * UPPI + 4.087 * OPPFE\$$

(37.289) (4.086)

0.997/0.022/1.04

(33) $UPG = -4.0446 + 0.1376 * UPPI + 0.1051 * \frac{UYW}{UGNP} + 0.4105 * UPG_{-1}$

(5.6959) (6.1348) (6.2979)

0.991/0.45/1.77

(34) $UGNPV = UC * UPC + UIF * UPIF + UIH * UPIH + UG * UPG$

$+ UJ * UPPI + UE * UPE - UM * UPM$

(35) $UPGNP = \frac{UGNPV}{UGNP}$

(36) $UYW = UW * ULW$

$$(37)\quad UW = EXP(-0.8065 + 0.50215 * \log UPC - 0.1807 * \frac{UU}{ULW}$$

(11.513) (-2.5413)

$$+ 0.50145 * \log UW_{-1})$$

(12.244)

0.999/0.0044/1.49

$$(38)\quad ULW = EXP(3.7258 + 0.64075 * \log UGNP - 0.2324 * \log \frac{UW}{UPGNP}$$

(10.619) (-2.2635)

$$+ 0.1828 * \log ULW_{-1}$$

(2.5106)

0.995/0.0069/1.49

$$(39)\quad UKF = 75.995 + 0.94925 * UKF_{-1} + UIF$$

(623.74)

$$(40)\quad UU = 2535 + 0.6806 * ULF - 0.77957 * ULW$$

(31.601) (-27.816)

0.987/203/1.61

$$(41)\quad UKH = -14.465 + 0.9938 * UKH_{-1} + UIH$$

(439.83)

C.3 EC Model

$$(42)\quad ECC = -17.92 + 0.33099 * ECGDP * \frac{ECPGDP}{ECPC} - 328.3 * (\frac{ECPC}{ECPC_{-1}})_{-1}$$

(11.258) (-4.346)

$$+ 0.4847 * ECC_{-1}$$

(13.12)

0.999/3.69/1.86

(43) $ECINV = 801.65 + 0.5585 * ECGDP - 0.13242 * ECGDP_{-1}$

(9.555) (-1.2569)

$- 21.089 * TIME + 0.3361 * ECINV_{-1}$

(3.4521) (1.5004)

(44) $ECE = -10.8187 + 1.32456 * ECFE$

(83.043)

0.998/4.79/1.21

(45) $ECM = EXP(-6.2112 + 1.61175 * \log ECGDP - 0.174 * \log \frac{ECPM}{ECPGDP})$

(17.454) (-2.3703)

0.981/0.016/1.97

(46) $ECGDP = ECC + ECINV + ECGC + ECE - ECM$

(47) $ECPC = -219.18 + 0.1796 * ECPM + 3.182 * TIME + 0.5195 * ECPC_{-1}$

(9.1195) (4.743) (7.0677)

0.999/698/1.44

(48) $ECPE = -129.999 + 86.01 * ECPFE + 1.809 * TIME$

(22.67) (7.0097)

0.999/0.95/0.59

(49) $ECPM = ECPM\$ * ECEX$

(50) $ECPGDP = -237.44 + 0.09975 * ECPM + 3.4755 * TIME$

(4.6186) (4.6186)

$+ 0.5457 * ECPGDP_{-1}$

(5.3593)

0.999/0.78/2.08

C.4 Canada Model

(51) $CAC = 21.853 + 0.29392 * CAGDP\frac{CAPGDP}{CAPC} + 0.62074 * CAC_{-1}$

(2.0646) (2.8783)

0.962/3.53/1.87

(52) $CAM = EXP(-6.7473 + 1.9418 * \log CAGDP)$

(21.373)

0.976/0.032/1.67

(53) $CAE = -5.1197 + 1.1765 * CAFE + 0.64 * (CAE_{-1} - CAFE_{-1})$

(19.21) (4.2121)

0.995/1.42/1.33

(54) $CAGDP = CAC + CAGDI + CAGC + CAE + CAZ - CAM$

(55) $CAPC = -4.2837 + 0.39396 * CAPM + 0.06149 * TIME$

(1.8063) (6.2922)

0.984/0.036/1.28

(56) $CAPE = 0.13617 + 0.8756 * CAPFE$

(69.773)

0.998/0.008/1.26

(57) $CAPM = CAPM\$ * CAEX$

(58) $CAPGDP = 0.11282 + 0.87885 * CAPC$

(47.286)

0.995/0.018/2.30

C.5 Asia NIES Model

(59) $ANC = 16.800 + 0.18373 * ANGDP * \frac{ANPGDP}{ANPC} + 0.66747 * ANC_{-1}$

(4.8359) (8.542)

$- 10.349 * \frac{ANPC}{ANPC_{-1}}$

(-1.8124)

0.998/0.98/1.59

(60) $ANM = EXP(-1.1066 + 0.86655 * \log ANGDP + 0.26843 * \log ANM_{-1})$

(4.3223) (1.6715)

0.981/0.046/1.40

(61) $ANE = 14.568 + 0.8889 * ANFE$

(26.622)

0.985/4.43/1.64

(62) $ANINV = 62.618 + 0.05768 * ANGDP + 0.63675 * ANINV_{-1}$

(1.8924) (6.0826)

$- 55.794 * \frac{ANPM}{ANPGDP}$

(-4.1054)

0.990/0.108/2.44

(63) $ANGDP = ANC + ANINV + ANGC + ANE + ANZ - ANM$

(64) $ANPC = -0.01964 + 0.68 * ANPM + 0.4038 * ANPC_{-1}$

(6.873) (5.0286)

0.995/0.021/0.82

(65) $ANPE = -2.1489 + 0.9689 * ANPFE + 0.02718 * TIME$

(5.8181) (3.3727)

0.982/0.035/0.92

(66) $ANPM = ANPM\$ * ANEX$

(67) $ANPGDP = -0.07972 + 0.59165 * ANPM + 0.54895 * ANPGDP_{-1}$

(3.0244) (4.0661)

0.991/0.030/1.57

C.6 ASEAN Model

(68) $ASC = 18.372 + 0.33583 * ASGDP * \frac{ASPGDP}{ASPC} - 17.524 * \frac{ASPC}{ASPC_{-1}}$

(4.6483) (-1.2529)

$+ 0.50063 * ASC_{-1}$

(4.7660)

0.998/1.68/1.57

(69) $ASINV = -32.6644 + 0.20265 * ASGDP + 46.9938 * \frac{ASPFE}{ASPM}$

(6.066) (4.2726)

0.876/3.25/1.13

(70) $ASM = EXP(-3.6445 + 1.5235 * \log ASGDP)$

(15.737)

0.957/0.056/0.74

(71) $ASE = 7.823 + 0.8979 * ASFE + 0.8172 * (ASE_{-1} - ASFE_{-1})$

(19.090) (3.2461)

0.973/2.78/1.53

(72) $ASGDP = ASC + ASINV + ASGC + ASE + ASZ - ASM$

(73) $ASPC = -0.12887 + 0.45677 * ASPM + 0.78407 * ASPC_{-1}$

(3.5253) (10.616)

0.992/0.036/2.15

(74) $ASPGDP = -0.18163 + 0.633 * ASPM + 0.63494 * ASPGDP_{-1}$

(3.8855) (6.2339)

0.989/0.038/1.58

(75) $ASPM = ASPM\$ * ASEX$

C.7 Trade Linkage Sector

(76) $USXFE = 0.17404 * \frac{JAM}{226.74} + 0.0846 * ECM + 0.6754 * \frac{CAM}{1.1692}$

$+ 0.1907 * ANM + 0.1538 * ASM$

(77) $JAXFE = 0.128 * UM + 0.0242 * ECM + 0.0391 \frac{CAM}{1.1692} + 0.2553 * ANM$

$+ 0.2184 * ASM$

(78) $ECXFE = 0.1522 * UM + 0.0593 * \frac{JAM}{226.74} + 0.5035 * ECM + 0.0776 * \frac{CAM}{1.1692}$

$+ 0.0934 * ANM + 0.1882 * ASM$

(79) $CAXFE = 0.1701 * UM + 0.0335 * \frac{JAM}{226.74} + 0.0213 * ECM + 0.0122 * ANM$

$+ 0.0087 * ASM$

(80) $ANXFE = 0.0657 * UM + 0.0416 * \frac{JAM}{226.74} + 0.0154 * ECM$

$+ 0.0217 * \frac{CAM}{1.1692} + 0.0582 * ANM + 0.0601 * ASM$

(81) $ASXFE = 0.0508 * UM + 0.1514 * \frac{JAM}{226.74} + 0.0136 * ECM$

$+ 0.0054 * \frac{CAM}{1.1692} + 0.0816 * ANM + 0.1504 * ASM$

(82) $USPFI = 0.128 * JAPFE + 0.1701 * CAPFE\$ + 0.1522 * ECPFE\$$

$+ 0.0508 * ASPFE\$ + 0.0657 * ANPFE\$$

(83) $JAPFI\$ = 0.174 * USPFE + 0.0335 * CAPFE\$ + 0.0593 * ECPFE\$$

$+ 0.1514 * ASPFE\$ + 0.0416 * ANPFE\$$

(84) $ECPFI\$ = 0.0846 * USPFE + 0.0242 * JAPFE\$ + 0.0123 * CAPFE\$$

$+ 0.5035 * ECPFE\$ + 0.0136 * ASPFE\$ + 0.0154 * ANPFE\$$

$$(85)\quad CAPFI\$ = 0.6754 * USPFE + 0.0391 * JAPFE\$ + 0.0776 * ECPFE\$$$

$$+ 0.0054 * ASPFE\$ + 0.0217 * ANPFE\$$$

$$(86)\quad ANPFI\$ = 0.1907 * USPFE + 0.2553 * JAPFE\$ + 0.0122 * CAPFE\$$$

$$+ 0.0934 * ECPFE\$ + 0.0816 * ASPFE\$ + 0.0582 * ANPFE\$$$

$$(87)\quad ASPFI\$ = 0.1538 * USPFE + 0.2184 * JAPFE\$ + 0.0087 * CAPFE\$$$

$$+ 0.1882 * ECPFE\$ + 0.1505 * ASPFE\$ + 0.0601 * ANPFE\$$$

$$(88)\quad ECPM\$ = -13.11 + 170.24 * ECPFI\$ + 2.071 * OPPFE\$$$

(40.822) (1.5863)

0.995/1.025/1.54

$$(89)\quad UPM = -14.597 + 117.042 * USPFI + 9.0468 * OPPFE\$ + 0.43214 * UPM_{-1}$$

(11.102) (3.5665) (10.528)

0.993/1.42/1.99

$$(90)\quad CAPM\$ = 0.5733 + 0.4258 * CAPFI\$ + 0.08078 * OPPFE\$$$

(13.335) (5.2216)

0.982/0.0099/1.67

$$(91)\quad ANPM\$ = 0.0449 + 1.1155 * ANPFI\$ + 0.17121 * OPPFE\$$$

(19.602) (8.8128)

0.991/0.013/0.08

$$(92)\quad ASPM\$ = 1.7019 + 0.44327 * ASPFI\$ + 0.40658 * OPPFE\$$$

(2.4924) (10.255)

$$- 0.01787 * TIME$$

(-4.2262)

0.952/0.027/1.65

(93) $JPMBOJ\$ = -0.2384 + 2.3382 * JAPFI\$ + 0.16298 * OPPFE\$$

$$(7.1851) \qquad (2.1923)$$

0.976/0.029/1.32

(94) $USPFE = 0.05993 + 0.01087 * UPPI - 0.02786 * ECEX$

(95) $$JAPFE\$ = \frac{0.3826 + 0.009928 * JAWPI + 0.14366 * JAEX}{JAEX} - \frac{0.00625 * TIME}{JAEX}$$

(96) $$ECPFE\$ = \frac{-1.7358 + 0.7142 * ECPFI\$ * ECEX}{ECEX} + \frac{0.06013 * OPPFE\$ * ECEX + 0.02752 * TIME}{ECEX}$$

(97) $$CAPFE\$ = \frac{2.48305 + 1.55206 * CAPFI\$ * CAEX - 0.034656 * TIME}{CAEX}$$

(98) $$ANPFE\$ = \frac{0.33264 + 0.53995 * ANPM + 0.11806 * ANPFE}{ANEX}$$

(99) $$ASPFE\$ = \frac{0.25180 + 0.58637 * OPPFE\$ * ASEX}{ASEX} + \frac{0.0009939 * UPM * ASEX}{ASEX}$$

(100) $JAPFE = JAPFE\$ * JAEX$

(101) $ECPFE = ECPFE\$ * ECEX$

(102) $CAPFE = CAPFE\$ * CAEX$

(103) $ANPFE = ANPFE\$ * ANEX$

(104) $ASPFE = ASPFE\$ * ASEX$

(105) $$USPWM = 0.1683 * JPMBOJ\$ + 0.3989 * \frac{ECPM\$}{100} + 0.2824 * CAPM\$ + 0.0837 * ANPM\$ + 0.0666 * ASPM\$$$

$$(106)\ JAPWM = 0.3855 * \frac{UPM}{100} + 0.2081 * \frac{ECPM\$}{100} + 0.0298 * CAPM\$$$

$$+ 0.2042 * ANPM\$ + 0.1723 * ASPM\$$$

$$(107)\ ECPWM = 0.5424 * \frac{UPM}{100} + 0.1236 * JPMBOJ\$ + 0.0699 * CAPM\$$$

$$+ 0.0884 * ANPM\$ + 0.1756 * ASPM\$$$

$$(108)\ CAPWM = 0.7385 * \frac{UPM}{100} + 0.0853 * JPMBOJ\$ + 0.1521 * \frac{ECPM\$}{100}$$

$$+ 0.0141 * ANPM\$ + 0.0100 * ASPM\$$$

$$(109)\ ANPWM = 0.4237 * \frac{UPM}{100} + 0.1570 * JPMBOJ\$ + 0.2825 * \frac{ECPM\$}{100}$$

$$+ 0.0353 * CAPM\$ + 0.1014 * ASPM\$$$

$$(110)\ ASPWM = 0.2504 * \frac{UPM}{100} + 0.4964 * JPMBOJ\$ + 0.1567 * \frac{ECPM\$}{100}$$

$$+ 0.005 * CAPM\$ + 0.0912 * ANPM\$$$

$$(111)\ USFE = \frac{FEuo}{1000} + EXP(0.45125 + \underset{(18.642)}{0.85902} * \log USXFE$$

$$- \underset{(-7.7849)}{0.87715} * \log \frac{USPFE}{USPWM})$$

0.969/0.023/1.56

$$(112)\ JAFE = \frac{FEjo}{1000} + EXP(-2.1273 + \underset{(20.386)}{1.42598} * \log JAXFE$$

$$- \underset{(-2.2492)}{0.46673} * \log \frac{JAPFE\$}{JAPWM})$$

0.972/0.059/1.18

$$(113)\, ECFE = \frac{ECFEO}{1000} + EXP(-1.8370 + 1.2590 * \log ECXFE$$

$$(33.741)$$

$$- 0.14057 * \log \frac{ECPFE\$}{ECPWM})$$

$$(\text{-}3.0432)$$

0.990/0.020/1.06

$$(114)\, CAFE = \frac{CAFEo}{1000} + EXP(-1.05517 + 1.14908 * \log CAXFE$$

$$(15.862)$$

$$+ 0.13650 * \log \frac{CAPFE\$}{CAPWM})$$

$$(0.7614)$$

0.981/0.033/1.03

$$(115)\, ANFE = \frac{FEano}{1000} + EXP(-4.66724 + 2.14973 * \log ANXFE$$

$$(17.975)$$

$$- 0.8285 * \log \frac{ANPFE\$}{ANPWM})$$

$$(\text{-}4.4796)$$

0.989/0.057/1.14

$$(116)\, ASFE = \frac{FEaso}{1000} + EXP(-1.60478 + 1.31645 * \log ASXFE$$

$$(16.896)$$

$$- 0.17651 * \log \frac{ASPFE\$}{ASPWM})$$

$$(\text{-}1.7602)$$

0.980/0.040/1.84

1. Values in the parenthesis indicate t-values.
2. Values at the end of structural equations are R^2 , standard errors and D-W ratios, respectively.

Chapter 15

The Growth of the Korean Economy and the Foreign Capital

Noriyoshi Oguchi[1]

1 Introduction

The Korean economy has grown very rapidly during the last two decades. The GNP increased by a factor of seven between 1970 and 1989. From 1970 to 1978, the average annual growth rate was 9.9 percent. Although the Korean economy had suffered a set back after the second energy crisis, the growth rate recovered in the late 1980's. Throughout the period, exports increased faster than GNP. As a result, the share of exports in GNP increased from 15 per cent in 1970 to 42 percent in 1987. At the same time, imports also increased very rapidly, resulting in a perpetual trade deficit for most of the period. The deficits in the current account were covered by surplus in the capital account. Import of foreign capital helped the development of manufacturing industry, but it also resulted in a relatively large foreign debt. The burden of servicing this debt became a problem during the negative growth period after the second energy crisis. In this paper we will evaluate the role of foreign capital in the development of the Korean economy after 1970. We will also analyze the effects of direct foreign investment (DFI) on the Korean economy. The amount of DFI was relatively small compared to the volume of foreign loans. DFI, however, has larger impacts on the receiving economy. Its direct effects are obvious: New employments, new production activities, increase in exports imports, etc.

However, it is not easy to obtain statistical data for these. Also, it is obvious that these economic activities generate secondary repercussions in the economy. The significance of these secondary effects are even more difficult to see in statistical data.

In this paper, we will estimate a macroeconometric model for Korea and use it to analyze the effects of foreign capital as well as thoseof DFI. Although there have been studies on the roles of foreign capital and of DFI , only a few used quantitative approaches. (See for example Healey [2], Grionoles and Bhagwati [1].) Also, most quantitative analyses use a single equation analysis, where the economic variables which were considered to be affected, are regressed on the amount of foreign capital or DFI. This approach may make the estimation of the overall effects possible, but it does not clarify how those effects are being generated. With macroeconometric models, we can develop theoretically meaningful relations

[1] School of Commerce, Senshu University, Tokyo, Japan

more explicitly. Importation of foreign capital and DFI affect various aspects of the economy and a macroeconometric model is a very useful tool to capture those effects. The exogenous shock of a foreign direct investment ripples through the economy and this process can be seen by simulation analysis if the econometric model captures interwoven relationships among the economic variables. Hong [3] gives us such an example whereby a fully developed macroeconometric model is used to estimate the effects of foreign debt on Korea. Oguchi and Fukuchi[8] too estimated the effects of Japanese investment on Thailand with a macroeconometric model of Thailand. A quantitative analysis with a macroeconometric model is also superior to the often-used single equation regression analyses with flow of for eign capital or DFI as a regressor. This is because in many respects, the stock of capital, rather than the flow of investment, has more important effects on the receiving economy. In our analysis, not only the flow of foreign capital but also the accumulated foreign debts are important variables. In the analysis of the effects of DFI, we treat the DFI, hence, the stock of foreign capital, differently from domestic investment and try to estimate the secondary effects. Also, we assume Cobb-Douglas type production functions and estimate production functions separately for domestic and foreign technology.

We will examine the difference in productivity between domestic capital and DFI, specifically Japanese DFI in section 2, before going into the detailed discussion of the macroeconometric model in section 3. In section 4, the results of the simulation analyses are examined and conclusions are presented in section 5.

2 A Comparison of Productivity

Before discussing the effects of DFI, it is worthwhile to have an overview of the role of foreign capital in the Korean economy. A rather small amount of DFI started in the late 1960's. At that time, the share of DFI in total long-term capital inflows was about 5 percent. This amounted to about 1.4 percent of total capital formation in Korea. The share did not increase during the 1970's. It stayed at less than 1 percent of long term capital inflows and at around 5 percent of total capital formation. Thus the role of DFI was rather limited, compared to the other forms of foreign capital inflow. This was because the other flows of foreign capital were of much larger scale, however 5 percent of total capital formation is still a significant amount. Thus we will first analyze here the effects of DFI.

The main reasons for treating DFI separately from the domestic capital stock is that production technologies associated with foreign capital are different from those widely used domestically. Here again, collecting data to estimate the productivity of foreign capital remains a difficult task. However, recent studies by the Korean Credit Rating Corporation [7] provides very detailed data for 1984 to 1987. They include the level of employment by foreign capital as well as value added. Since longer series of data regarding DFI are readily available, we can have a rough estimate of the production technology.

Production Data of DFI in Korea

	accumulated DFI (million $)	employment (thousand)	value added (million $)	1980 price
1984	3122.79	196	1040.42	
1985	3278.44	190	1089.29	
1986	3461.44	214	1335.59	

By assuming a Cobb-Douglas production function, we can determine the three parameters in $\log Y = a0{+}a1{*}\log K{+}a2{*}\log L$. The estimates we get are a1=1.572 and a2= 0.983. These results are unrealistically high. If we assume a technical progress of 2 percent per year, i.e., $\log Y = a0 + a1 * \log K + a2 * \log L + 0.02T$, then we get a1=1.1769 and a2=1.0082. The figures are still very large. This is because we have only three observations and the estimates we get are not very reliable. Also there is a very large increase in the value added while the levels of inputs do not increase very much. If we place a restriction of constant returns to scale with the technical change term, i.e., $\log \frac{Y}{L} = a0 + a1 * T + a2 * \log \frac{K}{L}$, a2 becomes negative and a1 is very large 0.0814. This again is not acceptable. If we assume the rate of technical change to be 0.01857, which is the estimate we obtain from the pooled data of Korean and Japanese secondary industries, then we obtain 0.2095 as the estimate for a2. This function is shown in Figure 1 by a dotted curve marked 'reference'. Yet these, of course, are not very reliable figures, since we have only three observations. Hence we use these estimates just as references and, for more reliable analysis, we have to use another method.

The majority of DFI in Korea is from Japan. As of 1987, 54.8 percent of total foreign investments were from Japan while 29.4 percent were from the US. Moreover the Japanese investments were mostly in the manufacturing sector. Hence we may roughly approximate the production technology of foreign capital in Korea by that of Japanese firms in Japan especially for the secondary sector. First, we look at the basic statistics on production in Korea and Japan. Table 1 gives the output(GNP) and capital stock and employment for the two countries in the secondary industry. The output and capital stock figures are in US dollars for easier comparison. In Table 2, we have figures for output per worker, and capital per worker. The capital-labor ratio in Korea in 1975 was 0.0062 billion dollars per 1,000 persons. That is 6,200 dollars per worker. The corresponding figure of output per worker was 5,800 dollars. Those figures for Japan for the same year were 19,000 and 12,000 dollars, respectively. Thus a Japanese worker was equipped with about three times more capital than his Korean counterpart and produced a little over twice as much. The capital per worker in Korea in 1985 was 8,600 dollars, which means about 3.3 percent growth rate a year during this period. The capital per worker in Japan increased at the much higher rate of 7.1 percent a year during the same period. Thus the difference in capital-labor ratios in the two countries widened. The difference in the output per worker widened even more as it rose at a 1.3 percent annually (from 1975 to1986) in Korea compared to 7.2 percent in Japan. Since these figures are compared in US dollars, they reflect changes in the exchange rates. This relative position of production relations can be easily seen in terms of production functions. We estimated a production function by pooling the data for the two countries. The difference should be captured by the dummy variables. The estimated production function for the period between 1970 and 1987 for Korea and between 1970 and 1986 for Japan are:

$$\log Y = -1.504 + 0.5226 * \log K2T - 1 + 0.3123 * \log E2 + 0.01856 * T$$

$$\qquad (2.5) \qquad\qquad (2.0) \qquad\qquad (0.9)$$

$$+ 0.0753 * \log E2 * DJ$$

$$(0.85)$$

R=0.993 SD=0.104

where DJ is the dummy variable for Japan. Although the t-values for variable T (which indicates time) and for the dummy variable for Japan are low in this particular equation, we judged these figures to be rather reliable from other estimation results.

The estimated production function is shown graphically in Figure 1. The graph represents the production relations for 1975. They shift upwards as time passes. Since the rates of the shifts for both countries (Korea and Japan) are the same, the relative position of the two curves does not change. Two x marks on the graph show the position of Korea for 1975 and 1980. Two o marks indicate the positions of Japan for the same years. Considering the graph, it is clear that the difference in technology is rather significant in explaining the difference in productivity between the two countries. With the 1975 figure, if the capital per worker in Korea had been at the same level as in Japan, it would have eliminated about 60 percent of the difference of labor productivity. This division is rather simplistic as technology and capital labor ratios are so closely related. Still, those figures give some indication of the relative importanse of capital and technology. This result coincides with the growth accounting literature where the contribution of capital itself is estimated to be rather small. As in growth accounting, we need more detailed examinations in order to have a more practical insight on differences in productivity.

The estimated production function we discussed earlier is also presented in the figure. As we said earlier, this estimation is based on only three observations, but it seems that the curve lies somewhere between the graphs, for Korea and Japan. Thus, it may be used as an approximation for a limited and small range of capital-labor ratios. For more reliable estimation, however, we need a larger set of data.

Figure 1   Comparison of Production Functions

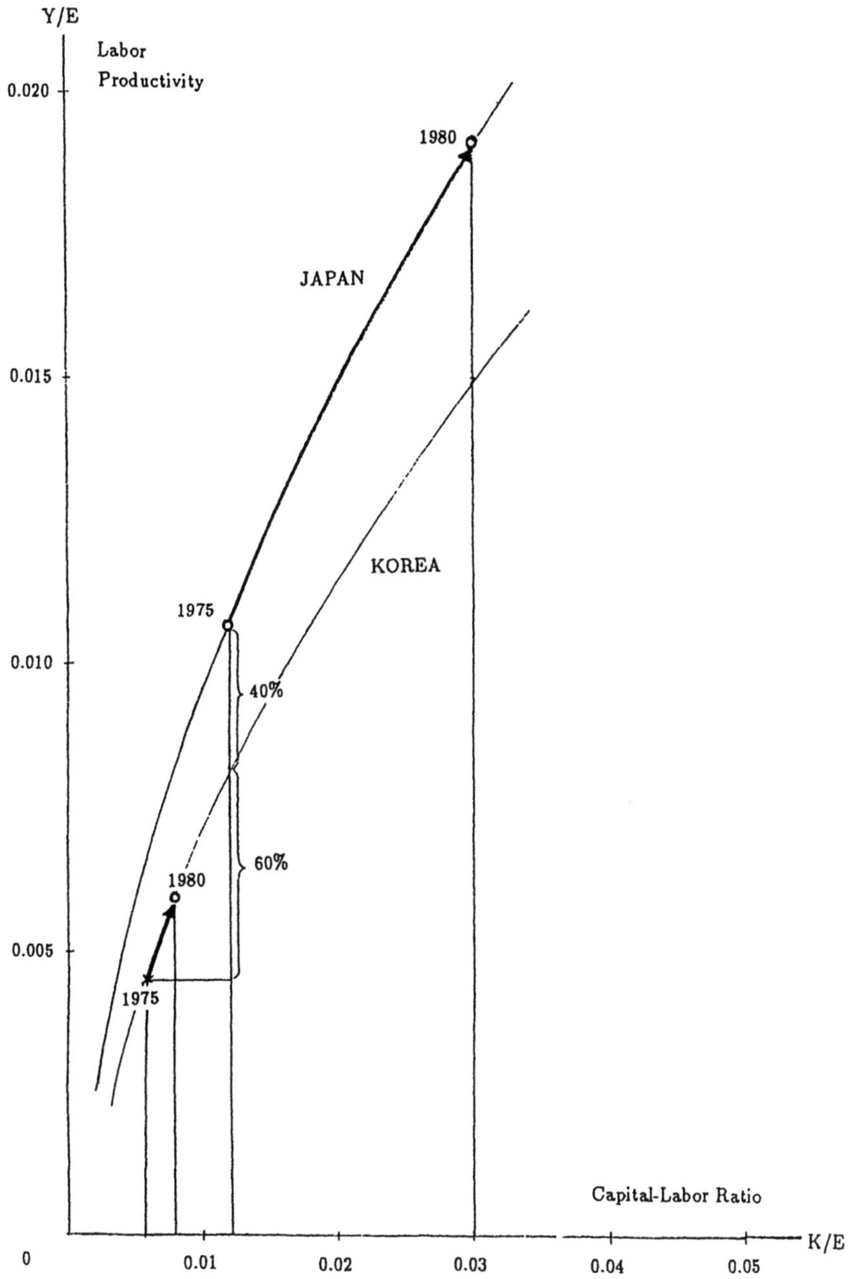

Table 1. Comparison of Productivity and Capital-Labor Ratio

KOREA

YEAR	Y2S	%	K2S	%	E2	%
1965	4.2519		0.0000		849.00	
1966	4.9156	15.6	6.6416		913.00	7.5
1967	5.9034	20.1	10.0934	14.2	1115.00	22.1
1968	7.0305	19.1	11.3349	12.3	1282.00	15.0
1969	7.7503	10.2	12.6468	11.6	1346.00	5.0
1970	6.9144	15.0	13.3823	5.6	1395.00	3.6
1971	9.2829	4.1	14.3554	7.3	1428.00	2.4
1972	9.7205	4.7	13.4355	-6.4	1499.99	5.0
1973	12.1679	28.3	13.6765	1.8	1621.00	21.5
1974	11.7864	-5.5	15.3469	12.2	2062.00	13.2
1975	13.2368	12.3	14.1183	-8.0	2265.00	9.8
1976	16.2138	22.5	15.7649	11.7	2743.00	21.1
1977	18.6548	15.1	17.7637	12.7	2901.00	5.8
1978	22.4459	20.3	20.1664	13.5	3123.00	7.7
1979	24.5934	9.6	23.8641	18.3	3237.00	3.7
1980	17.8659	-27.4	27.6906	16.0	3079.00	-4.9
1981	18.4294	3.2	22.8036	-17.6	2983.00	-3.1
1982	18.2826	-0.8	25.0400	9.8	3143.00	5.4
1983	19.8040	8.3	26.9277	7.5	3375.00	7.4
1984	22.2613	12.4	28.6678	6.5	3491.00	3.4
1985	22.1449	-0.5	31.6458	10.4	3659.00	4.8
1986	27.0951	22.4	33.8642	7.0	4013.00	9.7
1987	34.6293	27.8	40.4084	19.3	4602.00	14.7

JAPAN

YEAR	Y2S	%	K2S	%	E2	%
1970	160.7529		176.6179		19208.00	
1971	175.3168	9.1	204.6616	17.9	19531.00	1.7
1972	219.2832	25.1	239.6625	17.1	19703.00	0.9
1973	273.4656	24.7	304.6736	27.1	20613.00	4.6
1974	247.8140	-9.4	375.4134	23.2	20391.00	-1.1
1975	238.0181	-4.0	380.7987	1.4	19681.00	-3.5
1976	253.8965	6.7	397.8666	4.5	19737.00	0.3
1977	292.3798	15.2	417.3917	4.9	19650.00	-0.4
1978	400.8363	37.1	481.9988	15.5	19646.00	-0.6
1979	405.1880	1.1	639.7390	32.7	19763.00	0.6
1980	415.0190	2.4	646.4693	1.1	20117.00	1.8
1981	443.4067	6.8	662.0066	2.4	20219.00	0.5
1982	406.5074	-8.3	752.0811	9.5	20145.00	-0.4
1983	442.3852	8.8	678.4775	-6.4	20420.00	1.4
1984	481.0408	8.7	751.5906	10.8	20598.00	0.9
1985	506.1118	5.2	799.5960	6.4	20779.00	0.9
1986	724.6322	43.2	856.0766	7.1	20745.00	-0.2

Table 2.

	KOREA				JAPAN			
YEAR	YE2S	%	KE2S	%	YE2S	%	KE2S	%
1965	0.0050081		0.0000000					
1966	0.0053821	7.5	0.0096842					
1967	0.0052945	-1.6	0.0090524	-6.5				
1968	0.0054840	3.6	0.0088416	-2.3				
1969	0.0057580	5.0	0.0093958	6.3				
1970	0.0063902	11.0	0.0095931	2.1				
1971	0.0065006	1.7	0.0100528	4.8	0.0083691	11.2	0.0090388	2.9
1972	0.0064846	-0.2	0.0089630	-10.8	0.0089763	7.3	0.0104788	15.9
1973	0.0068467	5.6	0.0075115	-16.2	0.0111294	24.0	0.0121638	16.1
1974	0.0057160	-16.5	0.0074427	-0.9	0.0132667	19.2	0.0147807	21.5
1975	0.0058441	2.2	0.0062332	-16.3	0.0121531	-8.4	0.0184107	24.6
1976	0.0059110	1.1	0.0057473	-7.8	0.0120938	-0.5	0.0193485	5.1
1977	0.0064305	8.8	0.0061233	6.5	0.0128640	6.4	0.0201584	4.2
1978	0.0071873	11.8	0.0064574	5.5	0.0148794	15.7	0.0212413	5.4
1979	0.0075976	5.7	0.0073723	14.2	0.0204029	37.1	0.0245342	15.5
1980	0.0058025	-23.6	0.0089934	22.0	0.0205024	0.5	0.0323705	31.9
1981	0.0061781	6.5	0.0076445	-15.0	0.0206303	0.6	0.0321355	-0.7
1982	0.0058169	-5.8	0.0079669	4.2	0.0219302	6.3	0.0327418	1.9
1983	0.0058679	0.9	0.0079786	0.1	0.0201791	-8.0	0.0359931	9.9
1984	0.0063768	8.7	0.0082119	2.9	0.0216643	7.4	0.0332261	-7.7
1985	0.0060522	-5.1	0.0086487	5.3	0.0233538	7.8	0.0364885	9.8
1986	0.0067518	11.6	0.0084386	-2.4	0.0243569	4.3	0.0384810	5.5
1987	0.0075248	11.4	0.0087806	4.1	0.0349305	43.4	0.0412666	7.2

As is well known, an inflow of foreign capital by borrowing from abroad provides investment funds and the reserve of foreign exchange. At the same time, it accumulates as external debt, and drains the reserve of foreign exchange, as repayment is made in the future. By formulating this in the macroeconometric model, we analyze the effects of foreign borrowing. In Korea, as stated earlier, capital inflows from abroad in the form of borrowing was far larger than that in the form of direct investment. It was an important source of investment funds and of foreign exchange to finance current account deficits. We will analyze how significant were foreign borrowings in the growth of the Korean economy.

3 Macroeconometric Model

In this section we discuss a macroeconometric model for Korea, designed to analyze the effects of foreign borrowing and of DFI. The macroeconometric model for Korea consists of 51 equations. The entire model is presented at the end of this section together with a flowchart. The sample period is from 1968 to 1987. Since there are lagged explanatory variables, the estimation period is from 1970 to 1987. The model has the following basic features:

1. Since the model covers a relatively long period of time, the supply side determines the production level. The production functions are of the Cobb-Douglas type.

2. Productive activities are divided into three sectors, primary, secondary and tertiary industries.

3. Once the production, i.e., income determined, expenditures are determined.

4. Separate import functions are estimated for three categories of imports.

5. There is a rather detailed foreign sector.

6. Deflators are endogenously estimated.

For our expressed purpose of analyzing the effects of foreign capital, we have built the following features into the model. First, commercial foreign loans (endogenous) and official foreign loans explain investment. They are also accumulated to the outstanding foreign debts. A larger outstanding foreign debt discourages new foreign borrowing. It also requires larger repayments, part of which may accumulate to the debts. However, one notes a positive impact due to an increase in investment leading to a larger productive capacity, which in turn draws in more foreign capital.

DFI generates additional productive capacity and creates directly new employment. It also induces domestic investments. According to our estimated investment function, one won of direct foreign investment results in an increase of ten won of new investment during that year. This again raises the level of productive activities which in turn invites more direct foreign investments. On the other hand, the higher productive activity tightens the labor market and causes the wage rate to rise. A higher wage rate makes Korea less attractive as a target for DFI.

We will now briefly discuss the specification of the major functions. Employment is basically determined by the demand side. As in most developing countries, it is considered that there is labor force which is not employed efficiently. Thus, changes in demand for labor can be quickly accommodated. During the estimation period, we observed a large scale migration of labor from agriculture to secondary and tertiary sectors. Thus the labor supply for the primary sector is specified as the residual of the secondary and tertiary sectors. We specified a Phillips curve relation for wage determination in the manufacturing sector. Since the move from primary sector to manufacturing sector is not frictionless, the labor market conditions are reflected in the wage rate.

The availability of foreign capital is an important factor in determining investment. Thus we have the foreign loans and DFI in the investment function. Investment also depends on the demand side which reflects the firms' expectation regarding total demand. In order to determine the sectoral investments, we used a two step procedure. Total investment is determined by the factors which reflect the economy-wide conditions as we stated above. At the same time it is desirable to include sector-specific factors in the sectoral investment functions. For this purpose we estimated the economy-wide investment function as well as sectoral functions. Investment in each sector is then scaled up or down, so that the total equals the value indicated by the economy-wide investment function. Foreign capital was an important source of private investment. Also exports were one of the major engines of economic growth in Korea during the period. This is reflected in the investment function for secondary industry. Investment flows are related to the capital stock by statistical relations. Exports depend on price competitiveness and on world demand. The same two-step procedure as used for the investment functions was used for import functions as we divided imports into three categories.

The major transactions with foreign economies are endogenously explained. Most of the terms in the balance of payments are included. For current account, as we have mentioned earlier, exports and imports are endogenously explained. Interest payments in the invisible trade account are explained by the accumulated foreign debts, and by the interest rates in the international capital market. The accumulated foreign debts in return are given by the definition. DFI is explained by relative wage rates in Korea and Japan as well as by the exchange rate. The level of GNP is also adopted to indicate the activeness of the economy. We treated the holding of foreign reserves as exogenous, since it is more of a policy variable. The exchange rate is also left as exogenous, since this too was a policy variable during the period analyzed. In most of the international financial equations, we included dummy variables as they fluctuate rather widely. We opted for this route to maintain the relatively good explanatory power of the entire model. In fact, dummy variables are limited to the minimum necessity.

In our model the adjustment to short term business fluctuations is made through the labor market. A higher GNP level induces a larger demand for labor. This will cause a higher wage rate and higher price levels which will dampen total demand.

The results of the final test of the model is given after the model itself on page 30. Most of the major variables are within 10% in MAPE. The model follows the movement of the Korean economy fairly well, despite the considerable fluctuations during the period.

3.1 Korean Model 1970-1987

Rate of Change of Wage Rate in Manufacturing (GWN)

(1) $GWN = 0.514646980 + 0.344600667 * GPCP_{-1}$

(2.485)

$- 0.71814877 * UR - 0.166208824 * D37$

(-2.838) (-3.613)

$- 0.128917738 * D817$

(-5.145)

R^2=0.8458 RRB=0.7983 SD=0.043433346 DW=2.2221

Total Labor Force (L) (1,000 persons)

$$(2) \quad L = -8670.10553 + 0.633509352 * N - 302.618629 * UR_{-1}$$

(24.912) (-1.801)

R^2 =0.9793 RRB=0.9766 SD=299.779212 DW=0.9581

Employment in Tertiary Industry (E3) (1,000 persons)

$$(3) \quad E3 = 146.523598 + 0.821834464 * E3_{-1} + 1162.97827 * (\frac{GNP}{N})_{-1}$$

(8.614) (2.353)

R^2 =0.9934 RRB=0.9925 SD=138.529773 DW=1.7878

Employment in Secondary Industry (E2) (1,000 persons)

$$(4) \quad E2 = -1571.71367 - 0.015046748 * \frac{WMn}{PGNP_{-1}} + 0.376146192 * L$$

(-2.376) (5.678)

$$+ 0.124247216 * Y2_{-1}$$

(2.653)

R^2=0.9769 RRB=0.9719 SD=152.762640 DW=1.1756

Employment in Primary Industry (E1) (1,000 persons)

$$(5) \quad E1 = -399.110464 + 0.980173022 * (L - E2 - E3) - 144.238943 * D817$$

(21.278) (-1.910)

R^2=0.9898 RRB=0.9884 SD=74.0555338 DW=1.4042

Production in Primary Sector (Y1) (billion won)

$$(6) \quad \log Y1 = 2.62349545 + 0.431483407 * \log E1 + 0.299604570 * \log K1_{-1}$$

(2.103) (5.861)

R^2=0.8083 RRB=0.7828 SD=0.068230382 DW=1.3172

Production in Secondary Sector (Y2) (billion \$)

$$(7) \quad \log Y2\$ = -1.50397246 + 0.522574202 * \log K2\$_{-1} + 0.312314421 * \log E2$$

$$+ 0.01856832 * TIM$$

Production in Tertiary Sector (Y3) (billion won)

$$(8) \quad \log\frac{Y3}{E3} = 0.733385686 + 0.266245354 * \log\frac{K3}{E3}$$

(5.659)

R^2=0.6668 RRB=0.6460 SD=0.073084208 DW=0.5741

Unemployment Rate (UR) (%)

$$(9) \quad UR = \frac{L - E1 - E2 - E3}{L} * 100$$

GNP (billion won)

$$(10) \quad GNP = Y1 + Y2 + Y3$$

Fixed Investment (I) (billion won)

$$(11) \quad I = -1793.90469 + 0.22414025 * (LCN\$ + LPN\$) * \frac{RATE}{PI} * 100$$

(1.481)

$$+ 30.8724711 * (\frac{X\$}{GNP})_{-1} + 1.04249506 * DIN\$ * \frac{RATE}{PI}$$

(7.890) (1.892)

R^2=0.9521 RRB=0.9418 SD=1537.23492 DW=1.3067

Fixed Investment in Primary Industry (II1) (billion won)

$$(12) \quad II1 = -572.804535 + 0.099832109 * E1_{-1} + 0.185572837 * K1_{-1}$$

(1.384) (12.371)

R^2=0.9693 RRB=0.9652 SD=94.9191634 DW=1.9064

Fixed Investment in Secondary Industry (II2) (billion won)

$$(13) \quad II2 = -1451.82470 + 0.86832767 * YC80_{-1} + 0.211857143 * K2_{-1}$$

(1.812) (9.294)

$$+ 299.570120 * D702$$

R^2=0.9891 RRB=0.9867 SD=273.749341 DW=2.4585

Fixed Investment in Tertiary Industry (II3) (billion won)

(14) $II3 = -2890.15242 + 0.536840613 * Y3_{-1}$

(18.888)

R^2=0.9571 RRB=0.9544 SD=773.916491 DW=1.2507

(15) $I1 = \dfrac{II1 * I}{II1 + II2 + II3}$

(16) $I2 = \dfrac{II2 * I}{II1 + II2 + II3}$

(17) $I3 = \dfrac{II3 * I}{II1 + II2 + II3}$

Fixed Capital Stock in Primary Industry (billion won)

(18) $K1 = 44.9380500 + 0.939462064 * K1_{-1} + I1$

(304.822)

R^2=0.9998 RRB=0.9998 SD=37.891385 DW=1.1837

Fixed Capital Stock in Secondary Industry (billion won)

(19) $K2 = 324.838202 + 0.910559693 * K2_{-1} + I2$

(220.702)

R^2=0.9997 RRB=0.9997 SD=160.873803 DW=0.6942

Fixed Capital Stock in Tertiary Industry (billion won)

(20) $K3 = 42.6493343 + 0.946855123 * K3_{-1} + I3$

(585.316)

R^2=1.0000 RRB=1.0000 SD=157.862068 DW=2.1555

Total Imports (M\$) (100 million \$)

(21) $M\$ = -62.2068596 + 0.0074211 * GNP_{-1} + 0.725684212 * \dfrac{FEn\$}{PM_{-1}}$

(-1.410) (2.405)

$- 0.00033498 * PM * PATE$

R^2=0.9918 RRB=0.9901 SD=11.2420116 DW=2.5980

Imports of Investment Goods (MI$) (100 million $)

$$(22)\quad MMI\$ = 9.51743659 + 0.395500631 * MMI\$_{-1} + 0.010821984 * I2$$

(1.986) (3.804)

R^2=0.9579 RRB=0.9523 SD=8.63172759 DW=1.3596

Imports of Raw Material (MR$) (100 million $)

$$(23)\quad MMR\$ = 8.10041202 + 0.003510 * Y2 + 0.669830746 * MMR\$_{-1}$$

(3.953) (6.437)

R^2=0.9894 RRB=0.9880 SD=7.13219864 DW=1.516

Imports of Consumer Goods (MC$) (100 million $)

$$(24)\quad MMC\$ = 1.23021575 + 0.00084978 * GNP - TAX_{-1}$$

(11.822)

R^2=0.8973 RRB=0.8909 SD=3.33321509 DW=2.0853

$$(25)\quad MI\$ = \frac{MMI\$ * MS}{MMI\$ + MMR\$ + MMC\$}$$

$$(26)\quad MR\$ = \frac{MMR\$ * M\$}{MMI\$ + MMR\$ + MMC\$}$$

$$(27)\quad MC\$ = \frac{MMC\$ * M\$}{MMI\$ + MMR\$ + MMC\$}$$

Wholesale Price Index (PW) (1980=100)

$$(28)\quad PW = 3.38958454 + 0.00042412(\frac{WMn}{PGNP})_{-1}$$

(3.310)

$$- 13.4218340(\frac{Y2 + Y3}{E2 + E3})_{-1} + 0.0013381 * PM * RATE$$

(-1.842) (12.101)

R^2=0.9905 RRB=0.9885 SD=4.78958322 DW=1.2815

Total Tax Revenue of Government (TAX) (billion won)

$$(29)\quad TAX = -856.273043 + 0.173971272 * GNP$$

(32.830)

R^2=0.9854 RRB=0.9845 SD=334.572711 DW=0.4869

Rate of Change of Private Consumption Deflater (GPCP)

(30) $GPCP = 0.093280805 + 0.575386723 * GPW - 0.059650172 * D817$

(10.855) (-4.424)

R^2=0.9490 RRB=0.9422 SD=0.023080090 DW=2.0731

GNP Deflater (PGNP) (1980=1)

(31) $PGNP = 0.000216824 + 0.0099793 * PCP$

(85.019)

R^2=0.9978 RRB=0.9977 SD=0.023839671 DW=0.7653

Defator for Invertment Goods (PI) (1980=100)

(32) $PI = 4.57313773 + 64.6873028 * PGNP + 0.375275503 * PM$

(12.549) (3.771)

R^2=0.9880 RRB=0.9864 SD=4.76265849 DW=1.4657

Deflator for Exports (PX) (1980=100)

(33) $PX = 30.8609048 + 29.8241471 * PGNP - 0.063554802 * RATE$

(1.887) (-2.229)

$+ 0.824510470 * PX_{-1}$

(4.128)

R^2=0.9563 RRB=0.9469 SD=5.61737108 DW=1.6085

Exports (X\$) (100 million \$)

(34) $X\$ = -33296.3362 + 11.7134442 * WGNP + 22.39247658 * RATE$

(9.988) (4.596)

$- 60.7872241 * PX$

(-1.561)

R^2=0.9831 RRB=0.9795 SD=1729.24527 DW=1.4580

Corporate Income (YC80) (billion won)

(35) $YC80 = 12457.7517 - 0.124685576 * \frac{WMn}{PGNP} + 0.739098439 * (Y2 + Y3)$

(-3.303) (6.538)

R^2=0.9623 RRB=0.9573 SD=1151.30922 DW=1.1923

Revenue of Government (RG) (billion won)

(36) $RG = 428.772696 + 0.163415378 * RG_{-1} + 0.881301653 * TAX$

(1.468) (8.436)

R^2=0.9967 RRB=0.9962 SD=170.405174 DW=2.3695

Government Consumption Expenditure (CG) (billion won)

(37) $CG = -6511.12825 + 0.384426262 * RG + 0.216809410 * N$

(5.888) (3.580)

R^2=0.9921 RRB=0.9910 SD=162.685643 DW=1.8188

Private Consumption Expenditure (CP) (billion won)

(38) $CP = 3325.52705 + 0.712373963 * (GNP - TAX)_{-1}$

(27.903)

R^2=0.9799 RRB=0.9786 SD=1183.85320 DW=1.0827

Commercial Loan from Abroad (LCN\$) (million \$)

(39) $LCN\$ = -225.251415 + 0.086400131 * GNP_{-1}$

(2.556)

$- 0.067935003 * YCI_{-1} - 0.027188405 * FDN\$_{-1}$

(-1.218) (-1.666)

$- 433.859364 * D702 - 318.596961 * D734$

(-1.792) (-1.276)

$- 354.251311 * D835$

(-1.741)

R^2=0.8432 RRB=0.7576 SD=243.424305 DW=2.0712

Direct Foreign Investment (DIn\$) (million \$)

(40) $DIn\$ = -15.0269676 - 1163.03149 * WKJ_{-1}$

(-2.865)

$+ 0.596993076 * RATE_{-1} + 0.0047464 * GNP_{-1}$

(2.623) (1.600)

$+ 38.2320532 * D70 - 177.589020 * D75$

(0.788) (-3.361)

$- 74.1104254 * D768 - 200.858879 * D815$

(-2.491) (-5.416)

R^2=0.9547 RRB=0.9229 SD=41.2812887 DW=2.3246

Repayment of Foreign Loan (FLRP) (million \$)

(41) $FLRP = -754.998365 + 0.108273617 * FDN\$_{-1}$

$$(9.620)$$

$$+ 620.596988 * D704 + 320.761791 * D756$$

$$(1.950) \qquad (0.904)$$

$$- 1996.38947 * D836 - 1331.20844 * D82$$

$$(-5.884) \qquad (-3.128)$$

R^2=0.9315 RRB=0.9029 SD=379.988206 DW=1.5345

Investment Profit Payment Abroad (IRP\$) (million \$)

(42) $IRP\$ = -1050.26470 + 0.085761587 * FDN\$_{-1}$

$$(14.163)$$

$$+ 119.563259 * LIBO_{-1} + 173.743099 * D72$$

$$(3.736) \qquad (0.461)$$

$$+ 98.0033990 * D734 + 160.631864 * D789$$

$$(0.343) \qquad (0.589)$$

$$- 515.200730 * D87$$

$$(-1.247)$$

R^2=0.9732 RRB=0.9586 SD=333.167567 DW=1.9490

Foreign Debts (FDN\$)

(43) $FDN\$ = LCN\$ + LPN\$ - FLRP + FDN\$_{-1} * (1 + LIBO) + fdn$

Investment Fund from Abroad (ISUP)

(44) $ISUP = 100 * (LCN\$ + LPN\$)\dfrac{RATE}{PI}$

Nominal Wage Rate in Manufacturing Industry (WMn)

(45) $WMn = (GWN * WM_{n-1} + WM_{n-1}$

Production in Secondary Sector in US Dollars

(46) $K2\$ = K2 * RATE$

Capital Stock in Secondary Sector in US Dollars

(47) $K2\$ = K2 * RATE$

Relative Wage Rate in Korea and Japan (WKJ)

(48) $$WKJ = \frac{\frac{WMn}{RATE}}{\frac{JWMn}{JRAT}}$$

Corporate Invertment Fund (YCI)

(49) $$YCI = YC80\frac{PGNP}{PI}$$

Rate of Change of Wholesale Price Index (GPW)

(50) $$GPW = \frac{GPW - GPW_{-1}}{GPW_{-1}}$$

Private Consumption Deflation (PCP)

(51) $PCP = GPCP * PCP_{-1} + PCP_{-1}$

3.2 Exogenous Variables

PM	deflator for imports	1980=100
RATE	exchange rate	won/$
N	population	1,000
FEn$	foreign reserve	million $
LPN$	official forein loans	million $
fdn	errors and omissins in foreign debts	million $
JWMn	nominal wage rate in manufucturing sector in Japan	yen
JRAT	excahnge rate of Japanese yen to US dollar	yen/$
TIM	time	1964=1
LIBO	London Euro-Dollar rate	%
WGNP	world GNP	billion $

3.3 Result of Final Test

MAPE	variables
less then 5%	L,E3,Y3,CG,CP,FDN$
5-10%	WMn,E1,Y1.GNP,UR,M$,MR$,PW,TAX,PGNP K1,K2,K3,PI,RG
10-20%	Y2,I,I2,MI$,MC$,X$,YC80,DIn$,I1,PW,PCP,PX
over	LCN$,FLRP,IRP$,I3

MAPE: Mean Absolute Percentage Error

4 Simulation

We conducted simulation analyses with the estimated macroeconometric model in order to evaluate the role of foreign borrowings as well as the total economic effects of DFI. First we estimate the total effect of DFI by the simulation technique using the estimated macroeconometric model. For this, we dropped the estimated equation for DFI and treated it as exogenous. Then we set the value of DFI at the half of the actual amount. This is because about half of DFI was in the secondary sector. Then we subtracted the direct effect from the total effects, and obtained estimates of the secondary repercussions. We will present the results of the simulation analysis for three cases.

CASE (1). The first case is a straight evaluation of the effect of . Since the data figures are the result of past performance of the Korean economy with , the final test figures represent the reference value for FDI. We simulate the economy with the foreign investment set at half the actual value, and the difference is the effect of FDI. For this, we subtracted the employment associated with foreign capital as well as half of DFI from the corresponding Korean national figures, and let the model run its course. We also subtracted the reduced amount of DFI from the reserve of foreign exchange. The resulting differences are presented as the total effect of case (1) in Table 3. Here we assume that the productivity of foreign capital is the same as the Korean average. The difference in the production and emlpoyment resulting from the initial subtraction from the employment and capital stock in the production function alone gives the direct effects. The differences of the direct effects and the total effects are the indirect effects presented at the bottom of the table. In this table, we find that the indirect effects are rather large. As for employment, foreign ment invest increases the employment in the manufacturing sector but as it does so at the expense of the agricultural sector, total effects on employment is rather small. Most of the negative indirect effects on employment are in the primary sector. This aspect can be easily forgotten in the literature. It is one of the benefits of using a macroeconometric model to make such trade-off explicit. The negative indirect effect on GNP reflects this indirect effect on employment. As foreign investment takes workers away from agriculture, agricultural production declines. The total effect on other variables of interest are given in Table 6. The effect on investment grows gradually. This is due to the time lag involved in the investment. The accumulated foreign debts increases rather rapidly. This is because DFI makes the economy more active resulting in larger demand and opportunity for foreign capital.

CASE (2). The second simulation is of the case where the production technology associated with DFI is the same as that in Japan. With the assumption that Japanese direct investment comes with the Japanese production technology, we estimate the productive contribution of Japanese direct investment by applying the estimated Japanese production functions to the stock of the foreign capital. This approximation may be justified as the majority of foreign capital in Korea is from Japan and it is mainly in the manufacturing sector. This change in productivity from case (1) yields an immediate larger impact of the direct investment on GNP.

The results are given in Table 4. Since the capital-labor ratio of Japanese technology is much higher, the same amount of foreign investment creates a lower level of employment. Thus the effect on employment is much smaller than in the first case. This explains why the indirect effects are so different between case (1) and case (2). The total effect on GNP and other productive activities such as exports or investments are much larger as the same amount of foreign capital generates an increase in production.

The use of the estimated Japanese production function in calculation of the contribution of Japanese DFI to production differs from the method used by Ramstetter [9]. He regresses the value added in the manufacturing sector on employment and domestic and foreign capital stock in linear form. He takes the difference of the coefficients on the domestic and foreign capital stock as the difference of productivity of the two kinds of capital. In our analysis, we assume that Japanese direct investment in Korea has the same productivity as the investment made in Japan. Thus we estimate production functions for Japan and Korea. We also take into consideration the creation of new employment by DFI. Sekiguchi [11] emphasizes the technology transfer aspect of direct investment. This technology transfer includes managerial know how. Thus, in many DFI cases, it is as if a part of the investing country is transplanted into another country. The productive contribution in this case can be better estimated by applying the Japanese production functions where a separate estimation of the production function associated with foreign capital is not possible.

The third simulation analyses the role of foreign loans. Since the official foreign borrowings is exogenous, we control the value of this item in the model.

CASE (3). The levels of the official foreign borrowings were reduced by the amount of the reduction in DFI in simulation case (1). This is to compare the effects of DFI and of foreign loans. The results are given in Table 5. We can compare the results of this case to the result of case (1). It was expected that DFI would have a larger impact on the economy than a foreign borrowing of the same amount. The total effect on GNP for case (1) in 1987 is more than five times the amount of case (3). Also the effect on the level of employment in the case of DFI is about 8 times greater than that of foreign borrowings. This result shows that although the amount of DFI in Korea was rather small compared to that of foreign borrowings, the impact on the economy was rather significant. From Table 6 we see that changes in foreign debts in this case are smaller than those for case (1) and case (2). This is so, despite the fact that we reduced foreign borrowing directly in case (3) while in case (1) and (2) the foreign borrowings were not changed exogenously. This result indicates that secondary changes in the economy were more influential on the amount of foreign capital inflow. Since direct investment generates larger secondary repercussions in the economy, foreign debts also change more in these cases.

Table 3. Simulation Results Case (1)

Direct Effects

Year	E2	%	GNP	%	E	%
1970	27.88	2.13	98.22	0.56	27.88	0.28
1971	35.34	2.23	147.11	0.79	35.34	0.35
1972	51.33	3.30	208.72	1.07	51.33	0.48
1973	91.95	4.61	290.96	1.40	91.95	0.83
1974	116.17	5.71	480.11	2.05	116.17	1.01
1975	148.42	5.35	593.77	2.38	148.42	1.25
1976	175.50	7.32	660.34	2.45	175.50	1.43
1977	181.82	6.44	711.63	2.43	181.82	1.44
1978	190.08	7.39	774.03	2.44	190.08	1.46
1979	179.82	6.18	815.51	2.38	179.82	1.34
1980	154.69	5.47	1125.09	2.78	154.69	1.12
1981	190.66	4.98	1331.93	3.12	190.66	1.35
1982	189.71	5.34	1483.87	3.20	189.71	1.32
1983	195.70	4.91	1652.68	3.25	195.70	1.33
1984	199.62	4.81	1792.27	3.26	199.62	1.32
1985	200.11	4.43	2016.58	3.36	200.11	1.30
1986	226.66	4.70	2126.27	3.36	226.66	1.44
1987	244.51	5.25	2149.51	3.26	244.51	1.53

Total Effects

Year	E2	%	GNP	%	E	%
1970	27.88	2.13	7.86	0.04	0.55	0.01
1971	38.00	2.39	79.76	0.43	2.35	0.02
1972	64.07	4.12	107.98	0.55	3.57	0.03
1973	93.08	4.66	262.81	1.27	5.68	0.05
1974	143.54	7.06	543.44	2.32	8.43	0.07
1975	171.73	6.19	714.73	2.87	12.06	0.10
1976	216.79	9.04	816.62	3.03	15.25	0.12
1977	222.04	7.86	923.18	3.15	18.37	0.15
1978	244.28	9.50	1035.78	3.27	19.92	0.15
1979	231.47	7.96	1070.66	3.13	21.37	0.16
1980	211.58	7.49	1411.40	3.48	21.10	0.15
1981	274.13	7.15	1424.21	3.34	22.13	0.16
1982	267.81	7.54	1509.07	3.26	25.50	0.18
1983	281.94	7.07	1571.85	3.09	26.45	0.18
1984	281.81	6.79	1632.64	2.97	27.45	0.18
1985	283.80	6.28	1759.43	2.91	27.87	0.18
1986	309.93	6.43	1754.67	2.77	28.86	0.18
1987	314.07	6.74	1929.11	2.93	30.26	0.19

(continued)

Indirect Effects						
Year	E2	%	GNP	%	E	%
1970	0.00	0.00	-90.36	-0.51	-27.32	-0.28
1971	2.66	0.17	-67.34	-0.36	-32.99	-0.32
1972	12.74	0.82	-100.75	-0.52	-47.76	-0.45
1973	1.14	0.06	-28.15	-0.14	-86.26	-0.78
1974	27.37	1.35	63.33	0.27	-107.74	-0.94
1975	23.31	0.84	120.97	0.49	-136.36	-1.15
1976	41.29	1.72	156.28	0.58	-160.25	-1.30
1977	40.21	1.42	211.55	0.72	-163.46	-1.29
1978	54.20	2.11	261.75	0.83	-170.16	-1.30
1979	51.65	1.78	255.16	0.75	-158.45	-1.18
1980	56.89	2.01	286.31	0.71	-133.59	-0.96
1981	83.47	2.18	92.28	0.22	-168.53	-1.19
1982	78.10	2.20	25.20	0.05	-164.21	-1.14
1983	86.24	2.16	-80.83	-0.16	-169.25	-1.15
1984	82.19	1.98	-159.62	-0.29	-172.17	-1.14
1985	83.69	1.85	-257.16	-0.42	-172.24	-1.12
1986	83.27	1.73	-371.60	-0.59	-197.79	-1.26
1987	69.56	1.49	-220.41	-0.33	-214.25	-1.34

Table 4. Simulation Results Case (2)

Direct Effects						
Year	E2	%	GNP	%	E	%
1970	29.59	2.26	129.13	0.73	29.59	0.30
1971	33.90	2.14	189.33	1.01	33.90	0.33
1972	37.82	2.43	249.43	1.28	37.82	0.36
1973	46.73	2.34	314.59	1.52	46.73	0.42
1974	46.96	2.31	483.48	2.06	46.96	0.41
1975	47.81	1.72	557.76	2.24	47.81	0.40
1976	50.04	2.09	599.13	2.22	50.04	0.41
1977	52.42	1.86	650.15	2.22	52.42	0.41
1978	50.03	1.94	684.94	2.16	50.03	0.38
1979	40.95	1.41	679.45	1.98	40.95	0.30
1980	43.29	1.53	1003.87	2.48	43.29	0.31
1981	44.52	1.16	1125.40	2.64	44.52	0.31
1982	41.99	1.18	1227.65	2.65	41.99	0.29
1983	46.99	1.18	1414.48	2.78	46.99	0.32
1984	44.92	1.08	1498.12	2.73	44.92	0.30
1985	44.98	1.00	1685.05	2.78	44.98	0.29
1986	46.35	0.96	1728.96	2.73	46.35	0.29
1987	52.03	1.12	1785.14	2.71	52.03	0.32

Total Effects						
Year	E2	%	GNP	%	E	%
1970	29.59	2.26	8.35	0.05	0.59	0.01
1971	36.72	2.31	79.44	0.43	2.42	0.02
1972	50.86	3.27	103.01	0.53	3.24	0.03
1973	45.70	2.29	250.86	1.21	4.04	0.04
1974	69.02	3.39	508.70	2.17	4.47	0.04
1975	60.66	2.19	689.83	2.77	5.99	0.05
1976	77.11	3.21	762.14	2.83	6.88	0.06
1977	77.18	2.73	875.75	2.99	8.64	0.07
1978	82.71	3.22	963.24	3.04	9.70	0.07
1979	78.11	2.68	1008.07	2.94	10.73	0.08
1980	80.00	2.83	1292.46	3.19	11.35	0.08
1981	115.48	3.01	1336.26	3.14	12.89	0.09
1982	105.64	2.98	1383.29	2.99	15.12	0.11
1983	119.62	3.00	1440.39	2.83	15.91	0.11
1984	114.22	2.75	1486.09	2.70	16.89	0.11
1985	118.58	2.62	1600.38	2.64	17.25	0.11
1986	121.76	2.53	1602.18	2.53	17.91	0.11
1987	118.07	2.53	1766.95	2.68	18.38	0.11

(continued)

Indirect Effects						
Year	E2	%	GNP	%	E	%
1970	0.00	0.00	-120.78	-0.69	-29.00	-0.30
1971	2.82	0.18	-109.89	-0.59	-31.48	-0.31
1972	13.04	0.84	-146.42	-0.75	-34.58	-0.33
1973	-1.03	-0.05	-63.73	-0.31	-42.69	-0.39
1974	22.06	1.08	25.21	0.11	-42.49	-0.37
1975	12.85	0.46	132.07	0.53	-41.83	-0.35
1976	27.08	1.13	163.01	0.60	-43.16	-0.35
1977	24.77	0.88	225.60	0.77	-43.48	-0.35
1978	32.68	1.27	278.30	0.88	-40.33	-0.31
1979	37.16	1.28	338.62	0.96	-30.22	-0.22
1980	36.71	1.30	288.59	0.71	-31.94	-0.23
1981	70.97	1.85	210.86	0.49	-31.62	-0.22
1982	63.65	1.79	155.64	0.34	-26.87	-0.19
1983	72.63	1.82	25.90	0.05	-31.08	-0.21
1984	69.29	1.67	-12.02	-0.02	-28.04	-0.19
1985	73.61	1.63	-84.67	-0.14	-27.73	-0.18
1986	75.41	1.56	-126.78	-0.20	-28.44	-0.18
1987	66.04	1.42	-18.20	-0.03	-33.64	-0.21

Table 5. Simulation Results Case (3)

Year	E2	%	GNP	%	E	%
1970	0.00	0.00	0.00	0.00	0.00	0.00
1971	0.00	0.00	14.37	0.08	0.00	0.00
1972	0.49	0.03	38.48	0.20	0.02	0.00
1973	0.51	0.03	65.31	0.31	0.10	0.00
1974	1.15	0.06	128.74	0.55	0.21	0.00
1975	5.03	0.18	168.71	0.68	0.49	0.00
1976	3.94	0.16	181.09	0.67	0.91	0.01
1977	8.60	0.30	198.33	0.68	1.22	0.01
1978	5.97	0.23	216.73	0.68	1.60	0.01
1979	11.84	0.41	238.63	0.70	1.81	0.01
1980	9.31	0.33	293.03	0.72	2.18	0.02
1981	19.63	0.51	297.25	0.70	2.48	0.02
1982	16.52	0.47	308.20	0.67	3.05	0.02
1983	19.91	0.50	316.55	0.62	3.18	0.02
1984	18.52	0.45	317.78	0.58	3.40	0.02
1985	19.55	0.43	336.48	0.56	3.46	0.02
1986	19.78	0.41	333.91	0.53	3.58	0.02
1987	18.27	0.39	363.98	0.55	3.62	0.02

Table 6. Simulation Results: Effects on Major Variables

Simulation Case (1)

Year	Investment	%	Export	%	Foreign Debts	%
1970	190.50	34.52	0.00	0.00	0.00	0.00
1971	49.29	3.07	-1.46	-0.14	0.68	0.02
1972	492.44	15.99	0.76	0.01	7.52	0.20
1973	743.34	16.85	-2.31	-0.03	16.52	0.38
1974	740.50	14.47	5.54	0.06	38.81	0.67
1975	333.17	5.39	7.33	0.09	83.22	0.97
1976	523.69	7.18	16.15	0.17	138.33	1.30
1977	459.39	5.43	16.89	0.14	198.52	1.57
1978	292.97	3.35	24.04	0.15	268.96	1.89
1979	511.79	5.23	24.67	0.15	354.54	1.79
1980	391.95	4.12	36.43	0.18	449.32	1.72
1981	228.98	1.92	45.25	0.21	586.20	1.91
1982	220.82	1.59	49.16	0.24	707.75	1.97
1983	309.81	2.20	49.82	0.21	811.06	2.06
1984	418.10	2.68	46.74	0.17	925.73	2.05
1985	540.65	3.21	41.97	0.14	1019.14	2.02
1986	1308.16	6.69	30.71	0.08	1103.02	2.25
1987	1196.84	6.08	16.11	0.04	1184.40	2.83

Simulation Case (2)

Year	Investment	%	Export	%	Foreign Debts	%
1970	190.50	34.52	0.00	0.00	0.00	0.00
1971	49.11	3.06	-1.55	-0.14	0.72	0.02
1972	493.11	16.01	0.93	0.02	7.53	0.20
1973	744.40	16.88	-1.63	-0.02	16.10	0.37
1974	744.21	14.54	8.14	0.09	37.37	0.64
1975	341.61	5.52	12.95	0.16	78.87	0.92
1976	533.88	7.32	24.21	0.25	132.18	1.24
1977	481.59	5.69	30.96	0.26	188.12	1.49
1978	308.96	3.53	39.69	0.25	254.95	1.79
1979	540.12	5.52	47.47	0.29	334.46	1.69
1980	407.73	4.29	57.74	0.29	423.71	1.62
1981	258.79	2.17	69.45	0.32	549.47	1.79
1982	247.95	1.79	74.03	0.36	663.51	1.85
1983	346.82	2.47	78.42	0.33	757.64	1.92
1984	456.80	2.93	77.98	0.29	862.34	1.91
1985	586.03	3.48	77.70	0.26	946.36	1.87
1986	1361.78	6.96	72.34	0.20	1021.36	2.08
1987	1250.08	6.35	65.60	0.16	1094.77	2.62

(continued)

Simulation Case (3)

Year	Investment	%	Export	%	Foreign Debts	%
1970	40.96	7.42	0.00	0.00	0.00	0.00
1971	70.37	4.38	0.00	0.00	0.00	0.00
1972	87.89	2.85	0.30	0.01	1.24	0.03
1973	197.25	4.47	0.76	0.01	4.51	0.10
1974	156.58	3.06	1.23	0.01	10.04	0.17
1975	74.32	1.20	2.83	0.03	20.51	0.24
1976	82.69	1.13	2.61	0.03	33.45	0.31
1977	114.12	1.35	3.90	0.03	46.59	0.37
1978	107.48	1.23	2.38	0.01	61.53	0.43
1979	97.83	1.00	2.90	0.02	79.36	0.40
1980	56.52	0.59	-0.34	-0.00	100.49	0.38
1981	67.35	0.57	-1.02	-0.00	129.15	0.42
1982	38.59	0.28	-4.61	-0.02	154.50	0.43
1983	44.60	0.32	-6.78	-0.03	175.22	0.44
1984	80.69	0.52	-10.62	-0.04	198.00	0.44
1985	116.61	0.69	-13.95	-0.05	215.27	0.43
1986	274.22	1.40	-17.79	-0.05	229.95	0.47
1987	309.39	1.57	-21.98	-0.05	244.16	0.58

5 Conclusions

In this paper we tried to isolate quantitatively the effects of DFI and foreign loans in Korea. For the analyses of multi-dimensional effects of direct investment and foreign loans, we estimated a macroeconometric model for the Korean economy. Our experience indicates that simulation analyses using a macroeconometric model are pertinent. We found that production technology is quite different in Japan and Korea. Also, other data indicate that the productivity of foreign capital and of domestic capital may differ significantly. The large difference in labor productivity is a result derived from differences in capital labor ratio and from parameters of production functions. We find that about 60 percent of the difference in labor productivity is due to the capital labor ratio in the secondary industry while the remaining 40 percent is due to the difference in technology. Thus the difference in the parameters of the production functions are of considerable importance. Here we see the importance of technology transfer which explains partly the difference of the significance of DFI and foreign loans. The effects on GNP and employment due to DFI are more than 5 times larger than those due to foreign loans.

We will now summarize the major findings from the simulation analysis of the macroeconometric model.

1. The direct impact of DFI on the employment is rather small, which reflects thereby the high capital labor ratio of the production technology accompanying the foreign capital. The immediate impact on the production is larger than the share of capital, which indicates the high productivity of Japanese

investment.

2. The direct impact on employment and production increases more than proportionally as more capital accumulates.

3. The induced increase in production very largely depends on the production technology associated with foreign capital. If we assume the Japanese productivity, then, induced indirect effects are positive. If we assume relatively labor intensive Korean technology, then, induced effects are negative.

4. The induced increase in employment also depends on what production technology has adopted. In any case, the total effects on the employment are very weak.

5. About 40 percent of the difference in labor productivity in the secondary industry between Japan and Korea is due to the difference in technology and 60 percent is due to the difference in the capital labor ratio.

6. DFI has a favorable effect on the balance of international trade.

7. Foreign loans did help the growth of the Korean economy but in dollar figures, the effect of foreign loans on GNP was about one fifth of that of DFI.

References

[1] Grinoles, E. and J. Bhagwati (1976) "Foreign Capital, Savings, and Dependence," Review of Economics and Statistics

[2] Healey, D. T. (1973) "Foreign Capital and Exports in Economic Development: The Experience of 8 Asian Countries," Economic Records

[3] Hong, K. C. (1988) *Debt Projection Model,* Ph.D. Dissertation, Institute of Socio-Economic Planning, University of Tsukuba.

[4] Kojima, K. (1973) "A Macroeconomic Approach to Foreign Direct Investment," Hitotsubashi Journal of Economics, vol.16

[5] Kojima, K. (1985) "Japanese and American Investment in Asia: A Comparative Analysis," Hitotsubashi Journal of Economics, vol.26

[6] Komiya, R. (1969) "Direct Investment and Industrial Policy," in Niida, H. and A. Ono eds., *Industrial Organization In Japan,* Iwanami, Tokyo

[7] Korean Credit Rating Corporation (1987) *The National Economic Effects of Foreign Investment and the Management Analysis of the Foreign Firms,* Seoul, Korea (in Korean)

[8] Oguchi, N. and T. Fukuchi (1989) "Economic Effects of the Japanese Direct Investment to Thailand," Discussion Paper No. 273, Kyoto Institute of Economic Research, Kyoto University

[9] Ramstetter, E. D. (1988) "The Effects of Direct Foreign Investment on Taiwan: A Macroeconometric Investigation," Paper Presented at the First Meeting of East Asian Economic Association, Kyoto

[10] Ranis, G. and C. Schive (1975) "Direct Foreign Investment in Taiwan's Economic Development," in Galeson, W. ed., *Foreign Trade and Investment: Economic Growth in the Newly Industrializing Countries,* Univ. of Wisconsin Press, Madison

[11] Sekiguchi, S. (1977) "Direct Investment into Developing Countries," The Journal of Japan Economic Research, No.6

Appendix

Data for Korea 1963 - 1987

Year	WMn	L	E3	E2	E1	Y1	Y2
1963	3180	0	2158	667	4837	3727.67	753.84
1964	3880	8449	2284	690	4825	4325.86	977.28
1965	4600	8859	2547	849	4810	4284.09	1156.77
1966	5420	9071	2634	913	4876	4780.18	1333.91
1967	6640	9295	2791	1115	4811	4497.53	1603.36
1968	8400	9647	3072	1282	4801	4557.74	1979.09
1969	11270	9888	3243	1346	482	5036.79	2359.57
1970	14150	10199	3434	1395	4916	4989.60	2822.73
1971	16980	10542	3762	1428	4876	5157.90	3465.30
1972	20104	11058	3714	1499	5346	5262.30	3877.50
1973	22330	11600	3749	1821	3569	5636.40	4956.00
1974	30209	12080	3940	2062	5584	6036.70	5704.60
1975	38378	12340	4140	2265	3425	6289.10	6406.60
1976	51685	13061	4212	2743	5601	6927.50	7847.50
1977	69168	13440	4623	2901	5405	7132.40	9028.90
1978	92907	13932	5186	3123	5181	6426.60	10863.80
1979	119515	14206	5540	3237	4887	6899.10	11903.20
1980	146684	14431	3951	3079	4654	5677.40	11789.70
1081	176176	14683	6239	2983	4801	6487.80	12909.80
1982	202117	15032	6624	3143	4612	6970.80	13690.00
1983	226790	15118	6816	3375	4315	7510.10	15754.10
1984	245261	14997	7024	3491	3914	7397.90	18419.00
1985	269652	15592	7578	3659	3733	7675.70	19713.40
1986	294485	16116	7830	4013	3662	8029.90	23339.70
1987	328696	16873	8172	4602	3580	7487.10	27436.80

WMn : wage rate in manufacturing industry
L : total labor force
E3 : employment in tertiary industry
E2 : employment in secondary industry
E1 : employment in primary industry
Y1 : production in primary sector
Y2 : production in secondary sector

(continued)

Year	Y3	GNP	UR	I	I1	I2
1963	4024.26	8505.77	8.2	701.44	72.267701	179.79296
1964	4670.05	9973.19	7.7	679.10	80.468013	183.20023
1965	5112.25	10553.11	7.4	863.30	99.029210	253.18733
1966	5779.53	11893.62	7.1	1377.40	163.883470	465.71155
1967	6582.95	12683.84	6.2	1689.40	143.960440	471.12077
1968	7576.43	14113.26	5.1	2320.90	173.252820	646.32943
1969	8661.23	16057.59	4.8	2895.60	183.076230	681.87520
1970	9471.95	17284.28	4.5	2923.90	234.519980	625.69744
1971	9940.70	18563.90	4.5	3008.70	242.831490	640.31636
1972	10407.00	19546.80	4.5	3033.10	317.271400	652.10408
1973	11686.00	22278.40	4.0	3762.90	366.174500	978.45991
1974	12435.70	24177.00	4.1	4313.70	507.296330	1050.80540
1975	13120.00	25815.70	4.1	4640.30	416.704650	1100.21280
1976	14510.50	29285.50	3.9	5534.60	515.729650	1376.18400
1977	16246.60	32407.90	3.8	7091.30	627.332600	1631.76360
1978	18690.70	35981.10	3.2	9438.10	729.421010	2306.20810
1979	19699.70	38502.70	3.8	10259.00	685.711340	2433.80330
1980	19284.90	36752.00	5.2	12225.60	754.121090	2156.78650
1981	19529.40	38927.00	4.5	11726.40	1067.149900	3425.97830
1982	21056.20	41717.00	4.4	12940.30	1089.267300	3749.34190
1983	23713.80	46978.00	4.1	15242.20	1361.011000	3818.44590
1984	25522.10	51339.00	4.1	16909.40	1548.082800	5018.52620
1985	27524.90	54914.00	3.8	17702.80	1390.257100	6068.37130
1986	30653.40	62023.00	4.0	19634.00	1563.077200	7176.10450
1987	35011.10	69935.00	3.8	23055.50	1835.465400	8426.64140

Y3 : production in tertiary sector
GNP : GNP
UR : unemployment rate
I : fixed investment
I1 : fixed investment in primary industry
I2 : fixed investment in secondary industry

(continued)

Year	I3	K1	K2	K3	K
1963	449.37932	1082.3300	2149.1800	6325.4000	9556.9100
1964	451.43175	1126.2596	2249.1938	6552.1952	9927.6487
1965	511.08345	1187.3795	2405.4588	6867.6314	10460.4690
1966	747.80497	1305.0927	2739.9671	7404.7599	11449.8190
1967	1074.31870	1408.5542	3078.5523	8176.8516	12663.9580
1968	1501.31770	1537.6293	3560.0740	9295.3479	14393.0510
1969	2030.64850	1675.6799	4074.2494	10826.5800	16576.5090
1970	2063.68250	1852.3634	4545.6395	12381.3240	18779.3270
1971	2125.55210	2030.5477	5015.4893	13941.0070	20987.0440
1972	2063.72450	2245.0357	5456.3375	15336.1660	23037.5400
1973	2418.26550	2486.0597	6100.3811	16927.9210	25514.3620
1974	2755.59820	2839.8678	6833.2534	18849.7820	28522.9030
1975	3123.38250	3141.7197	7630.2238	21112.2930	31884.2370
1976	3642.68620	3504.2647	8597.6468	23673.0110	35774.9220
1977	4832.20370	3951.3385	9760.5367	27116.7200	40828.5960
1978	6402.47080	4517.3881	11550.2140	32085.2040	48152.8060
1979	7139.48520	5039.1861	13402.2370	37518.0570	55959.4810
1980	9314.69230	5614.6587	15048.0890	44626.1320	65288.8810
1981	7233.27170	6391.0152	17540.5040	49888.3720	73819.8910
1982	8101.69060	7153.0343	20163.4320	55556.0730	82872.5410
1983	10062.74200	8094.6529	22805.2330	62518.0050	93417.8920
1984	10342.79000	9136.8200	26183.6990	69480.7610	104801.2800
1985	10244.17100	10044.5490	30145.8690	76169.3990	116359.8100
1986	10894.81800	11059.9970	34807.8040	83247.1860	129114.9800
1987	12793.39300	12240.4660	40227.3460	91475.1770	143942.9900

I3 : fixed investment in tertiary industry
K1 : fixed capital stock in primary industry
K2 : fixed capital stock in secondary industry
K3 : fixed capital stock in tertiary industry
K : capital stock

(continued)

Year	M$	MI$	MR$	MC$	PW	CG	CP
1963	19.32	3.99	10.6830	4.6470	8.60	953.35753	10036.2970
1964	13.76	2.36	8.7109	2.6891	11.60	843.37016	8708.5635
1965	15.50	2.46	10.5520	2.4880	12.80	982.15223	9376.6404
1966	24.53	5.88	15.6200	3.0300	13.90	1201.16140	10019.7440
1967	33.77	10.52	19.2140	4.0360	14.80	1306.51950	10728.1840
1968	50.10	18.25	24.4320	7.4180	16.00	1503.31010	11409.4070
1969	63.32	20.60	29.8125	12.9075	17.10	1675.47450	12309.7940
1970	66.58	19.78	33.8990	12.9010	18.70	1615.95090	12661.9630
1971	80.62	23.08	40.9560	16.5840	20.30	1815.21730	14016.8470
1972	83.51	25.23	42.8110	15.4690	23.10	1987.38310	14471.9620
1973	105.48	28.78	58.2010	18.4990	24.70	1882.08330	15662.5000
1974	109.63	29.58	62.9680	17.0820	35.10	2346.00630	17163.5780
1975	113.13	29.96	64.7150	18.4550	44.40	2874.61530	18584.3580
1976	139.26	38.52	84.5130	16.2270	49.80	3221.61010	19565.2540
1977	167.86	45.84	103.2130	18.8070	54.30	3508.40950	20175.6850
1978	220.18	73.46	123.1150	23.6050	60.60	3761.20300	22409.0220
1979	244.75	74.05	141.5740	29.1260	72.00	3833.83450	24476.1900
1980	222.92	50.01	145.4200	27.4900	100.00	4386.60000	24584.7000
1981	247.93	57.28	154.3550	36.2950	120.40	4779.02940	26552.5120
1982	248.47	61.59	160.3320	26.5480	126.00	5080.99100	28069.8610
1983	284.70	82.49	170.7190	31.4910	126.26	5357.23220	30279.9840
1984	325.50	104.33	188.4280	32.7420	127.15	5468.82530	32530.7980
1985	345.20	118.05	194.7230	32.4270	128.31	5887.04770	34641.7510
1986	373.30	125.77	205.6150	41.9150	126.38	6648.30260	36775.4590
1987	451.30	151.96	250.4080	48.9320	127.03	7087.02840	38142.3560

M$: total imports
MI$: imports of investment goods
MR$: imports of raw material
MC$: imports of consumer goods
PW : wholesale price index
CG : government consumption expenditure
CP : private consumption expenditure

(continued)

Year	PGNP	PCP	PI	PX	X$	TAX
1963	0.0551	7.60	9.70	32.1	256.07477	932.84936
1964	0.0724	8.07	11.96	32.9	362.00608	564.91712
1965	0.0762	5.59	13.78	34.2	511.98831	783.46456
1966	0.0861	9.75	15.23	37.3	671.04559	1111.49820
1967	0.0997	11.16	16.25	39.0	821.02565	1416.24870
1968	0.1148	12.46	17.82	40.2	1132.83580	1849.30310
1969	0.1317	14.10	19.19	38.2	1629.58110	2179.95440
1970	0.1630	16.34	23.48	39.9	2093.23310	2238.03680
1971	0.1840	18.64	25.42	39.4	2709.64470	2462.50000
1972	0.2140	21.32	28.11	39.9	4070.42610	2225.70090
1973	0.2400	23.71	33.04	50.4	6398.80960	2410.41660
1974	0.3130	31.50	44.97	63.8	6991.22270	2919.16930
1975	0.3900	40.22	54.96	59.2	8582.77040	3566.66660
1976	0.4720	47.23	60.80	66.2	11654.53100	4433.68640
1977	0.5470	54.17	68.25	72.4	13876.38100	4794.69830
1978	0.6650	65.08	79.34	80.1	15868.41400	5492.18040
1979	0.7980	78.26	99.34	95.8	15715.55300	5967.04260
1980	1.0000	100.00	100.00	100.0	17504.90000	5807.70000
1981	1.1540	118.98	113.21	103.2	20594.76700	6289.34140
1982	1.2310	125.99	119.36	99.7	21919.15700	6820.79610
1983	1.2790	130.82	122.48	95.5	25596.96300	7858.24860
1984	1.3280	134.18	124.18	99.2	29480.74600	8207.60540
1985	1.3820	139.79	129.00	95.5	31710.05300	8593.63240
1986	1.4140	140.85	131.22	97.5	35604.61600	9622.56010
1987	1.5110	143.98	133.32	107.4	44023.18500	10816.47900

PGNP : GNP deflator
PCP : private consumption deflator
PI : deflator for investment goods
PX : deflator for exports
X$: exports
TAX : total tax revenue of government

(continued)

Year	YC80	RG	RATE	N	PM	LCN$
1963	0.0000	932.84936	130.00	27262	29.0	20.900
1964	7336.1878	1096.68500	256.02	27984	29.4	18.990
1965	7219.7322	1384.51440	272.06	28705	29.9	28.040
1966	7979.9070	1786.29500	271.46	29436	29.2	110.130
1967	7938.4152	1995.98790	271.60	30131	2.5	137.590
1968	8572.9094	2401.56790	281.50	30838	29.2	262.070
1969	9579.3470	2854.97340	304.45	31544	28.8	360.530
1970	9556.1349	2735.58280	316.65	32241	29.8	283.260
1971	10532.2280	2997.28260	373.30	32883	29.7	320.340
1972	11294.3450	3308.41120	398.90	33505	30.2	299.100
1973	13482.2910	2906.66660	397.30	34103	40.2	460.600
1974	14753.3220	3343.13090	484.00	34692	62.5	602.560
1975	15310.4610	4180.00000	484.00	35281	64.3	802.460
1976	15944.1520	5038.55930	484.00	35849	63.0	839.450
1977	16401.0230	5467.64160	484.00	36412	64.4	1241.060
1978	16746.0150	6075.93980	484.00	36969	68.0	1913.040
1979	16514.2850	6901.37840	484.00	37534	83.1	1577.710
1980	15213.9000	6635.20000	659.90	38124	100.0	1402.057
1981	16633.5350	7083.53550	700.50	38723	105.4	1246.790
1982	16657.1080	7738.34280	748.80	39326	97.6	904.380
1983	20127.4430	8407.58400	795.50	39910	92.0	972.510
1984	22519.4270	8907.30420	827.40	40406	94.1	857.720
1985	24451.4470	9413.09690	890.20	40806	90.2	963.930
1986	28152.4750	10395.54400	861.40	41184	84.6	1620.500
1987	29481.8660	11835.80400	792.30	41575	90.9	1558.240

YC80 : corporate income
RG : revenue of government
RATE : exchange rate
N : population
PM : deflator for imports
LCN$: commercial loan from abroad

(continued)

Year	WGNP	FLRP	FEn$	FDN$	LPN$	DIn$
1963	206.35648	0.0000000	131.5	0	24.261001	0.000
1964	1920.73070	3.7530001	131.7	177	11.088000	3.710
1965	2032.51370	4.9260001	141.6	206	11.209000	13.060
1966	2161.24410	9.4160003	239.2	392	62.758002	5.870
1967	2245.35340	19.6080000	350.6	645	79.755003	15.410
1968	2365.87100	29.8940010	409.7	1199	112.133000	17.930
1969	2460.01160	55.9930020	582.9	1800	148.092000	8.470
1970	2495.51250	96.2170040	586.9	2245	146.658000	30.740
1971	2485.90970	121.8020000	538.0	2922	324.535010	44.660
1972	2803.88610	185.2850000	697.9	3589	437.535020	58.900
1973	3035.99440	241.7780100	1038.8	4260	403.598010	152.400
1974	2966.51680	287.0930100	1054.0	5937	385.259010	156.440
1975	2943.68170	283.8640100	1546.3	8456	476.323020	66.540
1976	3087.53010	406.0450100	2952.8	10533	712.994030	101.550
1977	3309.16900	532.6300200	4306.4	12648	637.951030	142.940
1978	3708.10250	823.8530300	4937.1	14871	817.944030	180.960
1979	3785.79300	1197.8160000	5708.1	20500	1089.220000	195.290
1980	3789.40370	1091.8500000	6571.4	27365	1516.497000	130.943
1981	3912.00380	1317.1550000	6891.0	32490	1689.527000	150.210
1982	3742.66950	1431.6030000	6983.7	37295	1868.086000	128.620
1983	3924.69460	1622.1660000	6909.7	40094	1493.000000	122.490
1984	4171.71690	1768.2430000	7649.6	45285	1424.000000	193.280
1985	4324.50370	1831.7850000	7748.6	50588	1024.000000	236.070
1986	4964.01740	2531.9580000	7955.2	49018	880.000040	477.500
1987	5456.83720	5116.6062000	9192.9	40980	1109.000000	624.760

WGNP : world GNP
FLRP : repayment of foreign loan
FEn$: foreign reserve
FDN$: foreign debts
LPN$: official forein loans
DIn$: direct foreign investment

(continued)

Year	IRP$	JRAT	JWMn	JGNP	LIBO	TIM	fdn
1963	0.00	361.00	23986.75	74494.69	0.00	0	0.00000
1964	1.79	361.97	26389.50	83119.44	0.00	1	-165.40000
1965	2.01	361.49	28817.16	87991.62	0.00	2	5.10999
1966	3.25	362.35	32061.50	97379.44	6.12	3	-38.12000
1967	10.80	362.15	25740.33	108193.56	5.46	4	-143.04000
1968	17.50	360.55	40619.25	122071.81	6.36	5	-341.65000
1969	41.50	358.37	46694.83	137331.56	9.76	6	-420.83000
1970	81.20	358.07	53575.33	152112.62	8.52	7	-300.50000
1971	118.60	347.86	61189.75	158766.69	6.58	8	-516.15000
1972	160.80	303.17	70678.56	172317.62	5.46	9	-710.04000
1973	205.60	271.70	84529.25	185922.81	9.24	10	-674.83000
1974	320.60	292.08	105618.06	183285.12	11.01	11	-563.80000
1975	445.10	296.79	121885.12	188189.12	6.99	12	-1031.49000
1976	481.60	296.55	137566.56	197214.69	5.57	13	-1347.02000
1977	659.50	268.51	151222.00	207737.87	6.05	14	-2215.71000
1978	929.80	210.44	162671.87	218521.44	8.85	15	-2397.46000
1979	1432.50	219.14	170865.31	230073.56	12.09	16	-2590.07000
1980	2534.90	226.74	182291.25	239914.44	14.19	17	-2319.30000
1981	3554.20	220.54	193336.00	248725.81	16.87	18	-1324.65000
1982	3718.20	249.08	201621.12	256395.12	13.29	19	-1946.80000
1983	3272.90	237.51	209874.06	264703.62	9.72	20	-850.75000
1984	3994.60	237.52	220047.37	278139.94	10.94	21	-2694.48000
1985	3977.40	238.54	225640.75	291806.87	8.40	22	-3595.15000
1986	4020.20	168.51	230980.06	299023.94	6.86	23	-2732.86000
1987	3458.60	144.62	237422.81	312370.12	1.18	24	-2682.66000
1988		128.15	240850.56	330208.31	7.98	25	

IRP$: investment profit payment abroad
JRAT : excahange rate of Japanese yen to US dollar
JWMn : nominal wage rate in manufucturing sector in Japan
JGNP : Japanese GNP
LIBO : London Euro-dollar rate 1963-88
TIM : time
fdn : errors and omissions in foreign dedts

(continued)

Year	D702	D73	D801	D72	D734	D789	D87	D704	D756
1963	0	0	0	0	0	0	0	0	0
1964	0	0	0	0	0	0	0	0	0
1965	0	0	0	0	0	0	0	0	0
1966	0	0	0	0	0	0	0	0	0
1967	0	0	0	0	0	0	0	0	0
1968	0	0	0	0	0	0	0	0	0
1969	0	0	0	0	0	0	0	0	0
1970	1	0	0	0	0	0	0	1	0
1971	1	0	0	0	0	0	0	1	0
1972	1	0	0	1	1	0	0	1	0
1973	0	1	0	0	1	0	0	1	0
1974	0	0	0	0	0	0	0	1	0
1975	0	0	0	0	0	0	0	0	1
1976	0	0	0	0	0	0	0	0	1
1977	0	0	0	0	0	0	0	0	0
1978	0	0	0	0	0	1	0	0	0
1979	0	0	0	0	0	1	0	0	0
1980	0	0	1	0	0	0	0	1	0
1981	0	0	1	0	0	0	0	1	0
1982	0	0	1	0	0	0	0	1	0
1983	0	0	0	0	0	0	0	0	0
1984	0	0	0	0	0	0	0	0	0
1985	0	0	0	0	0	0	0	0	0.
1986	0	0	0	0	0	0	0	0	0.
1987	0	0	0	0	0	0	1	0	0.

(continued)

Year	D836	D82	D70	D75	D768	D815	D817	D835
1963	0	0	0	0	0	0	0	0
1964	0	0	0	0	0	0	0	0
1965	0	0	0	0	0	0	0	0
1966	0	0	0	0	0	0	0	0
1967	0	0	0	0	0	0	0	0
1968	0	0	0	0	0	0	0	0
1969	0	0	0	0	0	0	0	0
1970	0	0	1	0	0	0	0	0
1971	0	0	0	0	0	0	0	0
1972	0	0	0	0	0	0	0	0
1973	0	0	0	0	0	0	0	0
1974	0	0	0	0	0	0	0	0
1975	0	0	0	1	0	0	0	0
1976	0	0	0	0	1	0	0	0
1977	0	0	0	0	1	0	0	0
1978	0	0	0	0	1	0	0	0
1979	0	0	0	0	0	0	0	0
1980	0	0	0	0	0	0	0	0
1981	0	0	0	0	0	1	1	0
1982	0	1	0	0	0	1	1	0
1983	1	0	0	0	0	1	1	1
1984	1	0	0	0	0	1	1	1
1985	1	0	0	0	0	1	1	1
1986	1	0	0	0	0	0	1	0
1987	0	0	0	0	0	0	1	0

Index

MIX
Papier aus verantwortungsvollen Quellen
Paper from responsible sources
FSC® C105338

If you have any concerns about our products,
you can contact us on
ProductSafety@springernature.com

In case Publisher is established outside the EU,
the EU authorized representative is:
Springer Nature Customer Service Center GmbH
Europaplatz 3, 69115 Heidelberg, Germany

Printed by Libri Plureos GmbH
in Hamburg, Germany